SAFETY AND RISK IN SOCIETY

RISK MANAGEMENT

SAFETY AND RISK IN SOCIETY

Chemical Safety Board
Robert W. Talford (Editor)
2009. ISBN 978-1-60692-586-7

Consumer Product Safety Issues
Peter A. Varga and Mate D. Pinter
2009. ISMN 978-1-60456-826-4

Fire Safety
Ingmar Søgaard and Hans Krogh (Editors)
2009. ISBN: 978-1-60741-490-2

Fire In The United States: A Reference Work on the Nation's Fire Problem
Ciro Bouchard and Marco Fortin (Editors)
2009. ISBN: 978-1-60741-746-0

Accidents: Causes, Analysis and Prevention
Henri Bédard and Geraud Delashmit (Editors)
2009. ISBN 978-1-60741-712-5

Accidents: Causes, Analysis and Prevention
Henri Bédard and Geraud Delashmit (Editors)
2009. ISBN 978-1-61668-510-2 (E-book)

Protective Devices: Types, Uses and Safety
Victor E. Argosyan (Editor)
2010. ISBN: 978-1-60876-223-1

Risk Management
Benigno Jordão and Emilio Sousa (Editors)
2010. ISBN: 978-1-60876-011-4

Consumer Product Safety Commission Issues
Isaac E. Bowman (Editor)
2010. ISBN: 978-1-60876-766-3

A Look at School Crime Safety
Maegan E. Hauserman (Editor)
2010. ISBN: 978-1-61668-773-1

Rehab, Protection and Safety Measures for Firefighters and Emergency Responders
Andreo Rios
2010. ISBN: 978-1-60741-566-4

Rehab, Protection and Safety Measures for Firefighters and Emergency Responders
Andreo Rios
2010. ISBN: 978-1-61728-051-1 (E-book)

SAFETY AND RISK IN SOCIETY

RISK MANAGEMENT

BENIGNO JORDÃO
AND
EMILIO SOUSA
EDITORS

Nova Science Publishers, Inc.
New York

For permission to use material from this book please contact us:
Telephone 631-231-7269; Fax 631-231-8175
Web Site: http://www.novapublishers.com

LIBRARY OF CONGRESS CATALOGING-IN-PUBLICATION DATA

Risk management / editors, Benigno Jordão and Emilio Sousa.
p. cm.
Includes index.
ISBN 978-1-60876-011-4 (hardcover)
1. Risk management. I. Jordão, Benigno. II. Sousa, Emilio.
HD61.R56883 2009
338.5--dc22

2009041936

Published by Nova Science Publishers, Inc. ✦ New York

CONTENTS

PREFACE

Risk management is the discipline of identifying, monitoring and limiting risks. In some cases, the acceptable risk may be near zero. Risks can come from accidents, natural causes and disasters as well as deliberate attacks from an adversary. In businesses, risk management entails organized activity to manage uncertainty and threats and involves people following procedures and using tools in order to ensure conformance with risk-management policies. Risk management is also used in the public sector to identify and mitigate risk to critical infrastructure. Some traditional risk management programs are focused on risks stemming from physical or legal causes (e.g. natural disasters or fires, accidents, ergonomics, death and lawsuits). Financial risk management, on the other hand, focuses on risks that can be managed using traded financial instruments. In ideal risk management, a prioritization process is followed whereby the risks with the greatest loss and the greatest probability of occurring are handled first, and risks with lower probability of occurrence and lower loss are handled in descending order. This new book gathers the latest research from around the globe in this field.

Chapter 1 presents data for the quali-quantitative assessment of perioperative risk for anesthesia and surgery. Major adverse outcomes are considered, including risks of mortality and morbidity deriving from cardiac and respiratory complications. Also, other relatively minor morbidities are discussed: risk of postoperative nausea and vomiting, headache following dural puncture, postoperative cognitive dysfunction, hypotension following spinal anesthesia among others.

The most important independent and dependent variables are discussed, including age, weight, presence of comorbidities—especially cardiac and pulmonary disease—hypertension, hyperglycemia, hypoalbuminemia. The main guidelines are presented with special emphasis on the most recent AHA/ACC classification of risk. This paper mentions the more useful surgical risk scores which include the variables linked with surgery, such as site, duration, complexity, malignancies, and emergency.The more validated scores are discussed: surgical Possum, P Possum, M-Possum, Surgical Apgar Score, E-Pass—all quoted with their web sites for online calculations.

With the help of these references and clinical scenarios the anesthesiologist confronted by the preoperative assessment of a patient should be able to estimate on a scientific basis the relative risk of mortality and morbidity and consequently to adapt the perioperative approach with the aim to reduce the overall risk (anesthetic+ surgical) incurred by the patient.

Enterprise Resource Planning (ERP) systems are extremely complex information systems, whose implementation is often unsuccessful. In recent years these systems have received much attention both from academic literature and practitioners, so that various methods were proposed to try improving success rate of ERP introduction or implementation efficiency.

However, ERP projects still continue to be considered complex and risky to implement in business enterprises. A possible explanation for high ERP project failure rate is that managers do not take prudent measures to assess and manage risks involved in these projects (Wei et al., 2005).

In literature few authors promoted a structured risk management approaches in facing this kind of projects, but dealing with risk management for Enterprise Resource Planning (ERP) introduction projects is a difficult task, so that an effective and efficient risk management methodology is still a wish.

The scope of the present chapter is to discuss the main challenges, opportunities and shortcomings related to the development of a risk management methodology for Enterprise Resource Planning (ERP) projects.

In this aim, the structure of Chapter 2 is the following one:

- *Introduction* - It presents a general description of the ERP systems, risk management perspective, its peculiarities in ERP introduction projects and specifies main objectives of the chapter.
- *ERP risk management framework* - It reports the authors' perspective on the issues, introducing and discussing around an ERP Risk Management Framework driving the next stages of the review.
- *ERP risk management review* - It reports the review results comparing specific methodological works on ERP risk management. The identified contributions are described and analyzed according to the previous presented risk management framework.
- *Discussion* - The paragraph discusses main evidence from the critical review of the literature, analyzing main gaps and shortcomings in the field and suggesting future directions.
- *Conclusion* - It resumes the discussions about the overall coverage of the topic, utility for managers and researchers and main open issues.

In Chapter 3, the issue of effective land use planning around planned or existing industrial establishments with potential for major accidents involving hazardous substances is explained in a detail. The domains of process safety risk assessment and spatial/land use planning procedures, policies and levels are discussed at suitable level of details in order to demonstrate existing processes, procedures and pertaining uncertainties. Next, typical current approaches to incorporate risk assessment's results into land use planning process are discussed with emphasis on their difficulties and shortcomings. Considering levels of spatial planning for new establishments (new developments), the modifications of both risk assessment methodologies and spatial planning process are suggested in order to bridge the gap between both domains. First, risk assessment methodologies should provide information about suitable separation distances through threat index, explicitly considering vulnerability of the surroundings of the hazardous industrial establishment and also threat tolerability criteria set. Second, spatial/land use planning process should be revised in order to add additional iterations in the planning at various levels each considering available information about risks/threats anticipated or assessed (related to the levels of technical data about planned development/investment). Among other things, the approach and method elaborated succeeded in integration of two domains related to risk informed land use planning. The approach asks for interaction of different technical backgrounds, methods and approaches in terms of incorporation of technical risks/threats as integrative component into spatial/land use planning process.

In several developed countries, the markets have already matured and shown a relatively low level of growth. Thus, many multi-national corporations desiring to expand further their profits are turning into the emerging markets in hope of new promising businesses. Consequently, the main purpose of Chapter 4 is to identify and analyse the types of risks in European emerging markets, including new entrants to European Union and evaluate the way of managing (financial, operational, political, natural, procedural, technical etc.) in order for a company to be able to invest and establish its businesses in countries which often have complex regulations and difficult bureaucracies. The decision processes that businesses go through in order to accept the risks in entering these markets will be explored to identify the strategies that will produce effective risk management. The contribution of this research to the knowledge will be concentrated on the challenges for a firm to enter into these emergent European member states. This will take into account the risks and how effective risk management can lead to competitive advantage. The analysis will have a qualitative approach.

Climate risk management or governance is a new and evolving area. China also proposed to establish climate risk governance system in its 11th five-year plan period (2006~2010). Given that Climate change-related risks are messy, including numerous known and potential hazards, the most urgent task is to group these climate risks into a manageable number of categories. In Chapter 5, the authors adopt a new risk categorisation system brought forward by Renn in a framework of International Risk Governance Council (IRGC) to classify climate change risks, which may be instrumental in a better governance of climate risks. The authors first investigate the post-normal nature of IRGC's categorisation system and propose that "the degree of uncertainty in the risk-related knowledge" might be used as the classifying criteria. Then the authors use "confidence" and "likelihood", quantitative terms for uncertainties description in the IPCC Fourth Assessment, to establish a quantitative classification approach based on fuzzy set theory. Finally, the authors analyse this categorisation's implication for climate risk governance in China. However, this climate risk categorising approach is still a very preliminary one. There are some limitations in the method per se and its application, which need to be studied further in the future.

The objective of this article is to analyse factors influencing the sustainability performance of different energy sources in order to come to an effective decarbonisation of the fuel mix in a competitive manner. This is of course in the light of the new climate and energy policy of the EU and shall consider the most important energy sources currently used in Europe.

Neither a single current or future energy source – be it nuclear, fossil, renewables or hydrogen – nor a single support technology, such as carbon capture and storage, can alone represent the remedy to cope with the challenges of increasing energy demand, increasing levels of greenhouse gas emissions and increasing dependence on fuel supply from outside Europe.

However, the different sources and related technologies can effectively complement each other. Nuclear power should thus be seen in combination with its alternatives. How the mixture is done in order to achieve an appropriate, "sustainable" energy mix depends on the resources and local conditions of each country or region. There are, nevertheless, some basic commonalities and inevitable limiting conditions related to the specificities of the use of the various sources which should form the basis of any such decision-making and which will be introduced in Chapter 6.

Getting eventually to a decarbonised, non-fossil world will demand great determination, huge financial burden and true patience. But there is hope on the short- and mid-term horizons by means of effectively complementing and synchronising existing technologies, such as nuclear baseload electricity generation with other low CO_2-intensive sources, e.g. some of the renewables.

On the long-term horizon, only large-scale technological innovation will help, including advanced nuclear technologies in combination with significantly improved renewables and technologies to store energy, to largely replace fossil fuels also as power source for non-electrical applications.

Carroll, Ruppert, and Stefanki [1] emphasize potential dangers in using estimated parameter values in an independent-study for analysis of the primary study, and introduce the concept of "transportability". Transportability means "not only the model but also the relevant parameter estimates can be transported without bias". As far as we know, however, a mathematical definition and statistical considerations of the transportability have not been fully developed yet. Chapter 7 defines the transportability of a regression model, presents a sufficient condition, describes a necessary assumption and examines the transportability of the regression model with real data. The motivation of the study comes from the fact that the authors have to wait for the results of an over ten-year cohort study to know the epidemiological significance of the waist circumference (WC) in the definition of the metabolic syndrome. The authors considered it would be possible to estimate the risk associated with WC if an unbiased estimate of WC for each subject ten years previous would be obtained based on the transportability arguments. Since the transported estimates inevitably subject to measurement errors, this chapter develops a method for correcting for the measurement errors to obtain asymptotically unbiased estimates for relative risks associated with WC.

The two-stage clonal expansion (TSCE) model has been developed to investigate the mechanistic processes in cancer development on carcinogenesis based on the knowledge of molecular biology and considerable interest has been shown regarding the model's use in risk assessment. The model assumes three states of cells (normal, intermediate, and malignant) and four transition rate parameters to describe the rate at which a cell changes its state: the first initiation rate μ_1 for normal to susceptible cells, the proliferation rate β, death rate δ, and second initiation rate μ_2 for an intermediate cell.

Major issues exist concerning the application of the TSCE model. Since the likelihood derived from the two-stage model is complicated and the four parameters are not jointly identifiable with survival data, sophisticated reparametrizations are necessary to obtain statistically efficient and biologically useful parameters. Heidenreich *et al.* (2000) observed that different studies have used different parameters with different assumptions and reached different conclusions from the same data set. Hornsby *et al.* (2007) also found that different studies using slightly different methods or data sets yielded different conclusions. Despite the need for statistically sound and biologically meaningful estimation methods (Portier and El Masri, 1997), no standard parameterization or inference method has yet been established. These inconveniences deter comparison of the results among studies and broader applications of this model.

Regarding the problem, Nakamura and Hoel (2003) propose the conditional likelihood method and Baker *et al.* (2006) and others use the method. The conditional likelihood is much simpler than the original likelihood, yet, maximum-likelihood estimates (MLEs) of the most interesting parameters for assessing the initiation and the promotion effects are obtained from it. Chapter 8 compares the conditional likelihood method and other techniques used frequently in the literature from both mathematical and practical perspectives.

The authors conducted extensive simulation studies with small sample sizes to assess the performance of the MLE obtained using the conditional likelihood and the ability to distinguish between initiation and promotion effects. Based on the results, the authors propose a standard cancer-risk estimation method using the conditional likelihood approach and the authors applied it to some experimental data.

Safe drinking water supply is one of the most notable modern engineering achievements in the 20th century. It is a centerpiece of the U.S. environmental protection effort under the federal Safe Drinking Water Act (SDWA) and its amendments. In Chapter 9, water quality changes are analyzed for chlorine disinfectant as a reactive solute transporting in the drinking water distribution pipes. The solute fate and transport phenomena under discussion fall into two broad categories: chlorine decay throughout a distribution network, and dispersion-reaction of "foreign" contaminants in discrete volumes. Common to the two categories are their convection-dispersion-reaction (CDR) process. From here, the role of pipe flow hydrodynamics in kinetics of chlorine decay and water quality changes is reviewed in a stepwise theoretical analysis of the Dankwerts CDR model and its simplifications. The analysis is also supported by field observations reported in literature and by the testing results of controlled pilot-scale experiments. Through the analysis, complexities in chlorine's physiochemical interactions with other solutes and pipe walls begin to emerge in light of a flow hydrodynamic field, pointing to the challenge as well as potentials to prevent excessive quality deterioration and achieve simultaneous multi-criteria compliance required by the SDWA regulations. The effects of pipe flow properties (e.g, Reynolds number) on the reaction kinetics of chlorine and other solutes in water are quantified, the current state of knowledge and future research needs are identified for optimization of the water distribution process design and operations.

The purpose of Chapter 10 is to examine the key forms of perceived risks of organizational buying, and the effectiveness of procedural control methods in managing various dimensions of perceived risk. This study was conducted using a structured interview method among Finnish companies during 2008. The results suggest that personal level psychological risk, company level psychological risk, time-loss risk, and product performance risk are the most strongly present risks in organizational buying. The use of a procedural control method by which organizations can make provision for problems was found to be as the most effective method for managing company-level psychological risks. In turn, in the case of time-loss and product performance risks, this method was perceived as excessively bureaucratic, and thus, decreasing its use was found to be the most effective way of decreasing these risks. Process standardization was found to have a very limited influence on perceived risks.

In Chapter 11, the authors present an integrated approach of catastrophic risk management based on data from geographic information systems (GIS). The methodology enables the analysis of the spatial and temporal heterogeneity of various agents (stakeholders) and offers solutions for coherent, comprehensive and robust policy responses. Using the spatial adaptive Monte Carlo (stochastic) optimization procedure allows to analyze a variety of complex interactions between decisions and risks in order to find robust optimal portfolios of risk management measures for decreasing regional vulnerability with regard to economic, financial, and human losses. The model addresses the specifics of catastrophic risks, including the lack of information, the need for long-term perspectives and geographically explicit models, and a multi-agent decision making structure. The approach is illustrated with a case study of earthquake risk management in the Tuscany region of Italy.

Safety culture is a very relevant topic for high reliability organizations. In most models safety culture is defined as being basic assumptions, attitudes or values concerning organizational safety issues. When measuring safety cultures many researchers were primarily focussed on explicit safety-critical attitudes and generally relied on specific survey instruments. However, it is questionable whether self-report measures can capture all aspects of organizational safety culture. Chapter 12 deals with the relationship between implicit safety-critical attitudes and safety culture. Based on an implicit social cognition approach and conceptual models of safety culture it is asked whether implicit safety-critical attitudes may be a better predictor for the various safety culture indicators compared to explicit attitudes. In this study explicit and implicit safety-critical attitudes of 70 participants working at a German production unit for gearbox manufacturing were measured. The author used the Implicit Association Test (IAT) to measure implicit safety-critical attitudes. Questionnaires were used to assess explicit safety attitudes and various indicators of safety culture. The results of this study show that implicit safety-critical attitudes were superior in the prediction of safety culture indicators on an individual level. Moreover, recommendations for future research in the field of safety culture assessment are made.

Chapter 13 develops an expected utility model of an exporting firm in a developing country where currency derivative markets do not exist. The firm faces exchange rate risk exposure to a foreign currency cash flow. To cross-hedge against this risk exposure, the firm uses currency futures and options between the foreign currency and a third currency. Since a triangular parity condition holds among the three given currencies, this available hedging opportunity, albeit incomplete, is proved to be useful in reducing the firm's exchange rate risk exposure. The authors show that currency options are redundant under two rather restrictive conditions: (i) logarithmic utility functions and/or (ii) independent spot exchange rates. In a more realistic cross-hedging environment, the authors show that currency options are optimally used by the firm to incompletely span the missing currency futures between the domestic and foreign currencies. The authors also estimate the benefits of using currency options for cross-hedging purposes. The improvement in hedging effectiveness can be substantial.

In: Risk Management
Editors: B. Jordão and E. Sousa, pp. 1-53

ISBN: 978-1-60876-011-4

Chapter 1

PERIOPERATIVE RISK ASSESSMENT: AN ANESTHESIOLOGIST'S PERSPECTIVE FOR PATIENTS UNDERGOING NONCARDIAC SURGERY

Claudio Melloni
Consultant in Anesthesia at Villa Torri Private Hospital, Bologna; Villa Chiara Private Hospital, Bologna; Gynepro, Day Surgery Center, Bologna, Italy

Abstract

This review presents data for the quali-quantitative assessment of perioperative risk for anesthesia and surgery. Major adverse outcomes are considered, including risks of mortality and morbidity deriving from cardiac and respiratory complications. Also, other relatively minor morbidities are discussed: risk of postoperative nausea and vomiting, headache following dural puncture, postoperative cognitive dysfunction, hypotension following spinal anesthesia among others.

The most important independent and dependent variables are discussed, including age, weight, presence of comorbidities—especially cardiac and pulmonary disease—hypertension, hyperglycemia, hypoalbuminemia. The main guidelines are presented with special emphasis on the most recent AHA/ACC classification of risk. This paper mentions the more useful surgical risk scores which include the variables linked with surgery, such as site, duration, complexity, malignancies, and emergency.The more validated scores are discussed: surgical Possum, P Possum, M-Possum, Surgical Apgar Score, E-Pass—all quoted with their web sites for online calculations.

With the help of these references and clinical scenarios the anesthesiologist confronted by the preoperative assessment of a patient should be able to estimate on a scientific basis the relative risk of mortality and morbidity and consequently to adapt the perioperative approach with the aim to reduce the overall risk (anesthetic+ surgical) incurred by the patient.

Abbreviations

BAV:	atrio ventricular block
Bpm:	beats per minute
CABG:	coronary artery bypass graft
CI:	confidence interval
COPD:	chronic obstructive pulmonary disease
DVT:	deep vein thrombosis
GA:	general anesthesia
HF:	heart failure
HR:	heart rate
IBW:	ideal body weight
ICU:	intensive care unit
LOE:	Level of evidence:
MI:	myocardial infarction
mandm:	morbidity and mortality
NYHA:	New York Heart Association
PE:	pulmonary embolism
PONV:	postoperative nausea and vomiting
VTE:	venous thrombo embolism

Introduction

Are we able to estimate the overall risk incurred by a patient undergoing an operation? Could we estimate the individual risk of mortality and morbidity, at least major morbidity? The problem consists not only in deciding if this particular patient would be able to tolerate anesthesia and surgery, but even to choose the best anesthetic and surgical approach, because if surgery is elective, one of the most important goals of risk assessment is to avoid surgery and anesthesia altogether or defer them while an attempt is made to reduce the risk with interventions—again medical or surgical—before the main procedure. Therefore, accurate risk assessment could lead one to proceed, postpone or cancel surgery. Assessment of risk constitutes an integral part of the informed consent since only when all the odds are presented to the patient can we presume that he/she has been actually informed about the procedure.

Unfortunately understanding risk is difficult, both for the patient and the professional, and therefore it's no wonder that confusion arises about risks and in the comparison between risks and benefits. Many decisions are based more on emotions than facts and both can be manipulated and could be influenced by the possibility of financial interest.

The main components of risk are probability—the statistical likelihood that an event will happen—and bad outcome, i.e. injury, harm, loss, all indicating severity of damage. We cannot delve into the perception and understanding of risk nor can we explore ways of presentation and contextualization of risks: our goal would be to quote the more recent statistical data on mortality and morbidity offering a flow chart (when available) or scientific-evidence-based data for decision making for the anesthesiologist and the patient.

Prediction of difficult intubation is not covered; the reader interested in this topic has a tremendous amount of information available elsewhere!

Cardiac Evaluation

Perioperative cardiovascular evaluation for noncardiac surgery has been extensively reviewed by many authors and by the American College of Cardiology and the American Heart Association (ACC/AHA) [1] so that today there is a broad database of recommendations based on an impressive amount of top quality clinical evidence.

Aims of the preoperative cardiac evaluation are (and not necessarily limited to) the following:

1) identify patients with high procedural, not acceptable, risk;
2) identify patients with heart disease that can be improved or cured preoperatively
3) identify patients who can benefit from a preemptive CABG or other operation.

The stratification of cardiac risk and the ensuing risk modification algorithms include patient and surgical factors and are continuously evolving from clinical trials and advancements in revascularization procedures. Cardiac risk stratification could lead to the most appropriate perioperative choice; in the preoperative period, consideration could be applied to the possibility to improve the physical status of the patient, e.g. with an appropriate medical therapy; then surgical indications could be examined, including choice of procedure and degree of invasiveness. As far as the intraoperative period is concerned, the choice will be which anesthesia, which monitoring, which drugs, and finally which anesthesiologist. For the postoperative period, the choices will be which surveillance, which monitoring, and which follow up. The patient could be sent to ICU, which requires the choices of what type of monitoring and support would be deemed necessary. This last decision has heavy implications in the sense of resource utilization.

Cardiac Risk Index in Noncardiac Surgery

Criteria	Finding	
Age (yr)	>70	5
Cardiac status	MI within 6 mo	10
	Ventricular gallop or jugular venous distention (signs of heart failure)	11
	Significant aortic stenosis	3
	Arrhythmia other than sinus or premature atrial contractions	7
	≥5 premature ventricular contractions/min	7
General medical condition	$Po_2 < 60$ mm Hg, $Pco_2 > 50$ mm Hg, $K < 3$ mmol/L, HCO_3 <20 mmol/L, BUN > 50 mg/dL, serum creatinine > 3 mg/dL, elevated AST, a chronic liver disorder, or bedbound	3
Type of surgery needed	Emergency surgery	4
	Intraperitoneal, intrathoracic, or aortic surgery	3

*Risk is based on the total number of points:
Level I: 0–5
Level II: 6–12
Level III: 13–25
Level IV: >25

The older schemes incorporated mainly the condition of the patient and so were useful only in stratifying an overall risk and were unable to offer indications about specific treatments; one of the most widely applied is that proposed by Goldman's[2].

Goldman and coll. reviewed and criticized the New York Heart Association Functional classification, that is however so well-known that it has to be remembered here:

New York Heart Association Functional Classification:

Class I: Patients with cardiac disease but without resulting limitations of physical activity. Ordinary physical activity does not cause undue fatigue, palpitation, dyspnea, or anginal pain.

Class II: Patients with cardiac disease resulting in slight limitation of physical activity. They are comfortable at rest. Ordinary physical activity results in fatigue, palpitation, dyspnea, or anginal pain.

Class III: Patients with cardiac disease resulting in marked limitation of physical activity. They are comfortable at rest. Less than ordinary physical activity causes fatigue, palpitation, dyspnea, or anginal pain.

Class IV: Patients with cardiac disease resulting in inability to carry on any physical activity without discomfort. Symptoms of cardiac insufficiency or of the anginal syndrome may be present even at rest. If any physical activity is undertaken, discomfort is increased

The last release of the ACC/AHA is a real assessment tool and provides a model for algorithm-based-data driven evaluation. The most important factors are the clinical active conditions, the functional capacity and the surgical operation. Active cardiac conditions for which the patient should undergo evaluation and treatment before noncardiac surgery, since these are associated with a high risk of perioperative cardiovascular complications, are the following:

1) unstable coronary syndrome, i.e. unstable or severe angina, recent MI (>7 days but< 30 days);
2) decompensated HF, classified as NYHA class IV or worsening or new onset HF;
3) significant arrhythmias: high grade BAV (Mobitz 2,BAV3), symptomatic ventricular arrhythmias, atrial fibrillation) with uncontrolled ventricular rate (HR greater than 100 bpm at rest); symptomatic bradycardia; newly recognized ventricular tachycardia;
4) severe valvular disease: severe aortic stenosis (means a pressure gradient greater than 40 mm Hg, aortic valve area less than 1.0 cm2, or symptomatic), symptomatic mitral stenosis (progressive dyspnea on exertion, exertional presyncope, or HF).

All these conditions should lead to further patient evaluation and treatment before the planned procedure and are defined as "major clinical predictors", class I, level of evidence (LOE)B [1].

Another major indicator is the patient functional capacity, measured in MET (metabolic equivalents), energy equivalents correlated with the maximum oxygen uptake. A Met < 4 suggests very low cardiac reserve. The scale of Met can be verified by simple questions like "Can you take care of yourself— Can you eat, dress, or use the toilet (MET 1)?; Walk indoors around the house (met 2)? Walk a block or 2 on level ground at 2 to 3 mph (3.2 to 4.8 kph) (met 3)? Can you do light work around the house like dusting or washing dishes (met 4)?; can you climb a flight of stairs or walk up a hill (met 5)? Walk on level ground at 4 mph (6.4 kph)(met5)? Run a short distance? Do heavy work around the house like scrubbing floors or lifting or moving heavy furniture (met6)?Do recreational activities like golf, bowling, dancing, doubles tennis, or throwing a baseball or football (met 8-9)? Participate in strenuous sports like swimming, singles tennis, football, basketball, or skiing? (met 10)?

Simple application of the MET, like the Shuttle walking test[3] demonstrated a higher mortality after oesophagectomy in patients unable to walk > 350 m.

Other clinical risk factors were derived from RCRI (Revised Cardiac Risk Index) (RCRI factors [4]: stable mild angina, MI by history or Q wave in the ECG > 30 days, history or presence of compensated CHF, diabetes mellitus and chronic renal insufficiency defined by a serum creatinine > 2.0 mg/dl.

The last major indicator concerns high risk surgery, defined as surgery having a perioperative risk of serious cardiovascular accident > 5%. Among the high risk procedures are included only the vascular surgery of the aorta and of the peripheral arteries; intermediate risk surgery (cardiac risk between 1–5%) comprises intraperitoneal and intrathoracic, carotid endoarterectomy, head and neck, orthopedic, prostate; low risk (<1% cardiac risk) endoscopic procedures, body surface, cataract surgery, breast, and ambulatory.

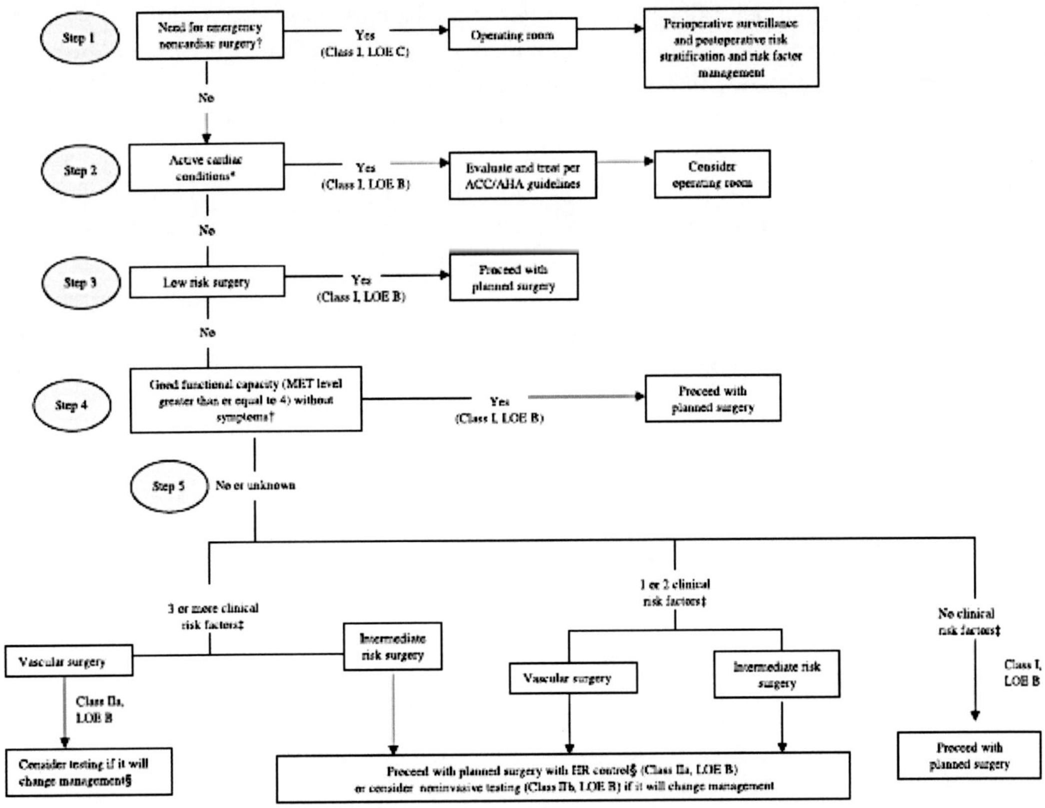

The complete algorithm including the decisional tree for testing strategies is subdivided as follows:

- The guideline indicates when supplementary tests are indicated, but this topic will not be treated here. It is interesting to note that preoperative hypertension does not contraindicate to proceed with the operation, unless new symptoms show, like a headache during a hypertensive crisis [5].
- These suggestions were anticipated even in the past [6] noting that a history of hypertension was a prognostic indicator for perioperative mortality, while high blood pressure at admission was not.The study indicated that the end organ damage secondary to hypertension was the main killer, not hypertension per se, concluding that without disease of the main organs, like renal insufficiency or ventricular hypertrophy with strain, the literature does not contraindicate the surgical procedure. It has been shown that betablockers should be continued in the perioperative period for patients already taking them because of angina, symptomatic arrhythmias, hypertension or other clinical indications following the guidelines ACC/AHA, class I.

Betablockers should be administered to high cardiac risk patients with preoperative signs of ischemia undergoing vascular surgery (LOE B).

Betablockers are indicated for patients undergoing vascular surgery for whom the perioperative evaluation identifies coronaropaties and/or a high cardiac risk, defined from the presence of > 1 clinical risk factor, even if undergoing intermediate risk surgery.Viceversa betablockers' utility remains uncertain in patients undergoing intermediate or vascular surgery with only 1 risk factor (LOE C) and for patients scheduled for vascular surgery without risk factors who are not taking drugs (LOE B).Note that patients undergoing peripheral vascular surgery have a worse long-term outcome, principally because of cerebrovascular and cardiac complications, than patients with a risk factor matched population of coronary artery disease patients without peripheral arterial disease [7].

It is obvious that betablockers should not be administered to patients for whom they are contraindicated (e.g., asthmatics). In conclusion, therapeutic dosages of betablockers should be administered to patients with high-intermediate cardiac risk. The work of [8] demonstrates these concepts very clearly.

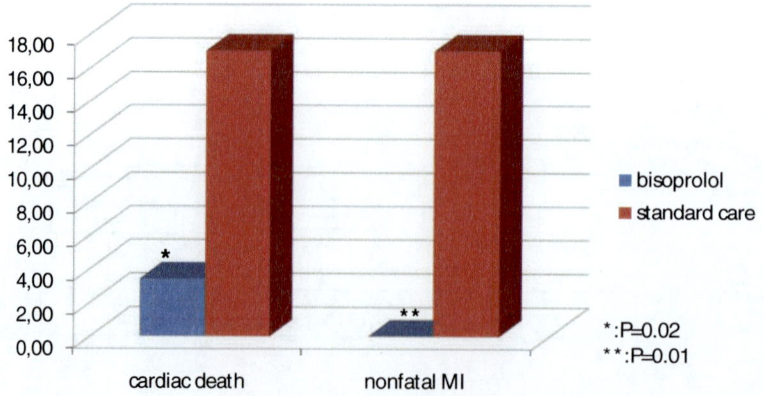

In order to make the most of the betablocker therapy, heart rate must be strictly controlled; only if and when the heart rate remains < 100 bpm can therapy be considered adequate, as outlined in [9]. Beside the high heterogeneity of the data in the literature, only with bpm<100 was there a significant protective effect—no efficacy was shown not attaining this target. Their metaregression demonstrates a linear association between the betablocker effect on the heart rate (mean, max and its variation) and the incidence of MI ($r2=0.63$; $P=0.001$)—a greater efficacy of the betablocker therapy was accompanied by a significant reduction of perioperative MI incidence.

However, the role of betablockade remains controversial in the light of new clinical evidence [10, 11] and it has been suggested that the AHA/ACC should soften their point of view about the need for betablocker therapy, at least in the intermediate and low risk group of patients.The careful reader is referred to other ongoing studies.

A recent hypothesis has shed new light on the possibility that it is not the perioperative bisoprolol therapy but the adrenergic receptor genotype which is the determinant of the cardiovascular outcome of at-risk patients undergoing surgery [12]. Carriers of at least one Gly allele of the beta1-adrenergic receptor polymorphism Arg389Gly showed a higher number of adverse events than Arg homozygous (32.4% vs. 18.7%). Since patients were anesthetized with spinal blockade; there is the possibility that regional anesthesia poses less risk to cardiac patients in comparison with GA.

Statin preoperative therapy should be continued for patients already on them (LOE B); their administration is reasonable for patients undergoing vascular surgery with or without clinical risk factors (LOE B).Their usage can be considered for patients with at least 1 clinical risk factor candidates for intermediate risk surgery (LOE C). An important clinical trial is underway to establish if statines + betablockers exert an additive or synergic effect in the reduction of complications in major noncardiac surgery, confirming the hypothesis of [13] where it was shown that the more at risk patients (3 or more risk factors) benefited most in terms of reduction in mortality and recurrence of MI.

Mortality in coronary patients undergoing noncardiac surgery depends from the invasiveness of the procedure: [14]:

High risk surgery >=4%	Low risk surgery<=4%
Abdominal 4%	Urologic 1.8
Vascular 11.3	Orthopedic 1.2
Thoracic 7.7	Skin 0
Head neck 7.3	Miscellaneous 3

Heart Failure as a Risk Factor

Ejection fraction (EF) is a critical determinant of cardiac morbidity and mortality. [15]

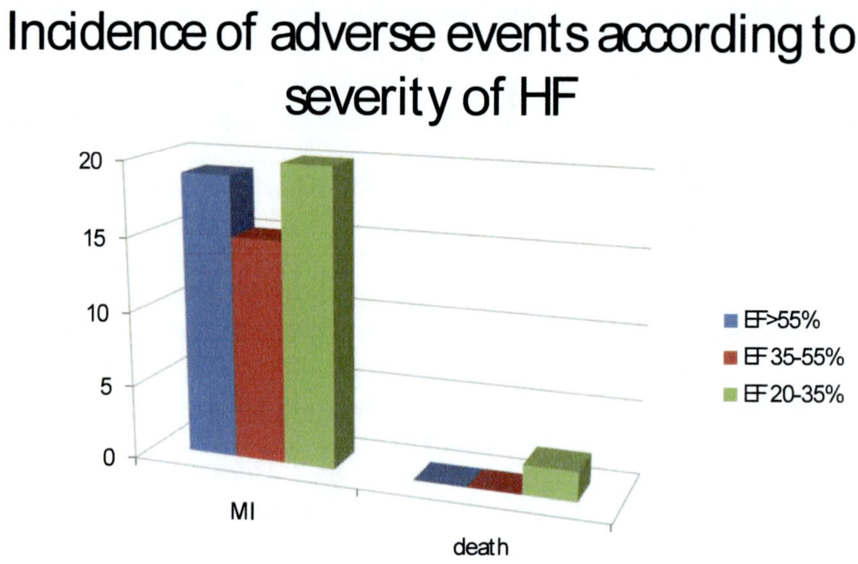

Perioperative mortality in patients with chronic heart failure in comparison with coronary artery disease is shown in the following table according to intervention type (data from Hammill et al. [16])—the frequency of a second admission within 30 days follows the same pattern:

Perioperative mortality	***Heart failure***	***Coronary artery disease***	***Comparison group***
Operative mortality tot	8	3.1	2.4
>knee amput	25.8	18	16
< knee amput	12.8	10.4	7.2
Carotid endoarterect	2.5	1.2	0.9
Colon cancer resection	11.9	6.3	5.4
Hip replacement	8.4	3.9	2.8
Knee replacement	0.9	0.4	0.3
Lap cholecystectomy	5.6	2.1	1.8
Lower extremity bypass	8.1	3.7	4.1
Open AAA	10.3	5.6	4.8
Open cholecyst.	15.9	7.7	6.9
Other abdominal cancer resection	11.8	4.3	4.9
Pulmonary cancer resection	10.2	6	5.1
Spinal fusion	3.8	2.1	1.3

Frequency of a second admission within 30 days	Heart failure	Coronary artery disease	Comparison group
Total	17.1	10.8	8.1
>knee amput	25.2	21.6	18.9
< knee amput	24.1	23.4	19.9
Carotid endoartcrect	15.2	10.8	8.7
Colon cancer resection	18	13.2	10.5
Hip replacement	16.6	10.3	8
Knee replacement	9.9	6.2	4.7
Lap cholecystectomy	16.4	10.1	8.4
Lower extremity bypass	27.2	18.2	16.2
Open AAA	14.8	11.3	10.4
Open cholecyst.	17.3	12.6	11.8
Other abdominal cancer resection	20	17.4	13.3
Pulmonary cancer resection	17.4	15.5	11.3
Spinal fusion	13.3	9.4	

In conclusion, elderly patients > 65 years with heart insufficiency undergoing major noncardiac surgery constitute a group at high risk of mortality and morbidity; the risk of perioperative mortality is greater than 63% and readmission rate for any cause is 51%. These data were obtained from a metaanalysis conducted on a very large population of Medicare patients older than ≥65 operated for 13 major types of surgery between the years 2000–2004.Renal insufficiency and subscription to Medicare < 1 year were exclusion criteria. Outcome targets were perioperative mortality and 30 days readmission. Among 159.327 operations, 18% were done on cardiac insufficiency patients and 34% on patients with coronary ischemia .Odds for mortality and readmission for patients with heart insufficiency and ischemia were 1.63 (CI 95%: 1.52–1.74) and 1.51 (CI 95%: 1.45–1.58), respectively:corrected relative risk 1.08 (CI 95%: 1.01–1.16) and 1.16 (CI 95%: 1.12–1.20), respectively.These effects were statistically significant and showed that cardiac insufficiency patients had a higher risk of mortality and morbidity compared with coronary patients.

The short-term outcome of these patients is dramatically improved if they (patients with stable heart failure) could be optimized before the procedure by an expert team of internists (Internal Medicine Preoperative Assessment Consultation and Treatment (IMPACT) Center at the Cleveland Clinic); only the mortality at 1 year is worse in comparison with normal healthy patients [17] at the expense of 1.4 days longer stay.

These findings contrast with the aforementioned and previous studies [18] that have focused on the perioperative outcomes of patients with HF; data from these studies are summarized in the figure:

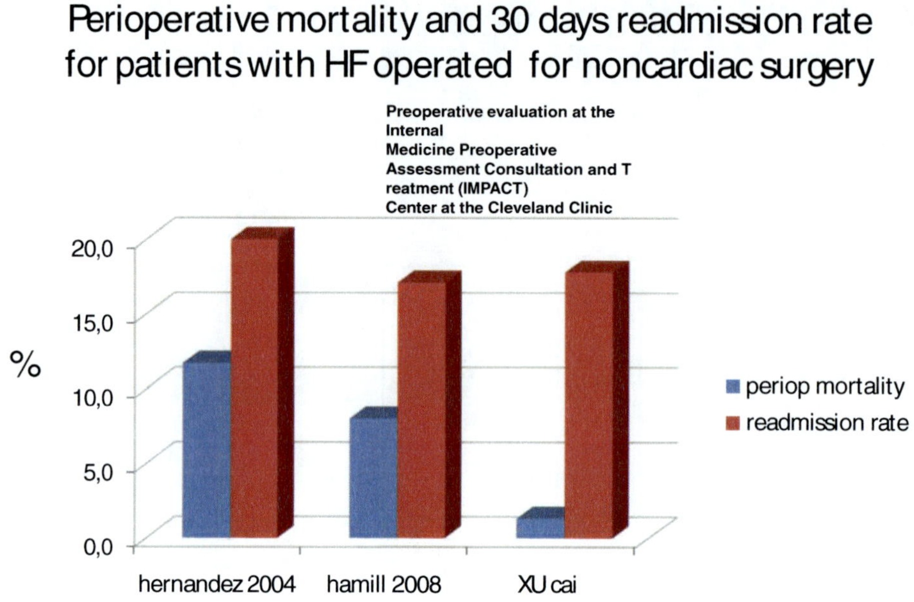

Adverse intraoperative haemodynamic effects impact on postoperative outcome [19] with higher mortality (2.1% vs 1.0%); however these risks were not anticipated by the ASA PS classification nor by the Revised Cardiac Risk Index (RCRI).

In order to avoid cheating by the anesthesiologists intraoperative data should be collected automatically, since very often the anesthesiologist does not register adverse effects on the chart for fear of the medicolegal consequences.

One of the major problem in the perioperative treatment of the cardiac (and noncardiac) patients resides in the fact that MI and ischemia often go unrecognized (unrecognized MI determined by rest wall motion abnormalities in the absence of a history of MI and silent myocardial ischemia, defined by stress-induced wall motion abnormalities in the absence of angina pectoris); according to [20].

This happens in 23 and 28% respectiverly in patients undergoing major vascular surgery.

Laboratory markers for cardiac risk after noncardiac surgery have been developed: N-terminal pro-brain natriuretic peptide (NT-proBNP), endogenous nitric oxide synthase inhibitor asymmetric dimethylarginine (ADMA), polymorphisms in platelet glycoprotein (GP) IIIa and GPIb [alpha] are three new entries.

Elevated NT-proBNP levels are independently associated with an increase in the risk of perioperative cardiovascular complications [21, 22].

Per 0.1-micromol/L increment in plasma ADMA concentration, the odds ratio to experience the primary end point increased by 1.26 [23].

Polymorphisms in platelet glycoprotein (GP) IIIa and GPIb[alpha] Pro33 and Met145 genotypes were independent predictors of composite ischemic outcome [24].

All these studies are promising, but included a small number of patients; they need to be validated in a much larger population. If they show to be sensitive and specific enough, they could substitute many of the laboratory tests that we do now which seem to be totally useless, at least from the point of view of prospective risk adjusted analysis.

The Risk of Loss of Vision

Ocular damage attributed to the anesthesiologists comprises about 3% of all claims collected by the ASA Closed claims [25]. Two distinct injuries are known: corneal damage (35%), rarely permanent (16%), and global ocular damage (30%) due to sudden patient movement during anesthesia or sedation for ophtalmic surgery. While the etiology of eye damage during opthalmic surgery is clear, much more intriguing is the etiology of the eye damage during other types of surgery [26], mainly cardiac, spine, head and surgery done in the prone position, with an average incidence from 0.002 to 0.2%.The cause is unknown and has been attributed to optic nerve ischemia, hypotension, asoconstriction, increase in the venous pressure, hypoxia and local anatomical and physiological peculiarities of the patient.

Perioperative Risk in Mentally Ill Patients

Little scientific evidence is available on this group of patients: schizophreny seems correlated with increased mortality and morbidity, and is characterized by ileus and mental confusion.These patients seem to be resistant to pain. Severely depressed patients exhibit a high incidence of postoperative delirium and mental confusion: these complications seem more frequent when the usual therapy is suspended in the postoperative period [27]. All in all, we recommed the continuation of psychotropic drugs in the perioperative period, but we suggest to contact the psychiatrist in charge of the patient as soon as possible in order to choose a therapeutic approach presenting the minimal risk of drug interactions. This opinion is based on case reports and small case series, but case reports of rare events, such as life-threatening interactions between psychotropic drugs and anaesthetics, do not provide reliable data on the frequency of such events and may lead to a rather defensive approach. Recommendations were published recently based on expert opinion from a multidisciplinary group[28][29].

The vast majority of anesthetic problems related to psychiatric disease are drug related: however not infrequently mental illness is accompanied by other medical problems that can compound the risk, like tabagism in schizophrenics [30].

Mentally ill patients could be found difficult when trying to obtain an accurate history or cooperation; information has often to be collected from several sources, such as family members, staff of group homes, primary physician, and psychiatrist. Because drug treatment of psychiatric disease is complex, it is necessary for the anesthesiologist to have a good knowledge of the mechanism of action and potential interactions of the most common antidepressants, anxiolytics, neuroleptics, anticonlvusants: this topic is beyond the scope of this book and the interested reader is referred to the excellent review done by [31] .

Risk of Perioperative Acute Ischemic Stroke

Perioperative acute ischemic stroke risk factors were identified in 372,000 adults subjected to major operations, which included hemicolectomy, hip replacement, and lung resections. Renal disease, atrial fibrillation, history of stroke, and cardiac valvular disease were the most significant risk factors for perioperative stroke[32]. The incidence varied between 0.2–0.7% of all procedures and rose to 0.3–1% for patients older > 65 years.

Thromboembolic Risk

The thromboembolic risk without prophylaxis has been summarized by [33]:

	DVT %	DVT %	PE %	PE %	
Risk level	calf	Proximal	Clinical event	fatal	Successful preventive strategy
low: minor surgery in patients . <40 anni without risk factors	2	0.4	0.2	<0.01	No prophylaxis,early deambulation, aggressive management
Moderate: minor surgery in patients with added risk factors Surgery in patients 40-60 years without added risk factors	10-20	2-4	1-2	0.2-0.4	Hep(q. 12 h),LMWH <3400,GCS,IPC
High: surgery in patients >60 or age 40-60 with risk factors(VTE,cancer,hipercoa gulability)	20-40	4-8	2-4	0.4-1	HEP q. 8 h,LMWH>3400,Ipc
Very high : Surgery in patients with multiple risk factors:: Hip or knee prosthesis, hip fracture major trauma spinal medullary trauma	40-80	10-20	4-10	0.2-5	LMWH>3400,fondapa rinux, Vit K antag p os(INR 2-3), IPC or GCS+LMWH or Hep

IPC intermittent pneumatic compression: HEP: unfractionated heparin LMWH; low molecular weight heparin GCS: gradual compression stockings.

Data from the Patient Safety in Surgery (PSS) Study were used to develop and test a predictive model of VTE using multiple logistic regression analyses [34]; in 183,069 patients undergoing vascular and general surgical procedures VTE occurred in 0.63%, with a 30-day mortality in patients who suffered a VTE of 11.19%.15 variables independently associated with increased risk of VTE included patient factors: female gender, higher American Society of Anesthesiologists class, ventilator dependence, preoperative dyspnea, disseminated cancer, chemotherapy within 30 days, > 4 U packed red blood cell transfusion in the 72 hours before operation. Preoperative laboratory values for this increased risk were albumin < 3.5mg/dL, bilirubin >1.0 mg/dL, sodium >145 mmol/L, and hematocrit <38%; operative characteristics were emergency operation, work relative value units, and infected/contaminated wounds.

VTE risk index can be calculated by adding the point values for each risk variable present in a patient. For example, a 70-year-old male patient with ventilator dependence, ASA class 3, undergoing a thoracic operation, and a preoperative hematocrit of 35% has a VTE risk index score of 14 points (9 points for thoracic operation, 2 points for ASA class 3, 2 points for ventilator dependence, and 1 point for low hematocrit).

The following table shows the VTE complication risk index for general and vascular surgery :

Table showing VTE complication risk index :

Risk factors	**Risk score points**
Surgical procedure on the respiratory tract	9
Thoraco abdominal aneurysm,embolectomy,thrombectomy,venous reconstruction,endovascular repair	7
Aneurysm	4
Operations on Mouth,palate	4
Operations on Stomach,intestine	4
Operations on Integument	3
Operations for hernia	2
ASa physical status: 3,4,5	2
ASa PS 2	1
Work Relative Value Units >17	3
WRU 10-17	2
Disseminated cancer	2
Chemoterapy for malignancies within 30 days of operation	2
Preop.Na>145 mMol/lt	2
Ventilator depencency	2
Preoperative Hct ≤38	1
Preop bilirubin> 1 mg/dl	1
Dyspnea	1
Albumin ≤ 3.5 mg/dl	1
Emergency	1

The risk index score was divided into 3 discrete ranges based on the rate of VTE: low (risk score 1 to 6), medium (risk score 7 to 10), and high (risk score >10). The estimated risk of VTE complication for the patient with risk index 14 is 2.1%. As VTE risk indices increase, the rate of VTE shows logarithmic acceleration.

NSQIP methodology can underestimate the true incidence of VTEs in the postoperative period and the impact of operations and hospitalization on development of postoperative VTE; however, a large part of the data in this study was derived from VA medical centers and results might not accurately reflect the general population, as veterans are more likely to be male patients and have greater comorbidities.The importance of the study resides in the possibility to identify patients at highest risk for VTE at the time of preoperative evaluation so that timely VTE prophylaxis could be applied with aggressive surveillance for those at highest risk.

Glucose Control: Hyperglycemia as Risk Factor

Perioperative untreated hyperglicemia is an independent risk factor accompanied by a mortality 3–4 fold higher in comparison with treated hyperglicemia:

	Glucose controlled	Not controlled
van den Berghe [35], 2001	4,6 % mortality	8 % mortality
Ouattara [36]2005	2,4	11.4
McGirt [37] 2006		2.8-, 4.3-, and 3.3-fold increases in risk of stroke /TIA, MI, or death
Gandhi [38]2005		A 20-mg/dL increase in mean intraoperative glucose associated with a 30% increase in adverse events.
Krinsley [39] 2003		42.5% among patients with mean glucose values in excess of 300 mg/dL.
Finney [40]2003	Increased administration of insulin was an independent predictor of ICU mortality; regression models demonstrated a mortality benefit if blood glucose was maintained < 144 to 200 mg/dL.	
Furnary[41] 2003	Continuous iv insulin was an independent predictor of survival.	
McAlister [42] 2003		Hyperglycemia was an independent predictor of adverse outcomes.
Vriesendorp (43)		Elevated postoperative glucose levels are an independen risk factor for infection in patients undergoing infrainguinal vascular surgery

	Glucose controlled	Not controlled
Bilotta(44)	prospective randomized pilot trial comparing IIT (target BG 80–120 mg/dL) to conventional treatment (target BG 80–220 mg/dL) in patients with aneurysmal subarachnoid hemorrhage status after surgical clipping, IIT was associated with decreased infection rate (42 to 27%) but no difference in the incidence of vasospasm, neurologic outcome, or mortality.	
Ramos (45).	Postoperative hyperglycemia increased the risk of postoperative infections by 30% with every 40-point increase from normoglycemia. Longer hospitalization was observed for patients with postop glucose from> 110	
Pomposelli (46)	elective surgery a single blood glucose level >220 mg/dL on the first postoperative day was a sensitive (87.5%) predictor of postoperative infection. Patients with blood glucose values> 220 mg/dL had infection rates that were 2.7 times higher than the rate for patients with lower blood glucose values (31.3% versus 11.5%, respectively)..The relative risk for serious postoperative infection, including sepsis, pneumonia, and wound infections, was 5.7 times higher than those with glucose levels less than 220 mg/dL.	
McConnell(47)	Surgical site infections (SSI)higher when mean 48 hr capillary glucose(MCG) was >11.0 mmol/L or 200 mg/dL (29.7% vs. 14.3% if MCG <11). 48-h MCG >11.0 mmol/L was significantly associated with SSI (OR 3.6, p = 0.02), independent of the dose and regimen of postoperative insulin administration.	

Poor intra- and postoperative control of blood glucose was an independent predictor of severe morbidity; mortality rate was increased in patients with poorly controlled glucose vs those with tightly controlled glucose; therefore a strict glycemic control is mandatory aiming at normal values. The situation is quite different in the ICU environment, where a great debate exists, with studies indicating better outcomes with a strict glycemic control and contrary views demonstrating dangers and complications; an editorial summarizes the subject and calls for more uniform definitions and protocols [48].

The subject of perioperative glycemic control has been the topic of a very recent metaanalysis [49] which identified the favourable effect of the good glicemic control on mortality, but underlined the risk of hypoglycemia and of the requirements for confirmation in large and rigorous randomized controlled trials.

Since diabetes affects all systems, diabetic patients are at great risk and glucose homeostasis is just one of the many problems encountered. Diabetics share the same risks as patients with cardiac ischemia, renal insufficiency or cerebrovascular atherosclerotic disease [50]; they have autonomic dysfunction, i.e. a triad of orthostatic hypotension, loss to beat to beat heart rate variability and delayed gastric emptying. It is still debatable the potential for difficult intubation [51].

The control of perioperative glucose levels reveals an important knowledge deficit among surgical resident and attending physicians [52] since the majority of physicians ignored the more recent guidelines and the treatment protocols.

Preoperative Prediction of Perioperative Respiratory Complications and Insufficiency

A multifactorial index for prediction of postoperative respiratory insufficiency following major surgery has been validated for males [53]: postoperative respiratory insufficiency appeared in 3.4% of cases. The prognostic indexes were:

- abdominal aortic aneurysmectomy
- thoracic surgery
- neurosurgery
- major abdominal surgery
- peripheral vascular surgery
- neck surgery
- emergency surgery
- albumin levels < 30 g/L
- BUN > 30 mg/dL
- Functional dependency
- COPD (chronic obstructive pulmonary disease)
- age > 60.

The probability of postoperative respiratory insufficiency was graded in risk classes with a point score for developing a respiratory failure risk index score:

Risk class for respiratory failure	points	Predicted probability of respiratory failure
1	<=10	0.5%
2	11-19	2.2%
3	20-27	5%
4	28-40	11.6%
5	>40	30.5%

These scores derived from the results of a statistical regression based on the type of surgery, where operations for abdominal aortic aneurysm valued 27, thoracic surgery 21, neuro,upper abdominal or peripheral vascular 14, neck and emergency 11, low albumin<3.0 gr/dl 9, Bun >30 mg/dl 8, functional status partially or totally dependent 7, history of COPD 6, age > = 70 6 and 60–69 4.

Reasoning out of these data, a 72-year-old male with a history of mild COPD undergoing a major abdominal operation and BUN>30, has an expected risk of postoperative respiratory insufficiency around 10–11%,resulting from class IV (14+8+6+6=34). The usefulness of the index derives from the simultaneous inclusion of factors specific for the operation and the patient,giving a reasonable estimate of cumulative risk.

Postoperative pneumonia risk is similarly constructed but presents some different risk factors [54]:

- long term steroid administration
- age>60 years
- dependent functional status
- weight loss > 10% of the total corporeal mass within the previous 6 months
- recent alcohol use
- smoking recently
- history of COPD
- cerebrovascular accident history, with a residual deficit
- Consciousness disturbances
- Risk factors connected with the operation: aortic aneurysmectomy; thoracic surgery, upper abdominal surgery, neck surgery, peripheral vascular surgery, neurosurgery.

Other risk facors identified in [55] include age>65 years, smoking habit, FEV1, FVC, FEV1/FVC reduction, duration of anesthesia, history of COPD, daily productive cough, upper abdominal incision, anesthesia > 2.5 hr. presence of a NG (nasogastric) tube, but only 4 variables are independent descriptors after a multivariate analysis: age, cough test, preoperative NG tube, anesthesia duration.

OSA as a Risk Factor

Sleep apnea syndrome (SAS)or obstructive sleep apnea (OSA) is correlated with daytime somnolence, night snoring, resistant hypertension, quality of life disturbances, cardiovascular disease, road traffic accidents. Only recently it has been linked with perioperative complications while it has been known that these patients are particularly sensitive to opioids, sedatives, general anesthesia [56]. A very important contribution has been the implementation of a rapid and easily applicable screening questionnaire [57] under the name of STOP, corresponding to the initials of the main symptoms: S.T.O.P.:snore, tired, observed (stopped breathing), pressure. Before this simple test patients had to be identified by reviewing the medical record and interviewing the patient and the family; a questionnaire (Berlin questionnaire)was proposed and used with success identifying patients likely to have SAS [58]. Stop consists of 4 questions: (STOP Q1–4):

- S—"Do you **s**nore loudly (louder than talking or loud enough to be heard through closed doors)?
- T—"Do you often feel **t**ired, fatigued, or sleepy during daytime?"
- —"Has anyone **o**bserved you stop breathing during your sleep?
- " P—"Do you have or are you being treated for high blood **p**ressure?

An useful adjunct to the questionnaire is "Bang", 4 other questions incorporating BMI, age(A), neck circumference(N),sex (Gender) (STOP-Bang).These points increase sensitivity; the only data to be measured by the staff is the neck circumference. A high risk for OSA is given by 3 or + yes, low risk < 3 yes.

The postoperative period is a risk time for the OSA patients;oxygen should be administered since desaturation is related to the postoperative opioid analgesia (morphine)[59].After orthopedic prosthetic surgery frequency of reintubation, hypercapnia, hypoxemia was greater, albeit statistically not significant, in OSA patients [60].

Albumin as a Predictive Tool

Albumin serum levels and operative site are able to identify the risk for major surgery [61]; all procedures had more complications amd higher mortality rate with hypoalbuminemia with a higher complication rate following esophageal and pancreatic surgery versus colon surgery.With albumin values <25 g/dL, mortality rate increased progressively until 20% - 30% with the lower values;no difference existed among the different sites of operation with albumin levels = > 3.25 g/dL. Length of stay and ICU admission were also related to low albumin levels. Since one of the prerequisites of the study was the inclusion of elective patients, the obvious implications are that every effort should be undertaken in improving the nutritional status of the patient before major surgery.

Surgical Prognostic Indices

The more validated surgical prognostic scores add value to the aforementioned considerations, since anesthesia cannot be considered per se but has to be interpreted in the context of the surgical operation proposed.This is the arena where the patients conditions should be weighted with the likelihood that the surgical operation will be succesful because surgery may not be advised if the chance of success are slight and the risk of causing a worse outcome, either in terms of mortality or serious morbidity is considered greater by operating.In order to make these difficult decisions as objective as possible a number of scoring systems have been constructed and their importance lie not only in evaluating the risk but even in the possibility of auditing and serving as benchmarking in the quality assessment between different institutions all other variables being equally stratified .Generally speaking, data are entered retrospectively first and validated in a successive work with prospective data: The techniques employ sophisticated statistical methods. The ASA PS score (American Society of Anesthesiologists Physical status score) is the most commonly used [62].

Class definition

1) healthy patient without medical problems
2) patient with mild, well controlled medical disease
3) patient with severe systemic disease, not incapacitating
4) patient with a severe systemic disease that is a constant threat to life
5) moribund patient not expected to live 24 hr regardless of operation
6) Organ donor

The ASA physical status evaluation is independent of the operation; patients of similar physical health scheduled for widely different operations would have similar scores,but, of course, their outcome would be influenced by the invasiveness of the procedure. The ASA classification does not constitute a risk evaluation, being based on the subjective assessment of the general fitness of the patient .Being a subjective assessment of the patient's comorbidities it is prone to different class assignments by anesthesiologists of different experience. However with the passage of time it has been (improperly) used as an overall risk assessment and as a matter of fact it functions well evaluating the mortality risk [63]. As a classification does not work well at predicting complications and morbidity even though this relationships holds true for pulmonary complications [64]:

Relationship between ASA classification and postoperative pumonary complications rate.

class	definition	Postoperative pulmonary complications
I	healthy patient without medical problems	1.2%
II	patient with mild,well controlled medical disease	5.4%
III	patient with severe systemic disease,not incapacitating	11.4%
IV	patient with a severe systemic disease that is a constant threat to life	10.9%

However its value in stratifying patients for interventions has become widely accepted and serves at least as a preliminary tool comparing outcomes in many systems, including the Regional Health System of some regions of Italy.

Similarly to the ASA classification, The Johns Hopkins (JH) risk classification system grades surgical operations on invasiveness and amount of blood loss :

Johns Hopkins risk classification system

Category 1 Minimally invasive procedure: little or no blood loss. Often done in an office setting. Minimal risk to patient independent from anesthesia.

Category 2 Minimal to moderately invasive procedure.Blood loss<500 ml. Mild risk to patient independent from anesthesia.

Category 3 Moderate to significant invasive procedure.Blood loss potential 500–1500 ml.Moderate risk to patient independent from anesthesia.

Category 4 Highly invasive procedure. Blood loss> 1500 ml.Major risk to patient independent from anesthesia.

Category 5 Highly invasive procedure. Blood loss> 1500 ml. Critical risk to patient independent from anesthesia. Usual postoperative intensive care unit stay with invasive monitoring.

The JH classification suffers of the same shortages as the ASA classification scores;it does not consider patient's comorbidites and potential anesthetic difficulties and is applied beforehand, so that it may differ dramatically with the reality.

Since an assessment of surgical severity constitutes an integral part of any measure of perioperative risk, the integration of patient physical status and surgical severity is of some value[65]

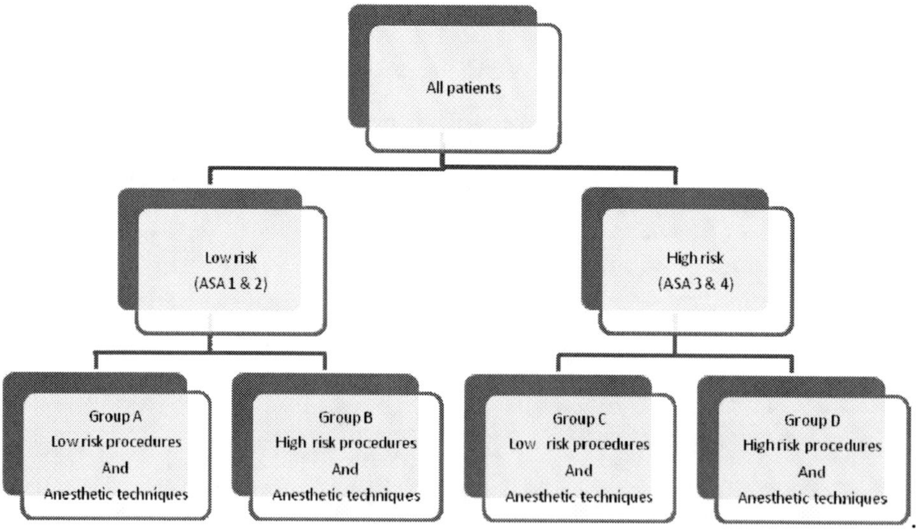

Invasiveness of surgery can be categorized; a table based on time points (T) can be used [66]:

In general surgery, postoperative morbidity rate ranges 15%–40%: these figures are higher among patients at the age of 80 years or more undergoing abdominal surgery, with mortality about 4% [67][68].While the range and types of operation continue to expand and the treatment guidelines for carcinoma change (progressively emphasizing radical treatment, safety and function), postoperative morbidity and mortality may be increasing. At the same time the welfare cost has increased including an escalation in the risk of medico-legal actions and, at least in the western world, this has prompted the medical associations and the national health systems to look for more efficient delivery of care without compromising quality.

Scoring systems are used to objectively assess and quantify the severity of illness, determine prognosis, guide patient monitoring and treatment, and avoid preventable deaths. Ideally, an effective scoring system should also be able to provide useful comparisons between surgeons, surgical units, hospitals and regions.

Operation	T Point (hrs)
Coronary artery bypass graft	5
Bile duct, liver or pancreatic surgery	4
Craniotomy	4
Head and neck surgery	4
Colonic surgery	3
Joint prosthesis surgery	3
Vascular surgery	3
Abdominal or vaginal hysterectomy	2
Ventricular shunt	2
Herniorrhaphy	2
Appendectomy	1
Limb amputation	1
Cesarean section	1

It seems logical that elderly patients with concurrent diseases are more likely to develop perioperative and postoperative complications and we have already shown that concurrent diseases associated with a higher morbidity included cardiac diseases,high blood pressure, coronary disease, chronic lung disease, diabetes hepatic cirrhosis.among others.But to these it is necessary to add the contribution of surgery, because the outcome of the patient depends from the interplay of patients condition, severity of surgery and possible complications from anesthesia.This is the main reason for the inclusion of surgical scores in our analysis.Using the scores we can obtain a numerical estimate of the health status of an individual patient prior to operation, enabling us to adjust the type and duration of operation and determine reasonably individualized intra and postoperative monitoring and treatment so as to decrease morbidity and mortality, especially in aged patients.

The Surgical Apgar Score

[68]collects preoperative risk variables with simple intraoperative events:

- lowest heart rate
- lowest mean arterial pressure
- estimated blood loss

A score built from these 3 predictors has proved strongly predictive of the risk of major postoperative complications and death in general and vascular surgery.

The score was thus developed using these 3 variables, and their beta coefficients were used to weight the points allocated to each variable in a 10-point score.Tthe 10 point Surgical Apgar score is build form the estimated blood loss (0 point > 1000 ml, 1 point for 601–1000, 2 points for 101–600, 3 points <100 ml); lowest mean arterial pressure in mmHG(<= 40, 0 points;40-54, 1 point;55-69, 2 points;=>70 , 3 points); lowest heart rate(bpm)(>85, 0 point; 76–85; 1 point; 66–75; 2 points; 56–65; 3 points; <=55, 4 points).

Graphically:

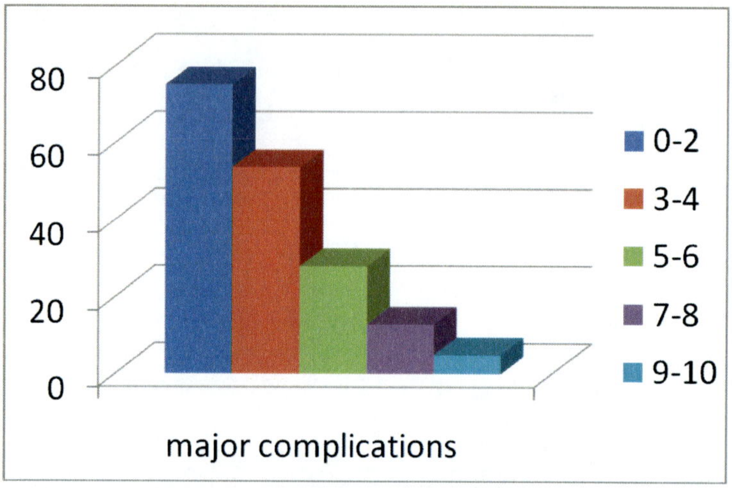

The score is linked with the preoperative conditions since with decreasing scores the cohort of patients appear more often elderly, male, non white with higher ASA scores, underweight and with more laboratory abnormalities, undergoing more complex operations and of emergent nature. The Surgical Apgar Scores were predictive of the postoperative course and the incidence of major complications rose from 5% for patients score 9–10 to 56% for patients score < 4.

Low scored patients were more prone to major complications and longer hospital stays. Complicated patients death probability was almost 20 fold higher if their Apgar scores were among 0–2 in comparison with patients whose score was 9–10.Major complications appeared well correlated with the intraoperative course.

The Surgical Apgar Score also may provide an immediate assessment of how well or poorly the operation has gone for a patient;in this cohort, surgical teams could cut a patient's risk-adjusted odds of major complications nearly in half with a score of 9 –10, or conversely, nearly triple the risk-adjusted odds with scores <4. The finding that simple intraoperative data are critical predictors of postoperative risk, is consistent with a variety of previous observations. Hemodynamic stability [69][70][71][72] and the amount of blood loss during surgery [73][74][75] have long been recognized as important independent factors in patient outcomes. What had not been recognized was the collective importance of these variables, and their potential contribution to an easily-implemented intraoperative performance metric.As an adjunct to surgeons' subjective impressions of the operation, the score may thus aid decision-making about unplanned admission after outpatient surgery, admission to the intensive care unit, or frequency of postoperative examinations by physicians and nurses, with the goal of preventing poor outcomes among low-scoring patients. More broadly, the Surgical Apgar Score provides a novel metric for evaluating the efficacy of safety interventions in the operating room—a much-needed tool for surgical safety initiatives because more than two-thirds of surgical adverse events involve complications in the operating room [76][77][78][79].

Possum Score

[80] has been proposed as a predictive index for complications and auditing since it incorporates the case mix; it is one of the most widely used, accepted and validated scores, its only drawback being a relative complexity since it requires 19 preoperative data, some of whom are not necessarily collected as a part of the clinical routine.

Generally speaking, Possum overestimates mortality in patients with the lowest scores and for these reason many corrections were made as Portsmouth-POSSUM(P-POSSUM) and specific POSSUM for different specialties,like the Vascular-POSSUM,O(rthopedic) Possum,etc.Please keep in mind that some data are not available before the operation;then they can be added and an estimate calculated adding some inaccuracy.

Possum Score.

	Score			
Variable	1	2	4	8
Age, y	≤60	61–70	≥71	NA
Cardiac signs	No failure	Diuretic, digoxin, antianginal, or hypertensive therapy	Peripheral edema; warfarin sodium therapy	Raised jugular venous pressure
Chest radiograph (heart)	NA	NA	Borderline cardiomegaly	Cardiomegaly
Respiratory history	No dyspnea	Dyspnea on exertion	Limiting dyspnea (1 flight)	Dyspnea at rest (rate, ≥30/min)
Chest radiograph (lung)	NA	Mild COPD	Moderate COPD	Fibrosis or consolidation
Mean systolic blood pressure, mm Hg	110–130	131–170 100–109	≥171 90–99	≤89
Pulse, beats/min	50–80	81–100 40–49	101–120	≥121 ≤39
Glasgow coma score	15	12–14	9–11	≤8
Hemoglobin, g/dL	13.0–16.0	11.5–12.9 16.1–17.0	10.0–11.4 17.1–18.0	≤9.9 ≥18.1
White blood cell count, ×10³/μL	4.0–10.0	10.1–20.0 3.1–3.9	≥20.1 ≤3.0	NA
Serum urea, mg/dL	≤21	22–28	29–41	≥42
Serum sodium, mEq/L	≥136	131–135	126–130	≤125
Serum potassium, mEq/L	3.5–5.0	3.2–3.4 5.1–5.3	2.9–3.1 5.4–5.9	≤2.8 ≥6.0
Electrocardiogram	Normal	NA	Atrial fibrillation (rate, 60–90)	Any other abnormal rhythm or ≥5 ectopics/min Q waves or ST/T-wave changes
Operative severity	Minor	Moderate	Major	Major plus
Multiple procedures	1	NA	2	>2
Total blood loss, mL	≤100	101–500	501–999	≥1000
Peritoneal soiling	None	Minor (serous fluid)	Local pus	Free-bowel content, pus, or blood
Presence of malignancy	None	Primary only	Nodal metastases	Distant metastases
Mode of surgery	Elective	NA	Emergency resuscitation within 2 h possible Operation <24 h after admission	Emergency (immediate surgery <2 h needed)

Abbreviations: COPD, chronic obstructive pulmonary disease; NA, not applicable; POSSUM, Physiological and Operative Severity Score for the Enumeration of Mortality and Morbidity.

SI conversion factor: To convert urea to millimoles per liter, multiply by 0.357.

To calculate the scores: R1:Mortality risk: Ln (R1/1 R1) = 7,04 + (0,13 x physiologic score) + (0,16 x operative score).

R2: morbility score: Ln (R2/1 R2) = 5,91 + (0,16 x physiologic score) + (0,19 x operative score).

For the patient shown above R: mortality risk Ln (R1/1 R1) = 7,04 + (0,13 x 21) + (0,16 x 14).=7.04+2.73+2.24=12.01=ln(12.01/1/12.01)=ln 12.01/0.083=ln 144,69=4,97; morbility risk: 5,91 +3,36+2,66=ln (11.93/1/11.93)=ln 142,36=4.95 .

Fortunately you do not need to calculate ;just go to http://www.riskprediction.org.uk/ppindex.php

Physiology Score	Operatorioerative Severity Score	Morbidity (%)	Mortality (%)
21	18	70.475	6.170

On that site you may choose what you prefer among a wide array of other scores!Another site easilyfound is the Societè Francais de Anestesie Reanimation (SFAR) site.

P-POSSUM has better accuracy ;it has shown high discrimination in pancreatic surgery [81]:with a predicted morbidity of 20% with a score =<15,30% with a score between 16-18,40% with a score 9-21,50% with a score 22-24,65-70% with a score >25.

Index	0	1	2	3	4
Age (yr)	< 60	60-69	70-79	⩾ 80	
Circulatory system	Normal Car Fun, BP, ECG	Car fun grade I, mild HP and abnormal ECG, sinoatrial bradycardia/tachycardia, low valtage of limb lead, BBB	Car fun grade II, Mod. HP, well controlled by med, occasional atrial premature beats	Car fun grade III, myocardial infarct < 3 mon, mod HP by med, ectopic, arythm, ST-T change, atrial fibrillation	Serious car, insuf, AHF, mal HP
Respiratory system	Normal	Long history of smoking, CB, asthma, URI, thick pulmonary markings	Mild COPD, mild PF change, mild pneumo	Mod COPD, Mod to serious abnormal PF	Respiratory failure
Liver function	Normal	History of hepatitis/ cirrhosis of liver, TB < 34.2 μmol/L	TB 34.2-51.3 μmol/L	TB > 51.3 μmol/L	
Renal function	Normal	BUN ⩽ 10.1 mmol/L, Cr ⩽ 170 μmol/L	BUN 10.1-15 mmol/L, Cr 170-300 μmol/L	Renal failure need dialysis	
Gastrointestinal tract	Normal	History of chronic gastroenteritis, controlled peptic ulcer	Active gastrointestinal diseases(hemorrhage/ perforation of ulcers, active Crohn's disease	Percutaneous intestinal fistula	Short bowel syndrome, transplantation of small bowels
Blood system	Normal	PLT/WBC decreased mildly, Hb (rectified) > 85 g/L	Hematopathy as stable leukemia, WBC ⩾ 14.5 × 10^9/L	Aplastic anemia, hypersplenism syndrome, leukemia *etc.*	
Endocrine system	Normal	Mild increased BG, UGLu (-), treated hyperthyroidism, hypothyroidism, acromegaly, gout, rheumatoid disease	Mild increased BG, UGLu (+ - + +), and controlled DM, by oral medicine, hormonotherapy, active gout	DM, astable with oral medicine	Diabetic nephropathy
Nutritional Status[2]	Normal	Slight malnutrition (albumin 30-35 g/L, weight decrease < 2.5 Kg/m)	Moderate malnutrition (albumin < 30 g/L, mass decrease 2.5-5 kg/m); Radiotherapy/chemotherapy	Cachexia	
GCS	15	12-14	9-11	⩽ 8	
Operative wound		Mino (OPT < 2 h/ hemorrhage volume < 300 mL)	Mod (OPT 2-4 h/hemorrhage volume 300-500 mL)	Major (OPT > 4 h/hemorrhage volume > 500 mL)/Palliative excision of Mal tumor	M Major[++] (excision > 3 organs) /Mal tumor can't excise
Anesthesia course				Arrhythmia/low BP < 1/2 h	continual low BP/ cardio-pulmonary resuscitation

Nor: Normal; Car: Cardiac; Fun: Function; BP: Blood pressure; HP: Hypertension; BBB: Bundle branch block; ECG: Electrocardiagram; Insuf: Insufficiency; AHF: Acute heart failure; Mod: Moderate; Med: Medicine; Mon: Month; CB: Chronic bronchitis; URI: Upper respiratory infection; PF: Pulmonary function; TB: Total bilirubin; BG: Blood glucose; UGLu: Urine glucose; DM: Diabetes mellitus; OPT: Operation time; Hm: Hemorrhage; Mal: Malignant; GCS: Glasgow coma score
[1]Liver function consul bilirubin in Child-Pough; [2]Nutritional status consider albumin

M POSSUM is a modified Possum score [82] with a slightly different equation and approach,which makes more sense from a general point of view.The significant factors influencing morbility and morbidity are represented by age, physiological functions(cardiovascular,respiratory,hepatic,renal,endocrine),lab results, nutritional status, duration of procedure, amount of blood loss, anesthetic course. Each function is assigned a score with increasing severity from 0 to 4 and their values are introduced into the final equation.

Morbility : lnR/1-R = -7.287 + 0.765M-POSSUM (P –0.000)

Mortality:lnR/1-R = -10.000 + 0.681M-POSSUM (P = 0.000).

Predictive precision is 83.6% for morbility and for mortality 94.1%,

The complete table is presented:

E-Pass

Estimation of Physiologic Ability and Surgical Stress (E-PASS) scoring system [83] contains a pre-operative risk score (PRS) + a surgical stress score (SSS);together they form a comprehensive risk score (CRS), sum of PRS+SSS, i.e.:

1) CRS=PRS+SSS
2) E-PASS=K*CRS
3) The equations are:
4) PRS = -0.0686 + $0.00345X_1 + 0.323X_2 + 0.205X_3 + 0.153X_4 + 0.148X_5 + 0.0666X_6$, where X_1 is age; X_2, the presence (1) or absence (0) of severe heart disease; X_3, the presence (1) or absence (0) of severe pulmonary disease; X_4, the presence (1) or absence (0) of diabetes mellitus; X_5, the performance status index (range, 0-4); and X_6, the American Society of Anesthesiologists' physiological status classification (range, 1-5).

2) SSS = -0.342 + $0.0139X_1 + 0.0392X_2 + 0.352X_3$, where X_1 is blood loss (in grams) divided by body weight (in kilograms); X_2, the operating time (in hours); and X_3, the extent of the skin incision (0 indicates a minor incision for laparoscopic or thoracoscopic surgery, including laparoscopic- or thoracoscopic-assisted surgery; 1, laparotomy or thoracotomy alone; and 2, laparotomy and thoracotomy).

3) CRS = -0.328 + (0.936 x PRS) + (0.976 x SSS).

Table 8. relationship between CRS and mortality, morbidity, hospital stay

CRS category	Mortality		Morbidity		Hospital Stay (d)*
	No.	Rate (95% CI)	No.	Rate (95% CI)	Median (interquartile range)
<.3	0/48	0% (0%–7.4%)	2/48	4.2% (1.2%–14.0%)	8 (7–9)
.3–<.5	0/63	0% (0%–5.7%)	28/63	44.4% (32.8%–56.7%)	9 (8–12)
.5–<1.0	6/76	7.9% (3.7%–16.2%)	74/76	97.4% (9.9%–99.3%)	11 (9–17)
>=1.0	7/17	41.2% (21.6%–64.0%)	17/17	100% (81.6%–100%)	13.5 (11.5–44)

* Calculated among living patients (ie, excluding the 13 patients in the upper 2 CRS categories who died as inpatients).

e.g.,

70 years, Copd, High blood pressure,gastrectomy 5 hours operation, estimated blood loss 800 ml.

- PRS = -0.0686 + 0.00345*70 $_{+}$0.323*0 $_{+}$0.205*1 $_{+}$0.153X_4 $_{+}$0.148*??X_5 $_{+}$0.0666*3, assuming X5=1…
- PRS=3,49
- SSS =0,4345
- CRS = -0.328 + (3,26) + (0,4240).=3,35, i.e. mortality 0-5%,morbility 44%.

The difficulty lies in the integration of this score with the cardiovascular risk score ;in fact the patient described above would have been assigned a mortality risk > 5%.

E-Pass could be better than POSSUM in digestive surgery and has been validated in the estimation of mortality and morbidity for hip prosthetic surgery [84], thoracic surgery [85]and elective aortic surgery [86].

Other simple scoring systems:

- Klotz et al.[87]identified few significant variables:
- ASA status,
- severity of operative procedure
- symptoms of respiratory disease
- Malignancy

Class A:score < 5 low risk of sistemic complications, around 5%;

- Class B:score 5-7 intermediate risk of sistemic complications, 17.9%
- Class C:score 8-10 punti, high risk of sistemic complications, 33.3%

Following retropubic prostatectomy major complications and mortality were associated with ASA class and amount of intraoperative blood loss. [88]

It is clear that the functional status(and not age per se) determines outcome;for a thorough discussion see [89]where the Performance status and Activities of Daily Living classification are connected with postoperative short term morbility,while a low score in the Mini Mental State Examination and a high score in the Geriatric Depression Scale are linked to the postoperative morbidity.These concepts should be studied in detail,but this information might not be collected during the preanesthetic visit nor done by our surgical colleagues….These points however mean that in order to evaluate scientifically the risk for the patient, assessment should be done early, long enough before the admission to the hospital or day surgery center.

Another simple score (The prospective perioperative risk assessment project)[90]utilizes for predictors:ASA physical status, age, surgical stress and a visual analogic scale(VAS) derived from a global risk estimate based on an intuitively appreciated evaluation(experience?),the so called "surgical eye" (RISK-VAS) The score varied from 0 (almost certain to go through procedure with no adverse outcome) to 10 (patient will almost certainly suffer a serious complication). Likewise on the basis of "gut-feeling", surgeons overpredicted morbidity in elective surgery, but underestimated the risk of complications in the emergency setting ; the overall estimate was fair. [91] .

All 4 classification systems were correlated with the incidence of adverse events,but the best was the RISK-VAS;patients scoring > 4 or +presented a 28 fold risk of serious postoperative event vs patients scoring < 4.Predictive value was 10% with RISK-VAS 7 or +. However the low number of cases, low mortality, absence of information about anesthesia render results difficult to interpret.It is interesting to note that the general impression of the anesthesiologist correlated with the results,confirming the role of experience and intuition .

Hermeneit and coll. [92] took another step examining influenceable intraoperative surgical and anesthesiological risk factors with the aim to identify influenceable risk factors for the development of post-operative morbidity applied to laparoscopic colonic resection .The authors were able to show that junior surgeons, change in anesthesia, treatment by an assistant in case of emergencies,intraoperative transfusion, operation lasting more than two hours, higher ASA status, intraoperative bleeding complications, procedures with a lower status of the anesthesiologist were discriminant factors in the incidence of postoperative adverse outcomes. This work raises organizational and ethical dilemmas,because it is true that factors such as overweight, ASA classification or urgency cannot be changed, but surgical factors can, such as a standardisation of the operative technique with reduction of the operating time and careful staunching of bleeding,avoiding a change of the anesthesiologist as well as preferring specialists in patients with higher ASA scores and in emergency cases.

A large restrospective survey conducted in Holland [93]examined 869,483 patients and discovered 807 cases of postanesthetic death(8.8 per 10,000 anesthetics) or coma(0.5 per 10000 anesthestics).within 24 hours Anesthesia management factors that were statistically significantly associated with a decreased risk were: equipment check with protocol and checklist, documentation of the equipment check, a directly available anesthesiologist, no change of anesthesiologist during anesthesia, presence of a full-time working anesthetic nurse, 2 persons present at emergence, reversal of anesthesia (for muscle relaxants and the combination of muscle relaxants and opiates), postoperative pain medication as opposed to no pain medication.

Therefore it is clear and logical that among factors impacting on the outcome of the surgical (medical) patient an important role is played by the general organization of the system and training of the entire staff. Unfortunately these variables are difficult to quantify but they constitute the main reason why every hospital should present its own data about mortality and morbidity with the purpose of auditing and presenting to the prospective patient a reasonable core data upon which he/she can make an informed choice;if not, is an informed consent truly “informed”?. A higher hospital and surgeon case volume has been repeatedly found associated with favorable surgical outcomes :risk-adjusted perioperative mortality and long-term conditional survival worsened as hospital surgical volume decreased for all cancer non metastatic surgery (colon, esophageal, gastric, liver, lung, pancreatic, rectal cancers[94].

Accordingly,I personally favor large institutions with heavy caseload because I am convinced that only having all specialties available in the same institution is a good quality service offered to patients, especially in case of unexpected adverse events .For instance: [95] as far as hepato-pancreatico-biliary surgery is concerned, institutions performing transplants demonstrated a 21% lower mortality in comparison with centers not doing transplants .Surgeons participation in transplants did not seem to count since the vast majority of procedures were done by non transplant surgeons .Operative mortality for cystectomy was also lower in high volume compared to low volume hospitals[96].

AFC score[97] shows that complications depends from 4 parameters :age> 70, neurologic comorbidity,weight loss > 10% within the last 6 months, emergency surgery. All these factors indicate a significant increase in the postoperative mortality following resection for cancer or diverticulitis .

Many publications favor SAPS and/ or APACHE scores for their predictive value;e.g. [98]prefers SAPS II and P Possum in patients with colorectal carcinoma undergoing surgery.

Note that the various systems have been adapted to the different types of surgery .Possum has been customized for Orthopedics(O-Possum) [99]Mortality after a femur neck fracture is higher than the local survival :observed morbility at 30 days 58%.mortality 12% [100]After 1 year the observed mortality was 38% for males(mean age 79), 29% for females(mean age 84). The use of the scoring systems in other institutions different from the parent ones needs adjustments [101];between 9 USA institutions collecting 890 major colonic procedures observed mortality varied between 0.8 and 15.4 %, 2.3 % on average while POSSUM, p-POSSUM,e Cr-POSSUM gave values 10.7 %, 11.2% e 4.9 % respectively Only Cr-POSSUM demonstrated a O/E (observed/estimated) ratio close to unity.

All the above studies emphasize the use of some surgical impact score on outcome. Like the APACHE scoring system in intensive care medicine, however, these scoring systems continue to lack sensitivity, specificity and have positive predictive values of only a few per cent. Although useful for population assessment, outcome scores suitable for application in individuals are still lacking.

Find on line calculations on :Risk prediction in surgery [http://www.riskprediction.org.uk/ppindex.php].

Which patients should be allocated to the ICU before the operation? Which should be sent to the ICU immediately after the operation?

Selected at risk patients [102]were classified on the basis of predefined criteria using POSSUM;among the outcome indexes ICU admission, ASA, oxygen availability, fluidotherapy,length of hospital and ICU stay, postoperative complications and mortality at 28 days were included .Patients admitted to the ICU presented higher values of ASA and Possum,but showed less complications as expected according to Possum equations. The study fails to show which are the patients likely to benefit of the ICU environment because it is not randomized and it is retrospective ;on the other hand it is obvious that selecting the more ill patients and optimizing their status they have a better outcome.

The Modified Early Warning Modified Score(MEWS 9[103]give us some clues about when,as early as possible,send patiens to intensive care after surgery,on the basis of a simple table :

Score	3	2	1	0	1	2	3
Respiratory rate (min^{-1})		≤ 8		9–14	15–20	21–29	> 29
Heart rate (min^{-1})		≤ 40	41–50	51–100	101–110	111–129	> 129
Systolic BP (mmHg)	≤ 70	71–80	81–100	101–199		≥ 200	
Urine output (ml/kg/h)	Nil	< 0.5					
Temperature (°C)		≤ 35	35.1–36	36.1–38	38.1–38.5	≥ 38.6	
Neurological				Alert	Reacting to voice	Reacting to pain	Unresponsive

The scores for each parameter are recorded at the time that observations are taken. If the total is 4 or more then the ward doctor is informed.

If the score is = > 4 the physician on duty is alerted.The index has shown a sesnibility of 75% and a specificity 83%. It is simple enough to offer an objective guide of vital signs to be adopted from unskilled personnel.

Specialized Surgery: Pulmonary Surgery

Max VO2 < 15 ml/kg suggests an increase in morbility following lung surgery [104]; while maximizing the oxygen availability with dobutamine improved prognosis in elderly patients[105] .

Preoperative PaO2 together with the determination of the areas at low intensity on the tridimensional tomography determines the incidence of postoperative hypoxemia following pulmonary surgery [106]Since the radiographs are done before surgery, this risk evaluation seems easy and better than the spirometric tests, which do not possess predictive value before laparotomy [107] but are useful to predict the risk of postoperative respiratory insufficiency or death following pneumonectomy [108].

Genomics and Risk Factors

Genomics is gaining importance in the risk assessment scenario:[109] Pro33 and Met145 genotypes are independ predictors of ischemic events as good as the presence of diabetes,abdominal aortic and thoracoabdominal surgery .They were synergististic improving the fitting of the probability of ischemia equations.The significance of relationship between GPIb[alpha] polymorphism and the ischemic results remained after having removed the ECG signs of ischemia fron the global score .

Postoperative delirium is linked with the apolipoprotein E E4 allele [110];patients having at least a couple of this allele had 28.3% incidence of postoperative delirium vs. 11.1% in patients without this modification.Other covariates important for the identification of patients at risk for postoperative delirium included old age, dependence in 1 or more daily functions,history of CNS disorders,lower diastolic pressure during the first postoperative day, more pain during Ist postoperative day.Which is the relationship between apolipoprotein and postoperative delirium is unknown; since the apolipoproteins modify the lipid transport into the regenerating neurons, mediate proinflammatory cytokines release from the activated microglia, interfere in the metabolism of the proteins precursor of the amyloid,substance involved in neurodegenerative disease like Alzheimer, increase the permeability of the blood brain barrier, alter the platelets function and interfere with the inflammation systematically, one of the hypothesis is that the allele APOE e4 decrease the repair ability in case of cerebral damage or interferes in the homeostatic mechanism .

Psicosomatic Traits

Anxiety does not seem to play a role in the field of noncardiac surgery;instead prospective data after cardiac surgery indicate a worse outcome for anxious patients operated upon valvular and/or coronary surgery. [111].

Laboratory Results

HCT(hematocrit) has shown a 1.6% (95% CI 1.1%-2.2%) mortality increment at 30 days for every deviation in % point from the normal range (39%- 51%.) [112].

Lower immunoglobulin M EndoCAb concentration[113] predicted increased risk of postoperative complication independent of POSSUM physiologic risk score;in contrast, total immunoglobulin M and total immunoglobulin G concentrations did not predict adverse outcome.

Hs CRP, high sensitivity reactive C protein, is inversely related to cardiorespiratory function [114] and has been able to predict the late complications following orthopedic surgery and the prolongation of hospital stay.

Tumor tissue Callicrein levels are important in the prognosis of the exeresis of ovarian tumors. [115].

Hyperuricemia, defined as serum uric acid >0.42 mmol/l for men and >0.36 mmol/l for women in patients undergoing open vascular surgery, was not predictive for perioperative adverse events but was associated with an increased risk of late mortality and major cardiac adverse event . [116]

Brain natriuretic peptide(BNP) levels predicted perioperative events in cardiac patients undergoing noncardiac surgery [117].There was a highly significant difference in the level of BNP for the incidence of cardiac postoperative complications with an optimal cutoff of >165 pg/ml (100% sensitivity, 70% specificity).

How to Improve Patients' Conditions

It is obvious that an aggressive approach toward improving the general health could improve his/her outcome ;this has been shown in patients candidate to peripheral vascular surgery with a [118] invasive haemodynamics tune up through PA catheterization,reducing the afterload,improving inotropy and optimizing the volemic status.Postoperative morbidity and mortality and graft thrombosis were all reduced ;total mortality was 3.4% ;9.5% in controls and 1.5% in the treated patients.

The correction of identified risk factors (malnutrition,encephalopathy,ascites,protrombin time,hypoalbuminemia,hyperbilirubinemia, deranged cardiovascular status) and avoidance of emergency surgery in patients with severe liver disease improves the outcome [119];advanced age was a negative factor.

A team approach with effective and prompt communication among all patient's caregivers is of paramount importance in orthopedic patients.[120] because these patients are most often affected by all sorts of comorbidities and every effort should be spent caring for the patient in its entirety.

Levosimendan infusion started 2 hrs before urgent hip fracture repair in elderly heart failure patients [121] improves haemodynamics, increasing cardiac index and decreasing systemic vascular resistance and B type natriuretic peptide plasma concentration. Similar findings were reported for elective abdominal surgery [122] with a longer follow up ;but surgery was minimally invasive consisting mainly of abdominal hernia repair .The 2 studies did not report complications within 30 days,but included few patients.

Nutritional Status Assessment

The assessment of the nutritional status is important because malnutrition is a recognized risk factor for perioperative morbidity .The Nutrition Risk Screening 2002 score was proposed to identify patients at nutritional risk who may benefit from nutritional support therapy, and has been officially adopted by the European Society of Parenteral and Enteral Nutrition.Schiesser and coll. [123] adopted the score in patients undergoing elective gastrointestinal surgery and were able to correlate the incidence and severity of postoperative complications. to the nutritional risk:complications were 40% in patients at nutritional risk, compared to 15% in patients with a normal score ;the incidence of severe complications was also significantly higher in patients at nutritional risk (54% versus 15%).

The severity of malnutrition is proportional to the level of surgical risk. [124].

Since no single test can accurately determine nutritional status, clinicians must look at several markers.and consider many variables :anthropometric measurements such as weight,height,BMI,mid-arm circumference (cm),triceps skin fold(mm),hand grip strength(kg), and laboratory tests such as serum albumin,prealbumin,transferrin,skin tests for delayed hypersensitivity. These markers can be used to help identify candidates for nutrition support and to follow patients' responses to nutrition .

The Prognostic Nutrition Index [125] combines nutritional markers: serum albumin, serum transferrin, triceps skinfold measurement, and skin tests for delayed hypersensitivity.

To evaluate the nutritional status a thorough history and physical examination are essential ;in this phase the use of simple questionnaires is very helpful,such as the short nutritional assessment questionnaire :did you lose weight unintentionally?Did you experience a decreased appetite over the past month?Did you use supplemental drinks or tube feeding over the past month?For every questions subgroups are created and points assigned from 0 to 3 .Patients who scored 0 or 1 points were classified as well-nourished and did not receive intervention; patients who scored 2 points were classified as moderately malnourished and received nutritional intervention:patients who scored >3 points were classified as severely malnourished and received nutritional intervention and treatment by a dietitian [126] More in depth questions about weight and percentage of weight loss are important,such as how much weight has been lost and in what time.Loss of more than 10% of usual body weight within 6 months is considered severe and is associated with increased morbidity and mortality,as is 7.5% in 3 months, 5% in 1 month,or 2% in 1 week. [127] .Another useful question concerns what is the patient's current weight as a percent of his or her ideal body weight or usual weight. Patients weighing less than 70% of their ideal weight or less than 80% of their usual weight are considered severely malnourished.

Muscle wasting,loss of subcutaneous tissue, and weight loss have been shown to determine rates of infection and antibiotic use and predicted longer hospital stay.[128] .

A simplification of nutritional assessment has based definition on 4 parameters: % weight loss from usual weight, percent IBW, serum albumin level, and inability to eat for $\geq$7 days (actual or predicted) [129]. Weight lost as a percentage of the patient's usual weight is considered mild if $\leq$10%, moderate between 10% and 20%, and severe if $\geq$20%.. Serum albumin levels are considered moderately depressed if < 3.2 g/dL, or severely depressed if < 2.5 g/dL(see also above for hypoalbuminemia). Thus, significantly malnourished patients defined by the parameters of > 10% weight loss and serum albumin level < 2.5 g/dL, with major surgery pending, should be considered for at least 7 days of preoperative nutritional repletion and early postoperative support.

Anesthesia as a Risk Factor?

Anesthesiological career and shifts have shown to have a certain importance [93]. Higher qualifications and overall quality influence morbidity and mortality [92].

Outcome from anesthesia is better when the direction is medical and doubts have been caste on the nurse governance [130]; the anesthesiological team directed by specialists in anesthesia is safer and more cost efficient [131] because mortality and impossibility of rescue were higher when care was not directed by anesthesiologists.

Pain Susceptibility Forecasts

It is possible to foresee postoperative pain? Is is possible to recognize patients who are "pain prone" with some simple test? The aim would be that, having recognized them, we would be prepared to treat them more efficiently, anticipating the suffering. [132] has shown that after cesarean section patients who exhibited a lower pain threshold suffered more pain.The preoperative evaluation was reasonably simple, conducted with the method of electrically induced pain (Pain Matcher). If this observation could be extended to other type of patients, it could be of great practical help.

Predictability of Minor Morbidities

PONV (Postoperative Nausea and Vomiting)

The issue of PONV is very important and has gained even more impact with the tremendous increase in day and ambulatory surgery. As a matter of fact PONV is a limiting factor in the early discharge of ambulatory surgical patients and the leading cause of unanticipated hospital admission.PONV may increase recovery room time, expand nursing care, increase total health care costs, cause high level of patient discomfort, cause high level of patient dissatisfaction, bring in other complications, like increase in pain, hematoma, and wound dehiscence [133] [134].

The risk factors for ponv have been identified and can be classified in groups: non anesthetic, anesthetic, postoperative. Among the factors patients related:

- Age, inversely correlated
- Female sex > male
- Weight: obese> normals
- Previous history of kinetosis
- Previous history of PONV
- Anxiety
- Comorbidities; diabetes(?)
- Surgery: some procedures are more related to ponv than others, particularly procedures on the extraocular muscles(strabismus),gynecological operations,plastic reconstructive surgery, cholecystectomy, middle ear surgery;
- Duration of operation

Anesthetic risk factors include: premedication, gastric, suction, anesthesia choice (inhalation > total intravenous anestesia).

Postoperative risk factors include: pain, dizziness, early deambulation, early oral intake, opioid administration.

Apfel and coll. [135] have proposed a simple scoring scheme presented below:

Risk Factors	Points
Female Gender	1
Non-Smoker	1
History of PONV	1
Postoperative Opioids	1
Sum =	0 ... 4

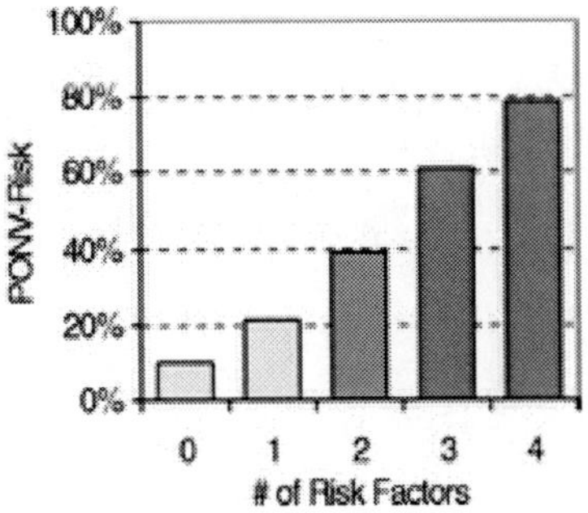

When 0, 1, 2, 3,of the independent risk predictors are present the PONV risk increases respectively from 10% to 20% to 40% to 60% to 80%.

For kids there are minor changes [136] when 0, 1, 2, 3, or 4 of the independent predictors are present the approximate POV risk (postoperative vomiting) is respectively 10%, 30%, 55%, 70%.

Risk Factors	Points
Surgery ≥ 30 min.	1
Age ≥ 3 years	1
Strabismus surgery	1
History of POV or PONV in relatives	1
Sum =	0 . . . 4

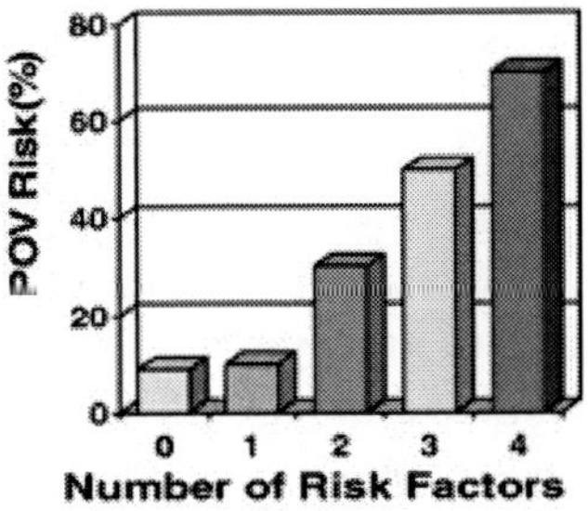

Recently [137] the prognostic value of these simplified models has been questioned and a calculation made by [138] has been proposed. The independent risk factors were:

- Age: for every 10 years increment the probability of PONV decreases by 13% ;
- Gender: male have 1/3 risk compared to females;
- Smoking: 1/3 less risk compared to non smokers;
- History of previous PONV; 3 fold increase in comparison with patients not having had the problem;
- Anesthesia type: general anesthesia increases the risk of PONV 11 times in comparison with other anesthesia types.
- Duration of anesthesia: for every 30 min increase there is a 59% increase in the PONV incidence;

- Surgery type: plastics has a 7 fold increase. Other procedures at risk include; shoulder, ophtalmology, ENT, with 4-6 fold increase .Orthopedics(non shoulder) and gynecological surgery(except D&C)have a 3 fold risk.

The authors compiled a terrible equation P=1/1+e $^{exp\ e}$

Where Exp=-5,97+(-0,14 *age)+(-1,03*sex)+ (-0,42*smoke)+(1,14*PONV history)+(0,46*duration)+(2,36*GA)+(1,48*ENT)+(1,77*ophtalm)+(1,90*plastic)+(1,20 Gynecol non DC)+(1,04 ort.knee)+(1,78*ortshoulder)+(0.94 ort other);

where Age = age in years/10; Sex = 1 if male and 0 if female; Smoke = 1 if smoker and 0 if nonsmoker; PONV History = 1 if previous PONV and 0 if no previous PONV; Duration = duration of surgery in 30-min increments; GA = 1 if general anesthesia and 0 if other type of anesthesia; ENT = 1 if ENT and 0 if other type of surgery; Ophthalm = 1 if ophthalmology and 0 if other type of surgery; Plastic = 1 if plastic surgery and 0 if other type of surgery; GynNonDC = 1 if gynecologic non DandC procedure and 0 if other type of surgery; OrtKnee = 1 if orthopedic procedure involving knee and 0 if other type of surgery; OrtShoulder = 1 if orthopedic procedure involving the shoulder and 0 if other type of surgery; OrtOther = 1 if orthopedic procedure involving neither knee nor shoulder and 0 if other type of surgery.

If you like math or use a computer, this equation is more precise in assessing the PONV probability;otherwise observe the factors recommended by Apfel and proceed according to the most recently published guidelines about prevention and /or treatment of PONV [139].

Predictability of Difficult Spinal

The authors [140]developed a predictive test for difficult spinal on the basis of objective criteria related to the technique: table:

Table 1. Scoring the categories of the difficulty variables. The spinous processes of the lumbar vertebrae were assigned as easy palpable (clear) or difficult to palpate (unclear); spinal bony deformities included kyphosis, scoliosis and lordosis. Difficult radiological characteristics included osteophytes, ligament calcification or narrow intervertebral spaces.

	0	1	2	3
Age (yr)	20–40	41–60	>60	
BMI (kg m^{-2})	<22	22–27	>27–34	>34
Spinal bony landmarks	Clear	Unclear		
Spinal bony deformity	No	Yes		
Radiological characteristics of lumbar vertebrae	Easy	Difficult		

Since bony landmarks and radiological images constitute the independent variables of the difficulty grade and the score 4 is the cutoff point above which difficulties could be expected, with this approach and including the radiological findings, at least 2/3 of patients are correctly stratified .Since the odds of a difficult score are higher than a facility score, this approach is a valid performance descriptor. The application of this scheme allows for the assignment of cases to the different levels of experience of the anesthesiological staff , reducing the number of attempts and improving performances;it also may reduce complications of regional anesthesia, since many depend from the technical performance, in the sense of repeated attempts and ensuing trauma [141].

Hypothermia Predictability in GA

The authors [142] have developed a model represented by an equation:

Z = -15.014 + 0.097 x (Age) + 0.263 x (Height) - 0.323 x (Weight) - 0.055 x (Preoperative systolic blood pressure) - 0.121 x (Preoperative heart rate). Hypothermia probability could be estimated by: = $1/(1 + e^{-Z.})$.Core temperature decreases significantly in patients with P >0.7. Increasing age and height and a decrease in the product (weight * sistolic pressure and heart rate)are able to estimate the occurrence of intraoperatiove hypothermia during major surgery .It has to be noted that these data were obtained from patients kept warm with a underneath 38 ^{0} circulating water mattress, kept covered by surgical drapes and that a heat moisture exchanger was attached to the endotracheal tube.All intravenous fluids were maintained at 37 $^{0.}$

Probability of the Oculo-Cardiac Reflex During Strabismus Surgery in the Child

The oculocardiac reflex is a response characterized but not limited to bradycardia in response to eye compression or extraocular muscle traction, especially related to squint surgery, less frequently evoked during cataract surgery. Because it may be accompanied by significant arrhythmias and respiratory abnormalities [143]and it is not always responsive to anticholinergics like glycopirrolato or atropine, its predictability could offer significant advantages..Linear and non linear analysis of the heart rate variability [144]derived from the RR interval, is correlated with the frequency and severity of the oculocardiac reflex and the ensuing arrhythmias(severe bradycardia,ectopic rythms,etc). PpNN50, rMSSD, from high frequency power analysis, are significantly lower in the group positive for the reflex;the discriminant analysis yelds a predictivity of 72%.

Hemorrhage Predictability During Operations: C Section and Hip Prosthesis

The study [145] has shown as risk factors for hemorrhage, defined as blood loss > 1500 ml or HB < 10 gr or transfusion of 2 or + PRBC during the procedure: the presence of preeclampsia (probability 3.6, 95% , CI 1.8-7.4), disorders of labor activity, (probability 4.4, 95% CI 1.4-13.7), native american race (probability 6.4, 95% CI 1.8-22.4), previous postpartum hemorrhage (probability 8.4, 95% CI 1.9-37.4), obesity > 120 Kg (probability 13.1, 95% CI 1.7-102.7).Combination of 2 or + factors increased risk (18 folds or +).

Predicting the need for allogenic blood transfusion during total joint arthroplasty_[146]is based on a simple score derived from age,gender,weight,Hb,ASA class, surgery revision or not:

Table 2. Clinical prediction Rule for Allogeneic Transfusion in Total Joint Arthroplasty

Variable	Value	Score
Age (yr)	<65	0
	65–79	20
	80+	30
Sex	Male	0
	Female	20
Weight (kg)	≤60	65
	61–70	40
	71–80	25
	81–90	20
	>90	0
Hemoglobin (g/dL)	≤120	140
	121–130	95
	131–140	40
	141–150	35
	>150	0
ASA Classification	I or II	0
	III or greater	15
Revision surgery?	No	0
	Yes	25

Scores for each variable are added together. The predicted risk of allogenic transfusion based on total scores is as follows: total score of 0–100, 10% or less; total score of 100–150, 10%–30%; total score of 150–200, 30%–50%; total score more than 200, >50%.

After having added together the scores for each variable the transfusion risk could be estimated :

score	Transfusion risk %
0-100	10 or less
100-150	10-30
150-200	30-50
>200	>50

Risk of Headache Following Dural Puncture

Incidence of post dural puncture headache (PDPH) depends on the needle caliber, female sex, young age,obstetrics, repeated attempts[147].

Hypotension /Tachycardia Risk

Heart rate variability, espressed in terms of preoperative total power, is able to forecast episodes of bradycardia or hypotension during the operation in patients at high risk [148]: variability and low/high frequency ratio is a prognostic index for hypotension following spinal anesthesia [149]. Since hypotension and bradycardia are associated with the incidence of serious postoperative complications these studies should help in the adoption of preventive measures .

The Supine stress test applied to pregnant women before the operation has allowed the identification of the group at risk of more serious hypotension following spinal anesthesia, so that hypotensive episodes could be reduced with a more aggressive prophylactic therapy [150]; positivity for hypotension during the supine stress test gave 4 folds more hypotensive episodes and 3 folds more vasopressor use in a praevious study too [151].

Age

Almost all studies agree with a risk increase with increasing age; e.g. odds of pulmonary complications is 2.09 fold (95% CI, 1.70–2.58) for ages 60–69 and 3.04 fold (CI, 2.11 to 4.39) for ages 70–79 in comparison with patients < 60 years .Similarly the presence of COPD increases the risk RI 1.79. fold [CI, 1.44–2.22]. [152].However it is not age per se the major determinant of outcome, but the past medical history, prior surgery, site of surgical incision among other factors as outlined in major gynecological surgery at extremes of age [153] [154].

Smoking Cigarettes

Smoking habit has already been quoted many times above; overall the risk of complications increases 1.26 fold (CI, 1.01 to 1.56).

In 2 retrospective studies smokers were found to have three- to six-fold increased risk of intra-operative pulmonary complications [155][156].The infection rate may be attributed to the reduction in immune function as as been suggested in a retrospective study in patients undergoing pulmonary surgery[157].The risk of postoperative pulmonary complications was significantly higher in smokers compared to non smokers [158].

Smoking impairs wound healing after surgery [159][160][161][162]and has been shown to increase the risk of anastomotic leakage after colorectal surgery [163].A recent metaanalysis [164]including trials with significantly reduced preoperative smoking [165]on the effect of smoking cessation on postoperative complication found that studies were rather heterogenous, with a significant reduction in wound-related complications, cardiopulmonary complications and the overall risk of any complication in one trial, and no evidence of a difference in complications in the other. The effect on longer term smoking cessation was not significant in either of the two trials with follow up beyond the perioperative period..Therefore so far direct evidence that reducing or stopping smoking reduces the risk of complications requires more studies .

In any case,because smoking is a factor that can at least be partly corrected, the value of an early patient visit by the anesthesiologist is corroborated.It is always time to improve the patient's bad living habits.

Alcoholism

Drinking alchol increases the risk for postoperative complications and has been included as a covariate in many studies.

Tønnesen and Kehlet [166]have reviewed eight previous reports analysing pre-operative alcoholism and postoperative morbidity. The most frequent complications were infection, followed by bleeding problems and cardiopulmonary insufficiency requiring intensive care, intensive care itself was not analysed.

Heavy male drinkers(72 g/day) had an increased risk of being admitted to ICU, the effect being stronger for week-day drinking A significant association was also seen between week-day drinking and death and frequency of admission to intensive care and inhospital mortalityafter general surgery procedures[167].

However minimizing alcohol consumption prior to elective surgery failed to demonstrate a beneficial effect on post-operative complications[168].

Liver Disease

The preoperative assessment of the patient with liver disease is facilitated by the use of well known classification of Child-Turcotte-Pugh (CTP) score formulated originally as a predictive formula for patients with liver disease undergoing portosystemic surgery but soon adopted in the estimation of risk for both hepatic and nonhepatic surgery for such patients [169]. This score quantifies a patient's status with respect to laboratory parameters(serum albumin level, serum bilirubin level) and clinical observations,like ascites, encephalopathy, nutritional status. The patient is placed in classes: A (good, 4% 3 month mortality), B (intermediate, 14% 3-month mortality), or C (poor, 51% 3-month mortality [170] [171].

Later on Pugh substituted the most subjective factor, nutritional status, and replaced it with prothrombin time and then with INR,a parameter less influenced by local standardization.

parameter	1 point	2 point	3 point
Total bilirubin concentration(micromol/lt)	<34	34-50	>50
Serum albumin concentration(gr/lt)	>35	28-35	<28
INR	<1.7	1.7-2.2	>2.2
Ascites	no	Controlled with therapy	Refractory with therapo
encephalopathy	no	Grade !-II or controlled by therapy	Grade III-IV or uncontrolled by therapy

The score is calculated adding the points for each component and then grading in 3 classes of increasing gravity:A 5-6,B 7-9,C 10-15.A correction is made for patients with chronic cholestatic disease.

CTP classes A, B and C are associated with mortality of 10%, 30–31% and 76–82%, respectively.

The score still relied on subjective assessment of ascites and encephalopathy so that the controversies on its prognostic value produced the Model for End-Stage Liver Disease (MELD) score;this score was initially developed for patients undergoing transjugular intrahepatic portosystemic shunting (TIPS),and calculated from patient's serum bilirubin level, creatinine level, international normalized ratio for prothrombin time, and the cause of liver disease (alcohol induced, cholestatic, viral, or other) [172] .The cause of liver failure was dropped from the MELD score because it proved prognostically insignificant [173].The final version is:

MELD score = (9.6 × loge[creatinine mg/dl]) + (3.8 × loge[bilirubin mg/dl]) + (11.2 × loge[INR]) + 6.4.

The final score is rounded off to the nearest whole number and the maximum score is 40 . For any laboratory values less than 1.0 a value of 1.0 is used. The maximum creatinine concentration is 4.0 mg/dl.

At a Meld score > 8 the postoperative complication rate rose from 10 to 44% following cholecistectomy [174].A Meld score > 14 predicted 77 % of death at 90 days following abdominal surgery [175].

In a study by Northup *et al.* [176] the 30-day mortality from nontransplant surgery in cirrhotic patients increased by 1% for MELD scores between 6 and 20, with an additional 2% per point for scores above 20:the Meld score discriminated well patients who died from survivors(.mean admission MELD score for the patients who died 23.3, 95% CI 19.6-27.0)vs patients surviving beyond 30 days (16.9, CI 15.6-18.2). However it has become clear that mandm depends heavily form the type of operation involved,with abdominal surgery,emergency surgery, cardiac surgery with bypass being the most dangerous.

In summary patients with Child Turcotte Pugh class C cirrhosis and MELD scores >14 represent higher risk and are generally not considered for surgical intervention;patients with Child Turcotte Pugh class B cirrhosis and MELD scores >8-14 have an increased perioperative risk and the indication for surgery should be assessed carefully; patients with Child Turcotte Pugh class A cirrhosis and MELD scores of <or= 8 present acceptable risk with low perioperative mortality .Besides these risk evaluation scores other tests have been validated, particularly those dynamic in nature,like the indocyanine green (ICG) clearance and the monoethylglycinxylid (MEGX) clearance: their use seems promising.

For a more detailed insight into the approach to the liver diseased patient we recommend the algoritm drawn by Hanje and Patel [177].

Obesity

The overall risk of the obese patient is probably more dependent on his/her physical status and /or comorbidities than on increase of BMI per se, since in many large studies the mandm risk has been limited to an increased risk of anastomotic leakage in the field of colorectal surgery [178].This is not to say that obesity does not represent a problem from the anesthetic or surgical point of view, but mandm evaluation of risk is something different,so much so that in a recent metaanalysis on the relationship between BMI and mortality in heart failure, overweight and obesity were associated with lower cardiovascular mortality also after having -adjusted sensitivity analysis so that the authors concluded for a protective effect of obesity against mortality!.[179].Stratifying patients in classes according to BMI, a metanalysis conducted on patients with coronary artery disease defined as history of percutaneous coronary intervention, coronary artery bypass graft, or myocardial infarction, followed up for at least 6 months[180]found that patients with a low body-mass index (BMI) (ie, <20) had an increased relative risk (RR) for total mortality and cardiovascular mortality; overweight (BMI 25-29.9) had the lowest risk for total mortality and cardiovascular mortality compared with those for people with a normal BMI. Obese patients (BMI 30-35) had no increased risk for total mortality or cardiovascular mortality Patients with severe obesity (> or =35) did not have increased total mortality but they had the highest risk for cardiovascular mortality.

Obesity was a risk for wound complication,but not for death or other major complications[181];more importantly the risk of postoperative death was greatest in underweight patients undergoing major intra-abdominal cancer surgery.

In conclusion,it is my personal opinion, at the moment corroborated by a single study [182]that only severe obesity presents a greater risk of perioperative adverse events, without forgetting the technical difficulties of surgical and anesthesiological access to the most important body structures .

Final Considerations

In order to evaluate the usefulness of a scoring system for the assessment of the risk for a patient a few questions must be answered:

Is it accurate?
Is it able to predict the perioperative events?
Could it predict the absence of perioperative adverse events?
Is it able to influence outcome?
Is it able to identify subgroups of patients for which it could be preferable to postpone or cancel surgery?
Is it able to identify subgroups of patients which may benefit from a risk reducing therapy?

One of the major problems utilizing databases resides in the incorporation of variables often not independent, but already dependent from other factors. Also the estimate of mandm in the single patient is still fraught with ample uncertainty. Nothwithstanding these difficulties the experience of surgical outcome registries in adult surgery allowed hospitals to be ranked in terms of unadjusted and risk adjusted outcome performances using the calculation of observed to expected ratios of predicted morbidity [183]. These seminal studies initiated outcome improvements through performances comparisons and were able to stimulate a decrease in surgical mortality and morbidity[184].

The quality programs originated in the Veterans Administration grew up in the National Surgical Quality Improvement Program (NSQIP);this approach demonstrated its superiority over other methods of data collection improving the capture of adverse events in both the hospital and after discharge and was able to feedback its participants so that they could foster quality and safety strategies by means of practice changes [185]. Thanks to the data obtained by the NSQIP the participating hospitals obtained reductions in surgical site infections, wound complications and postoperative urinary infections. It is my hope that with the amount of good data gathered by NSQIP and other quality assessments, the actual practice of risk evaluation could be adjusted to a prospective risk adjusted analysis done in real time and customized for the single patient with a reasonable accuracy.

References

[1] Fleisher LA, Beckman JA, Brown KA, Calkins H, Chaikof E, Fleischmann KE, Freeman WK, Froehlich JB, Kasper EK, Kersten JR, Riegel B, Robb JF, Smith SC, Jr., Jacobs AK, Adams CD, Anderson JL, Antman EM, Faxon DP, Fuster V, Halperin JL, Hiratzka LF, Hunt SA, Lytle BW, Nishimura R, Page RL, Riegel B: ACC/AHA 2006 guideline update on perioperative cardiovascular evaluation for noncardiac surgery: focused update on perioperative beta-blocker therapy: a report of the American College of Cardiology/American Heart Association Task Force on Practice Guidelines (Writing Committee to Update the 2002 Guidelines on Perioperative Cardiovascular Evaluation for Noncardiac Surgery): developed in collaboration with the American Society of Echocardiography, American Society of Nuclear Cardiology, Heart Rhythm Society, Society of Cardiovascular Anesthesiologists, Society for Cardiovascular Angiography and Interventions, and Society for Vascular Medicine and Biology. *Circulation* 2006; 113: 2662-74.

[2] Goldman L et al: Multifactorial index of cardiac risk in noncardiac surgical procedures. *New England Journal of Medicine* 1977;297:845–850.

[3] Murray, P., Whiting, P.,Hutchinson, S. P,Ackroyd, R.,Stoddard, C. J., Billings, C. . Preoperative shuttle walking testing and outcome after oesophagogastrectomy. *British Journal of Anaesthesia*.2007; 99:809-811.

[4] Lee TH, Marcantonio ER, Mangione CM, Thomas EJ, Polanczyk CA, Cook EF, Sugarbaker DJ, Donaldson MC, Poss R, Ho KK, Ludwig LE, Pedan A, Goldman L: Derivation and Prospective Validation of a Simple Index for Prediction of Cardiac Risk of Major Noncardiac Surgery. *Circulation* 1999; 100: 1043-1049.

[5] Weksler N, Klein M, Szendro G, Rozentsveig V, Schily M, Brill S, Tarnoperlski A, Ovadia L, Gurman GM: The dilemma of immediate preoperative hypertension: to treat and operate, or to postpone surgery? *J. Clin. Anesth.* 2003; 15: 179-83.

[6] Howell SJ, Sear YM, Yeates D, Goldacre M, Sear JW, Foëx P. Hypertension, admission blood pressure and perioperative cardiovascular risk. *Anaesthesia* 1996;51:1000-1004.

[7] Welten GM, Schouten O, Hoeks SE, Chonchol M, Vidakovic R, van Domburg RT, Bax JJ, van Sambeek MR, Poldermans D.Long-term prognosis of patients with peripheral arterial disease: a comparison in patients with coronary artery disease. *J. .Am. Coll Cardiol.* 2008 ;51:1588-96.

[8] Poldermans D, Boersma E, Bax JJ, Thomson IR, van de Ven LL, Blankensteijn JD, Baars HF, Yo TI, Trocino G, Vigna C, Roelandt JR, van Urk H The effect of bisoprolol on perioperative mortality and myocardial infarction in high-risk patients undergoing

vascular surgery. Dutch Echocardiographic Cardiac Risk Evaluation Applying Stress Echocardiography Study Group. *NEJM* 1999;341;1789-94.

[9] Beattie WS, Wijeysundera DN, Karkouti K, McCluskey S, Tait G . Does tight heart rate control improve beta-blocker efficacy? An updated analysis of the noncardiac surgical randomized trials. *Anesth. Analg.* 2008;106:1039 –48

[10] Bangalore S, Wetterslev J, Pranesh S, Sawhney S, Gluud C, Messerli FH Perioperative beta blockers in patients having non-cardiac surgery: a meta-analysis. *Lancet.* 2008;372:1962-76.

[11] Wiesbauer F, Schlager O, Domanovits H, Wildner B, Maurer G, Muellner M, Blessberger H, Schillinger M.Perioperative beta-blockers for preventing surgery-related mortality and morbidity: a systematic review and meta-analysis. *Anesth. Analg.* 2007 104:27-41.

[12] Zaugg M, Bestmann L, Wacker J, Lucchinetti E, Boltres A, Schulz C, Hersberger M, Kälin G, Furrer L, Hofer C, Blumenthal S, Müller A, Zollinger A, Spahn DR, Borgeat A Adrenergic receptor genotype but not perioperative bisoprolol therapy may determine cardiovascular outcome in at-risk patients undergoing surgery with spinal block: the Swiss Beta Blocker in Spinal Anesthesia (BBSA) study: a double-blinded, placebo-controlled, multicenter trial with 1-year follow-up. *Anesthesiology.* 2007 ;107:33-44.

[13] Kertai MD, Boersma E, Westerhout CM, Klein J, Van Urk H, Bax JJ, Roelandt JR, Poldermans D.A combination of statins and beta-blockers is independently associated with a reduction in the incidence of perioperative mortality and nonfatal myocardial infarction in patients undergoing abdominal aortic aneurysm surgery. *Eur. J. Vasc. Endovasc. Surg.* 2004 ;28:343-52.

[14] Eagle KA, Berger PB, Calkins H, Chaitman BR, Ewy GA, Fleischmann KE, Fleisher LA, Froehlich JB, Gusberg RJ, Leppo JA, Ryan T, Schlant RC, Winters WL, Jr., Gibbons RJ, Antman EM, Alpert JS,Faxon DP, Fuster V, Gregoratos G, Jacobs AK, Hiratzka LF, Russell RO, Smith SC, Jr.: ACC/AHA guideline update for perioperative cardiovascular evaluation for noncardiac surgery---executive summary a report of the American College of Cardiology/American Heart Association Task Force on Practice Guidelines (Committee to Update the 1996 Guidelines on Perioperative Cardiovascular Evaluation for Noncardiac Surgery). *Circulation* 2002;105: 1257-67.

[15] Franco CD, Goldsmith J, Veith FJ, Ascer E, Wengerter KR, Calligaro KD, Gupta SK.Resting gated pool ejection fraction: a poor predictor of perioperative myocardial infarction in patients undergoing vascular surgery for infrainguinal bypass grafting. *J. Vasc. Surg.* 1989;10:656-61.

[16] Hammill BG,Curtis,LH,Bennett-Guerrior E,O'Connor,CM,Jollis JC,Schulman KA,Hernandez AF.Impact of heart failure on patients undergoing major noncardiac surgery.*Anesthesiology* 2008;108:559-67

[17] Xu-Cai,YO. Brotman DJ. Phillips C O, Michota FA, Tang WHW,. Whinney C M, Panneerselvam A, Hixson ED, Garcia M, Francis GS, Jaffer AK. Outcomes of Patients with Stable Heart Failure Undergoing Elective Noncardiac Surgery.*Mayo Clin. Proc.* 2008;83:280-288.

[18] Hernandez AF, Whellan DJ, Stroud S, Sun JL, O'Connor CM, Jollis JG.Outcomes in heart failure patients after major noncardiac surgery. *J. Am. Coll Cardiol.* 2004;44:1446-1453

[19] Röhrig R, Junger A, Hartmann B, Klasen J, Quinzio L, Jost A, Benson M, Hempelmann G.The incidence and prediction of automatically detected intraoperative cardiovascular events in noncardiac surgery. *Anesth. Analg*. 2004; 98:569-77.

[20] Feringa HH, Karagiannis SE, Vidakovic R, Elhendy A, ten Cate FJ, Noordzij PG, van Domburg RT, Bax JJ, Poldermans D. The prevalence and prognosis of unrecognized myocardial infarction and silent myocardial ischemia in patients undergoing major vascular surgery. *Coron Artery Dis*. 2007;18:571-6.

[21] Yun KH, Jeong MH, Oh SK, Choi JH, Rhee SJ, Park EM, Yoo NJ, Kim NH, Ahn YK, Jeong JW.Preoperative plasma N-terminal pro-brain natriuretic peptide concentration and perioperative cardiovascular risk in elderly patients.*Circ. J.*2008;72:195-9.

[22] Leibowitz D, Planer D, Rott D, Elitzur Y, Chajek-Shaul T, Weiss ATBrain natriuretic peptide levels predict perioperative events in cardiac patients undergoing noncardiac surgery: a prospective study. *Cardiology*. 2008;110:266-70..

[23] Maas R, Dentz L, Schwedhelm E, Thoms W, Kuss O, Hiltmeyer N, Haddad M, Klöss T, Standl T, Böger RH.Elevated plasma concentrations of the endogenous nitric oxide synthase inhibitor asymmetric dimethylarginine predict adverse events in patients undergoing noncardiac surgery. *Crit Care Med*. 2007 ;35:1876-81.

[24] Faraday, Nauder, Martinez, Elizabeth A. Scharpf, Robert B. Kasch-Semenza, Laura ; Dorman, Todd ; Pronovost, Peter J. Perler, Bruce ; Gerstenblith, Gary Bray, Paul F. Fleisher, Lee A. Platelet Gene Polymorphisms and Cardiac Risk Assessment in Vascular Surgical Patients. *Anesthesiology*.2004; 101:1291-1297 .

[25] Gild W,Posner K,Kaplan R,Cheney F. Eye Injuries Associated with Anesthesia A Closed Claims Analysis. *Anesthesiology*. 1992;76:204-208.

[26] Newmann J.Perioperative Visual Loss After Nonocular surgery.*Amer.J.Ophtalmology* 2008,145:604-10.

[27] Copeland LA, Zeber JE, Pugh MJ, Mortensen EM, Restrepo MI, Lawrence VA. Postoperative complications in the seriously mentally ill: a systematic review of the literature. *Ann. Surg*. 2008;248:31-8.

[28] Kalkman CJ.. Perioperative use of psychotropic drugs; advice based on casuistic and 'expert-based medicine. *Ned. Tijdschr. Geneeskd*. 2007;151:342-4.

[29] Huyse FJ, Touw DJ, van Schijndel RS, de Lange JJ, Slaets JP. Psychotropic drugs and the perioperative period: a proposal for a guideline in elective surgery.*Psychosomatics*. 2006;47:8-22.

[30] Dalack GW,Healj DJ,Meadow-Woodruff JH.Nicotine dependence in schizophrenia:clinical phenomena and laboratory findings.*Am.J.Psychiatry* 1998;155:1490-1501.

[31] Ballantyne JC. “Psychiatric disease,chronic pain and substance abuse” chapter 12, pp. 281-301,In: Sweitzer BJ,*Preoperative assessment and management*,Wolters Kluwer-Lippincott William s and Wilkins,IInd edition,2008.

[32] Bateman BT, Schumacher HC, Wang S, Shaefi S, Berman MF.. Perioperative acute ischemic stroke in noncardiac and nonvascular surgery: incidence, risk factors, and outcomes. *Anesthesiology*. 2009 ;110:231-8.

[33] Geerts Wh,Pineo GF,Heit JA.Prevention of venous thromboembolism: the seventh ACCP conference on Antithrombotic and thrombolytic therapy.*Chest* 2004;126: 338s-400.

[34] Rogers SO Jr, Kilaru RK, Hosokawa P, Henderson WG, Zinner MJ, Khuri SF Multivariable predictors of postoperative venous thromboembolic events after general and vascular surgery: results from the patient safety in surgery study. *J Am Coll Surg.* 2007 ;204:1211-21.

[35] van den Berghe G, Wouters P, Weekers F, et al. Intensive insulin therapy in the critically ill patients. *N .Engl. J. Med.* 2001;345:1359–67.

[36] Ouattara A, Lecomte P, Le MY, et al. Poor intraoperative blood glucose control is associated with a worsened hospital outcome after cardiac surgery in diabetic patients. *Anesthesiology*. 2005;103:687–94.

[37] McGirt MJ, Woodworth GF, Brooke BS, et al. Hyperglycemia independently increases the risk of perioperative stroke, myocardial infarction, and death after carotid endarterectomy. *Neurosurgery*. 2006;58:1066–73.

[38] Gandhi GY, Nuttall GA, Abel MD, et al. Intraoperative hyperglycemia and perioperative outcomes in cardiac surgery patients. *Mayo Clin. Proc.*2005;80:862– 6.

[39] Krinsley JS. Association between hyperglycemia and increased hospital mortality in a heterogeneous population of critically ill patients. *Mayo Clin. Proc.* 2003;78:1471– 8.

[40] Finney SJ, Zekveld C, Elia A, Evans TW. Glucose control and mortality in critically ill patients. *JAMA*. 2003;290:2041–7.

[41] Furnary AP, Gao G, Grunkemeier GL, et al. Continuous insulin infusion reduces mortality in patients with diabetes undergoing coronary artery bypass grafting. *J. Thorac. Cardiovasc. Surg.* 2003;125:1007–21.

[42] McAlister FA, Man J, Bistritz L, Amad H, Tandon P. Diabetes and coronary artery bypass surgery: an examination of perioperative glycemic control and outcomes. *Diabetes Care*. 2003;26:1518 –24.

[43] Vriesendorp TM, Morelis QJ, Devries JH, Legemate DA, Hoekstra JB: Early post-operative glucose levels are an independent risk factor for infection after peripheral vascular surgery. A retrospective study. *Eur. J. Vasc. Endovasc. Surg*.2004; 28:520–5

[44] Bilotta F, Spinelli A, Giovannini F, Doronzio A, Delfini R, Rosa G: The effect of intensive insulin therapy on infection rate, vasospasm, neurologic outcome, and mortality in neurointensive care unit after intracranial aneurysm clipping in patients with acute subarachnoid hemorrhage: A randomized prospective pilot trial. *J. Neurosurg. Anesthesiol.* 2007; 19:156–60.

[45] Ramos M, Khalpey Z, Lipsitz S, Steinberg J, Panizales MT, Zinner M, Rogers SO.Relationship of perioperative hyperglycemia and postoperative infections in patients who undergo general and vascular surgery. *Ann. Surg*. 2008;248:585-91.

[46] Pomposelli JJ, Baxter JK, 3rd, Babineau TJ, et al. Early postoperative glucose control predicts nosocomial infection rate in diabetic patients. *J. Parenter Enteral. Nutr.* 1998;22:77–81.

[47] McConnell YJ, Johnson PM, Porter GA.J Gastrointest Surg.. Surgical Site Infections Following Colorectal Surgery in Patients with Diabetes: Association with and Postoperative Hyperglycemia. *J Gastrointest Surg*. 2008 Nov 11. [Epub ahead of print .

[48] Finfer S, Delaney T. Tight Glycemic Control in Critically Ill Adults. *JAMA* 2008;300: 963-64.

[49] Gandhi GY, Murad MH, Flynn DN, Erwin PJ, Cavalcante AB, Bay Nielsen H, Capes SE, Thorlund K, Montori VM, Devereaux PJ.Effect of perioperative insulin infusion on

surgical morbidity and mortality: systematic review and meta-analysis of randomized trials. *Mayo Clin Proc.* 2008 ;83:418-307.

[50] HaffnerSM,Lehto S,Ronnemaa T,Mortality form coronary artery disease in subjects with type 2 diabetes and in non diabetic subjets with and without prior myocardial infarction, *N.Engl.J. Med* 1998;339:229-234.

[51] Warner ME, Contreras MG, Warner MA, Schroeder DR, Munn SR, Maxson PM..Diabetes mellitus and difficult laryngoscopy in renal and pancreatic transplant patients. *Anesth. Analg.* 1998 86:516-9.

[52] Costantini TW, Acosta JA, Hoyt DB, Ramamoorthy S Surgical resident and attending physician attitudes toward glucose control in the surgical patient. *Am. Surg.* 2008;74:993-6.

[53] Arozullah AM, Daley J, Henderson WG, Khuri SF,for the National Veterans Administration Surgical Quality Improvement Program Multifactorial Risk Index for Predicting Postoperative Respiratory Failure in Men After Major Noncardiac Surgery. *Annals of Surgery* 2000 ;232: 242–253.

[54] Arozullah AM, Khuri SF, Henderson WG, Daley J. Development and Validation of a Multifactorial Risk Index for Predicting Postoperative Pneumonia after Major Noncardiac Surgery.*Ann. Intern Med.* 2001;135:847-857.

[55] McAlister FA, Bertsch K, Man J, Bradley J, Jacka M. . Incidence of and risk factors for pulmonary complications after nonthoracic surgery. *Am. J. Respir Crit. Care Med.* 2005;171:514-7.

[56] Jain,S,Dhand R.Perioperative treatment of patients with obstructive sleep apnea. *Curr. Opin. Pulm. Med* .2004;10:482-488.

[57] Chung F, Yegneswaran B, Liao P, Chung SA, Vairavanathan S, IslamS, Khajehdehi A, Shapiro CM. STOP Questionnaire. A Tool to Screen Patients for Obstructive Sleep Apnea .*Anesthesiology* 2008; 108:812–21.

[58] Netzer SC,Stolls RA,Netzer CM.Using the Berlin questionnaire to identify patients at risk for the sleep apnea syndrome.*Ann Intern.Med.* 1999;131:485-491.

[59] Blake DW, Chia PH, Donnan G, Williams DL. Preoperative assessment for obstructive sleep apnoea and the prediction of postoperative respiratory obstruction and hypoxaemia.*Anaesth Intensive Care.* 2008 ;36:379-84.

[60] Gupta RM, Parvizi J, Hanssen AD, Gay PC. Postoperative complications in patients with obstructive sleep apnea syndrome undergoing hip or knee replacement:a case-control study. *Mayo Clin. Proc.* 2001;76:897-905.

[61] Kudsk KATolley EA, DeWitt RC, Janu PG..Preoperative Albumin and Surgical Site Identify Surgical Risk for Major Postoperative Complications. *Journal of Parenteral and Enteral Nutrition* 2003; 27: 1-9.

[62] ASA Physical status . available at http://www.asahq.org/clinical/physicalstatushtm

[63] Vacanti CJ,VanHouten RJ,Hill RC.A statistical analysis of the relationship of physical status to postoperative mortality in 63.388 cases.*Anesth.Analg* 1970;49:654-566.

[64] Qaseem, A Fitterman S,, Rodney Hornbake E, Lawrence VA;. Smetana GW, Weiss K, Owens DK ; for the Clinical Efficacy Assessment Subcommittee of the American College of Physicians Risk Assessment for and Strategies To Reduce Perioperative Pulmonary Complications for Patients Undergoing Noncardiothoracic Surgery: A Guideline from the American College of Physicians.*Annals of Internal Medicine* .2006; 144:575-580 .

[65] Pasternak LR.Risk assessment in ambulatory surgery: challenges and new trends.*Can.J.Anesth*.2004;51:R4.

[66] Preoperative Risk Factors and Surgical Complexity Are More Predictive of Costs than Postoperative Complications: A Case Study Using the National Surgical Quality Improvement Program (NSQIP) Database .*Ann. Surg* .2005;242:463-471.

[67] Unalp HR, Kamer E, Kar H, Bal A, Peskersoy M, Ali Onal M. Urgent abdominal re-explorations. *World J .Emerg. Surg.* 2006; 1: 10.

[68] Martin RC 2nd, Brennan MF, Jaques DP. Quality of complication reporting in the surgical literature. *Ann. Surg.* 2002;235: 803-813.

[69] Regenbogen, Scott E., Lancaster, R, Todd, Lipsitz, Stuart R., Greenberg, Caprice C., Hutter, Matthew M., Gawande, Atul A..Does the Surgical Apgar Score Measure Intraoperative Performance? *Annals of Surgery*. 2008; 248:320-328.

[70] Mauney FM Jr. Ebert PA, Sabiston DC Jr. Postoperative myocardial infarction: a study of predisposing factors, diagnosis and mortality in a high risk group of surgical patients. *Ann. Surg.* 1970;172:497–503.

[71] Monk TG, Saini V, Weldon BC, et al. Anesthetic management and one-year mortality after noncardiac surgery. *Anesth. Analg.* 2005;100:4–10.

[72] Fillinger MP, Surgenor SD, Hartman GS, et al. The association between heart rate and in-hospital mortality after coronary artery bypass graft surgery. *Anesth. Analg.* 2002;95:1483–1488.

[73] Hartmann B, Junger A, Rohrig R, et al. Intra-operative tachycardia and peri-operative outcome. *Langenbecks Arch. Surg.* 2003;388:255–260.

[74] Copeland GP, Jones D, Walters M. POSSUM: a scoring system for surgical audit. *Br. J. Surg.* 1991;78:355–360.

[75] Wolters U, Wolf T, Stutzer H, et al. ASA classification and perioperative variables as predictors of postoperative outcome. *Br. J. Anaesth.* 1996; 77:217–222.

[76] Wolters U, Mannheim S, Wassmer G, et al. What is the value of available risk-scores in predicting postoperative complications after aorto-iliac surgery? A prospective non randomized study. *J. Cardiovasc. Surg* .(Torino). 2006;47:177–185.

[77] Gawande AA, Thomas EJ, Zinner MJ, et al. The incidence and nature of surgical adverse events in Colorado and Utah in 1992. *Surgery*. 1999;126:66 –75.

[78] Gawande AA, Zinner MJ, Studdert DM, et al. Analysis of errors reported by surgeons at three teaching hospitals. *Surgery*. 2003;133:614–621.

[79] Rogers SO Jr, Gawande AA, Kwaan M, et al. Analysis of surgical errors in closed malpractice claims at 4 liability insurers. *Surgery*. 2006;140: 25–33.

[80] Copeland GP, Jones D, Walters,M.POSSUM: a scoring system for surgical audit. *Br. J. Surg*. 1991 ;78:355-60.

[81] Tamijmarane A, Bhati CS, Mirza DF, Bramhall SR, Mayer DA, Wigmore SJ, Buckels JA Application of Portsmouth modification of physiological and operative severity scoring system for enumeration of morbidity and mortality (P-POSSUM) in pancreatic surgery. *World J. Surg. Oncol.* 2008 ;6:39.

[82] Ding LA, Sun LQ, Chen SX, Qu LL, Xie DF. Modified physiological and operative score for the enumeration of mortality and morbidity risk assessment model in general surgery. *World J. Gastroenterol.* 2007; 13: 5090-5095.

[83] Haga Y, Wada Y, Takeuchi H, Kimura O, Furuya T, Sameshima H, Ishikawa M. Estimation of physiologic ability and surgical stress (E-PASS) for a surgical audit in elective digestive surgery. *Surgery*. 2004 ;135:586-94.

[84] Hirose J, Mizuta H, Ide J, Nakamura E, Takada K.E-PASS for Predicting Postoperative Risk with Hip Fracture: A Multicenter Study. *Clin. Orthop. Relat. Res*. 2008 466: 833-41.

[85] Yamashita S, Haga Y, Nemoto E, Nagai S, Ohta M. E-PASS (The Estimation of Physiologic Ability and Surgical Stress) scoring system helps the prediction of postoperative morbidity and mortality in thoracic surgery. *Eur. Surg Res*. 2004;36: 249-55.

[86] Tang T, Walsh SR, Fanshawe TR, Gillard JH, Sadat U, Varty K..Estimation of physiologic ability and surgical stress (E-PASS) as a predictor of immediate outcome after elective abdominal aortic aneurysm surgery, *Am .J. Surg*. 2007 ;194:176-82.

[87] Klotz, H. P.; Candinas, D.; Platz, A.; Horvath, A.; Dindo, D.; Schlumpf, R.; Largiader, F. Preoperative risk assessment in elective general surgery. *British Journal of Surgery* 1996. 83:1788-1791 .

[88] Dillioglugil, Ozdal; Leibman, Bryan D.; Leibman, Neville S.; Kattan, Michael W.; Rosas, Alejandro L.; Scardino, Peter T. Risk Factors for Complications and Morbidity After Radical Retropubic Prostatectomy. *Journal of Urology*.1997 ;157:1760-1767.

[89] Audisio RA, Gennari R, Sunouchi K, Nair HR, Sestini A, Poperatorioe D, West Preoperative assessment of cancer in elderly patients: a pilot study.*Support Cancer Ther*. 2003 ;1:55-60.

[90] Arvidsson S, Ouchterlony J, Sjosted L, Svardsudd K. Predicting postoperative adverse events. Clinical efficiency of four general classification systems. *Acta Anaesthesiol. Scand*. 1996;40:783-791.

[91] Markus PM, Martell J, Leister I. Predicting postoperative morbidity by clinical assessment. *Br. J. Surg*. 2005;92:101–106.

[92] Hermeneit S, Müller M, Terzic A, Rodehorst A, Schamberger M, Böttger T Influenceable surgical and anesthesiological risk factors for the development of cardiac and pulmonary complications in laparoscopic surgery of the colon.*Zentralbl. Chir*. 2008; 133:156-63.

[93] Arbous, M S, Meursing AEE,van Kleef JW, de Lange JJ, Spoormans HHAJM, Touw P,Werner FM, Grobbee DE.; Impact of Anesthesia Management Characteristics on Severe Morbidity and Mortality.*Anesthesiology* 2005;102: 257-268.

[94] Bilimoria KY, Bentrem DJ, Feinglass JM, Stewart AK, Winchester DP, Talamonti MS, Ko CY.Directing surgical quality improvement initiatives: comparison of perioperative mortality and long-term survival for cancer surgery. *J. Clin. Oncol*. 2008 ;26:4626-33.

[95] Csikesz NG, Simons JP, Tseng JF, Shah SASurgical specialization and operative mortality in hepato-pancreatico-biliary (HPB) surgery. *J. Gastrointest Surg*. 2008 12:1534-9.

[96] Hollenbeck BK, Wei Y, Birkmeyer JDVolume, process of care, and operative mortality for cystectomy for bladder cancer. *Urology*. 2007 ;69:871-5.

[97] Alves A, Panis Y, Mantion G, Slim K, Kwiatkowski F, Vicaut E. The AFC score: validation of a 4-item predicting score of postoperative mortality after colorectal resection for cancer or diverticulitis: results of a prospective multicenter study in 1049 patients. *Ann. Surg*. 2007 ;246:91-6.

[98] Can MF, Yagci G, Tufan T, Ozturk E, Zeybek N, Cetiner S.. 5. Can SAPS II predict operative mortality more accurately than POSSUM and P-POSSUM in patients with colorectal carcinoma undergoing resection? *World J. Surg.* 2008; 32:589-9.

[99] Kurita M, Ichioka S, Oshima Y, Harii K.Orthopaedic POSSUM scoring system: an assessment of the risk of debridement in patients with pressure sores. *Scand J Plast Reconstr. Surg. Hand Surg.* 2006;40:214-8.

[100] Young W, Seigne R, Bright S, Gardner M.. Morbidity and mortality following neck of femur fracture using the POSSUM scoring system. *N Z Med. J.* 2006 ;119 (1234):U1986.

[101] Senagore AJ, Warmuth AJ, Delaney CP, Tekkis PP, Fazio VW.POSSUM, p-POSSUM, and Cr-POSSUM: implementation issues in a United States health care system for prediction of outcome for colon cancer resection. *Dis Colon Rectum.* 2004; 47:1435-41.

[102] Curran JE, Grounds RM). Ward versus intensive care management of high-risk surgical patients. *Br. J. Surg.* 1998; 85:956-61.

[103] Gardner-Thorpe J, Love N, Wrightson J, Walsh S, Keeling N.The value of Modified Early Warning Score (MEWS) in surgical in-patients: a prospective observational study.*Ann. R Coll. Surg. Engl.* 2006 ;88:571-5.

[104] Bayram AS, Candan T, Gebitekin C.. Preoperative maximal exercise oxygen consumption test predicts postoperative pulmonary morbidity following major lung resection. *Respirology* 2007;12:505-510.

[105] Lobo, SM. A., Salgado, PF., Castillo VG. T., Borim AA. Polachini, CA., Palchetti, JC., Brienzi, SL. A., de Oliveira, Granville G. Effects of maximizing oxygen delivery on morbidity and mortality in high-risk surgical patients. *Critical Care Medicine* 2000. 28:396-3404.

[106] Kaneda Y, Sudou M, Jinbo M, Li TS, Suga K, Tanaka N, Hamano K. Prediction of hypoxemia after lung resection surgery.Interact *Cardiovasc Thorac Surg.* 2005 4:85-9.

[107] De Nino LA,Lawence VA,Averyt EC.Preoperative spriromety and laparotomy:blowing away dollars.*Chest* 1997;111:1536-41.

[108] Celli BR,MacNee W. Standards for the diagnosis and treatment of patients with COPD: a summary of the ATS/ERS position paper.*Eur.Respir.J.*2004;23:932-946.

[109] Faraday, Nauder ; Martinez, Elizabeth A. ; Scharpf, Robert B., Kasch-Semenza, Laura, Dorman, Todd ; Pronovost, Peter J.; Perler, Bruce ; Gerstenblith, Gary, Bray, Paul F., Fleisher, Lee A. Platelet Gene Polymorphisms and Cardiac Risk Assessment in Vascular Surgical Patients. *Anesthesiology*. 2004; 101:1291-1297.

[110] Leung, JM, Sands LP, Yun Wang, Poon A, Kwok P, Kane JP, Pullinger CR Apolipoprotein E e4 Allele Increases the Risk of Early Postoperative Delirium in Older Patients Undergoing Noncardiac Surgery. *Anesthesiology* 2007; 107:406–11.

[111] Szekely A, Balog, P,, Benko E, Breuer T, Szekely J, Kertai MD., Horkay F, Koper, M S., Thayer JF. .Anxiety Predicts Mortality and Morbidity After Coronary Artery and Valve Surgery-A 4-Year Follow-Up Study. *Psychosomatic Medicine*. r 2007.;69:625-631,

[112] Wu, WC, Schifftner TL, Henderson WG, Eaton CB,Poses RM,Uttley G, Sharma SC, Vezeridis M, Khuri S F, Friedmann PD. Preoperative Hematocrit Levels and Postoperative Outcomes in Older Patients Undergoing Noncardiac Surgery. *JAMA* 2007; 297:2481-2488.

[113] Bennett-Guerrero E, Panah MH., Robin BG, Bodian CA, Winfree WJ, Andres Lewis A., Reich D L.,Mythen MG. . Decreased Endotoxin Immunity Is Associated with Greater Mortality and/or Prolonged Hospitalization after Surgery. *Anesthesiology* 2001;94:992-998.

[114] Ackland GL, Scollay JM, Parks RW, de Beaux I, Mythen MG..Pre-operative high sensitivity C-reactive protein and postoperative outcome in patients undergoing elective orthopaedic surgery. *Anaesthesia*. 2007 ;62:888-94.

[115] Dorn J, Schmitt M, Kates R, Schmalfeldt B, Kiechle M, Scorilas A, Diamandis EP, Harbeck N..Primary tumor levels of human tissue kallikreins affect surgical success and survival in ovarian cancer patients. *Clin. Cancer Res*. 2007 131742-8.

[116] Dunkelgrun M, Welten GM, Goei D, Winkel TA, Schouten O, van Domburg RT, van Gestel YR, Flu WJ, Hoeks SE, Bax JJ, Poldermans D.Association between serum uric acid and perioperative and late cardiovascular outcome in patients with suspected or definite coronary artery disease undergoing elective vascular surgery. *Am. J. Cardiol.* 2008;102:797-801

[117] Leibowitz D, Planer D, Rott D, Elitzur Y, Chajek-Shaul T, Weiss AT.. Brain natriuretic peptide levels predict perioperative events in cardiac patients undergoing noncardiac surgery: a prospective study.*Cardiology*. 2008;110 :266-70.

[118] Berlauk JF,Abrams JH, Gilmour IJ,O'Connor S. Rhiannon,Knighton, D R., Cerra, FB. Preoperative Optimization of Cardiovascular Hemodynamics Improves Outcome in Peripheral Vascular Surgery. *Annals of Surgery*.1991; 214:289-299.

[119] Wiklund, RA. Preoperative preparation of patients with advanced liver disease. Critical surgical illness :preoperative assessment and planning. *Critical Care Medicine*.2004; 32, Supplement:S106-S115,

[120] Bushnell BD, Horton JK, McDonald MF, Robertson PG..Perioperative medical comorbidities in the orthopaedic patient. *J. Am. Acad. Orthop. Surg*. 2008 ;16:216-27.

[121] Ponschab M,Hochmair N,Ghazwinian N,Mueller T,Plochl W.Levosimendan infusion improves haemodynamics in elderly heart failure patients undergoing urgent hip fracture repair.*Eur. J. Anaesthesiol*. 2008;25:627-633

[122] Katsaragakis S, Kapralou A, Markogiannakis H, Kofinas G, Theodoraki EM, Larentzakis A, Menenakos E, Theodorou D.Preoperative levosimendan in heart failure patients undergoing noncardiac surgery. *Neth. J. Med.* 2008 ;66:154-9.

[123] Schiesser M, Müller S, Kirchhoff P, Breitenstein S, Schäfer M, Clavien PA.Assessment of a novel screening score for nutritional risk in predicting complications in gastro-intestinal surgery. *Clin. Nutr*. 2008 ;27:565-70.

[124] Detsky AS, Baker JP, O'Rourke K, et al. Predicting nutrition-associated complications for patients undergoing ga strointestinal surgery. *J.Parenter Enteral. Nutr.* 1987; 11:440–446.

[125] Buzby GP, Mullen JL, Matthews DC.Prognostic nutritional index in gastrointestinal surgery. *Am. J. Surg*. 1980; 139:160–167.

[126] Kruizenga HM, Van Tulder MW, Seidell JC, Thijs A, Ader HJ, Van Bokhorst-de van der Schueren MA.Effectiveness and cost-effectiveness of early screening and treatment of malnourished patients.*Am. J. Clin. Nutr*. 2005;82:1082-9.)

[127] Windsor JA, Hill GL. Weight loss with physiologic impairment: a basic indicator of surgical risk. *Ann Surg* 1988; 207:290–296.

[128] Baker et al7 Baker JP, Detsky AS, Wesson DE, et al. Nutritional assessment. A comparison of clinical judgment and objective measurements. *N Engl.J Med* 1982; 306:969–972.

[129] Stack JA, Babineau TJ, Bistrian BR. Assessment of nutritional status in clinical practice. *Gastroenterologist* 1996; 4:S8-S15

[130] Abenstein JP, Warner MA: Anesthesia providers, patient outcomes, and costs. *Anesth Analg* 82:1273-83, 1996.

[131] Silber JH, Kennedy SK, Even-Shoshan O, Chen W, Koziol LF, Showan AM, Longnecker DE Anesthesiologist direction and patient outcomes. *Anesthesiology* 2000;93:152-163.

[132] Nielsen PR, Nørgaard L, Rasmussen LS, Kehlet H.Prediction of post-operative pain by an electrical pain stimulus. *Acta Anaesthesiol. Scand.* 2007 ;51:582-6.

[133] Macario A, Weinger M,Carney S, Kim A.Which clinical anesthesia outcomes are important to avoid?*Anesth.Analg.*1999;89:652-8.

[134] Jenkins, K.; Grady, D.; Wong, J.; Correa, R.; Armanious, S.Chung, F.Post-operative recovery:day surgery patients' preferences.*Br. J. Anaesth.* 2001; 86:272-274.

[135] Apfel CC, Kranke P, Eberhart LH.Comparison of surgical site and patient's history with a simplified risk score for the prediction of postoperative nausea and vomiting.*Anaesthesia.* 2004 ;59:1078-82.

[136] Eberhart LH, Geldner G, Kranke P, Morin AM, Schäuffelen A, Treiber H, Wulf H .The development and validation of a risk score to predict the probability of postoperative vomiting in pediatric patients. *Anesth. Analg.* 2004;99:1630-7.

[137] Engel JM, Junger A, Hartmann B, Little S, Schnöbel R, Mann V, Jost A, Welters ID, Hempelmann G. ..Performance and customization of 4 prognostic models for postoperative onset of nausea and vomiting in ear, nose, and throat surgery. *J Clin Anesth* .2006 ;18:256-63.

[138] Sinclair DR, Chung F, Mezei G.Can PONV be predicted?*Anesthesiology* 1999;91:109-18.

[139] van den Bosch JE, Kalkman CJ, Vergouwe Y, Van Klei WA, Bonsel GJ, Grobbee DE, Moons KG.Assessing the applicability of scoring systems for predicting postoperative nausea and vomiting. *Anaesthesia.* 2005 ;60:323-31.

[140] Atallah MM, Demian AD. Shorrab AA.Development of a difficulty score for spinal anaesthesia.*Br J Anaesth.* 2004 ;92:354-60.

[141] DeTommaso O, Caporuscio A, Tagariello V. Neurological complications following central neuraxial blocks: are there predictive factors? *Eur J Anaesthesiol* 2002; 19: 705-16.

[142] Kasai T, Hirose M, Yaegashi K, Matsukawa T, Takamata A, Tanaka Y. Preoperative risk factors of intraoperative hypothermia in major surgery under general anesthesia. *Anesth Analg.* 2002 ;95:1381-3.

[143] Blanc VF, Jacob JL, Milot J, Cyrenne L. The oculorespiratory reflex revisited . *Can J Anaesth.* 1988 ;35:468-72.

[144] Kim HS, Kim SD, Kim CS, Yum MK.Prediction of the oculocardiac reflex from pre-operative linear and nonlinear heart rate dynamics in children. *Anaesthesia.* 2000; 55:847-52.

[145] Naef RW 3rd, Chauhan SP, Chevalier SP, Roberts WE, Meydrech EF, Morrison JC. Prediction of hemorrhage at cesarean delivery. *Obstet Gynecol.* 1994 ;83:923-6.

[146] Rashiq S, Shah M, Chow AK, O'Connor PJ, Finegan BAPredicting allogenic blood transfusion use in total joint arthroplasty. *Anesth Analg*. 2004 ;99:1239-44.

[147] Kuczkowski KM.Post-dural puncture headache in the obstetric patient: An old problem. New solutions. *Minerva Anestesiol.* 2004 ;70):823-30 .

[148] Hanss R, Renner J, Ilies C, Moikow L, Buell O, Steinfath M, Scholz J, Bein B.Does heart rate variability predict hypotension and bradycardia after induction of general anaesthesia in high risk cardiovascular patients? *Anaesthesia*. 2008;63:129-35.

[149] Hanss R, Bein B,Weseloh H, Bauer M, Cavus E, Steinfath M, Scholz J, Tonner PH. .Heart rate variability predicts severe hypotension after spinal anesthesia. *Anesthesiology*. 2006;105:1281.

[150] Dahlgren G, Granath F, Wessel H, Irestedt L.. Prediction of hypotension during spinal anesthesia for Cesarean section and its relation to the effect of crystalloid or colloid preload.*Int J Obstet Anesth*. 2007;16:128-34.

[151] Kinsella SM, Norris MC. Advance prediction of hypotension at cesarean delivery under spinal anesthesia. Int J Obstet Anesth. 1996 5:3-7.

[152] Qaseem A, Snow V, Fitterman N, Hornbake ER, Lawrence VA, Smetana GW, Weiss K, Owens DK, Aronson M, Barry P, Casey DE Jr, Cross JT Jr, Fitterman N, Sherif KD, Weiss KB; Clinical Efficacy Assessment Subcommittee of the American College of Physician.Risk Assessment for and Strategies To Reduce Perioperative Pulmonary Complications for Patients Undergoing Noncardiothoracic Surgery: A Guideline from the American College of Physicians *Annals of Internal Medicine* 2006; 144: 575-580.

[153] Mains LM, Magnus M, Finan M.Perioperative morbidity and mortality from major gynecologic surgery in the elderly woman. *J Reprod Med*. 2007 ;52:677-84.

[154] Ben-Ami I, Vaknin Z, Schneider D, Halperin R. Perioperative morbidity and mortality of gynecological oncologic surgery in elderly women.*Int J Gynecol Cancer*. 2006; 16:452-7.

[155] Akrawi W, Benumof JL. A pathophysiological basis for informed preoperative smoking cessation counseling. *Journal of Cardiothoracic and Vascular Anesthesia* 1997;11:629–40.

[156] Schwilk B, Bothner U, Schraag S, Georgieff M. Perioperative respiratoryevents in smokers and non-smokers undergoing general anaesthesia.*Acta Anaesthesiologica Scandinavica* 1997;41:348–55.

[157] NakagawaM, TanakaH, TsukumaH, Kishi Y. Relationship between the duration of the preoperative smoke-free period and the incidence of postoperative pulmonary complications after pulmonary surgery.*Chest* 2001;3:705–10.

[158] Warner MA, Offord KP,Warner ME, Lennon RL, Conover A, Jansson-SchumacherU.Role of preoperative smoking cessation and other factors in postoperative pulmonary complications: a blinded prospective study of coronary artery bypass patients.*Mayo Clinic Proceedings*1989;64:609–16 .

[159] Haverstock BD,Mandracchia VJ. Cigarette smoking and bone healing:implications in foot and ankle surgery. *Journal of Foot and Ankle Surgery* 1998;37:69–74.

[160] Jorgensen LN, Kallehave F, Christensen E, Siana JE, Gottrup F. Less .collagen production in smokers. *Surgery* 1998;123:450–5.

[161] Silverstein P. Smoking and wound healing. *American Journal of Medicine* 1992;93 Suppl 1A:22S–24S.

[162] Sorensen LT, Horby J, Friis E, Pilsgaard B, Jorgensen T. Smoking as a risk factor for wound healing and infection in breast cancer surgery.*European Journal of Surgical Oncology* 2002;28:815–20.

[163] Sorensen LT, Jorgensen T, Kirkeby LT, Skovdal J, Vennits B, Wille-Jorgensen P. Smoking and alcohol abuse are major risk factors for anastomotic leakage in colorectal surgery. *British Journal of Surgery* 1999;86:927–31.

[164] Møller A, Villebro N. Interventions for preoperative smoking cessation (Review), *The Cochrane Collaboration* and published in The Cochrane Library 2008, Issue .1

[165] Moller AM, Villebro N, Pedersen T, Tonnesen H. Effect of preoperative smoking intervention on postoperative complications: A randomised clinical trial. *Lancet* 2002;359:114–7.

[166] Tønnesen, H., Kehlet, H. Preoperative alcoholism and postoperative morbidity. *British Journal of Surgery*.1999, 86, 869–74.

[167] Delgado-Rodríguez M,, Gómez-Ortega A,, MOrtiz, M Palma-Pérez S, Sillero-Arenas M.. Alcohol drinking as a predictor of intensive care and hospital mortality in general surgery: a prospective study.*Addiction* ;2003;98: 611–616.

[168] Shourie, K M,. Conigrave EM. Proude JE, Ward SE, Wutzke PS.,Haber . The effectiveness of a tailored intervention for excessive alcohol consumption prior to elective surgery. *Alcohol and Alcoholism* 2006; 41: 643–649, 2006.

[169] National Institutes of Health. NIH consensus statement on management of hepatitis C. *Hepatology* 2002;19:1– 46

[170] Child CG and Turcotte JG . Surgery and portal hypertension. *Major Probl. Clin. Surg.* 1964;1: 1–85 .

[171] Pugh RN, Murray-Lyon IM, Dawson JL, Pietroni MC, Williams R .Transection of the oesophagus for bleeding oesophageal varices. *Br. J. Surg* .1973; 60:646–64.

[172] Forman L, Lucey M. Predicting the prognosis of chronic liver disease: an evolution from CHILD to MELD. *Hepatology* 2001;33:473–5

[173] Pagliaro L. MELD: the end of Child-Pugh classification? *J Hepatol* 2002;36:141–2.

[174] Perkins L, Jeffries M, Patel T.(Utility of preoperative scores for predicting morbidity after cholecystectomy in patients with cirrhosis. *Clin. Gastroenterol. Hepatol.* 2004;2: 1123–1128.

[175] Befeler AS Palmer DE, Hoffman M, Longo W, Solomon H, Di Bisceglie AM . The safety of intra-abdominal surgery in patients with cirrhosis: Model for End-Stage Liver Disease score is superior to Child–Turcotte–Pugh classification in predicting outcome. *Arch. Surg* . 2005; 140:650–654.

[176] Northup PG, Wanamaker RC, Lee VD, Adams RB, Berg CL . Model for End-Stage Liver Disease (MELD) predicts nontransplant surgical mortality in patients with cirrhosis. *Ann. Surg* .2005; 242: 244–251,

[177] Hanje AJ, Patel T. Preoperative evaluation of patients with liver disease. *Gastroenterology and Hepatology* .2007 ;4:266-276.

[178] Gendall KA, Raniga S, Kennedy R, Frizelle FA.The impact of obesity on outcome after major colorectal surgery.*Dis. Colon. Rectum*. 2007 ;50:2223-37.

[179] Oreopoulos A, Padwal R, Kalantar-Zadeh K, Fonarow GC, Norris CM, McAlister FA. Body mass index and mortality in heart failure: a meta-analysis. *Am. Heart. J.* 2008; 156:13-22.

[180] Romero-Corral A, Montori VM, Somers VK, Korinek J, Thomas RJ, Allison TG, Mookadam F, Lopez-Jimenez FAssociation of bodyweight with total mortality and with cardiovascular events in coronary artery disease: a systematic review of cohort studies. *Lancet.* 2006;368 :666-78.

[181] Mullen JT, Davenport DL, Hutter MM, Hosokawa PW, Henderson WG, Khuri SF, Moorman DW Impact of body mass index on perioperative outcomes in patients undergoing major intra-abdominal cancer surgery. *Ann Surg Oncol.* 2008 15:2164-72.

[182] Davenport DL, Xenos ES, Hosokawa P, Radford J, Henderson WG, Endean ED.The influence of body mass index obesity status on vascular surgery 30-day morbidity and mortality. *J. Vasc. Surg.* 2009;49:140-7.

[183] Khuri S, Daley J, Henderson W, et al. Risk adjustment of the postoperative mortality rate for the comparative assessment of the quality of surgical care:results of the national Veterans Affairs Surgical Risk Study. *J. Am. Coll. Surg.* 1997; 185:315–327.

[184] Daley J, Khuri SF, Henderson W, et al. Risk adjustment of the postoperative morbidity rate for the comparative assessment of the quality of surgical care:results of the National Veterans Affairs Surgical Risk Study. *J Am Coll Surg* 1997; 85:328–340.

[185] Rowell KS, Turrentine FE, Hutter MM, et al. Use of National Surgical Quality Improvement Program data as a catalyst for quality improvement. *J. Am. Coll.Surg.* 2007; 204:1293–1300.

In: Risk Management
Editors: B. Jordão and E. Sousa, pp. 55-87
ISBN: 978-1-60876-011-4

Chapter 2

DIRECTIONS FOR AN ERP RISK MANAGEMENT METHODOLOGY: RESULTS FROM A LITERATURE REVIEW

Davide Aloini, Riccardo Dulmin and Valeria Mininno
Electric Systems and Automation Department, University of Pisa,
Via Diotisalvi 2, Pisa, Italy 56126, Italy

Abstract

Enterprise Resource Planning (ERP) systems are extremely complex information systems, whose implementation is often unsuccessful. In recent years these systems have received much attention both from academic literature and practitioners, so that various methods were proposed to try improving success rate of ERP introduction or implementation efficiency.

However, ERP projects still continue to be considered complex and risky to implement in business enterprises. A possible explanation for high ERP project failure rate is that managers do not take prudent measures to assess and manage risks involved in these projects (Wei et al., 2005).

In literature few authors promoted a structured risk management approaches in facing this kind of projects, but dealing with risk management for Enterprise Resource Planning (ERP) introduction projects is a difficult task, so that an effective and efficient risk management methodology is still a wish.

The scope of the present chapter is to discuss the main challenges, opportunities and shortcomings related to the development of a risk management methodology for Enterprise Resource Planning (ERP) projects.

In this aim, the structure of the chapter is the following one:

- *Introduction* - It presents a general description of the ERP systems, risk management perspective, its peculiarities in ERP introduction projects and specifies main objectives of the chapter.
- *ERP risk management framework* - It reports the authors' perspective on the issues, introducing and discussing around an ERP Risk Management Framework driving the next stages of the review.
- *ERP risk management review* - It reports the review results comparing specific methodological works on ERP risk management. The identified contributions are described and analyzed according to the previous presented risk management framework.

- *Discussion* - The paragraph discusses main evidence from the critical review of the literature, analyzing main gaps and shortcomings in the field and suggesting future directions.
- *Conclusion* - It resumes the discussions about the overall coverage of the topic, utility for managers and researchers and main open issues.

Introduction

IT (or IS – Information Systems) projects may be considered an interesting area for action and potential development of risk management practice. Risk management is a relatively new trend in this field (Sauer, 1999; Lyytinen and Ropponen, 2000), and, with the growing complexity of systems and the fast pace of technology change, the expected utility and relevance of this topic is continuously growing.

This chapter, in particular, focuses the attention towards a specific class of IS enterprise projects: the introduction of Enterprise Resource Planning (ERP) systems. They are accepted to be one of the most important developments in the world of Information Technology (IT) and are also the most popular standard business software of the last decade (Davenport, 1998; Robey, Ross and Boudreau, 2002).

ERP Systems

ERP systems are sets of integrated applications that can provide a total solution to the informative needs of an organization by addressing a large proportion of business functions including financial, accounting, human resources, supply chain and customer information.

The Eleventh Edition of the APICS Dictionary (Blackstone and Cox, 2005, p. 38) defines ERP as a "framework for organizing, defining, and standardizing the business processes necessary to effectively plan and control an organization so that the organization can use its internal knowledge to seek external advantages".

Although components of the main ERP solutions are at the highest level organized in different functional modules like financial accounting or sales, they all follow a process-oriented view of enterprises. ERP modules are integrated through a set of common definitions and a shared database. When data, such as an order from the customer, becomes available at one point in the business, the impact of this information is immediately reflected in all other areas, such as accounting, production scheduling, purchasing, and logistics. In other words, they bridge the information gap across the organization, synchronizing inter-dependent processes and help in eliminating most of the business problems related to errors in data entry and batch data processing. Finally, they support companies in laying down Decision Support Systems (DSS), Management Information System (MIS), Reporting, Data Mining and Early Warning Systems to the organization.

Reason for Adopting

There are some major reasons why companies undertake ERP.

1) *Integrate financial information*—As the CEO tries to understand the company's overall performance, he may find many different figures. Finance has its own set of revenue numbers, sales has another version, and the different business units may each have their own version of how much they contributed to revenues. ERP creates a single version of the truth that cannot be questioned because everyone is using the same system.
2) *Integrate customer order information*—ERP systems can become the place where the customer order lives from the time a customer service representative receives it until the loading dock ships the merchandise and finance sends an invoice. By having this information in one software system, rather than scattered among many different systems that can't communicate real time with one another, companies can keep track of orders more easily, and coordinate manufacturing, inventory and shipping among many different locations at the same time.
3) *Standardize and speed up manufacturing processes*—Manufacturing companies often find that multiple business units across the company make the same widget using different methods and computer systems. ERP systems come with standard methods for automating some of the steps of a manufacturing process. Standardizing those processes and using a single, integrated computer system can save time, increase productivity and reduce head count.
4) *Reduce inventory*—ERP helps the manufacturing process flow more smoothly, and it improves visibility of the order fulfillment process inside the company. That can lead to reduced inventories of the stuff used to make products (work-in-progress inventory), and it can help users better plan deliveries to customers, reducing the finished good inventory at the warehouses and shipping docks.
5) *Standardize HR information*—Especially in companies with multiple business units, HR may not have a unified, simple method for tracking employees' time and communicating with them about benefits and services. ERP can fix that.

ERP Project

Before going on and explaining the expected utility of a risk management approach to support the ERP system introduction, it is useful to clarify the meaning of ERP implementation and to describe the several phases through an organization moves dealing with an ERP project.

In a broad sense, implementation refers to all that must be done by a specific organization for it to be able to harness the capabilities of a particular information technology as envisioned (Sarker, 2000). Implementation essentially refers to anticipating and strategically managing the impacts of the change of the technology component (Robey, 1987) so that the IS becomes "organizationally valid" (Schultz and Slevin, 1975; Markus and Robey, 1983) as the organization comes to a post-implementation steady-state.

Researchers have described ERP life cycle using different, sometimes incomplete or overlapping models according to the target application. Some of them are characterized by few general phases, like the three stage model of Deloitte Consulting's (1998) (pre-implementation, implementation and post-implementation), while others are more analytic having five or more phases, such as Markus and Tanis (2000) (four stages model), Ross and Vitale (2000) (five stages model) or Rajagopal (2002) (six stages model).

In this section, the five-phase Implementation roadmap of SAP ERP is used to model the project life cycle (figure 1).

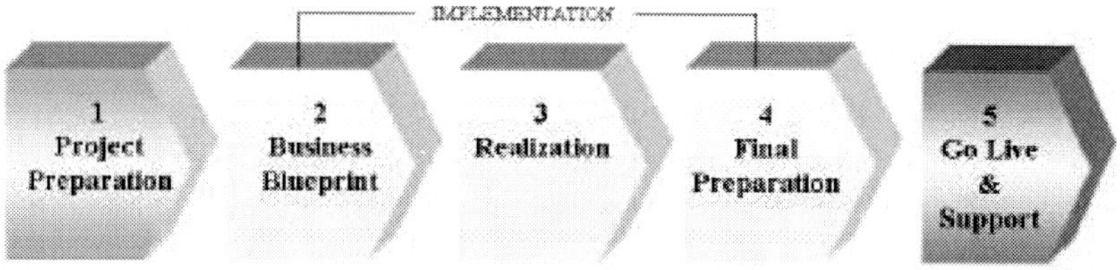

Figure 1. Project life cycle (SAP Implementation Roadmap).

In the *"Project Preparation"* phase main decisions regard project approval and funding. Goals, objectives and scope (what the ERP is to accomplish) of the project must be carefully defined. Typical tasks include: organizing the project team, selecting the package - hardware and database vendors, identifying and prioritizing the business process, communicating the objectives and impacts of the new system, evaluating the investment and fixing the budget, starting a risk management process and the preliminary activities of risk assessment and treatment. Defining the project's scope, for example, is a vital issue since a typical problem is the "scope creep", i.e an unplanned expansion of the project's goals and objectives. Scope creep causes the project go over time and budget, and increases the risk of unsuccessful implementation (Monk and Wagner, 2009). Key actors are IT specialists, line of business managers (cross-functional competences are required), ERP systems vendor and integrators, consultants.

The main objective of the *"Business Blueprint"* phase is to develop a detailed documentation about how the business processes have to be managed and supported by the enterprise system. Typical tasks include: the development of a detailed project plan, the definition of Key Users (KUs), the education of KUs and project team, the acquisition of supporting skills, the detailed process mapping (AS IS) and the definition of process reengineering needs (TO BE according to the procedures incorporated in the system, gap analysis and action plan to solve variances), the identification of the legacy systems treatment (elimination, integration, method of data retrieval, clean up and transfer to the ERP database). In this phase, as well as in the previous one, the Risk Management Process is central and risk management activities (such as risk identification, analysis, quantification and treatment, see next sections for further details) should be formalized through the project. Key actors are organizational cross-functional managers, project team, vendor, consultants, system integrators and business analysts.

The *"Realization"* phase covers the core activities to get the system up and running, through its configuration and hardware – network connection, actual reengineering of processes, execution of change management plan (if any). Typical tasks, besides configuration, are system integration, data clean up and conversion, education of KUs - IT staff - executive, development of standard prototype without detailed interfaces and reports. In this phase Risk Management activities involve the identification and development of risk response actions and the monitoring and control processes (further details will be provided in the next sections). Key actors are the same of the previous phase plus end users which begin their training.

The *"Final Preparation"* phase encompasses critical tasks as the system throughput testing for critical business processes (determining whether it can handle the volume of transactions), prototype completion with reports and interfaces, users enablement and final training, setting the Help Desk where end users can get support, bugs – fixing, final tuning and optimization of data and parameters, ending the data migration from legacy systems, setting the Go Live date. Key actors are the same of the previous phase. It is in this phase, for example, that the scope creep problem becomes usually evident. The team begins to miss deadlines and the costs to exceed the budget; moreover, at this time, the management can only plan marginal corrections to the problem, as most of the time and budget have been spent (Monk and Wagner, 2009).

The final phase of *"Go Live and Support"* starts from Go Live and ends when "normal operations", with processes fully supported and without any external support, have been achieved. Most of end users problems arise during the first few weeks; so monitoring the system is critical in order to quickly arrange changes if the performance are not satisfactory. Typical tasks are: supporting the Help Desk by project team skills, final bug fixing and rework, monitoring the operative performances of the new system, adding capacity. Key actors are: IT specialists and members of the project team staffed to Help Desk, operations managers, external technical support personal.

Importance, Complexity and Risk

Marcus and Tanis (2000) resume the several reasons why ERP systems are an important topic for IS research:

- *Financial Costs and Risks.* First of all installing an enterprise system is an expensive and risky adventure. The investment is in both software itself and in related services such as consulting, training and system integration. Large companies have been spending hundreds of million dollars to make the technical and business changes associated with enterprise systems. Consequently, successful deployment and use of ERP systems are critical to organizational performance and survival (Markus et al., 2000b). This increases the overall impact and risk of a project failure. Furthermore, the return on investment provided by an ERP can be difficult to estimate because some benefits are "intangible" - there is not a direct correlation between the system functionality/benefit and the firm functionality - and low quantifiable (i.e. "more availability of information"). Also, some changes take place over such a long period of time that they are difficult to track because of other business factors that may affect the company's costs and revenues, making it difficult to isolate the impact of the ERP system alone.
- *Technical Issues.* Enterprise systems are technically challenging. Among the more important technical areas of research around enterprise systems are the "development" life cycle for enterprise system packages; software selection approaches; enterprise modeling and software configuration tools and techniques.

- *Managerial Issues.* Enterprise system projects are managerially challenging since they may involve parties from many different organizations and cut across the political structures of the organization. Furthermore, enterprise systems have important implications for how companies should organize and manage their information systems functions.
- *IT Adoption, Use, and Impacts.* These systems have large potential impacts at different levels of analysis: individual and societal (employment, occupational structure, skills required, and quality of work), work system (cooperation, business process efficiency), organizational (competitive advantage, business results), and inter-organizational (impact on supply chain, industry structure). The existing environmental mix between what is done manually and what is done by the system will swing dramatically after implementation; many more tasks can be automated and automation will significantly reduce the flexibility of how the company operate in the business. Data integrity, for example, becomes critical since the computer cannot make human judgments. ERP systems tend to replace old systems and this happens at a Technical level as well as a Business Level. New ways of operating need to be learnt in short time. However, if appropriately managed, this can lead to high cost savings.
- *Integration.* Enterprise systems promise "seamless integration of all the information flowing through a company—financial and accounting information, human resource information, supply chain information, and customer information" (Davenport, 1998, p. 121). However, it is extremely important to note that achieving this integration depends on "configuring" (setting up) the system in particular ways. The word "Enterprise" in ERP means that whatever happens in one area has a ripple effect in other areas, but understanding the implications of actions of one area, on other areas of the company, is not something that happens overnight. Training tends to focus on how do I do my job and it should also focus on what are the impacts of my job in other areas.

Relevance of ERP Project Risk Management

Evidence shows that implementation difficulties still affect complex IT projects like ERP introduction (Champy and Hammer, 1993; Hammer, 1999). According to the estimation of the Standish Group International (SGI), 90 percent SAP R/3 ERP projects run late (Baki and Cakar, 2005); an other SGI study on 7400 IT project confirm that 34 percent were late or over budget, 31 percent were abandoned, scaled or modified, and only 24 percent were completed on time and on budget. A possible explanation for high ERP project failure rate is that managers do not take appropriate measures to assess and manage risks involved in these projects (Wei et al., 2005). In this field a gap in scientific literature yet exists (Aloini et al., 2007).

In particular, the OTR Group (1992) found that only 30% of organisations applied risk analysis in their IT investment and project management processes. Likewise, Willcocks (1996) found organisations undertook little formal risk analysis, except when undertaking financial calculations. In this perspective, it is prudent for organisations to improve their ability to manage their IT risks so that projects can be successfully delivered (Gobeli et al., 1998; Willcocks and Graeser, 2001; Jiang and Klein, 2001; Hartman and Ashrafi, 2002).

According to literature (Ward and Chapman, 2003), risk management can lead to a range of project and organizational benefits including:

- identification of favourable alternative courses of action;
- increasing confidence in achieving project objectives;
- improving chances of success;
- reducing surprises;
- more precise estimates (through reduced uncertainty);
- reducing duplication of effort (through team awareness of risk control actions).

Final Remarks

In conclusion, it could be argued that different factors, concerning different categories of problems, impact on the successful implementation of ERP systems, according to several distinct but complementary perspective of analysis.

Enterprise-wide/ERP projects are among the most critical IS project and pose new opportunities and significant challenges in risk management field.

Without question, effective management of these large IT projects is a new and unique challenge which requires the use of project management and control methods that have not been extensively used in the past. The sheer size of these projects requires centralized control, strict discipline and extensive monitoring of project outcomes.

So, in this field risk management should be more than a process or methodology, but a real-time threat management capability that is developed within an organization, through learning, practice and other mechanisms, over a long period of time, to apply in complex IT projects. It is not just about identifying and assessing risks, and putting in place mitigation and contingency strategies; it is also about being able to quickly and effectively respond to realized threats as they arise. Threats, in fact, may or may not have been foreseen, but they have the capability to significantly impact the project and its outcomes.

Research Relevance

The importance of a risk management approach in ERP projects is recognized both in theory and in business practice. In an extended review of the literature, Aloini et al. (2007) analyzed and classified a number of key contributions about ERP introduction projects in order to define the main issues and research approaches taken, and to identify which areas needed ERP risk management deployment and most relevant risk factors assessed. Authors underpin that, despite of the great importance reserved by literature for factors tied up to project management, including risk management, and change management areas, only a few articles dealt explicitly with these topics.

This chapter presents an useful roadmap of the literature assessing the current state of the art on project risk management as regard to ERP introduction projects (figure 2). Authors, in particular, identify and analyze relevant contributions proposing risk management approaches supporting ERP introduction.

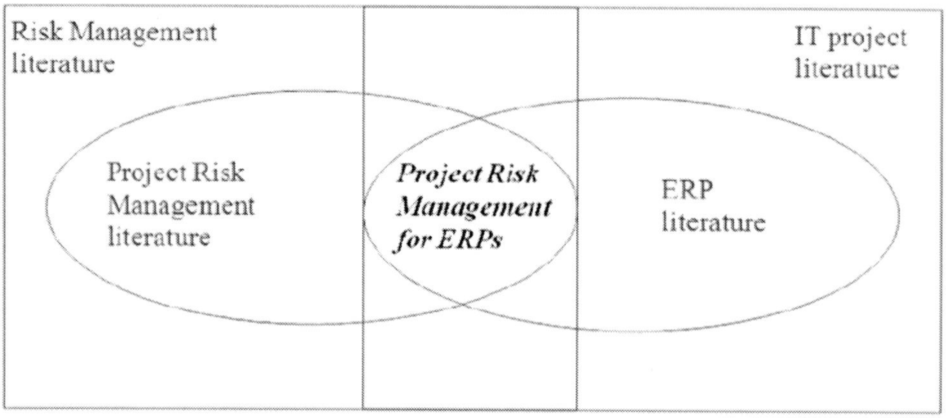

Figure 2. Literature review map.

Thus, the main objectives of the chapter are:

- to discuss relevant and recent developments in a new emerging topic in Risk Management field (Risk Management and ERP systems introduction);
- to present results from a literature review around ERP risk management methodologies addressing dimensions and issues for future directions.

The current body of literature in ERP Risk Management field is analyzed according to a specific Risk Management framework showing more and less explored areas, current gaps and open issues.

Risk Management Framework

Frameworks provide a guide for the development of the best practice and formality is desirable because it provides structure and discipline, which efficient facilitates an effective risk management making sure the right questions get asked and answered, making sure everyone understands the answers and help people to develop the right answers (Chapman and Ward, 2003).

Numerous Risk Management research projects are concurrently ongoing in this field and different framework proposals are available in literature. Some of the most established RMP (Risk Management Planning) frameworks are outlined in the PRAM Guide (Simon et al., 1997), the PMBOK Guide (PMI, 2000), the RAMP Guide (Simon, 1998; see also Lewin, 2002), Australian Standard (1999) and SHAMPU (Shape, Harness, And Manage Project Uncertainty) process (Chapman and Ward, 2003), PRINCE2 manual (Bentley, 2002) and SAFE approach (Meli, 1998). These are useful representative samples of alternative of generic Risk Management Process frameworks. Each approach tries to systematize, in an overall framework, risk management processes, establishing a taxonomy about risk, uncertainty and risk management and finally offering a compendium of useful techniques (both qualitative and quantitative) to be used during the different stages of the Risk Management process. Comparing these generally accepted approaches, however, not homogeneous and overlapping activities often emerge since they are adapted to different views and needs. In this section we present our proposal for an ERP risk management framework which tries to homogenize discrepancies revealed in the existing literature. The framework will be adopted as a guide for the next research stages. As follows, we first propose our definitions of Risk, Risk assessment and Risk management which will clarify the suggested approach dealing with risk during the introduction of enterprise resource planning systems.

Definition 1: Risk is an uncertain event or condition that, if it occurs, has a positive or negative effect on a project objectives.

Definition 2: Risk assessment is the process of quantitatively or qualitatively assessing risks. It involves an estimation of both the uncertainty of the risk and of its impact.

Definition 3: Risk management is the practice of using risk assessment to devise management strategies and deal with risk in an effective and efficient way.

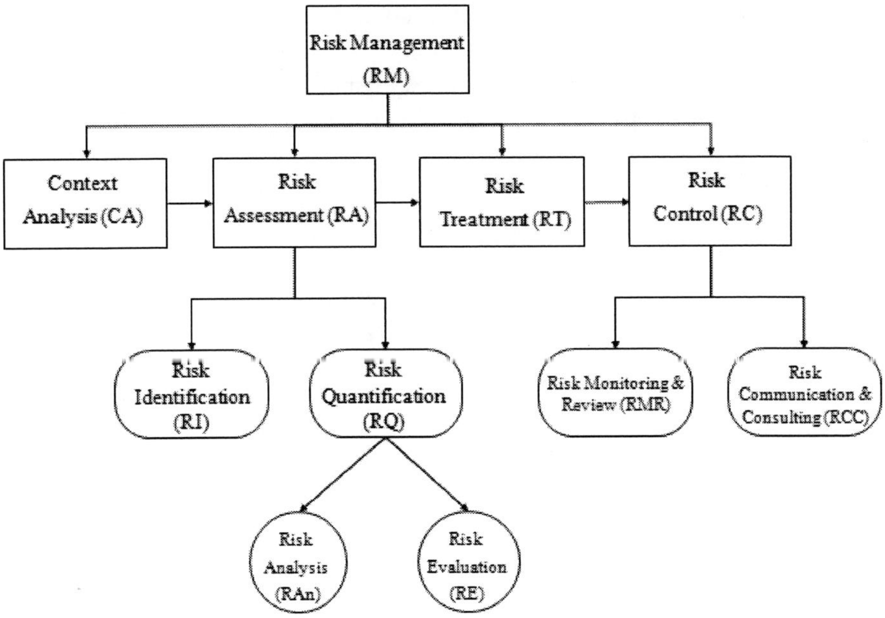

Figure 3. A schematic view of a general Risk management process.

According to this perspective, a general risk management framework can be drawn for ERP projects. It consists of 7 basic activities and 4 main stages, as figure 3 shows.

i) *Context analysis* – aims to define the boundaries of the risk management process: which processes have to be analyzed, the desired outputs, the expected performance etc., in order to support the definition of a correct risk model approach.

ii) *Risk assessment* – is a core step of the risk management process and includes:

a) *Risk identification* – which allows the organization to early determine potential threats (internal and external risk factors) and their impact (effects) on the project success.
b) *Risk quantification* – which aims to prioritize risk factors according to their risk levels and consists of two main phases:

- *Risk analysis (or estimation)* – provides inputs to the risk evaluation phases for the final quantification. The typical inputs are: the occurrence probability of a risk factor, the links (weight) with potential effects, the severity of these effects and the detection difficulty if needed.
- *Risk evaluation* – which defines risk classes. It selects an appropriate and effective risk aggregation algorithm and synthesizes the risk level for each identified risk factor.

iii) *Risk treatment* – targets toward the selection of an effective strategy to manage the risks related to the different risk classes identified. Risk management strategies consist of four classic approaches: the first aims to reduce risky circumstances, the second deals with risk treatment after a risk factor appears, while the third and fourth deal to risk externalization or acceptation.
iv) *Risk Control* – the final aim of risk management is managing project risk in order to perform a better control on the project and increase its probability of success. The principal issues of the risk control phase are:

a) *Monitoring and Review* – each step of risk management process is a convenient milestone for reporting, reviewing and action taking.
b) *Communication and Consulting* – aims to effectively communicate hazard to the project managers and the people involved into the project in order to support the managerial actions.

Background and Methodology

This work deepens results from a previous review (Aloini et al., 2007) in which authors collected and analyzed a number of key articles discussing and analyzing ERP implementation and in particular investigating risk factors in the ERP life cycle. Evidence showed that Risk Management is one of the less populated areas; works, in fact, are very limited and mainly concern to considerations about organizational and business impact of ERP on the organization or general risk assessment models. Few articles propose specific risk management methodologies and treatment strategies, moreover most of them remand to specific literature which is too general and not ERP focused.

For these reasons, in this work the analysis focused specifically on the erp risk management area. That is also in order to provide a complete and deeper overview of the risk management approach proposed in this field (and particularly on works related to the introduction and implementation project of erp systems in the company).

With this aim, we extended the reviewed literature including also contributions previously kept out from the general selection criteria since they were: a) out of the selected timeline; b) no peer-reviewed or c) not presented in the web facilities by selected list of editors. So that all the related works in literature, including both academic and practitioners initiatives, could be identified and analyzed.

The selected contributions were deeply analyzed and classified according both to the adopted research methodology and tools. In the discussion, moreover, according to the suggested erp risk management framework, a "vertical" key of interpretation is provided in order to show the coverage degree works response to specific needs in the different Risk Management phases and to put in evidence benefits, gaps of each approach highlighting directions to improve each phase.

Literature Review

In this section we report output from the literature review. In table 1 we report the main academic contributions in the ERP Risk Management field in relation to their aid ("low, middle or high" degree) in supporting different phases of the risk management process. Then some observations about the practitioner initiatives will be presented.

Table 1. Classification of articles

	Context Analysis	Risk Assessment			Risk treatment	Risk Control	
		Identification	Quantification			Monitoring and Review	Communication and Consulting
			Analysis	Evaluation			
Sumner (2000)		***			*		
Wright and Wright (2001)		**					
Scott and Vessey (2002)	*	**	*				
Tatsiopoulos et al. (2003)		*	*	*			
Huang et al. (2004)		**	*				
Zafiropoulos et al. (2005)		**	*	*	**	*	*
Leopoulos et al. 2005		**					
Yang et al. (2006)		*	*	**	*	*	*

Note: * low, ** middle, ***high degree.

What is clear, at a first view, is that most of the contributions are concentrated on the identification and analysis phases, while just few of them suggest operative models to support the global quantification phase or the selection of appropriate treatment strategies. Moreover, just one work provides a computer-assisted tool supporting the different stages of the process.

In the following sub-sections we report a critic overview of the works according to the several phases of the framework. For each phase, the main objectives and needs will be clarified; finally the different approach suggested by the authors will be described and analyzed.

Context Analysis

The *Context Analysis* (figure 4) is an important activity which should be preliminarily assessed in each risk management process. Establishing the context means setting boundaries within which risks must be managed and defining the scope, as well as the budget, for the following risk management activities.

This area is critical for the review proposal since the context analysis represents a fuzzy border line in the RM process so that it is difficult to classify the related contributions.

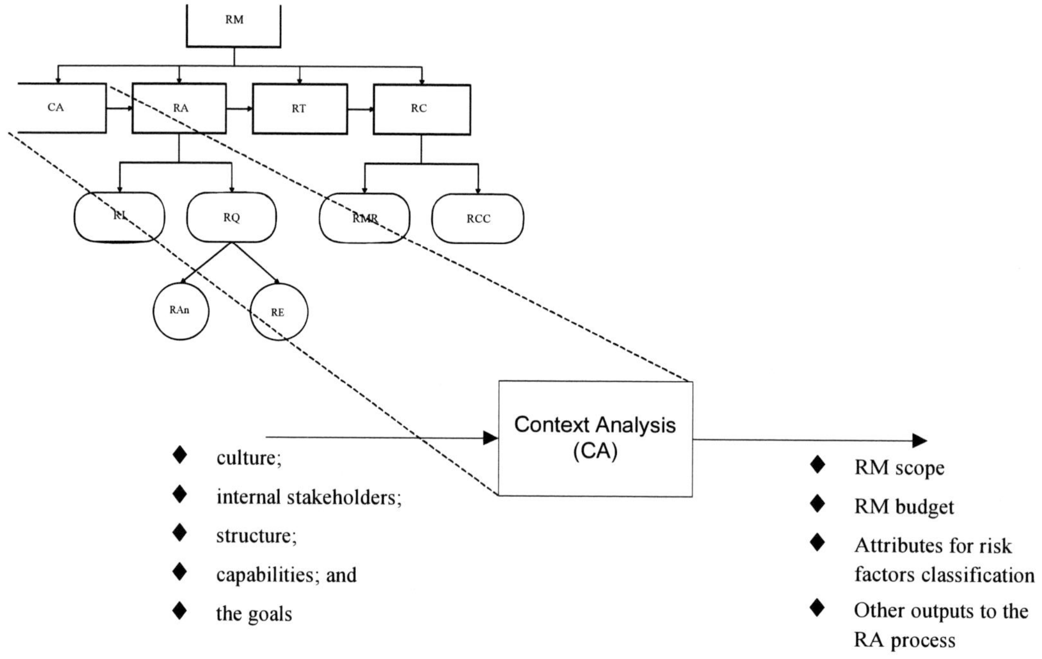

Figure 4. Context Analysis.

Context analysis concerns to both the *Process* dimension and the *Risk factor* dimension. Within the first, the context definition in the risk management process involves the representation of project units (functional, process, data, etc.) and their inter-relationships (Ahmed et al., 2003a, b). Before a risk management activity starts, in fact, it is necessary to understand the project/organization.

The key areas include for example:

- culture;
- internal stakeholders;
- structure;
- capabilities in terms of resources such as people, systems, processes, capital; and
- the goals, the objectives and the strategies put in place to achieve them.

Project modeling tools and techniques useful for this activity are generally well known, such as Project Network Diagrams, Precedence Diagramming Method (PDM), Generalized

Activity Networks (GANs), Design Structure Matrices (DSM), IDEF3 process modeling and IDEF0 functional modeling. Project and Risk Management literature is full of works which suggest one or more supporting techniques, as well IS literature reports a lot of contribution investigating on contextual variables affecting success in EPR projects.

Ahmed et al. (2007), for example, present a very complete review of tools and techniques supporting the context analysis in respect of the process dimensions. Likewise, Sarker (2000) offers a useful model of the implementation process (the socio-technical view of IS implementation) in order to understand the involved dimensions and key actors. It seems to be currently one of the most appropriate model for framing relevant variables in the process.

As for the Risk factor dimension, instead, the attention is on the features of the risk factors which could influence the Risk Management Process, and on developing risk criteria. Deciding the criteria against which risk has to be evaluated is essential in RMP. Decisions concerning whether risk treatment is required may be based on operational, technical, financial, legal, social, environmental, humanitarian or other criteria. The criteria should reflect the context defined above. These criteria often depend on the internal policies, goals and objectives of an organization and on the interests of stakeholders. It is important for the appropriate criteria to be determined at the outset. The risk criteria must correspond to the type of risks and the way in which risk levels are expressed.

Few contributions suggest techniques for a "risk oriented" context analysis targeted on ERP projects. Performing the context analysis in ERP projects is not a simple task and standard models are difficult to draw. This is mainly due to the complexity of such projects and their high specificity, secondly for the lack of standardization of the implementation processes which companies undertake.

Just Scott and Vessey (2002a) marginally approach the problem introducing a context diagram for ERP project in a number of case studies. The context diagram is a circle-shaped graphic tool that stimulates the search for critical elements that may affect the project especially, but not exclusively, in its relationship with the external context. Other contributions to the comprehension of phases and roles in the implementation process are given by the several schemes of the ERP project life cycle which are proposed in literature and by the Vendors or Business Integrator practices.

Risk Assessment

Risk assessment (figure 5) is a central phase in the risk management process. This stage aims to understand the nature of risk in terms of which factors could impact on project success, their interactions, probability of occurrence, detection difficulty and potential impact on the project, in order to quantify their risky and prioritize them. It consists of two principal steps: Risk Identification and Risk Quantification, which we will separately discuss.

Identification and quantification (which includes analysis and evaluation) of threats and vulnerabilities are the only way to understand and measure the impact of the risk involved and hence to choose the appropriate measures and controls to manage them. These processes are highly interactive; although they are here presented as discrete elements with well defined interfaces, in practice they influence each other and may overlap.

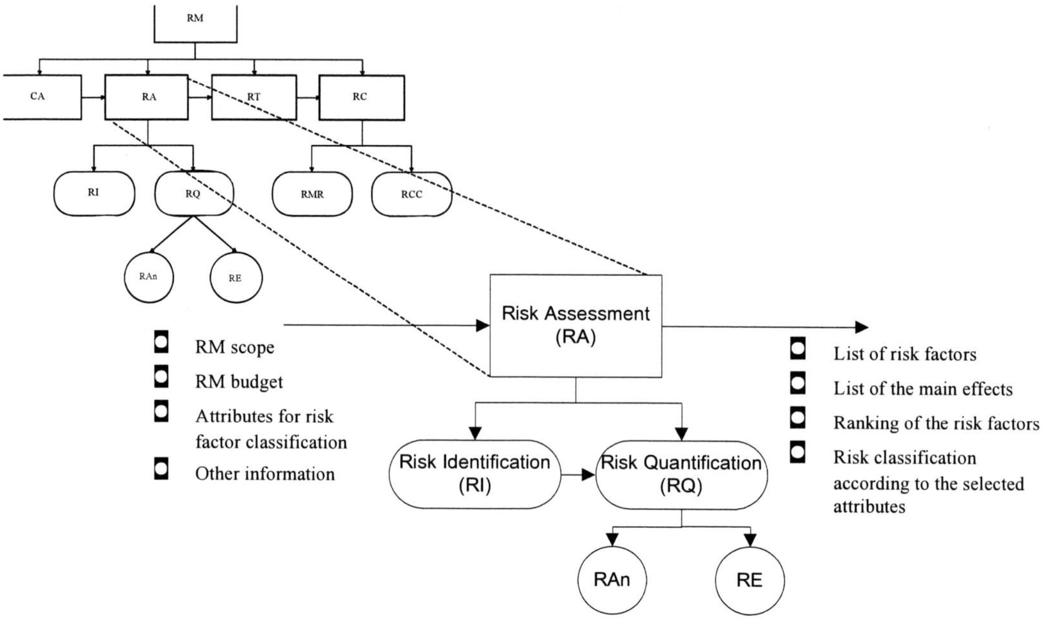

Figure 5. Risk Assessment.

Risk Identification

A key deliverable for an effective risk management is a clear, common understanding of the sources of uncertainty facing the project and what can be done about them. The "real" sources of risk are the un-identified ones, so that the identification phase can be considered as an initial risk response action (Chapman and Ward, 2003). Hence, a comprehensive identification using a well-structured systematic process is critical for the RMP, because a risk not identified at this stage may be excluded from further analysis (Australian Standard AS/NZS 4360:2004). Identifying issues involves two specific tasks:

- *Search* - for sources (and then responses), employing a range of techniques;
- *Classify* - to provide a suitable structure for defining sources (and then responses), aggregating or disaggregating particular issues as appropriate.

Within this purpose, the first aim is to understand what project success or failure mean in this kind of project. This is an essential step which links the Context Analysis with the Risk Assessment since risk factors and effects are strongly dependent from the definition of "success" and the context in which the project moves.

The identification of sources, effects and responses can be assessed in a variety of ways, by individual activity or involving other people, in order to stimulate imaginative thinking and draw on the experiences of different individuals.

A lot of potential useful techniques and tools are available in Risk Management literature such as interviewing individuals, interviewing groups or group processes such as brainstorming and decision conferencing, based on experience and records, flow charts, systems and scenario analysis, engineering techniques (diagrams, cause-effects diagrams, event or fault trees, Quality Function Deployment QFD), checklists, judgments. The best approach to use depends on the nature of the activities under review, the types of risk, the organizational context and the purpose of the analysis.

Many authors in literature have paid their attention on the identification of risk factors in ERP project. This area, in fact, is the most crowded of works; moreover the boundaries are not so well defined and sometimes overlapping with the Critical Success Factors area.

Looking at the existing contributions, mainly empirical researches based on interviews and questionnaires (Sumner, 2000; Tatsiopoulos ct al., 2003), different research approaches can be isolated. Some authors adopt more intuitive methods of recognizing a situation of risk aiming to stimulate the creativity in the user mind; others instead propose more structured techniques.

In the former class, works are mainly explorative and the identification tools presented are general in nature and usually use collaborative approaches to examine all the risky aspects of the project. Here we provide some details about the most interesting work in the risk identification area. Findings report mainly a description of the major risk factors concerning with an ERP project and some attemps of classification more than a methodological guide to the identification process.

Sumner (2000), for example, is among the first to suggest a guide for the identification phase in ERP risk management fields. Using case studies, she held an investigation to a better understanding of the major risk factors associated with enterprise-wide/ERP projects. In particular, she described and identified the risk factors in ERP projects which are unique to these projects. The findings report the project justification and risk factors identified by the project managers, then the risk factors uniquely associated with ERP systems implementation mentioned by senior project leaders are identified according to six main categories (Organizational fit, Skill mix, Management structure and strategy, Software systems design, User involvement and training, Technology planning/integration). After that, risk factors are organized within the ERP project life cycle (Planning, Requirements analysis, System design, System implementation and maintenance, Technology integration and implementation). The list of risks is quite complete and the risk factors are well defined and discussed; despite this, some improvements are still desirable to identify other relevant risk factor categories.

Wright and Wright (2002) present an exploratory study of the nature of ERP risks collecting detailed information about the risk perception of participants to the project. The study identifies pervasive ERP implementation and operating risks examining them by application (e.g., payroll, supply-chain management, business intelligence) and by vendor (e.g., SAP, PeopleSoft, Oracle). In particular authors focus on the impact of business-process reengineering and ERP customization on system reliability. The work appears a first attempt to identify critical factors for ERP risk management.

Scott and Vessey (2002a) evaluated the utility of a model (Scott and Vessey, 2002b) for risk factor identification in ERP implementation, applying it to SAP R/3 projects of two big corporations. They distinguished 4 levels to categorize ERP risk factors (external business context, organizational context, information system context and enterprise system context) and also investigated the interrelationships among these levels. Even if the authors suggest a frame to classify the different risk factor which could guide the identification phase for managers and practitioners, they did not explicitly deal with any structured risk management methodology useful for this scope.

Yang et al. (2006) contribution referring to the risk identification is quite marginal. No support is in fact provided for risk identification, except in the case study where nonetheless identified risk factors are not exhaustive and sometime overlapping.

The second group of works mainly contributes to the methodological issue of the identification process suggesting to managers useful approach and technique for risk factor identification and classification.

Checklist approaches, as well as influence diagrams, cause-effects diagrams, event or fault trees, can be very effective in focusing the attention of managers even if strongly caution should be adopted against over-reliance on checklists and similar approaches to drive the identification of sources and responses.

In this aim, Huang et al. (2004) suggested a concern-driven (i.e. perception based) assessment of risk factors using a Delphi method. Authors selected and contextualized the main ERP project risk factors using Delphi method which started from those identified in literature mainly by Sumner (2000) and Wright and Wright (2001). The research invited seven experts, all experienced and well performed in ERP projects, to participate in this study; after obtaining consensus from Delphi method, authors extracted 28 proper risk factors and then categorized them basing on their attributes: organization fit, skill mix, project management and control, and software system design user involvement, technology planning.

Table 2. Risk factors and their frequency rate in literature

ID	Risk factor	Frequency
R1	Inadequate selection of the ERP package	✓✓✓
R2	Poor project team skills	✓✓
R3	Low commitment of the top management	✓✓
R4	Ineffective communication system	✓✓
R5	Low involvement of the key users	✓✓
R6	Inadequate training	✓✓
R7	Complex ERP system architecture	✓
R8	Inadequate Business Process Reengineering	✓✓
R9	Bad managerial conduction	✓✓
R10	Ineffective project management techniques	✓✓
R11	Inadequate change management	✓✓
R12	Inadequate legacy system management	✓
R13	Ineffective consulting services	✓
R14	Poor leadership	✓
R15	Inadequate performance of the IT system	✓✓
R16	Inadequate IT system maintainability	✓
R17	Inadequate stability and performances of the ERP vendor	✓
R18	Ineffective strategic thinking and planning	✓✓✓
R19	Inadequate financial management	✓

Note: The frequency rate is related to the scientific literature.
Source: Aloini et al. (2007).

Leopoulos et al. (2005) sustain the utility of a structured model of risk factors in ERP implementations and create a Risk Breakdown Structure (RBS) of five categories and eight classes. Risks have been identified through published risk catalogues and return from experience related to ERP installations concerning three companies in the (para)pharmaceutical industry. The innovative outcome is the Risk Breakdown Structure specifically for implementation projects of ERP systems with e-commerce modules.

Finally, Zafiropoulos et al. (2005) presented a qualitative risk management application for modelling, optimal adaptation and implementation of a generic ERP system in small or medium-sized enterprises. The tool supports project managers also in risk identification suggesting a structured list of potential risk areas (Project definition; project management structure; project size; software package selection; sponsorship and commitment; staffing; technology; user organization) and a number of relevant risk factors.

In the following table a ranking of the most frequent risk factors reveled in literature is suggested (for further details see Aloini et al., 2007).

Risk Quantification

Risk Quantification aims to evaluate the risk level of the identified factors to synthesize a ranking which could drive and prioritize the selection of the appropriate treatment strategies. In this approach, the definition of risk quantification entails two essential components: uncertainty (i.e the probability of occurrence of a risk factor) and exposure (i.e the impact or effect of the occurrence of a risk factor on the project). The risk quantification process consists of two sub-phases: *Risk Analysis* and *Evaluation.*

The objective of the *Risk Analysis* is to investigate on the risk factors in order to provide a deeper understanding of the risk features which can enables a more reliable estimation of the probability of occurrence, their interrelationships and impact on the project in order to determine the influence of each risk factor on the system as a whole. Risk analysis strategies and methodologies may vary according to the risk, the purpose of the analysis and the required protection level of the relevant information, data and resources. Some theories include in risk analysis also the estimation of the probabilities of occurrence of the risk factors, the entity of effects that we, instead, include in risk evaluation phase. Anyway, as stated above, the type of performed analysis should be consistent with the criteria developed as part of the definition of the Risk Management context.

In the *Risk Evaluation* phase, instead, the final aim is to elaborate a ranking or a classification in order to assess the priority and severity of each. Then the effects, their likelihoods and hence the level of risk should be estimated (this activity is sometimes assessed during the analysis phase). Finally a comparison between the levels of risk against the pre-established criteria (i.e. in the risk criteria identification stage) and a balance between potential benefits and the adverse outcomes should be performed. This process enables us to make decisions about the extent and nature of required treatments and about priorities. In some cases the risk evaluation may lead to the decision of undertaking further analysis.

As for risk analysis and evaluation, literature is not so clear, and contributions can not easily interpreted and clusterized according to these two stages. Often authors unconsciously deal with the two phases simultaneously and in an integrated way, other times they ignore one of them. Since this reason, contributions are difficult to analyze and here we report and discuss literature evidence at once without distinction. What is clear is however that the risk analysis is at a preliminary development stage, just few authors deal explicitly with it. Some of them introduce general scheme for risk factor classification and analysis (Scott and Vessey, 2002a), but usually no one propose structured methodologies useful for this purpose.

Other authors join the risk analysis stage, which is usually preliminary and scarcely detailed, together with the phase of evaluation. In Tatsiopoulos et al. (2003), for example, the risk analysis is performed by the use of a qualitative methodology for the assessment of the probability of occurrence and impact. This work is one of the first contributions of applying a structured risk management process on a real ERP implementation. However, attention should be addressed in the risk analysis to the connection of the low-level risks with the strategic ones and to the inter-dependences between risk factors. Quantitative evaluations of risks are very difficult to be accomplished in this kind of models, expecially since the risk factors are not detailed and remain at an high level of definition.

Huang et al. (2004) used an AHP-based methodology to perform a very preliminary analysis (just aggregate) and the prioritize ERP risk factors. However, authors did not perform a formal risk quantification of effect severity or occurrence probability of risk factors but just ranks them according to a managers' global perception of risk. That is a clear weakness of the model since, assessing in the same time both the perceived impact and the probability of occurrence into a general "risk perception", concern-driven approach to risk management includes emotional and psychological reasons (drivers of concern) distinct from quantified cause-and-effect relations. Obviously, this could affect the effectiveness of the risk assessment processes.

Zafiropoulos et al. (2005) presented a qualitative risk management application for modelling, optimal adaptation and implementation of a generic ERP system in small or medium-sized enterprises. The tool supports project managers in assessing the importance and in evaluating potential impact of risk factors.

The risk management module has the following functionalities:

- Risk analysis: different categories of risk are assessed by questions to managers. The questions are generic and the manager has the chance of not to choose any answer, if this is not suitable for the specific project. Each category has sub-categories and each sub-category has one question with three possible answers.
- Risk evaluation: after having answered to various questions (on each category), the system calculates the resulting risk. Each question has a value, which range is between 0-10. The value depends on two elements: the importance the project manager and the consultants give to this subcategory and the possibility of risk manifestation.

Despite this is one of the most structured techniques appearing in literature for ERP rick management, some gaps occur. Authors, for example, did not explicit any risk effect on the project or explain how the tool proceed in risk evaluation. It seems that the evaluation assessed the risky of each risk category by itself without taking in consideration the probability of occurrence or the entity of the impact on the project goals. Moreover, in risk analysis, nothing is done to treat the potential interconnection between the risk factors.

Yang et al. (2006) suggest a systematic assessment of project risks in ERP introduction by the use of FMEA They introduce a standardized model to prioritize risk factors starting from risk factors severity, occurrence probability and detection difficulty. Authors create a performance evaluation matrix integrated with FMEA in order to select the strategies for improvement in each performance zone (increase resources to enhance satisfaction, decrease resources to reduce the cost of introducing the system, and maintain the present situation).

A standardized system based on the performance evaluation matrix is established in accordance with the locations of the three RPN indices Severity (S), Occurrence (O) and Detection (D). Performance levels will be assessed and the performance improvement strategy introduced by the system will be formulated. Finally, falling items within the non-appropriate performance zone will be specified through the Quality Function Development (QFD) method.

The data of risk priority number (RPN) are based on risk assessment. The multiplied risk factor indices refer to Severity (S), the outcome of a failure, Occurrence (O), the chance of a failure and Detection (D), the chance of a failure is not detected by customers or the difficulty level of detection. A ten point scale is used to build a comparison table for the evaluation of these three factors. RPN is the outcome of multiplying occurrence, detection and severity and can be represented as Formula 1. For the decision factor number of RPN, different decision factors and grade judgment principles can be formulated in accordance with FMEA applications.

$$RPN = S \times O \times D \quad (1)$$

Beside locating areas of abnormal coordinates through the performance matrix, a strategic improvement in crucial items is needed. The located abnormal areas would work with QFD for the development of the related matrixes to define the priority of critical improvement items as well as representing a reference point for the enterprises.

Main issues addressed by the research are concerning with the risk evaluation:

- An objective and convenient performance matrix to facilitate the evaluation of overall performance of implementing ERP.
- The utilization of three indices of FMEA to judge ERP performance level, including performance of implementing each ERP module.
- The use of QFD to determine critical ERP implementation items in addition to evaluating the strengths and weaknesses while establishing ERP objectives.

While the evaluation phase is formally well structured and defined, some observations should be moved about the risk analysis which remains more general and nothing is done to consider the inter-dependences among risk factors. Risk effects are not formalized and the meaning of project success functional to the identification of the main effect is not clearly defined.

Risk Treatment

The *Risk Treatment* (figure 6) phase is the process of selection and implementation of measures to modify risk. Risk treatment measures can include avoiding, mitigating, transferring or retaining risk.

(Definition adapted from ISO/IEC Guide 73)

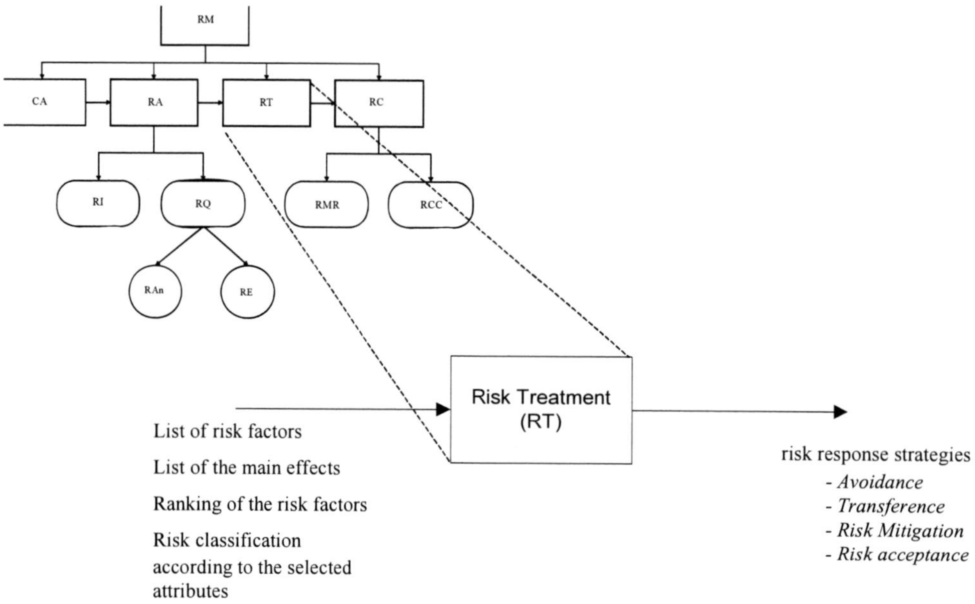

Figure 6. Risk Treatment.

According to this definition, the Risk Treatment closes the loop of the Risk Management process, managing the selection and implementation of risk response actions which should be included in a formal Risk Management Plan. In this phase, the cost evaluation is essential; in general, in fact, the cost of managing risks needs to be commensurate with the obtained benefits.

In this context a reactive (or feedback) approach refers to risk mitigation actions started after the occurrence of the risk events and it can be seen as the beginning of contingency plans. On the other hand, a pro-active (or feed forward) approach refers to actions started basing on the chance of a risk event occurring, such as insurance (Kartam and Kartam, 2001). A combination of these two approaches is applied in risk management to avoid risk, reduce the likelihood of risk, reduce the impact of risk, transfer risk, or retain risk (Australian Standard AS/NZS 4360, 1999).

In literature, in fact, different generic options for responding to project risks are suggested (e.g., DeMarco and Lister, 2003; Kerzner, 2003; Schwalbe, 2008). Four common risk response strategies are:

1) *Avoidance* strategy, which aims to prevent a negative effect occurring or impacting a project.
2) *Transference* strategy, which involves shifting the responsibility of a risk to a third party.
3) *Risk Mitigation* strategy, which is one of the most reinforcing actions designed to reduce a threat to a project by reducing its likelihood and/or potential impact before the risk is realized.
4) *Risk acceptance* strategy, which includes a range of passive and active response strategies: passively accepting that the risk exists or planning reaction (contingencies) to handle the conditions of when and if it occurs.

Risk treatment strategies responding to the risks of ERP system introduction are difficult to find in literature. Among all the contributions we considered in the review, only two authors introduce strategies to minimize risk. The first is Sumner (2000) in her work "Risk factors in enterprise-wide/ERP projects" while the second author is Zafiropoulos (2005) in his work "Dynamic risk management system for the modeling, optimal adaptation and implementation of an ERP system".

After having identified the main risk factors in the ERP context, Sumner maps them in a general life cycle scheme providing potential actions responding to specific risk classes and related responsibilities. The Sumner's work is among the first contribution in ERP risk treatment fields and summarizes general strategies for controlling risk factors in enterprise-wide/ERP projects. The suggested actions do not represent operative solutions but more often appear as a critical success factor. These strategies mainly refer to the development of commitment and support from the whole organization (top managers, managers and users), the selection of an appropriate project team (skilled) and communication.

Zafiropoulos (2005) instead, in presenting his supporting tool, accomplishes a risk mitigation form where specific strategies are suggested so that the manager had the necessary proposals for the tasks she/he needs. The form analyzes the possible risks and presents ways of dealing with each of them so that a mitigation strategy is proposed for each risk category and sub-category.

The Risk Treatment phase is characterized by a clear gap in literature. The proposed mitigating strategies are "standard", neither differentiated according to the type of risk treatment strategy (avoidance, mitigation, transference and acceptation) nor phased in the project life cycle (Zafiropoulos et al., 2005). When this happens (Sumner, 2000), strategies are too general, vague and do not provide any practical or effective solution. Often they only concern with resource allocation (Yang et al., 2006) or appear as general comments to critical success factors as many we have already studied in literature.

Furthermore, heuristics and best practices spread across all the ERP literature, have sometimes similar features to the risk treatment strategies, especially in case studies and researches in the field. However these strategies are not systematized or homogenized, resulting scarcely suitable for managers.

Risk Control

Risk Control (figure 7) phase includes structured and iterative procedures for the evaluation of the risk management effectiveness. In this phase, managers are required to determine the expected reduction in the risk level, the costs of actions undertaken, to report on the progress of risk treatments at regular intervals and to have the responsibility to iterate the process in order to identify new arising risks. It consists of two main sub-phases:

- *Risk Communication,* the process to exchange or share information about risk between the decision-makers and other stakeholders inside and outside an organization (e.g. departments and outsourcers respectively). The information can regard the existence, nature, form, probability, severity, acceptability, treatment or other aspects of risk. *(Definition adopted from ISO/IEC Guide 73)*

- *Monitor and Review*, the process for measuring the efficiency and effectiveness of the Risk Management processes, establishing an ongoing monitor and review process. This process ensures the specified management action plans remain relevant and updated. This process also implements the control activities including re-evaluation of the scope and compliance with decisions. *(ENISA)*

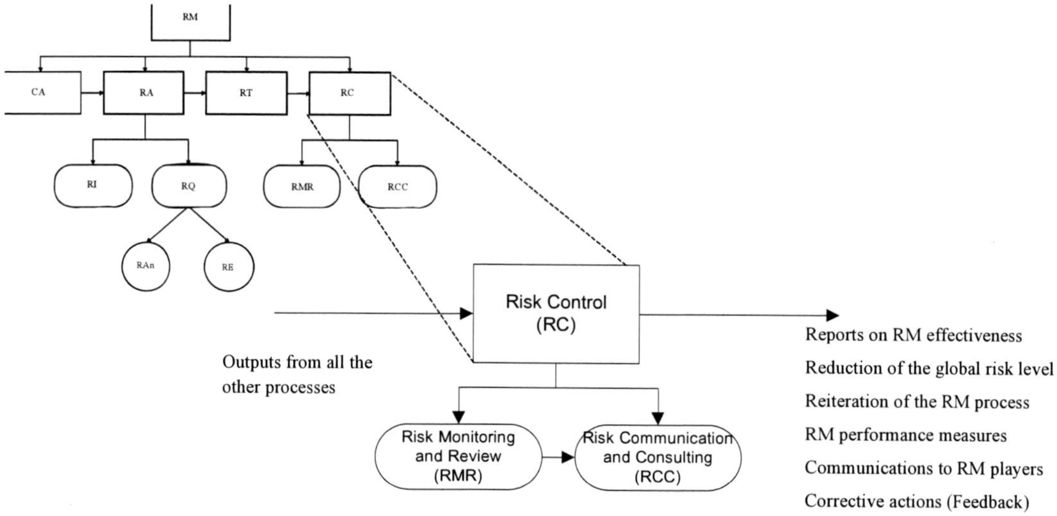

Figure 7. Risk Control.

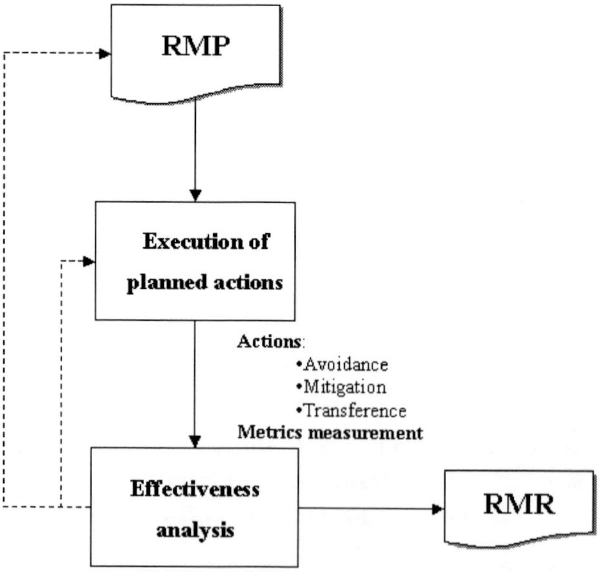

Figure 8. Control cycle.

It is important for the management and for all other decision makers to be well informed about the nature and extent of the residual risk (i.e. the level of risk which characterizes the project after the treatment measures). The organization should collect and document experience and knowledge through a consistent monitoring and review of events, treatment plans, results and all relevant records. For this purpose, residual risks should always be documented and subjected to regular monitoring-and-reviewing procedures.

The effectiveness analysis theoretically requires some metrics related to an evaluation of risk before the RMP (Risk Management Plan in figure 8) implementation (*unconditioned risk*, we suppose the risk factors free to occur) and after the RMP actions, along the life cycle (figure 8). To define such indicators is a complex and challenging task.

In literature just few specific contributions exist about risk monitoring and communication, authors often refer to more general risk management approaches. In particular, a clear gap emerges in the monitoring and review sub-stage where we found no authors promoting an iterative process to test the effectiveness of the RMP.

Zafiropoulos et al. (2005), in their computer-assisted tool, support actively the communication and reporting activities during all the project life cycle and suggest some risk treatment strategies. The system uses ASP pages and Microsoft Access 2000 so that the application is dynamic and accessible via network and supports three groups of users: project manager, consultants and system administrator. Specific modules comply with the communication needs during the phases of risk assessment (questions to managers, Graphical presentation of risk percentage) and treatment where a form analyzes each possible risk and the system dynamically presents the possible impacts and mitigation strategies according to the identified risks. The data management system, moreover, allows users to manage the risk; data is provided in the system to store the following fields in order to support the different stages of the risk management process: Category, Questions, Answers and Results.

Certainly, the knowledge repository and the dynamic structure of the application provide the team members with an immediate communication through the web both during the risk assessment and the treatment phases.

Yang et al. (2006) support performance measurement and the communication during the implementation process. The performance matrix they build represents an easily understandable report in order to guide manager in the project performance measurement and in risk monitoring. This could allow to better allocate resources and to follow-up improvements in ERP introduction projects.

Practitioner Initiatives (from Vendor or Business Integrators)

Contributions from practitioners are difficult to recover and available documentation is very fragmented and low detailed. This often happens because proprietary solutions are covered by patents and rarely disseminated, other times because their sectorial and ad hoc nature limits the audience interest towards these approaches. However, we know that relevant practitioners' initiatives, some more general and some other more specific for the ERP implementation process, exist.

In 1998, the IT Governance Institute (ITGITM) (*www.itgi.org*), established to advance international thinking and standards in directing and controlling an enterprise's information technology, has designed and created COBIT® 4.1 as an educational resource for chief information officers (CIOs), senior management, IT management and professional controls. COBIT supports IT governance providing a framework to ensure that, among the other goals,

IT risks are appropriately managed. However, the COBIT framework is quite general and does not extend to the operational level; neither suggests any tool or support to this phase.

Also some ERP vendors such as SAP and Baan have tried to provide methodologies and applications to conduct successful risk management. Specifically, SAP has a risk assessment application. The purpose of the application is to provide an objective measure of the degree to which the organization believes the R/3 implementation is credible and profitable for itself and for individuals. In addition, this application shows the change team how it could strengthen the credibility and perceived benefits of the R/3 implementation. This intelligence will be used to drive the change management initiative (SAP White Paper, 2003).

Baan provides a risk manager tool with which the project manager can conduct a risk assessment. In response, the system calculates the risks that may appear and suggests mitigation strategies. With the support of such systems, the project manager makes a more realistic estimation of costs and time, defining in a more accurate way the goals and the desired outcomes and avoiding the possible future problems, which may end in unwanted results.

Evidences and Suggestions

The review evidences that quite all the analyzed contributions in scientific literature present a rather qualitative and not integrated approaches to risk management. Although authors suggest to adopt integrated frameworks, often derived from Risk Management literature, they rarely propose methodologies and tools for the specific ERP case which could operatively drive or support the different stages of RM process. Moreover, the different phases are frequently approached as a single activity while, on the contrary, they are deeply interconnected and should be considered as a whole. By the literature analysis, the following alerts have been derived in order to support researchers and managers when a real ERP project has to be implemented.

Define Success Dimensions (Context Analysis)

The context analysis as well as other transversal phases, such as risk monitoring and communication, are scarcely supported by specific methods, and often, contributions remand to more specific works. However, the relevance of these activities for an effective risk management should drive the attention of managers and researches to assign more attention and resources to this task.

A first point for a proper approach to project risk management is to clearly define the meaning of success. The nature of the project success, and consequently performances, is in fact multidimensional. Marcus and Tanis (2003), for example, suggest that, among the others, a possible distinction of ERP project success is in terms of the implementation *project* (did the company succeed in getting the system up and running within some reasonable budget and schedule?) and *business results* (did the company succeed in realizing its business goals for the project?).

In some circumstances the measurement process is very simple, more commonly, as for example in complex project such as ERP implementation, it does not happen. For this reason the identification of the internal and external project stakeholders (employees, mangers, owner, consultants, providers, etc) and of the different processes taking part in the project activities is essential. If numerous attempts to define project stages (Life Cycle), objectives and players for ERP projects exist both in academic and practitioner literature, directions for a better comprehension of the success meaning in ERP project are less common. This is a very important topic for risk management since only a complete statement of the success dimensions can enable a correct identification of risk factors and effects.

Select Appropriate Risk Factor Attributes (Context Analysis)

A second critical point in Context Analysis is related to the selection of the appropriate attributes characterizing the risk factors. The context analysis, in fact, is functional both to the risk assessment and the treatment phases, since it can enable more complete risk identification, a better quantification and a more careful treatment.

Decisional attributes defined in the context analysis phase (such as control-ability, detect-ability, project life cycle, responsibility and dependence) can be used in the evaluation phase to assign different weights to the risk factors according to their features. The decisional attributes can also be used in the risk treatment and control phases to guide the resource allocation and the selection of suitable response strategies.

Standardization and Contextualization of Risk Factors (Risk Identification)

Looking at the risk assessment and analyzing how the previous works support the different phases of the process, we can argue that most of the collected contributions focus on the identification phase. Quite all the authors propose a more or less complete risk list in which risk factors are defined and discussed, however a lack of standardization is still evident. Moreover, sometimes terms such as ‘Risk Factors'', ‘‘Critical Success Factors'' and ‘‘Uncertainty Factors'' are used to convey also the same concept despite their significance is not ever overlapping.

What still lack is an attempt to identify how context variables impact on the risk factors “activation”. Different risk factors, in fact, could differently affect firms depending on their size, culture, organizational structure, stile of governance, sector, etc. In the same way, also the project life cycle plays an important role since the several project phases operate as trigger for specific risk factors. Hence, a direction for further researches is to investigate on which risk factors characterize the different stages of the project.

Explore the Way towards a More Quantitative Approach (Risk Quantification)

*R*isk assessment is a complex undertaking, usually based on imperfect information. Furthermore, the process can be perplexed by a number of factors (Chapman and Ward, 2003), including the following issues:

- Opportunities and threats can interact;

- A single risk factor can cause multiple effects;
- Opportunities for one stakeholder can be threats for another;
- The mathematical techniques used can create false impression of precision and reliability.

The above analysis demonstrates that the specification of the risk level is neither simple nor unique. Impact and likelihood may be expressed or combined differently, according to the type of risk, the scope and the objective of the Risk Management process; moreover quantification methods can considerably differ.

The Australian Standard (AS/NZS 4360:1999) distinguishes the approaches to risk quantification in: qualitative, semi-quantitative and quantitative.

a) *Qualitative* approach uses words to describe the magnitude of potential consequences and the likelihood those consequences will occur. It assumes that there is already a high degree of uncertainty in the likelihood and impact values so it defines them, and thus risk, in somewhat subjective or qualitative terms. Qualitative analysis may be used (Chapman and ward, 2003):

    - as initial assessment in order to identify risks which will be the subject for further detailed analysis;
    - where non-tangible aspects of risk are to be considered (e.g. reputation, culture, image etc.)
    - where there is a lack of adequate information and numerical data or resources necessary for a statistically acceptable approach.

b) *Semi-quantitative*, where the qualitative scales are set with given values. The aim is to produce a more expanded ranking scale than is usually achieved in qualitative analysis, but not to suggest realistic values for risk such as in quantitative analysis. It is an attempt to overcome the subjectivity of qualitative approach, when quantitative data are not completely available. The use of semi-quantitative analysis may lead to various inconsistencies due to the fact that the chosen numbers may not properly reflect the analogies between risks, particularly when either consequences or likelihood are extreme.
c) *Quantitative* approach uses numerical values (rather than the descriptive scales used in qualitative and semi-quantitative analysis) for both consequences and likelihood using data from a variety of sources. Mathematically, it gets very fast complicated, involving statistical techniques that are beyond the scope of this discussion.

Further researches in this topic should aim at allowing risk assessment to be repeatable and give consistent results especially in risk quantification, evolving toward more quantitative and structured approaches.

It is generally accepted, in fact, that quantitative risk assessment provides a logical framework with analytic and systematic procedures which allow to organize and apply scientific and engineering knowledge improving "rational" (consequence driven) decision making in uncertainty conditions. Using explicitly documented assumptions, knowledge, facts and available data (encapsulated in risk models) to assess risk and potential alternatives, it has many benefits in improving risk management process, because it makes possible to identify the specific areas of disagreement and either to resolve them or note which assumptions affect the result. Therefore moving towards more quantitative risk assessment and generally to more analytic and formal approaches is highly desirable, also in ERP projects.

Actually, some observations can also be moved about the suitability and cost effectiveness of a "quantitative" approaches. While, in fact, utilizing quantitative risk assessment seems straightforward and logical, there are troubles with using this approach with IT project. Likelihood, that is the other major element of risk, is often even less perfectly known. Therefore, a large margin of error is typically inherent in quantitative risk assessments for information systems. This might not always be the case in the future; as the body of statistical evidence becomes available, trends can be extrapolated from the past experience.

Moreover, to perform a quantitative risk assessment for an IT system is usually not cost-effective, due to the relative difficulty of obtaining accurate and complete information. However, if information is deemed reliable, a qualitative risk assessment is an extremely powerful tool to communicate risk to all levels of management.

Deal with Risk Factor Interdependences (Risk Analysis)

In order to support the risk quantification phase, most authors provide useful advices for the analysis of the risk factors, their potential impact and interesting suggestions for risk factor classification (risk analysis). A major issue, however, concerns the problem of the risk factors interdependence and the links between risk factors and effects.

Dependence, among the risk factors, is a critical aspect in ERP risk assessment since snowball effect can easily occur. In complex systems or projects, in fact, interdependence is a widespread phenomenon for risk management decision. We can interpret an ERP project as a complex networked project in which several "agents" (as class of homogeneous or correlated risk factors) have to be correctly managed for the project success. The risks of this kind of projects are typically interdependent: the potential consequence for a firm, in fact, not only depends on a specific agent choice but the failure of one "agent" also reduces the effectiveness of the measures that other agents may take to improve their security. Moreover, since interdependence does not require proximity, the antecedent to failure can be quite distinct and distant from the actual disaster. Therefore the occurrence of a specific event in the early stage of the ERP introduction life cycle could have a relevant impact on the whole project, and could be the cause of the effects that will be new risk factors for the latest stage of the project (for example the "inadequate selection of the ERP Software"). As well, an inadequate management of some risk factor in the latest stage of the project can equally have a disruptive effect on the whole project (Heal and Kunreuther, 2007).

The review shows that nobody in ERP/Risk Management literature propose any structured methodology useful to this scope and, in most of the contributions, it is revealed the absence of a structured phase for identifying significant linkages and interdependences between issues.

The main open issue in this topic is:

- How can the inter-relationship and dependences among the risk factors and effects be analyzed?

Caution in Input Elicitation/Estimation (Risk Analysis/Evaluation)

An objective difficulty in risk analysis affects in practice the estimation of the inputs and in particular of the risk factors probabilities. Quantitative likelihoods, in fact, can only be meaningfully determined for activities that are repeated many times, under controlled circumstances. A series of features make this estimation conceptually and operatively more complicated. First of all, the "one-shot" nature of many software project activities which mitigate against accurately estimating probabilities. Then, while it may be possible to generate metrics of low-level software engineering processes that enable probabilistic quantification of some important risk factors, there is likely to be many other critical software project risk factors that cannot be probabilistically assessed. Finally, since software projects are about enabling change through new applications using new technologies in dynamic environments, the degree to which past patterns are relevant to the future is basically uncertain in these projects.

As we discussed before, a wide dispute still exists in Risk Management literature between those who emphasize a formal quantitative assessment of the probable consequences caused by the recommended actions and a comparison to the probable consequences of alternatives, and people who emphasize perceived urgency (qualitative expert judgments) or severity of the situations motivating recommended interventions.

Sometimes good data are available to provide 'objective' probability estimates. Often there are aspects of a project where uncertainty is very important, but appropriate data are not available. Even where past experience is relevant, the required data may not have been collected, may not exist in a sufficient quantity or detail, or may not have been accurately or consistently recorded. In such situations, quantification may have to heavily rely on subjective estimates of probability distributions.

Another open issues is:

- Which are the best suitable techniques for the estimation/elicitation of the inputs in ERP risk management practice (probabilities of occurrence, entity of effects, weight of the links)?

Choose the Right Evaluation Algorithm (Risk Evaluation)

To achieve an effective evaluation of the risk level (ranking) of each risk factors, the evaluation methodology needs of both a computational algorithm which could keep in account all the crucial inputs (including risk factor interdependencies) and an accurate assessment of the informational inputs.

Some contributions, for example Huang et al. (2004) and Zafiropoulos et al. (2005), present an attempt of risk factor prioritization (risk evaluation). A common gap in their approach, however, is they assess in the same time the perceived impact and the probability of occurrence into a general risk perception, ignoring any inter-dependence. The main open issues for risk evaluation are:

- How defining an appropriate algorithm taking into account all the relevant inputs (Risk factor attributes, probabilities of occurrence, entity of effects, weight of links)?
- How should the risk acceptance threshold be set?

Set a Roadmap of Suitable Response Strategies (Risk Treatment)

As we stated, the risk treatment phase evidences a clear gap in literature. Methodologies and techniques for the definition of potential response actions are not available or lack and what we find are essentially heuristics.

Only two authors, among those we considered in our review, deal with strategies to minimize risk (Zafiropoulos et al., 2005; Yang et al., 2006) in ERP projects. However, the proposed response strategies are "standard", neither differentiated according to typical risk treatment strategy (avoidance, mitigation, transference and acceptation) or phased in the project life cycle. Furthermore, they often concern only with resource allocation and general comments to the most relevant Critical Success Factors so that they do not provide any practical solution.

Finally, the available heuristics and best practices which are spread across all the ERP literature (case study and on-field researches), sometimes have similar feature to potential risk treatment strategies. However these strategies are not systematized or homogenized, so that they are scarcely suitable to managers.

A roadmap of critical variables which could drive the selection of an appropriate and timely strategy in Risk Treatment phase is certainly so a desirable and difficult task.

Enable an Effective Communication and Control System (Risk Control)

A structured and iterative control of process effectiveness and a timely communication of needs and results are important in any Risk Management process.

Risk factors should progressively be monitored to detect, as early as possible, when they will appear or if the threat changes (in likelihood or impact). A progressive status of identified risk factors has to be maintained and periodically updated as well as fast communications should be given to all the involved managers. Any process feedback can lead to changes in the RMP end even to redefine the risk factors. Risk treatment itself sometimes introduces new risks that need to be identified, assessed, treated and monitored; risk response actions, in fact, can cause the rise of new risk factors or increase the probability of occurrence of the existent ones.

The effectiveness analysis requires some metrics related to a valuation of risk before the RMP implementation and after the RMP actions, along all the project life cycle. To define such indicators, the control and the evaluation of the expected risk reduction is a complex and challenging task.

These aspects should be carefully considered in the risk control phase; directions for the design of the control metrics as well systems and tools supporting the control and communication process are highly desirable.

Consider the Organizational Risk (Practitioner Initiatives)

As for practitioner initiatives, SAP and Baan, along with other ERP vendors have designed proprietary applications for the needs of their own ERP systems. These risk management applications are not generic and thus cannot be used at the implementation of any ERP system. Moreover they adopt more a technical perspective than an organizational one. The risk is seen from the vendor or business integrator point of view and despite these approaches could help in project resource planning, allocation and time forecasting, especially since they benefit of the large experience of these subjects, they fail to address other important dimensions of project success, such as the organizational one. For this reason, and for some other desired functionalities such as network access and dynamic content, the development of a more dynamic and generic risk management application is necessary (Zafiropoulos et al., 2005).

Conclusion

In this chapter we remarked the importance of a risk management approach for ERP introduction projects and presented a review of the state of the art about project risk management in ERP field. The attempt to identify gaps and shortcomings in the ERP risk management area is finalized to provide the basis for the development of an innovative risk management methodology tailored for ERP systems.

In order to contribute to both academic research and management practice, we have reviewed past and recent works and discussed new emerging techniques and tools supporting the different stages (context analysis, risk identification, risk analysis, risk evaluation, risk treatment and control) of a general ERP Risk management framework.

Findings show that works approaching the ERP field from a risk management point of view are very few in scientific literature and just a minority of them provide managers with structured process and methodologies giving a real operative support. Currently, formal Risk Management methods are rarely applied for risk management in complex projects like ERP introduction. Several generally accepted approaches to risk management exist but these are not diffused in ERP field. Moreover, numerous shortcomings were identified in the few proposed approaches.

In a few words, the most critical open issues converge in the following main themes:

- qualitative and not integrated approaches to risk assessment;
- operational difficulties to converge toward a more quantitative risk assessment;
- absence of a roadmap to suitable ERP risk response strategies;
- scarce support for the risk control process.

References

Ahmed, A., Amornsawadwatana, S., and Kayis, B. (2003). Application of ARENA simulation to risk assessment in concurrent engineering projects. *Proceedings of the 9th International Conference on Manufacturing Excellence*, October, 13-15. Melbourne, Australia.

Ahmed, A., Amornsawadwatana, S., and Kayis, B. (2007). A review of techniques for risk management in projects. *Benchmarking: An International Journal*, **14** (1), 22-36.

Ahmed, S. M. (2008). A comparison of usability techniques for evaluating information retrieval system interfaces. *Performance Measurement and Metrics*, **9**, 48-58.

Aloini, D., Dulmin, R., and Mininno, V. (2007). Risk management in ERP project introduction: Review of the literature. *Information and Management,* **44**, 547–567.

Ashrafi, R. A., and Hartman, F. (2002). Project management in the information systems and information technologies Management of risks in IT projects industries. *Project Management Journal*, **33** (3), 4-14.

Baki B., and Cakar, K. (2005). Determining the ERP package-selecting criteria: The case of Turkish manufacturing companies. *Business Process Management Journal*, **11** (1), 75-86.

Bentley, C. (2002). *Prince 2, Third Edition: A Practical Handbook.* Computer Weekly Professional.

Blackstone, J. H. Jr., and Cox, J. F. (2005). *APICS dictionary* (11th ed.). APICS: The Association for Operations Management.

Champy, J., and Hammer, M. (1993). *Reengineering the cooperation: a manifesto for business revolution*. New York, NY.

Chapman C., and Ward S. (2003). *Project risk management: processes, techniques and insights*. John Wiley.

Cobit 4.1, Framework Control Objectives Management Guidelines Maturity Models 2007, IT Governance Institute. Available at www.itgi.org

Davenport, T. H. (1998). Putting the enterprise into the enterprise system. *Harvard Business Review*, **76** (4), 121-131.

Deloitte Consulting's (1998). ERP's second wave: maximizing the value of ERP-enabled processes.

DeMarco, T., and Lister, T. (2003). Risk Management during Requirements. *IEEE Software*, **20** (5), 99-101.

ENISA Study (2007). *Emerging-risks-related Information Collection and Dissemination.* Available at www.enisa.europa.eu/rmra.

Graeser, J., and Willcocks, L. (2001). Delivering IT and E-business Value. *Computer Weekly Series*. Oxford: Butterworth and Heinemann.

Gobeli, D. H., Bechinger, I., and Koenig, H. F. (1998). Managing conflict in software development teams: a multilevel analysis. *Journal of Product Innovation Management*, **14** (4), pp. 323-334.

Hammer, M. (1999). Up the ERP revolution. *InformationWeek*, 186.

Heall, G., and Kunreuther, H. (2007). Modeling interdependent risks. *Risk Analysis*, **27** (3).

ISO/IEC Guide 73 (2002). Risk management. Vocabulary. *Guidelines for use in standards ISBN: 0 580 40178 2*, 1-28.

Jiang, J. J., and Klein, G. (2001). Software project risks and development focus. *Project Management Journal*, **32** (1), 3-9.

Huang, S.M., Chang, I., Li S.H. and Lin, M.T. (2004). Assessing risk in ERP projects: identify and prioritize the factors. *Industrial Management and Data Systems*, **104**(8), 681-688.

Kartam, N. A., and Kartam, S. A. (2001). Risk and its management in the Kuwaiti construction industry: contractors' perspective. *International Journal of Project Management*, **19** (6), 325-335.

Kerzner, H. (2003). *Project management: A systems approach to planning, scheduling, and controlling* (9th ed.). Chips.

Leopoulos, V., Kirytopoulos, K. and Voulgaridou, D. (2005). ERP systems as a component of the electronic supply chain: Classification of implementation risks. *Proceedings of the International Conference on Intelligent Agents, Web Technologies and Internet Commerce (CIMCA-IAWTIC'05)*

Lewin, C. (2002). *RAMP risk analysis and management for projects*. London, UK: Institution of Civil Engineers and the Faculty and Institute of Actuaries in association with Thomas Telford.

Lyytinen, K., and Ropponen, J. (2000). Components of software development risk: How to address them? A project manager survey. *IEEE Transactions on Software Engineering*, **26** (2), 98-112.

Markus, M. L. (1983). Power, politics and MIS implementation, *Communications of the ACM*, **26**, 430-444.

Markus, M. L., and Robey, D. (1988). Information technology and organizational change: Causal structure in theory and research. *Management Science*, **34**, 583−598.

Markus, M. L., and Tanis, C. (2000). The enterprise system experience – From adoption to success. In M. F. Price *and* R. W. Zmud (Eds.), *Framing the domains of it management: Projecting the future through the past.* Pinnaflex Educational Resources.

Markus, M. L., Axline, S., Petrie D., and Tanis, C. (2000). Learning from adopters' experiences with ERP: problems encountered and success achieved. *Journal of Information Technology*, **15**, 245-265.

Meli, R. (1998). SAFE: a method to understand, reduce, and accept project risk. *ESCOM-ENCRESS 98, Project Control for 2000 and Beyond* (1998, May 27-29). Rome, IT.

Monk, E. and Wagner, B., (2009), *Concepts in Enterprise Resource Planning,* Third Edition, Course Technology Cengage Learning, Boston, USA.

PMI, 2001. *A guide to the project management body of knowledge (PMBOK Guide)* (2000 ed.). Project Management Institute Publications.

PRAM project risk analysis and management guide. (1997). Norwich, UK: Association for Project Management.

Rajagopal, P. (2002). An innovation-diffusion view of implementation of enterprise resource planning systems and development of a research model. *InformationandManagement*, **40**, 87–114.

Robey, D. (1987). Implementation and the organizational impacts of information systems, *Interfaces*, **17**, 72-84.

Robey, D., Ross, J. W., and Boudreau, M. C. (2002). Learning to implement enterprise systems: An exploratory study of the dialectics of change. *Journal of Management Information Systems*, **19**, 17−46.

Ross, J. W., and Vitale, M. R. (2000). The ERP revolution: surviving vs thriving. *Information System Frontiers*, **2**, 233–241.

SAP White Paper (2003). Change Management. Retrieved from http://www.digitalglobalsoft.com/services/whitepapers/asap-change-management-whitepaper.htm.

Sarker, S. (2000). Toward a methodology for managing information systems implementation: A social constructivist perspective. *Informing Science*, **3** (4), 195-205.

Sauer, C. (1999). Deciding the future for IS failures: Not the choice you might think. In W. L. Currie and B. Galliers (Eds.), *Rethinking management information systems* (pp. 279-309). New York, USA: Oxford University Press.

Schultz, R. L., and Slevin, D. P. (1975). A program for research in implementation. In R. L. Schultz and D. P. Slevin (Eds.). *Implementing Operations Research/Management Science*. New York, NY: American Elsevier.

Schwalbe, K. (2008). *Information technology project management* (5th ed.). Cengage Learning.

Scott, J. E., and Vessey, I. (2002). Managing risks in enterprise systems implementations. *Communication of the ACM*, **45** (4).

Scott, J. E., and Vessey, I. (2002). *Toward a multi-level theory of risks in enterprise systems implementations*. Working Paper.

Simon, O. (1998). *RAMP Risk Analysis and Management for Projects: RAMP Guide*. London, UK: Institution of Civil Engineers and the Faculty and Institute of Actuaries in association with Thomas Telford.

Standard Australia (1999). *Risk Management*. (AS/NZS 3360) Strathfield.

Sumner, M. (2000). Risk factors in enterprise-wide/ERP projects. *Journal of Information Technology* (Routledge, Ltd.), 15(4), 317-327.

Tatsiopoulos, I. P., Panayiotou, N. A., Kirytopoulos, K. and Tsitsiriggos, K. (2003). Risk Management as a Strategic Issue for the Implementation of ERP Systems: A Case Study From the Oil Industry. *International Journal of Risk Assessment And Management*, **4**(1).

Wei, C. C., Chien, C. F., and Wang, M. J. (2005). An AHP-based approach to ERP system selection, *International Journal of Production Economics*. **96**, 47–62.

Willcocks, L. (1996). *Investing in information systems: Evaluation and management*. London, UK: Thomson Business Press/ Chapman and Hall.

Willcocks, L., and Graeser, J. (2001). Delivering IT and E-business Value. *Computer Weekly Series*. Oxford: Butterworth and Heinemann.

Wright, A. M., and Wright. S. (2001). Information system assurance for ERP systems: Unique risk considerations. *Journal of Information Systems*, **16**, 5-15.

Yang, C.-C., Huang, J.-T., Lin, M.-Y. and Lin, W.-T. (2006). A study on applying FMEA to improving RP introduction: An example of semiconductor related industries in Taiwan. *International Journal of Quality and Reliability Management*, **23** (3), 298-322.

Zafiropoulos, I., Askounis, D. and Metaxiotis, K. (2005). Dynamic risk management system for the modelling, optimal adaptation and implementation of an ERP system. *Information Management and Computer Security*, **13** (3), 212–234.

In: Risk Management
Editors: B. Jordão and E. Sousa, pp. 89-124

ISBN: 978-1-60876-011-4

Chapter 3

Bridging the Gap Between Risk Assessment and Land-Use Planning

Davor Kontić and Marko Gerbec
Jožef Stefan Institute, Jamova 39, 1000 Ljubljana, Slovenia

Abstract

The issue of effective land use planning around planned or existing industrial establishments with potential for major accidents involving hazardous substances is explained in a detail. The domains of process safety risk assessment and spatial/land use planning procedures, policies and levels are discussed at suitable level of details in order to demonstrate existing processes, procedures and pertaining uncertainties. Next, typical current approaches to incorporate risk assessment's results into land use planning process are discussed with emphasis on their difficulties and shortcomings. Considering levels of spatial planning for new establishments (new developments), the modifications of both risk assessment methodologies and spatial planning process are suggested in order to bridge the gap between both domains. First, risk assessment methodologies should provide information about suitable separation distances through threat index, explicitly considering vulnerability of the surroundings of the hazardous industrial establishment and also threat tolerability criteria set. Second, spatial/land use planning process should be revised in order to add additional iterations in the planning at various levels each considering available information about risks/threats anticipated or assessed (related to the levels of technical data about planned development/investment). Among other things, the approach and method elaborated succeeded in integration of two domains related to risk informed land use planning. The approach asks for interaction of different technical backgrounds, methods and approaches in terms of incorporation of technical risks/threats as integrative component into spatial/land use planning process.

Keywords: process safety, risk assessment, spatial planning, land-use planning, threat analysis

Introduction

20th century was among other things marked by a number of infamous large scale industrial disasters involving hazardous substances. Historical cases such as Oppau (Germany, 1921), Flixborough (UK, 1974), Seveso (Italy, 1976), Bhopal (India, 1984), Mexico City (Mexico, 1984), and more recent Enschede (Nederland, 2000), Toulouse (France, 2001), Texas City (USA, 2005), Gerdec (Albania, 2008) represent only a minor and clearly an incomplete list from literature (Mannan, 2005) on the subject. Large industrial accidents are related to the system safety aspects, usually referred to the process safety aspect, being one of the types of the safety (the rest are usually referred as occupational, product and third party safety). Majority of historical cases mentioned above resulted (in addition to the on-site damage) also in the substantial damage to the surrounding environment and fatalities among humans in the vicinity of the industrial establishments of a concern. Needless to say, headlines in the media reporting about the disaster(s) resulted in public and political upset and a society responded by goal oriented legislation in terms of minimum process safety management requirements.

Examples of such legislation are European directive 96/82/EC (EC, 2003; recognized also as "Seveso II directive") and in the USA the OSHA - 29 CFR 1910.119, both requesting process safety management system to be demonstrated by the operators. In European Union, Seveso II directive is transposed into national legislations of the member states and thus being subject of national policies, approaches, guidelines, solutions, etc.

Considering specific obligations set to the management of establishments by national legislations, same principal obligations apply in all member states:

- notification to the authorities on legal status (based on maximum quantities of hazardous substances at the establishment).
- Adoption of the Major Accident Prevention Policy (process safety policy) and its operational implementation as Safety Management System (into company's management system).
- Preparation (and submission to the competent authority for approval) of the Safety Report (operational document describing previous two topics and process safety risk assessment results and safety measures present regarding on-site activities).
- Preparation of the site's internal Emergency Planning (plan) for the foreseeable emergencies due to on-site activities. The planning shall be done according to potential major accident hazards (scenarios) as revealed by the Safety Report.
- Preparation and submission of the information to the public about legal status of the company (establishment) and safety measures that are in place in order to prevent and in mitigate consequences of potential major accidents. This obligation applies to the potentially affected population in the proximity of the establishment and is thus related to the results of the Safety Report.
- In addition to all above mentioned obligations, establishment's management must assure and demonstrate cooperation of internal Emergency planning/services with external emergency planning/services (usually at local community level).
- Last, but not least, establishment's management must provide a suitable data based on Safety Report's risk assessment results about suitable separation distances between

establishment and neighbouring public and residential areas. The idea is to assure "buffer zones" or exclusion zones in order to prevent damage to the public in a case of the major accident occurrence. This shall be done through land-use planning and related policies, usually bound to the local community authorities.

This contribution aims to provide an insight into difficulties arising while trying to bring land-use planning principles down to the practical use. It should be understood that developing a land use plan brings together domains of the risk assessment and the procedure of preparation of land use plan, both subjects of their specific issues, steps and uncertainties. As risks arising from establishment's activities reflect specifics of the hazards present there, they should be identified and quantified in the risk assessment procedure and results.

Technically speaking, risks (term *risk*: probability of the loss; or: risk combines the probability of an event occurring with the impact of that event) need to be translated into the meaningful interpretations in terms of expected impact distances due to foreseeable accidental events, considering developments/changes such as new establishments ("Greenfield investments"), modifications at existing establishments and developments in neighbourhood around existing establishments. The article 12 of the Seveso II directive sets clear land use planning policy goals to be reached (Figure 1).

LAND-USE PLANNING

1. Member States shall ensure that the objectives of preventing major accidents and limiting the consequences of such accidents are taken into account in their land use policies and/or other relevant policies. They shall pursue those objectives through controls on:

(a) the siting of new establishments,

(b) modifications to existing establishments covered by Article 10,

(c) new developments such as transport links, locations frequented by the public and residential areas in the vicinity of existing establishments, where the siting or developments are such as to increase the risk or consequences of a major accident.

Member States shall ensure that their land-use and/or other relevant policies and the procedures for implementing those policies take account of the need, in the long term, to maintain appropriate distances between establishments covered by this Directive and residential areas, areas of public use and areas of particular natural sensitivity or interest, and, in the case of existing establishments, of the need for additional technical measures in accordance with Article 5 so as not to increase the risks to people.

2. Member States shall ensure that all competent authorities and planning authorities responsible for decisions in this area set up appropriate consultation procedures to facilitate implementation of the policies established under paragraph 1. The procedures shall be designed to ensure that technical advice on the risks arising from the establishment is available, either on a case-by-case or on a generic basis, when decisions are taken.

Figure 1. Contents of the article 12 of EU directive 96/82/EC ("Seveso II"; EC, 2003).

The problem of successful integration of risk assessment and spatial/land-use planning encompasses multiple issues such as the pressure of the investors, absence of communication between stakeholders, absence of communication between planners and risk assessors, long administrative procedures in land-use planning field and the lack of a methodology that would effectively integrate risk assessment and spatial/land-use planning. The latter is being addressed to within the framework of this paper.

In this paper we will describe the sources of the gap between risk assessment (specifics and appropriate understanding of the results) and land use planning steps, followed by discussion and suggested approach in order to close the gap.

Description of the Current Gap

Seveso II directive requires member states to resolve risk related land-use planning issues to be solved through appropriate spatial/land-use planning (EC, 2003), however it does not provide explicit guidelines on how risk assessment and spatial planning should be integrated. Member states are therefore searching for their own best and specific approaches (Papazoglou et al. 2000; Rasmusen et al. 2000; Spadoni et al. 2000; Smeder et al. 1996; Hauptmanns, 2005; Basta and Struckl, 2005; Kontić et al., 2006).

Currently available methods for risk assessment with spatial representation of results serve predominantly for emergency planning, rarely are the results applied for land-use planning purposes (Shape-Risk, 2005). The latter is due to the form of the result of risk assessment which is not directly applicable in land-use planning, mainly because of its probabilistic character. The methodology that would effectively integrate risk assessment and spatial/land-use planning is lacking (Kontić and Kontić, 2009).

It has been observed that the gap between risk assessment and land-use planning exists due to the inappropriate form of risk assessment results to be used effectively in land-use planning as well as the procedural issues of adopting a risk-informed land use plan (Kontić and Kontić, 2009). It is assumed that risk assessment and spatial/land-use planning can be successfully integrated by modifications of both the existing risk assessment and the spatial/land-use planning methods. In relation to the latter, in the following chapters we discuss the issues in risk assessment process and land-use planning which may be the cause for the existing gap between the two disciplines.

Risk Assessment Process and Related Uncertainties

Industrial risk assessment in its broad definition is a structured procedure that evaluates qualitatively and/or quantitatively the level of risk imposed by the hazard sources identified within the industrial establishment. Its scope is recognised to be to assess the safety of the establishment and to determine the risk imposed on the surrounding population and environment, with aim of improving safety and minimising risks. It is noteworthy that although the various risk assessment methods, qualitative or quantitative, may differ in the results provided, they all have the same scope. The emphasis in a risk assessment should not necessarily be placed on the absolute accuracy of its predictions, but rather on its success or failure in demonstrating or improving the safety of the establishment.

The comprehensive risk assessment process that involves all necessary steps is schematically presented in Figure 2 (Kontić and Kontić, 2009; Gerbec and Kontić, 2008).

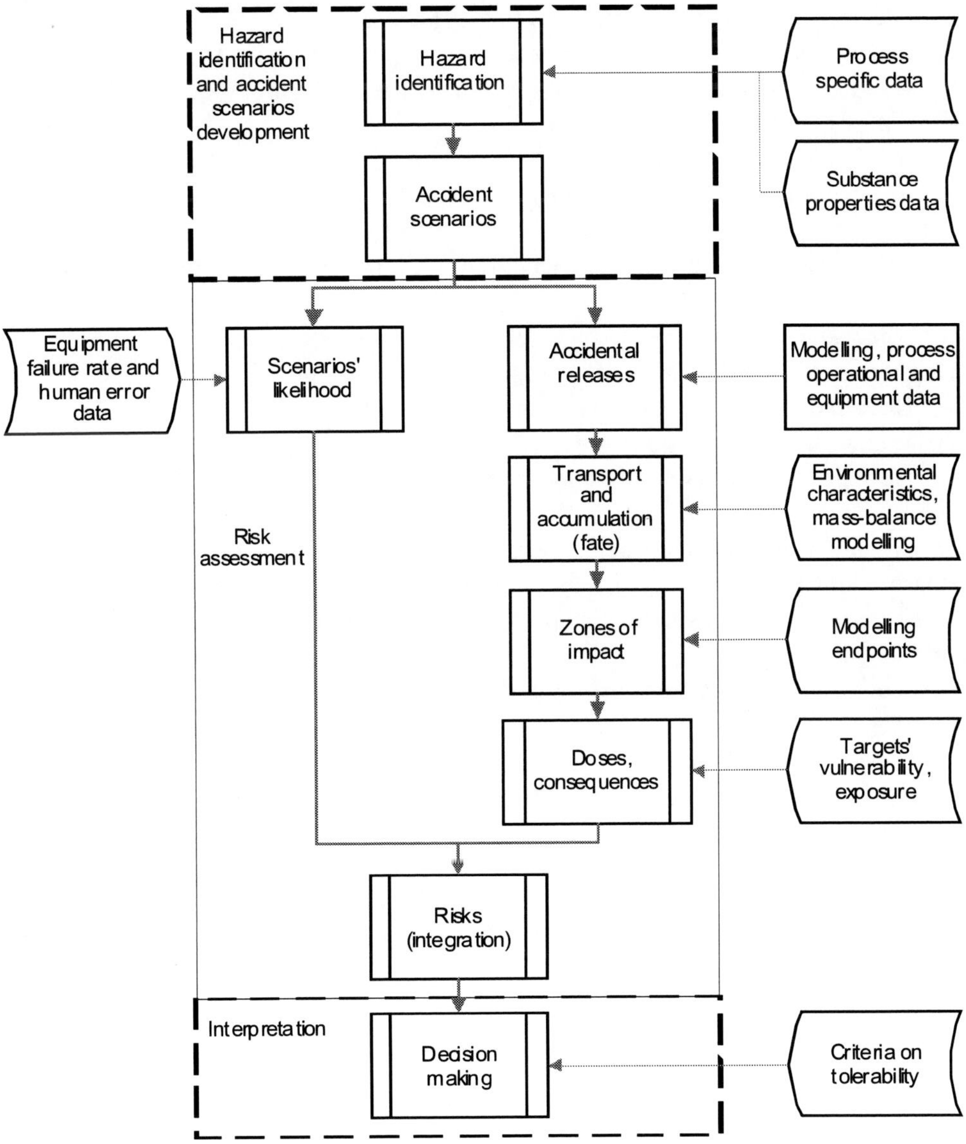

Figure 2. Graphical presentation of the risk assessment process.

The risk assessment shall provide results in terms of risk levels present due to certain industrial activities involving hazardous substances. The principal interest in terms of adverse consequences is usually about human fatalities, injuries, negative health effects, as well as on process losses (plant destruction, economic damage/losses) and damage to the environment. Related to the dimension of likelihood (probability), we are interested in expected future frequency (number of accidental events per unit of time) or probability (dimensionless) of adverse outcome out of certain mission (operation).

It is of a benefit to clarify the definition of the term major accident (EC, 2003), being an event involving dangerous substance in terms of:

- occurrence of the major emission, fire, explosion,
- uncontrolled event from the operation,
- leading to serious danger towards human health and/or environment (casualties, injuries, negative health impacts,
- immediate or delayed,
- inside or outside the establishment.

To put risk assessment in simple, it shall provide answer to the questions:

1) what can go wrong?
2) How bad is it going to be (if it happens)?
3) How likely is it to happen (what must go wrong)?
4) What is necessary to do to prevent it?
5) How shall we respond if it happens anyway?

Continuing with risk assessment, there is a number of methods, tools and approaches differing in required level of details, knowledge, data (not to mention required resources and time), providing results ranging from qualitative, through semi-quantitative to fully quantitative ones.

Related to the risk assessment process and its steps and results obtained, the related uncertainties should be always explicitly considered (Paté-Cornell, 1996). There two principal types of uncertainties, epistemic and aleatory. The epistemic ones are related to some level of imperfection in the knowledge used. The aleatory ones are related to the variability of the conditions/properties considered of the system under assessment. This kind of uncertainty is often also referred as statistical uncertainty, suggesting that it can be managed using statistical methods.

The existing risk assessment methods related tor land-use planning may be considered as a specific subdivision of those risk assessment methods used in the context of the safety of industrial establishments; some examples show a more integrated character that links risk assessment with land-use planning purposes (ARAMIS, 2004).

Risk Assessment Steps

Here we will explain general approach to carry out quantitative risk assessment as a process (Mannan, 2005; AIChE, 2000; Uijt de Haag, 1999) being graphically presented in Figure 2. Each step within the process is prone to the uncertainty, which in summary influences the overall trustworthiness of the analysis and is a subject of specific consideration in decision-making. An overview of these issues is given below.

1. Hazard Identification

Starting with detailed understanding of the process/plant/equipment subject of concern, the purpose is to identify all cause consequence relationships. The point is that any adverse outcome is a consequence of some cause(s), which are usually subject of safety or preventive measures in order to prevent or mitigate them. The hazard identification is usually done by a team (involving also experienced process engineers, line personnel, maintenance staff, etc.) using tools and methods ranging from simple ones like Check Lists, What-If Analysis, etc., to the more advanced methods (generally applicable, more resource demanding) like HAZOP (Hazard and Operability Study). The purpose is to obtain a comprehensive list of all hazards present.

Related issues/uncertainties at this step: it should be understood on a common sense basis that results of hazard identification can be biased by the potentially limited information/knowledge of the team involved, or on the other side by the deficiency of the particular e.g., check list questionnaire used. Practically speaking, certain hazards (consequences) or their cause(s) could be missed and lost at the start. Usually we are concerned at this step about epistemic type of uncertainty.

Example: this kind of uncertainty is probably most important considering a new process/plant/product, where previous experience does not yet exist. Alternatively, regarding some hazardous substance, some relevant properties or conditions could not be adequately known, understood, or considered in design or operation of the plant. It should be evident that such uncertainty is difficult to describe quantitatively.

2. Development of Accidental Scenarios

Starting with a list of hazards present, the representative hazards are to be sorted out in terms of severity and likelihood for adverse serious enough consequences. Usually, a limited representative list of hazards and their causes is prepared in terms of the accidental scenarios in terms of anticipated development of the events. Being representative means that for example, one scenario can consider (include) also a number of related, or similar, but less severe hazards (risks). The description of the scenarios shall should consider and clearly state assumptions in terms of anticipated, most likely or worst possible conditions leading to specific scenario. The purpose is to end up with a limited list of accidental scenarios list (typically from three to ten) and their detailed descriptions, considering worst probable, worst credible and worst possible cases (in terms of severity of consequences, leaving probability dimension of the risk to a separate issue).

Related issues/uncertainties at this step: First, uncertainty is inherited from previous step. However, usually, the related uncertainty comes from the required assumptions about actual propagation (progress) of the events from basic failures/mistakes to the realization of the adverse effect (e.g., release of the hazardous substance out of the equipment into the open air) and damage likely encountered (e.g., safe dispersion, ignition and fire/explosion). The issue is that assumptions are needed as all the details can not be exactly known at the time of the analysis, and some judgement is needed. The general approach here is that uncertainty is traded for the more conservative assumptions in order to be on a safe side, meaning that more severe outcomes are extremely unlikely or even impossible to occur.

Example: Considering an LPG (Liquefied Petroleum Gas) storage and distribution facility, one would quickly come to the scenarios involving potential releases of LPG from transportation (car tanker, railway car tank) and storage tanks (e.g., horizontal cylinders, storage spheres). A good approach would be to consider all tanks in terms of maximum quantities of LPG present, or expected duration of the LPG release, or maximum diameter of process pipeline connected, etc. This could lead to three representative scenarios:

1) worst probable case: LPG release from 2" hose from car tanker (capacity 30 m^3).
2) worst credible case: LPG release from 3" hose from railway car tanker (capacity 80 m^3)
3) worst possible case: LPG release from storage sphere (capacity 1000 m^3) due to vessel collapse or compromised in a fire.

3. Scenario's Likelihood

Assessment of the likelihood of certain scenario is usually done either using historical data or through elaboration of a model of accidental events sequences and considering likelihoods for all events (again using some kind of historical data). The later approach is usual, as historical data are usually available only for basic events (failures, errors, mistakes) and suitable methods such as fault tree and event tree are used. The purpose of the step is to assess the likelihood dimension of the risk pertaining to the specific accidental scenario.

Related issues/uncertainties at this step: The uncertainties in terms of assessed accidental event likelihood figure pertains from potentially inherited uncertainties from previous steps (epistemic due to deficiencies in detailed understanding of accidental causes and consequences relationships; not to mention potentially missed causes), and from basic event/failure/error rates data used. The issue of data used is related to the availability of field data (plant specific equipments failure rates and/or personnel error rates), or alternatively to use the generic (literature equipment failure rates and/or personnel error rates). While the first choice is preferred, it is seriously limited by the availability of the data, especially having in mind planning phase for the new plants. On the other side, there is a number of suitable literature data sources available, however, subject of serious issues about their applicability (many sources are from 1980s), vagueness (e.g., only generic type of certain equipment), related process conditions, and not to mention the issue of potential less than perfect maintenance in real world.

It shall also be noted that failure rates are usually reported not only as point values, but also (more suitable) as confidence intervals for values (5 and 95 percentile values are common). This means that as a result of accidental event frequency assessment one shall expect at least a confidence interval for value. Thus, realistically we can expect an order of magnitude accuracy.

Example: some cases of the aleatory uncertainty pertaining from equipment failure rates from given literature source are given in Table 1. Note however, that various literature sources can give significantly different figures. Generally speaking, uncertainties in figures used are linearly propagated to the results obtained. However, considering overall uncertainty of the likelihood assessment step, the benchmark exercises done and reported in the literature show results ranging over many orders of magnitude as obtained by different teams – for illustration, refer to the benchmark exercise in (Lauridsen et al., 2002).

Table 1. Example of uncertainties in failure rate data for equipment (from literature)

Equipment	Failure mode	Failures (per 10^6 hours)		
		low	mid	high
Hoses flexible	rupture	0.0099	0.570	2.20
Compressors el. driven	catastrophic failure	27.9	2470	9690
Fire detector	catastrophic	0.0198	1.14	4.41
Safety relief valves spring loaded	open prematurely	0.275	1.68	4.80
Valves pneumatic	Spurious operation	0.274	3.59	12.3

Note: low and high figures are related to 5 and 95 percentile values.

4. Accidental Releases (Source Term Conditions)

Usually, but not necessarily, hazardous substance must be first released from certain process equipment into the open space in order to obtain inherently hazardous situation. Obviously, substances in gaseous and liquid states are of a main concern here. Leaving the type of the hazard pertaining from the chemical and physical properties of the substance in question, obviously, larger the quantity released within certain time period renders larger hazard, and that is the answer to be obtained at this step. This issue is usually analysed using process specific (field) situation/data, such as capacities of the storage vessels, dimensions of process piping, assessed/tested response times for closing down the suitable valves, etc. At the end it is up to risk assessor(s) good engineering judgement what is to be considered.

Related issues/uncertainties at this step: At this point we are at the issue of mainly aleatory uncertainty in terms of minimum likelihoods (in terms of the release event) to be considered credible within a certain scenario. In some cases, worst case scenarios in terms of the catastrophic releases (instantaneous release of the whole inventory) from vessel(s) are suitable in order to be on a safe side. For some scenarios, e.g., compromised pipelines with leaks ranging in size from minor crack to full bore rupture, are to be evaluated on a basis for a likelihood for a certain leak size to occur (can be related to the quality of the safety measures present). In addition, process conditions need to be considered. This can lead to a set of sub-scenarios to be analysed.

Example: let us consider a generic case of a potential LPG leak from a storage vessel (250 m^3, 80 % full) from liquid phase output pipework connection. Considering a pipe with length 10 m to the leak point, diameters 50, 28 and 16 mm, respectively, using a suitable calculation procedure or programme tool (DNV PHAST 6.53 in our case) one could get for the first hour of duration average release rates of 5.9, 1.6 and 0.41 kg/s, respectively. The practical meaning of such release rates is shown on Figure 3 presenting relationship between LPG concentrations in open air against distance downwind from the release point for all three cases respectively.

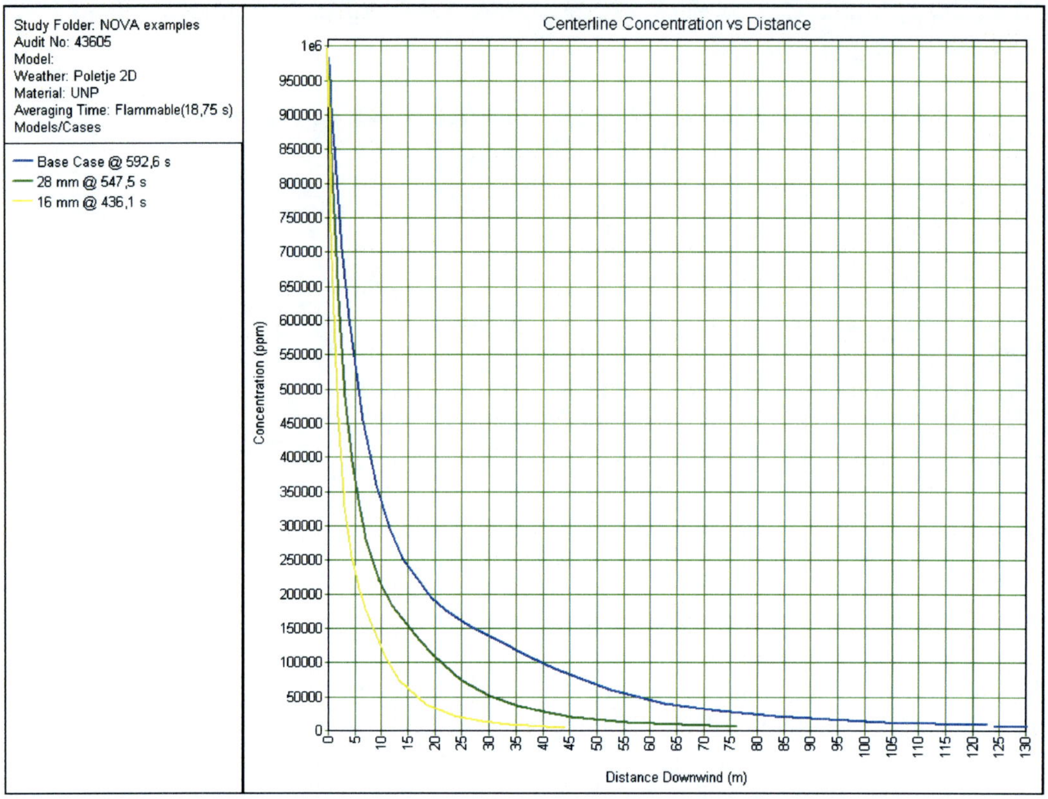

Figure 3. Example of the impact of the assumptions used at the source term step: LPG concentrations in open air against distance downwind from the release point considering release from 250 m^3 storage vessel, through 10 m pipe and alternative diameters: 50 mm (base case), 28 mm and 16 mm, respectively.

5. Transport and Accumulation (Fate)

Released substances are usually carried away by environmental media such as air, water stream, sloped terrain, etc., being also affected by the physical state (gas, liquid, solid). Considering land use planning issues, transport and fate of substances in gas or liquid states into the air is of a prime importance. The general approach is to apply source term substance release conditions as input to the modelling of the transport through the environmental media, e.g., air, and obtaining dispersion (fate) rate while substance is carried away. In that respect detailed environmental characteristics are needed, e.g., applicable wind conditions (speed, stability class), air temperature and similar.

Related issues/uncertainties at this step: Needless to say, uncertainties from previous steps are inherited. However, there are two main uncertainties present at this step: epistemic due to limits in the accuracy of the models/tools applied for assessment of transport/fate and the aleatory due to the statistical variability of the environmental data to be used. Generally speaking, the variability and predictability of the environmental data is more important and is usually considered through a set of sub-scenarios.

Example: let us consider further elaboration of the example from previous step - dispersion of LPG in air from 50 mm size leak and three weather situations (e.g., considering summer temperature 30°C, wind speeds 1.5, 2, and 4 m/s, respectively, corresponding wind stability categories according to Pasquill-Gifford, can provide situations named Summer 1.5F, Summer 2D and Summer 4D, respectively). Results of the modelling are shown on Figure 4. For the presentation purpose the LPG cloud is shown as an border line corresponding to the specific constant concentration (0.85 % by volume) in terms of top-to bottom view (footprint) of the cloud and distances. It can be seen for example, that maximum distances downwind to concentration of interest in this example are about 135, 120 and 100 m, considering weather situations named Summer 1.5F, Summer 2D and Summer 4D, respectively.

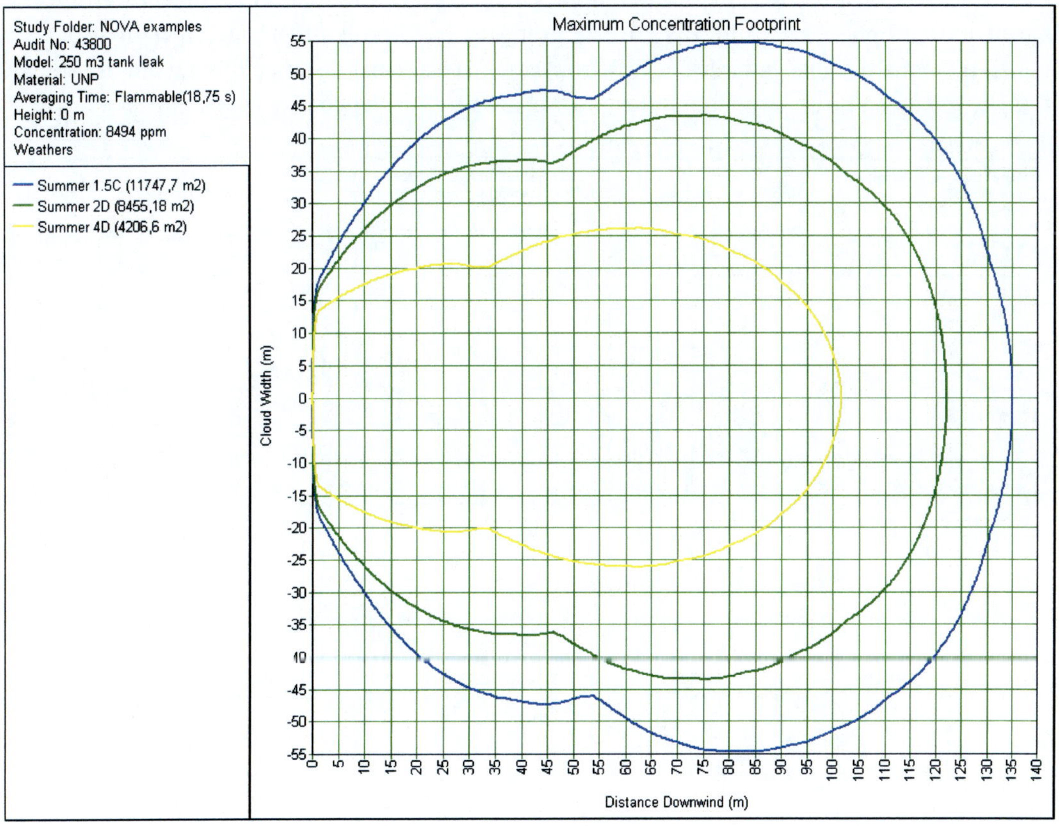

Figure 4. Example of environmental conditions (weather situations) impact on the extent of LPG cloud dispersion downwind. Border lines for specific concentration (0.85 % by volume) in terms of top-to bottom view (footprint) are shown considering situations Summer 1.5F, Summer 2D and Summer 4D, respectively.

6. Zones of Impact

The source term release and dispersion/fate assessment for hazardous substance can already provide needed results if we are concerned about toxic properties/damage. In a case of and/or flammable substance released additional dangerous phenomena such as flash fire (burning cloud), jet fire, pool fire and vapour cloud explosion are to be considered. The main issue regarding the fires is the related thermal radiation emitted, regarding explosion the issue is overpressure (shock) wave produced. The approach is again to use suitable models (implemented in programme tools) in order to predict thermal radiation level and/or peak overpressure levels over distances.

Related issues/uncertainties at this step: Needless to say, uncertainties from previous steps are inherited. There is epistemic uncertainty present due to limits in the accuracy and applicability of the models/tools applied, however, generally speaking this is not a major issue. In some cases aleatory uncertainty pertaining from environmental conditions (e.g., wind speed, location of ignition sources, etc.) can affect the results, however, that is usually resolved through built-in conservatism and elaboration of sub-scenarios.

Example: Considering previous example, let us assume LPG cloud is subject of ignition. One of the fire phenomena in this case is going to be a pool fire. The effect of leak size diameters on the thermal radiation levels from pool fire against distance downwind are shown on Figure 5. It can be concluded that results are strongly influenced by leak sizes.

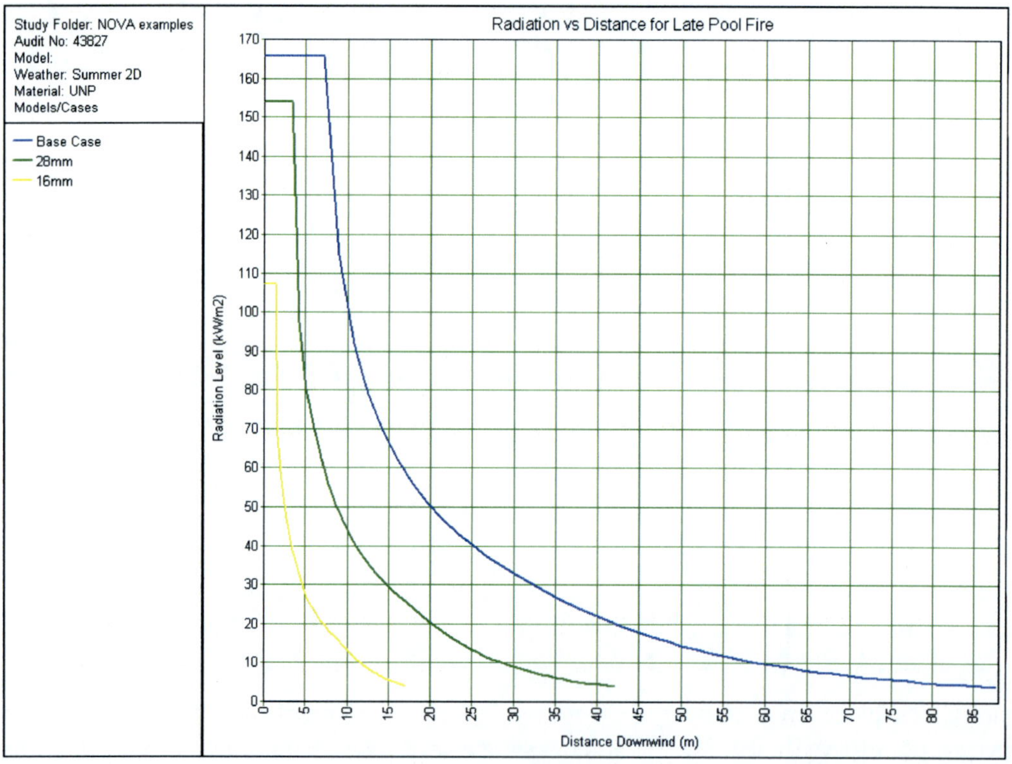

Figure 5. Example of the impact of the leak size diameter (50 mm (base case), 28 mm and 16 mm, respectively) on the thermal radiation levels due to LPG pool fire against distance downwind.

7. Doses, Consequences

Considering effects of the dangerous phenomena and vulnerability of the targets (e.g., humans) this step provides assessment of the expected level of damage (consequences). Performing this step, thus concludes determination of both components of the risk. The general approach is to compare actual (anticipated) exposure of exposed targets (if present) from the dangerous phenomena pertaining from specific scenario (dose received), against reference doses for certain levels of damage (e.g., fatalities, serious or minor injuries, damage to the buildings, process equipment, etc.). Thus, related to the damage level of a concern, corresponding reference doses are used in order to obtain zones of impact (impact distances). Considering given dangerous phenomena the following main approaches usually apply:

- considering exposure of humans to toxic substances via inhalation route, reference dose approaches differ in complexity. One of the simplest is Emergency Response Planning Guideline (ERPG) considering unprotected humans exposed to a certain concentration in ambient air up to 1 hour: not developing life threatening (ERPG-3), not developing non-reversible health effects (ERPG-2) and only developing smell/discomfort (ERPG-1) at the exposed.
- Considering exposure of humans to the thermal radiation from fire, simplest approach is to apply reference thermal radiation levels (in kW/m^2) at given location (distance) in order to obtain related anticipated damage levels. Excerpt from figures reported in the literature is given in Table 2. Note that figures implicitly consider exposure duration.
- Considering exposure of humans to the impacts of the explosion, usually reference peak overpressure levels at given location (distance) are applied in order to obtain anticipated damage levels.

Related issues/uncertainties at this step: Needless to say, uncertainties from previous steps are inherited. Considering this step only, limitations in the suitability and availability of the dose-consequence models/data used are usually considered low, but not absent (epistemic uncertainty). The aleatory uncertainty is more subtle in terms of actual exposure of the targets/humans. This means that it is difficult to be exact, and usually the approach is to be conservative (too pessimistic, but on a safe side).

Example: of interpretation of zones of impact and dose/consequences is given. Using previous example, detail of the thermal radiation levels against distance downwind is shown on Figure 6 in terms of thermal radiation level of 1.6 kW/m^2, as endpoint corresponding to the discomfort of humans at long exposures. It can be concluded that depending on leak sizes considered (16, 28 and 50 mm), impact zones to the endpoint used are approximately 25, 60 and 120 m, respectively, which can be interpreted as significant differences.

Table 2. Excerpt from literature data on the thermal radiation levels and damage caused

Thermal Radiation (kW/m^2)	Type of Damage Caused
37.5	Sufficient to cause damage to process equipment.
25	Minimum energy required to ignite wood at infinitely long exposures (non-piloted).
12.5	Minimum energy required for piloted ignition of wood, melting plastic tubing, etc.
4.5	Sufficient to cause pain to personnel if unable to reach cover within 20 seconds, however, blistering of skin (first degree burns) is unlikely.
1.6	Intensity sufficient to cause discomfort for long exposures.

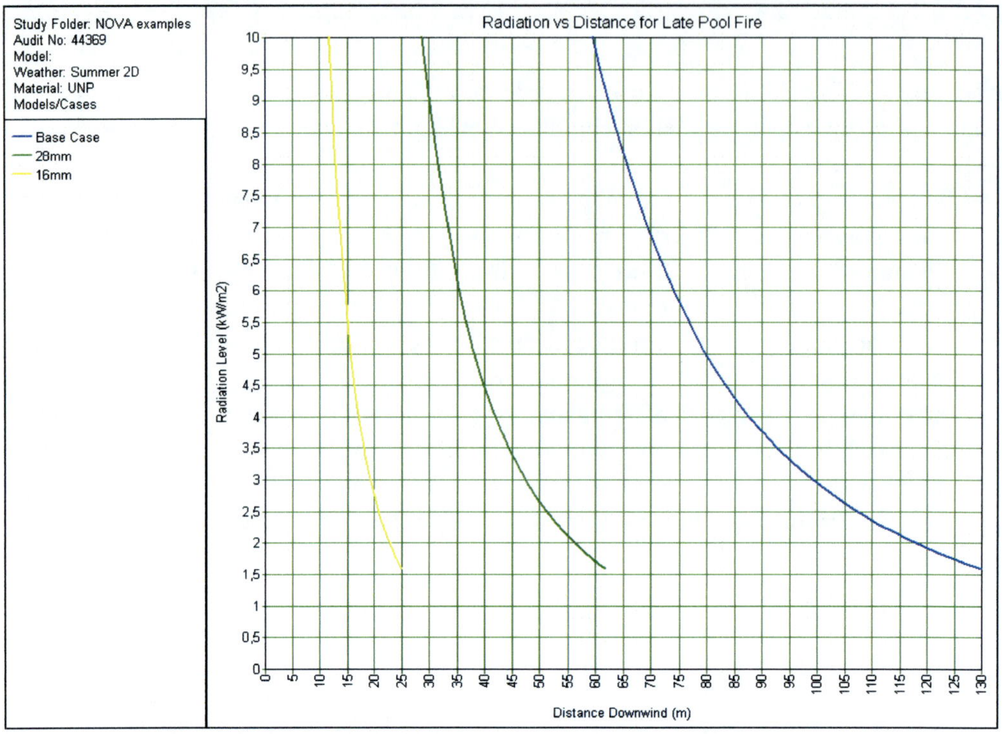

Figure 6. Detail from example in Figure 5. Impact zones (distances) down to thermal radiation level endpoint at 1.6 kW/m^2 are shown considering three leak sizes (50 mm, 28 mm, 16 mm, respectively). This endpoint represents discomfort to exposed humans for long exposures.

8. Risk Assessment Integration

Risk assessment usually results with a number of the elaborated scenarios and related results. The scenarios differ in terms of their likelihoods and consequences (severity of the damage). Considering application of the risk assessment's results for land use planning purposes, one must recall that we want to prevent damage to the surroundings, meaning that no person or object should be exposed beyond tolerable level of consequences, meaning certain tolerable doses, thus resulting in certain zones (distances) of exclusion ("exposure not allowed"). Technically speaking this means that we are not really interested in risk levels, but in related zones of impact in order to (ideally) remove the risk. Practically speaking, considering all scenarios analysed, the worst major accident scenario is usually screened out in terms of its maximum zones (distances) of impact related to tolerable (usually minor) level of the consequences. Alternatively, major accident scenarios subject of their very low (tolerable) likelihood could be skipped in such a screening. Anyway, thus obtained maximum zones (distances) are to be considered as a minimum distance from the risk source (major accident scenario's geographical location) to the surroundings to be protected by land use planning measures.

Land Use Planning Procedures, Policies and Levels

1. General

Land-use planning is defined as "a systematic assessment of land and water potential, alternative patterns of land use and other physical, social and economic conditions, for the purpose of selecting and adopting land use options which are most beneficial to land users without degrading the resources or the environment, together with the selection and implementation of measures most likely to encourage such land uses…" (FAO, 1976).

A plan is an intellectual anticipation of a desirable situation in the future, or in more simple words: a plan describes how a situation will exist. Planning is therefore the procedure for elaborating a plan. Actually this term covers a range of activities, from procedures of a purely technical type to administrative or governmental arrangements.

The EC provides a definition of "spatial planning" in its 1997 Compendium of Spatial Planning Systems and Policies (EC, 1997):

> "Spatial planning refers to the methods used by the public sector to influence the future distribution of activities in a space. It is undertaken with the aim of creating more rational territorial organisation of land uses and linkages between them to balance demands for development with the need to protect the environment and to achieve social and economic objectives. Spatial planning embraces measures to co-ordinate the spatial impacts of other sectoral policies to achieve more even distribution of economic development between regions than would otherwise be created by market forces and to regulate the conversion of land and property uses".

Spatial planning is thus a process of decision making, weighing between social, ecologic and economic demands. It is a steering instrument and also a regulatory procedure that:

- supports the economic development of the society
- safeguards environmental sustainability, including the safety of people
- achieves a reduction of regional disparity, and
- supports the development and stability of resources.

Spatial planning has also the character of a common generic term for the national physical/land use/territorial planning systems. The latter describe government action to regulate development and land uses in pursuit of agreed objectives. This form of planning is one policy sector within government, alongside policy sectors such as transport, agriculture, environmental protection and regional policy, although it may incorporate mechanisms to coordinate other sector policies.

The general plans are in essence models of a possible reality (Steinitz, 1976, 1990). Their service in connection with hazard mitigation is primarily in guiding future states of the environment against the identified scenarios of accidents (natural or technological in origin).

Many land-use planning methods are based on environmental impact assessment, whose basis is analysis based on interaction between environmental qualities and the activity (development) which is to be introduced. This interaction undergoes the evaluation process and the output result is a set of suitable locations for proposed development. However, such evaluation is conducted exclusively for normal operation (taking in consideration continuous point source pollution and nuisance), and excludes the incident scenarios. Risk is, therefore, not implemented in planning process when new industrial sites are developed.

Land use planning is commonly based on zoning process derived from spatial and economic analysis (structural analysis, urban analysis, acceptability analysis, feasibility analysis, etc.). An important part is played by environmental impact assessment (environmental vulnerability) for a given activity (considering primarily normal operation) in a certain (designated) study area. At the end of the process, zones are identified in which activities are, through the later licensing process, permitted to operate. As is clearly stated in the process of zoning, no risk assessment is taken into consideration.

2. Spatial/Land-Use Planning for Hazardous Industrial Establishments

The most effective preventive approach for reducing the consequences of industrial accidents is provision of appropriate separation distances between hazardous installations and residential areas (Christou and Papadakis, 1998; Christou et al, 1999; Christou and Mattarelli, 2000; Papazoglou et al. 2000).

In the context of spatial plan development this can be assured in one of the following phases:

a) in the phase of spatial plan development, where the proposed/chosen location is reserved for new/proposed hazardous installation and is properly distanced from vulnerable areas which are subject of protection (urban areas – hospitals, schools; natural areas, etc.)
b) in the phase of spatial plan revision/change where by changing the land-use plan – predominantly urban use – further proximity of hazardous and vulnerable areas is disabled; in this phase additional social and economic disagreements and conflicts occur associated with desires for closing-down or relocation of existing installations.

There are currently three main approaches to risk-informed land-use planning (Christou and Porter, 1999; Christou and Mattarelli, 2000; Christou et al., 2006):

a) the approach of generic separation (safety) distances,
b) the consequence-based approach, which focuses on the assessment of consequences of a number of conceivable event scenarios and shows the consequence area for lethal effects and serious injuries resulting from the scenarios assessed,
c) a risk-based approach which focuses on the assessment of both consequences and probabilities of occurrence of the possible event scenarios; it defines an area within which there is a given probability of a specified level of harm resulting from the large number of possible accident scenarios

Besides these main categories, a hybrid approach is also in use which is a combination of the last two; however, integration with the land-use planning process has not yet been established with any of the approaches. However, the praxis worldwide is risk-based conformity assessment of a development proposal or an existing situation coupled with the land-use planning goals, rather than integration into the land-use planning process as it is usually stated.

Generic Safety Distances

The determination and use of generic separation distances is based on the type of activity rather than on a detailed analysis of the risks. These safety distances are usually derived from expert judgments and are mainly based on historical factors, experience from operating similar plants, rough consequence calculations or information regarding the environmental impact of the plant. The approach of generic separation distances has been established and used in Germany and Sweden (Christou et al, 1999; Christou and Mattarelli, 2000; Hauptmanns, 2005).

Tables of appropriate distances are often used because of the limited relevance/knowledge of the case. The distance depends mainly on the type of industrial activity or on the quantity and type of hazardous substances present. Design characteristics, safety measures and particular features of the establishment under question are not explicitly taken into account. "Look-up" tables of generic distances can be very useful for standardised installations, especially for screening purposes. However, their conservative nature should always be taken into consideration and wherever practicable a detailed analysis is preferred.

The "Consequence-Based" Approach

The consequence-based approach focuses on assessment of the consequences of a number of reference scenarios obtained from a quantitative risk assessment study. Damage threshold values for accident physical effects (overpressure, thermal radiation, toxic concentration) are determined with respect to undesired consequences (fatalities, irreversible effects, reversible effects, etc.) (Christou, and Mattarelli, 2000). The method has generally been used in France, Finland, Luxembourg, Spain, Belgium and Austria (Christou et al, 1999; Hauptmanns, 2005; Cozzani et al., 2006; Stangl, 2006; Besi et al., 1996, Salvi et al., 2005) for existing hazardous installations or in the licensing procedures for specific development proposals.

The "consequence based" approach is based on the assessment of consequences of credible (or conceivable) accidents, without explicitly quantifying the likelihood of these accidents.

A basic concept is the existence of one or more "worst case scenario(s)", which are defined using expert judgment, historical data and qualitative information obtained from hazard identification. The underlying philosophy is based on the idea that if measures exist that are sufficient to protect the population from the worst accident, there will be sufficient protection for any less serious incident. Therefore, this method evaluates only the extent of the accident's consequences, and not their likelihood, which is taken into account only implicitly. Extremely unlikely scenarios may not be considered as "credible" or "conceivable" and may be excluded from further analysis.

The pre-selected "reference scenarios" can be chosen in various ways, either by a numerical or non-numerical consideration of the likelihood of occurrence or by simple expert judgement. Then, the more conceivable/reasonable of these reference scenarios (based on consideration of specific limiting conditions such as barriers or initiating events) are identified and taken into account for land-use planning purposes. Other, more serious, scenarios may not be considered for land use planning purposes, but possibly for emergency planning.

In this approach, the efficacy of measures (or barriers) is estimated qualitatively, semi-quantitatively, e.g., also judging on the character of representing an "independent layer of protection" (LOPA, 2001). The qualification for these measures, defined by norms, standards, national legislation, testing, etc., is usually taken as sufficient proof in this respect.

Zones defining restrictions in terms of land-use planning are determined by the calculation of distances at which the magnitude of the hazard (e.g. toxic concentration) reaches the threshold value for undesired effects (e.g. irreversible health effect/harm or fatality). An example of such zones is presented in Figure 7.

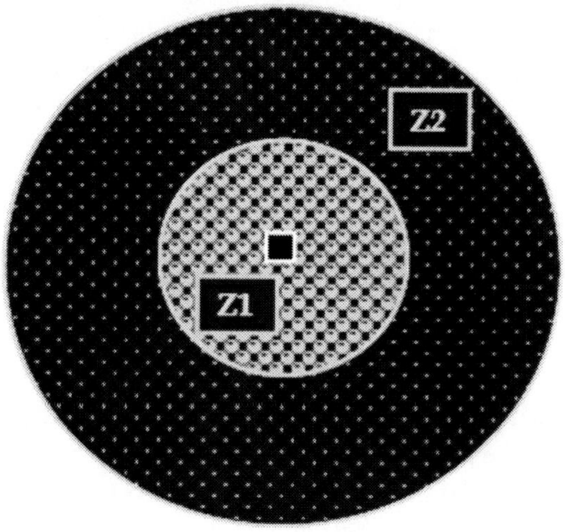

Figure 7. The land-use restriction zones according to the consequence-based approach. The zones correspond to pre-defined health effect thresholds Z1 and Z2.

This approach corresponds to the deterministic principle where safety, and thus undesirable consequences, are defined by a discrete value. The situation which is subject to planning restrictions is uniform (in terms of likelihood and severity) for the whole area within the calculated distance.

The Risk-Based/Probabilistic Approach

The risk-based approach (also known as the probabilistic approach) focuses on the assessment of both consequences and expected occurrence frequency or probability of possible accident scenarios. To estimate the likelihood of scenarios, various methods are in use, ranging from simple selection of scenarios and frequencies from the relevant databases to the application of sophisticated tools.

In general, the risk based approaches define the risk as a combination of the consequences derived from the range of possible accidents, and the likelihood of these accidents. The risk assessment process has been elaborated in chapter 2.1.

The results are represented as:

- the individual risk, defined as the probability of the reference damage (e.g. fatality, or "receiving a dangerous dose or worse"), due to an accident in the installation, for an individual located at a specific point near the installation, and
- the societal risk, defined for groups of people, which is the probability of occurrence of any single accident resulting at reference damage (e.g. fatalities) greater than or equal to a specific figure. Individual risk is usually presented by the iso-risk curves, while F-N curves provide a visualisation of the societal risk (Christou and Mattarelli, 2000; AIChE, 2000; Kletz, 1992) (examples of criteria are presented in Figure 8).

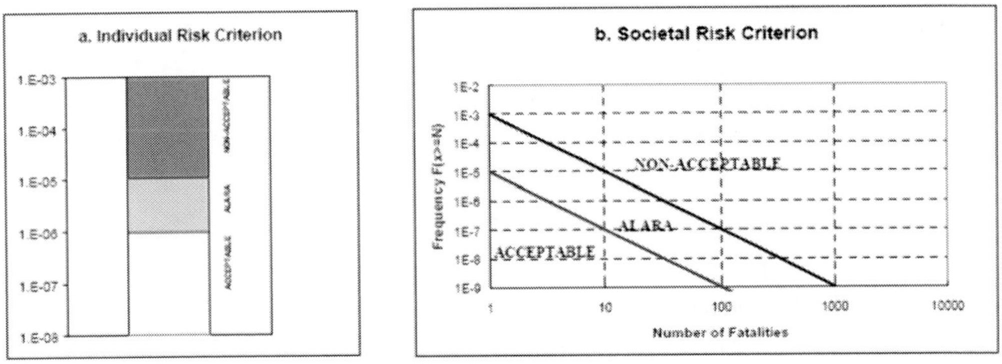

Figure 8. Examples of criteria for (a) individual and (b) societal risk.

The general idea of establishing individual and societal risk criteria is given below. Usually there are three categories of risk; one that is acceptable (or "tolerable", or "desirable"), one that is non-acceptable, and a category where the risk can be considered as affordable, however its reduction is strongly desired (according to the national policy for the status of the "acceptability" criteria, such as the ALARA principle – As Low As Reasonably Achievable, or the ALARP principle – As Low As Reasonably Practicable).

Land-use planning criteria are based on specific acceptability criteria with respect to the calculated risk. In terms of land-use planning, the results are used as the basis for risk reduction measures in terms of lowering the probability of incidents, as well as being a guideline for determining the acceptability of proposed development in the vicinity of hazardous sites. This approach is used in the United Kingdom and in the Netherlands (Cozzani et al. 2006; HSE, 1989, 2006; Laheij, 2000; Basta et. al, 2007) and is usually performed in the licensing stage, not in the land-use planning stage.

Hybrid Methods

A hybrid approach combining the last two has been devised and used is in Italy. It is based on a consequence-based approach, but takes frequencies into account (Cozzani et al. 2006). The method requires the identification of four damage zones. Threshold values for each of the three accidental cases (toxic release, fire and explosion) are supported by legislation. The vulnerability of surrounding land-uses is also taken into consideration (Carpignano et al., 2001).

The frequency values calculated for each scenario are considered as mitigating factors for land-use planning restrictions and are not used to express the individual or societal risk.

Within the hybrid approach two sub-categories are distinguished:

- Deterministic approach with implicit judgment of risk
- Semi-Quantitative Method

3. Issues Associated with Land-Use Planning

General

The problem of successful integration of risk assessment and spatial planning encompasses multiple issues in terms of land-use planning. The key two are:

- First, the absence of detailed and specific information about the new hazardous industrial installations at the stage of preparing and adopting a land-use plan. Namely, at this stage only generic data is available about hazardous installations which will be situated in an industrial zone. Such generic data are inadequate for preparing specific and quantitative risk assessment which could be the basis for designing a preventive policy with effective risk reduction measures/strategies at the stage of land-use planning. On the other hand detailed risk assessment for existing hazardous installations is possible; however its results have not been applied effectively in a land-use plan.
- Second, changes which appear due to the implementation of a land-use plan. This is illustrated in Figure 9. The message is that neither conformity assessment (confirmation against the selected risk criteria at the stage of land-use plan adoption), nor any kind of environmental impact assessment guarantees that risk will remain low (acceptable) throughout the land-use plan implementation, i.e. no matter what changes occur in urbanisation or other uses of the environment in the surrounding of hazardous installation.

Part a) of the Figure 9 illustrates current situations: ten or twenty years after the plan approval, and due to urbanisation development in the surroundings of the industrial zone where a hazardous industrial installation, i.e. Seveso II plant[1] is situated, the situation is no longer satisfactory or acceptable (high risk) as it was at the time of plan adoption (at t=0). Possible land-use planning safety improvement measures (risk reduction) are: relocation or shut down of the Seveso II plant; relocation of the population from the residential objects in proximity to the plant if the risk situation is extreme; implementation of additional preventive measures at the plant (e.g., safety improvement by installing additional safety devices) as well as more effective protective measures in the surroundings (e.g., additional technical barriers

[1] Seveso II plant/establishment is a common term for hazardous industrial installations from the Seveso II Directive.

against direct exposure of the population or improvement of the external emergency plan by assuring an effective evacuation).

Part b) of the Figure 9 illustrates how the conformity assessment is to be understood. Such an assessment at t=0, i.e. at the time of adopting a plan, may show that the situation in terms of risk is acceptable (low risk).

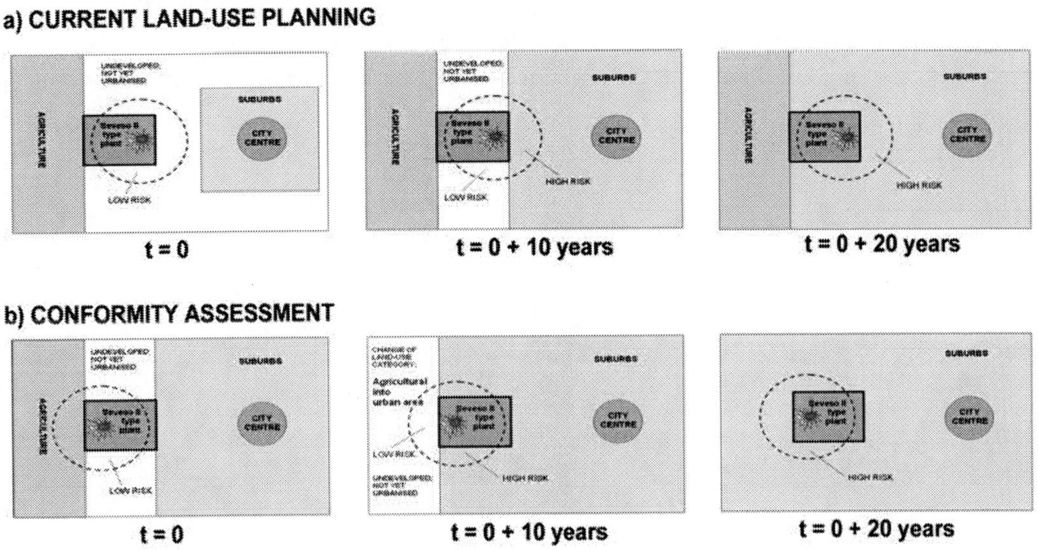

Figure 9. Illustration of risk related land-use planning issues.

However, if the conformity assessment is done again after ten or twenty years, the result may no longer be satisfactory or acceptable. This would mean that only the "frozen" land-use state, as shown at t=0, assures conformity and low risk. If such a "freezing" of the current state of a land-use plan would indeed be applied it would fundamentally change the existing philosophy and practice of land-use planning. It would basically countermand what the plan (the society) was initially saying should happen as land-use development in the future, so a question about the very purpose of the land-use planning would arise.

Spatial/Land-Use Planning Process

Land use planning focuses on zoning policy, i.e., dedication of a particular piece of territory to a certain purpose/use. Plan implementation is assured through the licensing process. Licensing relates to the implementation of a plan and is not, strictly speaking, a component of the planning activities (see Figure 10). Licensing basically consists of two stages: i) confirming whether the location of a proposed development project is in accordance with the zoning plan, and ii) confirming whether environmental acceptability standards will be met during operation of the proposed activity (emission and imission standards, nature protection goals and targets, etc.). The latter is to be demonstrated in the framework of an Environmental Impact Assessment (EIA). It is important to note that, at present, no specific quantitative safety standards are available for both stages. However, the approaches are under development.

Existing vs. New Hazardous Industrial Establishments

There is a difference in planning for existing or new hazardous industrial installations. For existing installations the technology, safety management systems, operational records, compliance status, standardization, etc. are known. The determination of impact zones associated with particular accidents is thus relatively accurate. On the other hand, at the stage of preparation of a land-use plan for a new industrial zone, little is known about the particular establishment and specific industries which will occupy the zone in the future. In such cases determination of impact zones is uncertain, thus this is clearly an issue that needs attention.

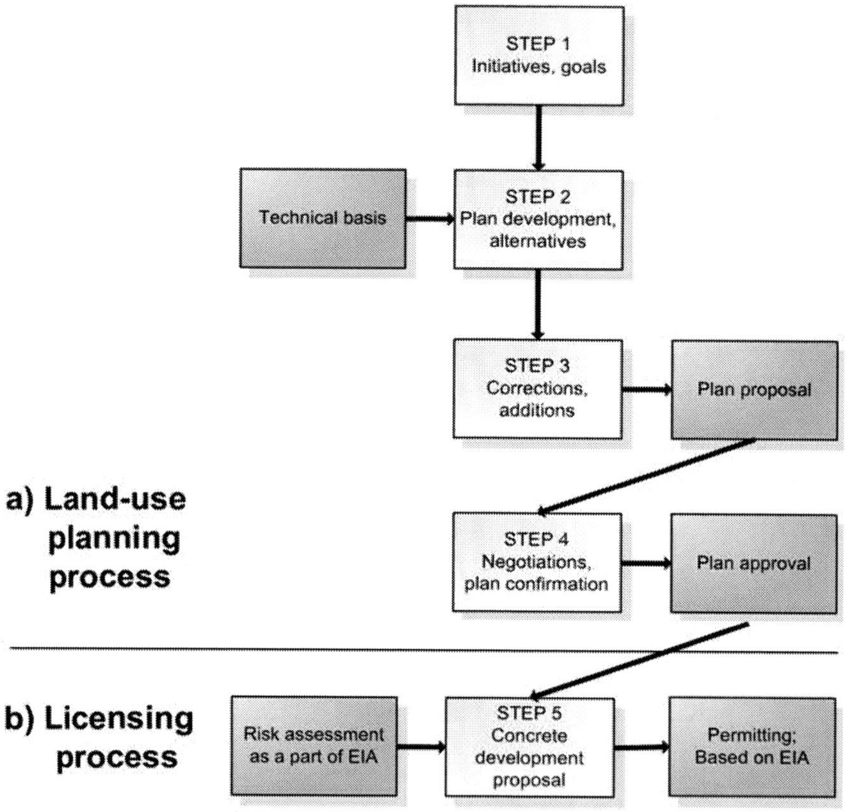

Figure 10. Schematic presentation of a spatial planning process: a) land-use planning process; b) licensing process. The scheme illustrates that at present risk assessment is applied within the licensing process and not in the planning stage.

Discussion about Closing the Gap

We assume that risk assessment and spatial/land-use planning can be successfully integrated by modifications of both the existing risk assessment and the spatial/land-use planning methods.

The modification/improvement of a risk assessment methodology should include its transformation to yield results in a form useful for land-use planners.

Modifications of spatial/land-use planning methodology are required to successfully implement risk assessment into the plan development process. These include improvement of the spatial/land-use planning procedure, which would allow discussion and optimisation of industrial risk from the early beginning of a plan development process.

The main reasons why planning process for hazardous industrial installations should be modified are:

- Implementation of the concept of proper safe distances is possible only if a hazardous installation is known and specified, i.e. if the impact/risk area can be determined. This is achievable only for existing installations and those for which licensing process is taking place. At the level of preparing a new zoning (land-use) plan, precise information on new hazardous occupants of the zones are not available, so the concept of proper distances based on accurate risk assessment is not possible at this stage.
- Licensing means that a development project is in its final planning stage. No developer would start the licensing process during preparation of a new land use plan, i.e., without assurance that the proposed location for the project is in accordance with the approved land-use plan – acceptable in terms of administrative procedure and social/economic development;
- In order to make land-use planning successful, the participation of all stakeholders must be established in a plan developing process, not only in a plan implementation process. This is difficult to achieve in the case of lack of information or ineffective presentation of information.

1. How to Bridge the Gap – Modification of Risk Assessment Methods

This chapter discusses bridging the gap between risk assessment and land-use planning by the modification of risk assessment methods to provide results applicable in land-use planning. The proposed approach (method) suggests the use of indexing as a form of results which allow distinguishing between different consequences expected on the targets (Kontić and Kontić, 2009; ARAMIS, 2004). The approach is addressed to as threat analysis. Such indexation is devised from the distances acquired as an endpoint of risk assessment process (i.e. severity of an incident – spatial distribution of expected effects – expressed as threat intensity level) and the expected vulnerability of the targets within distances in question. This approach has been described in detail by Kontić and Kontić (2009). A diagram of the threat analysis – a process of developing threat index – is presented in Figure 11.

Threat intensity level: a measure oriented to represent the magnitude and spatial distribution of the consequences associated with selected physical effects of incident outcomes (overpressure, thermal radiation, toxic concentrations in air and water). It takes into account a set of threshold levels concerning these consequences. At its core it is conceptually similar to risk severity, which allows the assessment of the risk level originated by a given installation over the affected zone (ARAMIS 2004, Planas et al., 2006).

The threat intensity level is devised from the accidental release data (see chapter 4. Accidental Releases) transformed into a series of GIS based maps for selected physical effects, where each cell carries a value on a scale of 1-5 according to the threshold level (1-low, 5-high). It represents one of the two main components (the second being the vulnerability of targets) of risk assessment that are to be used in spatial/land-use planning.

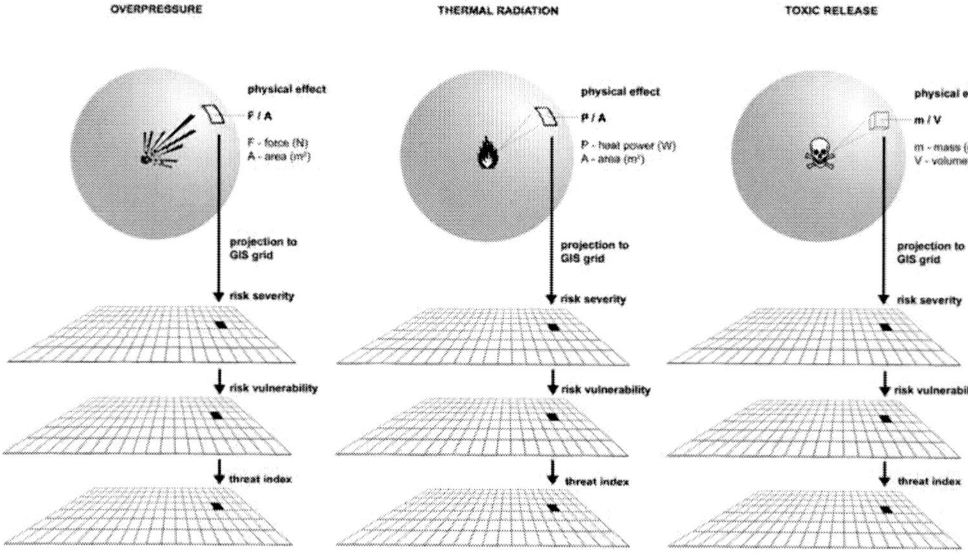

Figure 11. A diagram of the process of developing threat index.

Vulnerability of targets: a state or characteristic of the environmental component which is the receptor of a negative change (effect) due to an accident involving hazardous materials (Kværner, et al., 2006; Tixier et al., 2005, 2006; Marušič, 1993).

Threat index: expresses the degree of threat to a specific environmental element in the case of an accident. It is expressed numerically (semi-quantitative) and represents different levels of potential harm. In its essence, it builds on a consequence-based approach of risk assessment and combines it with the vulnerability of targets, i.e. receptors of consequences. As such, it requires the identification of accident scenarios with a consideration of the spatial distribution of physical effects.

An example of the application of the approach for a BLEVE scenario at LPG storage and handling facility is presented in Figure 12.

Threat analysis provides readily applicable information about hazard/risk/threat to be used in the framework of land-use planning (Kontić and Kontić, 2009). This information is beneficial in terms of:

- ensuring that no Seveso II plants are allocated in industrial zones surrounded by urban or in other vulnerable areas (e.g. surface and groundwater for drinking purposes, natural protected areas, etc.) (Figure 13 a).

- Limiting the development in the higher risk areas in order to minimise risk (Figure 13 b). The question posed in this regard is what regime would sustain the undeveloped land vis-à-vis ever-increasing pressure for development of open space.
- Providing conditions for siting hazardous installations in the initial stages of preparing a land-use plan, so that risk conflicts are avoided during the whole timeframe of implementing the plan. This results in the minimisation of risk/threat by separating human-made structures as far as possible from the source areas, and in the progressive inclusion of less vulnerable land uses or development towards the risk source (Figure 13 b). This conceptualisation is similar to the current praxis of appropriate distances (Christou et al., 2006). The application of this model could result in a slowdown in spatial development that would hardly be socially acceptable within the constraints of more sustainable development.
- Determination of the most appropriate development (urban design) in the vicinity of the risk/threat source by increasing the resilience of the objects to the effects/dangerous phenomena of incidents (by shape, orientation of buildings) (Figure 13 c).

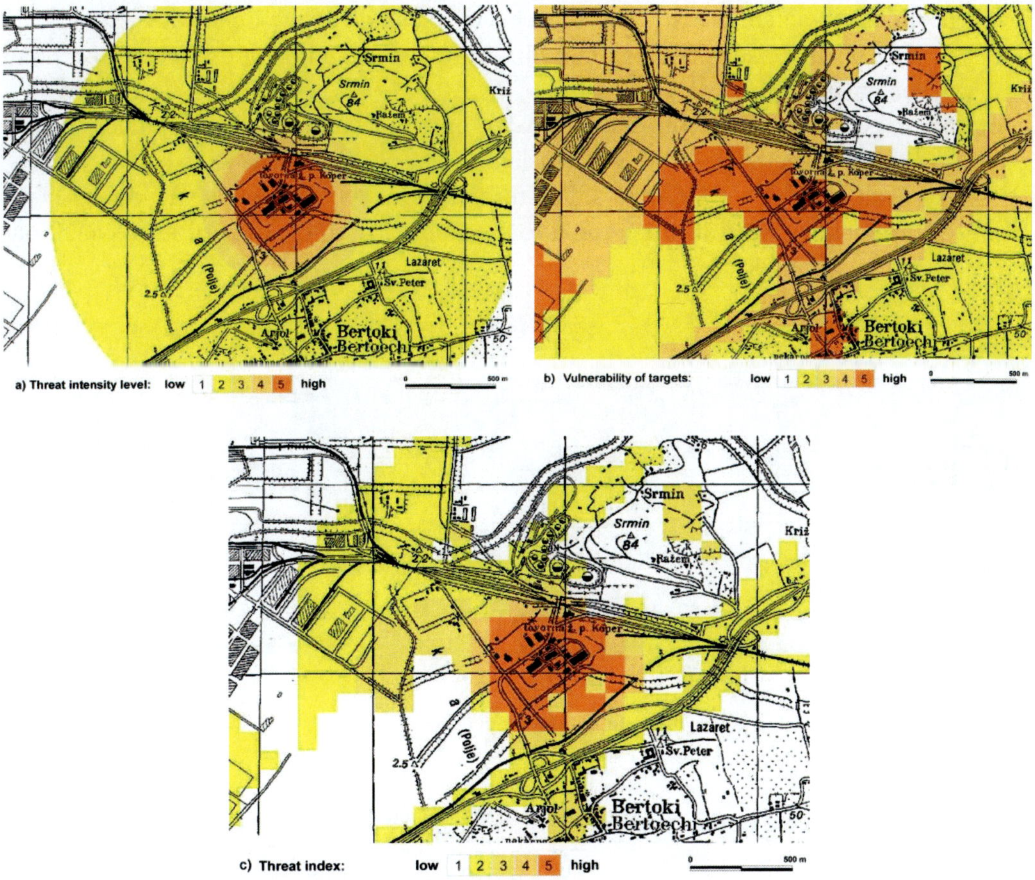

Figure 12. Example of threat analysis application for a LPG storage and handling facility; a) threat intensity level; b) vulnerability of targets; c) threat index.

The approach described above enables transparent and understandable interpretation of risk/threat for land-use planning purposes. The presentation of threat index in a GIS format is focused towards compatibility with other results of various spatial/environmental analyses conducted in the framework of land-use plan preparation.

Such analysis can be used as a basis for siting new hazardous industrial installations, as well as for controlling development around them. Moreover, the results can serve as guidelines for determining priorities for management within the impact area.

Three approaches for managing threat in terms of land-use planning are considered:

a) Standardisation – prohibition and/or control of development in areas of high threat (level 4 and 5), or conditionally allowing development in areas with medium threat (level 2-3). If such buffer zones are established, they would remain under constant development monitoring, where no development would be encouraged. Location, construction and operational permits (i.e. licensing) would be a question of case-by-case considerations by the authorities.
b) Technological optimisation – implementing technical measures on the installation to prevent or minimise the occurrence of incidents and associated consequences (an approach commonly used). The consequent reduction of the impact area could make future use of the surroundings more liberal and oriented towards stronger economic development.
c) Spatial development optimisation – based on the detailed threat index determination and the introduction of resilience (sustainability, probability of withstanding) index – a selection of uses of land and structures that would be able to withstand the severity of the consequences they are going to be exposed to in the case of an accident on a given/proposed location.

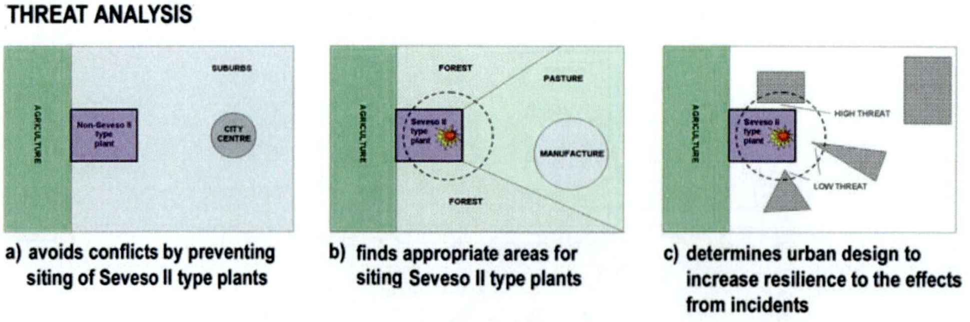

Figure 13. Utility of the threat analysis method for land-use planning.

2. How to Bridge The Gap – The Development of the Land Use Planning Process

In this chapter we address the development of the land-use planning process to allow or further support the integration of risk assessment and land-use planning.

Generalisation of a land-use planning process is schematically presented in Figure 14a. It consists of four main steps. It is evident that neither hazard, threat nor risk analysis are involved in this process. However, risk assessment is required in the implementation stage – step 5; after the plan making process – as part of the Environmental Impact Assessment (EIA) process during the licensing procedure (Kontić and Kontić, 2009; Kontić et al, 2006). The Environmental Impact Assessment of proposed development projects is an important base for the decision-making process in urban development, land-use planning, and other human activities related to altering the natural and built environments. Typically, environmental impact assessment comes "post factum", i.e. once the design of a project has been completed. Such an approach is not in accordance with the Seveso II Directive which requires consideration of risk assessment results in the land-use planning process as a means of minimising the consequences of accidents. A suggested improvement of the planning process so as to meet this requirement is presented in Figure 14b, requiring primary inputs to happen at early analytical stages of the plan-making process. The proposed modification extends the technical basis by general terms for siting hazardous installations, and provides preliminary determination of appropriate distances between a hazardous installation and vulnerable surrounding land-uses.

In the second step of the procedure (2a) general criteria and terms for allocation of hazardous installations are determined based on past experience for similar installations. In the new (proposed) sub-step (2b), a detailed allocation (within the industrial zone and in the surroundings) is determined, including safe distances, orientation, safety zones, etc. based on more detailed information about the proposed project. Additional detailed information about the hazardous industrial installation, including analysis of the resilience of the proposed installation/development, would also be included in this and the subsequent steps 3, 4 and 5. These steps would also provide the guidelines for architectural design, traffic infrastructure, locating new vulnerable objects (hospitals, schools, etc.), as well as other infrastructure (hydrant infrastructure, means of information in case of emergency, emergency infrastructure – fire escapes, routes of evacuation), which would contribute to more efficient evacuation in case of an accident.

In addition, the proposed alteration of the process requires continuous monitoring of the plan implementation (loop from step 5 to sub-steps 2a, 2b, 3, 4). Such feed-back loops enable prevention of conflicting spatial development around hazardous installations at all stages of the planning process by maintaining proper distances as long as needed. The fact that planning is seen as a process, is also one of the earliest and most essential factors to be recognised in the context of hazard and spatial/land-use planning integration. A continuous planning activity is more important than plans (Mušič, 1993; Kontić and Kontić, 2009).

Parallel to the modification of land-use planning process, threat analysis is divided into three sub-phases to be applied to different stages of land-use planning process, thus aiding to the success of the integrative approach.

These sub-phases are:

- *preliminary threat analysis* – early stage of LUP process; The main advantage of the approach is that it can provide preliminary guidelines for allocating new hazardous establishments, and act as a controlling instrument for development proposals around existing ones. Results in the form of the preliminary threat analysis also represent the basis for decision-making about allocation of future industrial zones featuring hazardous industrial installations. It is important to note that such maps can provide the basis for siting future installations, for which detailed specifications in the stage of developing zoning ordinances are not available.Preliminary threat analysis can serve as a tool for finding the most appropriate location for a proposed hazardous industrial installation for which the safety related information is available.

- *development of threat index* – intermediate stage(s) of LUP process; the analysis resulting in a definition of a threat index aims at the identification of threat in the vicinity of existing hazardous industrial establishments (or planned with known location).
- *resilience analysis (development of resilience index)* – latest stage of LUP process; in order to perform optimization in risk/threat informed land-use planning, it is necessary to reflect the resilience (sustainability, probability of withstanding) of the environmental components to the physical effects of the incidents. Resilience is to be properly considered in the framework of environmental threat-vulnerability analysis and is conducted for majority of environmental components. The optimization then is applied in the development of the surroundings of the hazardous industrial installation in question.

As described above, the suggested modification of the LUP process allows risk related information to be included at different stages of devising a land-use plan (i.e. when available), thus contributing to lesser conflicts in the final stages of LUP process.

The integration of different levels of spatial/land-use planning and risk information is presented in Figure 15.

The above methodological considerations can also be defined as efforts in developing a comprehensive interdisciplinary approach in land-use planning as a synergetic commitment of different professional perceptions and contributions, and all the agents involved in the land-use planning process.

The common practice of land-use planning and environmental management leaves little space for fear of disasters, and thereby for the necessary preparedness, as a special activity or concern. Therefore, risk assessment, expressed through this integrative approach, and the resulting measures for protection against the consequences of incidents are integrated into overall environmental planning and management activities.

As mentioned previously, a new spatial/land-use planning procedure, in order to successfully integrate risk/threat analysis, requires continuous monitoring of plan implementation. Different governmental agencies and sectors may incline to different styles of planning, since they all have their own form and approach to preparing plans. They may be oriented towards immediate and short-term results, while some might have a specific long-range view. The need for constant "development monitoring", by which the aforementioned differences of planning processes and results are brought to the same denominator must be emphasized again. As such, development monitoring would help to diminish the possible incoherence among local and hierarchically higher levels of planning (e.g. national). The results of such monitoring of plan or development proposals should be re-evaluated in terms of risk/threat analysis.

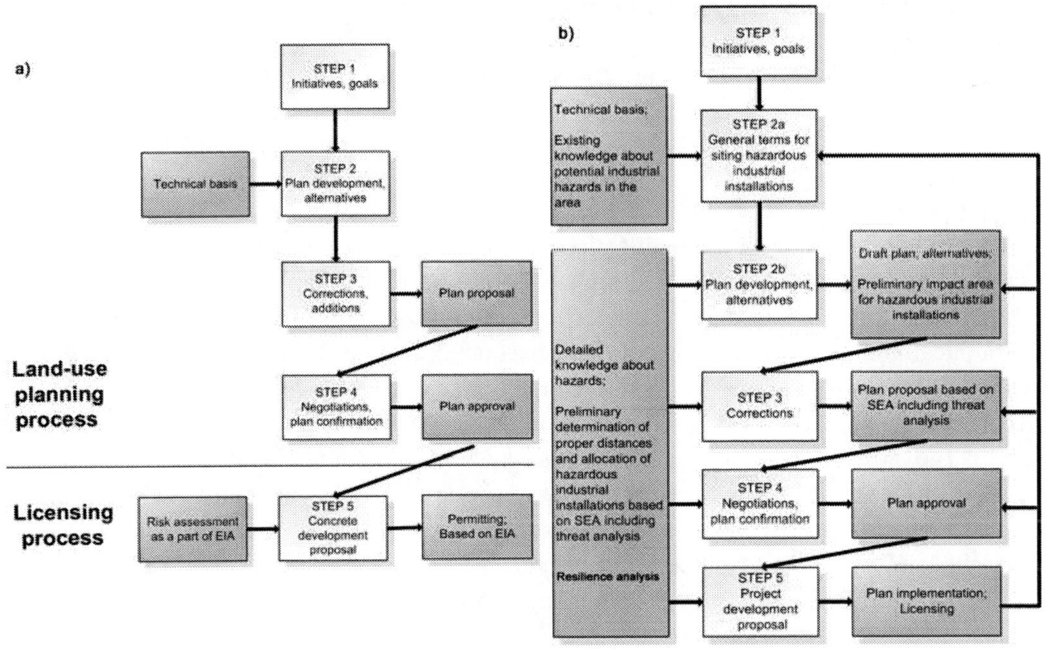

Figure 14. Schematic presentation of threat analysis and land-use planning integration; a) existing spatial/land-use planning process, b) proposal for modification of the spatial/land-use planning process.

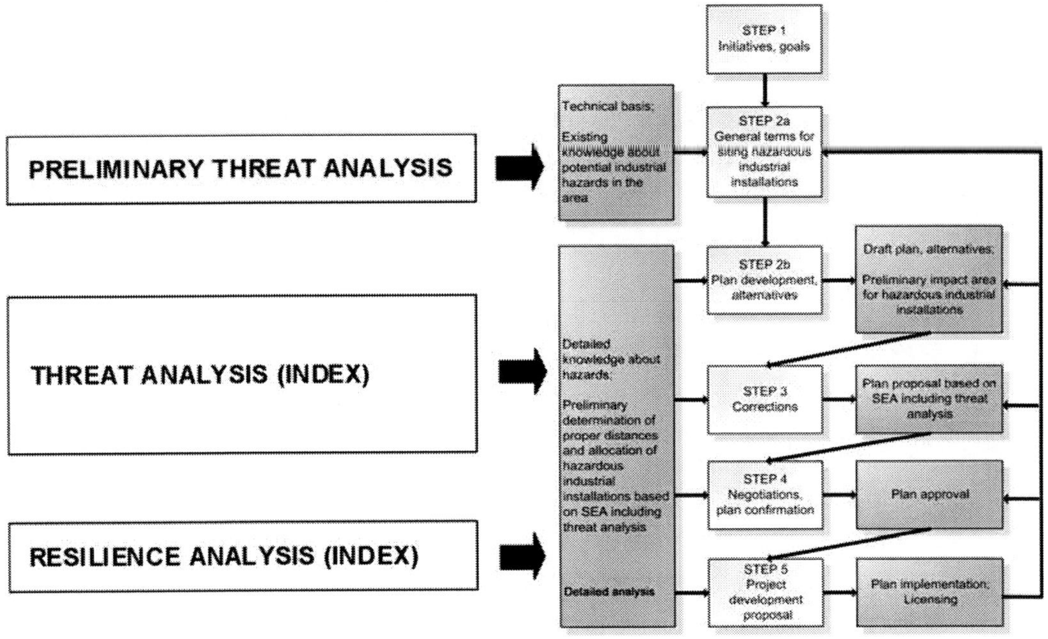

Figure 15. The integration of risk information in different levels of spatial/land-use planning.

3. Other Issues on Bridging the Gap

The Role of Accident Scenarios for the Determination of Impact Area

The role of scenario analysis is to provide important information regarding the selection of the reference accident scenarios to be used as a basis for risk informed spatial/land-use planning (Kontić and Kontić, 2007).

One should be aware of the implications of the accident scenarios at two levels. The first is selection of a scenario which has an impact on land-use planning. It is obvious that for this purpose some kind of preliminary risk or threat analysis should be made first, providing a geographical indication of the scope of the consequences before detailed risk/threat analysis is performed. In land-use planning, impacts of the scenario are relevant in terms of both human interests for land use and environmental protection. How much land a certain scenario "covers" (i.e. how big is the impact zone) and what environmental qualities may be degraded or lost in the case of an accident is ultimately a question of acceptability. Whether or not accident scenarios clearly and adequately associate these issues is a question to be identified during the land-use planning process.

The second level is accuracy or rather trustworthiness of the scenario. If the uncertainty of the selected scenario is too big and subsequent alteration of the impact area too significant, the land-use planning process may reject the approach as too vague or too sensitive. Namely, specific land uses in an actual land-use plan have sharp and static borders; there are no "grey" zones between neighbouring land uses, which would imply uncertainties of the scenario (e.g., alteration of the impact zone due to different modelling assumptions causing variations of the amount of involved substance). If scenario uncertainties are so big that they affect the land-use planning process, additional efforts should be made either to identify their sources, classify them into categories (e.g. epistemic or aleatory) and find the means for their reduction, or to investigate what additional safety measures could be applied (e.g., improvement of the safety management system at the plant) for the elimination of the scenario or diverting it into one with lower uncertainty, or to one non-relevant for land-use planning.

Consequence Thresholds

The difficult decision, in terms of planning for hazardous elements decision, rests primarily on the acceptable level of risk, which is related to many factors. A survey of threshold levels over diverse countries showed that uniform criteria concerning the values of thermal radiation, overpressure, etc. do not exist, even though several similar threshold values were found (ARAMIS, 2004).

Thresholds appear to be an important factor when determining the scope of the impact area. The selection of consequences, in relation to specific thresholds to be applied in the analysis, is of utmost importance.

Implication of Probabilities

Scenario likelihood/probability plays an important role in risk based decision-making (Slovic et al, 1984; Wynne, 1992; Laheij, 2000; Burger, 2001; Slovic, 2001). However, the implication of probabilities into land-use planning is a difficult task, because of a diametrical difference between the nature of risk and a land-use plan.

A land-use plan is a definite, static, and compulsory agreement between stakeholders about land uses in a particular area. Specific land uses in an actual land-use plan have sharp and static borders; there are no "grey" zones between neighbouring land uses, which would imply uncertain nature of risk.

Once a land-use plan is approved it only remains to be executed. In this perspective it appears that the best foundation for assuring proper incorporation of variable risk assessment results is the probability density function analysis of the outcomes of the scenario in question. Otherwise, uncertain and diverse results in terms of size of impact area should be considered only as an orientation; they do not represent exact basis for border drawing in an actual spatial/land-use plan.

The risk management literature examines acceptable risk as a function of management, which involves monetary gain, public participation in the siting process, and sometimes operational control as well as participation in reviewing operations at facilities (Shape-Risk, 2005). Risk management is an important element in the social acceptability of risk. Risk management includes reducing risk through improvements in the technology aimed at reducing the probability of an undesirable event, restricting land use near potentially hazardous facilities and creating emergency response capabilities aimed at the reduction of potential consequences (Hale et al., 2005).

In terms of land-use planning a discrepancy occurs, in that the safety management factors of the facility can be changed within a short time period, while general land-use plans are made for long (longer) time periods (10 or 20 years – a typical life of a land-use plan). Safety management system (EC, 2003) is the subject of regular safety auditing and inspection. If violation of safety policy and standards is recognised, which can be associated with conformity with the land-use plan, the responsible inspector is obliged to require improvements for the purpose of harmonisation of the safety management and overall safety of the installation with the land-use plan. The emphasis regarding the need for continuous development monitoring around hazardous industrial installations is again evident.

Application of the Method for New Hazardous Installations

The afore described threat analysis contributes to land-use management around existing hazardous installations, as well as to inform the search for suitable locations for new ones and to be used when preparing a new land-use plan. However, there are a number of issues related to the latter. The main problem here is lack of information about new installations (technology, capacity and safety measures) in the early land-use planning phases (Hauptmanns, 2005). The solution for the land-use planning process is being sought in an additional methodological step in land-use plan development, as well as revision (amendment) of existing steps (see Figure 14). The main idea here is that, through preliminary threat analysis and strategic environmental assessment (e.g. assessment of a municipal plan), the general terms and conditions for allocation of new hazardous installations are provided, while in the following steps a precise siting process is applied along with the determination of appropriate distances, orientation, eventual buffer zones and use of land in the vicinity of the establishment – based on more specific information provided by the developers.

4. Uncertainties

Risk and uncertainties are by definition inter-related terms (Petersen, 2002; Mlakar, 2006). The primary source of uncertainty concerning (risk-informed) land-use planning is the lack of data about the risk/threat source as well as about the receptors (humans, environment) on a designated level of analysis. Others include uncertainties associated with the understanding of the legislative framework, methodologies used, estimation of impacts to the environment, systems of values, etc. (Mlakar, 2006). To overcome these issues certain estimates must be made. When data is not available or of a quality which cannot be verified, generalised expert judgment and/or scenarios can be used (Mlakar, 2006). The issues of thereby related uncertainties are additionally problematical when following the EU Guidelines which require that risk-informed land-use planning is to be based on the selection of reference scenarios (Christou et al., 2006). As mentioned previously, in the land-use planning (predominantly for new hazardous industrial installations, zones) the details about the installations are not known, therefore the related uncertainties are so much greater.

In the context of land-use planning, risk assessment scenario and subjective uncertainty are of primary importance. Scenario uncertainty may be the reason for errors in consideration of type of consequences, while wrong expert judgements may bring erroneous interpretation of results. Both have potential for triggering conflicts and questionable decision-making, with long-term societal implications.

Risk impact area determination is also uncertain, which undoubtedly affects the perception and related decision-making. Distances presented in metre accuracy are an example of such uncertainty. Such results should be considered as an approximation and do not represent absolute values or background for possible border drawing in actual spatial/land-use plan. Generally the accepted level of uncertainty lies within an order of magnitude, while independent/individual components vary between 10% and factors of 2, 3 or more (AIChE, 2000; Kontić and Gerbec, 2008).

Conclusion

This paper demonstrates that risk assessment and spatial/land-use planning can be successfully integrated by modifying existing risk assessment and spatial planning methods. This was demonstrated by the introduction of threat analysis which includes the modification/improvement of the commonly used risk assessment methodologies to yield results in the form of threat index. Modifications of the spatial planning process are also a key factor for successful implementation of risk assessment into the plan development process. The latter thus allows discussion and optimisation of industrial risk at the beginning of a plan development process. The integration has proven successful due to the fact that the analysis is simultaneously scientifically accurate and flexible to the point that it can be used for existing as well as new establishments. The second important factor is that the method allows the preliminary identification of potential problems/issues when technological and/or spatial modifications are feasible. The third important factor of the method is that it is transparent, requiring the participation of all stakeholders in the plan developing, not only the plan implementation process.

The suggested approach succeeded in integrating two areas of concern regarding the risk-informed land-use planning. First, the interaction of different technical backgrounds, professional methods and approaches used in the preparation of plans (design and introduction of threat analysis), and second, the implementation of the technical basis concerning risk (hazard) into plans (changes to land-use planning process in order to accept threat analysis as an integrative component).

References

AIChE. 2000. *Guidelines for chemical process quantitative risk analysis*, Second Edition, AIChE, Center for chemical process safety, New York.

ARAMIS. 2004. ARAMIS project - Accidental Risk Assessment Methodology for Industries in the context of the Seveso II Directive. Final User Guide EVG1 – CT – 2001 – 00036.

Basta C., Neuvel J.M.M., Zlatanova S., Ale B. 2007. Risk-maps informing land-use planning processes; A survey on the Netherlands and the United Kingdom recent developments, *J. Haz. Mat.*, **145** (2007) 241–249

Basta C., Struckl M. 2005. Implementing art.12 of the Seveso II Directive: overview of procedures in selected member states and »Roadmap« proposals – draft version. *European working group on Land-use planning*. The Joint Research Centre of the European Commission.

Besi, S., Amendola F., Belloni V., Christou M.D., Smeder M., Amendola A., Poli U., 1996. *La pianificazione dell'uso del territorio in relazione ai rischi di incidente rilevante,* Report EUR 16412 IT, Institute for Systems, Informatics and Safety, JRC Ispra, Ispra, 1996.

Burger J., Sanchez J., Roush D. and Gochfeld M. 2001. Risk perception, future land use and stewardship: Comparison of attitudes about Hanford Site and Idaho National Engineering and Environmental Laboratory, *J. Env. Management* **61** (2001) 265–280.

Carpignano, A., Pignatta, G., Spaziante, G. 2001. Land use planning around Seveso-II installations: the Italian approach, in: *Proceedings of the European Conference on Safety and Reliability*, MG, Torino (I), p. 1763.

Christou M. D., Papadakis G.A. 1998. Risk Assessment and Management in the Context of the Seveso II Directive, in: Kirchsteiger, C. (Ed.), *Industrial Safety Series* **6**, Elsevier, Oxford

Christou, M. D., Amendola A., Smeder M. 1999. The control of major accident hazards: The land-use planning issue, *Journal of Hazardous Materials*, Elsevier Science B.V. 65 (1999) 151-178

Christou, M. D., Mattarelli M. 2000. Land-use planning in the vicinity of chemical sites: Risk-informed decision making at a local community level, *Journal of Hazardous Materials,* Elsevier Science B.V., 78 (2000) 191-222

Christou, M.D and Porter S. 1999. *Guidance on land use planning as required by Council Directive 96/82/EC (Seveso II)*. Institute for systems informatics and safety

Christou, M.D, Struckl M. Bermann T. 2006. *Land-use Planning Guidelines in the context of Article 12 of the SevesoII Directive 96/82/EC as amended by Directive 105/2003/EC.* European commission, Joint Research Centre, Major Accident Hazards Bureau.

Cozzani, V., Bandini R., Basta C. and Christou M. D. 2006. Application of land-use planning criteria for the control of major accident hazards: A case-study, *J. Haz. Mat.,* **136** (2006) 170-180

EC. 1997. *EU compendium of spatial planning systems and policies*: United Kingdom.

EC. 2003. Consolidated version of the Seveso II Directive, including the amendment 2003/105/EC, available at: http://eur-lex.europa.eu/LexUriServ/site/en/ consleg/1996/ L/01996L0082-20031231-en.pdf .

FAO. 1976. A framework for land evaluation. *FAO Soils Bulletin* **32**.

Gerbec M., Kontić B. 2008. *Types and sources of uncertainties in environmental accidental risk assessment: a case for a chemical factory in the Alpine region of Slovenia.* In: Martorell, S. (eds.), Soares, C.G., Barnett, J.; Safety, reliability and risk analysis: theory, methods and applications: *proceedings of the European Safety and Reliability Conference, ESREL 2008, and 17th SRA-Europe,* Valencia, Spain, September 22-25, 2008. Boca Raton; CRC Press, pp 2157-2165.

Hale A. R., Kontić B., Kontić D., Gerbec M. 2005. Management influences on major hazard prevention: The ARAMIS audit, in; Kołowrocki K. (ed.) Advances in safety and reliability: proceedings of the European and Reliability Conference, (ESREL 2005), Tri City (Gdynia-Sopot-Gdańsk), Poland, 27-30 June, 2005. Taylor and Francis. pp. 767-773.

Hauptmanns U. 2005 A risk-based approach to land-use planning. *Journal of Hazardous Materials*, **125** (2005) 1-9

Health and safety executive (HSE). 1989. *Risk Criteria for Land Use Planning in the Vicinity of Major Industrial Hazards,* HMSO

Health and Safety Executive (HSE). 2006. The Buncefeld Investigation: Progress Report

Kletz T. 1992. Hazop and Hazan, *Identifying and Assessing Process Industry Hazards.* Third Edition. Institution of Chemical Engineers, Warwickshire

Kontić B., Kontić D. 2007. Weaknesses of accidental risk assessment scenarios in the context of spatial planning, in: Skanata D. and Byrd D.M. (Eds.), Computational models of risks to infrastructure - NATO science for peace and security series. *Information and communication security,* Vol. 13, 2007), IOS Press, Amsterdam, 2007, pp. 169-180.

Kontić D., Kontić B. 2009. Introduction of threat analysis into the land-use planning process, *Journal of Hazardous Materials*, **163**(2009) 683-700.

Kontić D., Kontić B., Gerbec M. 2006. How powerful is ARAMIS methodology in solving land-use issues associated with industry based environmental and health risks?. *J. of Hazardous Materials,* Elsevier B.V., 130 (2006) 271-275

Kværner J., Swensen G., Erikstad L. 2006. Assessing environmental vulnerability in EIA—The content and context of the vulnerability concept in an alternative approach to standard EIA procedure. *Environmental Impact Assessment Review* **26** (2006) 511–527.

Laheij G. M. H., Post J. G., Ale B. J. M. 2000. Standard methods for land-use planning to determine the effects on societal risk. *Journal of Hazardous Materials* , Elsevier Science B.V., 71 (2000) 269-282

Lauridsen K., Kozine I., Markert F., Amendola A., Christou M., Fiori M. 2002. *Assessment of Uncertainties in Risk Analysis of Chemical Establishments - The ASSURANCE project,* Risø-R-1344(EN). Risø National Laboratory, Roskilde, Denmark, May 2002. Available at: http://www.risoe.dtu.dk/rispubl/SYS/syspdf/ris-r-1344.pdf

LOPA. 2001. *Layer of Protection Analysis: Simplified Process Risk Assessment.* Center for Chemical Process Safety of the American Institute of Chemical Engineers, New York

Mannan S. 2005. *Lee's loss prevention in the process industries*, 3rd Edition, Elsevier.

Marušič J. 1993.Conservation planning within a framework of landscape planning in Slovenia. *Landscape and urban planning*, **23** (1993) 233-237.

Ministerial Decree. 2001. Ministerial Decree of 9 May 2001, *Requisiti minimi di sicurezza in materia di pianificazione urbanistica e territoriale per le zone interessate da stabilimenti a rischio di incidente rilevante*, Gazzetta Ufficiale della Repubblica Italiana, no. 138, Rome (I), 16.6.2001.

Mlakar A. 2006. *Uncertainty management in physical planning proceedings, doctoral dissertation* (in Slovenian). University in Ljubljana, Biotechnical faculty, Ljubljana.

Mušič V.B. 1993. Earthquakes and management of urban environment urban planning and design as a part of the preventive strategies. *Tectonic and Seismotectonic, 8th international seminar earthquake prognostics*, Iran, Teheran

Paté-Cornell M. E. 1996. Uncertainties in risk analysis: Six levels of treatment. *Reliability Engineering and System Safety*, **54** (1996) 95 - 111.

Papazoglou I. A., Bonanos G., Briassoulis H., 2000. Risk informed decision making in land use planning. *J. of Risk Research*, **1**(2000) 69 – 92

Petersen A. C. 2002. The precautionary principle, knowledge uncertainty, and environmental assessment. *Paper for the Netherlands Institute of Government Workshop on Knowledge* Uncertainty, Rotterdam, 30-31 October 2002.

Planas E., Arnaldos J., Silveti B., Vallee A., Casal J.. 2006. A Risk Severity Index for industrial plants and sites. *J. of Haz. Mat.* **130** (2006) 242-250.

Rasmussen B., Bertelsen I., Burchard V., Christensen P., Duijm N. J., Groenberg C.D., Markert F. 1999. *Multi-objective decisions in land use planning involving chemical sites*, Risoe National Laboratory, Roskilde, Denmark.

Salvi O., Merad M., Rodrigues N. 2005. Toward an integrative approach of the industrial risk management process in France, *Journal of Loss Prevention in the Process Industries* **18** (2005) 414–422

SHAPE-RISK. 2005. *Synthesis document on WP3* – "Survey and comparison of common tools and service platforms"

Slovic P. 2001. The risk game. *Journal of Hazardous Materials*, **86** (2001) 17–24.

Slovic P., et al. 1984. Modelling the societal impacts of fatal accidents; Management Science, 30 (1984) 464-474.

Smeder M., Christou M.D., Besi S., 1996. Land use planning in the context of major accident hazards—an analysis of procedures and criteria in selected EU member states, Report EUR 16452 EN, Institute for Systems, Informatics and Safety, JRC Ispra, Ispra, 1996.

Spadoni G., Egidi D., Contini S. 2000. Through ARIPAR-GIS the quantified area risk analysis supports land-use planning activities. *Journal of Hazardous Materials*, Elsevier Science B.V., 71 (2000) 423-437

Stangl M.L., Land Use Planning in the context of Seveso II establishments in Austria, presented at *SRA-E 2006 conference*, Ljubljana, Slovenia 11-13 September 2006

Steinitz C. 1976. "On Hand-Drawn Map overlays: A Historical perspective and an Alternative approach" *Landscape Architecture*.

Steinitz C. 1990. A framework for theory applicable to the eduvcatiuon of landscape architects (and other environmental design professionals). *Landscape journal*, **9** (1990) 369-386.

Tixier J., Dandrieux A., Dusserre G., Bubbico R., Luccone L. G., Mazzarotta B., Silvetti B., Hubert E., Rodrigues N., Salvi O., Gaston D., 2005. Vulnerability of the environment in the proximity of an industrial site; In: Brebbia C.A., Bucciarelli T., Garzia F., Guarascio M. (Eds.), *Safety and Security Engineering (SAFE 2005),* WIT Transactions on The Built Environment, Vol 82.

Tixier J., Dandrieux A., Dusserre G., Bubbico R., Mazzarotta B., Silvetti B., Hubert E., Rodrigues N., Salvi O. 2006. Environmental vulnerability assessment in the vicinity of an industrial site in the frame of ARAMIS European project. *J. of Haz. Mat.* **130** (2006) 251–264.

Uijt de Haag P.A.M., Ale B.J.M. 1999. Guidelines for quantitative risk assessment "Purple Book", *Committee for the Prevention of Disasters*, CPR 18E, First Edition, ISBN 90 12 08796 1.

Wynne B. 1992. Risk and social learning. Reification to engagement, in; Krimsky S., Golding D. (eds.), *Social theories of risk,* pp.275-300. Praeger, Westport, CT.

In: Risk Management
Editors: B. Jordão and E. Sousa, pp. 125-151

ISBN: 978-1-60876-011-4

Chapter 4

THE EVALUATION OF BUSINESS RISK MANAGEMENT IN EUROPEAN EMERGING MARKETS

Christiana Arvaniti[1] ***and Athanasios A. Pantelous***[2]
[1] Hollings Faculty, Manchester Metropolitan University, UK
[2] Department of Mathematical Sciences, University of Liverpool, UK

Abstract

In several developed countries, the markets have already matured and shown a relatively low level of growth. Thus, many multi-national corporations desiring to expand further their profits are turning into the emerging markets in hope of new promising businesses. Consequently, the main purpose of this chapter is to identify and analyse the types of risks in European emerging markets, including new entrants to European Union and evaluate the way of managing (financial, operational, political, natural, procedural, technical etc.) in order for a company to be able to invest and establish its businesses in countries which often have complex regulations and difficult bureaucracies. The decision processes that businesses go through in order to accept the risks in entering these markets will be explored to identify the strategies that will produce effective risk management. The contribution of this research to the knowledge will be concentrated on the challenges for a firm to enter into these emergent European member states. This will take into account the risks and how effective risk management can lead to competitive advantage. The analysis will have a qualitative approach.

1. Introduction

Over the last two decades, European Community has change considerable, since new countries have started joining the European Union (EU). This expansion encompasses a large number of Eastern European Countries (EECs), which characterized by emergent and developing economies. These emerging markets, as well as the opportunity they represent for business growth and high returns, provide a greater risk than do most of mature markets. Nowadays, EECs are very important markets, which play significant role in the development

[1] E-mail address: C.Arvaniti@mmu.ac.uk.
[2] E-mail address: A.Pantelous@liverpool.ac.uk

of cross businesses in whole Europe and they present a unique profile of risks -geopolitical, regulatory, financial, currency and governance- among the others. Corporations investing in these countries must not only be able to protect themselves but they also need to develop their safeguards against the risks and fully understand the requirements of doing business in these entities by identifying also their own risk appetites. It is therefore important to look beyond traditional strategies that a business follows in order to meet the unique needs of each market and leverage effectively the diversification of each country at all levels. Considering and managing the risk, a private company is able to internationalised itself and build up a competitive profile by ensuring success in the new market place.

The main purposes of this chapter is to identify and analyze the types of risks in European Emerging Markets (EEMs), including new entrants to EU. Moreover, it tries to evaluate the way that a private company is able to invest and establish its businesses in new EU countries, where the regulations are more complex and difficult, by managing efficiently and effectively all the types of important risks. The decision process, which is a very difficult and challenging task is further exploited. Thus, the main contribution of this research to our knowledge is concentrated on the challenges of a corporation to enter properly into these EEMs. Consequently, this work takes into account several kinds of risks (however, the most important), and it tries to answer how effective risk management can lead to competitive advantage. At this stage, our analysis has a *qualitative* approach and we are mainly focused on private companies, which have a more international profile. Moreover, it should be stress out that our research can provide a stepping-stone for the introduction of some quantitative methods for pricing the risks into a complete (or mostly, into an incomplete) market framework.

Effective risk management has the potentiality to safeguard the financial performance of a corporation by considering three ultimate principles -*growths*, *profitability* and *capital utilization*. Customers' demands, competition, labour cost and business environment volatility drive down returns on capital exposing in a big risk businesses. Every company is able to accept a specific level of risk and have to develop strategies that can help to mitigate this level of risk and ensure its competitiveness in the market place. Operating in emerging markets is riskier than doing business in the developed world. These countries are characterized by greater political and financial instability, being more vulnerable in external risk factors such as natural disasters. Consequently, risk management becomes the core activity across all the industries in the huge EEM.

2. Emerging Markets: A Global Approach

The last two decades, Europe has changed considerable, since it has become one of the largest blocs in the world after North America and Far Asia including both developed and developing countries. This Union is being characterized as a Single European Market, and it attracts the attention of politicians, business people and academics. The main objectives of EU (and by extension the unified European Market) may be stated by identifying the existing physical, technical and fiscal barriers between all the members states establishing at first four freedoms of movements and then abolishing systematic controls at the borders, see El Kahal (1998). Summarizing, we obtain:

- Free movement of goods, people, service and capital.
- The removal of physical, technical and fiscal barriers.
- The liberalization of internal competition through strict completion policies.

In order to compete effectively or merely to survive the competition in such a dynamic environment, the corporations have to straggle for opportunities in the Single Market as well as in local domestic markets. Note that the competition in today's environment takes an international face rather than concentrating only within the national boundaries. The community has established rules on companies' takeovers, mergers and acquisitions, joint ventures, licensing agreements etc. The common sense says that differences between countries in Europe will continue to persist even if Brussels have done a big effort for a homogenous market with a common legislation. This is obvious, since within the Union, simultaneously, the developed and the emerging economies exist.

An emerging country can be defined as a country in which its national economy grows rapidly, its industry is structurally changing, its marketing is promising but volatile, its regulatory framework favors economic liberation and the adoption of a free market system and its government is reducing bureaucratic and administrative control over business activities, see for further details Luo (2002).

Moreover, the term "emerging market" is commonly used to describe business and market activities in industrializing or emerging regions of the world. The term signifies a business phenomenon that is not fully described by (or constrained to) geography or economic strengthen; such countries are considered to be in a transitional phase between developing and developed status. Examples of emerging markets include China, India, Mexico, Brazil, Chile much of Southeast Asia, countries in Eastern Europe, parts of Africa and Latin America. Emphasizing the fluid nature of the category, political scientist *Ian Bremmer* defines an emerging market as *a country where politics matters at least as much as economics to the markets*, see Hacker et al (2004).

Another definition of the term of "emerging markets" refers to certain region of the world that seems rabidly to be entering into the world business system. This include most Asia countries, some Eastern European such as Hungary, Czech Republic and some Latin American. These countries have attracted a great attention for personal and institutional investors as well as for international corporations, see Millar et al (2000).

According to Kolodko (2003b), it is easier to define what not an emerging market than what is. Thus, *emerging markets do not include, by definition, either those highly developed market economies which have long evolved mature institutional systems or those countries which have yet set out on bath of market development.*

Sabal (2002) presents emerging markets as those that share some of the following attributes but not necessary are categorized within the ranks of the developing word by strictly applying them.

1) A significant percentage of the population either is illiterate or has low level of education.
2) The per capita gross national product is lower that levels experienced in developed countries.
3) The distribution of wealth tends to be uneven. A small minority controls a majority of assets, while the rest of the population lives in poverty.

4) The economic and political conditions tend to be unstable.

The term "rapidly developing economies" is now being used to denote emerging markets such as The United Arab Emirates, Chile and Malaysia that are undergoing rapid growth. In recent years, new terms have emerged to describe the largest developing countries such as BRIC and BRIMC. According to Hacker et al (2004), these countries do not share any common agenda, but some experts believe that they are enjoying an increasing role in the world economy and on political platforms.

There are 25 countries listed as emerging markets.

- 10 in Asia - China, Hong Kong, India, Indonesia, Malaysia, Philippines, Singapore, South Korea, Taiwan, Thailand.
- 6 in Latin America - Argentina, Brazil, Chile, Columbia, Mexico, Venezuela.
- 2 in Middle East - Israel, Turkey.
- 1 in Africa - South Africa.
- 2 no socialist in Europe - Greece, Portugal.
- 4 in former socialist in Europe - Czech, Hungary, Poland, Russia.

Keane (1993) assumes that the new and the emerging markets consist special cases in investment because:

- They present unusual growth.
- They exhibit above average risk characteristic.
- They have useful diversification.
- They have high transaction cost.

Lenartowicz and Johnson (2007) mention that emerging markets economies are characterized as transitional economies as they are in the process of moving from a closed to an open market economy. This which characterizes an emerging market is the application of economic reform programs that can lead a market to a better financial performance, stronger position among the other countries, transparency and efficiency in the capital market. Additionally the reform of the exchange rate can ensure local currency stability by giving confidence to local investors to keep their capital inside the domestic market and also attracting foreign investors. The implementation of reforms has a result the guidance and the support of the emerging markets from donor countries and organizations such as the World Bank and International Monetary Fund.

3. Globalization

3.1. Globalization the New Era

Globalization is the historical process of liberalization and integration of goods, capital and labor markets, which have hitherto functioned to certain extent in separation, into a single world marketplace. (Kolodko, 2002, 2003).

Global is claimed to be the natural order of affairs in today's technological driven world in which time -space has been compressed, the end of geography has arrived and everywhere is becoming the same (Dickens, 2003). Between the meaning of internationalization and globalization there is a difference. Internationalizing process involves the simple extension of economic activities across national boundaries but globalizing process involves not only merely the geographical extension of economic activities across national boundaries but also the functional integration of all these activities.

Historically, according to Kolodko (2001), there are three phases in the globalization process.

1) Globalization of the Age of Exploration (16th to mid -17th centuries).
2) Globalization of the Industrial Revolution (mid-18th to 19th centuries).
3) Globalization of the Age of the Computers and the Internet (last quarter of 20th century and beginning of 21st).

Soon the world will be characterized by a global homogenization in every aspect of life - the same restaurants, hotels, clothes, malls and superstores with the same streets crowded with cars, see Marber (1998). Today it is no longer possible for a country to insulate itself from the rest of the world. Financial, technological and ideological developments, no matter if they are good or bad, have a global impact. The production and assembly have been shifted from the cheaper labour away from the multi-national home countries. Trade arrangements and organizations such as NAFTA, GATT and WTO have intensified the trends.

If we want to summarize our thoughts, there are six characteristics of the modern globalization.

1) The volume of the world trade increases very fast, nearly twice as fast as output-reduction of customs barriers.
2) The capital flow has been steadily increasing.
3) Dissemination of new technologies-technological and scientific revolution.
4) Population migration.
5) Post-socialist systemic transformation.
6) Cultural change- the phenomenon of Internet characterized the world as a "global village".

3.2. Globalization and Development

In today's changing environment Multi-National Corporations (*MNCs*) play superior role in the global growth sifting their business in new, alluring markets called emerging. These markets seem to be really promising if the companies understand what the customers want, develop distinctive and affordable offers, marketing them effectively and overcoming internal organizational barriers. The challenges in these volatile markets are many as decision-making process and communication with the headquarters of the corporations are not so flexible or the subsidiaries are not able to react quickly and efficient in the fast-changing conditions.

According to Olsen et al (2005) MNCs must develop a management model which can ensure flexibility in these unstable markets and also apply practices that can be accommodated from market to market during the passing time.

These practices are

1) Establishing and reviewing long-term directions.
2) Fitting emerging markets business within the organizational structure.
3) Defining roles and decision rights between headquarters and the local leadership.
4) Prioritizing local decisions.
5) Managing resource allocation flexible.
6) Monitoring and managing performance.

In emerging markets long-term direction and objectives are significantly more difficult due to the great uncertainty and macroeconomic volatility. The competitiveness is built upon the high, low and mid-range assumptions about market growth, pace of deregulation and other economic conditions.

Developing countries comprise approximately 85% of the world's population, 77% of the earth's land mass and 63% of global commodity but their economies constitute less than 22% of world income and only 12% of the global stock market capitalization. Moreover developing economies are growing at more than 6% per annum, more than double the 2,5% growth rate for the western developed world. There are many reasons for this difference in economics such as long terms trends in labor and technology, demographics shifts and political reorientations. The developed work can prosper from having new markets and cheaper production cost, see Marber (1998). Moreover, good another example of the increasing interest in EMs is the fact that investments into EMs was U.S. $13 billion in 1985 and has risen to $267 billion in 2003, see Rosling (2005). Companies from Western Europe have realized this potential and see Eastern Europe (which includes emerging markets such as the Czech Republic and Poland) as their future primary market of growth, closely followed by China. India and Russia are also expected to generate great growth possibilities, see Accenture (2005).

The entrance of developing countries in the global economy reflects a differentiation in the cost structures of weather and poorer nation. These countries have attracted great attention as they export competitive products-low skill, labour intensive goods or commodities; see Marber (1998). The root for the aggressive expansion of the MNCs into developing countries is the hard economic intensity as they are driven by profits and nothing else.

It is obvious for these markets that big risks are hidden for foreign corporations which have decided to develop their operations in such a way that they can flexible switch their production according to the markets needs. The main problem for them was the restrictions concerning the transfer of profits outside the country. This now has been improved and foreign enterprises are permitted to transfer their profits to their origin country, see Koldoko (2003a).

The increased demand of technological products reduces the importance of primary low-technological activities raising with this way more the skill-intensive activities. Corporations are able to disperse their business more efficiently as new information and communication technologies intensify competition; see Luo (2002). Location decision is based on the ability of the host country to provide skills, infrastructure, suppliers and institutions to operate technologies efficiently and flexibly. The core of a country competitiveness centers on productivity. Productivity is the value of the output produced by a unit of labor or capital. It is the superior element of a long-term standard of living and is the root source of national per capita income. Productivity depends on quality and features of products and services and the efficiency with which they are produced or provided. With this way countries productivity can be enhanced.

However, developed countries export those things in which they have a comparative advantage and importing those in which they do not. Countries no longer have a relative advantage in manufacturing and other labor-intensive industries because of the huge increase in living standards and wages. They succeed in developing comparative advantage in high technology and service sector. Emerging markets have discovered their own comparative advantage based on manufacturing. This allows them attract and generate capital and reinvest it back to their own economies, see Marber (1998).

Industrialized countries produce several kinds of manufactured goods. Simultaneously non-industrialized countries supply materials and agricultural products to industrialized countries and they act as a market for some manufactured goods. This is a result of a new global division of labour and the transformation of the old geographical patterns of specialization. The developments of technologies, of transportation and of communication between a corporation and production process lead the industrial production to new industrialize economies enforcing the idea of a global economic map without national boundaries, see Dickens (2003).

4. New Challenged Markets in Eastern Europe

Since 1986, thousand of enterprises established their businesses in many countries in Eastern Europe (*EE*). At the end of 1989 had climbed to 3,000 and at the end of 1990 to over 7,000. This had as a result the volume of capital investment to grow considerably to 2 billion in 1990 and passed the 4.5 billion dollars at the end of 1991, see Kolodko (2003a).

The reason that many companies did their first steps investing in EE was the possibilities of economies of scale, exploitation of technological advantages, security and assured market, enhance the companies position and many immigrants from EE started living in West. The majority of these immigrants were unskilled workers looking for a job to survive. But their descendant has become qualified and started their own business; see Kolodko (2003a).

Thus the opening of EE to foreign investment at the end of 1980's coincided with the emergence of sizeable and relatively affluent expatriate communities. The expatriate returned forceful back to their countries, doing business which involved a wide variety of fields such as production of goods as building materials, clothing, lingerie, cosmetics, metal ware, furs, leather ware, and electronic equipment. Also there was a small investment in hotels and pensions; see Dobosiewicz (1992).

EEc in 1988 and 1989 started changing the regulations concerning the rate of income taxes and relaxed also some of the restrictions on small businesses facilitating with this way the consolidation of a corporation in their market, giving the opportunity for further development.

In 1990, EE did the first step in following the same tax systems as those in West Europe and lift-transfer restrictions. This governmental maneuver gave a new air in the market from both sides; the sellers and the buyers. Foreign enterprises were able for first time to introduce products that were also sold in West meeting the demands and tastes of EE consumers, see Dobosiewicz (1992). Poland, Hungary and Czech Republic have now liberated themselves from communism and most of the analysts reclassified them as developing countries.

The political collapse of the Soviet Union produced a group of countries so-called *transitional economies* which have played a significant role in the development of the global economy. These countries, from central planned economies have changed their entities to capitalist markets economies. This process was quite painful as they had to pay attention on basic manufacturing industry and also leaded themselves to a potential growth, see Dickens (2003). Now, they are important strategic locations for corporations which seek lower-cost production sites insight the EU.

Many developing nations have started to take important steps to adapt their economies to the impact of the international capital flow and globalization making their countries more attractive to foreign investment. There are three areas where basically are taken action

1. Macroeconomic
   - Managing the Net Inflows of Foreign Exchange.
   - Reducing the impact of Reverse Fluctuations' on Monetary Aggregates.
   - Reducing the impact of Capital Flow on Aggregates Demand.
2. Banking System Reform
   - Modernization of banking laws and regulations.
   - Strengthening bank supervisory agencies.
   - Improvements on credit risk controls of bank portfolios.
   - Increasing the capitalization of banks.
   - Implementation of better mechanisms to deal with banking crises promptly and effectively.
3. Capital Market Reform
   - Infrastructure.
   - Property Rights.
   - The regulatory Framework.

International business and global expansion are now driven by more than 60,000 multi-national enterprises concentrated in electronics and electrics equipment, automobiles, petroleum, chemicals and pharmaceuticals, with over subsidiaries 80,000 overseas. The top ten in 2008 are Google, Apple, Toyota, Coca-Cola, IBM, INTEL, Nokia, Disney, General Electric and Microsoft (Infotech, 2008).

The main vehicle for a global expansion is the *Foreign Direct Investment* (*FDI*) for MNCs and it has reached more than 50 countries among them 24 developing. FDI in manufacturing industry is still growing during the past ten years. Nowadays, they are expected to account more than half of the total stock of inward FDI in developed countries and one third of that in developing countries.

According to Rugman and Collinson (2006), the triad countries are these three trading and investment blocs in the international arena which includes United States, EU and Japan. Triad-based and non-triad-based corporations have the same objectives when exploring market-seeking investment. They want to increase sales in each other territories by customizing products and services following markets' requirements, establish distribution and sales network and raise their profiles and brands. MNCs invest in production-related activities to benefit cheaper or better sources of inputs in particular locations. These activities can include raw materials, components or labour and expertise (resource-seeking FDI). On the other hand, MNCs can invest in distribution sales or marketing operations in order to sell products or services in particular country markets (Market-seeking FDI). Around 70% of all the FDI flows in the developed countries are mainly captured by the Triad. The other 30% is going to the developing countries and the major share to the Southeast Asia. Central and Eastern Europe (*CEE)* attracts only the 3-4% of the global FDI flow. Poland, Czech Republic and Hungary receive larger shares of FDI than the other countries in the region, but now they have experienced a decline.

The idea of FDI argues that companies choose their structure and location with main purpose to minimise overall transaction costs and also focuses on the decision making process for investment without providing any information about the motivations or the reasons for the possible success of the internationalization. It includes modes such as licensing, international joint ventures partnering and wholly owned subsidiaries, see Freeman and Reid (2006).

In some industries, MNCs have set up integrated international division of labour spanning region (as in automobiles) or continents (as in semi conductors). Within this complex systems the function transferred to different locations vary greatly. It is obvious that less industrialised locations are assigned simpler tasks like assembly and packaging while more skilled and technology intensive is allocated to more developed locations, see Luo (2002).

Cross-boarder Mergers and Acquisitions (MandA) remain popular in recent FDI. Most of these industries are horizontal aiming at economies of scale, technological synergies, increasing market power, eliminating excess capacity or consolidating and streamlining innovation strategies. The leading industries of MandA are telecommunications, energy and financial services.

According to Klonowski (2007) investing capital in CEE hides a number of challenges. First of all local venture capitalists often confuse venture capital with other types of financing. So, they have to act as educators and negotiators opposite to the entrepreneurs. Secondly, local entrepreneurs are not ready to receive venture capital as they do not have a documentation described their business and also they do not have even a business plan or financial forecasts. Thirdly, it is really difficult to make deals in the region of CEE as the legal infrastructure is not well established so the venture capitalist have to face many problems in many transactions.

The investment process as presented in Klonowski (2007) paper is as follows.

- Deal origination.
- Screening.
- Evaluation.
- Deal structuring.
- Post investment activities.

FDI inflows into CEE emerging markets also raised reaching $27 billions in 2000. Privatization is the key determinant of FDI inflows throughout the region with exception of

Hungary where the privatization process has by and large run its course. FDI flow into these markets can be facilitated when changes in emerging markets governments' policies are occurred.

Trade and investment liberalization allows MNCs to specialize more and to search for competitive locations, see Luo (2002). Privatization in developing countries accounts for 85% of all privatizations in the world from 1988 to 1993, see Marber (1998). However, a superior problem that the wealthy countries face is the growing number of older people and a shrinking number of youths. So they have to look for new markets for sales growth, see Marber (1998).

Koldoko (2003b) presents some figures from the World Bank (2002) which indicate that within the time span of a single generation, the economies that participating more actively in the globalization managed to double their real income per head while the income of other societies that involved less in this trend of international trade, did not increase.

There are countries that can not manage to attain a satisfied development level and reduce the gap with the western developed world. These are economies of CEE and the former Soviet Union which are on the way in time to full integration with the global economy. Specifically out of the total number of 28 post -socialist economies only Hungary has found its way to the more globalized group.

5. Risk Management Issues

5.1. The Elements of Risk

Risk management is a core part of any financial institution, company and organization's strategic management. It can be considered as the process whereby they methodically address the risks attaching to their actions with the goal of achieving sustained benefits within each activity and across the portfolio of all actions.

When the commercial activity increased, see Olsson (2002), and the people started doing new ventures further away from their domestic limits the meaning of risk was starting to be shaped. The developments in the field of science and mathematics made the people to understand that risk was associated with human actions and that they have to be able to control it. It takes them time to develop the key elements of risks which are used from today's risk managers. These elements were:

- The Laws of Probability (Pascal/Fermat).
- Utility Theory (Bernoulli).
- An understanding of Regression to the Mean.
- Diversification Theory (Galton).
- Strategy/Game Theory (von Neuman).

Today the term risk has become a commonplace and appears in many different ways in the everyday life. The definition, which has been adopted according to Olsson (2002), is:

Risk is the uncertainty of future outcomes.

According to Spekman and Davis (2004), risk on a very general level is defined as the probability of variance in an expected outcome or better it is seen as a negative consequence since the inference is the downside affect of an outcome. However through their research they conclude that the definition of risk is context, specific and also has objective or subjective nature. For instance, playing cards or throwing dice hides an objective risk, while subjective risk is an individual's assessment of a situation that motivates a person to action or not.

Additionally risk can be determined either on personal or organizational level and can be hidden everywhere. It is not easy to recognize it as it is something intangible and will be considered differently by different people. Not only in terms of what the risks are but also what the results would be and probabilities they attach to theses outcomes. The factors that will influence everyone's perceptions are the experience, knowledge, culture, position, financial status, ability to influence the outcome asymmetry, complacency, inadequate time horizons, single believes and preferences. The risk assessment literature has concentrated on technical and methodological issues, concerning the quantification of risks and a comparative neglect of important perspectives from sociology, economics, political science, anthropology and psychology. Especially, in the field of economics and politics, the risk is quite high that the policy maker must be able to manage it by promoting human welfare such as health, safety, environmental quality as well as the consumption of goods and services, see Kraft and Freeman (1989).

In the environment of businesses, the risk managers must be able to identify effectively the risk for the good of their businesses. The lack of identification means that there would be difficulties in managing the business processes. All businesses seek to take advantages through taking risks, but first they have to set a framework within they have to deal with the risk and after that to list the main risk types. A company before entering in a market must assess the market opportunities, understand the factors which set the size and nature of demand and also consider which competitors has to face and how.

The key areas are

- *Economic environment*- interest rates, exchange rates, inflation, taxation level, growth level.
- *Physical resources*- availability of agriculture products, mineral resources, geographical position of a country.
- *Social Factors*- population size, education levels, religion, social stability, work ethic, production basis and labour availability.
- *Political climate*- who runs the country, the degree of political freedom, the economical stability and development.

To summarize this subsection, we would like to stress that the focus of an effective risk management is the good identification (which is something really hard to be considered) and the handling of these risks. Consequently, its main objective is to add maximum sustainable value to all the activities of the organisation. It marshals the understanding of the potential upside and downside of all those factors which can affect the organisation. Moreover, efficient management increases the probability of success, and it reduces both the probability of failure (or ruin) and the uncertainty of achieving the organisation's overall objectives. Finally, risk management should be a continuous and always developing process which runs throughout the organisation's strategy and the implementation of that strategy. It should address methodically all the risks surrounding the organisation's activities past, present and in particular, future.

Furthermore, the risk management procedure should consider the culture of the organisation integrated with an effective policy and a programme led by the most senior management. It must interpret the strategy into tactical and operational objectives, assigning responsibility throughout the organisation with each manager and employee responsible for the management of risk as part of their job description. It supports accountability, performance measurement and reward, thus promoting operational efficiency at all levels; see for more details AIRMIC et al (2002).

5.2. Types of Risks

In the business game, the managers have to face different types of risk and they must be always alerted to face any kind of disruption. The following table presents the types as Olsson (2002) have described them in his book.

Table of Risks (Olsson, 2002)

Strategic Risks	The risk of fail to achieve business targets due to inappropriate strategies, adequate resources or changes in the economic or competitive environment.
Credit Risks	The risk that a counterparty may pay amounts owed, when they fall due.
Sovereign Risks	The credit risk associated with lending to the government itself or a party guaranteed by the government.
Market Risks	The risk of loss due to changes in the market prices. This includes: ▪ Interest rate ▪ Foreign exchange risk ▪ Commodity price risk ▪ Share price risk
Liquidity Risks	The risk that amounts due for payment cannot be paid due to a lack of available funds.
Operational Risks	The risk of loss due to actions on or by people, processes infrastructure or technology or similar which have an operational impact including fraudulent activities.
Accounting Risks	The risk that financial records do not accurately reflect the financial position of an organisation.
Country Risks	The risk that a foreign currency will not be available to allow payments due to be paid because of lack of foreign currency or the government rationing what is available.
Political Risks	The risk that there will be a change in the political framework of the country.
Industry Risks	The risk associated with operating on particular industry.
Environmental Risks	The risk that an organisation may suffer loss as a result environmental damage caused by themselves or others which impacts on their business.
Legal/regulatory Risks	The risk non-compliance with legal or regulatory requirements.
Systematic Risks	The risk that small event will produce unexpected consequences in local, regional or global systems not obviously connected with the source of disturbance.
Reputational Risks	The risk that the reputation of an organization will be adversely affected.

Some types of risk are easy to be considered and measured such as credit risk, market liquidity and some other which are much more difficult, such as reputation and systematic risk. The ability to measure risk in developed countries is clearly more advance than in emerging markets. So, in today's changeable environment managers not only need to be clearer about types of risk that they face but also about what information they need to measure those risk, considering always the most important elements of measuring which is time and cost. However, as we can see in *figure 1*, the above abundant categories of risk can be emerged into four basic categories. This categorization is based on the risk management standards of the Association of Insurance and Risk Management (AIRMIC), the National Forum for Risk Management in the Public Sector (ALARM) and the Institute of Risk Management (IRM) in UK.

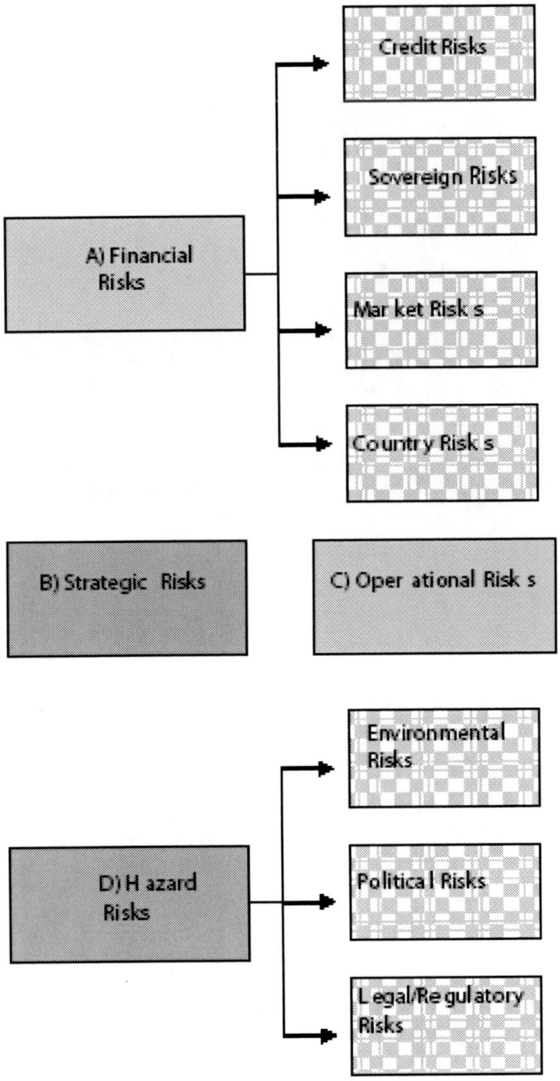

Figure 1. Basic Categories of Risks.

Prevention can be achieved by obtaining good quality data and then to turn it into useful information. After that the next step is to deliver that information to the appropriate person in the most meaningful format so to be able to make the right decision. The frequency of reporting these details varies depending on what situation the business has to deal with.

However, the danger to misunderstand the risk or not assess it correctly is high and may have negative results. These can occur in two levels:

1. *Internal* -business units or managers fail to inform their line managers or Head Offices of what they are doing.
2. *External* -failure to disclose the shareholders, the public or regulators the true nature or the level of risks a business is facing.

The risks facing an organization and its operations can result from factors both external and internal simultaneously to the organization (see the intersections in figure 2).

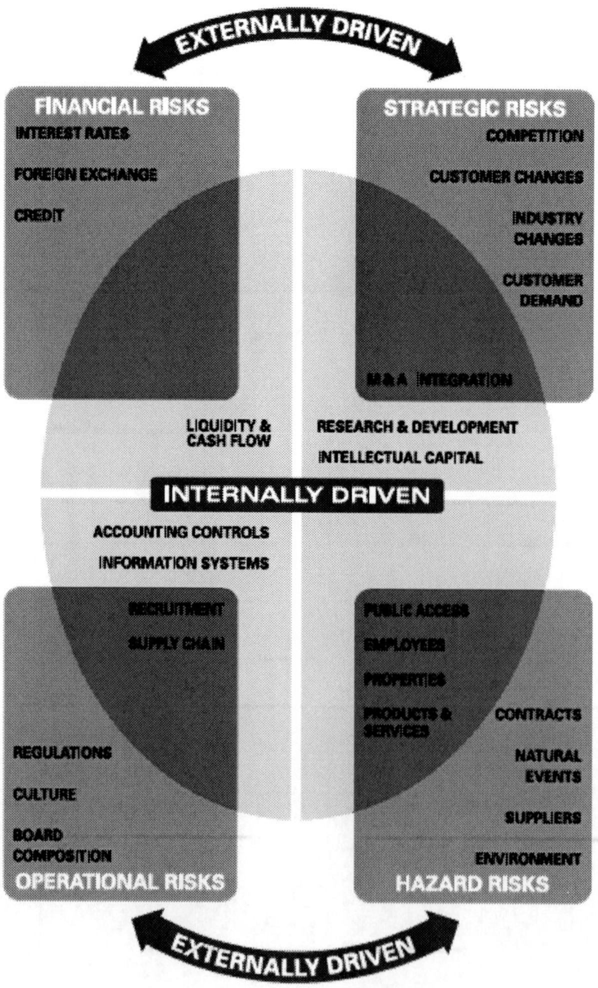

Figure 2. Examples of the Drivers of Key Risks (Source: AIRMIC et al., 2002).

Consequently, it is necessary to balance providing too much and too little information taken into considerations also the cultural barriers. With way the failure of managing the risk can be prevented giving the opportunity to the risk managers to take the appropriate action in time.

The last decades probabilistic risk analysis techniques have been applied to create new challenges for risk managers, who was struggle with decision-making. The Risk analysis, see Thompson (2002), evolves three basic elements of risk assessment, risk management and risk communication. Risk assessment has an impact to both risk management, and risk communication and highlights remaining research issues associated with using improved sensitivity and uncertainty analyses in risk assessment. The concept of variability and uncertainty can easily confuse. Uncertainty differs significantly from uncertainty as it arises from the lack of perfect knowledge. The uncertainty can be reduced by obtaining better information something which is a little bit impossible.

The *figure* **2** summarises examples of key risks in these areas and shows that some specific risks can have both external and internal drivers and therefore overlap the two areas. They can be categorised further into types of risk such as strategic, financial, operational, hazard, etc.

The National Research Council states: "*Uncertainty forces decision makers to judge how probable it is that risks will be overestimated or underestimates for every member of exposed population whereas variability forces them to cope with certainty that different individuals will be subjected to risk both above and below any reference point one chooses.*"

Improvement on risk can be made if the risk is not below the applicable decision-making, if there is no inimical change on the scientific knowledge and if the stakes are not high to warrant further analysis.

5.3. Steps to the Risk Management Process

Borge (2001) defines risk management as:

> "The taking of deliberate actions to shift the odds in our favor. To increase the odds of good outcomes and to decrease the odds of bad outcomes"

A business can be successful, surviving and growing in the market place by taking risk and adopting and responding to the changing environment. It is obvious to achieve this; it must have a coherent strategy, an effective risk management framework and robust but flexible implementation.

The risks factors, advice Carroll et al (2001), that a business faces are arisen from numerous and different issues. These can be grouped as following and can further sub-divided in other categories which are relevant to each organization or industry, knowledge and background.

1. The technological factors
   - Development of computer software.
   - Communication techniques.
   - Buyers increasing technological knowledge.

2. The human factors
   - Knowledge.
   - Responsibility.
   - Accountability.
3. The environmental factors
   - Ever-increasing need to protect the environment.
   - Buyers' knowledge of current environmental issues.
   - Investors' awareness.
   - The authoritarians' factors.
   - Central European Government Dictate.
   - Health and safety legislation.
   - Influence of media campaign.
4. The political factors
   - EU-Membership and the Euro.
   - Differences between politics in different countries.
5. The organizational factors
   - Continual change to organizational structure.
   - Reflecting evolving working practices.
   - Responding quickly to change.
6. The legal factors
   - Compliance with the latest laws.
   - Demonstration of compliance.
   - Balancing differing demands whilst satisfying all requirements.
7. The economic Factors
   - Changes in standards of service reflecting buying power.
   - Fashion, fads, trends.
   - Links with sport, media and leisure.

Every organization, private or public, can experience a numbers of risks which the most of them are based on ignorance and abdication.

Roehrig (2006) has mentions in his article that the list of uncertainties is endless. Politics, economics, environmental issues, technology, compliance regulations, privacy laws, physical security requirements, impact on credit, reputation are factors that characterized as risk to a business. As risk is ubiquitous in business, leaders are seeking a way to increase predictability. For corporation which sources products from abroad, it is necessary to be considered how to purchase and manage this outsourcing service. It is essential to identify which risks pass to the service provider, which risks the buyer retains and finally how both can jointly manage the risks. Nothing in business is free and typically whatever protection is given will not fully cover the business cost.

Some outsourcing customers view outsourcers as a king of insurance policy and if something goes wrong, there is an agreement assigning blame to them. A contract can be a way to offer security for the customers. However, every contract is different and there are certain risks that the vendor can absorb. A contract is not enough to manage business risk as it is not easy to cover all the aspect of risk management. Close collaboration, good governance and effective communication can ensure the best business performance and minimize the risks. The risk of service delivery which can have as a result penalty charges and a future pricing risk such as the fluctuation cost are the most important uncertainties a vendor can face.

The rewards of following an effective risk management are, see Culp (2001) and AIRMIC et al (2002), as follows:

- Provide the appropriate framework for higher sales or/and profits.
- Increase the share prices, the dividends and the satisfaction of the shareholders of the organization.
- Improve the decision-making, the planning and the prioritization.
- Increase the market share.
- Contribute to more efficient use/allocation of capital resources within the organization.
- Earn the industry awards and recognition.
- Reduce volatility in the non-essential areas of business.
- Provide high public esteem-customer satisfaction.
- Optimize the operation efficiency.
- Provide and increase the good reputation.

Risk management is a *strategy* which has a main purpose to reduce the negative effects of risks. So, the managers must be able to establish a specific context in order to develop the right risk management process, see also *figure 3*. This includes:

1. Definition of the organisation's strategic objectives.
2. Risk assessment in a selected domain of interest:
    a) Risk analysis,
    b) Risk identification,
    c) Risk description,
    d) Risk estimation,
    e) Risk evaluation.
3. Risk reporting: Planning the remainder of the process (Threats and Opportunities). Mapping out the following:
    - The social scope of risk management.
    - The identity and objectives of stakeholders.
    - The basis upon which risks will be evaluated, constraints.
1. Decision (i.e. defining a framework for the activity and an agenda for identification).
2. Risk treatment (i.e. developing an analysis of risks involved in the process).
3. Residual risk reporting (i.e. mitigation of risks using available technological, human and organizational resources).
4. Monitoring (i.e. final presentation and documentation).

Moreover, in order to be able to determine the objective of risk description, we should try to display the identified risks in a structured format, for example, by using the following table, see for more details AIRMIC et al. (2002).

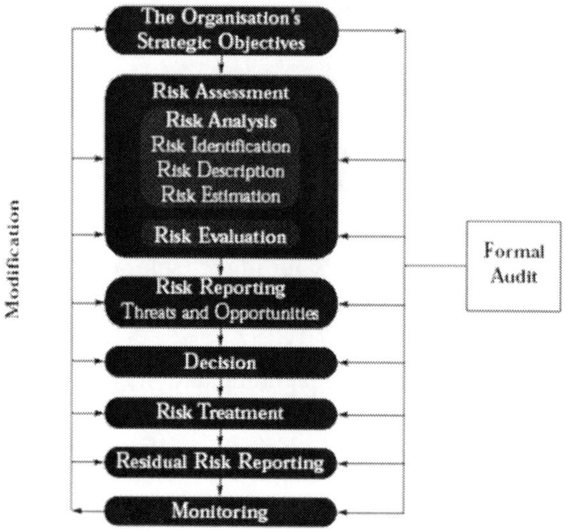

Figure 3. The risk management process (Source: AIRMIC et al., 2002).

Table. Risk Description

1. Name of Risk	
2. Scope of Risk	Qualitative description of the events. Moreover, the size, the type, the number, their dependencies.
3. Type of Risk	Financial, Strategic, Operational, Hazard etc.
4. Stakeholders	Stakeholders and their expectations.
5. Quantification of Risk	Significance and Probability (Mathematical Tools)
6. Risk Tolerance/ Appetite	Loss potential and financial impact of risk. Value at Risk. Probability and size of potential losses/gains. Objective(s) for control of the risk and desired level of performance.
7. Risk Treatment and Control Mechanisms	Primary means by which the risk is currently managed. Levels of confidence in existing control. Identification of protocols for monitoring and review.
8. Potential Action for Improvement	Recommendation to reduce risk.
9. Strategy and Policy Developments	Identification of function responsible for developing strategy and policy.

The assessment of risk gives the opportunity to evaluate the potential severity of the impact. Educated opinions and available statistics are the primary sources of information. According to Dorfman (1997) once the risks have been identified and assessed, all the techniques to manage risks are divided into four major categories which are the *risk avoidance*, *reduction*, *retention* and *transfer*.

The next step is to identify the potential risk (see Risk Reporting) which can start with the source analysis and problems' analysis. The source analysis can be internal or external (or both) to the system that is the target of risk management. Examples of risk sources are: stakeholders of a project, employees of a company or the weather over an airport. On the other hand, problem analysis risks are related to identify threats, for example the threat of losing money; the threat of abuse of privacy information; the threat of accidents and casualties etc. The threats may exist with various entities, most important with shareholders, customers and legislative bodies such as the government.

6. Risk and Emerging Markets in Eastern Europe

There are a large number of emerging markets each of which has a unique combination of characteristics that make them attractive or unattractive to different companies' which want to expand their business abroad. The word business, see Ansoff (1986), means that a corporation is and economically or money motivated, purposive, social organization which its success has been linked with profits. The risk characteristics, see Keane (1993), of emerging markets may obscure low relevant risk if the security returns happen to have a low correlation with those of established markets.

The main purpose is that these new formed markets to increase their efficiency and to be able to accept new investments, offering a secure and stable environment for new companies to run their business. The term efficiency can be used to describe several aspects of a security market such as the institutional infrastructure, the cost of transaction, the financial disclosure system and the markets' pricing behaviour. There is a possibility an emerging market to be inefficient in the three first senses but efficient in its behavior.

Emerging markets, see Keane (1993), present a unique problem in investment. They need time to develop their market and became attractive to new investors who before making any decision they must consider some implicit assumptions about the nature of each emerging market. The emerging markets present excess return opportunities, have distinctive diversification advantages, possess above average risk and are subject to high transaction costs and thin market conditions. These markets are really attractive to investors who are very well inform for the conditions there and also are probably avoided from investors who do not have the knowledge or the tolerance for risk. In emerging markets data problems are scientifically greater than in developed countries in terms of quality and quantity.

According to Griffy-Brown (2003) in current uncertain political and economic environment companies have to deal with many supply chain disruptions. For this reason, they need to adopt particularly ways of managing their business and gain competitive advantage which is driven by speed delivery and cost reduction. Efficiency nowadays is the key word for success. The existing supply chain technologies were designed to reduce the risk in the flow of materials component and finished goods across the global supply chain. But this system was introduced many years ago when the conditions were different. Especially the catastrophic event of 11th September and the continuing threat of deliberate disruption have changed the business environment.

Also Ericson (2001) mention that companies must readdress the issues of unforeseen supply chain disruption. Each industry or better corporation has a unique challenge related with supply chain risk. Cost of carrying inventory is not considered when a business has to face a disruption. It is really difficult to foreseen what will happen in the future, but by developing an effective connectivity in the entire supply chain ad collaborate through the tools then can ensure a faster recovery. The implementation of specific regulations inside the chain can ensure better collaboration between the members which consists the supply chain.

Risk in supply chain context is the inability of a company to reach customers demands. The dimensions of risks inside the supply chain as Zsidisin (2003) has developed them in his paper '*Managerial perceptions of supply risk*'. These are:

1. The physical movement of goods.
2. The flow of information.
3. The flow of money related with stable pricing, hedging, letters of credit timely, and payments of bills.
4. The corporation's internal information systems' security. The threat from an unknown third part who may be or not member of the supply chain network and whose purpose is to steal information or knowledge and destroy or upset or disable a corporation's operation.
5. Relationships forged among supply chain partners. This is related with the degree of independence among partners.
6. Notion of corporate social responsibility and supply chain members reputation.

According to Spekman and Davies (2004), every individual corporation has to consider the need for disaster recovery or crisis management particularly in areas such as information technology and production. Business risk and continuity management are two fields that many companies pay big attention in regards of the loss of market share, the time and the cost of re-entering a market after a disruption. The main concept of a supply chain network is customers' satisfaction. So, while the chain is tending to increases, higher are the levels of risk and vulnerability. The risk insight the supply chain can be increased from interactions between the associated organizations. The supply chain risks are generated from lack of visibility, lack of ownership, self-imposed 'chaos', the misapplication of *Justin* time practices and inaccurate forecasts.

Supply chain management aims to identify areas of potential risk and implement appropriate actions to face this risk. It can be defines as

> "The identification and the management of risks within the supply chain and risks external to it, through coordinated approach amongst supply chain members, to reduce supply chain vulnerability as whole" Chapman et al (2002).

While international business hide a lot of risk and easy can be failed. Managers are responsible to take into account some specific factor in order to guide their corporation to a successful course, see Gentle (2002). These are:

- Successful managing of the headquarters - country relations.
- Not letting headquarters have free access to country data.
- Limiting the number of international software version people.
- Keeping the initial architecture simple.
- Ensuring that level one support is in local language.
- Ensuring that he key project have international experience.

Supply chain disruptions can play important role upon industrialised, advance economies. The internal efficiency can be improved by reduced supply chain vulnerability to 'everyday' commercial supply chain risk. It is true that supply networks connect business, industries and economies. Chapman and al (2002) develop a model called *"The 3-P Approach of: Philosophy: Principles; Processes"*, see *figure 4,* which plays the role of a managerial 'toolkit' which is required to change the management approach and also give the opportunity to managers to deal with vulnerability.

- The philosophy drives change in a consistent manner.
- Principles exist to extend the use of supply-chain risk management throughout the organization.
- Processes, techniques and tools to identify and manage supply-chain risk in a holistic and systematic manner.

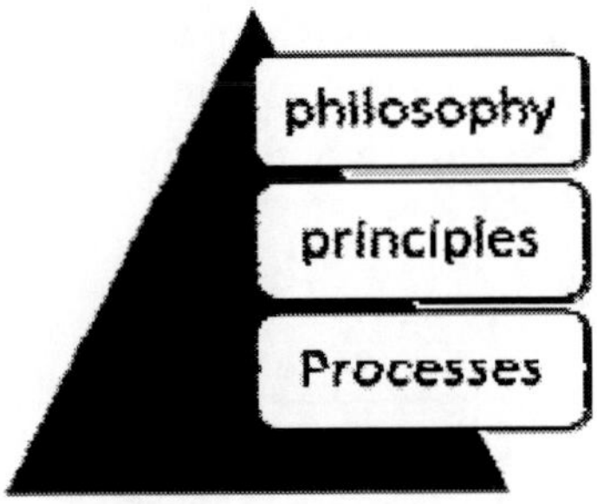

Figure 4. The '3-P' Approach of: Philosophy; Principles; Processes (Source: Chapman et al, 2002).

Failure to consider these three 'P's and develop the right techniques for managing the Supply Chain vulnerability will be a banner for the successful performance of a corporation in the market. All the organisations which are part of the same network must be sufficient agile to respond quickly, facing any disruption whatever their source or nature would be.

Whenever a company is doing businesses or international projects obtains inherently risks. Also, it presents an entirely new set of challenges to the managers. Multi-national business, see Gentle (2002), obviously are characterized by a hotchpotch of different systems and consolidation of headaches. Standardized international solutions are very appealing. The most important for a corporation is to reduce costs, consolidate its existence and keep the international synergy.

Risk management technique mixes a wide variety of investments within a portfolio. The most important aspect is in what level a market is integrated, as that implies high correlation between expected returns in different countries. The portfolio of different kinds of investments will, on average, attract higher returns at a lower risk than any individual investment found within the portfolio. This can be happened when investors improve the risk -return characteristics through the strategy of international diversification. Up to this point, diversification strives to smooth out unsystematic risk events in a portfolio so that the positive performance of some investments will neutralize the negative performance of others. Therefore, the benefits of diversification will hold only if the countries in the portfolio are not perfectly correlated and intergraded, see Patev et al (2006). Emerging markets in EE are able to face the requirement for the diversification process and according to many contemporary studies as Mishra and Akbar (2007) have presented the diversification is beneficial in emerging markets, while in developed countries can be a reason for a valued discount of the diversified company.

As it known Igor Ansoff, see Hindle (2008), is the father of modern strategic thinking according to who part of the four main marketing strategies.

- Defensive strategies.
- Intensive strategies.
- Diversification strategies.
- Integration strategies.

Ansoff has pointed out that a diversification strategy stands apart from the other three strategies as these three strategies are usually pursued with the same technical, financial, and merchandising resources used for the original product line, whereas diversification usually requires a company to acquire new skills, new techniques and new facilities. Therefore, diversification is meant to be the riskiest of the four strategies to pursue for a corporation.

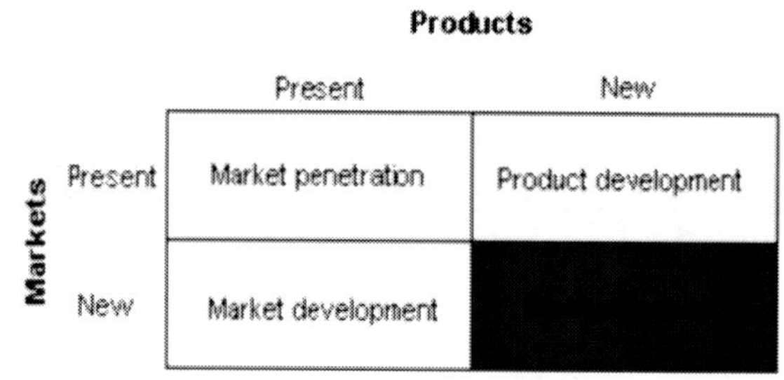

Figure 5. Ansoff's Matrix (Source: Ansoff, 1986 p99).

Diversification, as presents in Ansoffs' Matrix, see *figure 5*, seems to be the riskiest of the four strategies and requires the most careful investigation. Going into a new market with an unfamiliar product offering means a lack of experience in the new skills and techniques required and the company puts itself in a great uncertainty. Moreover, diversification might necessitate significant expanding of human and financial resources, which may detracts focus, commitment and sustained investments in the core industries. Therefore a corporation should choose this option only when the current product or current market orientation does not offer further opportunities for growth. In order to measure the chances of success, different tests can be done:

- The attractiveness test: the industry that has been chosen has to be either attractive or capable of being made attractive.
- The cost-of-entry test: the cost of entry must not capitalize all future profits.
- The better-off test: the new unit must either gain competitive advantage from its link with the corporation or vice versa.

Because of the high risks explained above, many attempts of companies to diversify led to failure. However, there are a few good examples of successful diversification:

- Virgin Media moved from music producing to travels and mobile phones
- Walt Disney moved from producing animated movies to theme parks and vacation properties
- Canon diversified from a camera-making company into producing whole new range of office equipment.

Product innovation and diversification are important management techniques for safeguarding future sales and earning. As Hake (1971) presents people, product and cultures have their own life cycles and even the most 'stable' product will one day be replaced by a new one. This is the law of growth and change following always the new trends and requirements. In recent year consumers and industrial buyers are more sophisticated and more difficult to be satisfied, while foreign companies enter in new market and have to compete with the domestic corporations which have been penetrated by the new international corporations. The competition and the technological progress will bring significant changes in the markets demands.

Freathy and O'Connell (1998) mention that the achievement of differentiation is through the development of a coordinated marketing strategy. Even if Freathy and O'Connell research is concentrated on airport retailing, their result can be generalized in other aspects of businesses. The four possible ways to undertake a strategy that differentiates can be applied in any business.

These possible ways are:

- *Product differentiation:* The main purpose is to understand what customers expect from a fashion retailer.
- *Promotional differentiation:* It includes all the promotional methods and technology in order to create a strategy of difference.
- *Distribution differentiation:* It identified alternative channels of distribution for a product or services.
- *Price differentiation:* It can be occurred in a cost advantage organization or where there are barriers preventing the organization with lower cost structure.

The European market has changed and each company is responsible to develop specific strategies to detect these changes in time and adopt measures which will enable profitable operation. The textile industry is a very good example of such changes which often occur without apparent warning and suddenly threaten the existence of entire industries, the investment of their owners and the jobs of their employers. Threats such as foreign competitors, consumers' habits, and technological change must be considered and companies must apply their objectives for the future. The diversification planning must be concentrated on research and product development, manufacturing, marketing, financing and personnel. Company should be always ready to introduce new products in order to be able to provide its customers with up-to-date programs.

7. Conclusion

Efficient risk management in corporations with multiple business units and different, some times contradictory, risk sources involves deep analysis of a complex, multi dimensional "physical" environment. Effective decision making in that conditions is very challenging, considering several type of risks, different kinds of internal as well as external factors. In our approach we have four main objectives:

1. Assess the characteristics of European emerging markets.
2. Analyse the types of risks within the European emerging markets.
3. Evaluate the risk management develop in doing business in emerging markets.
4. Identify risk appetite of a business in transitional entities.

It is also clear that risk management has the potentiality to safeguard the financial performance of a corporation by considering three ultimate principles - *growths*, *profitability* and *capital utilization*. Customers' demands, competition, labor cost and business environment volatility drive down return on capital exposing in a big risk businesses. Every company is able to accept a specific level of risk and have to develop strategies that can help to mitigate this risk and ensure its competitiveness in the market place. Operating in emerging markets is riskier than doing business in the developed world. These countries are characterized by greater political and financial instability, being more vulnerable in external risk factors such as natural disasters. Risk management becomes the core activity across all the industries as the main purpose for a firm is to survive and prosper. Finally survivors will be those that are looking for the best but they are prepared for the worst.

References

Accenture (2005) http://www.accenture.com/Countries/Sweden/About_Accenture/Newsroom/%C3%96steuropaAccenture.htm [Accessed 30th November 2006].

AIRMIC, ALARM and IRM (2002), *A risk management standard*, Report by the Association of Insurance and Risk Management (AIRMIC), the National Forum for Risk Management in the Public Sector (ALARM) and the Institute of Risk Management (IRM) in UK, pp. 1-14.

Ansoff, I. (1986), *Corporate strategy*, McGraw-Hill, New York, USA.

Best, M. (2001), *The new competitive advantage*, Harvard University Press, Cambridge.

Borge, Dan. (2001), *The book of risk*, Wiley, New York, USA.

Carrol, T. and Webb, M. (2001), *The risk factor,* Harrogate: Take That.

Cecchini, P. (1992), *The European challenge: the benefits of the single market.* The Cecchini Report Wilwood House, Aldershot.

Chapman, P., Christopher, M. Juttner, U., Peck, H., and Wilding, R. (2002), *Identifying and Managing Supply-Chain Vulnerability, Available* [online] www.iolt.org.uk.

Culp, C.L. (2001), *The risk management process [electronic resource]: business strategy and tactics*, Wiley, New York, USA.

Deschamps, E. *The European idea* [online] http://www.ena.lu [Accessed 15th March 2008].

Dickens, P. (2003), *Global shift: reshaping the global economic map in the 21st century,* (4th edition), London, SAGE.

Dobosiewicz, Z. (1992), *Foreign investment in Eastern Europe,* Routledge, London, UK.

El Kahal, S. (1998), *Business in Europe*, London- McGraw-Hill.

Ericson, J. (2001), *Addressing supply-chain disruptions*, 4th October, Available online: http://www.line56.com/print/default.a sp?ArticleID=3015andTopic ID=2, [Accessed 22nd May 2006].

Freathy, P. and O'Connell, F. (1998*), European airport retailing: growth strategies for the New Millennium,* Basingstoke: Macmillan Press.

Freeman, S. and Reid, I. (2006), Constraints facing small western firm in transitional markets, *European Business Review* Vol.18, No. 23, pp.187-213.

Gentle, M. (1957), *The CRM project management handbook: building realistic expectations and managing risk,* London: Kogan Page.

Gerbet, P. *The collapse of the Communist* [online] http://www.ena.lu [Accessed 15th March 2008].

Griffy-Brown, C. (2003) 'Just-in time to just –in case: Managing a supply chain in uncertain times', *Graziadio Business Report* Vol.6, No.2.

Guinipero, L.C. and Eltantawy, A.R. (2004) 'Security the upstream supply chain: a risk management approach', *International Journal of Physical Distribution and Logistics Management* Vol. 34, No. 9, pp. 698-713.

Hacker, S., Johansson, B. and Karlsson, C. (2004), *Emerging market economies and European economic integration,* Cheltenham: Edward Elgar.

Hake, B (1971), *New-product strategy: innovation and diversification techniques* London: Pitman.

Hindle, T. (2008) Guru: Igor Ansoff, *The Ecomist*, June 18th Available online: http:// www.economist.com/displaystory.Cfm?story_id=11701586 [Accessed 18th August 2008].

Infotech (2008), *Google joins Top ten global brands*, 19th September, [online] http://infotech.indiatimes.com/articleshow/3503782.cms [Accessed 17th December 2008]

Juttner, U. (2005), Supply Chain Risk Management: Understand the business requirements from a practitioner perspective, *The International Journal of Logistics Management* Vol.16, No.1, pp. 120-141.

Keane, S. (1993) *Emerging markets: the relevance of efficient theory* London: Technical and Research Committee of the Chartered Association of Certified Accountants.

Klonowski, D. (2007) The venture capital investment processing emerging markets: Evidence from Central and Eastern Europe. *International Journal of Emerging Markets* Vol. 2, No. 4, pp. 361-382.

Kolodko, W.G. (2002), *Globalization and Catching-up in Emerging Markets Economies*, Rochester, N.Y.; Woodbridge: University of Rochester Press.

Kolodko, W.G. (2003a), *Emerging markets economies: globalization and development*, Adershot: Ashgate.

Kolodko, W.G. (2003b), *Globalization and catching-up in emerging markets economies*, Proc. of the International Conference on Development Cooperation in an Enlargement European Union, Vienna, 3-4 November 2003.

Kraft, E.M. and Freeman, A.E. (1989), Introduction: economic and political issues in risk analysis, *Risk Analysis* Vol. 9, No. 3, pp. 279-281.

Kraljic, P. (1983), Purchasing must become supply management, *Harvard Business Review* Vol. 61, No. 5, pp.109-117.

Lenartowicz, T. and Johnson, J. (2007), Staffing managerial positions in emerging markets: a cultural perspective. *International Journal of Emerging Markets* Vol. 2, No. 3, pp. 207-214.

Luo, Y. (2002), *Multinational enterprises in emerging markets*, Copenhagen Business School Press.

Mitchell, V.W. (1995), Organizational risk perceptions and reduction: a literature review, *British Journal of Management* Vol. 6, No. 2, pp. 115-133.

Mishra, A. and Akbar, M. (2007), Empirical examination of diversification strategies in business groups: Evidence from emerging markets, *International Journal of Emerging Markets* Vol. 2, No. 1, pp. 22-38.

Morgan, E. J. (1980), *Growth, diversification and mergers,* Business economics, (The D324 course team), Unit 11, Social sciences: a third level course Milton Keynes: Open University Press.

Marber, P. (1998), *From third world to world class: the future of emerging markets in the global economy*, Oxford: Perseus.

Millar, C.J.M, Grant, R. and Choi, C.J. (2000), *International Business: Emerging Issues and Emerging Markets*, Macmillan Press: London, UK.

Ollson, C (2002), *Risk Management in emerging markets: how to survive and prosper*, London: Financial Times Prentice Hall.

Olsen, T.A., Pinto, M. and Virji, S. (2005) Navigating growth in emerging markets: six rules for improving decision making between corporate and local leadership, *Journal of Business strategy* Vol. 26, No. 6, pp. 37-44.

Pavet, P., Kanaryan, N. and Lyroudi, K. (2006) Stock Market Crisis and Portfolio Diversification in Central and Eastern Europe, *Managerial Finance* Vol. 32, No. 5, pp. 415-432.

Roehrig, P (2006), Bet on governance to manage outsourcing risk, Available online: http://www.btquarterly.com/?mc=bet-governanceandpage=ss-viewresearch [Accessed 12th August 2008].

Rosling, A. (2005), Mantras for emerging markets http://www.tata.com/0_media /features/speakers_forum/20050125_mantra.htm [Accessed 13th December 2006].

Sabal, J. (2002), *Financial decisions in emerging markets,* New York; Oxford: Oxford University Press, UK.

Spekman, E., R. and Davis, W. E. (2004), Risky business: expanding the discussion on risk and the extended enterprise, *International Journal of Physical Distribution and Logistics Management* Vol. 34, No. 5, pp. 414-433.

Steele, L.R. and Court, B.H. (1996), *Profitable purchasing strategies: a manager's guide for improving organizational competitiveness through the skills of purchasing*, McGraw-Hill, London, UK.

The World Factbook: European Union [online] https://www.cia.gov/library/publications /the-world-factbook/print/ee.html [Accessed 11th May 2008].

Thompson, K.M. (2002), Variability and uncertainty meet risk management and risk communication', *Journal of Risk Analysis* Vol. 22, No. 3, pp. 647-654.

Zsidisin, G.A. (2003), Managerial perceptions of supply chain, *The Journal of Supply Chain Management: A global Review of Purchasing and Supply* Vol. 29, No. 1, pp. 14-26.

Zsidisin, G.A. (2002), Defining supply chain risk: a grounded theory approach, Proc. from the Decision Science Institute Annual Meeting, San Diego, CA.

Zsidisin, G. A., Panelli, A. and Upton, R. (2000), Purchasing's organization involvement in risk assessments, contingency plans, and risk management: an exploratory study, *Supply Chain Management* Vol. 5, No. 4, pp. 187-198.

In: Risk Management
Editors: B. Jordão and E. Sousa, pp. 153-170
ISBN: 978-1-60876-011-4

Chapter 5

CATEGORISING RISKS FROM CLIMATE CHANGE UNDER IRGC'S RISK GOVERNANCE FRAMEWORK

Yuehong Zhang[1], Shaohong Wu[1], Dengwei Liu[2] and Erfu Dai[1]
[1] Institute of Georgaphic Sciences and Natural Resource Research,
CAS, Beijing 100101, China
[2] Development Research Center, Ministry of Water Resources,
Beijing 100038, China

Abstract

Climate risk management or governance is a new and evolving area. China also proposed to establish climate risk governance system in its 11th five-year plan period (2006~2010). Given that Climate change-related risks are messy, including numerous known and potential hazards, the most urgent task is to group these climate risks into a manageable number of categories. In this article, we adopt a new risk categorisation system brought forward by Renn in a framework of International Risk Governance Council (IRGC) to classify climate change risks, which may be instrumental in a better governance of climate risks. We first investigate the post-normal nature of IRGC's categorisation system and propose that "the degree of uncertainty in the risk-related knowledge" might be used as the classifying criteria. Then we use "confidence" and "likelihood", quantitative terms for uncertainties description in the IPCC Fourth Assessment, to establish a quantitative classification approach based on fuzzy set theory. Finally, we analyse this categorisation's implication for climate risk governance in China. However, this climate risk categorising approach is still a very preliminary one. There are some limitations in the method per se and its application, which need to be studied further in the future.

Keywords: Climate Change; Risk Categorisation; Uncertainty; Risk Governance

1. Introduction

Climate change problem has emerged over the last two decades. Many social, biological, and geophysical systems are at risk from climate change. As the climate system is definitely a complex one, containing multiple interactions and feedbacks between its subsystems and a component of inherent irreducible unpredictability in its behaviour (Rind, 1999), this can easily lead to divergence among the scientists and create a feeling of despair and helplessness in front of the threats and risks of climate change (Cohen, 1999). Considering the advantages of risk management, such as the use of formalised methods to manage uncertainty, stakeholder involvement, use of methods for evaluating policy options without being policy prescriptive, integration of different disciplinary approaches etc. (IPCC, 2007), risk management of climate change might be a very effective way to cope with these problems properly.

In view of this, IPCC also brought in the concept of risk in the Fourth Assessment Report (IPCC, 2007), and deemed risk management a useful framework for decision-making. Although climate risk management is a new and evolving area (Connell, 2005), the use of risk management or governance for climate change is expanding rapidly (IPCC, 2007). World Bank has proposed strategies addressing climate risk management in its Global Environment Facility Program (World Bank, 2006); UK and Australia also integrated risk management into climate change adaptation and mitigation, forming *Climate Change Impacts and Risk Management - A Guide for Business and Government* (Australian Greenhouse Office, 2006) and *UK Climate Impacts Programme (UKCIP)* (Willows and Connell, 2003) respectively.

In recent years, China has also taken a series of measures to respond to the challenges of climate change. Just in 2007, China has finished *National Assessment Report on climate change* (2007), and proposed *China National Plan for Coping with Climate Change* (National Development and Reform Commission, 2007). However, there is still not any integrated climate risk management system in China, other than some sporadic risk analyses and management scattered in several climate-related fields. Realizing the importance of the role of climate risk management or governance in sustainable development, China also proposed to establish climate risk governance system, which is a kernel part of the integrated risk governance programme during the 11th five-year plan period (2006~2010).

Here we defined the climate change risk as the possibility of impacts on natural ecosystems and socio-economic systems resulted from or aggravated by climate change, particularly the negative aspects, based on the definition of risk defined by "Australian/New Zealand Standard on Risk Management" (AS/NZS,1999). Given that Climate change-related risks are messy (Roger, 2004), including numerous known and potential hazards, the most urgent task at present is to group these climate risks into a manageable number of categories (Morgan, 2000). Climate-related risks have been categorised by gross measures of danger (e.g., population at risk, dollar cost), geographic (e.g., local, regional, global impact) and temporal (e.g., reversible or irreversible) scope, and the distribution of consequences over a variety of groups (e.g., location, income), among others (Oppenheimer, 2005; Patwardhan *et al.*, 2003; Oppenheimer and Petsonk, 2005). Different categorisations will best serve different objectives (Morgan, 2000).

In this paper we adopt a new risk categorisation system brought forward by Renn in a framework of International Risk Governance Council (IRGC), which is based on the different states of knowledge about each particular risk, distinguishing between "simple", "complex", "uncertain" and "ambiguous" risk problems (Renn, 2005). The reason we pitch on this risk categorisation system is that it is a problem-solving oriented system and can deal with the new challenges for the risk professionals in an era of post-modern confusion (Renn, 2006). IRGC's framework provided for each category with different routes of appraisal, characterisation, evaluation, management measures and tools, and even different ways for stakeholder participation, which will be instrumental in a better governance of risks. So we apply this categorisation system to the classification of climate change risks, aiming at boosting the management efficiency and facilitating the transformation from "risk analysis" to "risk governance" (Renn, 2006) in China.

However, there is not any specific or quantitative classifying method for this new categorisation system. Our main intention is to find a proper way to classify the climate risks quantitatively. In section 2, we investigate the post-normal nature of IRGC's categorisation, and propose that "the degree of uncertainty in the risk-related knowledge" might be treated as the classifying criteria. Section 3 analyses uncertainty of climate change and description method in IPCC. In section 4, we establish a quantitative classification system based on fuzzy set theory and degree of membership method. Section 5 presents its implications for climate risk governance in China. In section 6, we discussed the limitations in the categorising method and its application.

2. Irgc's Risk Categorisation System and Its Essence

IRGC's new risk categorisation system is based on the different states of knowledge about each particular risk, distinguishing between "simple", "complex", "uncertain" and "ambiguous" risk problems, which is characterised in Table I. The characterisation of a particular risk depends on the degree of difficulty of establishing the cause-effect relationship between a risk agent and its potential consequences, the reliability of this relationship and the degree of controversy with regard to both what a risk actually means for those affected and the values to be applied when judging whether or not something needs to be done about it (Renn, 2005). This qualitative description of the classifying criteria is somewhat abstract and people with different knowledge structure might have different understanding about it.

Considering this, Renn maintained that "a screening board" should be established involving members of the risk and concern assessment team, risk managers and key stakeholders (such as industry, NGOs and representatives of related regulatory or governmental agencies) to perform this challenging task (Renn, 2005). However, the establishment of the board also posed a great challenge: who should be involved in, how to organize and manage it, in which way to negotiate and who finance it, etc. Therefore, the practical application of this screening board may be very limited. It is essential to find a more feasible and relative impersonal way to categorise risks. And the primary thing we need to do is to analyse the essence and gist of this new categorisation system.

The motivation that Renn proposed the new "risk governance framework" is to deal with the new challenges for the risk professionals in an era of post-modern confusion (Renn, 2006). Scientific, economic, social, and cultural aspects and the effective engagement of stakeholders were integrated into this system. In this sense, the framework embodied many elements of post-normal science (Funtowicz and Ravetz 1993), and the categorisation system seems to be related to the "Communities of knowledge construction" proposed by Funtowicz and Ravetz (1992, 1993) (Figure1). They use "systems uncertainties" and "decision stakes" as attributes to distinguish between problem types. The first type is applied science (which includes as a subtype core science), the second professional consultancy, and the third post-normal science. These problem - solving approaches are represented in Figure 1 as concentric segments with increasing uncertainty and disagreement.

Table I. Characterisation of the Risk Categorisation by risk-related knowledge

Categorisation	Characteristics and Definition		Examples
"Simple" risk problems	Referring to those risks that have a clear cause-and-effect connection. simple risks should not be equated with small or negligible risks. The major issues here are that the potential negative consequences are obvious, the values applied are non-controversial and the remaining uncertainties are low.		Car accidents; Known food and health risks; Regularly reoccurring natural disasters
Complexity- induced risk problems	Complexity refers to the difficulty of identifying and quantifying causal links between a multitude of potential causal agents and specific observed effects. The nature of this difficulty may be traced back to interactive effects among these agents (synergism and antagonisms), long delay periods between cause and effect, inter-individual variation, intervening variables, and others.		Sophisticated chemical facilities; Synergistic effects of potentially toxic substances
Uncertainty- induced risk problems	Uncertain knowledge refers to the incompleteness of knowledge, with the available knowledge relying on uncertain assumptions, assertions and predictions. uncertainty often results from an incomplete or inadequate reduction of complexity in modelling cause-effect chains.		Earthquake; Terrorism
Ambiguity- induced risk problems	Referring to which give rise to several meaningful and legitimate interpretations of accepted risk assessments results. A condition of ambiguity emerges where the problem lies in agreeing on the appropriate values, priorities, assumptions, or boundaries to be applied to the definition of possible outcomes.	Interpretative ambiguity: different interpretations of an identical assessment result (e.g. as an adverse or non-adverse effect)	Electromagnetic radiation
		Normative ambiguity: different concepts of what can be regarded as tolerable referring e.g. to ethics, quality of life parameters, distribution of risks and benefits etc.	Nuclear power; Genetically modified food

*Adapted from White Paper No.1 of IRGC. (Renn, 2005).

The traditional "core" science is concentrated around the origin of Figure 1, in which decision stakes and uncertainties are low. The problem is likely to be solvable using a normal, puzzle-solving approach. When both uncertainty and disagreement are small, "applied science" can be used, where expertise is fully effective.

The outcomes of both applied science and core science have the features of reproducibility and prediction, for they operate on isolated, controlled natural systems. When there is an intermediate level of either uncertainty or disagreement, the application of routine techniques requires supplementation with skill, judgment, and sometimes even courage, and the "professional consultancy" would be applicable. Professional consultancy includes applied science, but deals with problems that require a different methodology for their complete resolution. When either uncertainty or disagreement is high, "post-normal science" applies, and the problem enters the societal/political arena. An issue in post-normal science is characterised as one where facts are uncertain, values in dispute, stakes high and decisions urgent (Funtowicz and Ravetz, 1992, 1993).

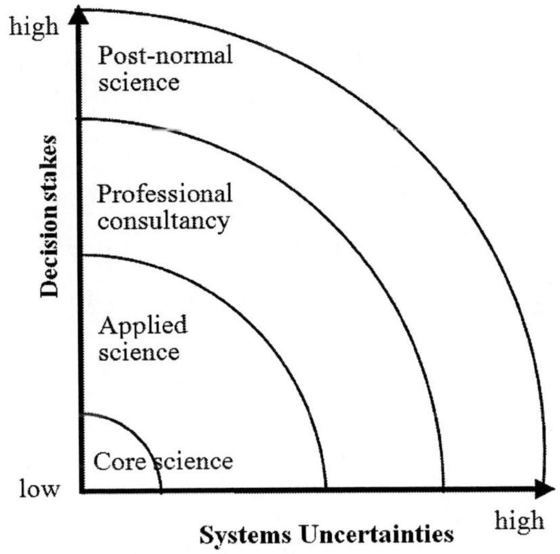

Figure 1. Communities of knowledge construction, from Funtowicz and Ravetz (1992, 1993).

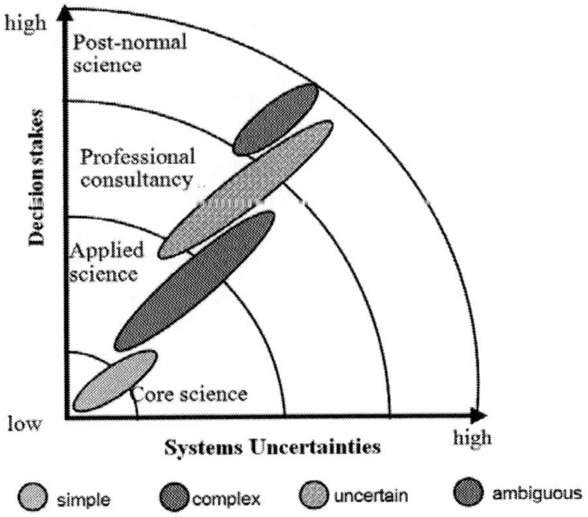

Figure 2. The relationship of the IRGC's new risk categories and Communities of knowledge construction.

According to the definition (Table I) and different strategies and instruments (Table II) IRGC proposed for each risk category, we could parallel the four risk categories to this "Communities of knowledge construction" roughly (Figure 2). "Simple risk" problems are those that the values applied are non-controversial and the remaining uncertainties are low. "Traditional" decision-making is assigned in IRGC's framework (Table II), which is similar to the problem-solving strategies of "core science" and "applied science" in "Communities of knowledge construction". For Complexity-Induced risk problems, although they have complicated potential causal agents and intervening variables due to the increased uncertainty, the traditional method, such as expert consensus seeking and some buffer capacity improving method are still applicable. So, "applied science" and "professional consultancy" are both needed in this category. Uncertainty-induced risk problems are those that knowledge is incomplete, with the available knowledge relying on uncertain assumptions, assertions and predictions. Their degrees of uncertainty are comparative high.

Table II. Risk Characteristics and their Implications for Risk Management

Knowledge Characteris-ation	Management Strategy	Appropriate Instruments	Stakeholder Participation
"Simple" risk problems	*Routine-based:* (tolerability/ Acceptability judgement) (risk reduction)	Applying "traditional" decision-making • Risk-benefit analysis • Risk-risk trade-offs • Trial and error • Technical standards • Economic incentives • Education, labelling, information • Voluntary agreements	Instrumental discourse
Complexity-Induced risk problems	*Risk-informed:* (risk agent and causal chain)	Characterising the available evidence • Expert consensus seeking tools: * Delphi or consensus conferencing * Meta analysis * Scenario construction, etc. • Results fed into routine operation	Epistemological discourse
	Robustness-focused: (risk absorbing system)	Improving buffer capacity of risk target through: • Additional safety factors • Redundancy and diversity in designing safety devices • Improving coping capacity • Establishing high reliability organizations	
Uncertainty-induced risk problems	*Precaution-based:* (risk agent)	Using hazard characteristics such as persistence, ubiquity etc. as proxies for risk estimates. Tools include: • Containment • ALARA (as low as reasonably achievable) • ALARP (as low as reasonably possible) • BACT (best available control technology), etc.	Reflective discourse
	Resilience-focused: (risk absorbing system)	Improving capability to cope with surprises • Diversity of means to accomplish desired benefits • Avoiding high vulnerability • Allowing for flexible responses • Preparedness for adaptation	
Ambiguity-induced risk problems	*Discourse-based:*	Application of conflict resolution methods for reaching consensus or tolerance for risk evaluation results and management option selection • Integration of stakeholder involvement in reaching closure • Emphasis on communication and social Discourse	Participative discourse

*From White Paper No.1 of IRGC, (Renn, 2005).

Although they still need the applied science and professional consultancy to control risk, the "Reflective discourse" (Table II) method indicates that they have stepped into the post-normal fields. For "Ambiguous" risk problems, there are different viewpoints about the relevance, meaning and implications of factual explanations and predictions for deciding about the tolerability of a risk as well as management actions. Specific measures or methods were not assigned to this risk type, except the way for stakeholder involvement and communication, which is a fully fledged post-normal science problem.

It should be clarified here is that the correlation (Figure 2) between the two systems is not a strict one. It only serves to illuminate that IRGC's risk categorisation system is virtually related to the "knowledge construction", by which we expect to find some clues and information for risk categorisation. The "knowledge construction" is distinguished by "systems uncertainties" and "decision stakes", it seems that we could also categorise risks by these two criteria. However, through the above analyses, we found that IRGC's risk categorisation system is mainly pertinent to "systems uncertainties". And considering "decision stakes" generally results from and varies with "systems uncertainties", using these two criteria simultaneously might have some unnecessary overlaps. Thus we only use "uncertainty" as the criteria for IRGC's new categorisation system, while, of course it may have a suspicion of reductionism.

That is to say we could narrow down IRGC's criteria - different states of knowledge to different "uncertainty" states of knowledge. Uncertainty may originate from ignorance, randomness, imprecise observation, immeasurability, lack of knowledge and ambiguity etc. From this broad sense, different degrees of uncertainty can cover all the four risk categories of IRGC. So "uncertainty" can be used to differentiate "simple", "complex", "uncertain" and "ambiguous" risk problems. However, it should be noticed that uncertainty here is a nonobjective measurable dimension, which is different from the "uncertain" risk that is one of specific risk types distinguished by it.

3. Uncertainty of Climate Change and Description Method in IPCC

In view of the novel, complex, uncertain, variable, and social-relevant nature of climate problems, Science cannot always provide well-founded theories based on experiments for explanation and prediction (Funtowicz and Ravetz, 1990), and sometimes the facts given by the scientists are diverging and inherently uncertain (Saloranta, 2001). This kind of climate change issue is considered clearly fulfills Funtowicz and Ravetz's criteria for Post-Normal Science (Saloranta, 2001; Funtowicz and Ravetz, 1990; Bray and Von Storch, 1999). Accordingly, different risks induced from climate change also show various degrees of complexity, uncertainty and disputes. If all the climate risks are assessed and managed in the traditional reductive methods indiscriminately, they will not only get low management efficiency, but even worse, may be irrational, unscientific and potentially misleading (Stirling, 2007). In this case, we need to find out what kinds of risks are appropriate for the traditional methods, and what kinds not. This exactly justified the application of IRGC's categorisation system, which could provide a more specific division in the approaches used in different uncertainty states.

Studies of climate change have paid careful attention to identifying and quantifying uncertainties from the outset, perhaps more so than in any other area of science (Manning, 2006). Describing uncertainty honestly is an important part of communicating science in a balanced way and is essential to maintain trust between scientists and the broader community, which has been recognized in the IPCC assessments (McBean, 2004) that has been a central actor in the global climate change issue. The sequence of the last four IPCC reports from 1990 to the present time provides an increasing formal and mature way for uncertainty description.

In the IPCC First and Second Assessment Reports, uncertainty was not addressed systematically, in which there was very limited use of standardized language to express uncertainties. The attempt by the IPCC in the Third Assessment Report (TAR) to quantitatively address uncertainty was an important and positive step forward, largely following the approach set out by Moss and Schneider (2000). Based on the method established for TAR, the Fourth Assessment Report (AR4) has developed an approach including many new considerations (Manning, 2006 ; Manning *et al.*, 2004). AR4 described the up-to-date uncertainty assessment, which is most relevant to "the present state of risk-related knowledge" (IRGC, 2005). Moreover, In AR4, the scientific uncertainty description in climate change was stressed to support analysis of risk and of options, especially Working Group II mainly dealt with the climate change impacts, adaptation and vulnerability research, which were also closely linked to the risks of climate change. Thus we could categorise climate-relate risks applying uncertainty description of Working Group II, AR4, in which "confidence" and "likelihood" are the quantitative terms for uncertainty description.

"Level of confidence" refers to the degree of belief or confidence in a science community that available models or analyses are accurate and will generally be determined by a combination of the amount of evidence or information available and the degree of consensus in the interpretation of that information, while "likelihood" indicates the chance of a defined occurrence or outcome and it can be a valuable construct where results are available from formal probabilistic analyses or can be expressed in a probabilistic way (Manning *et al.*, 2004, IPCC, 2007). It should be noticed that likelihoods can be interpreted in two ways. The first is the frequentist/classical view and ignores or downplays subjective uncertainty. The second view of likelihood assessments acknowledges that any likelihood assessment would contain subjective elements. So likelihood may be either based on quantitative analysis or an elicitation of expert views. However, the more subjective the likelihood assessment, the more the need to evaluate that subjectivity, and the more the assessment would be improved by adding information on confidence levels as well (Risbey and Kandlikar, 2007).

Many people have noted that the concepts of "confidence" and "likelihood" often appear to be closely linked. However, there are important differences between the two terms, which are recognized that each term provides a complementary aspect of describing uncertainties in AR4 (Manning, 2006 ; Manning *et al.*, 2004). Figure 3 depicts the inter-relationship between likelihood and confidence represented by two separate axes increasing towards the top and right, respectively. The shaded area represents the region in which findings are most sensibly expressed. If one has low confidence then any assigned likelihoods should be moderate rather than extreme (C). High confidence can rationally associate with all kinds of likelihood, in which Manning especially stressed that for medium likelihood, For example, we could have very high confidence that tossing a coin will turn up heads about 50% of the time (D). And this situation is very different from one where we might be forced to assign a medium likelihood due to lack of knowledge and low confidence (C). A and B marked in Figure 3 shows the irrational cases of assigning high or low likelihood when there is only low confidence (Manning, 2006). The combination of likelihood and confidence provides more powerful means for analysts to express uncertainty.

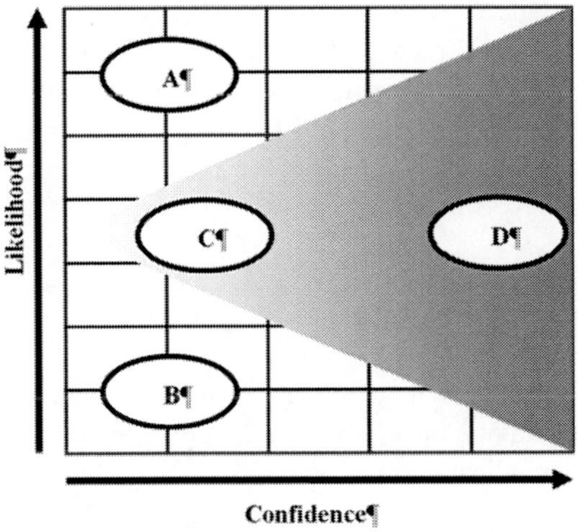

Figure 3. Schematic depicting inter-relationship between likelihood and confidence represented by two separate axes increasing towards the top and right, respectively. The shaded area represents the region in which findings are most sensibly expressed. Cases denoted by A and B, i.e. where one might associate very high or low likelihood with a very low confidence in the science, are not normally encountered. The distinction between the two dimensions of confidence and likelihood can be clearly seen by contrasting cases C and D as discussed in the text.(from Manning, 2006).

Recognizing the advantages of using both likelihood and confidence information, the IPCC AR4 has provided schemes for both these concepts in communicating uncertainties (Allen *et al.*, 2004; IPCC, 2005; Manning, 2006).

Thus "confidence" and "likelihood", the quantitative terms for uncertainty description in AR4 could both be used as the uncertainty criteria for climate risk categorization. Furthermore, given the authoritative, comprehensive and timely nature of IPCC assessment and its open and peer-reviewed process, we can minimize the disagreement and disputes in the categorisation which heavily depend upon our experience and cognition.

4. Quantitative Method of Risks Categorisation of Climate Change

The risk types (simple; complex; uncertain; ambiguous) are neither clear-cut nor mutually exclusive – the need is to find the dominant class (Bunting, 2006). That is to say, the change near the boundary is a gradual transition, rather than a sharp one. It is difficult to draw a clear demarcation line between the four types. This blurred character of the categorisation could be portrayed by the concept of fuzzy set theory and degree of membership.

Climate change risks are assumed as a problem domain $U=\{x_1,x_2,...,x_n\}$, in which, simple risk (R_1), complex risks (R_2), uncertain risks (R_3) and ambiguous risk (R_4) can be see as four fuzzy Sets. In traditional set theory something either belongs to a set or does not, depending on whether it fits the definition for that set (i.e. it has a degree of membership (μ) to the set either equal to one (μ=1) or equal to zero (μ=0)). In fuzzy set theory, something can partially belong to a set and have a degree of membership anywhere between zero and one (i.e. $0 \leq \mu \leq 1$). Each element (x) in this climate change risk domain may belong to all the four fuzzy set in different degrees. This different belonging degree (degree of membership) could be obtained according to the fuzzy membership function characterised by feature parameters. Finally according to the maximum principle, we can fix on the dominant category it should belong to. This classification approach could be divided into three steps: feature extraction; constructing the fuzzy membership function for the four risk categories; categorising by maximum principle.

4.1. Feature Extraction and Analysis

Feature extraction means that suitable feature parameters should be selected to sufficiently describe the traits of uncertainty in different risk categories of climate risks. As the previous sections have indicated, there is no doubt that "likelihood" and "confidence" are the most befitting feature parameters for uncertainty description of climate change risks. However, particular attention needs to be paid in two aspects.

First, when involving a certain climate risk, we should clarify its risk agents and potential consequences related. On one hand, risk agents and consequences are the intrinsic attributes of risks. IRGC's categorising criteria - different states of current knowledge just mainly focus on the cause-effect relationship between risk agents and their potential consequences (Renn, 2005). On the other hand, for a same event or risk, we may have very different levels of confidence in various probabilistic statements. If we do not emphasize the agents and outcomes for a specific risk, it may be diverging and confusing in screening the confidence and likelihood level from the report.

Second, Confidence may be divided into five degrees: Very high confidence (At least 9 out of 10 chance of being correct); High confidence (About 8 out of 10 chance); Medium confidence (About 5 out of 10 chance); Low confidence (About 2 out of 10 chance); Very low confidence (Less than a 1 out of 10 chance). "Likelihood" can be divided into seven degrees: Virtually certain (>99% probability of occurrence); Very likely(90 to 99% probability); Likely (66 to 90% probability); About as likely as not (33 to 66% probability); Unlikely (10 to 33% probability); Very unlikely (1 to 10% probability); Exceptionally unlikely (<1% probability)) (Manning *et al.*, 2004; IPCC, 2005; Manning, 2006). These classifications in "confidence" and "likelihood" promote expressions of expert judgment into broad categories rather than giving single point estimates or specific ranges for each issue addressed, which recognized fuzzy boundaries as done in the US National Assessment (USGCRP, 2000) so as to avoid a false sense of precision. However, here we need a specific numerical value that could be applied to the membership function. Thus, we have to choose its arithmetic mean value as the representative of the uncertainty range it assigned. For example, as to "Likely" (66 to 90% probability), we assign 0.78 as its representative value. This provisional alternative is just used for facilitating computing, and the specific value per se does not make any sense. Given that the overall fuzzy method we used, the specific value will not affect the final outcome.

4.2. Constructing the Fuzzy Membership Functions for the Four Risk Categories

According to the analysis of the essence of the four risk categories aforementioned and the relationship and distinction between “confidence” and “likelihood” proposed in the uncertainty workshop and described by Manning (Manning, 2006 ; Manning et al., 2004), we can roughly describe their relationship as follows:

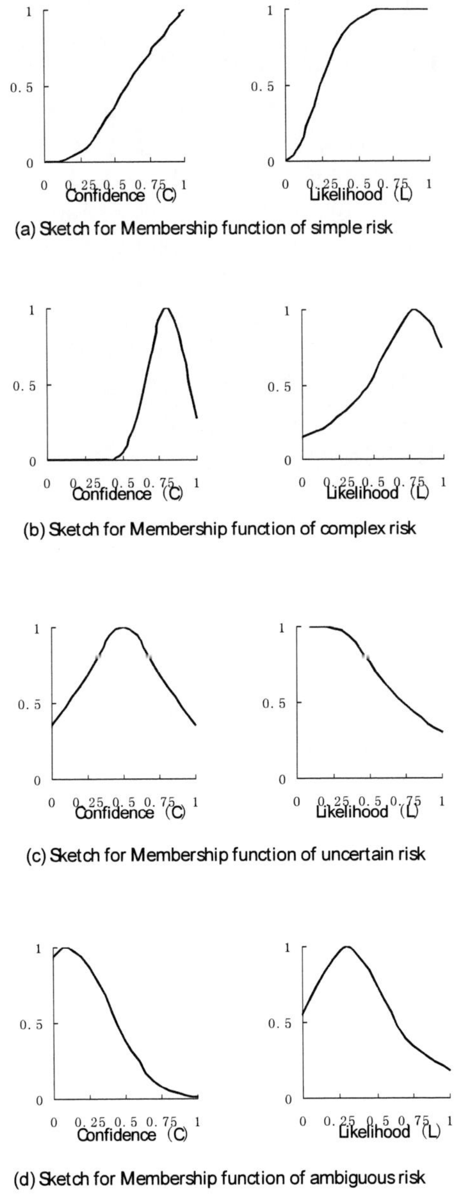

Figure 4. Schematic depicting for the membership function of four risk categories by ‘Confidence’ and ‘Likelihood’.

For "confidence", the higher the confidence level assigned is, the lower the degree of uncertainty becomes. With the increase of confidence, it should be corresponded to ambiguous, uncertain, complex and simple risk problems respectively. As to "likelihood", the relationship is much more complicated. When an event is said to be extremely likely (or extremely unlikely) it is implicit that we have high confidence (Risbey and Kandlikar, 2007). And the positive end (Virtually certain) may have lower uncertainties than the negative end (Exceptionally unlikely), since we generally have more knowledge and information on the high-probability events. For the medium likelihood, there are two circumstances as discussed before. First, when confidence is high, the uncertainty might lie between or same as the two ends. In this situation, likelihood generally has little effects on the degree of uncertainties. Second, when confidence is low, medium likelihood might be forced to be assigned due to lack of knowledge and low consensus (Manning, 2006). In this case, the uncertainty is commonly higher than the two ends.

The relationship above-mentioned could be expressed as Figure 4, in which we roughly sketch the possible varying trend of the degree of membership of the two feature parameters in each risk category. According to the common membership functions and their corresponding sketches Huang proposed (Huang and Wang, 1992; Wei and Chen, 2005), we can educe the general function type for each category based on Figure 4. And then through lots of trial calculations, we determine the sub-membership functions of the four risk categories characterized by "confidence"(C) and "likelihood" (L).

1) the membership function of simple risk:

The sub-membership function of Confidence: $\mu_{R_1}(C) = 2.72e^{-\frac{1}{C}}$ (C≠0)

The sub-membership function of Likelihood: $\mu_{R_1}(L) = 1 - e^{-(\frac{L}{0.3})^2}$

As above analysis, "confidence" is more relevant to the categorisation than "likelihood", so we assigned the weight for the two sub-functions: 0.6 and 0.4 respectively. Accordingly we establish the overall membership function of simple risk type:

$$\mu_{R_1} = 0.6(2.72e^{-\frac{1}{C}}) + 0.4(1 - e^{-(\frac{L}{0.3})^2})$$

2) Similarly, we define the membership function for complex risk type:

$$\mu_{R_2} = 0.6(e^{-33(C-0.8)^2}) + 0.4(\frac{1}{1+9(L-0.8)^2})$$

3) The membership function for uncertain risk type:

$$\mu_{R_3} = 0.6(\frac{1}{1+7(C-0.5)^2}) + 0.4(1 - e^{-(\frac{0.6}{L})^2}) \quad (L \neq 0)$$

4) The membership function for ambiguous risk type:

$$\mu_{R_4} = 0.6(e^{-6(C-0.1)^2}) + 0.4(\frac{1}{1+9(L-0.3)^2})$$

4.3. Categorising by Maximum Principle and the Case Study

Finally, according to the maximum principle: $\mu_{R_i}(x) = \max_{1\le j\le 4} \mu_{R_j}(C, L)$, climate change risk x_0 (C,L) is attributed to Ri, in which x_0 possesses maximum degree of membership.

Take the risk of "Marine life influenced by ocean acidity" as an example. The feature parameters that we extract from IPCC AR4 Working Group II were "medium confidence" and "likely" respectively. We adopt their arithmetic mean as the representative value of the uncertainty range: 0.5 (About 5 out of 10 chance), 78% (66 to 90% probability). According to the membership function of the four risk categories, we calculate the degree of membership respectively: the degree of membership to simple risk type is $\mu_{R_1} = 0.56$; for complex risk type, $\mu_{R_2} = 0.33$; for uncertain risk type, $\mu_{R_3} = 0.83$; for ambiguous risk type, $\mu_{R_4} = 0.55$. Finally according to the maximum principle: $\mu_{R_3} = \max_{1\le j\le 4} \mu_{R_j}(C, L) = 0.83$, the risk of "Marine life influenced by ocean acidity" is attributed to R_3, i.e. uncertain risk type.

5. Implications for Climate Risk Governance in China

Categorising various and messy climate change risks in this way could allocate climate change risks to different routes of appraisal, characterisation, evaluation and management that IRGC proposed for each category (Table II). This classification system will not only improve risk management efficiency, but also could make for better risk governance in climate change, which is especially useful for countries with little experience in risk management and governance, like China.

First, it could provide formalized methods to manage uncertainty in climate change risks. We have not paid enough attention in the uncertainty assessment of climate-related research in China for a long time. Since "the degree of uncertainty in the risk-related knowledge" is the criteria by which we classify climate risks, we could assess and manage risks according to different degree of uncertainties and complexities. The different routes of appraisal, characterisation, evaluation, management measures and stakeholder participation way for each category provided in IRGC's framework are just a good uncertainty management system for them. Thus, this categorisation could be expected to boost the uncertainty management in climate change research and risk management.

Second, categorising climate change risks in this way could facilitate stakeholder's involvement in the risk governance. IRGC's emphasis on governance is meant to underline the importance that it places on the inclusion of stakeholders and public groups within the risk handling process and, consequently, on the establishment of adequate public-private partnerships and participatory processes (Renn, 2005). In China, civil society, science communities, and NGOs related to climate and environment have been fostered and achieved great development in recent years, nevertheless not very mature. IRGC's new framework provided the concrete ways for these organizations and individuals' participation and involvement for the four classes of risk problems and the design discourse (Table II), which could facilitate risk communication and boost the development of the civil society and NGOs in China simultaneously.

Third, this categorisation could help integrate policy and social relevance research into climate risk governance. Climate change research would be shaped by both academic creativity and the needs of those outside academia (Turnpenny, 2003). Furthermore society is not an independent observer of the system but an intrinsic part of it (Manning *et al.*, 2004). This is known commonly as policy-relevant or social-relevant research. IRGC's new framework includes two types of contextual aspects. The first category include the structure and interplay of the different actors dealing with risks, how these actors may differently perceive the risks and what concerns they have regarding their likely consequences. the second category include the policy-making or regulatory style as well as the socio-political impacts prevalent within the entities and institutions having a role in the risk process, their organisational imperatives and the capacity needed for effective risk governance (Renn, 2005). These policy and social relevance researches are all contained in the strategies of the four risk categories. Involving these into climate change research and management may be a revolutionary one in our climate research fields, which will greatly contribute to the settlement of climate change problems and construction of climate risk governance system.

Fourth, this categorisation will advance multi-disciplinary approaches in climate change research. Climate change may have different impacts on ecological, economical, social and cultural fields, which definitely need multi-disciplinary or trans-disciplinary cooperation in this field. In China, we address the climate impact and risk research generally by sector and fields, among which there is a lack of cooperation and communication traditionally. These circumstances may lead to some unnecessary overlap in research and some transdisciplinary problems irresolvable. This new categorisation could classify problems of different sectors into the same category and use similar strategies, which might virtually promote the cooperation between different disciplines.

All in all, the use of formalised methods to manage uncertainty, stakeholder involvement, policy and social relevant research, and integration of different disciplinary approaches in IRGC's new categorisation are actually involves the skills of governance, which will provide a rudimentary and stepwise procedure for the construction of climate risk governance system in China.

6. Conclusions and Discussions

In this article, we investigated IRGC's new risk categorisation system based on post normal science, and probed into its relationship with the "Communities of knowledge construction system" proposed by Funtowicz and Ravetz. By analysis, we proposed that 'the degree of uncertainty in the risk-related knowledge' might be regarded as the classifying criteria for the four risk categories. And then we applied fuzzy set theory and degree of membership method, adopted 'confidence' and 'likelihood' in IPCC AR4 as feature parameters, constructed membership function for the four categories respectively, and determined the dominant type a certain risk should belong to according to the maximum principle. Thus, a new quantitative method for categorisation of climate change risks was established. By this method, we can allocate climate change risks easily to the four categories and follow their different routes of appraisal, evaluation and management measures and the way of stakeholder participation provided by IRGC's framework, which might contribute a lot to the establishment of climate risk governance system in China.

However, there are still some problems in this categorizing method and its application, which need to be discussed further and paid extra attention.

The first problem of this categorising method is the combination of confidence and likelihood. The IPCC AR4 had provided schemes for both these concepts in communicating uncertainties, considering the advantages of using both likelihood and confidence information (Allen *et al.*, 2004; IPCC, 2005; Manning, 2006). However, trying to describe both likelihood and level of confidence for the same issue may be confusing and there was no agreement on how to approach this (Manning *et al.*, 2004; Risbey, 2007). Thus, sometimes the two terms seemed not very compatible, which may lead to the inaccuracy in the categorisation. Besides this , some people still argue that the likelihood may not be assigned in fully quantitative way, especially in the condition of low confidence (Manning *et al.*, 2004). As to these problems, another approach of applying both likelihoods and levels of confidence is to be proposed using a progressive scheme that articulates the basis for the assessment of each attribute (Risbey *et al.*, 2002; Kandlikar *et al.*, 2005). This scheme allows analysts to use a sequential process that does not treat all uncertain variables as statistically quantifiable, and provides a mechanism for communicating uncertainty at a level appropriate to existing scientific understanding, which includes six steps: Full probability density function, Bounds, First order estimates, Expected sign or trend, Ambiguous sign or trend, Effective ignorance (Risbey and Kandlikar, 2007). Using this scheme to communicate uncertainty may be more reasonable and straightforward for the risk classification.

Another problem of this categorising approach is the construction of the membership functions. The membership functions of the four risk categories and the weight assigned to the sub-membership function are mainly out of our understanding and experience, which may lead to many subjective elements in this method. Thus, the classification method may be still very preliminary, which is not just because the imperfect categorization method, but is determined by the "uncertain" nature of this categorization system. Over the course of further analysis of risks and concerns, new data and information is being collected which may change the state of uncertainty about a certain risk. This might cause us to revise our estimates and necessitate a re-ordering of the risks (Renn, 2005).

With regard to the specific application of this climate change categorisation in the future, it should be noted that the risk management strategy for each category provided by the IRGC framework (Table II) is a universal standard for all risks. It is relatively abstract and recapitulative, may not very appropriate to the climate change risk evaluation and management. So next, we should integrate the study of climate change mitigation and adaptation measures, as well as some mature methods and techniques used in the traditional risk research into this system and establish the specialized risk evaluation and management strategy of each category for climate change risks governance.

In addition, it has been recognized that the distributions and impacts of possible climate-related risks might change over space and time. IPCC believed that across all areas of climate change, uncertainty tends to increase going from global to regional scales (Manning et al.,

2004). However, portraits of risk distributions can sustain a more informed understanding of climate-related risks than estimates of net global risks and adaptation and hedging is best done at a local or regional level where descriptions of risk can more accurately reflect characteristics that are path dependent and site specific (Yohe and Strzepek, 2007). Thus a careful balance is needed when this categorisation applied to the specific area. In the future, the case study will be carried out in Pearl River Delta located in the southeast of China, one of the most vulnerable areas IPCC assigned, to construct the climate risk governance system.

Acknowlegements

The work presented in this article is part of the Integrated Risk Governance program funded by key projects in the National Science and Technology Pillar Program during the 11th Five-Year Plan period, No. 2006BAD20B05. We thank professor YANG Qinye and WU Jianjun for enlightening discussions in some problems.

References

Allen, M., Booth, B., Frame, D., Gregory, J., Kettleborough, J., Smith, L., Stainforth, D., and Stott, P. (2004). Observational constraints on future climate: distinguishing robust from model-dependent statements of uncertainty in climate forecasting. In: *IPCC workshop on describing scientific uncertainties in climate change to support analysis of risk and of options*, Ireland, 11-13.

AS/NZS. (1999). *Australian/New Zealand Standard on Risk Management.*

Australian Greenhouse Office. (2006). *Climate Change Impacts and Risk Management: A Guide for Business and Government.* Prepared for the Australian Greenhouse Office by Broadleaf Capital International and Marsden Jacob Associates.

Bray, D., and Von Storch, H. (1999). Climate Science: An Empirical Example of Postnormal Science. *Bulletin of the American Meteorological Society*, **80**(3), 439-455.

Bunting, C. 2006. *Applying the IRGC Risk Governance Framework: What we have learned about risks and about the IRGC framework ESOF*, Munich. www.irgc.org.

Cohen, S. J. (1999). Out of the Lab and into the Frying Pan: The Need for Broader Conversations about Climatic Change. An Editorial Comment, *Climatic Change* **41**, 265–270.

Connell, R. K., Willows R. I., Harman J. etc. (2005). A framework for climate risk management applied to a UK water resource problem. *Water and Environment Journal*, **19** (4), 352–360.

Funtowicz, S. O. and Ravetz, J. R. (1990). Post-normal science: A new science for new times. *Scientific. European,* Supplement to Scientific American, 20-22.

Funtowicz, S. O. and Ravetz, J. R. (1992). The Emergence of Post-Normal Science, in von Schomberg, R. (ed.), *Science, Politics and Morality*, Kluwer Academic Publishers, Dordrecht, 25–123.

Funtowicz, S.O., andRavetz, J.R. (1993). Science for the post-normal age. *Futures*, **25** (7), 739-755.

Ha-Duong, M., Swart, R., Petersen, A., and Bernstein, L. (2007). Uncertainty management in the IPCC: Agreeing to disagree. *Editorial / Global Environmental Change* **17**, 8–11.

Huang, C. F., Wang, J. D. (1992). *Fuzzy Information Analysis and Application,Beijing*: Beijing University Normal press. (in Chinese).

IPCC, 2007. Climate Change 2007: *Impacts, Adaptation and Vulnerability- Working Group II Contribution to IPCC Fourth Assessment Report*. London: Cambridge University Press.

IPCC. (2005). The Guidance Notes for Lead Authors of the IPCC Fourth Assessment Report on Addressing Uncertainties. Geneva, Switzerland : IPCC. Available at: http://www.ipcc.ch/activity/uncertaintyguidancenote.pdf.

Kandlikar, M., Risbey, J., andDessai, S. (2005). Representing and communicating deep uncertainty in climate change assessments. *Comptes Rendus Geoscience*, **337** (4): 443–455.

Manning, M. R. (2006). The Treatment of Uncertainties in the Fourth IPCC Assessment Report. *Advances in Climate Change Research*, **2** (Suppl. 1): 13-21.

Manning, M. R., Petit, M., and Easterling, D. *et al.* (2004). IPCC Workshop on Describing Scientific Uncertainties in Climate Change to Support Analysis of Risk and of Options. Available at: http://www.ipcc.ch/.

McBean, G. (2004). Overview: Evolution in the Communication and Use of Scientific Uncertainties. IPCC Workshop on Describing Scientific Uncertainties in Climate Change to Support Analysis of Risk and of Options. Available at: http://www.ipcc.ch/.

Morgan, M. G., Florig, H. K., Dekay, M. L., and Fischbeck, P. (2000). Categorizing Risks for Risk Ranking. *Risk Analysis*, **20**(1), 49-58.

Moss, R., and Schneider, S. (2000). Uncertainties [M] // Pachauri R, Taniguchi T, Tanaka K. *Guidance Papers on the Cross Cutting Issues of the Third Assessment Report of the IPCC*. Geneva, Switzerland: IPCC.

National Assessment Report on climate change, China. (2007). Beijing: Science Press.

National Development and Reform Commission. (2007). *China National Plan for Coping with Climate Change*. Available at: http://www.sdpc.gov.cn.

Oppenheimer, M. (2005). Defining Dangerous Anthropogenic Interference: The Role of Science, the Limits of Science. *Risk Analysis*, **25**(6),1399-1407.

Oppenheimer, M., and Petsonk, A. (2005). Article 2 of the UNFCCC: Historical origins, recent interpretations. *Climatic Change*, **73**, 195–226.

Patwardhan, A., Schneider, S. H., and Semenov, S. M. (2003). Assessing the Science to Address UNFCCC Article 2: A Concept Paper Relating to Cross Cutting Theme Number Four. Geneva: Intergovernmental Panel on Climate Change. Available at: http://www.ipcc.ch/activity/cct3.pdf.

Renn, O. (2005). *White Paper on Risk Governance – towards an integrative approach*. White paper No.1 of the International Risk Governance Council. Available at: www.irgc.org.

Renn, O. (2006). From Risk Analysis to Risk Governance: New Challenges for the Risk Professionals in an Era of Post-Modern Confusion. *Risk newsletter*. Published by the SOCIETY for RISK ANALYSIS, 26, 1:6.

Rind, D. (1999). Complexity and Climate, *Science* **284**, 105–107.

Risbey, J. S., and Kandlikar, M.(2007). Expressions of likelihood and confidence in the IPCC uncertainty assessment process. *Climatic Change*, **85**:19–31.

Risbey, J. S., Lamb, P. J., Miller, R. L., Morgan, M. C., and Roe, G. H. (2002). Exploring the structure of regional climate scenarios by combining synoptic and dynamic guidance and GCM output. *Journal of Climate,* **15**(9):1036–1050.

Roger, N. J. (2004). When Do POETS Become Dangerous? *IPCC Workshop on Describing Scientific Uncertainties in Climate Change to Support Analysis of Risk and of Options.*

Saloranta, T. M. (2001). Post-normal science and global climate change issue. *Climatic Change*, **50**, 395–404.

Stirling, A. (2007) Risk, precaution and science: towards a more constructive policy debate. *European Molecular Biology Organization reports*, **8**(4):309-315

Turnpenny, J.(2003). Post-Normal Science and the Tyndall Centre: some critical issues. *Tyndall Briefing Note* No. **9**.

USGCRP. (2000). National Assessment Synthesis Team, Climate change impacts on the United States: *The potential consequences of climate variability and change*, US Global Change Research Program, Washington, DC.

Wei, C. Y., Chen, S. Z. (2005). *GIS modeling principles and methods*. Beijing: Science Press. (in Chinese).

Willows, R. I., and Connell R. K. (2003). Climate Adaptation: Risk, Uncertainty, and Decision-making. *UKCIP Technical Report, UK Climate Impacts Programme*, Oxford.

World Bank. (2006). Managing Climate Risk - Integrating Adaptation into World Bank Group Operations, *World Bank Group Global Environment Facility Program.*

Yohe, G., Strzepek, K., (2007). Adaptation and mitigation as complementary tools for reducing the risk of climate impacts. *Mitigation and Adaptation Strategies for Global Change*, **12**: 727-739.

In: Risk Management
Editors: B. Jordão and E. Sousa, pp. 171-185

ISBN: 978-1-60876-011-4

Chapter 6

THE NEW EU CLIMATE AND ENERGY POLICY – SUSTANABILITY PERFORMANCE OF THE DIFFERENT POWER GENERATION TECHNOLOGIES

Christian Kirchsteiger
European Commission, Directorate-General for Energy and Transport, Luxembourg

Abstract

The objective of this article is to analyse factors influencing the sustainability performance of different energy sources in order to come to an effective decarbonisation of the fuel mix in a competitive manner. This is of course in the light of the new climate and energy policy of the EU and shall consider the most important energy sources currently used in Europe.

Neither a single current or future energy source – be it nuclear, fossil, renewables or hydrogen – nor a single support technology, such as carbon capture and storage, can alone represent the remedy to cope with the challenges of increasing energy demand, increasing levels of greenhouse gas emissions and increasing dependence on fuel supply from outside Europe.

However, the different sources and related technologies can effectively complement each other. Nuclear power should thus be seen in combination with its alternatives. How the mixture is done in order to achieve an appropriate, "sustainable" energy mix depends on the resources and local conditions of each country or region. There are, nevertheless, some basic commonalities and inevitable limiting conditions related to the specificities of the use of the various sources which should form the basis of any such decision-making and which will be introduced in this article.

Getting eventually to a decarbonised, non-fossil world will demand great determination, huge financial burden and true patience. But there is hope on the short- and mid-term horizons by means of effectively complementing and synchronising existing technologies, such as nuclear baseload electricity generation with other low CO_2-intensive sources, e.g. some of the renewables.

On the long-term horizon, only large-scale technological innovation will help, including advanced nuclear technologies in combination with significantly improved renewables and technologies to store energy, to largely replace fossil fuels also as power source for non-electrical applications.

1. The Current EU Energy Mix

The current EU-27 energy mix can certainly not be considered sustainable[1]:

- *Environmental effects:* In the EU, CO_2 from energy makes up ~60% of Greenhouse gas emissions. On current trends, the ~4000 Mt total annual energy-related CO_2 emissions in 2005 will increase by more than 350 Mt for the year 2030. This is largely the consequence of continued burning of fossil fuel for energy generation (80% of the EU-27 total primary energy supply[2] in 2004 comes from gas, oil and solid fuels);
- *Security of supply:* Security of oil supply is threatened, with oil production in non-OPEC countries setting to peak and production being increasingly concentrated in a small number of countries (all of them outside of Europe). Gas security of supply is an increasingly growing concern as well, with Europe's gas production having peaked already and import dependency from non-European countries growing;
- *Competitiveness:* Facing the significant ageing of its energy infrastructures (generation, transmission, distribution), the EU-27 needs to invest € 900 billion up to 2030 only in the electricity sector, of which 65% are related to generation. The energy market reform needs to be finalised.

Due to different geographical conditions and historical developments, there are large differences in the energy mix of the individual Member States. As an example, in terms of the *total primary energy supply*, some Member States have a fuel mix[3]:

- *still being dominated*
    - by oil (Malta (100%), Cyprus (94%), Luxembourg (64%), Ireland (59%), Portugal and Greece (57%)),
    - by oil and gas (Luxembourg (90%), Netherlands (83%), Ireland (82%)), Italy (80%)),
    - by coal (Poland (58%)), or
- *with a strong contribution from nuclear (Lithuania (37%), France (40%)), or*
- *with a mix closely matching the one of the EU-27 (38% oil, 24% gas, 14% nuclear, 6% renewables), such as Germany (36% oil, 23% gas, 12% nuclear, 4% renewables).*

Whether or not the choices of energy technologies underlying these mixes are considered economical and acceptable to society has, for a long time, been left at the discretion and responsibility of the relevant stakeholders in each EU Member State.

---

[1] source: European Commission – DG TREN, Eurostat 2007

[2] Total primary energy supply shows the share of energy sources in the energy mix. It is the quantity of energy consumed within the borders of a country. It is calculated using the formula: primary production + recovered products + imports + stock changes – exports – bunkers (i.e. quantities supplied to sea-going ships).

[3] source: EU Energy Policy Data, SEC(2007) 12, Brussels, 10.10.2007.

Mainly due to the advent of the real possibility of climate change, the situation has changed and the Commission set the first measures for a European Energy Policy aiming at developing a low-carbon economy.

2. EU Energy Policy: Towards a Low-Carbon Economy

2007 marked a turning point for the EU's climate and energy policy:

The January 2007 European Commission Communication on "An Energy Policy for Europe"[4] identified four challenges to the sustainable, competitive and secure provision of energy for all Member States: climate change, increasing import dependence, higher energy prices and increasing interdependence in energy infrastructures.

At the March 2007 European Summit, the EU heads of states and governments endorsed the Commission proposal of a "20-20-20" strategy (i.e. EU-wide 20% less CO_2, 20% renewables, 20% efficiency increase) to be implemented by 2020. In case of an international post-Kyoto CO_2 agreement, the EU would even go for a 30% EU-wide CO_2 reduction. This challenge can only be met by promoting low-carbon energy sources: renewable and non-CO_2 intensive conventional ones. Currently, the EU-27 *electricity* mix is still dominated by ~57% fossil fuels, followed by ~29% nuclear and ~13% renewables (of which hydropower constitutes ~22%)[5].

The commitment to achieving a 20% EU-wide share of renewable energy use by 2020 was followed up on 23 January 2008 by a Commission proposal that featured differentiated targets for each Member State based on GDP, including a 10% mandatory increase in bio fuels for transport[6]. Measures in the January 2008 "Climate-Energy Package" include:

- an improved emissions trading system (ETS) covering more emissions and allowing firms in one EU country to buy allowances in any other;
- an emission reduction target for industries not covered by the ETS (e.g. buildings, transport, waste) so that everyone is contributing;
- legally enforceable targets for increasing the share of renewables in the energy mix – the targets will reflect each country's individual needs and its potential;
- new rules on carbon capture and storage and on environmental subsidies.

Now that the 2007 political commitments have been translated into a proposal for binding targets for the share of renewables in individual Member States, a debate is heating up about how the target of 20% (or even 30%) CO_2 reduction can be met. Predictably, environmental NGOs hail the political leaders for their overall courage to set a medium-term target and criticise their failure to set a long-term target, while industry warns against potential costs.

Advocates of renewable energy tend to agree that renewables like solar, wind, hydro and biomass can easily contribute 20% or more to the EU's energy mix by 2020 as long as certain

---

4 Communication from the Commission to the European Council and the European Parliament – An Energy Policy for Europe, COM(2007) 1, Brussels, 10 January 2007.

5 Eurostat 2007.

6 Communication from the Commission to the European Parliament, the Council, the European Economic and Social Committee and the Committee of the Regions, 20 20 by 2020 – Europe's Climate Change Opportunity, COM(2008) 30, Brussels, 23 January 2008.

conditions, especially related to financial support schemes for renewable energies, are met. The Commission, as part of its 23 January 2008 proposal, widened the scope of what is permissible under EU state aid rules in terms of subsidising renewable energies. The renewables industry confirms that, in the absence of a truly competitive internal energy market, state support is needed at least in the short term and that abandoning such schemes at this stage would spell disaster for achieving a low-carbon economy. Furthermore, private and commercial consumers need to use energy more efficiently and conditions for accessing electricity grids need to be improved so that power generation is no longer dominated by relatively few large entities but spreads to an increasing number of smaller electricity producers.

Sceptics of an overly ambitious push for renewable energies argue that renewables are an unreliable replacement for electricity generated from fossil or nuclear fuels, since energy sources like wind and sun can be neither controlled nor stored. A shift towards decentralised power generation with a high share of renewables raises concerns with respect to the stability of electricity grids: if electricity output from, for example, wind turbines suddenly increases dramatically over a short period of time, grids can become overloaded and shut down, leading to blackouts. Furthermore, renewables may not be able to respond quickly enough to sudden increases in demand, causing losses or significant decreases in power flows. Last but not least, there is a widespread feeling among sceptics that the financial assistance these projects currently get could result in a "subsidy-addicted" renewables industry and competitive economic advantages which would certainly not be sustainable.

Therefore, the key question is: What is the best set of measures to achieve an *effective* decarbonisation of the fuel mix in a *competitive* manner?

Are there a few "miracle technologies", such as renewables, carbon capture and storage (CCS) or hydrogen, which "can do the job"? – Or do we rather need a broad range of technologies, including the more "traditional" ones, such as fossil and nuclear power plants?

An answer to these questions must be based on a set of common criteria for an unbiased assessment.

3. Comparison of Energy Technologies

Costs will be compared in terms of generation costs, non-internalised costs (externalities) and other, technology and resource specific cost factors.

3.1. Generation Costs

It is well known and has been shown in many studies that the relative costs of electricity generation by "traditional technologies", such as coal, gas, nuclear and hydro power plants, vary from country to country and are highly dependent on local conditions, discount rates, and expectations regarding future fuel prices:

- *Coal* is and will remain an economically attractive option in a number of countries having access to cheap domestic resources as long as carbon emissions are essentially cost-free (e.g. Poland). As can be seen from Table 1, the costs of generating electricity from coal are in the range of € 30-50 /MWh (2005 estimate) and are expected to increase by ~10-50% under modest assumptions for future CO_2 costs (€ 20-30 /t CO_2).

- As a result of the development of highly efficient combined cycle technologies, *natural gas* has become competitive for baseload electricity generation in a number of countries, such as Germany, Netherlands and the UK (€ 35-45 /MWh; CO_2 costs sensitivity of ~10-50%). However, gas-generated electricity costs are very sensitive to gas prices that might increase significantly if market demand grows rapidly. Further, there is the issue of growing dependence on gas imports from outside Europe.
- Where favourable sites exist, *hydropower* projects offer opportunities for low-cost electricity generation (€ 25-95 /MWh). However, the number of additional sites is very limited, especially in Europe, and, in many countries, social and environmental impacts of large dams are preventing the implementation of additional hydropower plants (e.g. Austria).
- The competitiveness of energy generation from *other renewables*, such as wind, solar and biomass, is expected to be improved with the introduction of emissions trading. Although, over the last 20 years, the cost of electricity from utility-scale wind systems has dropped significantly due to improved technology, it is in the average still significantly higher than from fossil or nuclear sources (e.g. wind € 35-175 /MWh). Other, technology and resource specific factors which strongly influence the overall competitiveness, such as intermittency, will be discussed in section 3.3. Furthermore, the feed-in tariffs provided to renewable electricity generation sources bear the danger of not giving long-term signals to lower costs. In particular, the high feed-in tariffs for solar photovoltaics can be up to ten times higher than those provided to wind and even higher than investments in efficiency, diverting money away from other, possibly more effective policies to reduce greenhouse gas emissions.
- In spite of their high investment costs (~70% of total generation costs for nuclear in contrast to ~40% for coal and ~30% for gas) and the need to internalise all waste disposal and decommissioning costs, *nuclear* power plants compete favourably with fossil-fuelled units in most countries (€ 40-45 /MWh and no increases due to introduction of emissions trading). Improvements in plant performance over the last 10-15 years have resulted in significantly increased plant availabilities and power outputs, further lowering the costs for the generation of electricity from nuclear power plants. However, public acceptance is still lacking in quite a few EU Member States (especially Austria, Germany, Ireland and Spain).

In summary, in terms of generation costs, none of the traditional electricity generating technologies can be expected to be the cheapest in all situations. The preferred technology will depend on the specific circumstances of each country and on the degree to which technology-specific externalities are considered.

Table 1. The advantages and disadvantages of different sources of electrical energy (source: Communication from the Commission to the European Council and the European Parliament – An Energy Policy for Europe, COM(2007) 1, Brussels, 10 January 2007)

Energy sources	Technology considered for the cost estimate	2005 Cost (€ / MWh)	Projected Cost 2030 (€ / MWh with €20-30/tCO2)	GHG emissions (Kg CO2eq/MWh)	EU-27 Import dependency		Efficiency	Fuel price sensitivity	Proven reserves / Annual production
		Source IEA			2005	2030			
Natural gas	Open cycle gas turbine	45 – 70	55 - 85	440	57%	84%	40%	Very high	64 years
	CCGT (Combined Cycle Gas Turbine)	35 - 45	40 - 55	400			50%	Very high	
Oil	Diesel engine	70 - 80	80 - 95	550	82%	93%	30%	Very high	42 years
Coal	PF (Pulverised Fuel with flue gas desulphurisation)	30 - 40	45 - 60	800	39%	59%	40-45%	medium	155 years
	CFBC (Circulating fluidized bed combustion)	35 - 45	50 - 65	800			40-45%	medium	
	IGCC (Integrated Gasification Combined Cycle)	40 - 50	55 - 70	750			48%	medium	
Nuclear	Light water reactor	40 - 45	40 - 45	15	Almost 100% for uranium ore		33%	low	Reasonable reserves: 85 years
Biomass	Biomass generation plant	25 - 85	25 - 75	30	nil		30 - 60%	medium	Renewable
Wind	On shore	35 - 175	28 - 170	30			95-98%	nil	
		35 – 110	28 – 80						
	Off shore	50 - 170	50 - 150	10			95-98%		
		60 – 150	40 – 120						
Hydro	Large	25 - 95	25 - 90	20			95-98%		
	Small (<10MW)	45 - 90	40 - 80	5			95-98%		
Solar	Photovoltaic	140 - 430	55 -260	100			/		

3.2. Non-internalised Costs

An externality occurs when a decision causes costs or benefits to 3rd party stakeholders, typically the public at large. For example, electricity generation in coal fired power plants causes greenhouse gas emissions as well as "normal" air pollution which has a measurable effect on human health, resulting in lifetime lost for people living around the plant. Nuclear based electricity generation produces radioactive waste with potential health implications if not safely stored and disposed of.

The rather positive picture for nuclear based upon a comparison of generation costs is confirmed when the social, health and environmental costs related to the use of different energy technologies are included, which – in the case of other energy sources – are for the most part not yet integrated into the pricing system (externalities). Policy should aim to ensure that prices always reflect the total costs of an activity, incorporating the cost of damages caused by employing taxes, subsidies, or other economic instruments.

This internalisation of external costs is intended as a strategy to rebalance the social and environmental dimension with the purely economic one, accordingly leading to greater sustainability. Doing so is a clear objective for the European Commission, as, for example, expressed in recent EU Research Framework Programmes and in the 2001 Göteborg Protocol to the EU Constitutional Treaty on sustainable development[1], and reflected in the recently adopted EU Energy and Climate Change packages.

The probably most complete externalities evaluation performed so far for the use of the different energy technologies in Europe across their lifecycle was accomplished in the course of the EU-funded projects ExternE (External costs of Energy and their internalisation in Europe) and NEEDS (New Energy Externalities Development for Sustainability)[2]. The specific effects on human health and the environment were evaluated under both normal operation and accidental conditions together with the associated total costs.

Table 2. External costs for electricity production in the EU (in €-cent per kWh) (taken from ExternE project results (http://www.externe.info)**

Country	Coal & lignite	Peat	Oil	Gas	Nuclear	Biomass	Hydro	PV	Wind
AUT				1-3		2-3	0.1		
BE	4-15			1-2	0.5				
DE	3-6		5-8	1-2	0.2	3		0.6	0.05
DK	4-7			2-3		1			0.1
ES	5-8			1-2		3-5*			0.2
FI	2-4	2-5				1			
FR	7-10		8-11	2-4	0.3	1	1		
GR	5-8		3-5	1		0-0.8	1		0.25
IE	6-8	3-4							
IT			3-6	2-3			0.3		
NL	3-4			1-2	0.7	0.5			
NO				1-2		0.2	0.2		0-0.25
PT	4-7			1-2		1-2	0.03		
SE	2-4					0.3	0-0.7		
UK	4-7		3-5	1-2	0.25	1			0.15

* : biomass co-fired with lignites
** : sub-total of quantifiable externalities
(such as global warming, public health, occupational health, material damage)

[1] http://ec.europa.eu/archives/commission_1999_2004/wallstrom/pdf/psd.pdf.

[2] http://www.externe.info and http://www.needs-project.org.

Table 2 summarises the quantifiable external costs for electricity production in different EU Member States (in €-cent per kWh) in terms of global warming, public health, occupational health and material damages. Best performance is shown by wind, closely followed by nuclear, hydro and photovoltaics (PV). Fossil sources perform worst, mainly due to their impact on global warming and human health. Externalities for biomass differ strongly across different countries, mainly due to the different types of locally available biomass. Biomass externalities perform somewhere between the fossil and the nuclear/renewables groups.

Therefore, integrating external costs into the overall balance-sheet, further improves the competitiveness of nuclear and of certain renewables, mainly wind.

3.3. Other Factors and Summary Assessment

The above-derived conclusion that nuclear energy is one of the cheapest sources of low-carbon electricity that is presently produced in the EU and also has relatively stable costs[3] for baseload supply is reflected in the mentioned January 2007 Commission Communication on "An Energy Policy for Europe" in which a mapping of advantages and disadvantages of the different energy sources for electricity and heating is included. Table 1 summarises the results for electrical energy in terms of:

- generation costs with and without a price for CO_2 emissions,
- amount of greenhouse gas emissions across lifecycle (cradle to grave),
- EU-27 import dependency,
- technical efficiency,
- fuel price sensitivity, and
- proven reserves of fuel versus annual production.

The wide spread in the electricity generation costs for renewables is primarily a reflection of the wide discrepancies between Member States in terms of how renewable energies are financed. Even without considering future costs of CO_2 emissions, nuclear is clearly at the lower end of the generation costs, has very low CO_2 emissions across its entire lifecycle and is less vulnerable to fuel price changes than fossil or biomass-fired generation. This is because the supply of nuclear fuel represents only a limited part of the total costs of generating nuclear electricity (typically ~15%) and is based on natural resources which are sufficient for many decades and widely distributed around the globe. Nuclear power plants thus enhance EU security of energy supply, even though almost 100% of the uranium is currently imported[4] (but ~70% of the enriched uranium is originating from within the EU[5]). Recent high prices for uranium have stimulated exploration in EU Member States that could eventually be developed into local production sources.

---

[3] According to the IEA 2006 World Energy Outlook "new nuclear power plants could produce electricity at 4.9 to 5.7 $ cents per kWh [3.9 to 4.5 Euro cents at mid November 2006 exchange rates] if construction and operating risks are mitigated" and that is, at "a price of about 10 $ per tonne of CO2 emitted makes nuclear competitive with coal-fired power stations".

[4] ~50% of global mine production comes from reliable, politically stable trading partners (e.g. Canada, Australia).

[5] source: EU Energy Policy Data, SEC(2007) 12, Brussels, 10.10.2007.

Other factors which need to be taken into account for a final comparative assessment are:

- *Intermittency:* Nuclear and fossil thermal power plants with their easily storable high-energy density fuels operate at high load factors (up to >75% around the year for coal-fired plants and >90% for nuclear ones). In contrast, as wind and solar radiation are intermittent and far from being predictable, annual load factors of wind generation are even in countries with large capacities, such as Denmark or Germany, only ~20-25%, and in the case of photovoltaic solar generation much more further down the scale. This leads to the low-efficiency situation that – for the purpose of large-scale supply – renewables always need some backup supply present from "conventional" sources.
- *Land use:* New infrastructures for power production should fit as much as possible within the footprint of the old infrastructures, leaving land as much as possible for Nature. Replacing a typical 1000 MWe nuclear power plant with renewables would require more than 2500 square kilometres of prime land for the biomass option and ~770 square kilometres for the wind farm option[6]. Czech Republic President Václav Klaus calculated in his recent book "Blue Planet in Green Chains" that the replacement of the Temelín nuclear power plant alone would require 4750 windmills, resulting in a 150 meters high and 665 kilometres long "wall" between Temelín and Brussels.
- *Geographical distribution:* Not only the access to oil, gas and uranium resources is distributed in an uneven way across the planet, but also the access to the renewable flows from wind and solar radiation. In addition, many reliably windy or sunny sites are far from major load centres, which means that their large-scale exploitation would require creation of entirely new mega-infrastructures.
- *Resource consumption:* Apart from land, natural limits to the development and use of all energy technologies are given by their specific consumption across lifecycle of non-renewable resources (e.g. bentonite, copper, steel), renewable resources (e.g. wood), non-renewable energy ware (e.g. coal, oil, uranium, natural gas) and renewable energy ware (e.g. hydro-electricity, wood). Many comprehensive lifecycle assessments have shown that nuclear has a significantly smaller resource consumption than coal, wind and photovoltaics in terms of mass of resource consumed per kWh electricity produced (copper, steel) or volume of resource consumed per kWh produced (bentonite, water).
- A further dimension to the pressure on physical and economical resources is introduced by *Carbon Capture and Storage (CCS)*. Sequestering "merely" 50% of CO_2 emissions due to power generation would call for putting in place an industry that would have to force underground every year the volume of compressed gas larger than or (with higher compressions) more or less equal to the volume of crude oil extracted globally by petroleum industry whose infrastructures and capacities have been put in place over a century of development. Needless to say that such an endeavour could not be accomplished on a large scale, i.e. with a significant contribution to reducing greenhouse gas emissions, within a single generation.

[6] J.H. Ausubel, Renewable and Nuclear Heresies, Int. J. Nuclear Governance, Economy and Ecology, 2007.1(3).

Additional aspects to be considered when introducing CCS are the losses in fossil power plant efficiencies and related power output as well as the issue of public acceptability of long-term CO_2 storage (see section 4.2). Mainly due to the missing CO_2 infrastructure, CCS is expected to be more important only in the post-2020 period.

Together with generation costs and externalities, it is such limiting factors and physical realities which ultimately define the competitivity of any measure, i.e. of any investment intended to provide a significant contribution to the decarbonisation of the economy. – Nuclear, together with some renewables, shows best performance from such an overall comparative viewpoint. – What are then the obstacles to its continued present and its possibly increased future use?

4. The Role of Nuclear

Nuclear energy is currently the largest single source of low-carbon electricity in the EU, equivalent to 14% of the EU-27 total primary energy supply. There are currently 146 reactors producing a rough third of the total EU electricity. These nuclear power plants have delivered significant amounts of base-load electricity in a safe and cost-effective manner for decades. EU nuclear power plants are among the most efficiently operated reactors in the world (e.g. Finland, Germany, Netherlands). As the above comparative assessments have shown, nuclear power represents indeed a promising alternative for further reducing both CO_2 emissions and the dependence on fuel imports from certain regions of the world.

4.1. A Legacy of Past Problems

The history of the commercial use of nuclear energy is both relatively short and, in the eyes of many stakeholders, difficult:

It started in 1953 with the construction of Calder Hall in the UK, the world's first commercial nuclear power plant. This was only 11 years after the first man-made reactor, known as Chicago Pile-1, achieved criticality on December 2, 1942. The faith on the future of nuclear was untarnished in the 1950's and it was widely assumed that its use would result in an electricity bill "too cheap to meter". The 10 years between 1965 and 1975 saw the greatest number of new nuclear power plant orders. Expert consensus in the early 1970s foresaw a world shaped by ubiquitous and inexpensive nuclear energy. However, as we all know, societal expectations and industrial practices in the early 21st century in Europe are quite different. – Why has construction of nuclear power plants in Europe come to a practical standstill during the last two decades and started again only very recently and somewhat reluctantly in Finland, France and some of the "new" Member States?

At first glance, there are obvious reasons for the industry's long-time stagnation and retreat:

- the perceived problems of nuclear safety, and

- the lack of drive in many countries to implement a politically acceptable solution (from the set of technically already available ones) for managing the relatively small amounts of long-lived radioactive waste,

all this resulting in significant financial and regulatory risks for potential investors.

4.2. Current Practice, Challenges and Some Still Unresolved Issues

- Let us start with *nuclear safety*, a continuous challenge which is never "completely" won but which must always be considered a "work in progress". In retrospect, commercial development of the 1st Generation of nuclear power plants was perhaps too rushed (merely about one decade between Fermi's Chicago pile and the first commercial nuclear power plant!) and certainly not sufficient weight was initially given to public acceptability. A. Weinberg, one of the pioneers of the use of nuclear energy and former head of the Oak Ridge laboratories in the USA, assumed that had safety been the primary design criterion rather than compactness and simplicity that guided the design of the (originally submarine) Pressurised Water Reactors, we would have achieved inherently safe reactor designs already at "Generation I" rather than 5-7 decades later at today's "Generation III+" or at future "Generation IV" reactor development lines[7].
- *Plant optimisation:* In the EU, despite a 20% increase in electricity consumption over the last decade, despite very few new nuclear builds and despite continuing phase-out policies in some countries, the relative share of electricity generation from nuclear power plants has nevertheless remained practically constant (32% in 1994 and 31% in 2004). To accomplish this, significant efforts and investments were made by utilities into actions to optimise the performance of their plants. During the last 10-15 years, industry programs on capacity uprating and increasing of plant availability have resulted in >6000 MWe additional net power output in the EU-27, corresponding to 4-5 large new plants. Optimisation of nuclear power plant performance has greatly contributed to maintaining secure supply of electricity in Europe in a non-carbon-intensive way.
- *Plant ageing:* All operating plants, also improved ones in terms of operational performance, are continuously ageing and quickly approach the limits of their originally foreseen 30-40 years lifetime. The world's fleet of nuclear power plants is currently 20 years old on average; the one in the EU-27 is 23 years. 31% of the present nuclear generating capacity is from plants of 25 years age or older. Only 12% is 15 years old or less. Keeping the original 30-40 years limits of plant lifetime, about 44.000 MWe or 33% of the currently installed EU-27 nuclear net capacity would need to be taken from the grid over the next 10 years and somehow be replaced. Potential alternatives such as currently available renewable technologies can not fill such an enormous gap in a short period of time at competitive prices. New CO_2 emitting thermal power plants should be avoided as much as possible. New nuclear builds still face significant challenges: For the utilities, applications for new builds, if

[7] A. Weinberg, The First Nuclear Era, American Institute of Physics, Washington DC, 1994.

possible at all, involve investments with long break-even periods and a high risk profile. Therefore, under the existing conditions of large investment and regulatory risks, longer term operation is considered more economic than new nuclear construction and is therefore becoming practice in most EU Member States. From a safety perspective, there is no evidence that there would be a significant difference between normal and longer term operation. For many plants it can even be shown that safety levels have significantly improved after modernisation and life extension programs; in many cases to levels recommended by the IAEA as goal for new plants.

- *Radioactive waste management:* Solutions need to be implemented as a top priority for long term management of spent fuel and radioactive waste originating from the operation of nuclear power plants. Specifically, the actual implementation of the technically possible safe solutions to the management of radioactive waste, such as deep geological disposal, needs to progress. Such waste requires sophisticated treatment and management in order to successfully isolate it from interacting with the biosphere. This usually necessitates treatment, followed by a long-term management strategy involving storage and subsequent disposal in deep geological repositories. The process of selecting appropriate deep final geologic repositories for high level waste and spent fuel is now under way in several Member States with the first ones expected to be commissioned around 2020 (2018 for operation in Sweden, 2020 in Finland, 2025 in France). However, in other countries, such as Germany, the political standstill and deadlock remains. According to recent Eurobarometer results, 55% of Europeans are against the use of nuclear energy as a whole due to lack of implementation of solutions for radioactive waste, while 58% would be in favour if this problem were solved[8].
- *Governance:* In Europe, certainly until the aftermath of the 1980s' series of severe industrial accidents[9], the role of the public in decision-making processes on the use of major-hazardous industries was often largely ignored. In the meantime this has significantly been improved and many different means are now in place for the public to directly participate in decision-making processes. Yet, there is still a widespread feeling in some Member States that nuclear is an "undemocratic" technology with too many technical and organisational unknowns. For example, in the debates about the why's and where's of nuclear waste repositories it has always been demanded by NGOs to avoid specific technologies which generate hazardous end products that need to be safely stored away under enormous costs and uncertainties for centuries and millennia to come[10]. Informing people in a responsible way does, however, help: Eurobarometer results show that Europeans consider themselves not well informed about radioactive waste management. They tend to greatly overestimate the volumes of radioactive waste arisings compared with the volumes of other toxic waste, and to overestimate the risks associated with the storage and transport of even low level radioactive waste. Providing information on the facts results in clearly increased public support and diminishing fears. Still, there is a strong need to further enhance and improve communication and create an

[8] http://ec.europa.eu/public_opinion/index_en.htm

[9] i.e. 1982 Seveso (chemical process industry), 1984 Bhopal (bulk chemicals), 1986 Chernobyl (nuclear industry) and 1986 Basel (pharmaceuticals).

atmosphere of public confidence and trust which is stable beyond short-term political mandates.

4.3. A Future Role

Neither nuclear nor any of the other energy technologies, "traditional" or "new" ones (e.g. CCS, renewables), are by themselves the remedies which would solve all problems and eventually guarantee ever-lasting "green energy" in an ever-lasting "green world".

As already observed in 1939 by the Austrian economist Joseph Schumpeter[11], all technological innovations come in waves, and they diffuse, in the sense of filling markets with products or services. When the markets are saturated, production based on this technology maintains at current levels without further growth. Slowly and progressively, the introduction of a new set of technological innovations gives rise to a new pulse of growth. A classic example in the area of energy is that of relative market shares of primary energies. The International Institute for Applied Systems Analysis (IIASA) has impressively analysed the long-term stability of the substitution process of primary energy on a world-wide level: Wood and charcoal have been the staple fuels for humanity until the end of the 18th century. Coal then gradually substituted wood and its use peaked in ~1920, succeeded by oil (peaking in ~1975), natural gas (peaking in ~2030) and nuclear[12]. The probably most important result of this analysis is that all sorts of activities related to the use of a certain technology come to a standstill towards the end of its cycle, and constructions of current nuclear power plant designs are no exception.

Today's nuclear power plants are essentially limited to the production of electricity. Therefore, the production of non-electrical energy products, such as process-heat for industry, space heating and transportation, is likely to revolutionise the economics of nuclear power much more than standardising plants or building plants quicker due to reduced financial and regulatory risks. As it is essential to reduce emissions from fossil fuels, it is important to explore the feasibility of nuclear energy replacing fossil fuels as the power source for non-electrical applications. The most promising and realistic way to fulfil this need could be to use nuclear energy (together with strongly improved technologies to store energy) to produce *hydrogen*, an excellent energy carrier.

Using hydrogen as a source of energy for transport, electricity production and other applications is environmentally attractive. Currently, however, the most feasible methods of hydrogen production are linked with emissions to the atmosphere that negatively impact air quality and contribute to climate change. Therefore, hydrogen has today unfortunately only little advantage over conventional fossil fuels. This will change when nuclear and hydrogen join forces.

Hydrogen production will allow future nuclear power plants, which will not only be based on a less inter-dependent and more robust design, but also operate at higher temperature levels, to address the half of energy demand that is not met by electricity. Furthermore, as users demand electricity mostly during the day, it gives nuclear power plants

---

[10] For similar reasons, CCS technology is currently criticised by many NGOs.

[11] H. Schumpeter, Business Cycles – A Theoretical, Historical and Statistical Analysis of the Capitalist Process, McGraw-Hill, New York, 1939.

[12] C. Marchetti, Nuclear Energy and Its Future, Perspectives in Energy, 1992, Vol. 2, pp. 19-34.

the possibility to make valuable products 24 hours per day. Current nuclear power plants are limited to the production of baseload electrical power unless they reach out to hydrogen production to store and distribute their energy.

But this can only be one among various other longer term strategies. In the short term, what is urgently needed in the light of rising temperatures is a "quid pro quo" compromise to quickly move forward. An element in this solution could be that a large majority of stakeholders accept on the one hand the indispensable role of nuclear energy to ensure continued baseload electricity supply in Europe, while on the other hand renewables are given the chance they deserve by means of effective integration and synchronisation of renewables and existing baseload supply, including nuclear. Promising schemes in this direction are already under development, e.g. in Germany by means of wind power feed-in or in Scandinavia's Nord Pool electricity derivatives market. In this spot and futures market for electricity in the Nordic region, encompassing Norway, Sweden, Finland and Denmark, nuclear is successfully competing with hydroelectricity (where the production costs are very low) and via cogeneration with natural gas.

5. Summary and Outlook

Is Europe about to switch soon to conversion technologies relying on low carbon energy sources, largely replacing fossil and other carbon intensive fuels? Eventually, it will definitely have to, but impartial examination of some inevitable limiting conditions has shown that the transition to a decarbonised economy will be a difficult, costly and long-lasting task for the current and future generations[13]. The transition is highly desirable, but requires massive sustained capital expenditures on the development and implementation of improved energy technologies and infrastructures.

Nuclear should form an integral part of this long-lasting process of technological innovation towards sustainable energy mixes. Nuclear power plants require heavy investment but are profitable in countries where the cost of capital is relatively low[14]. Nuclear power's main advantages are a high degree of security of supply, very competitive electricity prices and the absence of greenhouse gas emissions.

Challenges for nuclear are:

- *Lifetime extension:* To ensure continued supply of baseload electricity in Europe in the face of ageing nuclear power plants and still very few new builds, extended economic operation of plants beyond the originally set plant life can for most plants be achieved while fulfilling safety and environmental requirements[15]. Of course, operating nuclear power plants over extended periods in a responsible way requires extensive resources to maintain the plants and ensure their safety, and in particular to prevent any risk of proliferation.

[13] V. Smil, Energy in the Twentieth Century: Resources, Conversions, Costs, Uses, and Consequences, Annu. Rev. Energy Environ. 2000. 25:21-51.

[14] Despite the advent of the single currency within the EU and the related changes in the cost of equity as a consequence of globalization, dispersion in the cost of capital remains: Country effects are becoming smaller and sector effects larger.

[15] Exceptions are RBMK, 1st generation VVER 440/230 and also old gas-cooled reactors.

- *Synchronising baseload nuclear and intermittent renewables:* To be able to cover current and medium-term future needs, concepts for effective synchronisation of baseload supply from nuclear and intermittent supply from renewables should be promoted. Promising attempts in this direction are underway, e.g. via wind power feed-in and grid restructuring, but need stronger encouragement and support.
- *Non-electrical energy products:* To provide in future an even more impressive contribution to decarbonising the economy, nuclear plants must in the longer run diversify to produce also non-electrical energy products, such as process heat and hydrogen. With appropriate reactors of "Generation IV" types, planned to be ready for deployment after 2040, hydrogen production can draw the nuclear power sector to a scale of operation an order of magnitude larger than today, meeting future demand for hydrogen and electricity for private consumers and industry.

With such a firm strategic view in mind, "the climate" in Europe and beyond has probably never been more favourable than now for a sustainable revival of nuclear power since the end of the 2nd oil price shock.

In: Risk Management
Editors: B. Jordão and E. Sousa, pp. 187-201
ISBN: 978-1-60876-011-4

Chapter 7

TRANSPORTABILITY OF REGRESSION MODEL REGARDING HEALTH RISK ASSOCIATED WITH THE METABOLIC SYNDROME

***Noriko Ishida*[1], *Shinichiro Ichimaru*[1,2], *Ayumi Hida*[2], *Midori Soda*[2], *Masazumi Akahoshi*[2] *and Tsuyoshi Nakamura*[1]**
[1] Nagasaki University, Nagasaki, Japan
[2] Radiation Effects Research Foundation, Nagasaki, Japan

Abstract

Carroll, Ruppert, and Stefanki [1] emphasize potential dangers in using estimated parameter values in an independent study for analysis of the primary study, and introduce the concept of "transportability". Transportability means "not only the model but also the relevant parameter estimates can be transported without bias". As far as we know, however, a mathematical definition and statistical considerations of the transportability have not been fully developed yet. This chapter defines the transportability of a regression model, presents a sufficient condition, describes a necessary assumption and examines the transportability of the regression model with real data. The motivation of the study comes from the fact that we have to wait for the results of an over ten-year cohort study to know the epidemiological significance of the waist circumference (WC) in the definition of the metabolic syndrome. We considered it would be possible to estimate the risk associated with WC if an unbiased estimate of WC for each subject ten years previous would be obtained based on the transportability arguments. Since the transported estimates inevitably subject to measurement errors, this chapter develops a method for correcting for the measurement errors to obtain asymptotically unbiased estimates for relative risks associated with WC.

Keywords: Transportability, Measurement Error, Corrected Score, Berkson Type, Metabolic Syndrome

1. Introduction

Forecast, or prediction, is an extrapolation of an observed trend to the future, which is not generally regarded as a proper inference among statisticians. For instance, values of stocks are not always correctly predicted. In other words, they are subject to error whose distributions are unknown. On the other hand, the recent weather report which presents the probability of rain is regarded as a reliable forecast by most people, including statisticians. Thus, there are reliable and not-reliable extrapolations. Carroll et al. [1] use "transportability", instead of extrapolability, to describe the situation when a prediction model developed from one population is applicable to another population. They argue that a naïve model that ignores measurement errors in variables may not be transportable. This chapter proposes conditions under which a regression equation observed in a sample may be transportable to another sample. The results have an application in a retrospective cohort study for the metabolic syndrome (MS).

MS is a significant and growing public-health problem [2]. While there are many different sets of symptoms to diagnose the syndrome [3], the critical element that they have in common is the accumulation of abdominal fat, which is evaluated by measurement of waist circumference (WC). The role for abdominal fat accumulation has been strongly implicated in the development of disorders such as impaired glucose tolerance, hypertension, and dyslipidemia, all of which contribute to the process of atherosclerosis [4].

This chapter examines the transportability of a regression equation for determining WC ten years previous from current measurements. As an application of the results, we demonstrate a retrospective cohort study for the relationship between WC and the mortality using a cohort database administered by the Radiation Effect Research Foundation (RERF).

We call the estimates obtained from a regression equation observed in a different sample as "transported estimates". Even when the transported estimates are unbiased, they are subject to measurement errors. Measurement error is one of the major causes of bias in epidemiological studies [1]. There are several ways to characterize measurement errors, and the methods for correcting biases depend on the type of statistical models employed. It is discussed in this chapter that the measurement errors involved in the transported estimates is of the non-differential Berkson type [1]. One of the objectives of this chapter is to develop a proportional hazards model to correct for this type of error, based on the corrected score method [5-6], that is originally developed exclusively for the classical type of measurement errors.

2. Statistical Methods

2.1. Transportability of Regression Model

Let y be a response variable and $\mathbf{x} = (x_1, \ldots\ldots, x_p)$ be a vector of explanatory variables and consider a population Γ that follows a regression model

$$y = \alpha + f(\mathbf{x}) + \varepsilon, \ \varepsilon \sim N(0, \sigma^2) \tag{1}$$

We also consider a different population Λ and a random sample $S = \{(y_1, \mathbf{x}_1), \ldots\ldots, (y_m, \mathbf{x}_m)\}$ of Λ and let a regression equation on S be

$$\hat{y} = \alpha^* + f^*(\mathbf{x}) \tag{2}$$

Definition (Transportability)

If $\mathrm{E}[f^*(\mathbf{x})] = f(\mathbf{x})$ holds for any $\mathbf{x}$ in Γ, the regression model (2) is transportable to Γ. The definition implies, $\mathrm{E}(y - \hat{y})$ is a constant independent of $\mathbf{x}$.

Proposition (A Sufficient Condition for Transportability)

Let us assume that $(y, \mathbf{x})$ in the Eq(1) follows a multivariate normal distribution Γ and $(y, \mathbf{x})$ in the Eq(2) follows a multivariate normal distribution Λ, too. Then, $f(\mathbf{x})$ is written as $\beta^T \mathbf{x}$ where β is determined by the variance matrix of Γ [7]. Therefore, if the variance matrix of Γ is equal to that of Λ, the regression model (2) is transportable to Γ. In other words, it is a sufficient condition for the transportability that the variance matrices of the multivariate normal distributions are mutually equal.

Although the Proposition is mathematically simple, it is not directly applicable to statistical analysis, since y is unavailable. To surmount the difficulty, we need certain practical assumptions. Let y denote the unknown WC value of an individual ten years previous, $\mathbf{x} = (x_1, \ldots\ldots, x_p)$ be a vector of p test results for him/her ten years previous, and let S be a random sample consisting of $(y, \mathbf{x})$ obtained from currently performed test results. Since a sample of $(y, \mathbf{x})$ ten years previous is not observable, the following hypothesis is necessary to construct a transportable equation.

Definition (y Homogeneity Hypothesis)

Let $\tilde{\Gamma}$ denote the marginal distribution of $\mathbf{x}$ in Γ and $\tilde{\Lambda}$ that of $\mathbf{x}$ in Λ. We consider the following two conditions:

(A) $\tilde{\Gamma}$, $\tilde{\Lambda}$, and Λ are all multivariate normal distributions and the variance matrices of $\tilde{\Gamma}$ and $\tilde{\Lambda}$ are mutually equal.

(B) Γ is a multivariate normal distribution and the variance matrices of Λ and Γ are mutually equal.

We say y Homogeneity Hypothesis holds from Λ to Γ if (A) is a sufficient condition for (B), or (B) always holds whenever (A) holds. The condition (A) is observable but (B) is not. Hereafter, y Homogeneity Hypothesis will be abbreviated to y HH; for instance, like WC-HH or Weight-HH.

To extrapolate estimates, we must make an assumption about relationships between variables beyond the limit of the observations [8]. The y HH implies that if the relationships among the components of $\mathbf{x}$ ten years previous hold now and the relationships between y and $\mathbf{x}$ is normal, then the latter relationships also hold ten years previous. Since WC was not measured ten years previous, the direct verification of the WC-HH is difficult. Instead, Weight-HH will be investigated in detail and the results will be extrapolated with medical considerations to WC-HH.

The previous definition is mathematically clear, however, may not be suitable to statistical applications. In fact, the equality of the variance matrix between $\tilde{\Gamma}$ and $\tilde{\Lambda}$ is examined by hypothesis testing using samples, and therefore even if the null hypothesis of the equality is not rejected, it does not ensure the mathematical equality. The result of the test depends on their sample sizes, too. Similarly, Carroll et al. [1] require transported estimates to be unbiased but not to be exact. Furthermore, since the magnitude of errors in the transported estimates also depends on the sample size, it should be confirmed if the sample size is large enough to present the transported estimates with sufficient accuracy to be used for risk analysis.

2.2. Measurement Error Models for Transported Estimates

Let y and $\mathbf{x} = (x_1, \ldots\ldots, x_p)$ denote WC and a vector of other measurements, respectively, and assume that $(y, \mathbf{x})$ follows a multivariate normal distribution. Then it holds [7] that

$$y = \alpha + \beta^{\mathrm{T}}\mathbf{x} + \varepsilon,\ \varepsilon \sim N(0, \sigma^2) \tag{3}$$

where α, β and ε denote a scalar constant, a vector of regression coefficients and a random variable following $N(0, \sigma^2)$, respectively. Let $\mathrm{D} = \{(\mathrm{y}_1, \mathbf{x}_1), \cdots, (\mathrm{y}_n, \mathbf{x}_n)\}$ denote a random sample following (3). Put $1 = (1, \cdots, 1)^{\mathrm{T}}$, $\mathrm{y} = (\mathrm{y}_1, \ldots\ldots, \mathrm{y}_n)^{\mathrm{T}}$, $\bar{\mathrm{y}} = (\mathrm{y}_1 + \ldots\ldots + \mathrm{y}_n)/n$, $\boldsymbol{y} = (\mathrm{y}_1 - \bar{\mathrm{y}}, \ldots\ldots, \mathrm{y}_n - \bar{\mathrm{y}})^{\mathrm{T}}$, $\bar{\mathrm{x}} = (\mathrm{x}_1 + \ldots\ldots + \mathrm{x}_n)/\mathrm{n}$, $\boldsymbol{x}_i = \mathbf{x}_i - \bar{\mathbf{x}}$, $\boldsymbol{X}^{\mathrm{T}} = (\boldsymbol{x}_1, \ldots\ldots, \boldsymbol{x}_n)$, $\mathbf{b} = (X^{\mathrm{T}}X)^{-1}X^{\mathrm{T}}\boldsymbol{y}$, $\hat{\alpha} = \bar{\mathrm{y}} - \beta^{\mathrm{T}}\bar{\mathbf{x}}$ and $f(\mathbf{x}) = \beta^{\mathrm{T}}\mathbf{x}$. Then it holds that $\mathrm{E}(\mathbf{b}) = \beta$ and $E(y \mid \mathbf{x}) = \alpha + f(\mathbf{x})$ [9].

Let us denote WC and the other measurements ten years previous by y^* and $\mathbf{x}^*$, respectively. We assume that $\mathbf{x}^*$ is known but y^* unknown, and $(y^*, \mathbf{x}^*)$ follows the regression model (3). Let's put $w^* = f^*(\mathbf{x}^*)$, then y^* and w^* are mutually independent and $y^* - w^*$ follows a normal distribution with mean 0 and variance

$$V(y^* - w^*) = V(y^*) + V(w^*) = \sigma^2\left\{1 + (1/n) + \boldsymbol{x}^{*T}(X^T X)^{-1}\boldsymbol{x}^*\right\},$$

where $x^* = \mathbf{x}^* - \overline{\mathbf{x}}$. When n is large and x^* is not extremely large, inside the bracket $\{\ \}$ is approximately equal to 1. Thus it approximately follows that $V(y^* - w^*) = \sigma^2$ and

$$y^* = w^* + \varepsilon^*,\ \varepsilon^* \sim N(0, \sigma^2) \tag{4}$$

This equation indicates that the unknown y^* given w^* is a random variable approximately following a normal distribution with mean w^* and the common variance σ^2. Thus, it is shown that the measurement errors in y^* is approximately a non-differential Berkson type.

As far as the authors are concerned, correcting methods for Berkson type measurement errors in non-linear models have not been well developed [1]. Therefore, we have developed a correction method for the transported estimates as follows.

Since $w^* = f(\mathbf{x}^*)$ is a linear combination of the components of $\mathbf{x}^*$ and therefore (w^*, y^*) is normally distributed. Thus, w^* also follows a linear regression model with covariate y^*, written as

$$w^* = \alpha_0 + \alpha_1 y^* + \varepsilon,\ \varepsilon \sim N(0, \sigma^{*2}) \tag{5}$$

When the sample size of D is large, α_0, α_1 and σ^* are approximately equal to their population values. Put $u = (w^* - \alpha_0)/\alpha_1$ then we have

$$u = y^* + \varepsilon^*,\ \varepsilon^* \sim N(0, (\sigma^*/\alpha_1)^2) \tag{6}$$

The last model indicates that u is subject to the classical type measurement error. Thus, it is now possible to apply the corrected score method [6, 10-11] to a various non-linear models with covariate u.

3. Dataset

3.1. RERF Cohort Sample

A total of 3,374 men in Nagasaki have received biennial health examinations since 1958 as part of a follow-up program associated with the Radiation Effects Research Foundation (RERF), formally the Atomic Bomb Casualty Commission. A detailed description of this program has been published elsewhere [12-13]. The examination records for 667 men who were younger than 75 years [14] with valid height and weight measurements in 1994-96 (the 19th examination period) and 323 men satisfying the same condition in 2004-06 (24th examination period) were analyzed in the present study. The examination items included height, weight, temperature, systolic blood pressure (SBP), diastolic blood pressure (DBP), asparate aminotransferase (AST), alanine aminotransferase (ALT), glucose (GLU), alkaline phosphatase (ALP), cholinesterase (ChE), serum urea (UA), triglyceride (TG), total cholesterol (T-Cho), albumin (Alb), iron (Fe), high-density lipoprotein (HDL), white blood cell counts (WBC), red blood cell counts (RBC), thymol turbidity test (TTT), hemoglobin (Hb), hematocrit (Ht), platelet count (PLT). Waist circumference (WC) has been measured only since 2004.

In Japan, MS was defined, among men with a WC in excess of 85 cm and women with a WC in excess of 90 cm, as having 2 or more components from among the following; 1) Dyslipidemia: triglycerides ≥ 150 mg/dl and/or HDL cholesterol < 40 mg/dl, 2) Hypertension: blood pressure ≥ 130/85 mmHg, 3) Impaired glucose tolerance: fasting plasma glucose ≥ 110 mg/dl. In this chapter, those with at least two of these three criteria will be referred to as semiMS.

4. Analysis of Data

4.1. Verification of Transportability of Regression Model

Using Weight which is strongly associated with WC, we will first examine whether the underlined conditions, the italic conditions for Weight-HH in the Definition in 2.1 and also whether transportability of Weight from the current sample to the sample ten years previous holds. Based on the results, we will consider the transportability of WC. Henze-Zirkler test, Bartlett test and Chow test [15] will be used to test the multivariate normality, the equality of two variance matrices and the equality of the regression coefficients, respectively. Two sided p-values less than 0.05 were considered statistically significant. The stepwise variable selection method was applied to obtain linear regression equations for Weight and WC. Analyses were performed using SAS 9.1 (SAS Institute, Cary NC).

4.2. Risk Estimation for Death Using Transported Estimates

We first construct a linear regression equation for WC on the current sample. Secondly, the assumption for WC-HH will be examined with the variables used in the equation. Then, a transported estimate of WC is obtained for each examinee in the sample ten years previous. Finally, we will apply the Cox regression model with the transported estimate of WC, *semiMS* (1 for semiMS, 0 otherwise) and Age as covariate. The follow-up period is ten years and the endpoint is either MS-related death or death due to cancer. To treat possible non-linearity in WC for relative risk function, the following piecewise linear functions will be employed:

$$<WC - C> \; = \max(WC - C, 0)\,,\ \mathrm{C} = \ln(70), \ln(75), \ln(80), \ln(85), \ln(90), \ln(95)$$

where ln denotes log-transformation [16]. Interactions between selected variables will be also employed.

5. Simulation Studies

The sample size for the simulation is 600 in accordance with that of data used for the Cox-regression analysis. The effect of the measurement errors and the performance of the correction method mainly depend on four parameters: the number of failures (d), SD of w^* denoted by $SD(w^*)$, SD of the measurement errors in w^* denoted by $SD(\varepsilon^*)$ and the true regression coefficient β [6]. For the sake of simplicity, we set $SD(w^*)=1$ and the values of d, $SD(w^*)$ and $SD(\varepsilon^*)$ will be varied. For each combination of the parameters, 1000 independent samples are generated and consequently 1000 independent estimates are obtained. Newton-Raphson iretarion was performed to search for MLE. The simulation goes as follows:

a) Generate 600 random numbers following $N(4.5,1)$. The mean value 4.5 comes from $\ln(WC)$ in Table1 and does not affect the results. These numbers correspond to w^*.
b) Generate 600 random numbers following $N(0, SD(\varepsilon^*)^2)$, where $SD(\varepsilon^*)$ is either 0.2, 0.4 or 0.6. These numbers correspond to ε^*.
c) Obtain a sum $y^* = w^* + \varepsilon^*$ corresponding to a true WC.
d) Generate random numbers $T = -\ln(U)/\exp(\beta y^*)$ following an exponential distribution with mean $\exp(\beta y^*)$, where U denotes a uniform random number in $(0,1)$ and T corresponds to the failure time. β is either 0.7, 0.9, 1.1, 1.3 or 1.5.
e) Assume the smallest d values of T are regarded as failures and otherwise censored.
f) Apply the Cox regression model with a covariate w^* to the sample to obtain MLE β^+ (naïve estimate) and an asymptotic variance estimate $SD(\beta^+)^2$ based on the observed information.
g) Apply the Cox regression model with correction for the measurement error to obtain the corrected estimate β^* and the sandwich variance estimate $SD(\beta^*)^2$.
h) Repeat a)-g) for 1000 times to obtain 1000 independent estimates β^+, β^*, $SD(\beta^+)$, $SD(\beta^*)$ and their averages. The average of $SD(\beta^+)$ and $SD(\beta^*)$ will be denoted by $Est\_SD(\beta^+)$ and $Est\_SD(\beta^*)$, respectively. Also calculate the sample variance of 1000 β^+ and β^*, denoted by $Emp\_SD(\beta^+)$ and $Emp\_SD(\beta^*)$, respectively.

6. Results

6.1. Normalization

Since the variables are all continuous, Box-Cox transformation [17] was applied to normalize each variable. Normality was tested using the skewness, kurtosis and Shapiro-Wilk tests. We excluded extreme measurements and some variables that were difficult to transform to normal. The basic statistics of the variables remained for statistical analyses are shown in Table 1.

Table 1. Normalization

	Current					Ten years previous				
	Max	**Min**	**Mean**	**SD**	**N**	**Max**	**Min**	**Mean**	**SD**	**N**
Height	179.3	148.7	163.7	5.789	323	179.4	138.0	163.4	5.917	667
ln(Weight)	4.66	3.68	4.12	0.165	323	4.70	3.63	4.09	0.160	667
ln(SBP)	5.32	4.38	4.85	0.136	323	5.34	4.50	4.87	0.145	667
ChE	1.47	0.55	1.01	0.175	309	1.47	0.51	0.99	0.185	602
UA	9.40	1.00	5.56	1.302	319	9.70	0.70	5.95	1.325	615
T-Cho	304.0	78.00	197.5	33.30	320	327.0	90.00	192.0	33.34	620
ln(HDL)	4.56	3.18	3.91	0.253	318	4.85	3.20	3.95	0.275	614
RBC	568.0	356.0	458.8	42.93	315	580.0	360.0	466.4	42.04	609
Hb^2	313.3	118.8	210.7	36.09	312	320.4	123.2	213.6	36.14	609
$PLT^{1/2}$	5.87	3.02	4.40	0.511	313	5.87	2.74	4.45	0.578	609
ln(WC)	4.83	4.09	4.43	0.107	323	-	-	-	-	-

6.2. Transportability of Regression Model for Weight and WC

The regression equation for weight on the current sample is as follows:

$$\ln(Weight) = 1.108 + 0.0139Height + 0.186\ln(SBP) + 0.188ChE + 0.0135UA \\ -0.144\ln(HDL) + 0.000656Hb^2 \tag{7}$$

Table 2 denotes the results of the tests descrived in Section 4.1.

Table 2. The results of the test for the Weight-HH

sample	Henze-Zirkler T			Bartlett test			
	T	**n**	**p**	X^2	**n1**	**n2**	**p**
Current (**x**)	0.060	299	0.9502	24.463	299	581	0.2712
Ten years previous (**x**)	-0.470	581	0.6350				
Current (y,**x**)	1.160	299	0.2468	30.271	299	581	0.3504
Ten years previous (y,**x**)	-0.680	581	0.4985				

The results support that the Weight-HH holds. On the other hand, the regression equation for Weight using the same variables as in Eq(7) with the sample ten years previous becomes

$$\ln(Weight) = 1.594 + 0.0133Height + 0.0801\ln(SBP) + 0.227ChE + 0.00708UA \\ -0.116\ln(HDL) + 0.000616Hb^2 \tag{8}$$

The Chow test for the equality of the regression coefficients between (7) and (8) was not significant ($\text{Chow F}=1.73$, $d.f.1=7$, $d.f.2=866$, $p=0.0995$) supporting the equality. The average of the residuals from Eq(7) in the current sample and those from Eq(8) in the sample ten years previous were both 0.00 with SD 0.1153 and 0.1137, respectively. Bartlett test for the equality of the variance of them was not significant ($X^2=0.0775$, $d.f.1=299$, $d.f.2=581$, $p=0.7807$). The test results support the transportability of Weight.

In this chapter, we verified the transportability of Weight that is strongly correlated with WC ($r=0.879$, $n=323$) in the current sample. Since WC is considered to represent the amount of "fat" and Weight is "fat and muscle", if the relationship between WC and Weight ten years previous was different from that in the current sample, it should be the change in the amount of muscle. Since the sample consists of 48-75 years old persons, the case seems unlikely for most of them. Therefore we assumed that the relationship between WC and Weight has not changed significantly. These considerations lead us to the WC-HH.

6.3. Analysis of Risk for Death Using Transported Estimates

The regression equation for WC on the current sample is as follows:

$$\ln(WC)=2.237-0.00369Height+0.628\ln(Weight)+0.0364\ln(SBP)+0.000172Hb^2$$

with the coefficient of determination 0.81 and SD 0.0467. Table 3 presents the results of the tests for the assumptions of WC-HH. It follows from the results and the WC-HH that the regression equation for WC on the current sample is transportable to the sample ten years previous. Thus, we obtained a transported estimate for each examinee in the sample ten years previous whose mean and SD are 4.42 and 0.094, respectively.

Table 3. The results of the for the assumptions of WC-HH

sample	Henze-Zirkler T			Bartlett test			
	T	n	p	X^2	n1	n2	p
Current (**x**)	1.120	312	0.2642	8.295	312	609	0.6000
Ten years previous (**x**)	0.940	609	0.3467				
Current (y,**x**)	0.760	312	0.4475	-	-	-	-

A follow-up of 608 subjects was performed until June 2008. The results of the Cox regression analysis are shown in Table 4 and illustrated in Figure 1 (MS-related causes of death), where $\ln(WC)^*$ is $\ln(WC)$ minus 4.496, or its average, for stabilization of estimates [18]. The naive estimate is approximately 30% attenuated from the corrected one. The results indicate that, for those of semiMS, the larger the WC, the smaller the risk of MS-related death.

On the other hand, the results of the Cox regression analysis for all cancer deaths are shown in Table 5 and illustrated in Figure 2. The results indicate that the risk of cancer death is increased as *WC* increases beyond 90 irrespective of semiMS or not.

Table 4. MS-related causes of deaths (Number of the endpoint observed is 37)

	Naive			Corrected	
	Estimate	SE	p	Estimate	SE
age	0.086	0.030	0.0039	0.086	
$\ln(WC)^{*} \cdot semiMS$	-11.70	1.976	<0.0001	-17.27	1.753

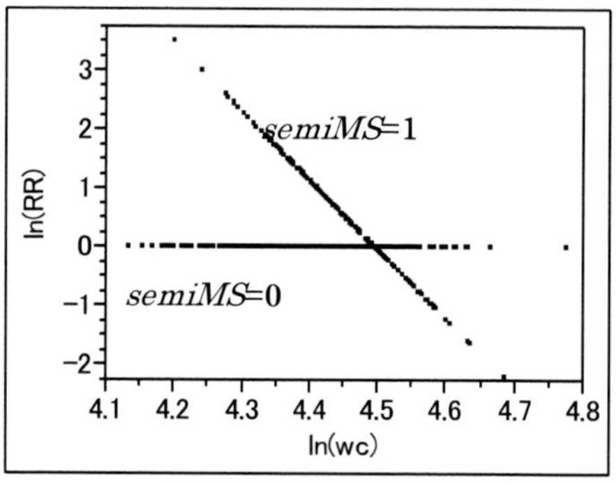

Figure 1. MS-related causes of deaths.

Table 5. Cancer causes of deaths (Number of the endpoint observed is 64)

	Estimate	SE	p
age	0.064	0.020	0.0015
$< \ln(WC) - \ln(90) >$	7.77	2.869	0.0068

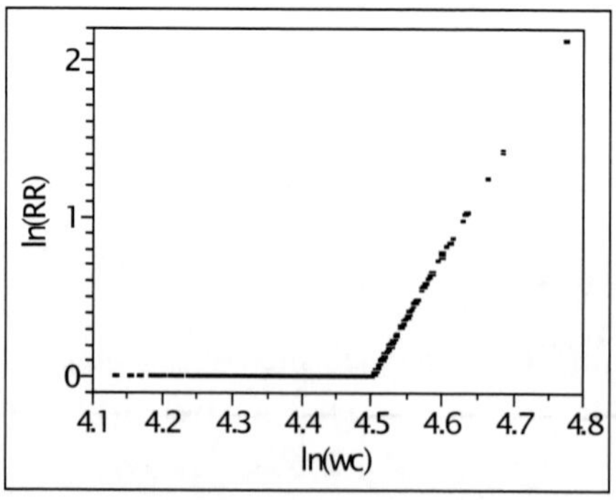

Figure 2. Cancer causes of deaths.

6.4. Results of Simulation

Table 6 shows the results of the naïve estimates and Table 7 the corrected estimates. The index $\beta SD(\varepsilon^*)$ for the effects of the measurement error [6] is also presented. As for the naïve estimates, the bias is approximately 3% when $SD(\varepsilon^*) = 0.2$, 15% when $SD(\varepsilon^*) = 0.4$ and 30% when $SD(\varepsilon^*) = 0.6$, irrespective of the values of d and β. The attenuation tends to be slightly smaller as β becomes large or d is increased. $Emp\_SD(\beta^+)$ and $Est\_SD(\beta^+)$ agree well with each other.

On the other hand, the corrected estimates were not attained when $SD(\varepsilon^*) = 0.6$ due to non-convergence within ten iterations or encounter of negative observed information. Except for the cases, they are approximately equal to the true values and $Emp\_SD(\beta^*)$ and $Est\_SD(\beta^*)$ agree well with each other. Numerical studies reveal that the corrected estimates are approximately unbiased with valid variance estimates for the small sample size.

7. Conclusion

We formally define the "transportability" introduced by Carroll et al. [1] and propose a sufficient condition for it and confirmed the feasibility of the condition with RERF follow-up data. The RERF sample is peculiar that they have been covered with free medical treatment and health insurance by Japanese Government. These conditions seem to contribute to keeping homeostasis condition for a long period.

As for the risk for MS-related death for those of semiMS, our results indicate that the larger the WC, the smaller the risk. The unexpected result might be due to the fact that each semiMS subject had at least two among the dyslipidemia, hypertension, and impaired glucose tolerance; in other words most of semiMS subjects may have been already ill at the baseline. This consideration suggests that it is necessary to exclude those who died of any cause within a few years after the baseline examinations [19] to estimate the risk associated with the examination results.

Since the transported estimates of WC used for the risk analysis were subject to measurement error, the naïve risk estimates may be biased [1]. This chapter reveals the measurement error involved in the transported estimates is the Berkson type and develops a method for correcting for the measurement errors based on the corrected score method [10-11]. The numerical study demonstrated that the correction method yields approximately unbiased estimates with valid variance estimates even for the small sample size data.

Table 6. The results of the naïve estimates (% attenuation)

death	β	SD ε(*)	β+	Emp SD	Est SD
	0.7	0.20	0.679(3)	0.192	0.196
		0.40	0.608(13)	0.173	0.175
		0.60	0.521(26)	0.150	0.150
	0.9	0.20	0.874(3)	0.195	0.199
		0.40	0.781(13)	0.175	0.178
		0.60	0.665(26)	0.153	0.152
	1.1	0.20	1.070(3)	0.200	0.203
25		0.40	0.951(14)	0.185	0.182
		0.60	0.802(27)	0.156	0.155
	1.3	0.20	1.262(3)	0.205	0.210
		0.40	1.113(14)	0.187	0.187
		0.60	0.929(29)	0.167	0.159
	1.5	0.20	1.456(3)	0.215	0.219
		0.40	1.276(15)	0.195	0.194
		0.60	1.045(30)	0.170	0.163
	0.7	0.20	0.677(3)	0.138	0.139
		0.40	0.605(14)	0.124	0.125
		0.60	0.514(27)	0.106	0.106
	0.9	0.20	0.871(3)	0.138	0.142
		0.40	0.775(14)	0.125	0.127
		0.60	0.654(27)	0.111	0.108
	1.1	0.20	1.065(3)	0.140	0.146
50		0.40	0.941(14)	0.128	0.131
		0.60	0.783(29)	0.111	0.111
	1.3	0.20	1.251(4)	0.143	0.152
		0.40	1.097(6)	0.130	0.135
		0.60	0.901(31)	0.117	0.114
	1.5	0.20	1.439(4)	0.152	0.159
		0.40	1.244(17)	0.140	0.140
		0.60	1.008(33)	0.123	0.117
	0.7	0.20	0.677(3)	0.111	0.114
		0.40	0.603(14)	0.101	0.103
		0.60	0.509(27)	0.088	0.087
	0.9	0.20	0.868(4)	0.114	0.117
		0.40	0.770(14)	0.103	0.105
		0.60	0.644(28)	0.091	0.089
	1.1	0.20	1.060(4)	0.115	0.122
75		0.40	0.931(15)	0.105	0.108
		0.60	0.769(30)	0.095	0.092
	1.3	0.20	1.247(4)	0.121	0.127
		0.40	1.083(17)	0.111	0.112
		0.60	0.881(32)	0.100	0.094
	1.5	0.20	1.432(5)	0.128	0.134
		0.40	1.228(18)	0.116	0.117
		0.60	0.979(35)	0.105	0.097

Table 7. The results of the corrected estimates

death	β	SD (ε*)	βSD (ε*)	β*	Emp SD	Est SD	fail
	0.7	0.20	0.14	0.707	0.201	0.202	0
		0.40	0.28	0.712	0.208	0.207	0
		0.60	0.42	0.726	0.226	0.222	1
	0.9	0.20	0.18	0.912	0.205	0.205	0
		0.40	0.36	0.920	0.218	0.214	0
		0.60	0.54	0.950	0.264	0.468	4
	1.1	0.20	0.22	1.119	0.214	0.212	0
25		0.40	0.44	1.134	0.247	0.230	0
		0.60	0.66	1.168	0.296	0.405	30
	1.3	0.20	0.26	1.324	0.223	0.222	0
		0.40	0.52	1.346	0.265	0.253	0
		0.60	0.78	1.367	0.325	0.417	103
	1.5	0.20	0.30	1.535	0.238	0.235	0
		0.40	0.60	1.584	0.319	0.319	1
		0.60	0.90	1.558	0.354	0.689	216
	0.7	0.20	0.14	0.705	0.145	0.145	0
		0.40	0.28	0.708	0.150	0.148	0
		0.60	0.42	0.719	0.162	0.157	0
	0.9	0.20	0.18	0.909	0.146	0.149	0
		0.40	0.36	0.915	0.157	0.154	0
		0.60	0.54	0.936	0.193	0.185	1
	1.1	0.20	0.22	1.115	0.150	0.154	0
50		0.40	0.44	1.126	0.171	0.164	0
		0.60	0.66	1.159	0.222	0.239	9
	1.3	0.20	0.26	1.316	0.156	0.162	0
		0.40	0.52	1.336	0.187	0.180	0
		0.60	0.78	1.393	0.288	0.372	45
	1.5	0.20	0.30	1.521	0.169	0.172	0
		0.40	0.60	1.553	0.231	0.223	1
		0.60	0.90	1.573	0.314	0.593	182
	0.7	0.20	0.14	0.706	0.117	0.119	0
		0.40	0.28	0.708	0.123	0.121	0
		0.60	0.42	0.713	0.135	0.128	0
	0.9	0.20	0.18	0.908	0.121	0.123	0
		0.40	0.36	0.913	0.130	0.127	0
		0.60	0.54	0.928	0.161	0.146	0
	1.1	0.20	0.22	1.112	0.124	0.128	0
75		0.40	0.44	1.120	0.141	0.136	0
		0.60	0.66	1.153	0.207	0.198	3
	1.3	0.20	0.26	1.314	0.132	0.136	0
		0.40	0.52	1.328	0.163	0.150	0
		0.60	0.78	1.376	0.253	0.335	42
	1.5	0.20	0.30	1.519	0.143	0.145	0
		0.40	0.60	1.546	0.192	0.170	1
		0.60	0.90	1.572	0.287	0.398	149

Acknowledgements

We thank Dr. Makie for helpful comments. RERF is a private, non-profit foundation funded by the Japanese Ministry of Health Labour and Welfare and the U.S. Department of Energy, with the latter funding provided through the National Academy of Sciences. This chapter was based on RERF research protocol RP A04-08.

References

[1] Carroll, RJ; Ruppert, D; Stefanski, LA. (1995). *Measurement Error in Nonlinear Models*. Chapman and Hall, London.

[2] Federspil, G.; Nisoli, E; Vettor, R. (2006). A critical reflection on the definition of metabolic syndrome. *Pharmacological Research* **53**, 449-456.

[3] Lefebvre, PJ. (2005). Prediabetes or what's in a name? *Diabetes and Metabolism* **31**(6), 519.

[4] Miyawaki, T; Hirata, M; Moriyama, K; Sasaki, Y; Aono, H; Saito, N; Nakao, K. (2005). Metabolic syndrome in Japanese diagnosed with visceral fat measurement by computed tomography. *Proceedings of the Japan Academy Series B: Physical and Biological Sciences* **81**, 471-479.

[5] Nakamura, T. (1990). Corrected Score Function of Errors-in-Variables Models: Methodology and Application to Generalized Linear Model. *Biometrika* **77**, 127-137.

[6] Nakamura, T. (1992). Proportional Hazards Model With Covariates Subject to Measurement Error. *Biometrics* **48**, 829-838.

[7] Cramér, H. (1937). *Random variables and probability distributions*, Cambridge.

[8] Ghani, AC; Donnelly, CA; Cox, DR; Griffin, JT; Fraser, C; Lam, TH; Ho, LM; Chan, WS; Anderson, RM; Hedley, AJ; Leung, GM. (2005). Methods for estimating the case fatality ratio for a novel, emerging infectious disease. *American Journal of Epidemiology* **162**(5), 479-786.

[9] Snedecor, GW; Cochran, WG. (1967), *Statistical methods. 6th Ed.* The State University Press, Ames Lowa, USA.

[10] Augustin, T. (2004). An Exact Corrected Log-Likelihood Function for Cox's Proportional Hazards Model under Measurement Error and Some Extensions. *Scandinavian Journal of Statistics* **31**(1), 43-50.

[11] Zucker, DM; Spiegelman, D. (2008). Corrected score estimation in the proportional hazards model with misclassified discrete covariates. *Statistics in Medicine* **27**(11), 1911-1933.

[12] Pierce, DA ; Vaeth, M ; Cologne, JB. (2008). Allowance for random dose estimation errors in atomic bomb survivor studies: A revision. *Radiat Res* **170**(1), 118-126.

[13] Akahoshi, M; Soda, M; Carter RL; Nakashima, E; Shimaoka, K; Seto, S; Yano, K. (1996). Correlation between systolic blood pressure and physical development in adolescence. *American Journal of Epidemiology* **144**, 51-58.

[14] Marrugat, J; Subirana, I; Comín, E; Cabezas, C; Vila, J; Elosua, R; Nam, BH; Ramos, R; Sala, J; Solanas, P; Cordon, F; Gene-Badia, J; D'Agostino,RB. (2007). Validity of an adaptation of the Framingham cardiovascular risk function: the VERIFICA study. *Journal of Epidemiology and Community Health* **61**(1), 40-47.

[15] Chow, G.C. (1960). Tests of Equality between Sets of Coefficients in Two Linear Regressions. *Econometrica* **28**, 591-605.

[16] Nakamura, T ; Akazawa, K ; Kinukawa, K ; Nose, Y. (1999). *Piecewise Linear Cox Model for Estimating Relative Risks Adjusting for the Heterogeneity of the Sample. Statistics for the Environment* Vol.4, Chap.16, 281-9, Wiley, New York.

[17] Box, GEP; Cox, DR. (1964). An analysis of transformations. *Journal of the Royal Statistical Society* **B26**, 211-252.

[18] Aikcn, LS; Wcst, SG. (1991). *Multiple Regressions: Testing and Interpreting Interactions*. CA: Sage, Thousand Oaks.

[19] Hida, A; Akahoshi, M; Toyama, K; Imaizumi, M; Soda, M; Maeda, R; Ichimaru, S; Nakashima, E; Eguchi, K. (2005). Do Glucose and Lipid Metabolism Affect Cancer Development in Nagasaki Atomic Bomb Survivors? *Nutrition and Cancer* **52**(2), 115-120.

In: Risk Management
Editors: B. Jordão and E. Sousa, pp. 203-224
ISBN: 978-1-60876-011-4

Chapter 8

CONDITIONAL LIKELIHOOD APPROACH FOR A TWO-STAGE CLONAL EXPANSION MODEL

Yushi Yoshida[1], Shuntaro Sato[1], Tsuyoshi Nakamura[1] and David G. Hoel[2]
[1] Nagasaki University, Nagasaki, Japan
[2] Medical University of South Carolina, Chaleston, U.S.A

Abstract

The two-stage clonal expansion (TSCE) model has been developed to investigate the mechanistic processes in cancer development on carcinogenesis based on the knowledge of molecular biology and considerable interest has been shown regarding the model's use in risk assessment. The model assumes three states of cells (normal, intermediate, and malignant) and four transition rate parameters to describe the rate at which a cell changes its state: the first initiation rate μ_1 for normal to susceptible cells, the proliferation rate β, death rate δ, and second initiation rate μ_2 for an intermediate cell.

Major issues exist concerning the application of the TSCE model. Since the likelihood derived from the two-stage model is complicated and the four parameters are not jointly identifiable with survival data, sophisticated reparametrizations are necessary to obtain statistically efficient and biologically useful parameters. Heidenreich *et al.* (2000) observed that different studies have used different parameters with different assumptions and reached different conclusions from the same data set. Hornsby *et al.* (2007) also found that different studies using slightly different methods or data sets yielded different conclusions. Despite the need for statistically sound and biologically meaningful estimation methods (Portier and El Masri, 1997), no standard parameterization or inference method has yet been established. These inconveniences deter comparison of the results among studies and broader applications of this model.

Regarding the problem, Nakamura and Hoel (2003) propose the conditional likelihood method and Baker *et al.* (2006) and others use the method. The conditional likelihood is much simpler than the original likelihood, yet, maximum-likelihood estimates (MLEs) of the most interesting parameters for assessing the initiation and the promotion effects are obtained from it. This chapter compares the conditional likelihood method and other techniques used frequently in the literature from both mathematical and practical perspectives.

We conducted extensive simulation studies with small sample sizes to assess the performance of the MLE obtained using the conditional likelihood and the ability to distinguish between initiation and promotion effects. Based on the results, we propose a standard cancer-risk estimation method using the conditional likelihood approach and we applied it to some experimental data.

1. Introduction

The two-stage clonal expansion (TSCE) model, also called a biologically-based mechanistic model, is so to speak a stochastic representation of gene mutations and clonal growth in carcinogenesis process (Moolgavkar and Venzon, 1979; Moolgavkar, 1986). It has been used not only to investigate the development of cancer in toxicology but also to guide the interpretation of epidemiological data to quantatively link the likelihood of a disease to environmental causes (Portier and Edler, 1990; Luebeck *et al.*, 1991; Leenhouts and Chadwick, 1994, Portier, 2001). The model involves four parameters: μ_1, β, δ, and μ_2 (Fig. 1).

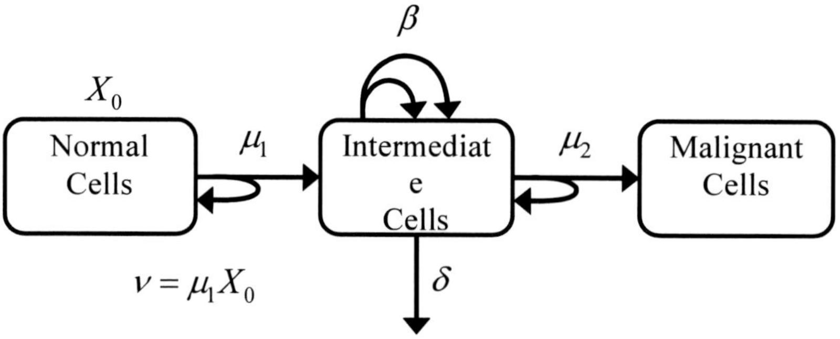

Figure 1. The two-stage clonal expansion (TSCE) model.

A normal cell is transformed into an intermediate cell at a constant rate μ_1 per unit time per cell. Each intermediate cell is subject to three events: birth, death or differentiation. Specifically, each intermediate cell undergoes clonal expansion by dividing into two intermediate cells at a rate of β divisions per unit time per cell, death at a rate of δ per unit time per cell, or division into one intermediate cell and one malignant cell at the rate of μ_2 per unit time per cell. Once a malignant cell has developed, it will replicate into a detectable tumor in a relatively short period of time; therefore, the formation of one malignant cell is usually associated with the development of detectable cancer (Moolgavkar and Luebeck, 1990; Portier *et al.*, 1995; Heidenreich *et al.*, 1997; Moolgavkar, 1999). It is commonly assumed that the number of normal cells is large and constant at X_0 throughout the observation period and that the normal cells create one intermediate cell at the rate of $\nu = \mu_1 X_0$ per unit time.

The probability of no malignant cells at time t, say $S(t)$, is obtained by solving a series of differential equations for the probability generating functions (Moolgavkar and Venzon, 1979; Kopp-Schneider *et al.*, 1994; Portier *et al.*, 1995; Heidenreich *et al.*, 1997) or for Poisson probabilities (Portier *et al.*, 2000). Since the four parameters are not jointly identifiable with survival data, reparameterization is necessary (Hanin and Yakovlev, 1996;

Heidenreich *et al.*, 1997; Sherman and Portier, 1997). It is frequently assumed that $\delta = 0$ (Leenhouts and Chadwick, 1994), $\mu_1 = \mu_2$ (Moolgavkar and Luebeck, 1992; Brugmans *et al.*, 2004; Schöllnberger *et al.*, 2006) or $\beta - \delta$ is independent of dose (Portier and El Masri, 1997; Bijwaard *et al.*, 2001). The value of X_0 is usually obtained from an independent source (Moolgavkar, 1999; Bijwaard *et al.*, 2001) because only $\nu\mu_2 = X_0\mu_1\mu_2$ is estimable from survival data. The effect of exposure is incorporated by assuming dose-response model for the parameters.

Heidenreich *et al.* (2000) compared the results obtained by three independent European groups, all of which applied the clonal expansion model to the same data set of lung tumors in rats exposed to radon, and found that the groups reached different conclusions. Hornsby *et al.* (2007) pointed out some problems of using different parametrizations of the TSCE model and other biologically based models. Despite the need for statistically sound and biologically meaningful estimation methods (Portier and El Masri, 1997), no standard parameterization or inference method for TSCE model has been established. This lack of a standard method hinders the comparison of results among researchers, as well as broader application of the TSCE model.

Our objective was to justify the conditional-likelihood approach used by Tessier *et al.* (2001), Nakamura and Hoel (2003), and Baker *et al.* (2006) mathematically. We also describe the relationships among parameterizations summarized by Heidenreich *et al.* (2000), the conditional likelihood, and the proportional hazards model. This chapter also uses extensive simulation studies to examine the performance of the conditional-likelihood approach for establishing a reliable, feasible inference method for the TSCE model. Particular interests in the simulation are the sensitivity of the TSCE model (Brugmans *et al.*, 2002) and its ability to discern the initiation and promotion effects (Portier and Edler, 1990). Finally, we applied it to some experimental data. The ultimate goal of this chapter is to contribute to establishing a standard cancer-risk estimation method using the TSCE model for a broader range of application.

2. Survivor Function and Likelihood

2.1. Derivation of the Survivor Function

Let $S(t)$ denote the survivor function, or the probability of no malignant cell at time t. Several methods are proposed to explicitly derive $S(t)$ (Kopp-Schneider *et al.*, 1994). In this chapter, we will demonstrate the derivation process following Portier *et al.* (2000), since the method seems most simple and general. They use the multistage models for event history (Andersen, 2002) to obtain a series of differential equations, and $S(t)$ is determined as a solution with certain initial conditions.

A simple k-stage model of carcinogenesis is illustrated in Figure 2. The model assumes that cells act independently as Markovian process and the k-th stage corresponds to the malignant cells. The model parameters are allowed to be time-dependent.

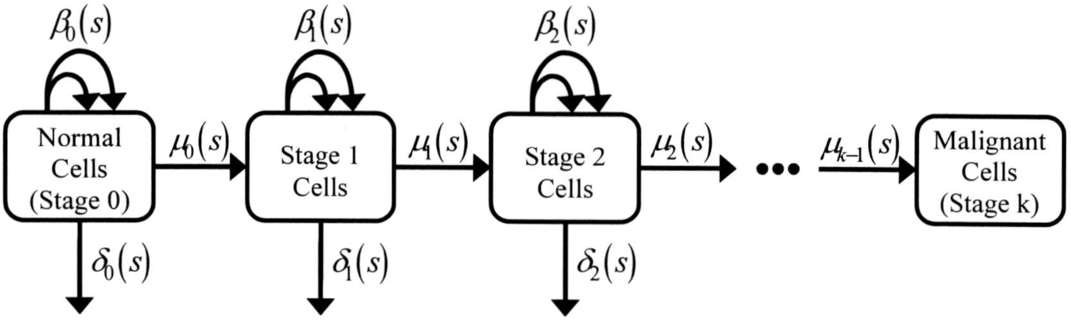

Figure 2. k-stage model with β, δ and μ the promotion, initiation and death rate, respectively, at each stage.

In an infinitesimal time period $[s, s+\Delta]$, a cell in stage i $(i = 0,1,2,\dots,k-1)$ can

[1] replicate into two cells with probability $\beta_i(s)\Delta + o(\Delta)$

[2] die with probability $\delta_i(s)\Delta + o(\Delta)$

[3] initiate with probability $\mu_i(s)\Delta + o(\Delta)$ resulting in one stage i cell and one stage $i+1$ cell

[4] or remain no change with probability $1 - [\beta_i(s) + \delta_i(s) + \mu_i(s)]\Delta + o(\Delta)$

where $o(\Delta)$ is small order of $\Delta \to 0$. Now, define for $t > s$

$$P_{ik}(s,t) = \Pr\{no \text{ progeny of a cell in stage } i \text{ at } (t - s) \text{ are in stage } k \text{ at } t\},$$

then $P_{02}(t,t)$ is the survivor function for one normal cell and $P_{02}^{m}(t,t)$ is that for m normal cells.

Let us consider $P_{ik}(s+\Delta, t)$ and let $j_0,\dots,j_i,\dots,j_{k-1}$ denote the number of cells in stage $0,\dots,i,\dots,k-1$, respectively, when there was one cell in stage i at $t-s-\Delta$. Then it follows from Markovian property and the independence of cells, that

$$P_{ik}(s+\Delta,t) = \sum_{j_0=0}^{\infty}\sum_{j_1=0}^{\infty}\cdots\sum_{j_{k-1}=0}^{\infty} \Pr\left\{\bigcap_{n=0}^{k-1} X_n(t-s) = j_n \mid X_i(t-s-\Delta) = 1, \bigcap_{\substack{n=0 \\ n\neq i}}^{k} X_n(t-s-\Delta) = 0\right\} \prod_{n=0}^{k-1} P^{j_n}{}_{nk}(s,t) \tag{1}$$

Since Δ is infinitesimally small, we may assume that only one transformation out of the four possibilities described above is possible between $t-s-\Delta$ and $t-s$. Then (1) is simplified to

$$P_{ik}(s+\Delta,t)=\beta_i(t-s-\Delta)\Delta\{P_{ik}(s,t)\}^2+\delta_i(t-s-\Delta)\Delta+\mu_i(t-s-\Delta)\Delta P_{ik}(s,t)P_{i+1,k}(s,t)$$
$$+\{1-\beta_i(t-s-\Delta)\Delta-\delta_i(t-s-\Delta)\Delta-\mu_i(t-s-\Delta)\Delta\}P_{ik}(s,t)+o(\Delta)$$

Rewriting, we have

$$\frac{P_{ik}(s+\Delta,t)-P_{ik}(s,t)}{\Delta}=\beta_i(t-s-\Delta)\{P_{ik}(s,t)\}^2+\delta_i(t-s-\Delta)+\mu_i(t-s-\Delta)P_{ik}(s,t)P_{i+1,k}(s,t)$$
$$-\{\beta_i(t-s-\Delta)+\delta_i(t-s-\Delta)+\mu_i(t-s-\Delta)\}P_{ik}(s,t)+o(\Delta)/\Delta$$

Putting $\Delta\to 0$, we have

$$\frac{dP_{ik}(s,t)}{ds}=\beta_i(t-s)\{P_{ik}(s,t)\}^2+\delta_i(t-s)+\mu_i(t-s)P_{ik}(s,t)P_{i+1,k}(s,t)$$
$$-\{\beta_i(t-s)+\delta_i(t-s)+\mu_i(t-s)\}P_{ik}(s,t) \tag{2}$$

As for the TSCE model in this study, k=2 and the four parameters associated with stage 1 are concerned and they are assumed time independent. Therefore, (2) is further simplified to

$$\frac{dP_{ik}(s,t)}{ds}=\beta P_{ik}{}^2+\delta+\mu_i P_{ik}(s,t)P_{i+1,k}(s,t)-\{\beta+\delta+\mu_i\}P_{ik}(s,t)$$

Since there are only three possibilities of the combination of i,k, the above equation leads to the following three equations:

$$\frac{dP_{01}(s,t)}{ds}=\beta\{P_{01}(s,t)\}^2+\delta-\{\beta+\delta+\mu_1\}P_{01}(s,t)$$

$$\frac{dP_{02}(s,t)}{ds}=\beta\{P_{02}(s,t)\}^2+\delta+\mu_1 P_{02}(s,t)P_{12}(s,t)-\{\beta+\delta+\mu_1\}P_{02}(s,t)$$

$$\frac{dP_{12}(s,t)}{ds}=\beta\{P_{12}(s,t)\}^2+\delta-\{\beta+\delta+\mu_2\}P_{12}(s,t)$$

where μ_0 and μ_1 are changed to μ_1 and μ_2, respectively, for the consistency of symbols. The simultaneous differential equations are solved with initial condition $P_{02}(0,t)=1$ and $P_{12}(0,t)=1$ to obtain the survivor function $S(t)=P_{02}(t,t)$ (Portier *et al.* 1994).

2.2. Original Parameterization

Kopp-Schneider *et al.* (1994), Portier *et al.* (1995), and Heidenreich (1996) obtained the survivor function $S(t)$ for the two-stage model as follows:

$$S(t) = \exp\{-\Lambda(t)\}$$

where

$$\Lambda(t) = \frac{\nu}{\beta}\left\{\frac{t(R+\beta-\delta-\mu_2)}{2} + \log\frac{R-(\beta-\delta-\mu_2)+(R+\beta-\delta-\mu_2)e^{-Rt}}{2R}\right\} \tag{3}$$

with

$$R^2 = (\beta+\delta+\mu_2)^2 - 4\beta\delta = (\beta-\delta-\mu_2)^2 + 4\beta\mu_2$$

Changing parameters (Moolgavkar, 1999) such that

$$\eta = \nu/\beta \quad \text{and} \quad \psi = \beta-\delta-\mu_2 \tag{4}$$

gives

$$\Lambda(t) = \eta\left\{\frac{t(R+\psi)}{2} + \log\frac{R-\psi+(R+\psi)e^{-Rt}}{2R}\right\} \tag{5}$$

The parameters η, ψ, and R are identifiable, as is

$$\rho = \nu\mu_2 = \eta(R^2-\psi^2)/4 \tag{6}$$

The parameters ψ and ρ are of interest in most applications and have been biologically interpreted as the net proliferation rate and the overall mutation rate, respectively (Moolgavkar, 1986; Luebeck *et al.*, 1991). By constructing the likelihood function based on (3), one can obtain the MLE of η, ψ, and ρ. We call this the *original likelihood method.* The complicated form of the likelihood based on this approach often causes convergence problems (Portier and El Masri, 1997).

2.3. Conditional Likelihood

To avoid computational difficulties, set $\delta = 0$ in (3) to obtain:

$$\Lambda^*(t) = \frac{\nu^*}{\beta^*}\left[\beta^* t + \log\frac{\mu_2^* + \beta^*\exp\{-(\beta^*+\mu_2^*)t\}}{\beta^*+\mu_2^*}\right] \tag{7}$$

To avoid confusion between the original parameters in (3) and those under the condition of $\delta = 0$, we use ν^*, β^*, and μ_2^* in (7). We call the likelihood based on (7) the *conditional likelihood.* Although the conditional likelihood is computationally much simpler than the original likelihood, the biological interpretation of ν^*, β^*, and μ_2^* and are unclear because they ignore the death of intermediate cells in the original two-stage model. In other words, the MLEs of ν^*, β^*, and μ_2^* that are obtained using the conditional likelihood based on (7) are considered biased estimates for the corresponding true parameters ν, β, and μ_2 in (3) because, in a biological sense, the true value of δ is not zero.

3. Theoretical Background for Conditional Likelihood

3.1. Variable Transformation

Let $\{(t_i, d_i), i = 1, \ldots, n\}$ be survival data from n subjects, where t_i denotes the elapsed time until an event for subject i is observed and $d_i = 1$ or 0 depending on whether the event is death or censored. For survival, the MLEs of the parameters using the original likelihood based on (3)–(6) and those of the conditional likelihood based on (7) are as follows:

$$\psi = \beta^* - \mu_2^*,\ \rho = \nu\mu_2 = \nu^*\mu_2^*, \text{ and } \eta = \nu/\beta = \nu^*/\beta^* \tag{8}$$

and

$$\frac{\beta}{\beta^*} = \frac{\nu}{\nu^*} = \frac{\mu_2^*}{\mu_2} \tag{9}$$

Proof: Consider a further parameterization of (5), namely

$$\eta = \nu/\beta,\ \alpha = (R+\psi)/2, \text{ and } \kappa = (R-\psi)/2, \tag{10}$$

which results in

$$\Lambda(t) = \eta\left[\alpha t + \log\frac{\kappa + \alpha\exp\{-(\alpha+\kappa)t\}}{\alpha+\kappa}\right]$$

If we set $\lambda(t) = \partial\Lambda(t)/\partial t$, then the log-likelihood of the survival data $\{(t_i, d_i), i = 1, \ldots, n\}$

is written as a sum of $\Lambda(t)$ and $\log\lambda(t)$ as

$$\ell(\alpha,\kappa,\eta)=\sum_i\{d_i\log\lambda(t_i)-\Lambda(t_i)\} \tag{11}$$

Applying the variable transformation

$$\alpha=\beta^*,\ \ \kappa=\mu_2^*,\text{ and }\eta=\nu^*/\beta^* \tag{12}$$

to (11) results in

$$\ell^*(\nu^*,\beta^*,\mu_2^*)=\sum_i\{d_i\log\lambda^*(t_i)-\Lambda^*(t_i)\}$$

where $\lambda^*(t)=\partial\Lambda^*(t)/\partial t$. This is exactly the conditional log-likelihood with $\{(t_i,d_i),i=1,\ldots,n\}$. Since the Jacobian of the transformation is

$$|J|=\begin{vmatrix}1&0&0\\0&1&0\\-\nu^*/\beta^{*2}&0&1/\beta^*\end{vmatrix}=1/\beta^*>0,$$

the transformation is one to one and is strictly monotone in the whole parameter space. Therefore, it follows from the chain rule, or the invariance under parameter transformations, of maximum likelihood estimation (Cox and Hinkley, 1974) that the relationships in (12) hold exactly between the MLEs of the original parameters and those of the conditional parameters.

Furthermore, it follows from (10) that

$$\psi=\alpha-\kappa\ \text{ and }\ \rho=\eta\alpha\kappa$$

and (8) and (9) follow from (4), (6), (10), and (12).

Thus, the parameters β^*, μ_2^* and ν^* in the conditional likelihood represent the same biological functions as do the parameters α, κ and $\eta\alpha$, respectively, in the original likelihood. In other words, the real biological parameters estimated by β^*, μ_2^* and ν^* are α, κ and $\eta\alpha$, respectively. It is an interesting coincidence that $\nu^*\mu_2^* = \nu\mu_2$ for the overall initiation rate, although the individual initiation rates ν^* and μ_2^* are not necessarily equal to ν and μ_2, respectively. As for the promotion rate, if β^* is much greater than μ_2^*, the following relationships hold approximately

$$\beta^*=\beta-\delta=\psi \tag{13}$$

Luebeck *et al.* (1999) and Moolgavkar (1999) regarded ψ as a net proliferation rate, whereas Luebeck *et al.* (1991) and Hazelton *et al.* (2001) defined $\beta-\delta$ as a net proliferation rate, and Leenhouts and Chadwick (1994) treated β^* as a net proliferation rate. Therefore, ψ,

$\beta - \delta$ and β^* are referred to as the net proliferation rates. Assigning (13) to (9) gives approximately

$$\frac{\beta}{\beta-\delta}=\frac{\nu}{\nu^*}=\frac{\mu_2^*}{\mu_2}$$

3.2. Dose-Response Model for Population Parameters

Let us assume log-linear models for each of the original parameters

$$\log \nu = a_1 + b_1 D$$

$$\log \mu_2 = a_2 + b_2 D$$

$$\log \beta = a_3 + b_3 D$$

$$\log \delta = a_4 + b_4 D$$

where D denotes a covariate such as the radiation dose, which may be continuous, ordinal, or binary. It follows that

$$\log \rho = \log \nu^* \mu_2^* = a_1 + a_2 + (b_1 + b_2) D$$

and

$$\log \mu_1 \mu_2 = \log \rho - \log X_0$$

That is, the dose-rate parameters for $\log\rho$, $\log\mu_1\mu_2$, and $\log \nu^* \mu_2^*$ are the same.

Section 3.2 indicates that the effect, given by $b_1 + b_2$, of dose D on the overall mutation rate $\mu_1\mu_2$ is exactly equal to the effect on $\nu^*\mu_2^*$. In other words, the dose-rate effect on the overall mutation rate can be obtained from the conditional likelihood alone.

3.3. Miscellanea

If $b_3 = b_4$ and if (13) holds, then it follows that

$$\log \nu^* = c_1 + b_1 D$$

$$\log \mu_2^* = c_2 + b_2 D$$

where c_1 and c_2 are constants that are not dependent on D.

These results indicate that b_1 and b_2, the dose-rate effects on ν and μ_2, are approximately equal to those on ν^*, μ_2^* respectively, if the ratio β/δ is independent of D, as assumed by Groos and Kopp-Schneider (2006).

4. Methods for Parameter Estimation

4.1. Dose-Response Model for Estimation

For each parameter θ, a simple log linear model is assumed:

$$\log\theta = \log\theta\_a + \log\theta\_b \times D \tag{14}$$

where $\log\theta\_a$ is a constant, $\log\theta\_b$ is a regression coefficient, and D is a covariate. The dose-response model (14) is assumed for each of the parameters ρ, ψ, η, ν^*, β^*, and μ_2^*.

The MLEs of the original parameters ρ, ψ, and η may be obtained by transforming the MLEs of ν^*, β^*, and μ_2^*. That is,

$$\log\psi\_a \approx \log\beta^*\_a$$

$$\log\psi\_b \approx \log\beta^*\_b$$

$$\log\rho\_a = \log\nu^*\_a + \log\mu_2^*\_a$$

$$\log\rho\_b = \log\nu^*\_b + \log\mu_2^*\_b \tag{15}$$

$$\log\eta\_a = \log\nu^*\_a - \log\beta^*\_a$$

$$\log\eta\_b = \log\nu^*\_b - \log\beta^*\_b$$

where $\approx$ denotes an approximate equality.

4.2. Initiation and Promotion Models

Each parameter of the TSCE model has its own role, which distinguishes it from empirical models like the Cox regression model or logistic regression model. Among the empirical models, those for generating simulation samples and those for estimating parameters are normally identical. In contrast, the TSCE model incorporates typical models that represent different biological mechanisms of carcinogenesis. This chapter defines three distinct models using the original parameters for generating samples. Regarding models for inference, a variety of models using the conditional likelihood parameters are treated to obtain biologically significant estimates.

i. Models for Generating Simulation Samples

Following three models are considered for generating survival data:

(a.) Simple initiation model: $\log\rho\_b > 0$ and $\log\psi\_b = 0$

(b.) Balanced initiation model: $\log\rho\_b > 0$ and $\log\psi\_b < 0$

(c.) Promotion model: $\log\rho\_b = 0$ and $\log\psi\_b > 0$

The balanced initiation model has a feature to prevent the number of intermediate cells from growing too large (Nakamura and Hoel 2003).

ii. Models for Estimating MLE

Following five models are considered for estimation of parameters, where each model implicitly includes the three basic parameters $\log\nu^*\_a$, $\log\beta^*\_a$, and $\log\mu_2^*\_a$:

a1. Overall initiation model: $\log\nu^*\_b$, $\log\mu_2^*\_b$
a2. First initiation model: $\log\nu^*\_b$
b1. Full model: $\log\nu^*\_b$, $\log\beta^*\_b$, $\log\mu_2^*\_b$
b2. Semi full model: $\log\nu^*\_b$, $\log\beta^*\_b$
c. Promotion model: $\log\beta^*\_b$

4.3. Algorithm Searching for MLE

We applied the Newton-Raphson iteration algorithm for searching for MLE. The convergence criterion was to satisfy the following three conditions simultaneously:

[1] The norm of the score vector was less than 0.01.
[2] The main diagonal elements are all positive.
[3] The Euclidean distance between the new and the old parameter vectors was less than 0.00001.

Estimated parameters $\log\nu^*\_a$, $\log\nu^*\_b$, $\log\beta^*\_a$, $\log\beta^*\_b$, and $\log\mu_2^*\_a$, $\log\mu_2^*\_b$ were transformed to $\log\psi\_a$, $\log\psi\_b$, $\log\rho\_a$, $\log\rho\_b$, and $\log\eta\_a$, $\log\eta\_b$ according to (15) in 4.1.

To obtain proper initial values for the Newton-Raphson iteration, we used to apply the so called "Grid table method" developed by Nogami *et al.* (2007). As an extension of it, we have developed a more efficient algorithm named "Dynamical method", the detail of which will appear elsewhere.

5. Numerical Study on the Sensitivity of the Conditional Likelihood

5.1. Parameter Setting and Data Generation

The objective of the simulation study in this section was to assess the performance of parameter estimation using the conditional likelihood. Three sets of parameter values are used to generate survival data and the MLE is obtained from the survival data using the conditional-likelihood method. For each combination of parameter values, 100 independent survival data were generated, thus producing 100 independent MLEs. The empirical variance and average of the 100 estimates of the asymptotic variances based on the information matrix were compared. The sample size was fixed at 500, of which 100 were censored. The three sets of parameter values used for generating data are shown below.

Table 1. Parameter setting

Model	$\log\psi\_a$	$\log\psi\_b$ $\times 100$	$\log\rho\_a$	$\log\rho\_b$ $\times 100$	$\log\eta\_a$	$\log\eta\_b$ $\times 100$
a. Simple Initiation	-4.9	-	-17.0	0.42	-0.08	0.72
b. Balanced Initiation	-4.9	-0.1	-17.0	0.42	-0.08	0.72
c. Promotion	-3.3	0.35	-35.0	-	1.7	-0.35

For the two initiation models, the parameter values are chosen based on the results obtained from the JANUS experimental data on radiation effects in mice (Nakamura and Hoel, 2003) where $\log\psi\_b$ was approximately equal to -0.001. The dose level is 0, 50, 100, 250 and 500 with 100 cases each. On the other hand, those for the promotion model were obtained from analyzing the Dioxin experimental data (Kociba *et al.*, 1978), which will be discussed in Section 6. The dose level for the model is 0, 1, 10 and 100 with 125 cases each.

The objective of this simulation is to assess the performance when the models for estimation and those for generating data are essentially the same. Therefore, we applied

[1] Overall initiation model (a1) to data generated from Simple initiation model (a),
[2] First initiation model (a2) to data generated from Simple initiation model (a),
[3] Full model (b1) to data generated from Balanced initiation model (b),
[4] Semi full model (b2) to data generated from Balanced initiation model (b),
[5] Promotion model (c) to data generated from Promotion model (c).

5.2. Results and Discussion

The results are presented in Table 2 (1 to 5). Convergence status is shown, since false convergence and non-convergence are serious concerns in fitting the TSCE model to data (Portier and El Masri, 1997). In the tables, the most significant parameters biologically are $\log\rho\_b$ and $\log\psi\_b$, followed by $\log\rho\_a$ and $\log\psi\_a$, while both $\log\eta\_a$ and $\log\eta\_b$ are of little concern. First, the Newton–Raphson algorithm converged within five to ten iterations on average, indicating that the new algorithm to search for initial values worked well. Second, the relative error (1 − Mean/True value) is less than 2% for $\log\psi\_a$ and 3% for $\log\rho\_a$, while for $\log\rho\_b$ and $\log\psi\_b$, the estimates and true values are approximately equal to each other. The relative error for the latter two is larger than that for $\log\rho\_a$ and $\log\psi\_a$, since their absolute values are smaller and the coefficients of variation (Emp.SD/True) are larger. The results indicate that the MLE obtained using the conditional likelihood method is approximately unbiased for small sample sizes with various models. Regarding the variance estimates, Est.SD and Emp.SD agree well with each other for only 100 replicates with a small sample size.

In particular, Table 2(2) reveals an important feature for application of the model. It emphasizes that a simple initiation model with a dose-dependent second initiation rate of

$\log\mu_2^*\_b = 0$ performs approximately the same as the full model in terms of the estimates of ρ and ψ.

Table 2. Simulation results for parameter estimation

(1) (a, a1) Average MLE: -2754.6, Average Iterations: 6.24

	$\log\psi\_a$	$\log\psi\_b \times 100$	$\log\rho\_a$	$\log\rho\_b \times 100$	$\log\eta\_a$	$\log\eta\_b \times 100$
True value	-4.9	-	-17	0.42	-0.08	0.72
Mean	-4.90	-	-17.3	0.427	-0.288	0.768
Mean / True value	0.999		1.02	1.02	3.60	1.07
Emp.SD	0.0835	-	0.365	0.0390	0.209	0.299
Est.SD	0.0764	-	0.350	0.0417	0.218	0.281

(2) (a, a2) Average MLE: -2756, Average Iterations: 4.97

	$\log\psi\_a$	$\log\psi\_b \times 100$	$\log\rho\_a$	$\log\rho\_b \times 100$	$\log\eta\_a$	$\log\eta\_b \times 100$
True value	-4.9	-	-17	0.42	-0.08	0.72
Mean	-4.86	-	-17.5	0.454	-0.237	0.454
Mean / True value	0.991	-	1.03	1.08	2.97	0.630
Emp.SD	0.0740	-	0.340	0.0336	0.209	0.0336
Est.SD	0.0688	-	0.321	0.0333	0.217	0.0333

(3) (b, b1) Average MLE: -2817.5, Average Iterations: 8.33

	$\log\psi\_a$	$\log\psi\_b \times 100$	$\log\rho\_a$	$\log\rho\_b \times 100$	$\log\eta\_a$	$\log\eta\_b \times 100$
True value	-4.9	-0.1	-17	0.42	-0.08	0.75
Mean	-4.89	-0.104	-17.3	0.444	-0.303	0.827
Mean / True value	0.997	1.04	1.02	1.06	3.79	1.10
Emp.SD	0.134	0.0375	0.572	0.142	0.307	0.314
Est.SD	0.111	0.0336	0.467	0.118	0.297	2.87

(4) (b, b2) Average MLE: -2818.5, Average Iterations: 7.62

	$\log\psi\_a$	$\log\psi\_b \times 100$	$\log\rho\_a$	$\log\rho\_b \times 100$	$\log\eta\_a$	$\log\eta\_b \times 100$
True value	-4.9	-0.1	-17	0.42	-0.08	0.75
Mean	-4.85	-0.109	-17.5	0.478	-0.294	0.587
Mean / True value	0.989	1.09	1.03	1.14	3.67	0.783
Emp.SD	0.121	0.0353	0.523	0.129	0.336	0.163
Est.SD	0.103	0.0340	0.440	0.116	0.305	0.148

Table 2. Continued

(5) (c, c) Average MLE: -2039.5, Average Iterations: 9.83

	$\log\psi\_a$	$\log\psi\_b$ $\times 100$	$\log\rho\_a$	$\log\rho\_b$ $\times 100$	$\log\eta\_a$	$\log\eta\_b$ $\times 100$
True value	-3.3	0.35	-35	-	1.7	-0.35
Mean	-3.30	0.350	-35.2	-	1.96	-0.350
Mean / True value	1.00	0.999	1.01	-	1.15	0.999
Emp.SD	0.0775	0.00500	2.02	-	1.52	0.00500
Est.SD	0.0641	0.00541	1.67	-	0.754	0.00541

6. Numerical Study for Establishing a Standard Inference Method

6.1. Discerning between the Promotion and Initiation Effects

The last section examined "sensitivity," while this one deals with "specificity." That is, several models are applied to the same data to see if the correct model is identified. In this section, the algorithm may not converge successfully when inappropriate models are applied. This is a peculiar feature of the TSCE model. For empirical models like the Cox or logistic regression models, the algorithm almost always converges, even when those models are inappropriate, except for the monotone-likelihood phenomenon (Heinze and Schemper, 2004). This is because log-likelihood functions are normally concave in the entire parameter space, *i.e.*, the second derivatives are positive definite. In contrast, in the TSCE model, the log-likelihood functions are concave only within a small neighborhood of the MLE.

The models used for generating survival data are the same as in the last section. As for the models for estimating parameters, we do not use $\log\mu_2^*\_b$, since Section 5.2 suggests that $\log\mu_2^*\_b$ is not necessary to obtain the MLE of the original parameters $\log\psi$ and $\log\rho$. Therefore, we have three models (a, b, and c) for generation and three models (a2, b2, and c) for estimation. The dose distribution, algorithm, and convergence criteria used in this section are exactly the same as in the last section. Model selection was performed based on either Akaike information criterion (AIC) (Akaike, 1971) or the likelihood ratio test.

6.2. Results and Discussion

Table 3 presents the parameter estimates and Table 4 shows the proportions of the selected models. The average MLE and average number of iterations for convergence are also given in Table 4. Non-convergence occurs when initiation models are applied to the promotion model (Table 4(3)). The error rate of incorrectly selecting the promotion model for the two initiation models is only 2% (4 out of 200). In contrast, the error rate of incorrectly selecting the initiation models for the promotion model is 7%. The worst case is for estimating the balanced initiation model, for which 30 out of 100 were identified as $\log\psi\_b = 0$. Nevertheless, regarding the ability to distinguish between the initiation and promotion effects, the error rate is 2% (2/100), since the 30 cases also indicate initiation effects.

In conclusion, the simulation results indicate that the conditional-likelihood approach is reliable, feasible, and has a high ability to distinguish between initiation and promotion effects with a small sample size. To our knowledge, simulation studies for the original likelihood with a small sample have not been published.

Table 3. Estimates of parameters

(1) a. Simple initiation model

	$\log\psi\_a$	$\log\psi\_b \times 100$	$\log\rho\_a$	$\log\rho\_b \times 100$	$\log\eta\_a$	$\log\eta\_b \times 100$
True value	-4.9	-	-17	0.42	-0.08	0.72
a2. First Initiation	-4.86	-	-17.5	0.454	-0.237	0.454
b2. Semi full	-4.81	-0.022	-17.7	0.537	-0.359	0.559
c. Promotion	-5.13	0.129	-16.5	-	0.701	-0.129

(2) b. Balanced initiation model

	$\log\psi\_a$	$\log\psi\_b \times 100$	$\log\rho\_a$	$\log\rho\_b \times 100$	$\log\eta\_a$	$\log\eta\_b \times 100$
True value	-4.9	-0.1	-17	0.42	-0.08	0.75
a2. First Initiation	-5.07	-	-16.7	0.132	0.313	0.132
b2. Semi full	-4.85	-0.109	-17.5	0.478	-0.294	0.587
c. Promotion	-5.13	0.0385	-16.4	-	0.558	-0.039

(3) c. Promotion model

	$\log\psi\_a$	$\log\psi\_b \times 100$	$\log\rho\_a$	$\log\rho\_b \times 100$	$\log\eta\_a$	$\log\eta\_b \times 100$
True value	-3.3	0.35	-35	-	1.7	-0.35
a2. First Initiation	-3.07	-	-36.9	8.16	0.794	8.16
b2. Semi full	-3.27	0.0812	-36.0	6.29	1.45	6.21
c. Promotion	-3.30	0.350	-35.2	-	1.96	-0.35

Table 4. Results of model selection

(1) a. Simple initiation model

Model	**Average MLE**	**Average Iterations**	**Convergence Rate (%)**	**Proportion of selection**
a2. First Initiation	-2756	4.97	100	91/100
b2. Semi full	-2755.6	6.02	100	7/100
c. Promotion	-2762.8	4.31	100	2/100

Table 4. Continued

(2) b. Balanced initiation model

Model	Average MLE	Average Iterations	Convergence Rate (%)	Proportion of selection
a2. First Initiation	-2822.1	4.01	100	30/100
b2. Semi full	-2818.5	7.62	100	68/100
c. Promotion	-2824.5	4.1	100	2/100

(3) c. Promotion model

Model	Average MLE	Average Iterations	Convergence Rate (%)	Proportion of selection
a2. First Initiation	-2059.3	29.3	78	7/100
b2. Semi full	-2048.8	28.7	39	0/100
c. Promotion	-2039.5	9.83	100	93/100

7. Comparison between the TSCE Model and Proportional Hazards Model (PHM)

7.1. Radiation and Dioxin Data

Based on the results obtained in the previous sections, we applied the conditional-likelihood method to the JANUS experimental data on radiation effects in mice. The mice were either controls or exposed to ^{60}CO gamma rays or fission neutrons (mean energy 0.85 MeV) over a range of predetermined total doses calculated in centigray (cGy) at the midline of the mouse. Four types of experiments were performed: a single gamma exposure, 60 once-weekly gamma exposures, a single neutron exposure, and 60 once-weekly neutron exposures. The mice were examined histologically at time of death, the endpoint of interest being death due to or contributed by cancer. See Grahn *et al.* (1992) for a detailed description on the experiments.

We also applied the method to a toxicity study on TCDD in rats (Kociba *et al.*, 1978). The Kociba data dealt with female Sprague-Dawley rats maintained for two years on diets supplying 0, 1, 10 and 100 pg/kg/day and observed for each animal the date of death, the presence or absence of hepatocellular carcinoma or adenoma.

Basic information on the data is shown in Table 5. Each data set was analyzed using six estimation models (no dose, first initiation, promotion, second initiation, semi-full, and overall initiation) and the results are presented in Table 6. The second initiation has not been treated previously, but was included in the analysis for reference purposes.

Table 5. Basic information on the data

Exposure pattern	Dose*	Endpoint		Number of subjects
		Death	Censored	
Single gamma (n = 838)	0	42	149	191
	86.31	36	153	189
	137.1	36	114	150
	197.6	46	262	308
60 once-weekly gamma (n =1360)	0	75	483	558
	100.02	54	508	562
	199.98	25	139	164
	300	8	68	76
Single neutron (n =2823)	0	235	791	1026
	0.942	160	501	661
	2.355	97	314	411
	4.71	90	222	312
	9.42	70	160	230
	18.84	35	148	183
60 once-weekly neutron (n =1702)	0	84	450	534
	2.052	91	429	520
	7.698	31	173	204
	13.848	38	181	219
	21.546	32	193	225
Daily dioxin (n = 236)	0	2	84	86
	1	1	49	50
	10	9	41	50
	100	18	32	50

*Unit of dosage is cGy for radiation and pg/kg/day for dioxin

7.2. Analysis Using TSCE Model

The best-fitted model was determined based on the AIC and the likelihood ratio test, as in the previous section. For example, for the single gamma exposure data, the first initiation model has the largest likelihood among the three one-dose-rate parameter models and neither $\log\beta^*\_a$ nor $\log\mu_2{}^*\_a$ are significant with the likelihood ratio test (the difference between the log-likelihoods is 0.11 and 0.1, respectively). The best-fitted models determined based on criteria are given in Table 6.

The dose-rate initiation effect of the fractionated gamma exposure per 100 cGy is approximately 0.92 = exp(0.116–0.199) times that of the single gamma exposure.

On the other hand, the relative biological effectiveness (RBE) between gamma and neutron exposures is calculated by 0.0234/0.00116=20.2, since the dose-effect relationship is expected to be linear for the neutron exposure as well as the low-dose, fractionated gamma exposure. The result coincides with the ratio of radiation weighting factors according to the recommendations of the International Commission on Radiological Protections (ICRP, 1991).

Table 6. Best fit model by exposure pattern

Exposure pattern	$\log\psi\_a$	$\log\psi\_b \times 100$	$\log\rho\_a$	$\log\rho\_b \times 100$	$\log\eta\_a$	$\log\eta\_b \times 100$
Single gamma	-4.83	-	-17.0	0.199	-0.0149	0.199
60 once-weekly gamma	-4.76	-	-17.3	0.116	0.125	0.116
Single neutron	-4.89	-	-16.8	2.34	0.325	2.34
60 once-weekly neutron	-4.75	0.685	-17.5	-	0.117	-0.685
Daily dioxin	-3.33	0.35	-34.81	-		-1.68

7.3. Analysis Using PHM

We assume the ordinary proportional hazards model (Cox, 1972)

$$\lambda(t \mid D) = \lambda_0(t)e^{\beta D}$$

Where $\lambda_0(t)$ is an unspecified baseline hazard function and β a regression coefficient for a covariate D. The results obtained from applying the model to the JANUS data are tabulated in Table 7. The estimated regression coefficients, which are regarded as relative risks, are approximately equal to those for $\log\rho\_b$ in Table 6. RBE between gamma and neutron exposures is calculated by 2.36 / 0.112 = 21.1 as explained in 7.2, nearly equal to that obtained for the TSCE model in 7.1. The reason for the coincidence is discussed in Section 8.

Table 7. Parameter estimates

Exposure pattern	$\boldsymbol{\beta}$	**SE**	**p**
Single gamma	0.00209	0.000523	<.0001
60 once-weekly gamma	0.00112	0.000342	0.0011
Single neutron	0.0236	0.00437	<.0001
60 once-weekly neutron	0.024	0.00354	<.0001
Daily dioxin	0.0285	0.00399	<.0001

8. Concluding Remarks

Recently, considerable attention has been paid to the promoting action of radiation observed in atomic-bomb survivors (Heidenreich *et al.*, 2007). Nevertheless, the observation was considered problematic, since the promotion effect has never been observed for low-dose ionizing radiation in cellular experiments (Brugmans *et al.*, 2002) and the results of analysis using the TSCE model are very sensitive to its assumptions (Hornsby *et al.* 2007). This prompted us to develop the conditional-likelihood approach to find the MLEs of the biologically most significant parameters in the TSCE model without any additional assumptions. We have conducted extensive simulations to determine inference methods for reliable results using the TSCE model. To the best of our knowledge, no simulation studies been reported that examined the performance of the TSCE model with a small sample size based on the original likelihood.

Our simulation results suggest that the conditional-likelihood approach with $\delta = 0$ shows a practically sufficient sensitivity and specificity for the net proliferation rate ψ and the overall initiation rate ρ. Setting $\delta = 0$ is not the same as assuming $\delta = 0$. Leenhouts and Chadwick (1994), Leenhouts (1999), and Bijwaard *et al.* (2001) studied the model assuming $\delta = 0$ and found that the likelihood using $\delta = 0$ and the original likelihood yielded similar results; a mathematical explanation of this coincidence is described in Section 3.1.

For the estimation of dose-rate effects, we used a log-linear model (14) that allows the estimation of the effects on $\log\mu_1\mu_2$ without knowledge of X_0. Similar log-linear models for dose-rate effects were used by Moolgavkar and Luebeck (1990), with certain additional assumptions. Groos and Kopp-Schneider (2006) assume that the ratio β/δ is constant and independent of the exposure dose D. Section 3.3 asserts that under the assumptions, $\log\nu^*\_b$ and $\log\mu_2^*\_b$ are asymptotically unbiased estimates of $\log\nu\_b$ and $\log\mu_2\_b$, which represent the effects of exposure D on the first and the second initiation rates, respectively.

Portier and El Masri (1997) point out that algorithms to determine the MLE using the original likelihood with identifiable parameters may fail to converge because the likelihood surface can have a long ridge or may be extremely flat. This phenomenon of unstable performance even in the neighborhood of the MLE is peculiar with the original likelihood. Therefore, certain restrictions among the parameters as described in Introduction are usually employed to find restricted MLEs, consequently the generalization of the results are limited. Heidenreich *et al.* (2000) perform an inter-comparison of the results obtained by three carcinogenesis modeling groups on the same experimental data and reported that they reached different interpretations on the radiation effect on the model, even when starting from the same type of multi-step model. A resolution of the conflicts is left for future work. Section 3 seems to partly resolve the issue. According to Eq (4) in their paper, the parameters Y and γ used by the GSF group in Germany are equivalent to ρ and ψ in this study. On the other hand, the RIVM group in the Netherlands fitted a model with $\delta = 0$ ($\beta = 0$ in their notation). Therefore, their estimates of μ_1 and μ_2 are equivalent to μ_1^* and μ_2^* in our notation in Section 3. However, they treat their estimates as if they were unbiased estimates for the original parameters μ_1 and μ_2 in contrast to what Section 3 concludes.

The fact that the estimates and standard errors for $\log\rho$ and $\log\beta^*$ in Table 2(2) are virtually equal with those in Table 2(3) suggests that we may set $\log\mu_2^*\_b = 0$ in the conditional likelihood function for inferences on $\log\rho\_b$. This was expected since $\log\rho = \log\nu^* + \log\mu_2^*$. On the other hand, if $\log\beta^*\_b = \log\mu_2^*\_b = 0$ and only $\log\nu^*\_b > 0$, then it follows from (5) in 2.3 that the dose effect follows the proportional hazards model (Cox, 1972). Therefore, it is suggested that the conditional likelihood and the proportional hazards model will yield similar results as far as the relative risk for radiation exposure is concerned. This would be so in general, if the radiation exposure acts as an initiator rather than a promoter, that is, $\log\beta^*\_b$ should be much smaller than $\log\nu^*\_b$. This explains the similarity between the two models in the estimation of the relative biological effect between the gamma and neutron exposures by Baker *et al.* (2006) and Section 7.

It would be interesting to transform the RIVM estimates to unbiased estimates of the original parameters ρ and ψ using the results of Section 3.1 and compare them with Y and γ

used by GSF. However the transformation from Table 4 (RIVM) to Table 2 (GSF) in Heidenreich *et al.* (2000) is not straightforward, since the two groups use different parameters and assumptions in their model building processes.

9. Conclusion

From the theoretical and numerical investigations, we conclude that the conditional-likelihood approach has a practically sufficient ability to distinguish between the initiation and promotion effects with a small sample size. Since this approach requires no additional assumptions, the results should promote broader application of the TSCE model. The conditional-likelihood method merits further study, with the goal of establishing a standard inference technique for the TSCE model.

Acknowledgements

One of the investigators D. G. H. received support from a Department of Energy grant DE-FG02-08ER64605

References

Akaike, H. (1971). Information theory and an extension of the maximum likelihood principle. *Research Memo.* No. **46**, *The Institute of Statistical Mathematics.*

Andersen, P. K. (2002) Multi-state models for event history analysis, *Statistical Methods in medical research*, **11,** 91-115

Baker, G. S., Nakamura, T., and Hoel, D. G. (2006). Comparison of two models of cancer risk estimation: A statistical analysis. *European Journal of Oncology*, **11**, 165-176.

Bijwaard H., Brugmans, M. J. P. and Leenhouts, H. P. (2001). A consistent two-mutation model of lung cancer for different data sets of radon-exposed rats. *Radiation and Environmental Biophysics,* **40**, 269-277.

Brugmans, M. J. P., Bijwarrd, H., and Leenhouts, H. P. (2002). The overrated role of "Promotion" in mechanistic modeling of radiation carcinigenesis. *Journal of Radiological Protection,* **22**, A75-A79.

Brugmans, M. J. P., Rispens, S. M., Bijwaard, H., Laurier, D., Rogel, A., Tomášek, L. and Tirmarche, M. (2004). Radon-induced lung cancer in French and Czech miner cohorts described with a two-mutation cancer model. *Radiation and Environmental Biophysics,* **43**, 153-163.

Cox, D. R. (1972). Regression models and life tables. *Journal of the Royal Statistical Society,* **B34**, 187-220.

Cox, D. R. and Hinkley, D. V. (1974). *Theoretical Statistics.* London, Chapman and Hall.

Grahn, D., Lombard, L.S. and Carnes, B.A. (1992). The comparative tumorigenic effects of fission neutrons and cobalt-60 γ rays in the B6CF1 mouse. *Radiation Research,* **129**, 19-36.

Groos, J. and Kopp-Schneider, A. (2006). Application of a color-shift model with heterogeneous growth to a rat hepatocarcinogenesis experiment. *Mathematical Biosciences,* **202**, 248-268.

Hanin, L. G. and Yakovlev, A. Y. (1996). A nonidentifiable aspect of the two-stage model of Carcinogenesis. *Risk Analysis*, **16**, 711-715.

Hazelton, W. D., Luebeck, E. G., Heidenreich, W. F. and Moolgavkar, S. H. (2001). Analysis of a historical cohort of chinese tin miners with arsenic, radon, cigarette smoke, and pipe smoke exposures using the biologically based two-stage clonal expansion model. *Radiation Research*, **156**, 78-94.

Heidenreich, W. F. (1996). On the Parameters of the Clonal Expansion Model. *Radiation and Environmental Biophysics,* **35**, 127-129.

Heidenreich, W. F., Luebeck, E. G. and Moolgavkar, S. H. (1997). Some properties of the hazard function of the two-mutation clonal expansion model. *Risk Analysis*, **17**, 391-399.

Heidenreich, W. F., Brugmans, M. J. P., Little, M. P., Leenhouts, H. P., Paretzke, H. G., Morin, M., Lafuma, J. (2000). Analysis of lung tumour risk in radon-exposed rats: An intercomparison of multi-step modeling. *Radiation and Environmental Biophysics*, **39**, 253-264.

Heinze, G., and Schemper, M. (2001). A solution to the problem of monotone likelihood in cox regression. *Biometrics,* **57**, 114-119.

Hornsby, C., Page, K. M., and Tomlinson, I.P. (2007). What can we learn from the population incidence of cancer? Armitage and Doll revisited. *Lancet Oncology,* **8**, 1030-1038.

ICRP. (1991). *ICRP Publication 60: 1990 Recommendations of the International Commission on Radiological Protection*, **60**. Oxford, Pergamon Press.

Heidenreich, W. F., Cullings, H. M., Funamoto, S. and Paretzke, H. G. (2007). Promoting Action of Radiation in the Atomic Bomb Survivor Carcinogenesis Data? *Radiation Research,* **168**, 750- 756.

Kociba, R. J., Keyes, D. G., Beyer, J.E., Carreon, R. M., Wade, C. E., Dittenber, D. A., Kalnins, R. P., Frauson, L. E., Park, C. N. (1978). Results of a two-year chronic toxicity and oncogenicity study of 2,3,7,8-tetrachlorodibenzo-p-dioxin in rats. *Toxicology and Applied Pharmacology,* **46** (2), 279-303.

Kopp-Schneider, A., Portier, C. J. and Sherman, C. D. (1994). The exact formula for tumor incidence in the two-stage model. *Risk Analysis*, **14**, 1079-1080.

Leenhouts, H. P. and Chadwick, H. C. (1994). A two-mutation model of radiation carcinogenesis: application to lung tumors in rodents and implications for risk evaluation. *Journal of Radiological Protection,* **14**, 2115-2130.

Leenhouts, H. P. (1999). Radon-induced lung cancer in smokers and non-smokers: risk implications using a two-mutation carcinogenesis model. *Radiation and Environmental Biophysics,* **38**, 57-71.

Luebeck, E. G., Moolgavkar, S. H., Buchmann, A. and Schwarz, M. (1991). Effects of Polychlorinated Biphenyls in Rat Liver: Quantitative Analysis of Enzyme-Altered Foci. *Toxicology and Applied Pharmacology*, **111**, 469-484.

Luebeck, E. G., Heidenreich, W. F., Hazelton, W. D., Paretzke, H. G. and Moolgavkar, S. H. (1999). Biologically based analysis of the data for the Colorado uranium miners cohort: Age, dose and dose-rate effects. *Radiation Research,* **152**, 339-351

Moolgavkar, S. H. and Venzon, D. (1979). Two-Event Models for Carcinogenesis: Curves for childhood and adult tumors. *Mathematical Biosciences,* **47**, 55-77.

Moolgavkar, S. H. (1986). Carcinogenesis modeling: From molecular biology to epidemiology. *Annual Reviews in Public Health,* **7**, 151-169.

Moolgavkar, S. H. and Luebeck, E. G. (1990). Two-event model for carcinogenesis: Biological, mathematical, and statistical considerations. *Risk Analysis,* **10**, 323-341.

Moolgavkar, S. H. and Luebeck, E. G. (1992). Multistage carcinogenesis: a population perspective on colon cancer. *Journal of the National Cancer Institute*, **84**, 610-618.

Moolgavkar, S. (1999). Stochastic Models for Estimation and Prediction of Cancer Risk. In V. Barnet, A. Stein, and K. F. Turkmen (Eds.), *Statistics for the Environment* **4** (pp.237-257). Chichester, Wiley.

Nakamura, T and Hoel, D. G. (2003). Comparing cancer risks between radiation and dioxin exposure based on two-stage model, *Environmetrics,* **14**, 203-211

Nogami, S., Yoshida, Y. and Nakamura, T. (2007). On the reliability of maximum likelihood estimates in the two-Stage clonal expansion carcinogenesis model. In L. Edler. (Ed.) *Programme and Abstracts of the International Conference on Statistical Methods for Risk Analysis* (pp. 43-44). Lisbon.

Portier, C. and Edler, L. (1990). Two-stage models of carcinogenesis, classification of agents, and design of experiments. *Fundamental and Applied Toxicology,* **14**, 444-460

Portier, C., Kopp-Schneider, A. and Sherman, D. (1995). Calculating tumor incidence rates in stochastic models of carcinogenesis. *Mathematical Biosciences,* **135**, 129-146.

Portier, C. and El Masri, H. (1997). Statistical research needs in mechanistic modeling for carcinogenic risk assessment. *Statistical Methods for Medical Research,* **6**, 305-315.

Portier, C., Sherman, C. D. and Kopp-Schneider, A. (2000). Multistage, stochastic models of the cancer process: A general theory for calculating tumor incidence. *Stochastic Environmental Research and Risk Assessment,* **14**, 173-179.

Portier, C. J. (2001). Linking toxicology and epidemiology: the role of mechanistic modeling. *Statistics in Medicine,* **20**, 1387-1393.

Schöllnberger, H., Manuguerra, M., Bijwaard, H., Boshuizen, H., Altenburg, H. P., Rispens, S. M., Brugmans, M. J. P. and Vineis, P. (2006). Analysis of epidemiological cohort data on smoking effects and lung cancer with a multi-stage cancer model. *Carcinogenesis,* **27**, 1432-1444.

Sherman, C. D. and Portier, C. (1997). The two-stage model of carcinogenesis: overcoming the nonidentifiability dilemma, *Risk Analysis,* **17**, 367-374.

Tessier, G. S., Lam, C. F., Nakamura, T. and Hoel, D. G. (2001). Two-stage models applied to gamma and neutron exposed mice. *European Journal of Oncology,* **6**, 297-301.

In: Risk Management
Editors: B. Jordão and E. Sousa, pp. 225-293

ISBN: 978-1-60876-011-4

Chapter 9

CHLORINE AND SOLUTE TRANSPORT AND REACTIONS IN DRINKING WATER DISTRIBUTION: THE ROLE OF FLOW HYDRODYNAMICS ON WATER QUALITY CHANGES AND MULTI-CRITERIA COMPLIANCE

***Y. Jeffrey Yang*[*,1], *Robert M. Clark*[≠,2] and *Audrey D. Levine*[†,3]**

[1] U.S. EPA, Office of Research and Development, National Risk Management Research Laboratory, Cincinnati, Ohio

[2] Environmental Engineering and Public Health Consultant, Cincinnati, Ohio, USA

[3] U.S. EPA, Office of Research and Development, Washington, D.C., USA.

Abstract

Safe drinking water supply is one of the most notable modern engineering achievements in the 20th century. It is a centerpiece of the U.S. environmental protection effort under the federal Safe Drinking Water Act (SDWA) and its amendments. In this chapter, water quality changes are analyzed for chlorine disinfectant as a reactive solute transporting in the drinking water distribution pipes. The solute fate and transport phenomena under discussion fall into two broad categories: chlorine decay throughout a distribution network, and dispersion-reaction of "foreign" contaminants in discrete volumes. Common to the two categories are their convection-dispersion-reaction (CDR) process. From here, the role of pipe flow hydrodynamics in kinetics of chlorine decay and water quality changes is reviewed in a stepwise theoretical analysis of the Dankwerts CDR model and its simplifications. The

---

[*] E-mail address: yang.jeff@epa.gov. Phone: (01)-513-569-7655. (Corresponding author). U.S. EPA, Office of Research and Development, National Risk Management Research Laboratory, MS 690, 26W Martin Luther King Dr., Cincinnati, Ohio 45268, USA

[≠] E-mail address: rmclark@fuse.net

[†] E-mail address: levine.audrey@epa.gov

analysis is also supported by field observations reported in literature and by the testing results of controlled pilot-scale experiments. Through the analysis, complexities in chlorine's physiochemical interactions with other solutes and pipe walls begin to emerge in light of a flow hydrodynamic field, pointing to the challenge as well as potentials to prevent excessive quality deterioration and achieve simultaneous multi-criteria compliance required by the SDWA regulations. The effects of pipe flow properties (e.g, Reynolds number) on the reaction kinetics of chlorine and other solutes in water are quantified, the current state of knowledge and future research needs are identified for optimization of the water distribution process design and operations.

1. Introduction

Solute transport and reactions in a flowing pipe can alter the physiochemical and biological qualities of drinking water in its distribution from a treatment plant to the consumer's tap. They are of fundamental interest to fluid dynamic research and drinking water engineering. As a principal physical asset of municipal water supply, a distribution network consists of interconnected pipes hundreds of thousand kilometers in length, storage tanks and reservoirs of various sizes, valves, pump stations, and other auxiliary structures (Walski et al., 2003). There are many factors that affect the water quality in the network. To address the water quality challenge and protect public health, U.S. Environmental Protection Agency (US EPA) has regulated drinking water quality under the 1974 landmark legislation Safe Drinking Water Act (SDWA) and subsequent amendments. Accompanying the legislation is a sustained research in areas of modeling, monitoring, and engineering control on water quality changes, network design and operations.

The first municipal water utility in the U.S. was established in 1652 in Boston (Massachusetts, U.S.) for domestic water supply and fire protection (Hanke, 1972). By 1860, there were 136 water systems in the U.S., most of which supplied water from springs low in turbidity and relatively free from pollution (Baker, 1948). By the end of 1800s, waterborne disease was recognized as a serious problem in industrialized river valleys. Subsequently, chlorine disinfection was adopted for better sanitary water supply in the U.S. after successful application and demonstration in England in 1908. The rate of common epidemics such as typhoid and cholera has dropped significantly since the time. For example, effective water treatment resulted in a decline of typhoid deaths in Pittsburgh (Pennsylvania, U.S.) from 158 per 100,000 in the 1880s to 5 per 100,000 in 1935 (Fujiwara et al., 1995). Similarly, both typhoid case and death rates for the City of Cincinnati (Ohio, U.S.) declined more than tenfold in the period 1898 to 1928 due to the use of sand filtration, disinfection via chlorination, and the application of drinking water standards (Clark et al., 1985). Maintaining residual disinfectant levels in water distribution was attributed to the success in water quality protections prior to the delivery at a consumer's tap.

In the U.S., a water distribution system serves dual functions of providing fire-fighting capacity and potable water for domestic consumptions. The water supply function requires prevention of water quality deteriorations during distribution. This chapter is devoted to review the subject and analyze relationships between water quality changes and pipe flow hydrodynamics. A pair of water quality variables – chlorine decay and disinfection by-products (DBP) formation – is used as an example to illustrate the role of pipe flow in a competitive chemical reaction system. Section 1.0 provides an introduction and gives an overview of the distribution system history, the evolution of water quality requirements and regulatory standards. Section 2.0 analyzes the hydrodynamic properties and other factors such as pipe materials that affect water qualities. Attention is paid to chlorine decay and DBP formation as an example of simultaneous compliance to the EPA's Total Coliform Rules (TCR) and the Disinfection / Disinfection By-Product (D/DBP) rules. Solute (e.g., chlorine) fate and transport in a flowing water pipe are examined to unearth the interdependency between water quality change and hydrodynamic properties. In Section 3.0, the fate and transport of a "slug" of foreign contaminant introduced into a flowing water pipe are described and examined to show how the hydrodynamic factors affect the contaminant transport and propagation. Foreign contaminants as a discrete "slug" of solutes are the other major category of process contributing to significant water quality deterioration in a distribution network. Because of distinct hydrodynamic properties, they deserve separate attention in this review.

1.1. The Dual Service Functions of a Distribution Network

Since the first commercial application in 1652, water distribution networks in the U.S. have carried two service functions in a single physical network: water supply and fire-fighting. A detailed understanding of "how water is used" in a distribution network is critical to the network design and operation. The manner in which industrial and residential customers use water drives the overall hydrodynamic properties of a network, and thus determines its design and operational attributes. Water demand and usage in a distribution network varies both spatially and temporally. This non-stationary water demand in the form of varying water withdrawal rates must be satisfied at every portion of the network. Furthermore, most U.S. distribution networks also serve to provide adequate standby fire-flow capacity (Fair and Geyer, 1971). Fire hydrants are installed in areas that are easily accessible to fire fighters but possess no obstacles to pedestrians and vehicles. The ready-to-serve flow and pressure requirements for fire fighting are governed by the National Fire Protection Association that establishes standards for fire-fighting capacity of a distribution network (NFPA, 2003). The extra volume reserved for standby fire-fighting capacity, however, can result in long water residence time in the network, which is unnecessary for domestic water supplies but nonetheless results in significant, yet unwanted, water quality changes.

A typical distribution network consists of several major hydraulic components, including storage tanks and reservoirs, water pipes, valves, pumps, hydrants and other auxiliary apparatus, network monitoring and control equipment. Among them, the storage tanks/reservoirs and water pipes are the two most important components (Fig. 1) where significant water quality changes may take place:

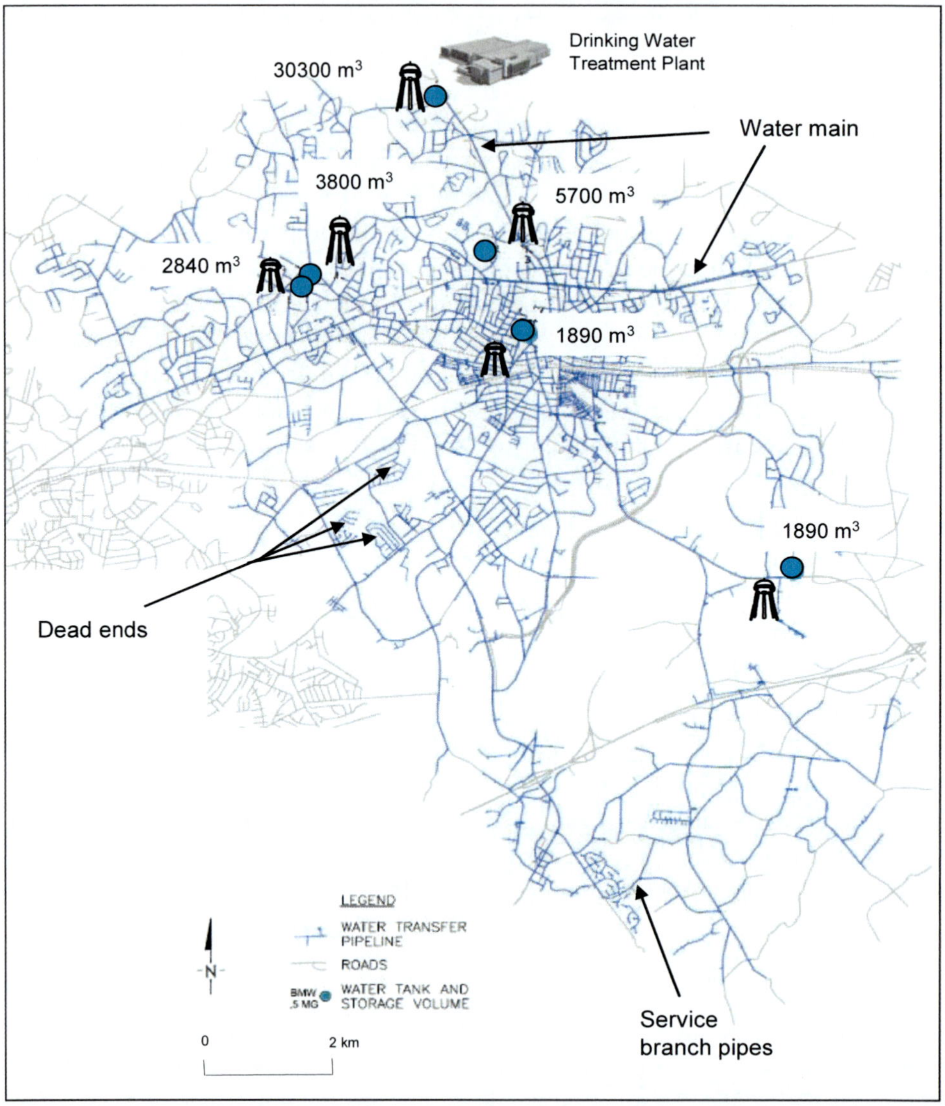

Figure 1. An example of municipal distribution system in a typical southeastern U.S. city. The distribution network transfers an average of 22700 m^3/day drinking water from the drinking water plant in the north to over 12000 customers in over 250 km^2 service areas. Six water storage tanks, each over 1890 m^3 storage capacity, and power equipment are used in managing network pressure and supplying water to commercial customers in the center business district, residential consumers in city perimeters, and the industries in the south. Examples of dead ends are marked, illustrating large hydrodynamic changes potentially in a distribution network.

Storage Tanks/Reservoirs

Tanks and reservoirs are used to provide storage capacity to meet flow fluctuations in demand, to provide reserves for fire-fighting and other emergency situations, and to equalize pressures in a distribution network. Elevated tanks are the most frequently used storage facility; other types of tanks and reservoirs include in-ground tanks and open or closed reservoirs. Construction materials are generally concrete and steel. An issue that has drawn a great deal of interest is the problem of water turnover within a storage facility (Clark et al., 1996b; Grayman et al., 2004). Because much of the water storage is allocated to fire protection, the stored water can become stagnant and experience aging and mixing problems leading to stratification and/or large stagnant zones within the water volume and thus the accelerated water quality deterioration.

Pipe Network

The networks of pipes or "mains" that carry water from the source such as a treatment plant to consumers are often categorized as transmission/trunk, distribution, and service mains (Fig.1). Transmission/trunk mains usually convey large amounts of water over a long distance from a treatment facility to a storage tank. Distribution mains are smaller in diameter and generally follow city streets. Service mains are pipes that carry water from a distribution main to the building or property being served (Fig.1). In general, even a medium-sized water utility may have thousands of kilometers of buried pipes constructed from various types of materials ranging from new and lined metal pipes, to plastic pipes, wood pipes of old construction, and to unlined pipes that are more than 50 years old. Over time, biofilms and tubercles attach to pipe walls. They often result in both loss of carrying capacity and a significant loss of disinfectant residual, thereby adversely affecting water quality (Clark and Tippen, 1990).

Water pipes and other distribution network components form a hydraulically connected flow field of varying hydrodynamic properties determined by how water flows into the network from a water treatment plant or a storage facility and how water is withdrawn at user points. Generally, turbulent flows prevail in major water mains while laminar, even stagnant, flows occur frequently in service branches and pipe dead ends (Walski et al., 2003; Rossman, 2000; Rossman and Boulos, 1996). As examined later in the chapter, there is a close relationship among hydrodynamic properties, water age, and water quality changes. This phenomenon deserves attention in drinking water distribution network operations and in water quality management.

In the section that follows, the evolution of distribution network buildup and water quality requirements is reviewed to place the discussions under a proper technological and regulatory background.

1.2. Water Quality Requirements for Water Supply

Since the late 1890s, concerns over waterborne disease and uncontrolled water pollution have regularly translated into legislation at the state and federal levels. The first federal water quality regulation was promulgated in 1912 under the Interstate Quarantine Act of 1893. At that time, interstate railroads provided a common drinking water cup to share among passengers while traveling on the train, a practice that the Act prohibited. Prior to 1962, several sets of federal drinking water standards were issued but applied only to interstate carriers (Grindler, 1967; Clark, 1978). By the 1960s, each of the states and trust territories had established its own drinking water regulations.

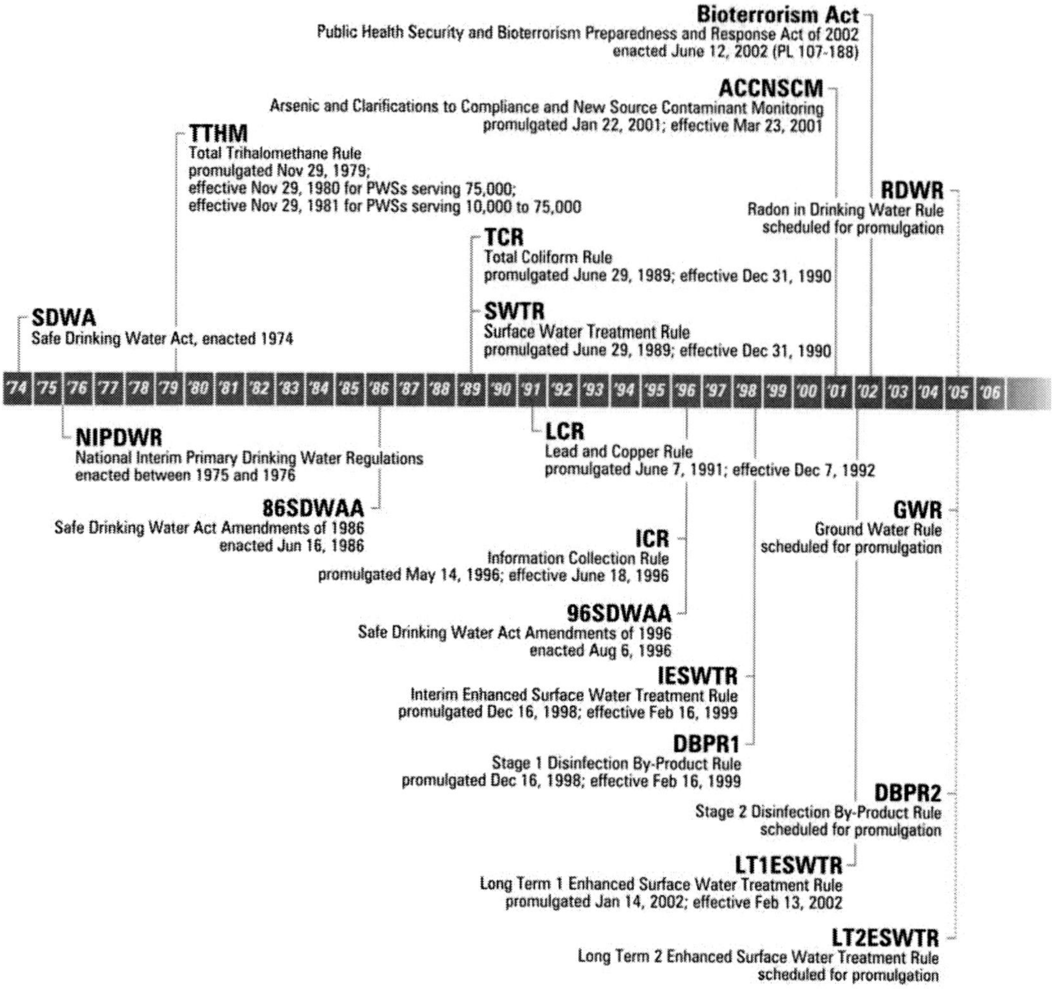

Figure 2. Time evolution of the U.S. federal Safe Drinking Water Act (SDWA) and amendments since the initial Act enactment on December 16, 1974. The SDWA amendments, notably in the 1990s, intend to regulate a various type of water quality constituents with a purpose to provide chemically and biological safe drinking water to consumers. A multi-barrier strategy is often required for simultaneous compliance to SDWA regulations; for example, the biological disinfection for TCR and SWTR compliance and the DBP controls under the DBPR1 and DBPR2 regulations.

As in many other developed nations, water utilities in the U.S. vary in size, ownership, and types of operation. A variety of water distribution networks were being developed for drinking water delivery, and public concerns over water safety became the driving force in demanding for close monitoring and regulatory oversight. This eventually led to the establishment of a set of drinking water regulations. Despite earlier success in reducing waterborne diseases, the annual number of outbreaks remained static around 1951 and may have increased slightly after that time (Clark, 1978). The stagnation in progress led, in part, to the passage of the Safe Drinking Water Act of 1974 on December 16, 1974. Through the landmark legislation, the U.S. Congress authorized US EPA to promulgate the first set of federal regulations which would "protect health to the extent feasible, using technology, treatment techniques, and other means, which the Administrator determines are generally available (taking costs into consideration)". As a result, a set of regulations was promulgated in 1975 and became effective on June 24, 1977. These were known as the National Interim Primary Drinking Water Regulations (NIPDWR). The NIPDWR established enforceable Maximum Contaminant Levels (MCLs) for 10 inorganic contaminants, six organic contaminants, turbidity, coliform, ^{226}Ra, ^{228}Ra, gross alpha activity, and other man-made radionuclides.

Regulations under the SDWA apply to all public water systems (PWSs); that is, to those systems that regularly serve 25 or more people at least 60 days out of the year or that have 15 or more service connections. The SDWA defines a PWS as one of community water supply (CWS) systems, transient, non-community water supply (TNCWS) systems, and non-transient, non-community water supply (NTNCWS) systems. The CWS systems provide year-round services to residents and range in size from those that serve as few as 25 people to those that serve several million. TNCWS systems serve areas such as campgrounds or gas stations where people do not remain for long periods of time. A NTNCWS system serves primarily non-residential customers, but must serve at least 25 of the same people for at least six months of the year. Examples include schools, hospitals, and factories that have their own water supply. It is estimated that as of 2005, there were 159,796 water systems in the U.S. that meet the federal definition of a PWS. Thirty-three percent of these systems were categorized as CWS systems, 55% are categorized as TNCWSs, and 12% are NTNCWS systems. Overall, PWSs served 297 million residential and commercial customers. Although the vast majority (98%) of PWSs served less than 10,000 people, almost three quarters of the U.S. population obtained water from community water supplies serving more than 10,000 people. Some water systems deliver water to other water supplies, or those known as water distributors, rather than directly to customers.

US EPA has promulgated a series of rules and regulations as a result of the SDWA that require drinking water utilities to meet specific guidelines and numeric standards for water quality. Some of the rules that specifically target water quality within a distribution network are the Lead and Copper Rule (LCR), the Surface Water Treatment Rule (SWTR), the Total Coliform Rule (TCR), and the Disinfectants/Disinfection By-Products Rule (D/DBPR). The LCR established monitoring requirements for lead and copper in tap water samples. The SWTR establishes the minimum disinfectant residual and the maximum allowable heterotrophic bacterial plate count within a distribution network. The TCR requires monitoring of the distribution networks for total coliforms, fecal coliforms, and/or *Escherichia coli* O157:H7 (*E. coli*). The D/DBPR addresses the maximum disinfectant residual and concentration of disinfection by-products such as total trihalomethanes (TTHMs) and total haloacetic acids in the distribution networks. Figure 2 illustrates the evolution of federal drinking water regulation since the passage of the SDWA in 1974. Table 1 shows the current SDWA Rules and Regulations governing distributed drinking water. At the center of regulations is drinking water disinfection at a water treatment plant and in a distribution network (LeChevallier et al., 2008)

In the U.S., chlorine and chloramines are most often used in drinking water disinfection because they are effective in pathogen inactivation and the residual concentrations can be maintained in the water distribution network at a level required by the SDWA regulatory standards. Some utilities in the U.S. and Europe use ozone and chlorine dioxide as the oxidizing agents for primary disinfection in water treatment prior to addition of chlorine or chloramines for residual disinfection. For example, the Netherlands identifies ozone as the primary disinfectant, as well as the common use of chlorine dioxide, but typically uses no chlorine or other disinfectant residual in the distribution network (Connell, 1998). While disinfectants are effective in controlling many microorganisms, they can also react with natural organic matter (NOM) in the treated and/or distributed water to form potentially harmful DBPs. To minimize the formation of DBP compounds and hence reduce their health risk, US EPA has promulgated regulations that specify maximum residual disinfectant level goals (MRDLGs) for chlorine (4 mg/L as chlorine), chloramines (4 mg/L as chlorine), and chlorine dioxide (0.8 mg/L as chlorine dioxide). In addition, MCLs for the TTHMs and five haloacetic acids (HAA_5) as the disinfection by-products have been established as 0.080 and 0.060 mg/L, respectively. The regulated TTHMs include chloroform, bromodichloromethane, dibromochloromethane and bromoform. The regulated HAA_5 are monochloroacetic acid, dichloroacetic acid, trichloroacetic acid, monobromoacetic acid, and dibromoacetic acid.

Table 1. Partial listing of rules and regulations governing water qualities in a drinking water distribution system.

Regulation	Key Distribution System Requirements
SDWA	Gives EPA the authority to establish national primary and secondary drinking water regulations (MCLs and MCLGs).
NIPDWR	The NIPDWR which was adopted at the passage of the SDWA required that representative coliform samples be collected throughout the distribution system.
TTHM	Established a standard for TTHMs as 0.1 mg/L.
86SDWAA	Established the MCLG concept.
TCR	Regulates coliform bacteria which are used as surrogate organisms to indicate whether or not treatment is effective and system contamination is occurring.
SWTR	Requires using chlorine or some other disinfectant.
LCR	Monitoring for compliance with the LCR is based entirely on samples taken at the consumer's tap.
ICR	Provided data to support the interim and long-term enhanced SWTR, and Stage 2 DBP rule.
96SDWAA	Has many provisions dealing with distribution systems, including the role that surface water quality can play in influencing the quality of distributed water.
IESWTR	Provisions to enhance protection from pathogens, including *Cryptosporidium*, and intended to prevent increases in microbial risk while large systems comply with the DBPR1.
DBPR1	This standard applies to all. Has lowered the standard for TTHMs from 0.1 mg/L to 0.08 mg/L. community water supplies in the U. S. and requires monitoring and compliance at selected points in the distribution system.
LT1ESWTR	Provisions to enhance protection from pathogens, including *Cryptosporidium*, and prevent increases in microbial risk for systems serving less than 10,000 people while they comply with the DBPR1.

Some epidemiological and outbreak investigations conducted in the last decade suggest that a substantial proportion of waterborne disease outbreaks, both microbial and chemical, are attributable to problems within distribution networks (e.g., Lee et al. 1991, Craun and Calderon, 2001; Blackburn et al., 2004). As shown in Figure 3, the proportion of waterborne disease outbreaks associated with problems in a distribution network is increasing after 1980 despite the decrease in total number of reported waterborne disease outbreaks. The decrease in numbers of waterborne disease outbreaks per year is probably attributable to improved water treatment practices and compliance with the SWTR, which reduced the risk from water borne protozoa (Pierson et al., 2001; Blackburn et al., 2004). Two extensively studied examples of waterborne disease in the U.S. were an *E. coli* outbreak in Cabool (Missouri, U.S.) in 1989 and a Salmonella outbreak in Gideon (Missouri, U.S.) in 1993. These two examples illustrate the importance of the multiple-barrier concept in which water quality protection in the distribution network is an essential component. In both case studies, the water source was non-disinfected groundwater and the utility's infrastructure was breached allowing contaminants to enter the system leading to the waterborne outbreaks. The deterioration in water quality and the resulting health risks were the results of multiple defects including source water contamination, inadequate treatment, and breeches in the distribution network (Clark et al., 1993a, b, and 1996a).

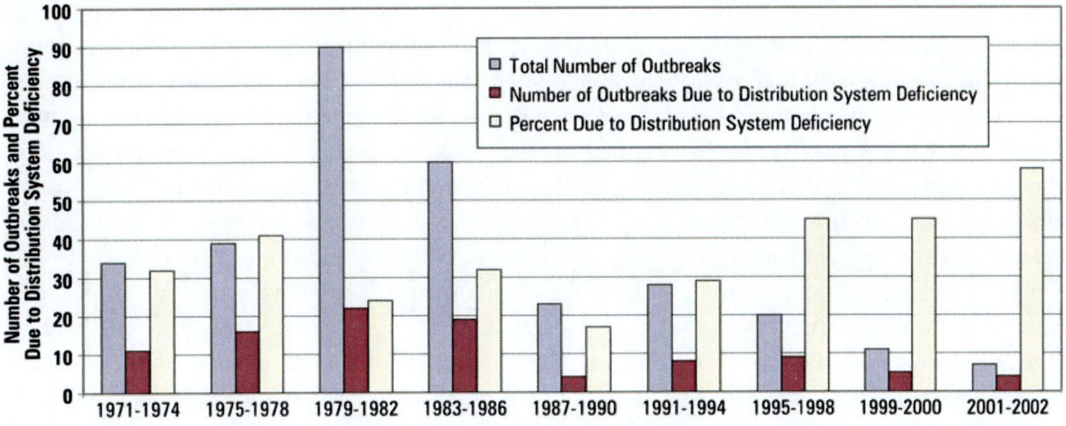

Figure 3. The change with time of waterborne disease outbreaks in CWS' and the proportion of outbreaks due to distribution system deficiencies. After the SDWA legislations and implementation, the outbreaks and those due to the system deficiencies both declined. The improvement ceased in the late 1980s when the fraction of system-failure related outbreak actually increased over time.

Recently, distribution network security has become an issue for the water utility industry in addition to the rules and regulations promulgated under the SDWA. Security of water systems is not new. The potential for natural, accidental, and purposeful contamination of water supplies has been the subject of many recent studies (Kunkel et al., 2008; WHO, 2004; Murray et al., 2006; Jain and McLean, 2006). In May 1998, the Presidential Decision Directive 63 was issued to outline a policy on protection of critical infrastructure including water supplies (PDD 63, 1998). It was not until after September 11, 2001, that the water industry focused on the vulnerability of the nation's water supplies to security threats. In recognition of these issues, the Public Health Security and Bioterrorism Preparedness and Response Act of 2002 (Bioterrorist Act) was signed into law (PL107-188, 2002) in June 2002 (See Fig.2). Under the requirements of the Bioterrorism Act, a CWS serving more than 3,300 people is required to prepare vulnerability assessments and emergency response plans.

In summary, both external and internal factors can result in water quality deterioration in a distribution pipe. External factors include the influx of contaminants into distribution pipes through breaks, leaks and cross-connections, or by intentional sabotage. This category of external contamination can also introduce nutrients and foreign contaminants, decrease disinfectant concentrations, and lead to a degradation of the drinking water quality. Internal factors include chemical and physical transformations that take place in the water distribution. Sometimes external and internal factors are difficult to differentiate for the observed quality deterioration in a water distribution network. For example, decreases in disinfectant concentrations associated with retention time in the distribution network might be due to intrusions of external contaminants or as the result of the disinfectant reactions that occur with pipe walls and with natural organic matter in the bulk water.

1.3. Factors Affecting Water Quality in Distribution Networks

Some important concerns over water quality deterioration in distribution networks include maintenance of proper disinfectant levels; minimization of DBP formation; turbidity, taste, color, and odor issues; distribution tank mixing and utilization; water main repair and pressure stabilization; flow management; cross-connection control and back-flow prevention. Depending on the design and operation of a particular system, there are many opportunities for water quality to change as water moves from treatment plant to the consumers. These unwanted changes may occur for various reasons such as failures at the treatment barrier, chemical reactions and transformations in the bulk water phase, corrosion and leaching of pipe material, biofilm formation, and mixing between different sources of water. It is extensively studied that bacteriological growth inside a flowing pipe can cause taste-and-odor problems, discoloration, slime buildup, and economic problems such as biological deterioration of pipe materials (Water Research Centre, 1976). Bacterial numbers tend to increase during distribution depending on factors such as bacterial quality of the finished water, water temperature, residence time, presence or absence of a disinfectant residual, construction materials, and availability of nutrients for growth (e.g., Geldreich et al., 1972; LeChevallier et al., 1987, 2008; Maul et al., 1985a,b; Zhang and DiGiano, 2002; Camper et al., 2003).

Maintenance of a disinfectant residual throughout a distribution network is considered an important element of water quality management in a multiple barrier strategy. Recently, LeChevallier et al. (2008) pointed out that water disinfection is at the center of multi-barrier water quality protections and calls for other forms of regulations such as D/DPB rules and LCR. Generally, the presence of a disinfection residual is desirable because it can inactivate pathogenic organisms. The absence of a disinfectant residual may indicate that the water quality integrity of a system has been compromised, possibly by intrusion, nitrification, or because of an excessive chlorine residual loss (also known as chlorine decay) from corrosion of iron pipes, pipe pitting and thinning, pipe leaks, or unusual biofilm growths. For example, US EPA (2002) evaluated the prevalence of foreign intrusions in water distribution due to pipe breaks and described several instances where the intrusions had resulted in severe public health impacts. These instances included the outbreak of hemorrhagic *E. coli* serotype 0157:H7 in Cabool (Missouri, U.S.) during December 1989 and January 1990, which led to 240 cases of diarrhea and 4 deaths (Geldreich, 1996).

In pipes, chlorine decay may occur in reaction with NOM in the bulk water phase and in interaction with pipe walls during the water distribution (Fig. 4). The pipe wall demand, possibly due to reaction with biofilm or pipe materials, may consume chlorine residual rapidly. Maintaining adequate levels of the disinfectant residual may require routine cleaning or replacement of pipes and intensive treatment (Clark et al., 1993a,b), and chlorine addition at boost stations within the distribution network (Boccelli et al., 1998, 2003). Prior to the SDWA passage, most drinking water utilities concentrated on meeting drinking water standards at the treatment plant, even though it had long been recognized that water quality could deteriorate substantially in a distribution network. After its passage, the SDWA requires that certain federal water quality standards be met at various points within a distribution network.

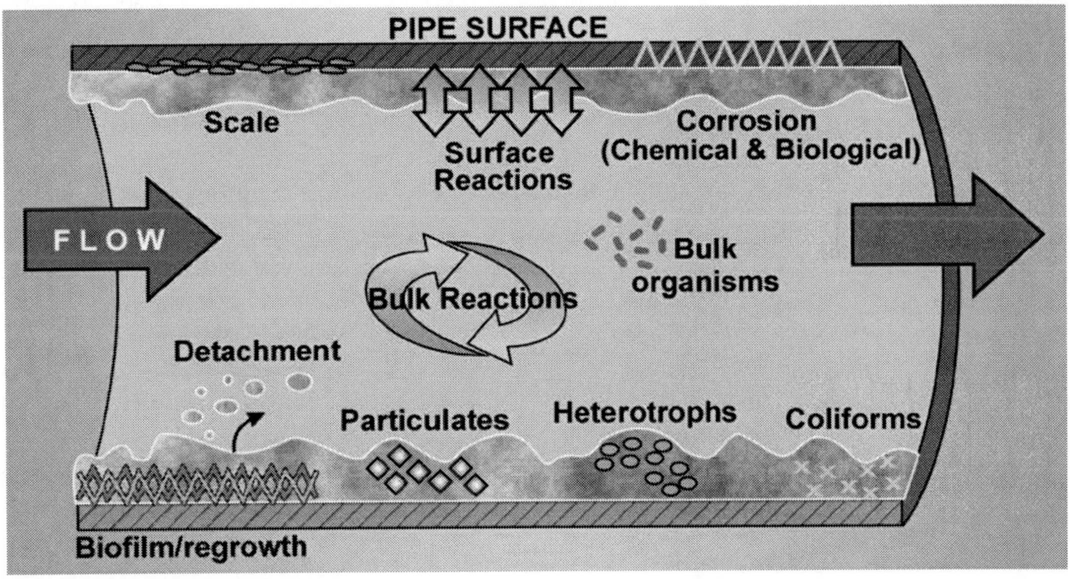

Figure 4. Schematics of principal factors that affect chlorine decay and transport in a flowing water pipe conceptualized as a complex plug flow chemical reactor. Pipe wall demand results from chlorine interactions with pipe scales of inorganic materials (e.g., iron oxide particulates), biological organisms (e.g., heterotrophy and coliforms), and absorbed organic contaminants. When detached, the pipe scale becomes a part of the chlorine bulk demand along with chemical and biological reactants (e.g., organisms) in the water bulk phase. In addition, chlorine is subject to hydraulic dispersion in a flowing pipe.

Bulk demand and wall demand are the two sources of chlorine decay in a flowing pipe. The phenomena have been extensively studied since the early time (e.g, Feben and Taras, 1951); yet the precise mechanism for chlorine consumption in a given distribution network is far from being well quantified. Some factors affecting chlorine fate and transport in a flowing water pipe include biofilm growth, nitrification, pipe leaching, internal corrosion, scale formation, and chemical reactions that include the loss of disinfectant residual or the DBP formation (Table 2). In broad terms, the loss of disinfectant residual is a result of chlorine reduction in the bulk water phase and at the pipe-water interface, although nitrification (in the case of chloramine) can also be a factor. In the bulk water phase, dissolved constituents including NOM and inorganic materials (e.g., Fe^{2+} and Mn^{2+}) act as reducing agents that react with the disinfectant These substances are present in the water either as a result of incomplete removal during treatment, the corrosion of pipe material (e.g., cast iron), or the reduction of existing insoluble iron and manganese deposits. As early as in 1953 (Williams, 1953), for example, it was found that the loss of both chlorine and chloramine residuals in the Brantford (New Hampshire, U.S.) water system was related to an increase in ferrous iron caused by corrosion in the distribution network pipes. Benjamin et al (1996) found that the accumulation of iron corrosion products at the pipe wall and the uptake of these products into the bulk water led to a deterioration of water quality. There also are several reports that the loss of chlorine residuals in corroded unlined metallic pipes, particularly cast iron, increases with increasing velocity (Powell, 1998; Powell et al., 2000; Grayman et al., 2002; Doshi et al., 2003). Evidence for the role of corrosion in reducing disinfectant residuals was described by Camper et al. (2003), who studied the interactions among pipe materials, organic carbon levels, and disinfectants using annular reactors with ductile–iron, polyvinyl chloride (PVC), epoxy, and cement-lined coupons at four field sites. They found that iron surfaces supported much higher bacterial populations than other materials, which serve as a line sink in the chlorine residual loss.

Table 2. Major factors affecting chlorine decay in a flowing drinking water pipe.

Process/factor	Chlorine Decay Mechanism	Major Factors	Reference
Biofilm growth	1) Attached biofilm as a chlorine sink in disinfection	Cl mass transfer to pipe wall Biological composition and regwoth, Temperature, pH, Eh	Clark and Haught (2005), LeChevallier et al. (1987), Rossman (2000), Camper et al. (2003)
	2) Detachment and suspension in bulk water phase	Hydraulic shearing force, Reynolds number, pipe surface tubercles	NRC (2006), Clark et al. (1993b)
Nitrification	Associated with nitrifying bacteria in the chloraminated system, which convert ammonia to nitrite and nitrate and increase the ratio of chlorine to ammonia nitrogen	Chloramines usage, nitrification bacteria, solute (chlorine) transfer to bacteria-hosting pipe wall	Wolfe et al. (1988, 1990)
NOM oxidation	Chlorine oxidation of NOM and other chlorine scavengers in bulk phase, producing chlorine decay and formation of disinfection by-products	NOM chemical properties and reactivity, chlorine level in bulk phase, effective contacts between reactants	Richardson (1998), Richardson et al. (2004), Yang et al. (2008b), Clark and Sivaganesan (2002)
Pipe leaching,	Releasing and diffusion of chemicals from pipes, linings, fittings, joints and sealing compounds into the bulk water producing taste and color problems	Chemical composition of pipe interior materials	Burlingame et al. (1994) Khiari et al. (2002)
Internal corrosion	Destruction of metal pipes through thinning and pit corrosions of metal pipes, in which chemicals and metallic inorganics are released into bulk water phase	pH, Eh, pipe materials, pipe interior coating, pipe age, biofilm built-up	Sarin et al. (2001, 2003, 2004)
Water age, flow hydrodynamics	Indirect controlling variable affecting the time and efficiency of chlorine reactions with contaminants in the pipe flow	Water residence time, pipe flow velocity, network pressure distribution	Rossman et al. (1994), Walski et al. (2003), Clark and Haught (2005), Yang et al. (2008b)

2. The Role of Hydrodynamics in Water Quality Changes: Chlorine Decay and DBP Formation

A multi-barrier strategy for water quality protection requires simultaneous multi-criteria compliance, which sometimes can be difficult to achieve. Take chlorine decay and DBP formation as an illustration. On the one hand, a distribution network is required to maintain a minimum level of disinfectant residual in order to protect against microbial contamination. The disinfection reduces risk of infectious diseases in water supplies and has dramatically reduced outbreaks of waterborne pathogens. On the other hand, the disinfection simultaneously produces DBPs as long as the disinfectant residual and NOMs are in contact in a water pipe. The identification of chloroform, a DBP, in drinking water (Rook, 1974; Bellar and Lichtenberg, 1974) has raised questions about possible health risks posed by these compounds. Since 1974, additional DBPs have been identified and concerns have intensified about health risks from exposures to DBPs (Richardson, 1998; Richardson and Krasner, 2003; and Richardson et al., 2004). For the very reason, risk managers have responded in the interest of protecting public health by developing alternative treatment systems and by issuing rules and regulations designed to maintain protective levels of disinfection and at the same time, reduce the potentially harmful levels of DBPs in drinking water.

The required simultaneous compliance in biological disinfection and reduction of DBP formation has invoked a sustained research effort for mechanistic determination of the chlorine decay and DBP formation in a distribution network. Such an understanding serves as the basis to investigate ways in which network design and operations are optimized for producing and delivering chemically and biologically safe drinking water. One outcome of this effort is the development of mathematical models to predict both the chlorine decay and the rate of DBP formation. These integrated kinetic models allow one to quantitatively evaluate alternative treatment options and operational strategies. Before examining these mechanistic models, a review of the basic chemistry and simple models for chlorine decay and DBP formation in bulk water phase is provided.

2.1. Chlorine Decay and DBP Formations

2.1.1. General Chemistry in Disinfection and DBP Formation

Chlorine is the most widely used non-selective oxidant in drinking water disinfection. Recent concerns over DBP formation have introduced the use of chloramines as an alternative. In the case of chlorine, chlorine gas dissolved in water forms hypochlorous acid $(HOCl)$ and hypochlorite ion (OCl^-):

$$Cl_2 + H_2O \rightarrow HOCl + H^+ + Cl^- \quad (1)$$

$$HOCl \overset{pK_a}{\Leftrightarrow} OCl^- + H^+ \quad (2)$$

As a weak acid, $HOCl$ dissociates to OCl^- at a dissociation constant (pK_a) as a function of the water pH in the pipe. At pH=6, a chlorine solution is about 95% $HOCl$ while at pH 9 it contains about 95% OCl^-; $HOCl$ has a stronger disinfection power than OCl^-. Overall chlorine is a strong oxidizing agent that readily reacts with a number of inorganic and organic constituents in water. Compared to the loss of chlorine residual, the loss of chloramine in distribution networks is less studied. In water, chloramine is unstable as it undergoes auto-decomposition through a complex set of reactions. The overall reaction in chloramine-based disinfection can be written as:

$$3NH_2Cl \rightarrow N_2 + NH_3 + 3Cl^- + 3H^+ \quad (3)$$

In a flowing pipe, chlorine residual from either free chlorine or chloramines is consumed by chlorine bulk demand and wall demand. A majority of the bulk demand comes from chlorine-reactive NOM present in most source waters. The NOM reactivity is a function of source water characteristics and the treatment process in drinking water plants. A major group of naturally occurring NOM is terrestrial or aquatic humic material (Richardson et al., 2004), which tends to be fairly stable in water until in contact with free chlorine, a powerful oxidant in drinking water. Humic materials are the dominant fraction, often 50-70% of the dissolved organic carbon (DOC). Other fractions of NOM components include hydrophilic acids, carbohydrates, carboxylic acids, and amino acids (Richardson et al., 2004). Overall, reactions between organic compounds and chlorine species fall into three categories (Brezonik, 1994): oxidation of organic functional groups, addition to double bonds, and electrophilic substitution. The chlorine-contaminant reactions rarely proceed to complete mineralization of the organic matter. Instead, the reaction adds or substitutes a chlorine atom into the structure of another molecule forming DBP compounds. In oxidation of the reactive NOM, the loss of chlorine residual over time is a gradual process; half-lives of chlorine residual in treated water can vary from several hours to several days.

The reactions between disinfectants (e.g., chlorine residual and hypobromous acid – the latter forms when bromide reacts with HOCl) and NOM in bulk water phase, or to a much lesser degree, in pipe deposits (Rossman et al., 2001), can produce literally hundreds of halogenated DBPs. Over 600 DBPs have been identified (Richardson, 1998) including both chlorinated and brominated compounds, most of which are present only in trace concentration levels. The by-products produced in greatest quantities are trihalomethanes (THMs). These are methane (CH_4) molecules in which any or all of the hydrogen atoms are replaced by chlorine or bromine atoms. THMs make up only 20% to 40% of the total halogenated organic halides produced by chlorination, however. Other classes of by-products of concern include HAAs, haloacetonitriles, cyanogen halides, halopicrins, and chloral hydrate.

The four THM compounds regulated under the D/DBP rule are trichloromethane (TCM), bromodichloromethane (BDCM), dibromochloromethane (DBCM), and tribromomethane (TBM), known collectively as the total THM (TTHM). The U.S. drinking water standard for TTHM is 80 μg/L. In chlorination, THM formation can be illustrated in a NOM-oxidation step followed by hydrolysis. Using model reactant propanone (CH_3COCH_3) as an example:

$$CH_3COCH_3 + (3-m)HOCl + m \cdot Br^- \rightarrow CH_3COCBr_mCl_{(3-m)} + (3-m)H_2O + m \cdot H^+ \quad (4)$$

$$CH_3COCBr_mCl_{(3-m)} + H_2O \rightarrow CH_3COOH + CHBr_mCl_{(3-m)} \quad (5)$$

m=0 Chloroform, $(CHCl_3)$

m=1 DCBM, $(CHBrCl_2)$

m=2 DBCM, $(CHBr_2Cl)$)

m=3 Bromoform, $(CHBr_3)$

The formation of HAA compounds is illustrated by taking acetic acid (CH_3COOH) as the model reactant, when hypochlorite or bromine ion reacts with the acid by replacing the hydrogen atoms in the methyl group:

$$CH_3COOH + n \cdot HOCl \rightarrow CH_{3-n}Cl_nCOOH + nH_2O \quad (6)$$

n=3 TCAA, (CCl_3COOH)

n=2 DCAA, $(CHCl_2COOH)$

n=1 MCAA, $(CH_2ClCOOH)$

$$CH_3COOH + m \cdot Br^- + m \cdot HO^- \rightarrow CH_{3-m}Br_mCOOH + m \cdot H_2O \quad (7)$$

m=1 MBAA, $(CH_2BrCOOH)$

m=2 DBAA, $(CHBr_2COOH)$

m=3 TBCAA, (CBr_3COOH)

$$CH_3COOH + n \cdot HOCl + m \cdot Br^- + p \cdot HO^- \rightarrow CH_{3-m-n}Br_mCl_nCOOH + (p+n) \cdot H_2O \quad (8)$$

n=1, m=1, p=1 BCAA, $(CHBrClCOOH)$

n=1, m=2, p=2 CDBAA, $(CBr_2ClCOOH)$

n=2, m=1, p=1 BDCAA, $(CBrCl_2COOH)$

Propanone and acetic acid as the model reactants represent only a small subclass of the NOM; NOM's chemical compositions and properties vary widely. To quantify DBP formation in practical applications, attempts have been made by using common surrogate parameters such as total organic carbon (TOC) and spectral absorbance (Sohn et al., 2004; Clark and Sivaganesan, 2002, and references therein). TOC concentration is indicative of the mass of organic material, whereas spectral absorbance relates to specific structure and functional groups. The most commonly used spectral absorbance for NOM is the ultraviolet absorbance at a wave length of 254 nm (UVA) that measures conjugated double bonds. The specific UVA (SUVA) is the ratio of UVA to the dissolved fraction (DOC) of the TOC. Its values indicate NOM's nature and reactivity with higher values for a more aromatic character (Amy, 1993).

Chlorine decay and the DBP formation are influenced by the condition of treatment as well as the constituents in the raw and treated water. Obviously, water treatment at a water plant changes the concentration and composition of drinking water constituents, and is likely to change the chlorine demand and DBP formation potential. In modeling chlorine decay and the DBPs formation, it is important to find the model input parameters that can reflect these changes of water quality characteristics. According to model reactions (4)-(8), relative chemical activities of free chlorine and bromine in the water disinfection can affect the compositions of brominated and chlorinated compounds. For chlorine-based disinfection, DBP formation is predominated by chlorinated THM and HAA compounds. Bromoform and brominated HAA formation is limited by the low concentrations of naturally occurring bromine ions in drinking water (Pourmoghaddas et al, 1993; Vikesland et al., 2001).

In addition to NOM, chlorine also reacts with various inorganic compounds; for example, with ammonia to form different species of chloramines. Aqueous chlorine converts Br^- into hypobromous acid ($HOBr^-$) which then attacks organic compounds to form brominated DBPs. Other examples are oxidization of soluble iron and manganese in water to the insoluble ferric and manganese chlorides. The general aqueous chemistry of drinking water chlorination can be found in various publications (e.g., Sarin et al., 2003, 2001, and 2004).

2.1.2. Kinetic Modeling of Chlorine Residual Decay

One of the primary purposes in chlorine decay studies is to establish models serving as a predictive tool in water quality management. In the early developments, chlorine decay models had primarily been empirical in nature or semi-mechanistic, most of which are weighted to address non-biological reactions. Later developments have been focused on relatively fast reactions of free chlorine in the aqueous phase and on prediction of chlorine decay variations with hydraulic residence time using a single system-specific decay coefficient. For example, Vasconcelos et al. (1996) developed several simple empirical mathematical models to describe free chlorine decay (e.g., first-order decay model, a parallel first-order decay model, and generic n^{th} order decay model). Clark (1998) proposed a chlorine decay and THM formation model based on a competitive reaction between free chlorine and NOM. The model was validated against the Vasconcelos et al. (1996) data sets and found to be as good or better, judged by the regression correlation coefficient R^2 values, than the models examined by Vascocelos et al. (1997).

Sophisticated predictive models incorporate true mechanistic descriptions and are useful in elucidation of the fundamental processes for water quality predictions. The earliest attempt to model chlorine decay is given by Feben and Taras (1951) in an exponential expression:

$$C_t \rightarrow C_1 t^n \tag{9}$$

where C_t is the chlorine consumed at time t (hr), C_1 is the chlorine demand after one hour, and n is a constant characteristic of a given water matrix. The one-hour chlorine demand and n must be determined experimentally for drinking water. The long-term chlorine decay, in both distributed drinking water and in natural waters receiving chlorinated discharges, has been typically calculated using the first-order reaction kinetics of Johnson (1978):

$$C_t \approx C_0 e^{(-kt)} \tag{10}$$

C_0 is initial chlorine concentration. The first-order chlorine decay constant, k, is dependent upon the source water chemical characteristics and the degree of treatment received by the water. Although simple to use, the first-order kinetic model is capable of reproducing neither the higher decay rate observed in the initial stages of chlorination, nor the slow tailing off of the decay rate in late reaction times. The departure from the ideal first-order decay of Johnson (1978) is illustrated in Figure 5a for a typical chlorine bulk decay curve (Yang, unpublished data). In experiments presented here, Cincinnati (Ohio, U.S.) tap water was de-chlorinated and then re-chlorinated for an initial concentration of approximately 0.85 mg/L free chlorine. Before the re-chlorination, the water was filtered using granular activated carbon followed by addition of inorganic humic acid to make up a TOC concentration of 0.64 mg/L. The re-chlorinated tap water with a new TOC content was monitored for variations of water quality parameters (free and total Cl, pH, turbidity, DO) and sampled for analysis of TTHM and individual compounds.

Haas and Karra (1984) investigated several kinetic models to better describe chlorine decay variations, including first-order decay, power law decay (n*th* order), first-order decay with stable components, power-law decay with stable components (n*th* order), and parallel first-order decay. They found that the parallel first-order decay model yielded the best results. The better performance is illustrated in Figure 5a. The parallel model assumes that there are two constituents in water reacting with chlorine: the fast reacting components that exert the initial chlorine decay, and the slow reacting components that become important in the late time.

Subsequent to the work of Haas and Karra (1984), chlorine decay models have evolved into different forms; all intended to characterize the rapid chlorine decay in the early time and the tailing effect in the late time where long-term chlorine demand dominates in the chlorine residual loss. In a crude classification, these kinetic developments can be grouped into four categories according to their mathematical and kinetic expressions. The first is the simplest first-order chlorine decay kinetics as described by Johnson (1978) in Eq.10. The second is a parallel reaction model, either the first- or the second-order (Qualls and Johnson, 1983; Gang et al., 2003; Clark and Siveganesan, 2002) that assumes simultaneous occurrence of a fast reaction and a slow reaction in chlorine residual loss. Another category is the second-order kinetics for the chlorine and its reactants, both in dilute concentrations. This approach was introduced in Clark (1998) who compared the representation of first-order reactions, first-order parallel reactions, second-order and second-order parallel reactions to typical chlorine decay curves observed in water treatment plants. The last type of kinetic model, comparatively empirical in nature, links the chlorine decay to an expression of water quality parameters such as UV_{254} (Sohn et al., 2004).

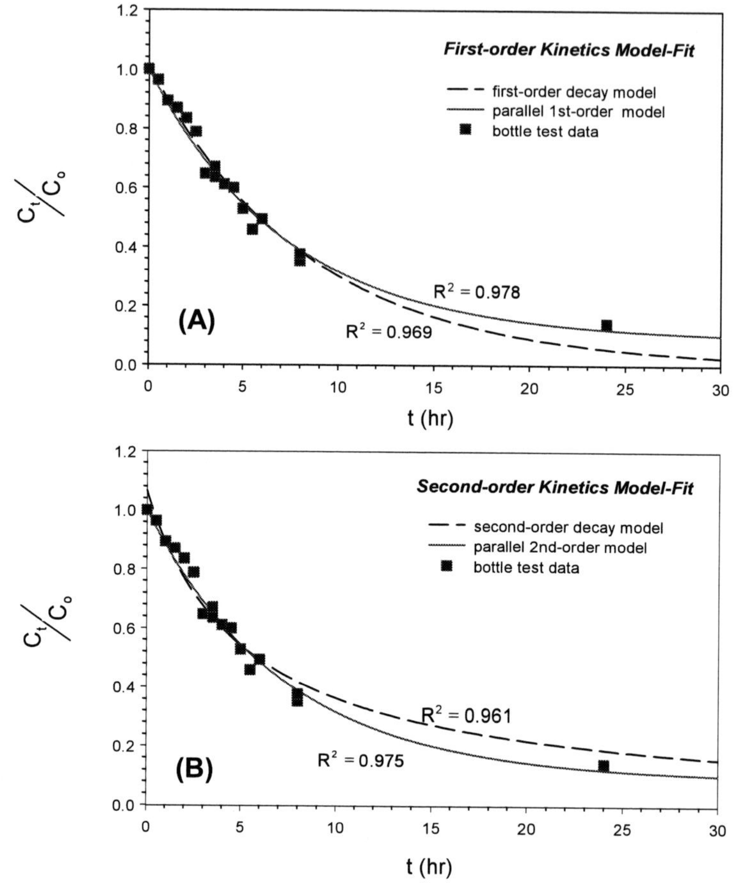

Figure 5. Curve fitting of the glass bottle testing data (Yang, unpublished) in determination of the chlorine bulk decay constant. (A) first-order kinetic models (Eqs.10,14), and (B) second-order kinetic models (Eqs.24, 29). Testing water was the dechlorinated Cincinnati city water with addition of hypochloride and humic acid for a target concentration of free chlorine Co=0.85 mg/L and TOC=0.64 mg/L. It is noted that the parallel first-order and second-order kinetic models outperform their single-stage equivalents in representing the late-time tailing effect of chlorine decay.

Parallel First-Order Reaction Kinetics

Based on Johnson's (1978) first-order kinetic model in Eq.10, parallel first-order reactions were proposed for the tailing effect of chlorine decay in the late time as shown in Figure 5a. A model of Qualls and Johnson (1983) described the short-term chlorine consumption by fulvic acids during the first 5 minutes of a reaction and then the long-term chlorine demand. This model was originally developed for cooling water systems and later applied to disinfection of natural waters. The governing equation is:

$$\frac{\partial C}{\partial t} = -k_f C \cdot F_1 - k_s C \cdot F_2 \qquad (11)$$

In Eq.11, the chlorine decay is composed of two parallel first-order decay components represented by fast and slow rate constants, k_f and k_s. The first term on the right hand side (RHS) of Eq.11 describes rapid chlorine decay within the first 30 seconds, and the second simulates a slower decay from 30 seconds to 5 min. In Eq.11, C is the chlorine concentration in water; F_1 and F_2 are the concentrations of reactive sites on the fulvic acids for the fast and slow reaction, respectively.

Similarly, Jadas-Hecart et al (1992) attempted to identify the organic compounds that react with chlorine for the Seine River water entering the final treatment stage at the Choisy-le-Roi water plant in France. They studied the chlorine consumption kinetics of water samples taken after overall treatment and found a two-phased chlorine decay process. An initial phase of immediate chlorine consumption in the first four hours, taken as the initial chlorine demand, was followed by the second phase of slower consumption defined as the long-term chlorine demand. The long-term chlorine demand was interpreted with the following kinetic equation:

$$\frac{\partial C'}{\partial t} = k(a - C')^{\alpha}\left(b - \frac{C'}{n}\right)^{\beta} \tag{12}$$

where C' is chlorine consumed after (t- 4) hours; k is the chlorine decay rate constant; a and b are the total residual chlorine at 4 hours and the maximum potential chlorine demand, respectively; n is stoichiometric coefficient, and α, β are partial orders of the reaction.

Most recently, Gang et al. (2003) simplified the representation of NOM reactive site fraction (F_1 and F_2) in Eq.11 and further demonstrated the use of parallel first-order reactions to study chlorine decay and DBP formations in natural water. By assuming a chlorine molar fraction f in fast chlorine decay and the fraction (1-f) in long-term demand, the overall chlorine residual loss is given by Eqs.13-14 (Gang et al., 2003):

$$\frac{\partial C}{\partial t} = -k_f \cdot fC - k_s \cdot (1 - f)C \tag{13}$$

$$C_t = C_o\left[f \cdot e^{-k_f t} + (1 - f)e^{-k_s t}\right] \tag{14}$$

Others describing the staged chlorine kinetics include the Water Treatment Plant model (US EPA, 1992) originally proposed for drinking water treatment plant evaluations. The model describes chlorine decay by dividing the decay curve into three components. These included an initial (t< 5 minutes) reaction, a second-order reaction (5 min< t <5 hours) and a first-order reaction (t > 5 hours). These three phases are represented in equations of sequentially hybrid first-order and second-order kinetics:

$$\ln\left(C_o - C_1 - 7.6C_{NH_3}\right) = -0.62 + 0.522\ln\left(\frac{C_o}{C_{TOC}}\right) + 0.302\ln(UV_{254}) + 0.842\ln(C_{TOC})$$

$$<5\text{min} \tag{15}$$

$$\frac{1}{C_t}-\frac{1}{C_1}=k_1 t \quad 5\text{min}< t <5 \text{ hours} \tag{16}$$

$$C_t = Ae^{-k_2 t} \quad t>5 \text{ hours} \tag{17}$$

In the multi-staged chlorine decay kinetics, C_1 is the chlorine residual at 5 minutes; k_1 and k_2 are second order and first order rate constants; constant A is obtained by solving for C_t using Eqs.15-16 at t=5 hours.

Chlorine Decay Model of Inhabitation

Dugan et al. (1995) proposed a saturation model based on the Michaelis-Menton equation to predict the entire chlorine decay curve. The Michaelis-Menton kinetic model, originally proposed in biological kinetic studies, simulates the reactions as zero-order in the early time of chlorine decay and the first-order reactions in the late time. When TOC concentration (C_{TOC}) was chosen as the predictive water quality parameter to represent chlorine demand, the governing rate equation and analytical solutions for chlorine concentration (C) can be written as:

$$\frac{\partial C}{\partial t}=\frac{k_1 C_{TOC}\cdot C}{K\cdot C_{TOC}-C} \tag{18}$$

$$\frac{K}{k_1}\ln\frac{C}{C_0}-\frac{C-C_o}{k_1\cdot C_{TOC}}=t \tag{19}$$

$$K=a+b\cdot\frac{C_0}{C_{TOC}}$$

$$k_1=c+d\cdot\frac{C_0}{C_{TOC}}$$

where a, b, c, d are empirical constants.

The chlorine decay comprises of two components in Eq.19. The first term on the LHS represents the first-order exponential chlorine decay, which becomes dominant in the late time. The second term is zero-order chlorine decay important in the early time of drinking water disinfection. Such a chlorine decay model is used in chlorine modeling in EPANET (Rossman, 2000) and commercial simulation platform PipeNet to account for the early-time and long-term chlorine decay phenomenon. Koechling (1998) further developed a modified version of the saturation model and expressed the chlorine decay as a function of the water's DOC and UVA, instead of the TOC concentration, for the easy use in practical applications:

$$\frac{\partial C}{\partial t} = \frac{k_2 \cdot SUVA_0 \cdot C}{k_1 - C} \tag{20}$$

$$k_1 = -0.32 \cdot UVA_0 + 1.91 \cdot C_{DOC}$$

$$k_2 = -0.32(UVA_0)^{1.365}$$

$$SUVA_0 = {UVA_0}/{C_{DOC}}$$

where C_{DOC} is dissolved organic carbon (mg/L); UVA_0 is UVA measurement at t=0. This model gave excellent results for a large range of waters tested.

Second-Order Kinetics of Chlorine Decay

Clark (1998) developed an equation for chlorine decay based on the concept of competing reactive substances and assumed a general chlorine reaction as:

$$a[Cl] + b[B] \rightarrow p[P] \tag{21}$$

where $[Cl]$ represents chlorine; $[B]$ is a collection of all reacting substances; $[P]$ is reaction products; and a, b, and p are stoichiometric coefficients. For reactants at a dilute concentration, the second-order kinetic law applies:

$$\frac{dC}{dt} = -k_A C^a C_B^b \tag{22}$$

$$\frac{dC_P}{dt} = k_P C^a C_B^b \tag{23}$$

In Eqs.22-23, k_A and k_P are second-order rate coefficients for reactant chlorine and the reaction product, respectively. By equating $[Cl]$ to the molar equivalent of $[B]$ reacted, the following analytical equation for chlorine at time t is obtained by integrating Eqs.22-23 (Clark, 1998):

$$C_t = \frac{K}{1 - R \cdot e^{-u \cdot t}} \tag{24}$$

$$u = \frac{k_A b}{a}\left(C_o - \frac{a}{b} C_{Bo}\right) = \frac{k_A b}{a} K \tag{25}$$

where, the model parameters R (dimensionless), K (mg/l), and u (min^{-1}) are estimated for a given water system; t is the time of reaction or water residence time in a pipe in minutes; C_o and C_{Bo} are, respectively, the chlorine concentration and the chlorine-equivalent reactants at $t = 0$.

Clark and Sivaganesan (1998) utilized Eqs.24-25 to predict chlorine decay and TTHM formation for a number of field and laboratory data sets. A two-stage least-square estimation procedure using the Marquardt-Levenberg method was adopted to estimate the model's coefficients (Clark and Sivaganesan, 1998). Predictive equations for the parameters K and R are empirical in nature, estimated from initial chlorine concentration (C_o), pH, TOC, and temperature (T in °C):

$$K = e^{0.32} C_0^{-0.44} TOC^{0.63} pH^{-0.29} T^{0.14} \tag{26}$$

$$R = e^{1.49} C_0^{-0.48} TOC^{0.18} pH^{-0.96} T^{0.28} \tag{27}$$

Parallel Second-Order Kinetics of Chlorine Decay

Clark and Sivaganesan (2002) expanded from the second-order chlorine decay kinetics and treated the chlorine decay in a water phase as a result of two parallel second-order reactions:

$$\begin{aligned} a[A] + q_1[Cl] &\xrightarrow{k_f} p_1[P_1] \\ b[B] + q_2[Cl] &\xrightarrow{k_s} p_2[P_2] \end{aligned} \tag{28}$$

where [A] and [B] are fast- and slow-reacting contaminants or chlorine demands, which react with chlorine [Cl] to produce reaction products [P_1] and [P_2] at rates k_f and k_s, respectively; constants a, b, q_1, q_2, p_1, p_2 are stoichiometric coefficients. These chemical reactions yield two second-order kinetic equations (Clark and Sivaganesan, 2002):

$$C \cong f_m C_o \cdot \left[\frac{(1-R_1)}{1-R_1 e^{-(1-R_1)k_f t}} \right] + (1-f_m) C_o \cdot \left[\frac{(1-R_2)}{1-R_2 e^{-(1-R_2)k_s t}} \right] \tag{29}$$

In Eq.29, f_m is the molar fraction of chlorine in reaction with fast-reacting contaminants, while ($1-f_m$) denotes all other chlorine consumption in the late-time slow reactions. Dimensionless parameters R_1 and R_2 are defined empirically as illustrated in Eq.27. It is apparent from Eq.29 that the fast reaction controls chlorine residual decay in the early phases and the residual concentration approaches a constant representing the long-term chlorine demand of the bulk water phase (Fig.5b).

Comparison of Chlorine Decay Kinetics

There is a general interest in comparing the chlorine decay models and identifying their advantages as well as limitations in representing and predicting chlorine decay for a given water system (e.g., Clark, 1998; Clark and Sivaganesan, 2002; Gang et al., 2003; Powell et al., 2000). The kinetic reaction of chlorine decay in the bulk phase is a function of NOM's chemical reactivity, the concentrations of NOM and chlorine residual in the bulk phase. They do not fully count for chlorine demand from pipe walls as described in later sections. Mechanistically, the reaction between chlorine and NOM follows the second-order kinetic law when both are present at diluted concentrations of similar levels. For water in a distribution network, the concentration of chlorine could be far smaller than those of NOM and other scavengers in the bulk phase. This condition validates the use of overall first-order kinetics in reference to free chlorine in the water. The inference does not exclude the other circumstances for which other orders of chlorine decay kinetics apply.

One empirical approach in selecting a kinetic model is by data curve fitting in which the bulk chlorine decay is mathematically described. Model performance is often evaluated by the regression correlation coefficient (R^2). This statistical criterion, however, is often inadequate to retrieve true chlorine decay kinetics for a given water system; the potential exists to yield misleading conclusions. Take the chlorine decay dataset in a glass bottle bulk decay testing as an example (Fig.5). The first-order parallel and the second-order parallel chlorine models yield higher R^2 of regression than their single-stage counterparts. The parallel reaction models slightly better represent the late-time chlorine decay behavior. Clark (1998) and Clark and Sivaganesan (2002) have arrived at similar conclusions. Mathematically, the fast and slow chlorine reactions respectively affect the position and geometry of the chlorine decay curve in the early and late times. Such mathematical flexibility makes the model capable of closely resembling the experimental data; there is no verification by the curve fitting itself on the validity of the kinetic determination. A preferable approach (Farinha et al., 1997, Wang and Hofmann, 1999) is the experimental kinetic testing and analysis of bulk chlorine decay in glass beakers free of wall demand. Unfortunately, a precise but potentially costly kinetic determination is not always available and the determined kinetic constant may not be representative due to the seasonal and daily variations in source water compositions and variance often found at a water treatment plant. One possible alternative is to use the simplest mathematical expression of acceptable predictive accuracy as a substitution for the water residence time of interest. This is shown in an example in Figure 5, for which the precise kinetics of chlorine decay is not known. The parallel first-order and the parallel second-order models represent the experimental data well in time up to 36 hours, a time range compatible to water residence in an actual distribution network. Thus both models are applicable for predictions.

2.1.3. Kinetic Modeling of by-Product Formation

Because DBP formation is accompanied with chlorine decay as shown in Eq.21, most kinetic models directly relate DBP formation to the loss of chlorine residuals. In the case of TTHM concentration (C_{TTHM}), Clark (1998) and later Boccelli et al. (2003) used a second-order kinetic model to quantify the THM formation in term of chlorine loss:

$$C_{TTHM} = C_{TTHM,0} + F_{THM}\left\{C_0 - \frac{C_0(1-R)}{1-R\cdot e^{-u\cdot t}}\right\} \tag{30}$$

or

$$\eta = \frac{\Delta C_{TTHM}}{C_0} = F_{THM}\frac{R\left(1-e^{-u\cdot t}\right)}{1-R\cdot e^{-u\cdot t}} \tag{31}$$

The second term on the RHS of Eq.30 describes THM formation proportional to the chlorine residual loss by a THM formation factor F_{THM}. F_{THM} is defined as the molar fraction of chlorine consumed in THM formation; other parameters and variables are defined in earlier sections. For $F_{THM} = 1$, chlorine decay is consumed entirely for DBP formation. $F_{THM} < 1$ when chlorine is also consumed by other chlorine demand producing no DBPs. In Eq.31, the specific DBP yield (η) increases with time asymptotically and is directly proportional to F_{THM} or the fraction of DBP-forming reactive NOM.

For chlorine bulk demand that follows the first-order kinetics in Eq.10 (Johnson, 1978), the parallel first-order reactions in Eq.14 (Gang et al., 2003), or the parallel second-order reactions in Eq.29 (Clark and Sivaganesan, 2002), the corresponding specific TTHM yield (η_{TTHM}) can be written as:

$$\eta_{TTHM} = \frac{\Delta C_{TTHM}}{C_o} = F_{THM}\cdot e^{(-kt)} \text{ First-order chlorine decay} \tag{32}$$

$$\eta_{TTHM} = \frac{\Delta C_{TTHM}}{C_o} = F_{THM}\left\{1-\left[fe^{(-k_1t)} + (1-f)e^{(-k_2t)}\right]\right\}$$

Parallel first-order chlorine decay (33)

$$\eta_{TTHM} = \frac{\Delta C_{TTHM}}{C_o} = F_{THM}\left\{1-f_m\cdot\left[\frac{(1-R_1)}{1-R_1e^{-(1-R_1)k_ft}}\right] + (1-f_m)\cdot\left[\frac{(1-R_2)}{1-R_2e^{-(1-R_2)k_st}}\right]\right\}$$

Parallel second-order chlorine decay (34)

Prior to these model developments and in one of the earliest attempts, Trusell and Umphres (1978) reviewed the effect of pre-ozonation, bromide, pH and chlorine dose on the formation of THMs in natural waters, and proposed a pseudo first-order kinetic model for THM formation. This early work was followed by others in mechanistic and statistical models that relate THM formation to specific variables such as molar stoichiometric reactions, TOC, and other water quality parameters. Harrington et al. (1992) developed a computer program to simulate DBP formation, removal of natural organic matter, inorganic water quality changes, and disinfectant decay in water treatment process. Equations were developed that simulate the

THMs formation, TOC removal, and reduction of ultraviolet absorbance by alum coagulation, as well as changes in alkalinity and pH. Model simulations were compared with limited sets of observed values. The central tendency of the model was to under-predict finished-water pH by 4%, finished-water TOC by 7%, and TTHM in the distribution network by 20-30%. Amy et al., (1987) discussed the formulation and calibration of several models for prediction of TTHM in untreated natural waters subjected to chlorination. Their general approach was to analyze specific portions of a large database derived from several natural water sources in order to isolate the effects of a given parameter on TIIM formations. Two general strategies were used in formulating the models. One used multiple linear regression models based on logarithmic transformations of both independent and dependent variables. The second relied on multiple nonlinear regressions. Both modeling strategies assumed that a level of chlorine residual is maintained throughout a 168-hr reaction period, and that TTHMs continuously increase with time. Quantities such as UVA, chlorine dose, temperature and TOC were used as the independent variables.

Following Trusell and Umphres' (1978) work, Kavanaugh et al. (1980) proposed the earliest mechanistic THM formation model in a distribution network following post-chlorination. The THM formation was described by an overall stoichiometric expression in a rate equation:

$$3[\mathrm{HOCl}] + [\mathrm{NOM}] \rightarrow [\mathrm{P}] \tag{35}$$

$$\frac{dC_{TTHM}}{dt} = k_n C_B \left(C_{A,0} - \frac{3C_{TTHM}}{\eta^*} \right)^m \tag{36}$$

In the above equations, three moles of hypochlorous acid react with one mole of NOM to form one mole of TTHM. The rate equation assumes the first-order kinetic law with respect to TOC and m-th order with respect to HOCl. Then the chlorine concentration C_A can be stoichiometrically related to C_{TTHM} by defining the TTHM yield (η^*) as the moles of TTHM formed per mole of chlorine consumed. When the free chlorine is exhausted, namely $\eta^* = 3C_{TTHM}/C_{A,0}$ where $C_{A,0}$ is the initial chlorine concentration, then the yield (η^*) can be determined by measuring C_{TTHM}. Thus the equation is a three-parameter kinetic model with k_n as the rate constant, m and η^* that must be determined empirically for the given water.

Clark (1998) followed his approach on chlorine decay modeling, and proposed a THM formation model in which THM formation was linearly proportional to chlorine consumption. See Eq.30. Schenck et al. (1998) investigated the applicability of the Vartiainen and Liimatainen (1988) model to source waters and water treatment practices in the U.S. The Vartiainen and Liimatainen (1988) model, developed for data collected in Finland, relates the mutagenicity as determined in the Ames assay to total organic carbon (TOC) concentration of the water, chlorine dose, and to a less extent, to the concentration of ammonia. It has been used as the basis for the later epidemiological studies conducted in Finland that have reported a positive correlation between the mutagenicity of chlorinated drinking waters and certain human cancers. In the work by Schenck et al. (1998), water samples were collected from three full-scale treatment plants and one pilot-scale plant in the U.S. All the plants used chlorine exclusively for disinfection. One full-scale plant used ground water while the other plants used surface water. Collected water samples from all three plants were concentrated by XAD resin adsorption for testing in the Ames assay. The observed levels of mutagenicity in the finished waters were 1.5 to 2 times higher than those predicted using the Vartiainen and Liimatainen (1988) model. The underestimation indicates the model vulnerability when DBP formation is simply assumed to correlate directly to chlorine consumption without considering other competitive chlorine consumption factors for a specific water chemical matrix.

2.2. Hydrodynamic Factors in Chlorine Decay and DBP Formations

The kinetic models for chlorine bulk decay and DBP formation described in Section 2.1 are appropriate in describing chemical reactions while discounting chlorine demand other than those in the bulk phase. Kinetic equations (29)-(34) on DBP formations, for example, clearly illustrate the kinetic assumption. Such an assumption is valid for chlorine decay and DBP formation in bulk water or for the glass bottle testing in which the bulk demand is predominant (Fig.5). In a field distribution network, it is now known that chlorine decay occurs in response to multiple sources of chlorine demand. Besides chemical reactions in the bulk phase, wall demand is another principal factor responsible for the loss of chlorine residual in a distribution network (Clark and Haught, 2005) particularly those comprised of aged metallic pipes (Sarin et al., 2003, 2004).

2.2.1. Competitive Chlorine Demand in Pipe Flows

Previous work has incorporated pipe wall demand into overall chlorine decay in a flowing water pipe. Rossman et al. (1994) developed a chlorine decay model based on the use of first-order bulk phase and reaction-limited wall demand coefficients; this model is the basis for the widely used EPANET network simulation model. Clark (1998) extended the concept to include a rapid and slow reaction component, and to study the effect of variables such as temperature and pH (Clark and Sivaganesan, 1998). Further extensions included the formation of brominated byproducts. McClellan et al. (1999) modeled the aqueous-phase loss of free chlorine due to reactions with NOM by partitioning the NOM into reactive and non-reactive fractions. Other mechanistic models have incorporated reactions with reactive pipe surfaces that may dominate the residual loss as compared to bulk-phase reactions (Lu et al., 1995; Vasconcelos et al., 1997). Clark and Haught (2005) were able to predict free chlorine loss in corroded, unlined metallic pipes subject to changes in flow velocity by considering chlorine mass transfer to the pipe wall where the chlorine was rapidly reduced.

Figure 6 illustrates the concept of competitive reactions in chlorine decay and DBP formation when chlorine wall demand is significant. The chlorine competitive consumption occurs between wall demand and bulk demand; a part of the latter produces the harmful DBP compounds. Overall, chlorine wall demand is a function of two major factors. One is chlorine reactivity with the pipe materials, biofilms, and inorganic pipe scales attached on the pipe surface. The other is the hydrodynamics of pipe flow that governs the rate and mechanisms of chlorine transport from bulk phase onto pipe walls where the chlorine reaction occurs.

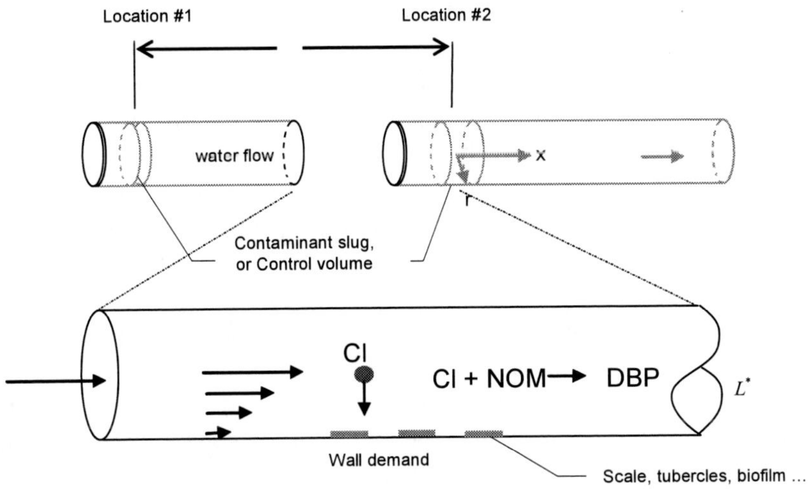

Figure 6. Schematics showing chlorine decay and DBP formation in a flowing pipe under a 3-D radial coordinate system. A water control volume or a finite contaminant slug hydraulically disperses along the axial *x* direction (upper graph). Shown in an amplified pipe section (lower graph), chlorine in bulk water reacts with NOM to form DBPs and simultaneously transfers to the pipe wall in wall demand reactions. Location #1 and #2 refer to sensor stations in modeling of contaminant "slug" CDR process in Section 3.0.

Mathematically, chlorine concentration change in a competitive reaction system of a flowing water pipe is given by a general Dankwarts equation in a radial coordinate system (Fig.6). Modified from Yang et al. (2008a) by the use of dimensional variables:

$$\frac{\partial C}{\partial t} + \overline{u}_x \frac{\partial C}{\partial x} = \frac{1}{Pe_L}\left(\frac{\partial^2 C}{\partial x^2}\right) + \frac{1}{Pe_D}\left(\frac{\partial^2 C}{\partial r^2}\right) - \left(\frac{\partial C}{\partial t}\right)_{wall} - \left(\frac{\partial C}{\partial t}\right)_{bulk,1} - \left(\frac{\partial C}{\partial t}\right)_{bulk,2} \quad (37)$$

$$Pe_D = \frac{r_o^*}{m \cdot D_{eff}} \overline{u}_{x'} = \frac{1}{m^2} Pe_L$$

where $\overline{u}_x$ is average flow rate across a pipe section; Pe_L and Pe_D are axial and radial Péclet number, respectively; D_{eff} is chlorine dispersivity in water. The scaling factor (m) allows for modeling at a pipe length of interest in the unit of pipe radius; m=2 for the characteristic pipe length. The first and second term on the RHS of Eq.37 are, respectively, the axial and radial dispersion of chlorine as a solute in a flowing pipe. The third term on RHS is attributed to radial diffusion-driven mass transfer onto the pipe wall, where chlorine is consumed at a rate $\left(\frac{\partial C}{\partial t}\right)_{wall}$; the third and fourth terms together depict the contribution of wall demand.

The terms of chlorine decay for bulk-1 and bulk-2 are used to distinguish, at least in theory, bulk chlorine reactions for DBP formations and all other chlorine demand in the bulk phase.

In Eq.37, the role of flow hydrodynamics on the chlorine decay rates is implicitly shown as the controlling factor for radial and axial dispersion of chlorine and its reactants in a flow water pipe. The general governing equation has been discussed in various forms of simplification for specific flow conditions. For example, Lu et al. (1993) assumed that under a steady-state pipe flow, axial dispersion of chlorine solute in the pipe is negligible for which the first term on RHS of Eq.37 approaches zero. An iterative mathematical procedure proposed by Lu et al. (1993; 1995) allows the calculation of steady-state chlorine concentration profiles in a pipe cross-section and to predict the growth of biofilm in drinking water distribution networks. Another approach to model the contaminant propagation in a water pipe was developed by Biswas et al. (1993). Their model used a transport equation for simultaneous convective transport of chlorine in the axial direction, diffusion in the radial direction, and consumption by a first-order reaction in the bulk-liquid phase. Islam (1995) and Islam et al. (1997) developed a model called QUALNET that predicted the temporal and spatial distribution of chlorine in a pipe network under slowly varying unsteady-flow conditions. Boulos et al. (1995) proposed a technique called the event-driven method, using a "next event" scheduling approach for significant reduction of computing times. Several different types of numerical methods have been proposed to solve these types of models by using either finite-difference or finite-element methods. Islam et al. (1997) used the finite difference scheme in numerical computation of chlorine decay in a flowing field. This approach was used in the models that were the basis for the early drinking water quality management studies (Grayman et al., 1988). Comprehensive evaluations on simulation computation methods in water modeling are available in Rossman and Boulos (1996).

The development of the EPANET hydraulic model has satisfied the need for a comprehensive public-sector prediction platform. It has been a key component in providing the basis for water-quality modeling in many utilities throughout the U.S. In establishing the predictive model, Rossman et al. (1994) simplified chlorine transport Eq.37 by assuming negligible radial and axial chlorine transport under steady-state flow conditions. The resultant governing equations used in EPANET and other commercial network modeling platforms are given below:

$$\frac{\partial C}{\partial t} + \bar{u}_x \frac{\partial C}{\partial x} = -\left(\frac{\partial C}{\partial t}\right)_{bulk} - \left(\frac{\partial C}{\partial t}\right)_{wall} \tag{38}$$

$$\left(\frac{\partial C}{\partial t}\right)_{bulk} = \left(\frac{\partial C}{\partial t}\right)_{bulk,DBP} + \left(\frac{\partial C}{\partial t}\right)_{bulk,2}$$

Here again the bulk chlorine decay rate for the DBP-forming reaction is distinguished from that for other reactions. Solving the governing chlorine transport equation (38) has been at the center of water quality modeling for a distribution network. A further simplification is the steady-state axial transport of chlorine in a fully developed pipe flow. Under this assumption, the axial advection term in Eq.38 can be neglected and the governing equation is rewritten in a general form:

$$\frac{\partial C}{\partial t} = -\zeta(k_b, C) - J_w \tag{39}$$

$$\frac{\partial C}{\partial t} = -k_b C - J_w \text{ (first-order bulk demand)} \tag{40}$$

where k_b is the overall bulk decay coefficient that includes the chlorine demand in DBP-forming and non-DBP forming reactions; J_w is chlorine radial flux to the pipe wall equal to consumption rate of wall demand. The bulk decay rate term $\zeta(k_b, C)$ is designated to represent chlorine bulk demand by one of the kinetics described in Section 2.1.2; Eq.40 is a special case of Eq.39 under first-order bulk reactions, a familiar form of kinetic equation in Rossman et al. (1994).

Comparing Eq.40 to Eq.10 of Johnson's (1978) first-order kinetic model shows that the difference is the incorporation of chlorine flux term J_w for a flowing water pipe. The flux J_w is controlled by the mass transfer of chlorine as the solute in water and by the reaction rate of chlorine consumptions at pipe wall. This relationship is a function of hydrodynamic properties, which defines the boundary condition of Eqs.39-40 and thus the analytical solution for chlorine variations. Possible scenarios in boundary conditions can be further identified by analyzing the relative magnitude between chemical reaction rate at pipe wall (k_w) and the chlorine flux (J_w).

Wall Reaction Limited (Epanet)

When $k_w << J_w$, chlorine wall demand is limited by the rates and types of wall reactions. Rossman et al. (1994) proposed a first-order kinetic wall reaction model in respect to chlorine concentration. By the kinetic definition, this model assumes that the wall reaction rate is only a function of chlorine concentration at the pipe wall surface for which the pseudo first-order reaction kinetics applies in respect to chlorine. In the EPANET model, the boundary condition of governing Eq.39 is the first-order chemical reaction at the pipe wall surface. The chlorine mass transfer rate onto the pipe wall equals to the chlorine reaction rate. By designating the term $2(C - C_w)/r_o$ as the chlorine concentration gradient from bulk phase to pipe wall, k_{mt} and k_w as the rate coefficient of mass transfer and wall reactions respectively, one can write:

$$J_w = k_{mt} \frac{2(C - C_w)}{r_o} \tag{41}$$

$$k_{mt}(C - C_w) = k_w C_w \tag{42}$$

Substituting Eqs.41-42 into Eq.39 yields the familiar overall first-order reaction kinetic equation for chlorine decay in a flowing water pipe:

$$\frac{dC}{dt} = -\left\{k_b - \left[\frac{2}{r_o}\right]\left[k_{mt}k_w/(k_{mt}+k_w)\right]\right\}C \tag{43}$$

then,

$$C_t = C_o e^{-K \cdot t} \tag{44}$$

$$K = k_b + 2\frac{k_{mt}k_w/(k_{mt}+k_w)}{r_o} \tag{45}$$

The first term on the RHS of Eq.45 is the bulk decay rate constant. The second term is the overall wall decay rate constant as a function of k_w, k_{mt}, and the pipe radius (r_o). Clark and Haught (2005) discussed the implications of this property. It is apparent in Eq.45 that the overall first-order chlorine decay constant K depends on the rate of chlorine mass transfer in water, which in turn is directly a function of the flow hydrodynamic parameters: Sherwood number (Sh) and molecular diffusion coefficient (D_{ab}) (Rossman, et al., 1994; Rossman, 2000):

$$k_{mt} = Sh \cdot D_{ab}/(2r_o) \tag{46}$$

$$Sh = 0.0149Re^{0.88}Sc^{0.333} \quad \text{for } Re > 2300 \tag{47}$$

$$Sh = 3.65 + \frac{0.0688\left(\frac{2r_o}{L}\right)Re\ Sc}{1 + 0.04\left(\frac{2r_o}{L}Re\ Sc\right)^{0.67}}$$

for

$$Re < 2300 \tag{48}$$

where L is the pipe length. The values for k_{mt} vary with flow hydrodynamics in form of Reynolds number (Re) and Schmidt number (Sc).

When $k_{mt} >> k_w$, Eq.45 becomes $K \approx k_b + 2\frac{k_w}{r_o}$. The overall kinetic constant is a sum of bulk decay constant and the wall reaction rate. It is not difficult to understand from this relationship that aged metallic pipes with large amounts of chlorine-reactive materials at the pipe wall surface could have different chlorine decay characteristics when compared with a PVC pipe. When $k_{mt} << k_w$, Eq.45 is reduced to $K \approx k_b + 2\frac{k_{mt}}{r_o}$ which is identical to the mass transfer limited model of Clark and Haught (2005) described below. In this special instance, the overall chlorine decay kinetic constant is directly related to the bulk decay rate and the chlorine mass transfer coefficient.

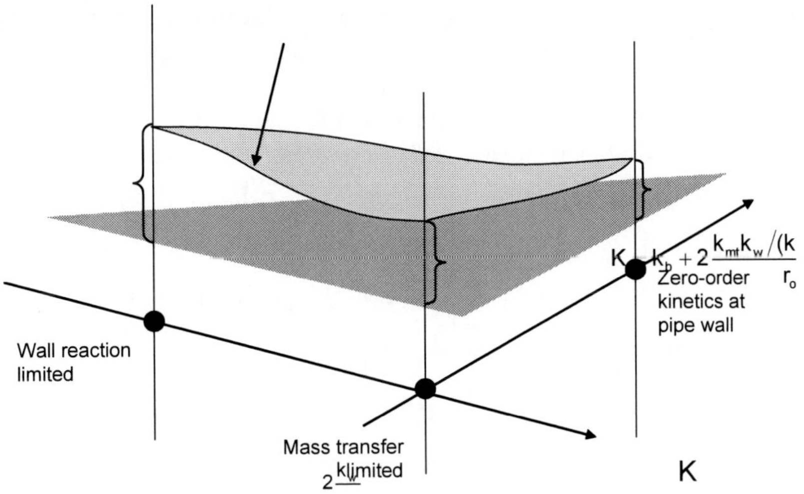

Figure 7. A schematic illustration of overall first-order chlorine decay constant (K) and the wall demand contributions under three end members of wall demand scenarios: wall reaction limited, mass transfer-limited, and the zero-order wall reaction kinetic. In the latter case, the contribution is also a function of time (See Eq.52).

A schematic diagram in Figure 7 illustrates the effect of water flow hydraulics in overall kinetic constants. Obviously, the designation of chlorine overall decay constant is supposed to vary as a function of pipe materials and the hydraulic properties in a water distribution pipe. It then follows that the wall demand reaction constant in EPANET model is essentially a fitting parameter as argued by Clark and Haught (2005) and later by Clark et al. (2008).

Mass Transfer Limited Model

An opposite boundary condition exists when $k_w >> J_w$. In this case, chlorine concentration at the pipe surface where the reaction takes place is effectively kept at zero by rapid chlorine reactions. Clark and Haught (2005) described the hydrodynamic-dependant chlorine decay phenomenon and discussed its implications. Chlorine decay rate at the pipe wall is limited by radial mass transfer rather than chlorine reaction rate. This mass-transfer-limited condition is the most pronounced under laminar and stagnant flow conditions. In the mass-transfer limited model, which assumed $C_w = 0$ due to instantaneous reaction, the flux expression becomes (Clark and Haught, 2005):

$$J_w = k_{mt} C \tag{49}$$

When Eq.49 is substituted into the general transport equation (39), the mass transfer limited case yields chlorine concentration in a flowing pipe as:

$$C = C_o e^{-\left(k_b + 2\frac{k_{mt}}{r_o}\right)t} \tag{50}$$

Clark et al. (2008) examined the model performance with experimental data of chlorine decay in a pilot-scale distribution pipe. They found that this model tends to consistently under-estimate the actual chlorine demand at low velocities (low mass transfer) and over-estimates chlorine demand for higher velocities (high mass transfer) in the unlined metallic pipe where significant wall demand existed. Furthermore, the mass transfer rate constant k_{mt} becomes meaningless in fully turbulent flow where chlorine concentration is homogeneous in pipe cross section. This is a special condition when $k_{mt} << k_w$ in the EPANET model (Fig.7), where mass transfer is no longer the limiting factor in the chlorine decay rate.

Wall Reaction Limited with Zero-Order Kinetics

A disinfectant transport model commonly mentioned in the literature is the "zero-order" chlorine decay kinetics (Digiano and Zhang, 2005; Vasconcelos et al. 1996). It is a special case of wall reaction limited model described above, where wall reaction is not dictated by the first-order, but zero-order reaction kinetics. The amount of chlorine transported to the pipe wall is assumedly limited by the reaction rate when both chlorine in water phase and the chlorine-reaction sites on the pipe surface are saturated. Under this kinetic assumption, radial flux of the disinfectant equals the rate of chlorine consumption at the pipe wall following the zero-order kinetic law:

$$k_{mt}(C - C_o) = k_o \tag{51}$$

By substituting Eq.51 into Eq.41 and integrating Eq.40, the chlorine concentration at a given time is given by:

$$C = C_o e^{-k_b t} - \frac{2k_o}{r_o k_b}\left(1 - e^{-k_b t}\right)$$

or

$$C/C_o = \left(1 + \frac{2k_o}{C_o r_o k_b}\right)e^{-k_b t} - \frac{2k_o}{C_o r_o k_b} \tag{52}$$

Apparently in Eq.52, the relative chlorine concentration change consists of first-order chlorine decay in the bulk phase and a time-independent chlorine sink by wall reactions. These two chlorine decay mechanisms are represented by the first and the second term on the RHS of Eq.52, respectively. The wall chlorine sink becomes significant relative to the bulk demand in the late time. Clark et al. (2008) argued that this combination can better explain the chlorine tailing effect after the rapid concentration decline in the early part of the reaction time. This observation is consistent with Digiano and Zhang (2005) in that the reaction coefficient increases with mass transfer but approaches an asymptote as mass transfer increases.

Caution is needed, however, when applying the zero-order kinetic law to chlorine decay in late time when chlorine concentration is significantly reduced. Under this condition, the model assumption that the wall demand is limited only by reaction rate needs to be reexamined. The kinetic rate depends on both the wall reaction rate and the diluted chlorine concentration at pipe wall surface. Depending on the relative magnitude of k_w and J_w, either the wall reaction limited (Eqs.44-45) or the mass transfer limited kinetics (Eq.50) is more characteristic of the late-time chlorine decay data (Fig.7).

Overall Decay Constant and Hydrodynamic Effects

The chlorine decay curve for all cases in the three models can be approximated using an overall first-order reaction constant (K). Re-arranging Eqs.40-49 leads to a solution for K in a flowing pipe. For the first-order wall reaction limited chlorine decay, substituting Eqs.46-48 into Eq.45 yields K as a function of pipe flow Reynolds number:

$$K = k_b + 2\frac{k_w}{r_o}\left(\frac{0.0149\,Re^{0.88}\,Sc^{0.333}D_{ab}}{2r_o k_w + 0.0149\,Re^{0.88}\,Sc^{0.333}D_{ab}}\right)$$

for turbulent flow $\quad Re > 2300 \quad$ (53)

$$K = k_b + 2\frac{k_w}{r_o}D_{ab}\left(\frac{3.65\left[1+0.04\frac{d}{L}(Re\,Sc)^{0.67}\right]+0.0688\frac{d}{L}Re\,Sc}{2r_o k_w\left[1+0.04\frac{d}{L}(Re\,Sc)^{0.67}\right]+0.0688\frac{d}{L}Re\,Sc}\right)$$

for laminar flow $\quad Re < 2300 \quad$ (54)

Similarly, the overall chlorine decay constant under the mass-transfer limited condition (Clark and Haught, 2005) is comprised of a bulk decay constant and a mass-transfer coefficient. From Eq.50,

$$K = k_b + 2\frac{k_{mt}}{r_o} \text{ Mass transfer limited model} \quad (55)$$

Lastly in the case of the zero-order wall reactions, chlorine concentration change in the flowing pipe is a combination of first-order chlorine decay and the wall chlorine sink. Chlorine concentrations under a zero-order wall demand consists of two parts in a $C-t$ chlorine plot. The early-time data follow the first-order kinetics, for which the first term on the RHS of Eq.52 dominates. The second-term on the RHS relates to the tailing effect of a typical chlorine decay behavior. For the early-time data, the exponential chlorine decay curve could yield the bulk decay constant, k_b :

$$K = k_b \text{ Zero-order wall reaction limited model} \quad (56)$$

All the three model conditions indicate that depending on the k_w and J_w relationships, chlorine decays in drinking water can be mathematically fit into a first-order chlorine reaction in a similar form as for bulk chlorine decay in Eq.10. The overall first-order kinetic constant, however, contains the factors of hydrodynamic properties (e.g., Eqs.53-55). The mass transfer in the hydrodynamic field is most important for the mass-transfer limited model, followed by the first-order wall reaction limited model when $k_w/(k_{mt}+k_w) \leq 1$. Under zero-order wall reactions, the early-time chlorine decay is independent of hydrodynamic properties. But the hydrodynamic effect becomes apparent in late-time of the chlorine decay.

First-order kinetics for chlorine bulk decay is assumed in deriving the overall kinetic rate expressions in Eqs 53-56. In Section 2.1.2, other bulk decay kinetic models capable of representing chlorine as the solute transporting in the water pipe and reacting with bulk demand. These include the parallel first-order, inhabitation model, second-order, and parallel second-order reaction kinetics. Now considering the three cases of wall demand, it is not difficult to postulate the possible physical conditions that can be represented by a combination of kinetic variations in the bulk decay (Eqs.10-23) and the wall demand (Eqs.32-42). Examples of possible kinetic combinations and the physical implications in pipe flows are listed in Table 3.

Table 3. Selected combinations of chlorine bulk demand and wall demand in a flowing water pipe and their related potential field conditions*

Bulk Demand	Wall Demand	Analytical Solution[1]	General Conditions
1st Order: $\varsigma(k_b, C) = k_b \cdot C$	MTL: $J_w = k_{mt}\frac{2C}{r_o}$	$C = C_o e^{-\left(k_b + k_{mt}\frac{2}{r_o}\right)t}$	Dilute Cl in bulk phase, laminar and stagnant flows, fast wall reactions or $\varsigma(k_b, C) > J_w$
1st Order: $\varsigma(k_b, C) = k_b \cdot C$	WRL: $J_w = k_{mt}\frac{2(C - C_w)}{r_o}$	$C = C_o e^{-\left(k_b + \frac{2}{r_o}\frac{k_{mt}k_w}{k_w + k_{mt}}\right)t}$	Dilute Cl in bulk phase, transitional and turbulent flows, slow wall reactions or $\varsigma(k_b, C) < J_w$
1st Order: $\varsigma(k_b, C) = k_b \cdot C$	ZOR: $J_w = k_o$	$C = C_o e^{-k_b t} - \frac{2k_o}{r_o k_b}\left(1 - e^{-k_b t}\right)$	High levels of Cl in bulk phase, slow wall reactions or $\left(\partial C_w / \partial t\right) << J_w$
2nd Order: $\varsigma(k_b, C) = k_b \cdot C^2$	MTL: $J_w = k_{mt}\frac{2C}{r_o}$	$C = C_o \frac{2k_{mt}}{(C_o k_b r_o + 2k_{mt})e^{\frac{2}{r_o}k_{mt}t} - C_o k_b r_o}$	High levels of Cl in bulk phase, laminar and stagnant flows, fast wall reactions or $\varsigma(k_b, C) > J_w$
2nd Order: $\varsigma(k_b, C) = k_b \cdot C^2$	WRL: $J_w = k_{mt}\frac{2(C - C_w)}{r_o}$	$C = \frac{C_o \frac{2k_w k_{mt}}{(k_w + k_{mt})}}{\left[r_o k_b C_o + \frac{2k_w k_{mt}}{(k_w + k_{mt})}\right] e^{\left(\frac{2}{r_o k_b}\frac{k_w k_{mt}}{(k_w + k_{mt})}t\right)} - r_o k_b C_o}$	High levels of Cl in bulk phase, transitional and turbulent flows, slow wall reactions or $\varsigma(k_b, C) < J_w$
2nd Order: $\varsigma(k_b, C) = k_b \cdot C^2$	ZOR: $J_w = k_o$	$\arctan\frac{C}{\sqrt{\frac{2k_o}{r_o k_b}}} - \arctan\frac{C_o}{\sqrt{\frac{2k_o}{r_o k_b}}} = -\sqrt{\frac{2k_o k_b}{r_o}}t$	High levels of Cl in bulk phase, slow wall reactions or $\left(\partial C_w / \partial t\right) << J_w$

Note: * - Only the types of first-order and second-order bulk demand kinetics are shown. Other types including the parallel first-order and second-order, logistic functions, are not analyzed.
1 – Solution of governing equation (39) for fully developed pipe flow, where longitudinal dispersion terms in Eq.38 is neglected.
Abbreviations: MTL – Mass transfer limited; WRL – Wall reaction limited; ZOR – Zero-order wall reaction kinetics.

These possible combinations illuminate the wide range of variations in chlorine decay potentially found in a water distribution network. This also indicates the possibility that a specific chlorine decay model in use may vary depending on pipe flow hydrodynamic properties. This theoretical conclusion explains the long-held field observation that one single model could not be universally applied. Distribution networks in different locations and even in different parts of a single network tend to have specific overall chlorine decay constants. Field observations of such large variations have been widely reported in literature; some are described in Section 2.4. Apparently in modeling chlorine decay, the exact model to select is a function of water chemistry, pipe materials, pipe ages in service, flow regimes, and hydrodynamic factors. How to select an appropriate model and apply it to a particular distribution network or its segments is a challenge to practicing engineers and a prominent subject for future research.

2.2.2. DBP Formation in Competitive Reactions of a Hydrodynamic Field

The hydrodynamic factors affecting chlorine decay also affect the rate at which individual DBP contaminants form in a flowing water pipe. Rossman et al (1999) investigated the factors that characterize the reaction conditions affecting water qualities in a distribution network, and further examined these factors in chlorine decay including pipe wall material, corrosion products, and biofilm slime. Much of the study was devoted to determining the rate at which DBPs form in a pipe as compared to that in a glass bottle. In conclusion, they found that the rate constants for chlorine decay in the pipe were an order of magnitude higher than in the bottle. The underlying cause is competitive chlorine consumption in bulk demand and wall demand. Only a fraction of the chlorine reactions is involved in DBP formation.

Let's first discuss how the stoichiometric reactions in DBP formation are affected by the hydrodynamics-dependent chlorine wall demand. In a conceptual model, chlorine reacts with $[NOM_{DBP}]$ to form DBP compounds and also reacts with other bulk demand $[NOM_{BCD}]$ with no DBP formation. Simultaneously chlorine consumption occurs with reactants $[WALL]$at the pipe wall surface. DBP formation only responds to a fraction of chlorine oxidation that targets on NOM in the multi-component competitive reactions (Fig.6):

$$[HOCl]+[NOM_{DBP}]\xrightarrow{k_1}[DBP_s]+[Cl^-] \tag{57}$$

$$[OCl^-]+[NOM_{DBP}]\xrightarrow{k_2}[DBP_s]+[Cl^-] \tag{58}$$

$$HOCl+OCl^-+[NOM_{BCD}]\xrightarrow{k_b'}\text{others} \tag{59}$$

$$HOCl+OCl^-+[Wall]\xrightarrow{k_w}\text{Scale}+\text{others} \tag{60}$$

The formation of chlorine disinfectants is illustrated in Reactions 1-2 in the preceding section. The hypochlorous acid dissociation constant $[pK_a]$ in Reaction 2 is pH-dependent for which Reaction 57-58 at a reaction rate k_1 and k_2 are distinguished to identify the role of water pH in DBP formations (Liu and Qi, in press). When pH <6.0, the free chlorine in water is predominantly hypochlorite OCl^- in a molar fraction >95%, which is less potent as an oxidant than hypochlorous acid $HOCl$. At pipe walls, anoxic conditions may occur as the results of excessive biofilm growth particularly in stagnant and pipe deadend zones where pH may become acidic. Nonetheless, the pH effects on hypochlorous acid dissociation and consequently the overall disinfection capacity and DBP formation rate are worthy of considerations. Following Liu and Qi (in press), a DBP formation kinetics is given with the water pH effect considered:

$$\left(\frac{\partial C}{\partial t}\right)_{bulk,1} = -k_{DBP}E_{DBP}C \tag{61}$$

$$k_{DBP} = \frac{k_2 + k_1 10^{(pH-pK_a)}}{1+10^{(pH-pK_a)}} \tag{62}$$

where $[E_{DBP}]$ is the molar concentration of chlorine equivalents for DBP-forming reactive NOM. Similarly, $[E_B]$ and $[E_{BCD}]$are designated respectively for chlorine molar equivalents of overall bulk demand and the other chlorine bulk demands without DBP formation. The second-order reaction kinetics equations for free chlorine and reactants at dilute concentrations in drinking water can be written as:

$$\left(\frac{\partial C}{\partial t}\right)_{bulk,2} = -k_b^{'}C\cdot[E_{BCD}] \tag{63}$$

$$\left(\frac{\partial C}{\partial t}\right)_{bulk} = \left(\frac{\partial C}{\partial t}\right)_{bulk,1} + \left(\frac{\partial C}{\partial t}\right)_{bulk,2} = -k_bC\cdot(E_{DBP}+E_{BCD}) = -k_bC\cdot E_b \tag{64}$$

$$k_b = \frac{E_{DBP}}{E_b}k_{DBP} + \frac{E_{BCD}}{E_b}k_b^{'} \tag{65}$$

$$\frac{\partial C_{DBP}}{\partial t} = k_{DBP}E_{DBP}C_A = \left(\frac{\alpha-1}{\alpha}\right)k_bE_bC_A \tag{66}$$

$$\alpha = \frac{k_bE_b}{k_b^{'}E_{BCD}}\ (\alpha \geq 1) \tag{67}$$

Parameters $k_b, k_{DBP}, k_b^{'}$ are, respectively, the kinetic rate constants for bulk chlorine decay, DBP formation, and other chlorine bulk demand with no DBP formation. The pseudo first-order reaction constant for bulk decay E_bk_b in Eq.65 comprises of those for DBP formation $E_{DBP}k_{DBP}$ and for the non-DBP forming bulk demand $E_{BCD}k_b^{'}$. Based on these designations, DBP yield factor α is in fact a ratio of the pseudo first-order reaction constant between overall bulk decay and the other bulk decay of non-DBP formation (See Eq.67).

For overall bulk demand primarily consisting of the DBP-forming NOMs, the proportionality constant in Eq.66 $\left(\frac{\alpha-1}{\alpha}\right)$ is approximately equal one. In a multi-species competitive reaction system for a flowing water pipe, simultaneous chlorine decay and DBP formation can be derived from Eqs.38 and 66 at the assumed pseudo first-order reaction kinetics. After chlorine concentration is solved from corresponding analytical solutions or from numerical computations, it is not difficult to quantitatively determine the corresponding DBP concentrations from two differential equations 68 and 69:

$$\frac{\partial C}{\partial t} = \overline{u}_x \frac{\partial C}{\partial x} - k_b C \cdot E_b - \frac{2}{r} J_w \qquad (68)$$

$$\frac{\partial C_{DBP}}{\partial t} = \left(\frac{\alpha-1}{\alpha}\right) k_b C \cdot E_b \qquad (69)$$

The DBP formation rate is generally described as a function of molar concentrations of free chlorine and DBP-forming NOM in water (Clark, 1998; Clark and Savigenesan, 2002; Bocelli et al., 2003; Gang et al., 2003). According to Eqs.68-69, the formation rate is also a function of chlorine decay in non-DBP forming bulk demand and wall demand, and of chlorine concentration variations from axial dispersion in multi-component competitive reactions inside a water distribution pipe. In Section 2.3 below, the results of controlled experiments will be used to identify principal factors that affect the DBP formation rate: hydraulic advection (the first term on the RHS of Eq.68), the reactive bulk demand in DBP formation (Eq.69 and the second term on the RHS of Eqs.68), and chlorine transfer in wall demand (the third term on the RHS of Eq.68).

2.3. Experimental Investigation of the Hydrodynamic Factors

A series of comparative experimental studies have been conducted in the EPA's Water Supply and Water Resources Division. The purpose was to isolate and quantify the effects of major variables including hydrodynamic properties on chlorine decay and DBP formation. These studies include hydraulic characterization using conservative tracers (Panguluri et al., 2007), chlorine decay and DBP formation in various flow conditions for Reynolds number of 0-55000 (Clark et al., 2008; Yang et al., 2008a, b). In this section, only those published results are cited and discussed to explore the role of pipe flow hydrodynamics in water quality changes. This limited discussion is intended to identify the hydrodynamic effects that were examined on a theoretical basis in the preceding sections. Readers, who are interested in the EPA's comparative studies including experimental devices, analytical methods, and other experimental results, are referred to other resources (http://www.epa.gov/nrmrl/wswrd/dw/dsr.html).

2.3.1. Comparative Studies

The experimental device in the EPA comparative studies is a pilot-scale water distribution simulator consisting of an aged ductile iron water pipe of 14.6-cm inside diameter and a new polyvinyl chloride (PVC) water pipe of 14.5-cm inside diameter (Panguluri et al., 2007). The experimental setup is illustrated in Figure 8. The aged unlined ductile iron and the new PVC pipes are contrasted to identify the effect of pipe wall demand on chlorine decay and DBP formation under simulated pipe flows. There was a 0.3-1 cm-thick pipe scale and tubercles attached to the ductile iron pipe surface where prevailing tubercles and biofilm growth were observed (Fig.8b). The new PVC pipe with clean interior, on the other hand, exhibited a minimal degree of wall demand (Clark et al., 2008).

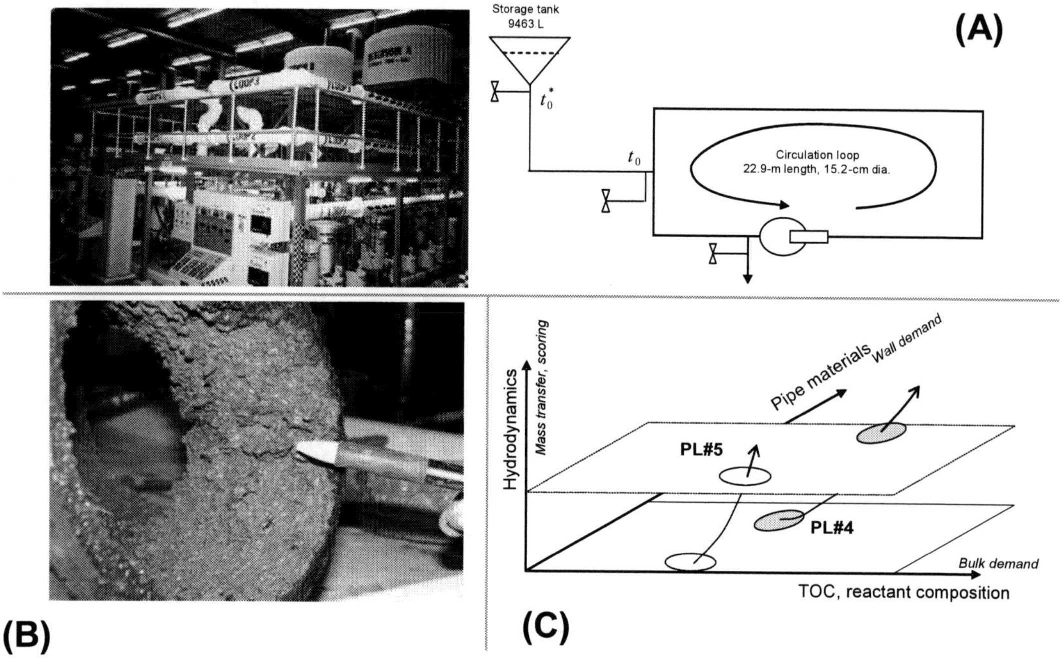

Figure 8. Experimental setup for chlorine decay and DBP formation comparative studies at EPA Testing and Evaluation facility. (A) pipe loops used in studies include one aged unlined ductile iron pipe (PL#4) and a new PVC pipe (PL#5); each is 22.9 meters in length and 15.2 cm in diameter. (B) An aged ductile iron pipe section showing significant pipe scale and tubercles build-up; and (C) Experimental design focused on isolation of the role of three principal variables in chlorine decay and DBP formation rates: hydrodynamics, pipe materials, and reactant (e.g., NOM) chemical properties and concentrations.

The contrasting experiments for each of and between the two pipe materials were conducted to isolate the potential hydrodynamic effects. The aged ductile iron pipe and new PVC pipe were selected for their large degree of difference in wall demand. The two pipe materials are also widely used in field distribution systems; the PVC is increasingly used in field because of the engineering and field installation convenience. In the experiments, while other variables were controlled as a constant, pipe flow conditions of the experiments varied from stagnant to fully turbulent conditions at which the chlorine decay rate and DBP formation rate were determined: stagnant (Q_p=0), laminar (Q_p=0.19 L/sec, Re=1500), transitional (Q_p=0.38 L/sec, Re=3100), and turbulent (Q_p=0.63 and 6.31 L/sec, Re=5100 and 51500). Hypotheses in this investigation included: 1) the higher wall demand and the greater flux, J_w, reduce chlorine concentrations in bulk water and thus reduce the DBP formation potentials (See Eq.68); 2) the pipe flow hydrodynamics affected the rate of chlorine decay and DBP formation through the effect on the radial chlorine flux term J_w. Three types of wall demands were tested: glass beakers free of wall demand, aged ductile iron pipe of strong wall demand, and new PVC pipe loop of some wall demand.

2.3.2. Chlorine Decay Constants

Clark et al. (2008) reported the chlorine decay experimental results. In the testing, experimental conditions were varied in pipe flow rate and pipe materials while initial chlorine and NOM concentrations remained fairly constant (Table 4). The initial free chlorine level in the testing water was modified by adding hypochlorite solution to a target initial concentration of approximately 2.5 – 2.6 mg/l. The water temperature ranged from 12.43 °C to 26.14 °C. The water pH ranged 8.19 to 9.06. For each of the pipe materials, five experimental runs were intended to characterize the loss of chlorine as a function of flow velocity at 0.19 L/sec., 0.38 L/sec., 0.63 L/sec., and zero flow or stagnant conditions. The corresponding Reynolds numbers were 1500, 3100, 5100, and 0, respectively (Table 4). In the experiments, chlorine and general water chemistry parameters were measured using online instruments. Grab samples were also collected in the test loops and a reservoir of 9.46-m^3 stainless steel mixing tank (Fig.8), for analysis of free chlorine, turbidity, temperature (in-line), pH (in-line) in the loop, total organic carbon (TOC), TTHMs, and HAAs. .

Table 4. Experimental conditions of chlorine decay comparative studies for unlined ductile iron pipe loop #4 and PVC pipe loop #5. #

Test	Q (L/sec)	V (m/s)	Re	#4 DI Pipe T (C°)	#4 DI Pipe $[TOC]_o$ (mg/L)	#4 DI Pipe $[Cl_f]_o$ (mg/L)	#5 PVC pipe T (C°)	#5 PVC pipe $[TOC]_o$ (mg/L)	#5 PVC pipe $[Cl_f]_o$ (mg/L)
4a	0.631	0.038	5,400	19.3±0.7	0.504	2.2	19.4±0.8	0.622	2.5
3a	0.379	0.023	3,200	19.5±0.4	1.061	1.9	19.3±0.5	1.073	2.1
2a	0.189	0.011	1,700	20.1±0.7	0.961	1.9	20.4±0.9	0.993	2.4
1a	0	0	0	23.7±0.7	0.88	2.1	24.3±2.1	0.924	2.3

Note: # - Modified from Clark et al. (2008).

Pipe flow rate (Q) and water temperature (T) were measured by reading an inline flow meter and thermometer.

Initial TOC and free chlorine concentrations, or $[TOC]_0$ and $[Cl_f]_0$, were measured at t=0 when the pipe loops (Fig. 8) were filled with testing water

As discussed in Section 2.2, chlorine decay in a flowing water pipe can be described by the overall first-order or parallel first-order kinetics (i.e., Eqs.54-56). The experimental differences among the three types of wall materials or wall demand can be discerned from the relationship among K, k_{mt} and k_w. For the mass transfer limited model, the overall first-order reaction constant in Eq.55 comprises a bulk decay constant (k_b) and a mass transfer constant (k_{mt}). The wall reaction limited model in Eq.45 also includes k_{mt} and a correction factor $k_w/(k_{mt}+k_w)$. For the physical conditions described in these two kinetic scenarios, the overall first-order chlorine decay constant determined from experiments differs from the chlorine decay rate in bulk water phase from the glass bottle tests in Figure 5. It is also a function of pipe flow Reynolds numbers and, in the case of wall reaction limited condition, the rate of chlorine wall reactions. For reaction-limited chlorine decay under zero-order reactions at k_0, the overall chlorine decay rate could be approximated by the bulk decay constant with a tailing effect expressed by the ratio of k_o/k_b. This possibility is mathematically shown in Eq.52.

In the presence of both chlorine bulk demand and wall demand, it is often difficult to quantify and isolate chlorine decay caused by one of these two potential kinetic-limiting factors. One approach in experimental testing is to determine overall chlorine decay rate constants, and then to analyze their dependence on other variables including the rate of mass transfer and wall reactions in pipe flows. One uncertainty in this empirical approach is the lack of precise understanding on the bulk decay kinetics when wall effect is an important component. Section 2.1.2 describes the potential kinetic expressions for chlorine bulk decay. Besides the simple first-order kinetics, other kinetic models such as parallel first-order and second-order kinetic laws are applicable and have been proposed. The potential combinations between the possible bulk decay kinetic models and wall demand scenarios are extensive; some representative and simple cases are listed in Table 3. No criteria are currently available to exclusively distinguish these kinetic possibilities. Data fitting guided by regression correlation constant (R^2) is the single most used criterion. However, such a statistical criterion is insufficient to replace mechanistic determination for the reaction orders and kinetic types.

Figure 9 shows the chlorine decay experiment data and their best-fit curves based on the first-order kinetics (Eq.10) and the parallel first-order kinetics (Eq.13) for the overall chlorine bulk decay. The determined kinetic constants are plotted in Figure 10 against the pipe flow rate and the flow Reynolds number. Determined decay constants for the new PVC pipe are similar under all tested flow conditions within the uncertainties of determined values; the rate at stagnant flow is only slightly higher. The values range from 0.011 ± 0.003 hr^{-1} to 0.025 ± 0.004 hr^{-1}. In contrast, the overall chlorine decay rates for the same testing water are much higher in the ductile iron pipe that contains significant chlorine wall demand. The overall decay constant ranges from 0.080 ± 0.011 hr^{-1} at stagnant flow to 0.304 ± 0.018 hr^{-1} at Q=3.81 L/sec hr^{-1}, an approximate 40 times increase as the flow becomes turbulent. This statistically significant positive correlation between the flow rate and the determined overall chlorine decay constant is further displayed in Figure 10.

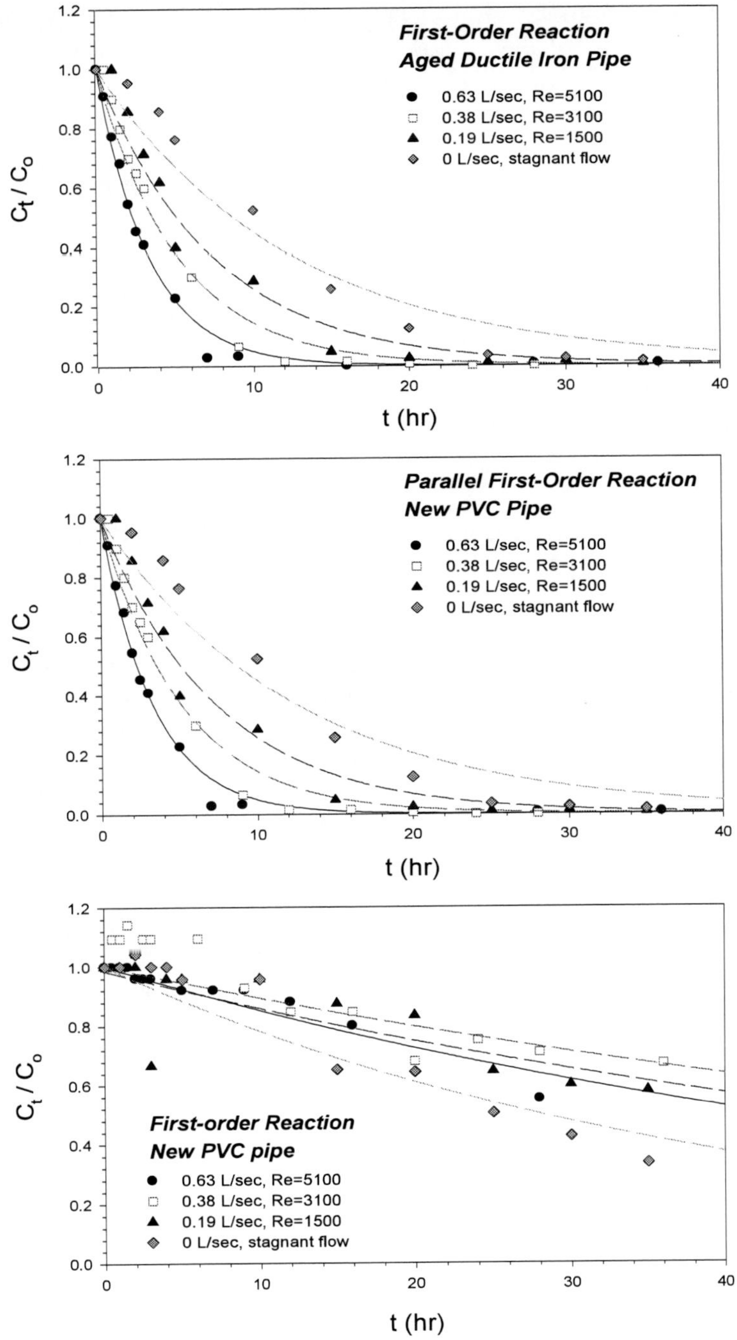

Figure 9. Model fits to chlorine decay experimental data for the aged cast iron pipe (A,B) and for the new PVC pie (C). Models used include first-order, parallel first-order, second-order, and parallel second-order kinetics. Both the first-order and second-order kinetic laws similarly, if not equally, represent the experimental data. It is only for the aged cast iron pipe of substantial wall demand that the chlorine reaction kinetic rate varies systematically with the pipe flow rate and Reynolds number. No systematic differences are discernible in the kinetic regression of the chlorine decay data for the new PVC pipe with negligible wall demand.

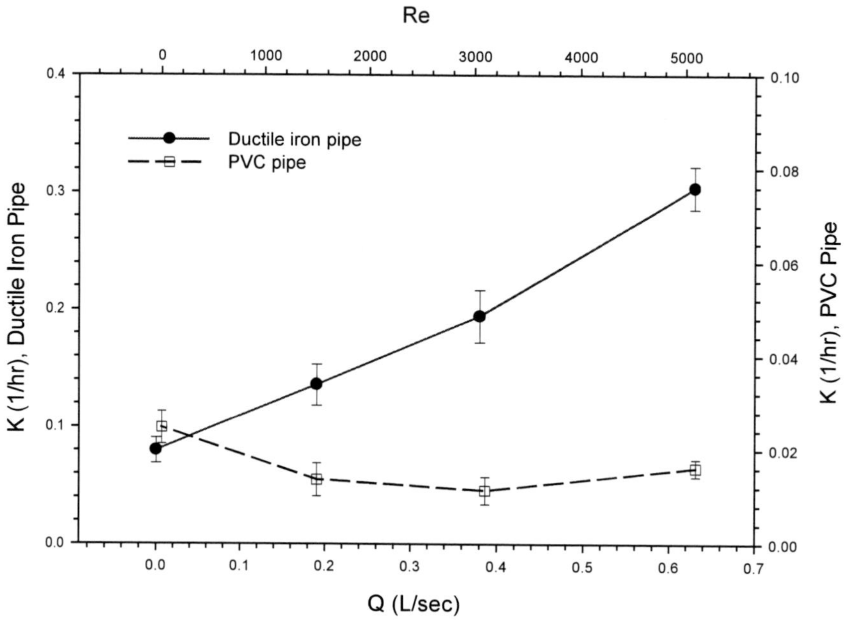

Figure 10. The overall chlorine decay constant K determined from the experiments increases with the pipe flow rate (Q) and Reynolds number (Re) in the aged ductile iron pipe. The variation of determined K values is significantly reduced for the new PVC pipe of negligible wall demand. At the stagnant flow conditions, the overall decay constants are similar for both types of pipe materials.

Clark et al. (2008) attributed the observed flow dependency of overall chlorine decay rate to the effect of increased chlorine mass transfer toward pipe walls in the aged ductile iron pipe that has a significant wall demand. Not accidentally, this phenomenon has been reported in field studies of water quality changes in drinking water distribution (See Section 2.4). Yet it is noted that hydraulic and kinetic mechanisms underpinning the observations are not fully understood in drinking water distribution. This flow-dependant phenomenon, however, has been studied extensively in pharmaceutical and chemical engineering (Baldyga et al., 1996; Levien and Levenspiel, 1999; Forney and Nafia, 2000; Chakraborty and Balakotaiah, 2002) where the potential impacts on product qualities in tubular flow reactors and in mass transfers. In drinking water quality management, the observation of flow dependency begins to attract research attention because of the implications on water quality deteriorations (e.g., Yang et al., 2008a,b; Clark and Haught, 2005; Panguluri et al., 2007).

2.3.3. Hydrodynamic Effects on DBP Formations

Yang et al. (2008b) reported the preliminary results of comparative experimental studies on THM formation rate and its relationships with pipe flow hydrodynamics. Their results show a strong correlation between chlorine decay and DBP formation, and further illustrate quantitatively the effects of hydrodynamics on the rate of THM formation. The theoretical basis for such a relationship has been described in the preceding section 2.2.2.

An example of correlated chlorine decay and DBP formation is given in Figure 11. Noteworthy is the timing and concentration relationships between free chlorine residual loss and the THM formation. At the turbulent flow condition (Q=0.63 L/sec, Re=5200), the free chlorine residual decayed rapidly to depletion within 3 hours and 7 hours for the ductile iron and PVC pipe, respectively. After that time, THM formation continued and reached a pseudo steady-state concentration at 44 μg/L in the ductile iron pipe loop #4. The rate of THM formation in loop #5 (PVC) is comparable with that in loop #4 before complete residual loss at t =3 hours (Fig. 11). This reflects the similar bulk chlorine demands of the same testing water used in the two experiments. In subsequent time periods at t >3 hours, water quality changes in the two loops became different. Because of smaller wall demand in the new PVC pipe, the chlorine residual remained present for t < 7 hours. After complete residual loss, the TTHM concentration continued to rise asymptotically to a pseudo steady-state concentration of approximately 78 μg/L, a level that is very close to the U.S. drinking water standard at 80 μg/L.

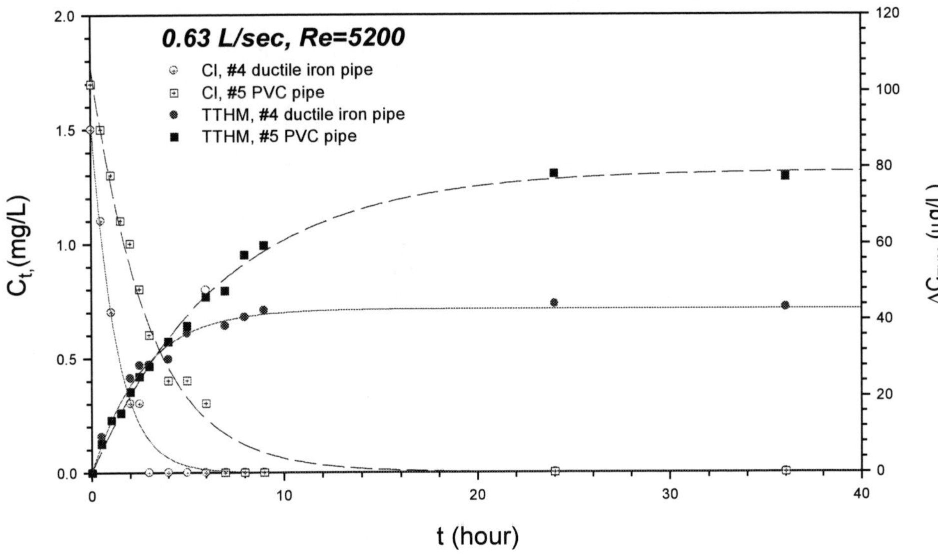

Figure 11. Time-series concentration plots for chlorine and TTHM in the 0.63 L/sec experiment under turbulent flow condition (Re=5100). Note the differences between loop #4 (ductile iron) and loop #5 (PVC) in both chlorine decay and THM formation. After exhaustion of free chlorine in water, the THM formation continued for up to 10 hours before reaching a pseudo-steady state condition.

The role of wall demand in the multi-species reactions of a flowing water pipe is analyzed not only in observed correlation between chlorine decay and DBP formation (Fig.11), but also quantitatively in the DBP formation kinetic rates between the two pipes. The correlation between chlorine decay and DBP formation has been described in previous publications (Clark and Sivaganesan, 2002; Boccelli et al., 2003; Warton et al., 2006). In Figure 12, the TTHM experimental data under various pipe flows are best-fit using the analytical solution for the parallel first-order DBP formation in Eq.69 (Clark, 1998). Alternatively, as described in Section 2.2.2, one also can examine first-order kinetics and other models of chlorine bulk decay in quantifying DBP formation. By the regression criteria along, the parallel first-order kinetic model is adequate to mathematically describe the experimental data.

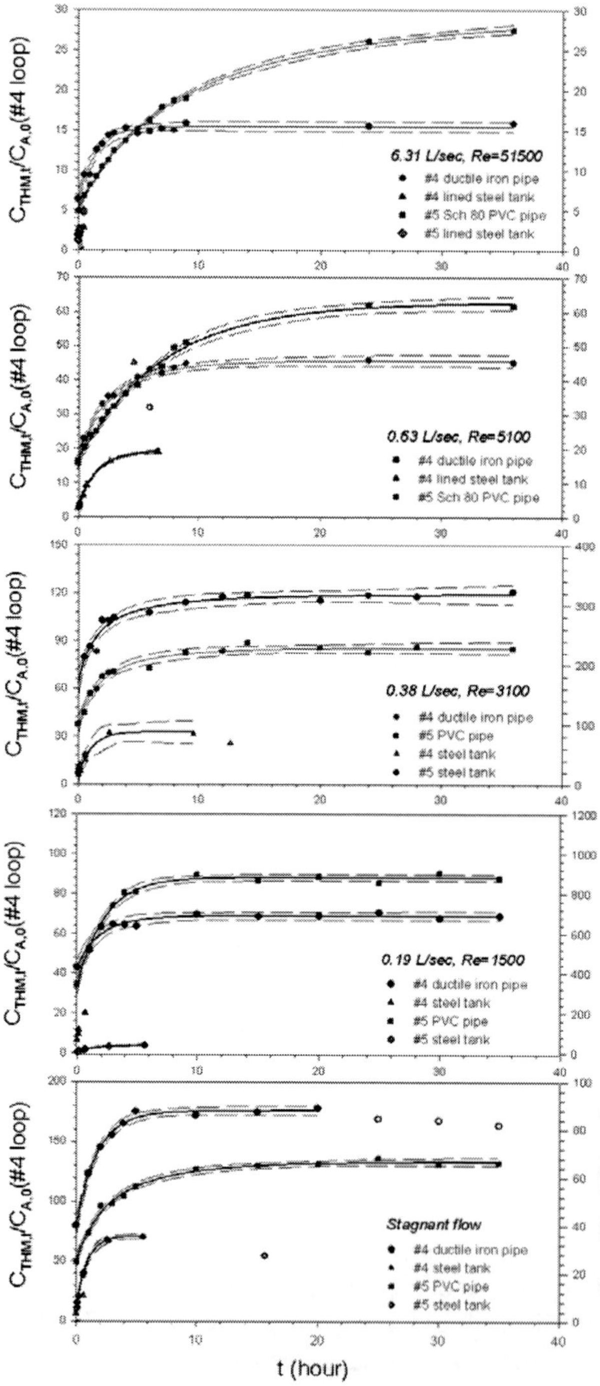

Figure 12. Time-series variation of normalized TTHM concentration against initial chlorine concentration for loop #4 (aged ductile iron), loop #5 (new PVC), and the steel tank shared by both loops. Non-linear regression lines (solid) and 95% CI bounds (dashed) are based on the DBP formation model of Clark (1998) in Eq.29. Regression constants range from 0.916 to 0.998. Modified from Yang et al. (2008b).

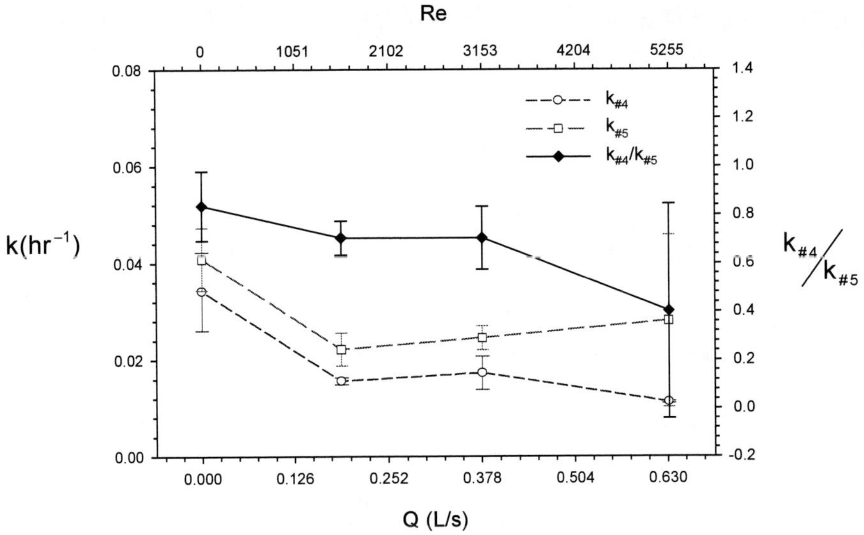

Figure 13. The overall first-order TTHM formation kinetic constants determined from the pilot-scale pipe loop experiments showing large variations with flow rate (Reynolds number). The TTHM formation constant negatively correlates with pipe flow rate for the aged ductile iron pipe (#4 pipe loop) of large wall demand. The new PVC pipe of minimal wall demand shows no statistically significant correlations with flow rate. The ratio of TTHM formation constants between the two pipes $\left(k_{\#4}/k_{\#5}\right)$ shows consistent variations with the flow rate. Error bars are one-standard deviation.

As for chlorine decay, the differences in THM formation kinetics between two pipe materials (Fig.12) is the result of competitive chlorine reactions in bulk demand and wall demand; the latter is related to pipe flow Reynolds number. Mechanistic principles for such a correlation have been described in Section 2.3.2. In the #4 aged ductile iron pipe, free chlorine residual decreased rapidly and DBP concentrations reached an asymptotic level within 7-10 hours (Fig. 11). Because of prevailing tubercles (Fig.8) and associated large wall demand in turbulent flow regimes, a significant fraction of chlorine loss in ductile iron pipe #4 is attributed to wall demand, not DBP formation from chlorine-NOM reactions in the bulk phase. In comparison, the new PVC pipe has negligible wall demand (Clark et al., 2008). A larger fraction of chlorine reacted with NOM leading to the higher DBP formation rate. This difference between the two pipes is clearly shown in the determined THMs formation kinetic constants when plotted against pipe flow rate (Fig.13). The ratio of kinetic rates between the ductile iron pipe and the PVC pipe $\left(k_{\#4}/k_{\#5}\right)$ indicates the difference in wall reactions because all other experimental conditions were maintained constant. For the ratio close to 1, the THM formation rate is similar between the two pipes. Conversely, the smaller the ratio, the smaller THM formation rate as observed in the #4 cast iron pipe and the larger fraction of chlorine consumption at the wall that yielded no THM formation.

As shown in Figure 13, the ratio is negatively correlated with Reynolds number. It decreases from 0.83 to 0.40 when the flow rate changed from stagnant to 0.63 L/sec. The change corresponds to a large decrease in THM formation rate in pipe #4 as the pipe flow rate increases, strongly indicating the role of wall demand in the competitive reaction system.

2.4. Field Observations in Previous Studies

In the sections above, we provided a theoretical analysis and described the controlled pilot-scale experiments to show the role of hydrodynamic factors in chlorine decay and DBP formation kinetic variations. In fact, there has been a long list of field observations that factors other than the bulk demand can cause water quality deterioration in a distribution network. One advantage in field studies is the opportunity of simultaneously observing hydrodynamic effects on chlorine decay, DBP formation and other water quality factors. Compared to experimental testing, however, the disadvantage is apparent in difficulties to isolate and quantify the hydrodynamic effects.

Previous investigations indicate that the chlorine residual loss in corroded unlined metallic pipes increased at higher pipe flow velocity. In one of the earliest studies, Williams (1953) found that the treatment plant in Brantford (Ontario, Canada) produced water that was acceptable from a taste and odor point-of-view. However, this study also found that while quality was maintained in high flow areas of the system, it deteriorated dramatically in low flow areas and in dead ends. It was further concluded that the loss of both chlorine and chloramine residuals in the Brantford water system was related to an increase in ferrous iron caused by corrosion in the distribution network pipes. In separate studies in collaboration with the South Central Connecticut Regional Water Authority (Clark, et al., 1991) and with the North Marin Water Authority in Northern California (Clark et al., 1994; Vasconcelos, et al., 1997), it was found that the total system decay rate of chlorine was much higher than the bulk decay rate. This additional demand was most likely due to pipe wall demand, biofilm, and tubercles. Benjamin et al. (1996) identified the accumulation of iron corrosion products at the pipe wall and the uptake of these products into the bulk water as the leading cause of water quality deterioration.

In a comprehensive study of chlorine residual losses in drinking water distribution networks, Powell (1998) and Powell et al. (2000) found a very large range of variation in wall demand for chlorine. The results suggest that cast-iron pipe typically has 10 to 100 times higher wall demand than PVC pipe. He also found an increase in wall demand with velocity which was most prominent in cast-iron pipe. These observations are consistent with the EPA comparative studies in the flowing ductile iron and PVC pipe loops described in Section 2.3. In a comprehensive field study by the Detroit Water and Sewerage Department, a series of 35 chlorine loss tests in pipe segments ranging in length from 153.5 – 614-m were conducted under varying flow conditions. The majority of the pipes were 70 to 135 year-old unlined cast-iron pipes ranging from 15.24 to 40.6 cm in diameter. The study showed that higher flow rates resulted in greater residual chlorine loss in the pipe (Grayman et al., 2002; Doshi et al, 2003).

In addition to water quality deterioration from corrosion by-products, there is evidence that corrosion scales support microbiological organisms. Camper et al. (2003) studied the interactions for different pipe materials, and found that, regardless of carbon levels, iron pipe had the highest numbers of bacteria. At the University of Illinois, Sarin et al. (2003) conducted a study of iron release from corroded, unlined cast-iron pipe using a pipe-loop system constructed from 100-year-old unlined cast iron pipes from the Massachusetts Water Resources Authority in Boston (Massachusetts, U.S.). The investigators concluded that iron release was closely linked to turbidity in positive correlations between iron and turbidity concentrations. Iron release was found to be sensitive to changes in alkalinity. Recent corrosion research by the University of Illinois has focused on characterizing the nature of scales in metal pipes (Sarin et al., 2004). The investigators found that corrosion has a number of negative effects on water quality in drinking water distribution networks, including the creation of scales on pipe walls.

Eisnor and Gagnon (2003) studied pipe wall demand for free chlorine on full-scale distribution networks. They have shown that free chlorine losses in system pipes were considerably higher than would have been predicted using the bulk water decay rate. Clark and Haught (2005) conducted a study to systematically assess the effect of free chlorine loss in corroded unlined metallic pipes subject to changes in velocity using the pipe loop in Figure 8. Results from the study supported the concept that the rate of free chlorine residual loss increased with velocity in unlined metallic pipe. Furthermore, Al-Jasser (2007) attempted to assess the service age of pipes on the effective chlorine wall decay constant. After examination of 302 pipe sections of different diameters and eight different pipe materials, it was found that the effect of pipe age was most evident in cast-iron pipes, whereas steel pipes were less affected.

To maintain a minimum threshold of chlorine residual throughout a distribution network, Tryby at al. (1999) examined the feasibility of using booster chlorination in distribution networks. They developed a conceptual model for bulk chlorine decay under booster conditions. The conceptual analysis demonstrated that the use of booster chlorination allows microbial inactivation and maintenance of a detectable residual to be viewed as separate treatment issues. Booster chlorination could allow dosages to be reduced at the water treatment plant without compromising treatment objectives. By reducing dosages, DBP yields at the water treatment plant may also be reduced and the disinfectant mass conserved can be more efficiently applied at points located in the distribution network. Their studies suggest that increasing residual concentrations alone will not eliminate the risks associated with pathogens and biofilm regrowth in problem areas. Several barriers against the entrance of contaminants are required.

Boccelli et al. (1998) studied disinfectants added at locations distributed throughout a water distribution network. Such a strategy can reduce the mass of disinfectant required to maintain a detectable residual at points of consumption in the distribution network, which may lead to reduced DBP formation, particularly in THM. An optimization model is formulated for the dynamic schedule of disinfectant injections which minimizes the total dose required to satisfy residual constraints over an infinite time horizon. This infinite-time problem is reduced to a solvable finite-time optimal scheduling model by assuming periodicity of mass injections and network hydraulics. Furthermore, this principle of linear superposition is shown to apply to disinfectant concentrations resulting from multiple disinfectant injections over time. A matrix generator code was developed to interface with the EPANET network water quality model. This code automatically generates the linear programming formulation for the optimal scheduling, which is then solved using simple algorithms. Results from application of the model suggest that booster disinfection can reduce the amount of disinfectant required to satisfy concentration constraints, when compared to conventional disinfection only at the source. The optimal booster schedule reduced the average disinfectant concentration within the distribution network and, in some cases, the variability of these concentrations. The number of booster stations, booster location, and distribution network hydraulics were all shown to affect the optimal scheduling.

Now the new understanding of hydrodynamic effects on the rate of chlorine decay and DBP formations points to the complex chlorine reaction kinetic scenarios in water distribution pipes, some of which are listed in Table 4. Because many distribution networks are extremely complex and difficult to study in the field, mathematical models that incorporate both chlorine bulk demand and wall reactions in a multi-component reaction system can provide a quantitative tool to better assess the water quality changes in distribution. This section has described the models, their evolution with time, and limitations for practical uses. Recent studies that have attempted to model chlorine residual in field hydrodynamic fields have been undertaken by Huang and McBean (2007) and Yang et al. (2008a). Huang and McBean (2007) suggested a two-component second-order chlorine bulk decay model and Yang et al. (2008a) suggested a modified one-dimensional Dankwerts convection-dispersion-reaction (CDR) model. Undoubtedly, incorporation of these mechanistic models and the inspection of potential kinetic scenarios in Table 4 can help improve the water quality management and network operations such as booster scheduling of Boccelli et al (1998; 2003). Such an operational optimization for simultaneous compliance of both chlorine decay and DBP formation is an example of model-based system control and management that require further studies and development.

3. Hydraulics and Mass Transport of Foreign Intrusions

In Section 2.0, chlorine decay and DBP formation in a flowing pipe are used to illustrate the difficulty and opportunities in predicting water quality changes and achieving simultaneous compliances over multiple water quality criteria. The focus is placed on water of relatively uniform quality that enters a distribution network from a treatment plant or a storage facility at $t=0$. Subsequent water quality changes in distribution are a function of chlorine reactions in the bulk water and at pipe walls. The second major category of water quality changes is the result of foreign intrusions into a water pipe. Such foreign intrusions are characterized by a finite volume of contaminants instantaneously introduced (or over a short-term time period) into the pipe due to failure of the closed pipe flow system due to a pipe line break, back-siphoning, and even intentional sabotage. Contaminant back-siphoning from pipe breaks, for example, usually only lasts but can repeat for <10 sec before the negative transient pressure dissipates (AWWA, 2004). Once entering into a flowing drinking water pipe, the identifiable contaminant body is then subject to convection, dispersion and reaction (CDR), a process mathematically described in Eq.37 (Yang et al., 2008a).

Compared to solute transport described in Section 2.0, contaminant transport as a "slug" of contaminants in water distribution network has been less discussed, but is of fundamental interest in practical applications. One application area is the protection of drinking water distribution networks from intentional sabotage. Accurate real-time detection of chemical and biological contaminants is required in planning and implementing security and mitigation measures (Hasan et al., 2004; ILSI, 1999; US EPA, 2005; Jain and McLean, 2006). As highlighted in the incidental contamination of potable water in Scotland (Gavriel et al., 1998), poisoning of water supplies in Japan (Yokoyama, 2007), and domestic bioterrorist acts (Stern,

2000), intentional sabotage remains a significant threat to the public health (WHO, 2004; Greenfield et al., 2002). The urgent need to protect water supplies as noted in Burrows and Renner (1999) has prompted numerous investigations into methodologies for detection, decontamination, public health preparedness, and threat scenario analysis (e.g., Murray et al., 2006; Iqbal et al., 2000; Greenfield et al., 2002; Khan et al., 2001; Meinhardt, 2005; Morse et al., 2003). In this section, fate and transport of an introduced "slug" of reactive and non-reactive contaminants are reviewed and discussed. Related to this brief overview is the real-time intrusion-related water quality anomaly detection and measurement for such a "slug" in a flowing water pipe.

3.1. Water Quality Changes Due to Contaminant Intrusions

3.1.1. Change Detections

Water quality changes at locations of pipe leaks, back-siphoning, and intentional sabotage have been reported (Kunkel et al., 2008; AWWA, 2004). Among the change of water quality parameters, the loss of chlorine residual is a primary indicator of hydraulic communication between the outside and the inside of a water distribution pipe. Recently, a series of controlled experimental studies have been conducted at the EPA's Testing and Evaluation (T&E) facility to detect and identify the presence of a contaminant "slug" and to document its fate and transport in a flowing water pipe (Li, 2000; Szabo et al., 2007; Yang et al., 2006, 2007; Haught et al., 2005). These investigations have led to a systematic understanding of water quality changes, most notably the geometry of chlorine concentration profiles in the solute propagation front. The profiles, as demonstrated in Yang et al. (2008a, 2009) can reflect the pipe flow hydrodynamics, contaminant-chlorine reaction kinetics, and the manner in which a contaminant "slug" is introduced into the pipe flow.

Solute transport in pipe flow has been studied extensively in the past century. The early experimental and theoretical work by Taylor (1953, 1954) and later by Aries (1956) and others (e.g., Ekambara and Joshi, 2004) have focused on the transport of tracers in a finite discrete volume in laminar and turbulent pipe flows. A familiar example is hydraulic testing using conservative sodium fluoride as a tracer in characterizing the pipe flow hydrodynamics (Levenspiel, 1972) such as solute dispersion coefficient. In a drinking water distribution pipe, however, the transport of foreign contaminant "slug" differs from the classic tracer experiments. The difference arises from the fact that because of the chlorine disinfectants in drinking water, a reactive foreign contaminant body is subject to simultaneous convection, dispersion and reaction (CDR). Unlike the conservative tracers, the CDR process is a function of the contaminant-disinfectant reactivity and the interactions with pipe walls (Yang et al., 2008a).

Monitoring the propagation of a foreign contaminant "slug" is essential to the study of contaminant CDR processes. In addition to the classic discrete sampling and analysis, the development and deployment of chemical and physical sensors provide extra capability by which contaminant transport in pipe flows can be fully traced and, notably, in real-time. In drinking water applications, compound-specific sensors are rare and expensive to deploy because of capital and operational costs and potentially thousands of chemical and biological contaminants to monitor. A common practice relies on the use of conventional water quality sensors and advanced sensor data treatment algorithms (See Yang et al., 2009; Klise et al., 2006; Kroll and King, 2006). Common water quality sensors include those for total chlorine, free chlorine, chloride, oxidation-reduction-potential (ORP), dissolved oxygen (DO), turbidity, pH, and specific conductivity. Among them, chlorine measurements are the most sensitive indicators of contamination because of chlorine's oxidation ability with a wide spectrum of contaminants (Haught et al., 2005; Szabo et al., 2007; Kroll and King, 2006). On the other hand, conventional water quality sensors have their marked disadvantages mainly due to their non-selectivity. How to relate the detection of a change in a conventional water quality parameter to the presence and levels of foreign contaminants in pipe flow is a daunting challenge and has been a subject of extensive research (Klise et al., 2006; Yang et al., 2006, 2007, 2009; Haught et al., 2005). Yang et al. (2009) outlined an adaptive monitoring approach, based on the continuity of characteristic signal variations at the contaminant (solute) propagation front, to reduce sensor signals other than those related to a moving contaminant "slug". They assumed that, in general, a water quality sensor signal output (I^t) consists of contributions from contaminants of interests (I_c^t), natural background (I_b^t), instrument noise (I_n^t), drifting (I_d^t), and random variance related to operations (σ). The background (I_b^t) is zero or negligible for compound-specific sensors, but can be significant for non-selective water quality sensors for which signal output and a target concentration (C_i) are related by:

$$I^t = I_c^t + I_b^t + I_n^t + I_d^t + \sigma \tag{70}$$

or

$$I_i^t = \beta \cdot C_i^t + \hat{m}F(t) + \nu(I_n^t, \sigma) \tag{71}$$

$$C_i = \beta I_c^t + \theta_i \tag{72}$$

where $\hat{m}$ is a constant matrix; the Taylor polynomial form $F(t)$ is a function of time and represents combined sensor response from background (I_b^t) and sensor drifting (I_d^t); $\nu(I_n^t, \sigma)$ is normally distributed and independent of time, accounting for instrumental noise and operation-related random variances, which can be eliminated using time-series signal processing techniques. The linear instrument response factor β is defined in calibration against a set of standard solutions and the intercept θ_i is often forced to zero. Eq.71 further indicates that the contaminant detection and its false rates are directly a function of relative strength between the time-dependant contaminant and background signals in a pipe flow system.

Yang et al. (2006, 2009) described an adaptive monitoring process for signal separation by sensor output normalization against those in an adaptive time window (T). The methodology helps identify the contaminant signal in form of water quality changes and separate it from background variations and instrument noises. When the adaptive period T is defined such that the constant $\left\lfloor \hat{m}_{(i,j)}F(t+1) - \hat{m}_{(i,j)}F(T) \right\rfloor << I_i^T$, the relative change (Δc) in sensor output is obtained from rearranging Eq.71:

or
$$\Delta C \cong -\frac{\left(C_i^t - C_i^T\right)}{C_i^T}\frac{1}{1+\kappa} \qquad (73)$$

$$\kappa = \frac{m_{(i,j)}F(T) + \nu(I_n^T, \sigma)}{\beta C_i^T} \text{ and } \lim_{T\to\infty}(\kappa) \to 0 \qquad (74)$$

In background monitoring, the relative change of sensor outputs converges to zero. $\Delta c < 0$ for parameters of a reactant, and $\Delta c > 0$ for parameters of a reaction product. The monitoring operator κ is a small constant in design of an adaptive monitoring program, a design requirement that can be difficult to achieve in the case of excessive background variations and instrument drift or failure.

3.1.2. Experimental Testing

Systematic studies of water quality sensor response to contaminant intrusions were conducted by several investigators at US EPA and its collaborators at the Battelle Memorial Institute for hundreds of conventional contaminants, chemical and biological agents. Most of these results were captured in a series of published reports (Szabo et al., 2007; Haught et al., 2005; Yang et al. 2006). At the EPA's T&E facilities, fate and transport of contaminant "slugs" were determined in experiments using the pilot-scale once-through water distribution pipe in Figure 14. To simulate external contaminant intrusions, a finite volume of contaminant solution was injected into pipe flow under a constant hydraulic pressure. Water quality changes responding to the intrusions were measured at two water quality sensor stations placed at 24.4-m and 335.4-m downstream from the contaminant injection port. Conventional water quality parameters were measured including total chlorine, free chlorine, chloride, oxidation-reduction-potential (ORP), dissolved oxygen (DO), turbidity, pH, and specific conductivity. The 15 contaminants injected in the experimental testing included pesticides and herbicides, laboratory chemicals, inorganic oxidants, *E.coli* and biological growth media.

The free chlorine and total chlorine concentration data (Szabo et al, 2007) show U-shape curves of residual loss on a concentration-time (c-t) plot for each sensor station (Fig.15). Yang et al. (2006) and Haught et al. (2005) considered the loss as the result of oxidation reactions between contaminants and the oxidant chlorine in the water. Chloride, as a final reaction product, shows a concentration increase curve and a characteristic dispersion tail extending beyond the downstream boundary of the chlorine residual loss (Yang et al., 2009). Similar V-shaped tails occurred for ORP that decrease as chlorine oxidants are depleted in contaminant oxidation. Furthermore, pH changes occurred at the same time periods as for the other measured parameters. Detected and qualified pH changes are as low as approximately 1% using the adaptive technique. Such adaptive monitoring during the experimental simulation generated consistent c-t variations that, as described in mathematical modeling of previous sections, reflect the combined effect of hydrodynamics and chemical chlorine-contaminant reactivity.

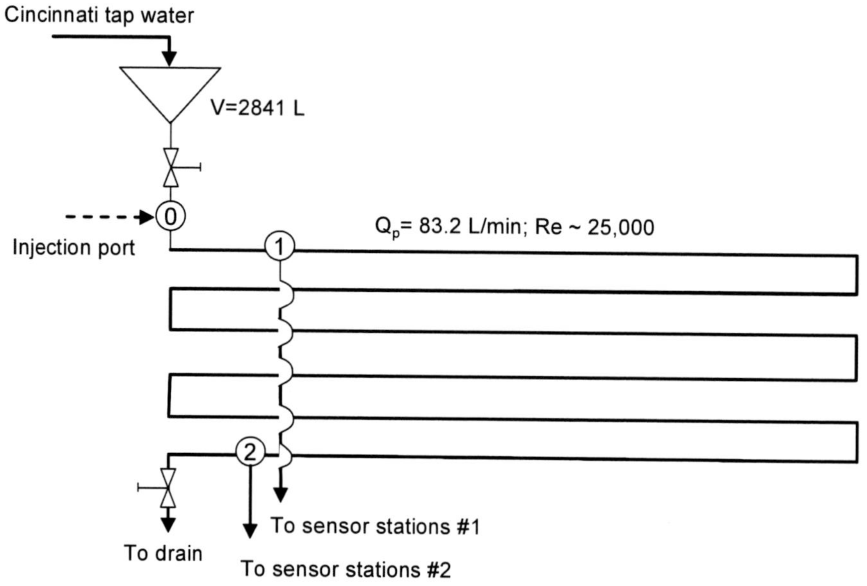

Figure 14. Experimental setup diagram for the fate and transport experimental studies. A 10-L contaminant "slug" was injected at Q_i=0.5 L/min at location O in the 426.8-m long drinking water distribution pipe. Water quality changes were measured using online water quality sensors at two sensor monitoring stations 22.4-m and 335.4-m downstream from the injection port.

On the c-t plots (Fig.15), contaminants aldicarb, glyphosate, *E.coli* with nutrient broth, anhydrous and pentahydrate sodium thiosulfate all showed >80% free chlorine loss at the position of a contaminant "slug". In the experiments, Yang et al. (2006) reported that the relative changes in total chlorine sensor responses (ΔC in Eq.73) as small as 3.15% were registered by monitoring sensors during the injection of several contaminants: dimethyl sulfoxide, nutrient broth, terrific broth, and trypticase soy broth. Compared to free chlorine, the composite sensor dataset for total chlorine (Fig.15) contains large background variations; some are due to sensor noise or background changes.

Based on the experimental results, there are marked differences in the pattern geometry that can be readily observed among the water quality parameters in a flowing water pipe. For example, chlorine residual loss at a reactive contaminant "slug" is detectable in the U-shape pattern on the time-series $\Delta c - t$ plots (Fig.15). In the curve geometry, the opening width marks the time-equivalent pipe length where residual loss has occurred; the relative change (Δc) is uniform in the flat curve bottom within the contaminant "slug". Sharp-sided curvature suggests a rapid recovery of chlorine residual level to the background where $\Delta c \cong 0$. Yang et al. (2008a) mathematically related the rate of recovery and the curve geometry principally to the chlorine-contaminant reaction kinetics and to a lesser degree to the pipe flow hydraulics and solute dispersivity. These characteristic associations are described in the subsequent sections. Once again the chlorine responses are used to illustrate and explore their relations with the flow hydrodynamic factors.

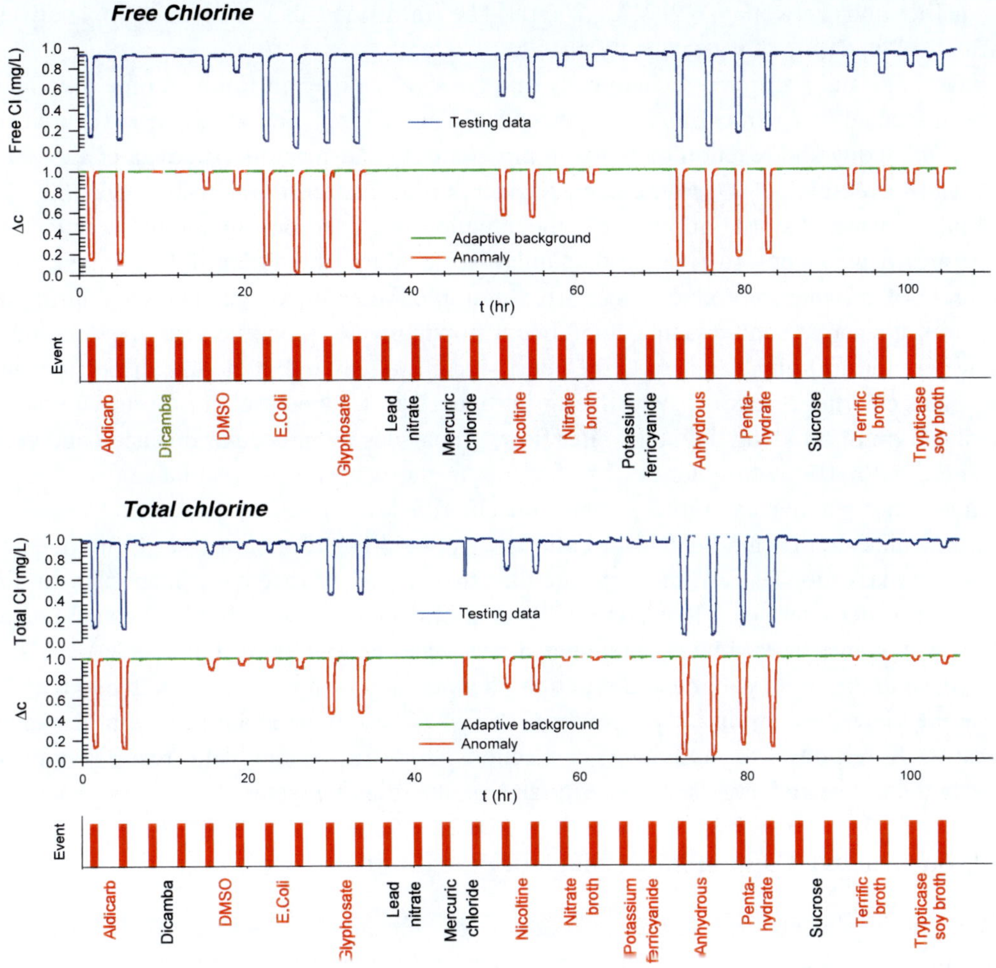

Figure 15. Adaptively treated sensor outputs on the *c-t* plot for a composite dataset, showing signal changes at the location of contaminant "slug" registered at the first monitoring station. The composite testing dataset is composed of individual tests for the 15 contaminants, each with two repeated injection events at 20-min duration; x-axis is an artificial accumulative testing time for the composite dataset. Positively detected contamination events are marked in Red.

3.2. Modeling of a Contaminant "Slug" Transport in Pipe Flow

The theoretical basis of describing the behavior of a finite contaminant "slug" in a water pipe is different from that of product water entering a distribution network from a water treatment plant. For the latter, chlorine decay and water quality changes are in response to the chlorine bulk demand and wall demand inside of a flowing water pipe. The theoretical basis, experiments and field observations are described in Section 2.0. In the case of a foreign contaminant intrusion, significant water quality changes may occur at the locations of intrusion and in pipe segments downstream. The intrusion brings "foreign" contaminants into a flowing pipe, which mix and react with chlorine and other chemical constituents in the drinking water. This is considered one of the primary water quality deterioration mechanisms in a distribution network (AWWA, 2004). The intrusion also creates complexity in mathematical modeling of water quality changes.

In fact, fate and transport of chemically and physically different fluids in pipe flow have long been studied in chemical and pharmaceutical engineering. The attention is focused on micro-scale mixing and reaction of fluids in pipes and tubular reactors (Baldyga et al., 1996; Levien and Levenspiel, 1999; Forney and Nafia, 2000; Chakraborty and Balakotaiah, 2002). In a drinking water distribution network, the attention is placed on mixing and reactions of two chemically different waters rather than micro-scale immiscible fluids. Whether it happens in the case of mixing of product water from multiple water treatment plants or during an intrusion of a reactive contaminant "slug" into a flowing water pipe, the resulting conditions in the water pipe are similar in nature: the macro-scale fluid mixing, hydraulic dispersion, and contaminant-chlorine reactions. After being introduced to a pipe flow, the finite volume of contaminant transport along the bulk water flow, propagates by molecular diffusion and axial dispersion, and reacts with chlorine disinfectants in the water. This simultaneous chlorine-contaminant fast reaction can rapidly reduce the chlorine level inside of the "slug", generating a chlorine concentration gradient from bulk water toward the contamination. Consequently, the chlorine mass transfer is in the opposite direction to that of reactive contaminants at the contaminant-water interface. The water quality changes in the water body of the contaminated "slug" and at its interface with uncontaminated bulk water phase (Yang et al., 2008a).

Because of the finite volume and duration, the intrusion of foreign materials into a water pipe can be viewed as an instantly introduced "slug" of reactive contaminants that disperses physically in response to hydraulic convections and dispersions and reacts with the disinfectant chlorine and other substances already in the drinking water.

3.2.2. Non-Reactive Contaminant "Slug" in Pipe Flows

When foreign contaminants are non-reactive to chlorine disinfectant, their behavior is similar to the process of a conservative tracer of Taylor (1953, 1954). Conservative constituents have no reactivity with chlorine and consequently differ in mass transport behavior than those chlorine-reactive contaminants in drinking water pipes. Injection of a conservative tracer such as sodium fluoride in pipe flow testing (e.g., Taylor, 1953, 1954; Aries, 1956; Ekambara and Joshi, 2004) can be viewed as a familiar example of non-reactive contaminant intrusion. When $k_b=0$, $J_w = 0$ and using the transverse averaged concentration, the Danckwerts CDR model in Eq.37 can be simplified into a governing differential equation that is identical to that of Levenspiel (1972) for non-reactive contaminant or tracer transport in water pipes. The dimensionless exit age (E*) for the contaminant residence time distribution is solved explicitly from Eq.76 and 77 (Levenspiel, 1972).

$$\frac{\partial C}{\partial t} = \frac{\partial C}{\partial x} + \frac{1}{m^2 Pe_D}\left(\frac{\partial^2 C}{\partial x^2}\right) \tag{75}$$

$$E^* = \frac{1}{2\sqrt{\pi Pe_L^{-1}}} \exp\left[-\frac{(1-t)^2}{4 \cdot Pe_L^{-1}}\right] \quad Pe_L > 100 \tag{76}$$

$$E^* = \frac{1}{2\sqrt{\pi \cdot tPe_L^{-1}}} \exp\left[-\frac{(1-t)^2}{4t \cdot Pe_L^{-1}}\right] \quad Pe_L \leq 100 \tag{77}$$

Li (2000) found these equations conformed to tracer experiment results under a wide range of flow conditions in a long water pipe. Both the numerical modeling (Eq.75) and the Levenspiel (1972) analytical solutions (Eq.76) provide E-curves consistent with the tracer experimental results of Li (2000) in turbulent flows (Fig.16). After approximately 202-m distance of transportation, the contaminant slug remains chemically distinctive. In another sodium chloride tracer experiment, Yang et al. (2007) observed that a chemically distinct "slug" remained as a discrete volume of water with axial expansion in accordance with the Eq.76 as first proposed in Taylor (1954). Similar observations were also made in Panguluri et al (2007) who studied the transport of a conservative tracer in a circulating pipe loop in Figure 8. Their results indicated that a "slug" of tracer became homogenized only when the water volume of tracer passed a boosting pump 3 to 5 times in the flow rate range examined.

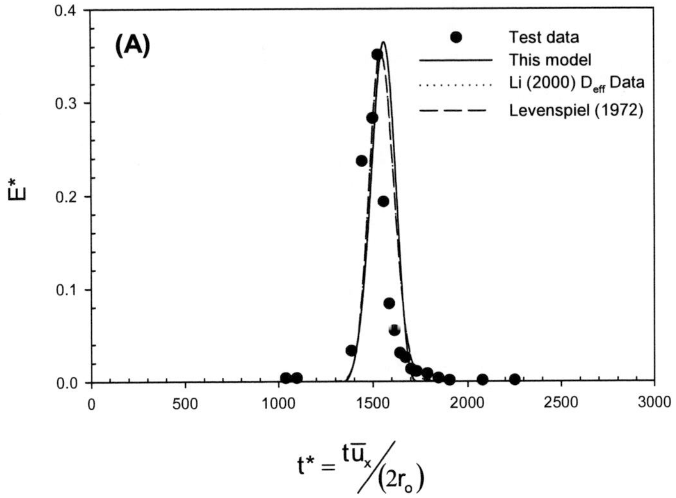

Figure 16. Model-simulated E*-curves and sodium fluoride experimental data for a 112.2-m long PVC water pipe under turbulent conditions (Q=18.3 L/sec, Re=9020). D_{eff}=33 was used for the CDR model calculation at k_f=0 and $J_w = 0$ and for the analytical solution of Levenspiel (1972). Also shown are E*-curves of the analytical model using D_{eff} experimental values of Li (2000). X-axis t* is dimensionless. Modified from Yang et al. (2008a).

3.2.3. Reactive Contaminant "Slug" in Pipe Flows

For a chlorine-reactive "foreign" contaminant slug, Yang et al. (2008a) proposed that upon introduction, the reactive contaminants in chlorinated drinking water produce a series of changes in both chlorine bulk demand and wall demand. Such a change alters the post-mixing chlorine residual level within the contaminant body, changes the chlorine mass transfer and reaction kinetics, and results in water quality changes within the "slug" and its interface with the uncontaminated bulk water.

Upon the introduction of a reactive contaminant "slug", the fast contaminant-chlorine reactions within the contaminated water create a new bulk demand in the contaminant "slug" after mixing. The concentration decrease leads to a smaller concentration gradient from the "slug" to the pipe wall than in the background bulk water, and thus reduces wall demand according to its definitions of Rossman et al. (1994) and Clark and Haught (2005). See Section 2.2.1 for discussions. In the CDR model by Yang et al. (2008a), the fast and slow reactions within the contaminated "slug" of water follow the stoichiometric reactions in Eq.28 and the parallel second-order reaction kinetics in Eq.29 (Clark and Sivaganesan, 2002).

The chlorine residual profile at the contaminant-water interface determines the shape and extent of the chlorine residual loss as recorded at the sensor stations in Figure 17. In a mathematical description of the chlorine loss curvature, the governing equation is given in Eq.37 subject to the following boundary and initial conditions specific to a contaminant "slug" in a flowing pipe:

$$C_{(\infty,t)} = C_o \qquad \text{at } t \geq 0$$

$$\left(\frac{\partial C}{\partial x}\right)_t = 0 \text{ at } x = 0$$

$$C/C_o \cong f_m \cdot \frac{(1-R_1)}{1-R_1 e^{-(1-R_1)k_f t}} + (1-f_m)\cdot\left[\frac{(1-R_2)}{1-R_1 e^{-(1-R_2)k_s t}}\right]$$

at
$$\left(\bar{u}_x t - \frac{h}{2r_o}\right) \leq x \leq \left(\bar{u}_x t + \frac{h}{2r_o}\right) \tag{78}$$

$$C = \begin{cases} \Gamma(C_{x=x_1}) \\ & \text{at } t = 0 \\ C_o \end{cases} \tag{79}$$

$\Gamma(C_{x=x_1})$ is a chlorine concentration input function at sensor station #1 (Fig. 6); $\Gamma(C_{x=x_1}) = C_o$ for the contaminant introduced at this location. Boundary conditions in the contaminant "slug" $\left(\bar{u}_x t - \frac{h}{2r_o}\right) \leq x \leq \left(\bar{u}_x t + \frac{h}{2r_o}\right)$ are given in Eq.78. In Eq.37 when the axial Péclet number ($Pe_L = m^2 Pe_D$) is sufficiently large, the axial dispersion becomes negligible and subsequent simplifications yield the governing equations of Rossman et al. (1994) for the EPANET model. The governing Eq.37 is valid to describe mass transport in a long and narrow pipe, for which the axial dispersion is fully developed (Taylor, 1953, 1954) and the axial dispersion term can be neglected.

In a period before the solute front propagates and chlorine-contaminant reacts to the extent to which the contaminant "slug" is homogenized with bulk water, the chlorine loss profile in Figure 17 remains distinctive at the water and contaminant "slug" interface. The profile curvature is given in governing Eq.37, initial and boundary conditions in Eqs.78-79. Inside of the contaminant "slug", the chlorine decay follows one of the chlorine decay models described in Section 2.1.2. The degree of chlorine loss is proportional to the initial chlorine concentrations. This proportionality is observed for the pilot-scale pipe flow experiments (Fig.17).

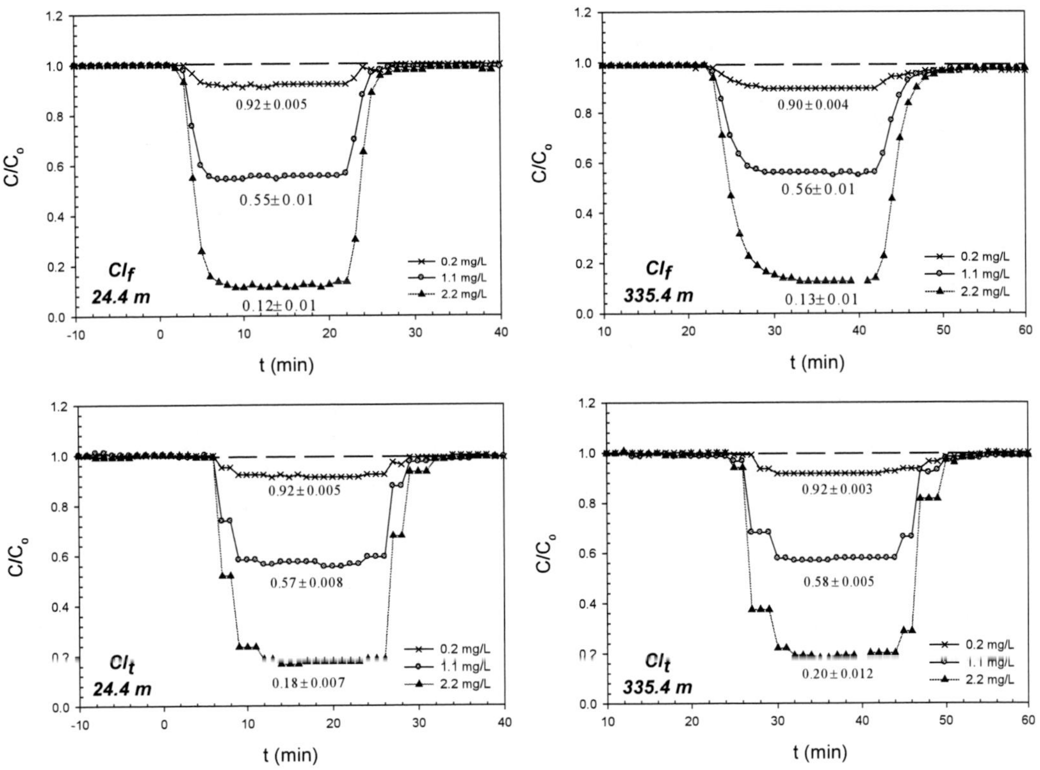

Figure 17. Progressive chlorine residual loss (c) at initial aldicarb concentrations 0.2 mg/L, 1.1 mg/L, and 2.2 mg/L. Average chlorine concentrations and one standard derivation $(\overline{m} \pm 1\sigma)$ are marked for the chlorine (cl_f) and total chlorine (cl_t). It is noted that the residual loss is proportional to the initial concentrations of aldicarb solution injected into the flowing water pipe.

3.3. Hydrodynamic Factors in Fate and Transport of Contaminant Intrusions

It is not difficult to find from governing Eq.37 that the chlorine residual consumption rates in wall demand and bulk demand are intrinsically related to axial and radial hydraulic dispersion. Because of this linkage, chlorine and other water quality parameters are characterized by concentration profiles associated with both hydraulic parameters of a pipe flow and the contaminant reactivity with chlorine disinfectants. Such a correlation was discussed in recent work by Clark and Haught (2005) and Yang et al. (2008a).

3.3.1. Quasi-Steady State Chlorine Decay and Hydrodynamics

Experimental testing has led to the observation that chlorine residual loss within the contaminant "slug" of reactive contaminants (e.g., aldicarb, E.coli, colchicine) displayed no significant change between the two sensor stations spaced at a 311-m flow distance. It follows that the contaminant "slug" must have reached a quasi-steady state in chlorine residual loss before reaching sensor station #1. After a rapid decay in the early time, chlorine concentration approaches a plateau in the late time under a quasi-steady state. This is observed in the contaminant intrusion experiments for the reactive contaminants, aldicarb (Fig.17), colchicine and *E.coli* (Fig.18).

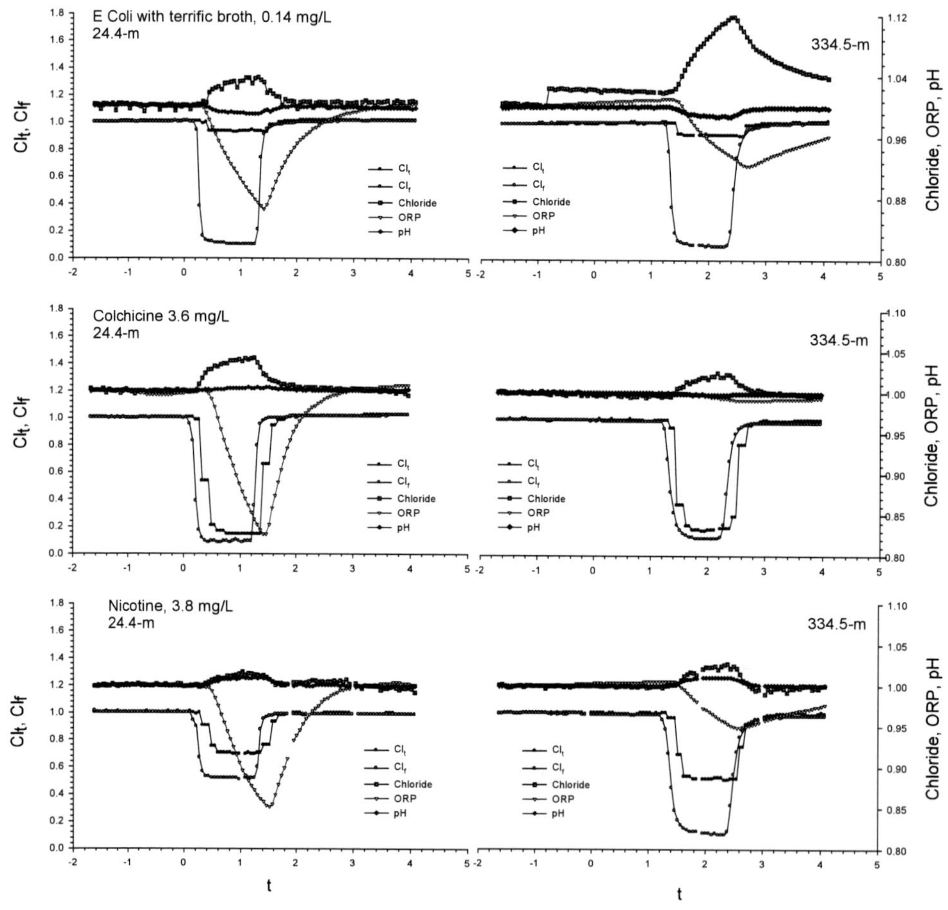

Figure 18. Sensor response patterns for *E.coli,* alkaloid colchicine and nicotine as detected at the two sensor stations 24.4-m and 334.5-m downstream from the contaminant intrusion location. The sensor station setup is shown in Figure 6. Y-axes are the measurements normalized against the background concentration free of contamination. X-axis is dimensionless time normalized to hydraulic retention time at the 334.5-m sensor station. Modified from Yang et al. (2007).

The time to reach a quasi-steady state is a function of pipe flow velocity, chlorine-contaminant reaction constant, and the distance between contaminant intrusion location and the first-sensor station for measurement. In the intrusion detection experiments, chlorine decay reached a quasi-steady state rapidly for the reactive contaminants aldicarb, glyphosate, colchicine, and *E.coli* in terrific broth. After the quasi-steady state was reached, further chlorine loss (Δc in Eq.73) between the two monitoring stations of a 311-m flow distance was too small for accurate measurement (See Fig. 17). The quasi-steady state shows the chlorine-contaminant reactivity and its rate relative to the water flow velocity between two monitoring stations marked as line "L" in Figure 6. Conversely, less-reactive contaminants tend to exhibit a non-steady-state chlorine loss curvature that changes between the two sensor locations. Examples were observed in the experiments for the contaminant nicotine, the water parameters pH and ORP, as well as the reaction byproduct chloride (Fig.18). In the extreme case of a conservative solute, the chlorine concentrations show no change. This is shown in the experiments for chlorine resistant dicamba in Figure 15.

3.3.2. Curve Geometry and Flow Hydrodynamics

In addition to the changes in chlorine and other parameters within the contaminant "slug", Yang et al. (2008a; 2009) have described the change in geometry of the solute propagation front. Their simulation and experimental results shows the geometry as an indicator of chlorine-contaminant reactivity, which can be used to reveal the effects of flow hydrodynamics on contaminant reaction and propagation in the pipes. One example for illustration is the aldicarb contaminant intrusion experiment shown in Figure 19, where experimental data for the 24.4-m sensor station are displayed along with the CDR numerical simulation results. The initial aldicarb concentrations was 2.2 mg/L in the experiments. The numerical simulation results were based on Eqs.37 and 78-79.

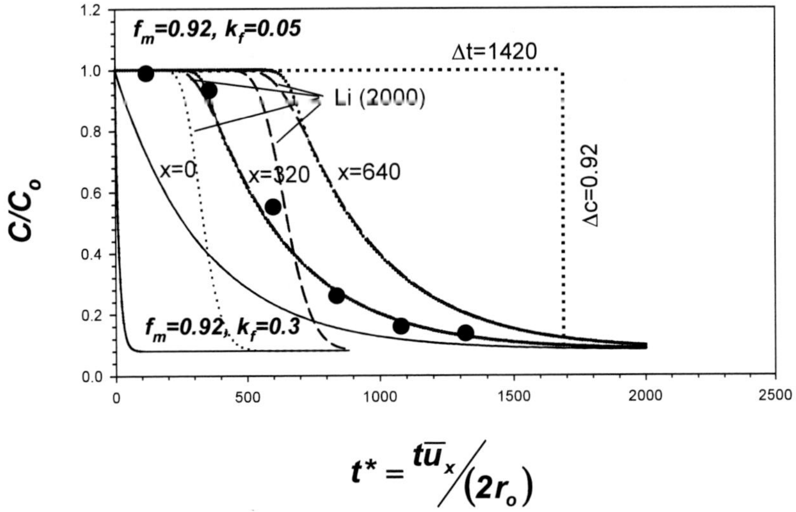

Figure 19. CDR numerical simulation results and free chlorine experimental testing data for a reactive aldicarb contaminant slug (C_o=2.2 mg/L) injected into a water pipe. Experimental results (solid circles) show chlorine concentration profile at the slug propagation front. Simulation results in solid and dashed lines show the impacts of k_f and D_{eff} at f_m=0.09: k_f=0.05 and 0.3 1/sec, and D_{eff} =33 cm^2/sec and 1400 cm^2/sec. The width (Δt) and depth (Δc) of chlorine residual loss curves are marked for the 24.4-m sensor station at x=320. Modified from Yang et al. (2008a).

Yang et al. (2008a) used the model results and further analyzed the hydrodynamic factors that affect the geometry of chlorine concentration profile at the contaminant "slug" propagation front. Dispersion coefficient (D_{eff}) affects the spread of a solute dispersion curve in pipe flows (Aries, 1956; Levenspiel, 1972). In reactive contaminant transport, this effect is shown by Péclet number Pe_L (= $m^2 Pe_D$) in the axial dispersion term of the CDR model (See Eq.37). It is also observed from the model equation that the effect is counterbalanced by chlorine-contaminant reaction at the contaminant-water interface. For fast-reacting contaminants such as aldicarb, the effect of Pe_L on the chlorine residual loss curve is negligible in turbulent flows. No substantial difference is observed in the simulated chlorine residual loss curves between D_{eff} =33 and D_{eff} =1400 at k_f =0.05 sec^{-1} (Fig.19). To identify any effect, the modeling used D_{eff}=1400 in calculations, which is one order magnitude larger than the average value Li (2000) determined from tracer experiments. Thus it appears that for fast-reacting contaminants, the residual loss curve geometry is insensitive to the Pe_L values that are often unavailable for a field distribution network or have unascertained accuracies from using different models (Ekambara and Joshi, 2004).

The geometry of the chlorine concentration profile is most sensitive to the chlorine-contaminant reactivity. When the fast reaction coefficient k_f increases 6 times from 0.05 sec^{-1} to 0.3 sec^{-1}, the residual concentration profile deepens marking a rapid chlorine residual loss inside of the contaminant "slug" (Fig.19). Thus the chlorine profiles measured in the field are useful evidence for assessing chlorine-reaction properties of the introduced contamination (Yang et al., 2009).

4. Summary

The roles of pipe flow hydrodynamics have been examined using the variations of chlorine and other water quality parameters in a drinking water distribution pipe. At most, these analyses explored only the surface of the subject on how hydrodynamics affects solute transport and reactions and thereby impacts the water qualities in a distribution pipe. It nonetheless supports the notion that the hydraulic effect is widespread in hydrodynamic regimes of a water distribution network – whether it is solute (e.g., chlorine, DBPs) transport and reaction in water entering the pipe network from a water plant, or it is an outside contaminant intrusion during distribution. A number of physiochemical scenarios and corresponding mathematical models could explain the relationships applicable to different sets of hydraulic and physical conditions in pipe flow, pipe characteristics, chemical composition and physiochemical properties of drinking water leaving a treatment plant, and the presence of contaminant intrusions. A sample of those possible ensembles is shown in Table 3. Only when such complexity is considered, can models and other predictive mathematical tools truthfully represent and describe the water quality changes in a distribution network. Then models as predictive tools can then be realized in assisting network design and operations in terms of water quality management.

In a stepwise fashion (Section 2.0), we have systematically described the role of bulk decay, wall demand, and the hydrodynamic factors in chlorine decay and DBP formation in a flowing water pipe. Experimental studies and theoretical analysis quantitatively link the reaction rate of chlorine as a reactive solute to the hydraulic dispersion and chemical reactions with bulk demand and wall demand. This analysis reaffirmed previous experimental and field observations that chlorine is consumed competitively in chemical reactions between the bulk demand and pipe wall demand; the latter is a function of pipe flow hydraulics. As a result, the chlorine decay rate is generally greater in field conditions than laboratory tests. These conclusions underscore the fact that the chlorine decay constant in all first-order chlorine models is an empirical fitting parameter, an argument elucidated previously by Clark and Haught (2005) and Clark et al. (2008). True mechanistic determinations of chlorine decay and DBP formation are flow-specific for a given pipe of wall demand characteristics. The combinations of the flow, pipe materials, and chemical reactivity could replicate a number of possible conditions that potentially exist in field conditions.

Intrusion of foreign contaminants into a distribution pipe is another important factor for water quality change and deterioration. Regardless of whether the intrusion is a result of purposeful acts or natural transit pressure suctions at pipe leaks and breaks, they share common attributes and hydrodynamic behaviors in a pipe flow. Common in the transport phenomenon are a finite volume, sudden introduction to a continuous pipe flow, and a wide range of potential contaminant compositions with different degrees of reactivity with disinfectants (e.g., chlorine). In Section 3.1, we have reviewed monitoring techniques to fully monitor and trace a contaminant "slug" moving through a water pipe. This evaluation arrives at the conclusion that adaptive monitoring and data analysis methods can suppress background noises and amplify sensor signals related to the water quality changes caused by "foreign" intrusions. Furthermore, based on experimental studies and numerical simulations, a discrete "slug" of foreign contaminants propagates in a pipe flow in accordance to a convection-dispersion-reaction (CDR) process described in the Dankwarts one-dimensional solute transport model (Yang et al., 2008a). The associated water quality changes are identifiable by, for example, the chlorine residual loss in the propagation front of a moving contaminant "slug". The chlorine concentration curvature is a function of the contaminant-chlorine reactivity and the pipe flow Reynolds number. Larger chlorine residual loss inside of the contaminant "slug" occurs with contaminants that are more reactive with chlorine in drinking water. This property, when fully characterized using the adaptive monitoring technique, can assist in recovery and reconstruction of contaminant chemical properties.

Incorporation of these complex hydraulic and kinetic factors into the modeling of water quality changes is a daunting challenge. Not one single model currently can fully represent all physiochemical scenarios in field conditions. For example, the six ensembles of chlorine decay scenarios in a flowing water pipe in Table 3 represent a small subset of the potential complexity in the field, which have not been fully examined. The current water distribution models are representative of certain conditions under which chlorine decay and other associated water quality changes take place. As drinking water disinfection has been the center of drinking water quality management, the linkage between hydrodynamic effects and water quality changes requires a closer examination.

Acknowledgement

The authors acknowledge the financial support to research projects by U.S. EPA National Homeland Security Research Center and U.S. EPA National Risk Management Research Laboratory. Many of the research results are described and published experimental data are used for illustrations in this manuscript. Any opinions expressed in this paper are those of the authors and do not necessarily reflect the views of the Agency, therefore, no official endorsement should be inferred. Any mention of trade names or commercial products does not constitute endorsement or recommendation for use. Finally but not least, internal reviews by Dr. Walter Grayman, Dr. Zhiwei Li, Dr. Stephen Buchberger, Dr. Chris Impellitteri, and Ms. Jean Dye, are acknowledged.

References

Al-Jasser, A.O., (2007). Chlorine decay in drinking-water transmission and distribution systems: Pipe service age effect. *Water Research*, **41**:387-396.

Amy, G.L., Chadik, P.A., and Chowdhury, Z.K., (1987). Developing models for predicting trihalomethane formation potential and kinetics", *J. AWWA*, **9** (7): 89-97.

Amy, G.L., (1993). Using NOM characterization for the evaluation of treatment. In *Workshop Proc. Natural Organic Matter in Drinking Water - Origin, Characterization, and Removal,* Sept. 19-22, Chamonix, France, p.19

Aries, R., (1956). On the dispersion of a solute in a fluid flowing through a tube. *Proc. Royal Soc. London*, **235**(1200): 67-77.

AWWA, (2004). Verification and control of pressure transients and intrusion in distribution systems. *Awwa Research Foundation*, Denver, U.S.A., 126p.

Baker, M. H, (1948). The quest for pure water. *AWWA*, Lancaster, PA: Lancaster Press.

Baldyga, J., J.R. Bourne, and S.J. Hern, (1996). Interaction between chemical reactions and mixing on various scales. *Chem. Engng. Sci.*, **52**(4): 457-466.

Bellar, T.A., and Lichtenberg, J.J., (1974). Determining volatile organics at microgram -per-liter levels by gas chromatography", *J. AWWA*, **66**: 739-744.

Benjamin, M. M., H. Sontheimer, and P. Leroy, (1996). Corrosion of iron and steel. In: *Internal Corrosion of Water Distribution Systems*. Denver, CO: AWWARF/DVGW-Technologiezentrum Wasser. 29–77

Biswas, P., Lu, C., Clark, R. M., (1993). A model for chlorine concentration decay in drinking water distribution pipes. *Water Research*, **27**(12):1715-1724.

Blackburn, B. G., G. F. Craun, J. S. Yoder, V. Hill, R. L. Calderon, N. Chen, S. H. Lee, D., A.Levy, and M. J. Beach, (2004). Surveillance for waterborne-disease outbreaks associated with drinking water—United States, 2001–2002. *MMWR*, **53**(SS-8):23–45.

Boccelli, D.L., Tryby, M.E., Uber, J.G., Rossman, L.A., Zierolf, M.L., and Polycarpu, M.M., (1998). Optimal scheduling of booster disinfection in water distribution systems, *J. Wat. Res. Planning Mngmt*, **124**(2): 99-111.

Boccelli, D.L., M.E. Tryby, J.G. Uber, and R.S. Summers, (2003). A reactive species model for chlorine decay and THM formation under rechlorination conditions. *Water Research*, **37**: 2654-2666.

Boulos, P.F., Altman, T., Jarrige, P.A., amd Collevati, F.C., (1995). Discrete simulation approach for network water quality models. *J. Wat. Res. Planning Mngmt*, **121**(1): 49-60.

Brezonik, P.L., (1994). Chemical kinetics and process dynamics in aquatic systems. Lewis Publishers, Inc.

Burlingame, G., J.Choi, M. Fadel, L. Gammie, J. Rahman, and J. Paran. (1994). Sniff new mains...before customers complain. *Opflow*, **20**:10:3.

Burrows W.D. and S.E. Renner, (1999). Biological warfare agents as threats to potable water. *Env Health Perspectives*, **107**(12): 975-984.

Camper, A.K., K. Brastrup, A. Sandvig, J. Clement, C. Spencer, and A.J. Capuzzi. (2003), Impact of distribution system materials on bacterial regrowth. *J. AWWA*, **95**(7):107-121.

Chakraborty, S. and V. Balakotaiah, (2002). Low-dimensional models for describing mixing effects in laminar flow tubular reactors. *Chem. Engng. Sci.*, **57**: 2545-2564.

Clark, R. M., (1978). The Safe Drinking Water Act: implications for planning. In D. Holtz and S. Sebastian (eds.): *Municipal Water Systems-The Challenge for Urban Resources Management*. Indiana University Press, Bloomington, pp. 117–137.

Clark, R. M., J. A. Goodrich, and J.C. Ireland. (1985). Costs and Benefits of Drinking Water Treatment. *J. Environmental Systems*, **14**(1):1–30.

Clark, R. M., and D. L. Tippen, (1990). Water Supply. In R. A. Corbitt (ed.): *Standard Handbook of Environmental Engineering*. McGraw-Hill Publishing, New York, pp. 5.173–5.220

Clark, R. M., W. M. Grayman, J. A. Goodrich, R. A. Deininger, and A. F. Hess, (1991). Field testing of distribution water quality models. *J. Amer. Water Works Assoc.*, **83**(7): 67–75.

Clark, R.M., Goodrich, J.A., and Wymer, L.J., (1993a). Effect of the distribution system on drinking water quality. *J. Water Supply Research and Technology*, **42**(1):30-38.

Clark, R. M., Grayman, W. M., Males, R. M., and Hess, A. F., (1993b). Modeling contaminant propagation in drinking water distribution systems. *J. Environmental Engineering*, **119**(2): 349-364.

Clark, R. M., Smalley, G., Goodrich, J. A., Tull, R., Rossman, L.A., Vasconcelos, J. and Boulos, P., (1994). Managing water quality in distribution systems: Simulating TTHM and chlorine residual propagation. *J. Water Supply Research and Technology*, **43**(4):182-191.

Clark, R.M., E.E. Geldreich, K.R. Fox, E.W. Rice, C.H. Johnson, J.A. Goodrich, J.A. Barnick, and F. Abdesaken, (1996a). Tracking a Salmonella serovar Typhimurium outbreak in Gideon, Missouri: Role of contaminant propagation modeling. *J. Water Supply Research and Technology*, **45**(4):171-183.

Clark, R.M., Abdesaken, F., Boulos, P.F., and Mau, R., (1996b). Mixing in distribution system storage tanks: Its effect on water quality. *J. Environmental Engineering*, **122**(9): 814-821

Clark, R. M. (1998). Chlorine Demand and TTHM Formation Kinetics: A Second- Order Model. *J. Environmental Engineering*, **124**(1): 16-24.

Clark, R. M., and M. Sivaganesan, (1998). Predicting chlorine residuals and the formation of TTHMs in drinking water. *J. Environmental Engineering*, **124**(12): 1203-1210

Clark, R. M., and M. Sivaganesan, (2002). Predicting chlorine residuals in drinking water: a second order model. *J. Wat. Res. Planning Mngmt*, **128**:1–10.

Clark, R. M. and R.A., Haught, (2005). Characterizing pipe wall demand: Implications for Water Quality. *J. Wat. Res. Planning Mngmt*, **131**(3), 208-217

Clark, R. M., Y. J. Yang, C. Impellitteri, R. C. Haught, D. Schupp, S. Panguluri, and E. R. Krishnan, (2008). Controlling disinfectant residual losses in drinking water distribution systems: Results from experimental and modeling Studies. *Water Distribution System Analysis*, South Africa, 17 - 20 August 2008.

Connell, G.F. (1998). European water disinfection practices parallel U.S. treatment methods. *Drinking Water and Health Quarterly.* http:// www.clo2.com/reading/waternews/european.html

Craun, G. F., and R. Calderon. (2001). Waterborne disease outbreaks caused by distribution system deficiencies. *J. AWWA.* **93**(9):64–75.

Digiano, F.A., and W. Zhang, (2005). Pipe section reactor to evaluate chlorine –wall reaction. *J. AWWA*, **97**(1): 74-85

Doshi, P. E., W. M. Grayman, and D. Guastella, (2003). Field testing the chlorine wall demand in distribution mains. *In:* Proceedings of the Annual Conference of the American Water Works Association. Denver, CO: AWWA. pp. 1–10

Dugan, N.R., R.S. Summers, R.J. Miltner, and H.M. Shukairy, (1995). An alternative approach to predicting chlorine residual decay, *Proc. AWWA-WQT Conference,* New Orleans, LA, pp. 1317-1338

Eisnor, J.D., and G. A. Gagnon, (2003). A framework for the implementation and design of pilot-scale distribution systems. *J. Water Supply and Technology-Aqua,* **52**(7): 501-519.

Ekambara, K., and J.B. Joshi, (2004). Axial mixing in laminar pipe flows. *Chem. Engng Sci,* **59**, 3929-3944.

Fair, G.M., and J.C. Geyer,. (1971). *Water supply and waste-water disposal.* John Wiley and Sons, Inc., NY.

Farinha, J.P.S., J.M.G. Martinho, and L. Pogliani, (1997). Non-linear least-squares and chemical kinetics: An improved method to analyse monomer-excimer decay data. *J. Mathematical Chemistry*, **21**: 131–139.

Feben, D., and M.J. Taras, (1951). Studies on chlorine demand constants. *J. AWWA,* **43**(11): 922-932

Forney, L.J. and N. Nafia, (2000). Eddy contact model: CDF simulations of liquid reactions in nearly homogeneous turbulence. *Chem. Engng Sci.*, **55**:6049-6058.

Fujiwara, M., J. M. Manwaring, and R. M. Clark, (1995). Drinking water in Japan and the United States: Conference Objectives. In R. M. Clark and D. A. Clark (eds.), *Drinking Water Quality Management.* Lancaster, PA: Technomic Publishing Company Inc.

Gang, D.C., T.E. Clevenger, and S.K. Banerji, (2003). Modeling chlorine decay in surface water. *J Env. Informatics*, **1**(1):21-27.

Gavriel, A.A., J.P.B. Landre, and A.J. Lamb, (1998). Incidence of mesophilic *Aeromonas* within a public drinking water supply in north-east Scotland. *J. Applied Microbiol,* **84**:383-392.

Geldreich, E.E., H.D. Nash, D.J. Reasoner, and R.H. Taylor. (1972). The Necessity of Controlling Bacterial Populations in Potable Water: Community Water Supply. *J. AWWA*, **64**:596-602.

Geldreich, E.E. (1996). *Microbial Quality of Water Supply in Distribution Systems.* Boca Raton, FL, Lewis Publishers.

Grayman, W.M., R.M. Clark, and R.M. Males, (1988). Modeling distribution-system water quality: Dynamic approach. *J. Wat. Res. Planning Mngmt*, **114**(3):295-312.

Grayman, W. M., L. A. Rossman, M. A. Gill, Y. Li, and D. E. Guastella. (2002). Measuring and modeling disinfectant wall demand in metallic pipes. In: *Proceedings of the EWRI Conference on Water Resources Planning and Management.* Reston VA: ASCE.

Grayman, W. M., L. A. Rossman, R. A. Deininger, C. D. Smith, C. N. Arnold, and J. F. Smith. (2004). Mixing and aging of water in distribution system storage facilities. *J. AWWA*, **96**(9): 70–80.

Greenfield, R. A., B.R. Brown, J.B. Hutchins, J.J. Iandolo, R. Jackson, L.N. Slater, and M.S. Bronze, (2002). Microbiological, biological, and chemical weapons of warfare and terrorism. *Am J. Med Sci*, **323**(6):326-340.

Grindler, B. J. (1967). Water and water rights: a treatise on the laws of water and allied problems: eastern, western, federal. *The Allan Smith Company*, Indianapolis, US.

Haas, C. N., and S.B. Karra, (1984). Kinetics of wastewater chlorine demand exertion. *J. WPCF,* **56**(2): 170-173

Hanke, S. H. (1972). Pricing urban Water. *In* S. Mushkin (ed.). *Public Prices for Public Products*. The Urban Institute. Washington, DC, pp. 283–306

Harrington, G.W., Z.K. Chowdhury, and D.M. Owen, (1992). Developing a computer model to simulate DBP formation during water treatment. *J. AWWA*, **84**(11):78-87

Hasan, J., S. States, R. Deininger, (2004). Safeguarding the security of public water supplies using early warning systems: A brief review. *J. Cont Wat Res Ed*, **129**: 27-33.

Haught, R., J. Hall, M. Rahman, R. Richardson-Coy, and H. Piao, (2005). The bench-scale minimum threshold experiment. WQTC, Toronto, Canada.

Huang, J.J., and E.A. McBean, (2007). Using Bayesian statistics to estimate the coefficients of a two-component second-order chlorine bulk decay model for a water distribution system. *Water Research*, **41**:287-294

International Life Sciences Institute (ILSI), (1999). *Early Warning Monitoring to Detect Hazardous Events in Water Supplies*. T.M. Brosnan (ed), Washington, D.C., 37p.

Iqbal, S.S., M.W. Mayo, J.G. Bruno, B.V. Bronk, C.A. Batt, and J.P. Chambers, (2000). A review of molecular recognition technologies for detection of biological threat agents. *Biosensors and Bioelectronics*, **15**: 549-578.

Islam, M.R., (1995). Modeling of chlorine concentration in unsteady flows in pipe networks. PhD Dissertation, Washington State University, Pullman.

Isalm, M. R., M. H. Chaudhry and R. M. Clark, (1997). Inverse modeling of chlorine concentration in pipe networks under dynamic conditions. *J. Environmental Engineering*, **10**: 1033-1040

Jadas-Hecart, A., A. El Morer, M. Stitou, P. Bouillot, B. Legube, (1992). Modelisation de la Demande en Chlore D'une Eau Traitee. *Water Research,* **26**(8): 1073.

Jain, S. and C. R. McLean, (2006). An integrating framework for modeling and simulation for incident management. *J. Homeland Sec Emerg Mngmt*, **3**(1), Art 9: 1-24.

Johnson, J.D., (1978). Measurement and Persistence of Chlorine Residuals in Natural Waters. *In* R.L. Jolley (ed), *Water Chlorination: Environmental Impact and Health Effects*, Ann Arbor Science, Ann Arbor, MI.

Kavanaugh, M.C., A.R. Trussell, J. Cromer, and R.R. Trussell, (1980). An empirical kKinetic model of trihalomethane formation: Applications to meet the proposed THM standard. *J. AWWA*, 578-582

Khan, A.S., D.L. Swerdlow, and D. D., (2001). Precautions against biological and chemical terrorism directed at food and water supplies. *Public Health Rep.*, **116**(1): 3-14

Khiari, D., Barrett, S., Chinn, R., Bruchet, A., Piriou, P., Matia, L., Ventura, F., Suffet, I. H., Gittelman, T., and Leutweiler, P. (2002). Distribution generated taste-and-odor phenomena. AwwaRF, Denver, CO.

Klise, K.A., and S.A. McKenna, (2006). Water quality change detection: multivariate algorithms. T.T. Saito, D. Lehrfeld, (eds.), *Proc SPIE,* **6203**, J1-J9.

Koechling, M.T., (1998). Assessment and modeling of chlorine reactions with natural organic matter: Impact of source water quality and reaction conditions. Ph.D. Thesis, University of Cincinnati, Cincinnati, Ohio.

Kroll, D., and K. King, (2006). Real world operational testing and development of an on-line water security monitoring system. *Proc. 8th Ann WDSA Symposium*, Cincinnati, U.S.A.

Kunkel, G., K. Laven, and B. Mergelas, (2008). Does your city have high-risk pipes? *J. AWWA*, April: 70-74

LeChevallier, M.W., T.M. Babcock, and R.G. Lee, (1987). Examination and characterization of distribution system biofilms. *Applied and Environmental Microbiology*, **53**: 2714-2724.

LeChevallier, M.W., M.J. Friedman, and J.C. Routt, (2008). Development of optimization criteria for distribution system operations. *Proc. AWWA WQTC*, Cincinnati, US.

Lee, B. H., R. A. Deininger and R. M. Clark, (1991). Locating mMonitoring stations in water distribution networks. *J. AWWA*, **83**(7): 60-66.

Levenspiel, O., (1972). Chemical reaction engineering. John Wiley & Sons, New York. 578p.

Levien, K., and O. Levenspiel, (1999). Optimal product distribution from laminar flow reactors: Newtonian and other power-law fluids. *Chem. Engng, Sci.*, **54**: 2453-2458.

Li, S.Y., (2000). *Chlorine transport and decay studies in a pilot scale drinking water distribution dead end pipe system.* Ph.D. dissertation, University of Cincinnati, Cincinnati, Ohio.

Lu, C., P. Biswas, and R. M. Clark, (1993). Modeling of breakpoint reaction in drinking water distribution pipes. *Environment International*, **19**(6): 543-560.

Lu, C., B., Pratim, and R.M. Clark, (1995). Simultaneous transport of substrates, disinfectants and microorganisms in water pipes. *Water Research*, **29**(3): 881-894.

Liu, W. and S. Qi, (in press). Modeling and Verifying Chlorine Decay and Chloroacetic Acid Formation in Drinking Water. *Frontiers of Environmental Science & Engineering in China*

Maul, A., A.H. El-Shaarawi, and J.C. Block, (1985a). Heterotrophic bacteria in water distribution systems - I. Spatial and temporal variation. *The Science of the Total Environment*, **44**: 201-214.

Maul, A., A.H. El-Shaarawi, and J.C. Block, (1985b). Heterotrophic bacteria in water distribution systems - II. Sampling design for monitoring. *The Science of the Total Environment,* **44**: 215-224.

McClellan, J. N., D. A. Reckhow, J. E. Tobiason, J. K. Edzwald, and D. B. Smith, (1999). An integrated kinetic model for chlorine decay and DBP formation. *American Chemical Society*, **217**:U728-U728.

Meinhardt, P.L., (2005). Water and bioterrorism: Preparing for the potential threat to U.S. water supplies and public health. *Annual Review of Public Health*, **26**: 213-237.

Morse, S.A., R. B. Kellogg, S. Perry, R. F. Meyer, D. Bray, D. Nichelson, and J. M. Miller, (2003). Detecting biothreat agents: the laboratory response network. *ASM News*, **69**(9): 433-437.

Murray, R., J. Uber, and R. Janke, (2006). Model for estimating acute health impacts from consumption of contaminated drinking water. *J. Wat. Res. Planning Mngmt*, **132**: 293-299.

National Fire Protection Association (NFPA), (2003). *Fire protection handbook,* 19th edition. A.E. Cotes (ed), National Fire Protection Association, Quincy, MA.

National Research Council (NRC), (2006). *Drinking water distribution systems: Assessing and reducing risks.* National Academies Press, 500 Fifth Street, N.W. Lockbox 285, Washington DC 20055.

Panguluri, S., Y.J. Yang, R.C. Haught, R.M. Clark, and E.R. Krishnan, (2007). Tracer dispersion studies for hydraulic characterization of pipes. *Proc. Water Environmental and Water Resources Congress*, Tampa, Florida

Pierson, G., K. Martel, A. Hill, G. Burlingame, and A. Godfree, (2001). Methods to prevent microbiological contamination associated with main rehabilitation and replacement. *AWWARF*, Denver, CO.

PDD 63, (1998). Critical Infrastructure Protection. The White House, Washington D.C. May 22, 1998.

PL107-188, (2002). *Public Health Security and Bioterrorism Preparedness and Response Act of 2002.*

Pourmoghaddas, H., Stevens, A.A, Kinman, R.N., Dressman, R.C., Moore, L.A., Ireland, J.C., (1993). Effect of bromide ion on the formation of HAAs during chlorination. *J. AWWA*, **85**(1): 82-87

Powell, J. C. (1998). *Modeling chlorine in water distribution networks.* Ph.D. Thesis. School of Civil Engineering, The University of Birmingham.

Powell, J. C., J. R. West, N. B. Hallam, C. F. Forster, and J. Simms, (2000). Performance of various kinetic models for chlorine decay. *J. Water Resources Planning and Management*, **126**: 3–20.

Qualls, R.G., and J.D. Johnson, (1983). Kinetics of the short-term consumption of chlorine by fulvic acid. *Environ. Sci. & Techn.*, **17**(11): 692-698

Richardson, S. D. (1998). Drinking water disinfection by-products, *In* R. A. Meyers (ed.)., *Encyclopedia of Environmental Analysis and Remediation.* New York: John Wiley & Sons. Pp. 1398–1421

Richardson, S. D., and S. W. Krasner, (2003). Disinfection by-products and other emerging contaminants in drinking water. *Trac-Trends in Analytical Chemistry*, **22**(10): 666–684.

Richardson, S. D., H. S. Weinberg, S. W. Krasner, and A. D. Thruston. (2004), Nationwide DBP occurrence study. *EPA-600-R02-068.* Athens, GA.

Rook, J.J., (1974). Formation of haloforms during chlorination of natural waters. *Water Treatment Exam*, **23**: 234

Rossman, L. A., R. M. Clark, and W. M. Grayman, (1994). Modeling chlorine residuals in drinking-water distribution systems. *J. Environmental Engineering*, **120**(4): 803–820.

Rossman, L.A. , and P.A. Boulos, (1996). Numerical Methods for Modeling Water Quality In Distribution Systems: A Comparison. *J. Wat. Res. Planning Mngmt,* **122**(2): 137-146.

Rossman, L.A., Brown, R.A., Singer, P.C., and J.R. Nuckols, (1999). Kinetics of THM and HAA production in a simulated distribution system. *Proc. AWWA WQTC*, Tampa, Florida

Rossman, LA.(2000). EPANET version 2 users manual. US EPA, Drinking Water Research Division, Ohio, US.

Rossman, L. A., R. A. Brown, P. C. Singer, and J. R. Nuckols, (2001). DBP formation kinetics in a simulated distribution system. *Water Research*, **35**(14): 3483–3489.

Sarin, P., V. L. Snoeyink, J. Bebee, W. M. Kriven, and J. A. Clement., (2001). Physico-chemical characteristics of corrosion scales in old iron pipes. *Water Research*, **35**(12): 2961–2969.

Sarin, P., J. Clement, V. L. Snoeyink and W. M. Kriven, (2003). Iron release from corroded, unlined cast-iron pipe. *J. AWWA*, **95**(11): 85–96.

Sarin, P., V. L. Snoeyink, D. A. Lytle, and W. M. Kriven, (2004). Iron corrosion scales: model for scale growth, iron release and colored water formation. *J. Environmental Engineering*, **130**(4): 364–373.

Schenck, K. M, Wymer, L. J. Lykins, B. W. Jr., and Clark, R. M., (1998). Application of a Finnish Mutagenicity Model to Drinking Waters in the U.S. *Chemosphere*, **37**(3): 451-464

Sohn, J., G. Amy, J. Cho, Y. Lee, and Y. Yoon, (2004). Disinfectant decay and disinfection by-products formation model development: chlorination and ozonation by-products. *Water Research*, **38**: 2461–2478

Stern, J., (2000). The prospect of domestic bioterrorism. *Emerging Infectious Diseases*, **5**(4): 517-523.

Szabo, J.G., J.S. Hall and G. Meiners, (2007). Water quality sensor responses to contamination in a single pass water distribution system simulator. *EPA/600/R-07/001*, Water Information Sharing and Analysis Center (WaterISAC) (www.waterisac.org).

Taylor, G., (1953). Dispersion of soluble matter in solvent flowing slowly through a tube. *Proc. Royal Soc. London*, **219**(1137):186-203.

Taylor, G., (1954). Conditions under which dispersion of a solute in a stream of solvent can be used to measure molecular diffusion. *Proc. Royal Soc. London*, **225**(1163):473-477.

Trusell, R.R. and Umphres, M.D., (1978). The formation of trihlomethanes. *J. AWWA*, pp 604-612

Tryby, M.E., D.L. Bocelli, M.T. Kocchling, J.G. Uber, R.S. Summers, and L.A. Rossman, (1999). Booster chlorination for managing disinfection residuals. *J. AWWA*, **92**(1): 96-108.

U.S. Environmental Protection Agency, (1992). *Water treatment plant simulation program user's manual,* version 1.21. Prepared by Malcolm Pirnie, Inc., US EPA, Cincinnati.

U.S. Environmental Protection Agency, (2002), New or Repaired Water Mains. Office of Water (4601M), Office of Ground Water and Drinking Water, *Distribution System Issue Paper*. Washington, DC., 13p.

U.S. Environmental Protection Agency, (2005). *Technologies and techniques for early warning systems to monitor and evaluate drinking water quality: State-of-the-art review.* ORD, NHSRC, Washington, DC.

Vartiainen, T., and A. Liimatainen, (1988). Relations between drinking water mutagenicity and water quality parameters. *Chemosphere*, **17**(1): 189-202.

Vasconcelos, J. J., P. F. Boulos, W. M. Grayman, L. Kiene, O. Wable, P. Biswas, A. Bhari, L. A. Rossman, R. M. Clark, and J. A. Goodrich, (1996). Characterization and modeling of chlorine decay in distribution systems. *AWWARF*, Denver, US.

Vasconcelos, J. J., L. A. Rossman, W. M. Grayman, P. F. Boulos, and R. M. Clark, (1997). Kinetics of chlorine decay. *J. AWWA*, **89**(7): 54–65.

Vikesland, P. J., K. Ozekin, and R. Valentine, (2001). Monochloramine decay in model and distribution system waters. *Water Research*, **35**(7): 1766–1776.

Walski, T. M, D.V. Chase, D.A. Savic, W.M. Grayman, S. Beckwith, and E. Koelle, (2003). Advanced water distribution modeling and management. Haestad Press, Waterbury, CT. pp 1-4.

Wang, S. and H. Hofmann, (1999). Strategies and methods for the investigation of chemical reaction kinetics. *Chemical Engineering Science*, **54**(11):1639-1647.

Warton, B., A. Heitz, C. Joll, and R. Kagi, (2006). A new method for calculation of the chlorine demand of natural and treated waters. *Water Research*, **40**:2877-2884.

Water Research Centre, (1976). Deterioration of bacteriological quality of water during distribution. *Notes on Water Research,* No. **6**.

Williams, D. B. (1953). Dechlorination linked to corrosion in water distribution systems. *Water and Sewage Works*, **100**: 106–111.

Wolfe, R. L., E. G. Means, M. K. Davis, and S. E. Barrett. (1988). Biological nitrification in covered reservoirs containing chloraminated water. *J. Amer. Water Works Assoc.* **80**(9):109−114.

Wolfe, R. L., N. I. Lieu, G. Izaguirre, and E. G. Means. (1990). Ammonia oxidizing bacteria in a chloraminated distribution system: seasonal occurrence, distribution, and disinfection resistance. *Appl. Environ. Microbiol.* **56**(2):451−462.

World Health Organization, (2004). Public health response to biological and chemical weapons WHO guidance. 2nd Ed., World Health Organization, Geneva. 340p.

Yang, Y.J., R.C. Haught, J. Hall, J.A. Goodrich, and J. Hasan, (2006). Adaptive monitoring to enhance water sensor capabilities for chemical and biological contaminant detection in drinking water system. *Proc. SPIE*, **6203**, 62030K-1 to K-12.

Yang, Y.J., R.C. Haught, J. Hall, J. Szabo, R.M. Clark, and G. Meiners, (2007). Adaptive water sensor signal processing: Experimental results and implications for online contaminant warning systems. *Proc.Water Environmental and Water Resources Congress*, Tampa, US.

Yang, Y. J., Goodrich, J.A., Clark, R.M., and Li, S., Y. (2008a). Modeling and testing of reactive contaminant transport in drinking water pipes: Chlorine response and implications for online contaminant detection. *Water Research*, **42**: 1397 – 1412

Yang, Y.J., C. Impelliteri, R.M. Clark, R.C. Haught, D. Schuppe, S. Panguluri, and E.R. Krishnan, (2008b), Chlorine decay and THMs generation under turbulent and laminar flow regions in PVC and ductile iron pipes: Preliminary results on the role of flow velocity and mass transport in water quality deteriorations. *ASCE/EWRI 2008 Water Environmental and Water Resources Congress*, Hawaii, US.

Yang, Y. J., R.C. Haught, and J. A. Goodrich, (2009). Testing and modeling of reactive contaminant transport in drinking water pipes: Real-time event detection and contaminant classification, *J. Environmental Management.* doi:10.1016/j.jenvman.2009.01.021.

Yokoyama, K., (2007). Our recent experiences with sarin poisoning cases in Japan and pesticide users with references to some selected chemicals. *Neurotoxicology*, **28**(2): 364-373.

Zhang, W., and F.A. DiGiano, (2002). Comparison of bacterial regrowth in distribution systems using free chlorine and chloramine: A statistical study of causative factors. *Water Research*, **36**(6):1469-1482.

In: Risk Management
Editors: B. Jordão and E. Sousa, pp. 295-305
ISBN: 978-1-60876-011-4

Chapter 10

PROCEDURAL CONTROL IN MANAGING PERCEIVED RISKS IN THE ORGANIZATIONAL BUYING CONTEXT

Pentti Järvi and Munnukka Juha
University of Jyväskylä, School of Economics and Business Administration, Finland

Abstract

The purpose of this paper is to examine the key forms of perceived risks of organizational buying, and the effectiveness of procedural control methods in managing various dimensions of perceived risk. This study was conducted using a structured interview method among Finnish companies during 2008. The results suggest that personal level psychological risk, company level psychological risk, time-loss risk, and product performance risk are the most strongly present risks in organizational buying. The use of a procedural control method by which organizations can make provision for problems was found to be as the most effective method for managing company-level psychological risks. In turn, in the case of time-loss and product performance risks, this method was perceived as excessively bureaucratic, and thus, decreasing its use was found to be the most effective way of decreasing these risks. Process standardization was found to have a very limited influence on perceived risks.

Keywords: risk dimension, risk management, procedural control

Introduction

Although organizational risks and risk perceptions have been studied broadly in recent years, little research has been conducted on identifying and managing specific risk forms perceived during the buying process (e.g. Bunn 1994, Mitchell 1995 and 1998, Newall 1977, Woodside et al. 1999). In particular the use of procedural control methods for managing risks lacks thorough empirical research (Newall 1977). However, information on the perceptions of different forms of risks occurring during the organizational buying process and the most effective ways of managing those forms are focal topics from both the research and practitioner perspectives. The purpose of this paper is to identify the key forms of risks perceived by members of buying organizations during the buying process, and find out how these risks are managed by procedural control methods. Furthermore, we explore how the use of procedural control is associated with the importance attributed to the purchase and buying situation.

Bunn (1994) applied a combination of various theoretical and empirical research methods in seeking to identify four constructs that underlie organizational buyer behaviour: procedural control, proactive focusing, use of analytical techniques, and search for information. Procedural control is understood as the extent to which organizations rely on policies, procedures, or informal 'rules of thumb' in decision making during the buying process. Bunn found that procedural control was significantly correlated with the length of the buying process and importance of the purchase. Further he discovered that the employment of established control mechanisms or the 'rules of thumb' is more frequent in simple and routine buying situations (Bunn 1993). Similarly, Woodside, Liukko and Vuori (1999) found in their study on capital equipment purchases that procedural control is often less relevant when purchases are unique occasions. The findings of Woodside and Sherrell (1980) in turn suggest that organizational buying is mostly done according to well defined procedures. This leads us to expect that purchases that are made less frequently and are more complicated will generally perceived as more important than those that occur more frequently, are done routinely, and are simple conditions in nature.

Thus procedural control, then has been found to play a focal role as a means of responding to the changes in the magnitude and the forms of perceived risks. Based on the findings of Woodside and Sherrell (1980), Bunn (1994) and Woodside, Liukko and Vuori (1999) we expect companies to be more inclined towards the use of procedural control methods in the purchases of lower importance. Thus, the first hypothesis states:

> H1: The importance of the purchase is negatively associated with the use of procedural control in the buying decision- making process.

Mitchell (1998) has noted that in the organizational literature the complexity of risk measurement in respect of risk forms has not been recognized. He also argues that any risk or risk reduction scale should consider both organizational and personal risk dimensions and the purchaser's professional and domestic dimensions. Therefore, we have chosen to apply the instrument originally proposed by Roselius (1971) and later improved by Stone and Grønhaug (1993) for measuring risks perceived during the organizational buying processes. According to the classification, five perceived risk forms are identified: performance risk, psychological risk, financial risk, and time-loss risk. The fifth dimension, physical risk, is excluded from this study as it is not-applicable for measuring perceived risks related to organizational buying.

Performance risk concerns the ability of a product to perform as anticipated. Psychological risk relates to the anticipation that participation and decisions made during the buying process will lower both self-image and perceived image from others' point of view (Mitchell and Greatorex 1990). Financial risk captures the financially negative outcomes for a company after the product is purchased. Time-loss risk relates to the perception that the adoption and the use of the product will take too much time. Mitchell (1998) argues that the temporal aspect is the most important risk perceived by companies.

Previous studies have found that risk perception is negatively associated with procedural control. For example, Madhok (1995) found evidence that in buying situations where the buyer and seller do not posses a strong customer relationship, tighter control procedures will be imposed in order to lower perceived risk. The results obtained by Parkhe (1993) and Kumar and Seth (1998) were similar: higher perceived risk in relational uncertain situations led to reliance on tighter controlling procedures. As the earlier studies on procedural control and risk perception do not distinguish different dimensions of risk, we expect the negative relationship observed between procedural control and risk perception to be valid all forms of perceived risk. Therefore we expect higher procedural control to lead to a lower level of perceived psychological, performance and time-loss risks. The following hypotheses were constructed:

H2: Psychological risk is negatively associated with the use of procedural control in the buying decision making process.

H3: Performance risk is negatively associated with the use of procedural control in the buying decision making process.

H4: Time-loss risk is negatively associated with the use of procedural control in the buying decision making process.

Research Methodology

The empirical study was carried out among Finnish business organizations in 2008. The data were collected by a structured interview method with companies from various industries: manufacturing (59%), construction (9%), accommodation and food services (8%), recreation services (3%), and other (20%). The companies represented in the study also varied in size as 61% had 250 personnel or less and 39% over 250. The buying situations covered in the interviews ranged from new tasks to modified rebuy situations, the emphasis on new task situations. The relative percentages of the different buying situations were simple modified rebuy (9%), complex modified rebuy (20%), judgemental new task (21%), and strategic new task (49%). The respondents were mostly from either middle management (40%) or top management (33%). Employees accounted to 19% and supervisors to 8% of the respondents. The respondents had been actively involved in the buying process. To find the best informants, companies' own judgements were trusted. The total number of interviews was 88.

To identify the buying situations we applied the classification proposed by Bunn (1993). According to Mitchell (1998) it is an accurate measure for studying the risks of organizational buying. Bunn identifies six buying situation categories: casual, routine low priority, simple modified rebuy, complex modified rebuy, judgemental new task, and strategic new task. This enables the accurate sorting of buying situations with differing levels of risk. We focused here on complex modified rebuy, judgemental new task, and strategic new task buying situations (i.e. 73 interviews) as the perceived risks are often notably less relevant and also more difficult to identify in straight rebuy or simple modified rebuy situations.

In the structured interview the measures of the risk forms were constructed on the basis of the instrument proposed by Roselius (1971) and Stone and Grønhaug (1993). Forms of perceived risk are measured by 20 items rated on 5-point Likert scale. Procedural control during the buying process 9 items, also rated on the same 5-point scale. Both buying situations and other buying information were measured on a nominal scale. In addition to the structured questions some topics were also discussed by means of open-ended questions, such as: "How has your company arranged risk management in the case of important purchases"? "How was the profitability of the purchase evaluated during the purchasing process"? "What were the main sources of information during the purchasing process"? These qualitative data were used to more specifically describe the procedures the companies employed during the buying process. The questionnaire was screened with two industry experts to ensure the validity and accuracy of the questions.

Hypotheses Testing

To test the hypotheses (figure 1), linear multiple-regression analysis was applied. Churchill (1995) among others suggests that a regression model is valid when the following assumptions are confirmed: (i) linearity of the relationship between dependent and independent variables, (ii) homoscedasticity, (iii) independence of the error terms, (iv) normality of distributions, and (v) multicollinearity. The F-test was applied to test the goodness-of-fit of the data and the model, in line with Cooper and Emory (1995), who stated that "in multiple regression analyses the F-test has an overall role for the model". Multicollinearity diagnostics (VIF) was employed to confirm that predictor variables did not inter-correlate, and skewness was employed to measure the degree of asymmetry of distributions. The adjusted squared multiple correlation coefficient (R^2) was used to determine the proportion of the variation explained by the regression line (Zikmund 1991).

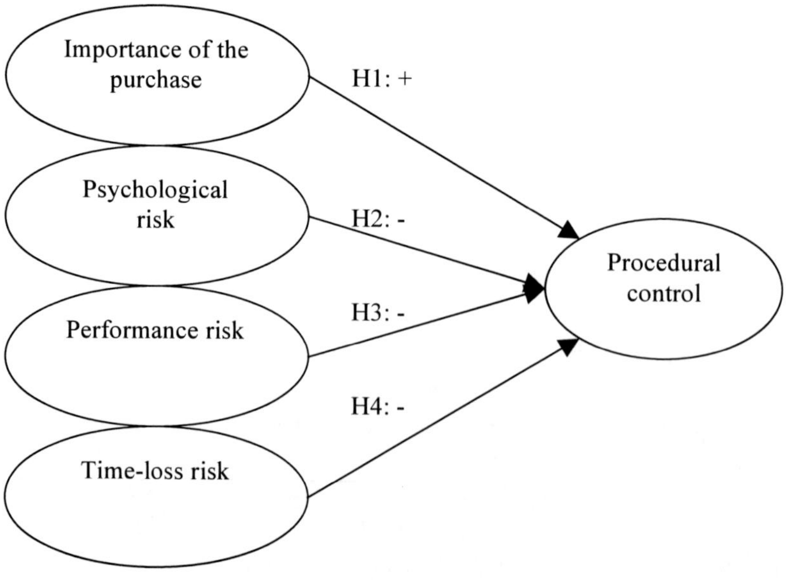

Figure 1. Research design.

Empirical Findings

The open-ended questions showed that risk management was generally perceived from a proactive planning perspective. Companies widely employed risk analytical methods to lower and protect against risks. The most frequently mentioned method of risk management was information gathering, that is, companies relyied on thorough information on supplier and customer backgrounds, especially when they had no prior experience of them, to lower the level of perceived risks. Partners outside and inside the company were regarded as important sources of information in reducing perceived risks associated with the purchase. The respondents mentioned that they also employed sanctions and guarantees and used more than one supplier to manage perceived risks. Also, specific methods of analysis were employed, such as: market analysis, profitability analysis, alternative calculations, certifications, cost analysis, simulation and repayment calculations.

The interviews also revealed that companies had a wide variety of specific procedural control methods in use. These methods consisted of formal and informal processes such as risk analysis processes, process specification, auditing processes, tender processes, risk mapping processes, and the SWOT process. The most significant differences between the companies was related to the use of written, formal procedures. This finding is presumably related to the fact that the interviewed companies varied significantly in size and organizational type. However, the most of the companies had some formal procedures for various stages of the buying process.

Factor Constructs

Exploratory factor analysis was employed to construct latent factors for the various forms of perceived risks associated with the buying process and on the procedural control methods need to manage those forms of risks. Principle component analysis was carried out, followed by varimax rotation with Kaiser Normalization. Variables with factor loadings over 0.5 were selected for the factors. The reliability of the factor constructs was confirmed by Cronbach's alpha (critical value 0.6; Nunnally 1967).

The factor analysis provided four dimensions of perceived risk and two dimensions of procedural control. In the original instrument, suggested by Roselius (1971) and Stone and Grønhaug (1993), only three risk dimensions were separated: psychological, performance, and time-loss risks. However, in our data psychological risk was divided into two sub-dimensions; these were named personal psychological risk (PPR) and company psychological risk (CPR). The factor constructs are presented in table 1. Four factors with eigen values exceeding 1 accounted for 58% of the total variance. Time-loss (explaining 9% of the variance) and performance risk factors (explaining 30% of the variance) corresponded to the original instrument. Of the two sub-dimensions of psychological risk factor, PPR accounted for 13% and CPR for 6 % of the variance.

To measure procedural control we applied the instrument proposed by Bunn (1994). The factor analysis extracted two sub-factors representing procedural control: process standardization, explaining 29% of the variance, and making provision for problems, explaining 20% of the variance. Together the two factors accounted for 49% of the total variance (table app. 2). The factors are defined in appendix 1.

Table 1. Factor analysis forms of perceived risks and risk management styles

Factor and component	Component loading	Cronbach alpha
Dimension of perceived risk		
Factor 1. Personal psychological risk (PPR)		.736
PPR 1 (B3.2f)	.739	
PPR 2 (B3.3f)	.701	
PPR 3 (B3.2e)	.624	
PPR 4 (B3.3e)	.553	
Factor 2. Company psychological risk (CPR)		.691
CPR 1 (B3.2c)	.817	
CPR 2 (B3.2d)	.723	
CPR 3 (B3.2a)	.568	
Factor 3. Time-loss risk (TLR)		.762
TLR 1 (B3.1d)	.805	
TLR 2 (B3.2b)	.759	
TLR 3 (B3.1c)	.666	
TLR 4 (B3.1b)	.559	
Factor 4. Product/Performance risk (P/PR)		.923
P/PR 1 (B3.4b)	.905	
P/PR 2 (B3.4c)	.886	
P/PR 3 (B3.4a)	.871	
P/PR 4 (B3.4d)	.859	
Dimension of procedural control		
Factor 1. Process standardization (RM/PS)		.593
RM/PS 1 (C1a)	.732	
RM/PS 2 (C1g)	.562	
RM/PS 3 (C1b)	.803	
Factor 2. Provision for problems (RM/PFP)		.757
RM/BP 1 (C1e)	.844	
RM/BP 2 (C1h)	.715	
RM/BP 3 (C1f)	.744	
RM/BP 4 (C1i)	.683	

Hypotheses Testing

The factor analysis extracted four factors corresponding to forms of risks the respondents' perceived during the buying process and two factors representing procedural control methods for managing the risks. Based on the findings of prior studies 4 hypotheses were formed suggesting that procedural control is applied more actively in the purchases of higher importance; and that the use of procedural control is negatively associated with the perceived level of specific risk forms.

The hypothesis 1 suggested that the importance of the purchase is positively associated with the level of procedural control methods the company applies during the buying process. The result of testing of this hypothesis is presented in table 2, and indicates that a very significant relationship to exist between the level of making provision for problems (RM/PP) and the importance of the purchase (IoP, β 0.432). The beta coefficient indicates a strong and positive relationship, that is, the higher the importance of the purchase the higher the level of preparation for potential problems. Unexpectedly, however, standardization of the process (RM/PS) was not found to have a statistically significant association with the importance of the purchase. Therefore, hypothesis 1 was only partly supported. The overall regression model was found to significantly explain16% (F 7.326, R^2 0.162) of the variance of the importance of the purchase dimensions. The acceptability of the regression result was examined at each stage of regression with tests for linearity, homoscedasticity, normality and multicollinearity. The results of these tests confirm that all the assumptions held. The multicollinearity diagnostics were examined with VIF values, which scored less than the critical value of 10.

Table 2. The influence of the importance of the purchase on the use of procedural control

Relationships	β coefficient	t-statistics	F statistics	Adjusted R^2
IoP → RM/PS	0.058	0.475	7.326***	0.162
IoP → RM/PP	0.432	3.564***		

Note: *** significant at the 0.001 level; ** significant at the 0.01 level; * significant at the 0.05 level.

Table 3. The relationship between forms of perceived risks and the use of procedural control methods during the buying process

Relationship	β coefficient	t-statistics	F statistics	Adjusted R^2
PPR→ RM/PS	0.100	0.737	1.595	0.032
CPR→ RM/PS	0.022	0.159		
TLR→ RM/PS	-0.308	-2.224*		
P/PR→ RM/PS	0.155	1.224		
PPR→ RM/PP	-0.009	-0.066	5.191***	0.218
CPR→ RM/PP	0.291	2.222*		
TLR→ RM/PP	-0.400	-3.117**		
P/PR→ RM/PP	-.0336	-2.720**		

Note: *** significant at the 0.001 level; ** significant at the 0.01 level; * significant at the 0.05 level.

The table 3 presents the results of the testing hypotheses 2, 3, and 4. The results show that only one statistically significant relationship exists between the occurrences of the different forms of risks and the level of process standardization (RM/PS). The result of the regression analysis suggests that process standardization is significantly associated with the existence of time-loss risk (TLR), β-value -0.308. The negative coefficient implies a negative relationship, that is, the lower the time-loss risk the higher the level of process standardization. The regression model was not found to significantly explain (F 1.595, R^2 0.032) the variance of the process standardization dimensions.

Making provision for problems (RM/PP) in managing specific forms of perceived risks during the buying process proved to be a more efficient method of risk management than process standardization. A statistically significant linear relationship was detected between the level of preparation made for potential problems occurring during the buying process and the company psychological risk (CPR, β 0.291), time-loss risk (TLR, β -0.400), and performance risk (P/PR, β -0.336). The relationships between procedural control and time-loss risk and product performance risk were especially strong. The relationships of both variables were negative, suggesting that the lower the level of perceived risk the higher the degree of making provision for problems. In the case of company psychological risk the relationship was positive. The higher level of company psychological risk explains the higher degree of making provisions for problems. No statistically significant relationship was found in the case of personal psychological risk. The regression model explains 22% of the variance in the dimensions of making provisions for problems (R^2 0.218). In order to confirm to overall explanation power of the model and to measure its robustness, the F-test was also performed. The result indicated that explanatory power of the model is statistically very significant.

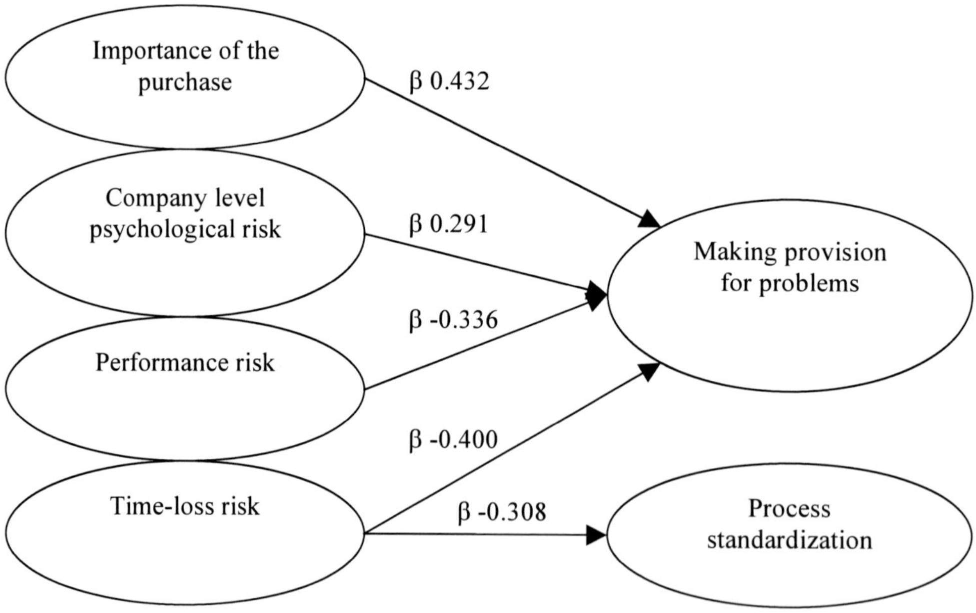

Figure 2. The results of hypothesis testing.

To conclude, the results of the tests of hypotheses are presented in figure 2. Support was found for hypothesis 4, partial support for hypothesis 1 and 3, while hypothesis 2 was not supported. The use of process standardization as a means of managing risks was not supported, although it had a significant negative relationship with time-loss risk. The use of procedural methods of making provision for potential problems was found to have an important role in managing the various forms of perceived risks in organizational buying.

Discussion

The results suggest that procedural control can be divided into two sub-dimensions, process standardization and making provision for problems. Four distinct dimensions of perceived risks were also found to exist: personal psychological risk, company psychological risk, product performance risk and time-loss risk. The analyses provided clear support for the first hypothesis which assumed a positive relationship between procedural control and the importance of the purchase. Throughout the analyses the two dimension of procedural control provided highly different results. Generally, process standardization had no relationship with the various risk dimensions, while making provision for problems showed significant relationships with all the risk dimensions except personal psychological risk. These divergent results might be caused either by problems in the factor construct, as the factor loadings were left on a rather low level and Cronbach's alpha was also relatively low, or that the companies did not perceive process standardization to be related to the risks associated with the purchase.

However, making provision for problems proved to be significantly associated with the importance of the purchase and perceived risks during the buying process. The analyses indicated that a higher level of either product performance risk or time-loss risk leads to the less intensive use of procedures by which companies make provision for potential problems. Formal and informal procedures and policies are avoided, as these are presumably perceived to be ineffective managing these forms of risks. These processes are thus obviously considered as bureaucratic that then intensify time pressure and hinder the buying centre's ability to choose the product that possesses the least product performance risk. The connection with psychological risks was surprisingly weak. Company psychological risk was the only risk form found to have an influence on the use of making provision for problems. The relationship was positive, contrary to our expectations, suggesting that making provision for problems is an efficient method of managing company psychological risks.

To conclude, procedural control should be separated into two dimensions, process standardization and making provision for problems. The results provide evidence that companies generally decrease the use of procedural control in buying situations characterized by high time-loss or high product performance risks. Thus, in buying situations with lower perceived risk levels procedural control is more intensively utilized. For managing psychological company risks, making provision for problems is, nevertheless, an effective method.

The few limitations were observed in relation to this study. First, the process standardization factor obtained rather low factor loadings and internal consistency values which in turn might have influenced the analyses of results. Another limitation relates to the sample size, which was rather small and was not delimited to a particular industry or size of company and thus restricts generalization of the results. Further studies should concentrate on exploring the status of process standardization in risk the management context and on specific industries with larger sample sizes.

Appendix 1. The dimension of perceived risk and procedural control

Factors	Explanation of the factors
Risk dimension	
Personal psychological risks (PPR)	The risk that the participation and decision made during the buying process will lower the self-image and the perceived image from others' point of view.
Company psychological risks (CPR)	The risk that the decisions and the process outcomes will lower the company's or department's image, lower the future potential for conducting similar purchases, and impair the department's position in the organization.
Time-loss risks (TLR)	The perceived risk that the adoption and the use of the product will take too much time.
Product/Performance risks (P/PR)	The risk that products will not perform as anticipated.
Procedural controlling methods	
Process standardization (RM/PS)	The extent to which buyers rely on simplifying policies, procedures, or informal rules when approaching a specific purchase decision.
Provision for problems (RM/PP)	The extent to which buyers make provision for working out problems occurring during the buying process through policies, procedures, or informal rules.

References

Bunn, M.D. (1993), Taxonomy of buying decision approaches, *Journal of Marketing*, **57**, 38-56.

Bunn, M.D. (1994), Key aspects of organizational buying: conceptualization and measurement, *Journal of the Academy of Marketing Science*, **22**(2), 160-169.

Churchill, G.A. (1995), *Marketing Research: Methodological foundations* (6th ed), the Dryden press, Forth Worth.

Cooper, D.R. & Emory, W.C. (1995), Marketing research methods, Irwin, Homewood.

Kumar, S. & Seth, A. (1998), The design of coordination and control mechanisms for managing joint venture-parent relationships, *Strategic Management Journal*, **19**(2), pp.579-99.

Madhok, A. (1995), Revisiting multinational firms' tolerance for joint ventures: a trust-based approach, *Journal of International Business Studies*, **26**(1), pp.117-37.

Mitchell, V.-W. & Greatorex, M. (1990), *Measuring perceived risk and its components across product categories*, Emac Conference, Innsbruck, 153-167.

Mitchell, V.-W. (1995), Organizational risk perception and reduction: a literature review, *British Journal of Management*, **6**, 115-133.

Mitchell, V.-W. (1998), Buy-phase and buy-class effects on organizational risk perception and reduction in purchasing professional services, *Journal of Business & Industrial Marketing*, **13**(6), 461-478.

Newall, J. (1977), Industrial buyer behaviour, *European Journal of Marketing*, **11**(3), 166-211.

Nunnally, J.C. (1967), *Psychometric theory*, New York.

Parkhe, A. (1993), Messy research, methodological predispositions, and theory development in international joint ventures, *Academy of Management Review*, **18**(2), pp.227-68.

Roselius, T. (1971), Consumer rankings of risk reduction methods, *Journal of Marketing*, **35**, 56-61.

Stone, R.N. & Grønhaug, K. (1993), Perceived risk: further considerations for the marketing discipline, *European Journal of Marketing*, **27**(3), 39-50.

Woodside, A.C., Liukko, T. & Vuori, R. (1999), Organizational buying of capital equipment involving persons across several authority levels, *Journal of Business & Industrial Marketing*, **14**(1), 30-48.

Woodside, A.G. & Sherrell, D.L. (1980), New replacement part buying, *Industrial Marketing Management*, **10**(2), 123-132.

Zikmund, W.G. (1991), *Business research methods*, Harcourt brace jovanovich college press, Forth Worth.

In: Risk Management
Editors: B. Jordo and E. Sousa , pp. 307-326
ISBN 978-1-60876-011-4

Chapter 11

Catastrophic Risk Management Using Spatial Adaptive Monte Carlo Optimization

Tatiana Ermolieva, Günther Fischer and Michael Obersteiner

Abstract

In this chapter, the authors present an integrated approach of catastrophic risk management based on data from geographic information systems (GIS). The methodology enables the analysis of the spatial and temporal heterogeneity of various agents (stakeholders) and offers solutions for coherent, comprehensive and robust policy responses. Using the spatial adaptive Monte Carlo (stochastic) optimization procedure allows to analyze a variety of complex interactions between decisions and risks in order to find robust optimal portfolios of risk management measures for decreasing regional vulnerability with regard to economic, financial, and human losses. The model addresses the specifics of catastrophic risks, including the lack of information, the need for long-term perspectives and geographically explicit models, and a multi-agent decision making structure. The approach is illustrated with a case study of earthquake risk management in the Tuscany region of Italy.

1. Introduction

The possibility of more frequent extreme natural disasters dominates the discussions of current global changes. A shift in the overall hazard exposure due to the occurrence of more frequent extreme events will lead to more frequent economic and social shocks at national and regional levels with consequences to the global economy. Under such conditions, the lack of proper risk management may significantly affect sustainability. An integrated catastrophic risk management approach, as presented in this chapter, offers solutions for developing coherent, comprehensive and robust policy responses. Coherence is needed when integrating different perspectives, e.g., of economists, development planners, natural scientists and disaster managers; and comprehensiveness in order to identify policy gaps between the existing measures in place compared to those needed to ensure economic development that is robust against shocks from possible future catastrophes. The presented approach uses the Adaptive Monte Carlo (stochastic) optimization procedure that allows the analysis of a variety of complex interactions between decisions and risks in order to find robust optimal portfolios of risk management measures for decreasing regional vulnerability with regard to economic, financial, and human losses. The approach is illustrated with a case study of earthquake risk management.

Global change induced by anthropogenic activities, rapid and increasingly powerful technological innovations, creation of densely populated locations with high concentration of industries and infrastructure, is increasing the vulnerability of modern societies thereby making them more exposed to human–made and natural disasters.

MunichRe reports that the losses from natural and human–made catastrophes are rapidly increasing: within the last three decades the direct damages from natural disasters alone have increased nine–fold (MunichRe 1999). It is estimated that within the next 50 years more than a third of the world's population will live in seismically and volcanically active zones (NRC 1999). One of the main reasons for this is current land use practices, which often ignore location–specific risks: analysis of insurance companies shows that because of economic growth in hazard–prone areas, damages due to natural catastrophes have grown at an average annual rate of 5 percent (Froot 1997). The growth of losses due to catastrophes is also likely to be further exacerbated by the increasing frequency and severity of weather related extreme events due to global climate warming (Milly et al. 2002; Palmer and Raisanen 2002).

Impacts of catastrophes cannot be properly evaluated on aggregate levels. For example, aggregate worldwide economic impacts of global warming may even be considered as beneficial whereas some regions and even countries may be wiped out. The consequences of disasters have spatial profiles and determine prospects for sustainable regional agricultural and rural development depending on the mitigative and adaptive capacities available to cope with them (Fischer et al. 2002). While the developed world has the financial and technological means to cope with extreme events, for many developing countries the impacts of catastrophes may cause major economic shocks and disruptions.

Catastrophic risk management is a complex transdisciplinary problem requiring knowledge of environmental, natural, financial and social systems. The burden on these systems is unevenly distributed, debatable in scope, and not yet well matched to the policy making apparatus. Costly losses involve various agents and stakeholders: individuals, governments, farmers, producers, consumers, insurers, investors, etc., their perception of catastrophes, goals and constraints with respect to these rare but high impact events. The scarcity of historical data is an inherent feature and a main challenge in dealing with rare catastrophes and new strategies. Purely adaptive, learning–by–doing approaches may be very expensive and dangerous. Thus, catastrophic risks create new scientific problems requiring integrated approaches, new concepts and tools for risk–based land use planning and risk management. The role of models enabling the simulation of possible catastrophes and estimating potential damages and losses becomes a central task for designing mitigation and adaptation programs.

In this chapter we discuss an integrated framework, which enables the analysis of the spatial and temporal heterogeneity of various agents (stakeholders) induced by mutually dependent losses from extreme events. The model addresses the specifics of catastrophic risks: the lack of information, the need for long–term perspectives and geographically explicit models, and the multi–agent decision making structure. The model combines geographically explicit data on the distribution of capital stocks and economic values in infrastructure and land use in a region with a stochastic model generating magnitudes, occurrences, and locations of catastrophes. Using advanced stochastic optimization techniques, the model, in general, allows the analysis of robust optimal portfolios of ex–ante (land use, structural mitigation, insurance) and ex–post (adaptation, rehabilitation, borrowing) measures for decreasing regional vulnerability measured in terms of economic, financial, and human losses as well as in terms of selected welfare growth indicators. The approach is illustrated in a case study of earthquake risks in the Tuscany region of Italy. A Monte Carlo catastrophe model generates location specific random losses from an infinite number of catastrophic earthquake scenarios. An embedded stochastic optimization procedure analyzes spatial and temporal heterogeneities of locations (individuals), insurers, and the government guiding the design of fair and sustained loss sharing programs. Discussions of similar issues regarding catastrophic risks can be found in (Amendola et al. 2000; Amendola et al. 2000; Ermoliev et al. 2000a; Ermoliev et al. 2000b; Ermolieva et al. 2000). As shown in these studies, the technique implied in the model may be important to governments, both central and local, to better negotiate risks and to make decisions on the allocation of properties, agricultural investments, and the implementation of mitigation and adaptation strategies. Also, it is important for insurance companies to make decisions on contracts, premiums, and re–insurance agreements in the case of highly dependent exposures. It is also useful for disaster planning agencies, because it provides a more realistic evaluation of the spatial and temporal distribution of the potential losses.

Section 2. introduces conceptual risk management models for coping with catastrophic events such as floods, earthquakes, windstorms, etc. It illustrates the necessity to capture the main feature of catastrophes — their abruptness in time and space similar to “spikes” that cannot be properly treated or modeled on “average”. Section 3. discusses the main features of an integrated geographic information system (GIS) –based catastrophe management model that, in the absence of historical data, simulates samples of dependent potential losses. Traditionally, insurance and finance quantify extreme events in monetary units. The catastrophe model deals with events, which are non–quantifiable in this sense, and with multivariate distributions of extreme values, i.e., with cases that are not treated within the conventional extreme value theory. This Section also discusses the shortcomings of the standard “if–then” scenario analyses for catastrophic risk management. Section 4. describes a spatial and dynamic stochastic optimization model developed for the evaluation of a catastrophe loss–spreading program (Ermoliev et al. 2000a; Ermolieva et al. 2000) and its possible extensions for designing risk reduction measures. This Section also outlines general ideas of the Adaptive Monte Carlo Optimization (AMCO) proposed in (Amendola et al. 2000; Ermoliev et al. 2000a; Ermoliev et al. 2000b; Ermolieva et al. 2000) to overcome the difficulties of a pure “if–then” approach. In order to stabilize the loss spreading (insurance) program the model uses economically sound risk indicators such as expected over–payments by “individuals” (cells of risk–prone areas) and an expected shortfall of the insurance. These indicators are used together with so–called stopping times to orient the analysis towards the most destructive scenarios. Section 5. specifies the model for a case study of catastrophic earthquakes. Numerical experiments are based on real and modified data from earthquake risk studies in the Tuscany region of Italy (Amendola et al. 2000). This Section illustrates that the “if–then” type of analyses, when based only on the intuition (opinions) of "stakeholders", may easily fail to produce robust strategies in the case of highly interdependent multivariate distributions of catastrophic losses. Section 6. summarizes the conclusions gained in designing catastrophe management models and their application in major case studies.

2. A Simple Risk Management Model

Catastrophic events such as floods, earthquakes, and windstorms occur abruptly in time and space as "spikes" that cannot be properly modeled on "average". The following risk management models address this "abruptness" feature of catastrophes.

Let us consider a simple model of growth under abrupt shocks, which is a stylized version of the insurance business (see, e.g., Borch 1962; Daykin et al. 1994; Grandell 1991). The main variable of concern is the risk reserve r^t at time t: $r^t = r_0 + \pi^t - A^t, t \geq 0$, where π^t, A^t are aggregated premiums and claims, and r_0 is the initial risk reserve. The process $A^t = \sum_{k=1}^{N(t)} S_k$, where $N(t)$, $t \geq 0$ denotes a random number of claims in interval $[0, t]$ (e.g., a Poisson process) with $N(0) = 0$, and $\{S_k\}_1^\infty$ is a sequence of independent and identically distributed random variables (claims) — in other words, replicates of a random variable S. In this model, the inflow of premiums π^t pushes r^t up, whereas the random outflow A^t pushes r^t down.

The main problem of catastrophic management is to avoid the situation when r^t drops abruptly below the "vital" level (ruin) in our example, equal to 0. It is only possible with a certain probability $\Psi = P\{r^t \leq 0 \text{ for some } t,\ t > 0\}$. The deterministic approach is

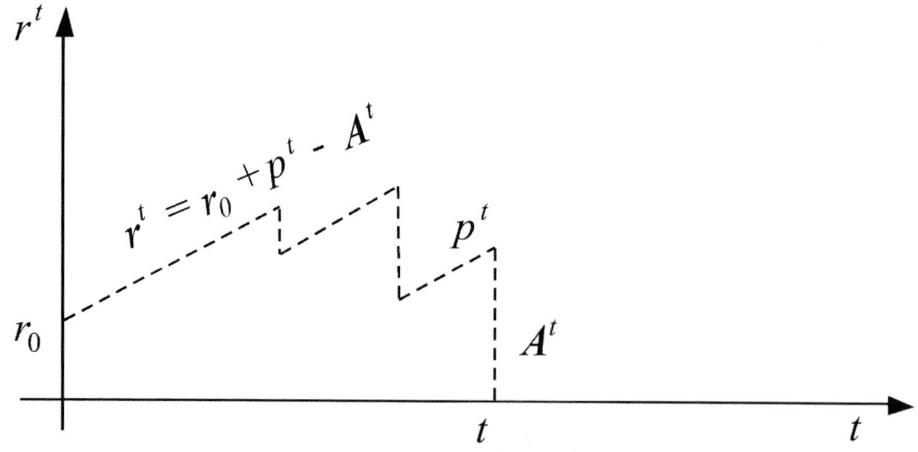

Figure 1. Trajectory of the risk reserve r^t subject to the random process of claims.

very simplified, as illustrated by the following calculations. Assume that $N(t)$, S_k, are independent, $N(t)$ has intensity α, i.e., $E\{N(t)\} = \alpha t$, and $\pi^t = \pi t$, $\pi > 0$. Then the expected profit over the interval $[0, t]$ is $(\pi - E(S)\alpha)\, t$, and the expected profit increases in time for $\pi - E(S)\alpha > 0$. Thus, the practical deterministic model ignores complex interdependencies among the timing of claims (temporal clustering), their sizes, and the subsequent possibility of ruin, $r^t \leq 0$. In this formulation the random process r^t is replaced by a linear function in t, $r^t = r_0 + (\pi - \alpha ES)\ t$. The difference $\pi - \alpha ES$ is the "safety loading". It follows from the strong law of large numbers that $\left[\pi^t - A^t\right]/t \to [\pi - \alpha ES]$ with the probability of 1. Therefore, in the case of positive safety loading, $\pi > \alpha ES$, we have to expect that the real random profit $\pi^t - A^t$ for a sufficiently large t would also be positive under the appropriate choice of premium $\pi = (1+\rho)\alpha ES$, where ρ is the "relative safety" loading $\rho = (\pi - \alpha ES)/\alpha ES$. However, this holds true only if ruin does not occur before time t.

As illustrated in Fig. 2, despite the fact that sustained growth of risk reserves r^t is guaranteed on average, the ruin of the real growth process may occur before sustained growth takes off. In other words, the substitution of the complex jumping process by a simple deterministic model (showing "robust" sustained growth) may lead to unforeseen collapses (surprises). Only a stochastic model is able to estimate the demand in such purely financial risk management measures as borrowing, contingent credits, or governmental bonds. It is also possible to reduce the severity of the distribution of claims by various loss reduction mitigation measures. However, all this is possible only by analyzing the probability of ruin Ψ. In general, various decision variables affect Ψ. The claim size S depends on the coverage of the insurer operating on geographically distinct locations. Important decision variables are r_0, ϕ, and re–insurance arrangements. The reduction of Ψ to acceptable levels can be viewed as the so–called chance constraint stochastic optimization problem (see Gilber and Gouy 1998; Prekopa 1995). The complexity is associated with the jumping process A^t with analytically intractable dependencies of A^t on decision variables, which requires specific stochastic optimization (STO) methods.

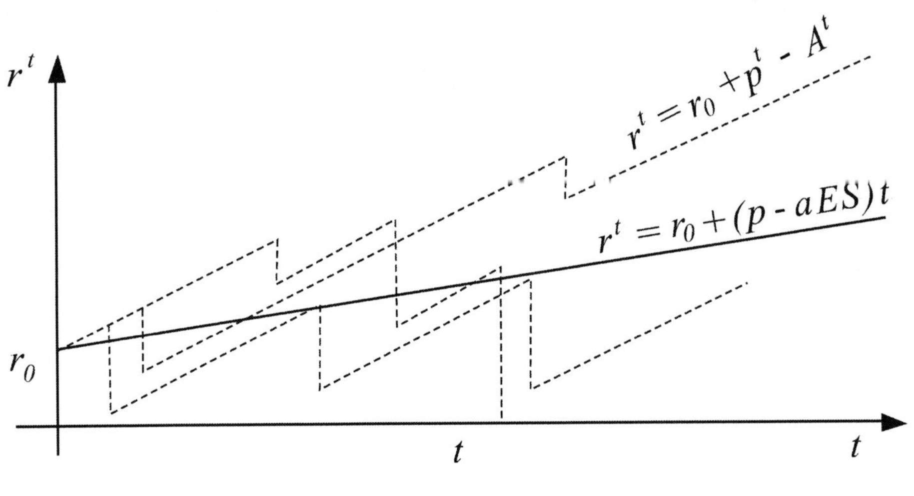

Figure 2. Expected and real growth of the risk reserve. There is an exit scenario due to an extreme event at time τ, which depletes the safety loading.

3. Stochastic Integrated Catastrophic Risk Management Model

Section 2. briefly outlined some methodological complexities of the catastrophe management model. This section aims at discussing them with more elements. A model for integrated catastrophe management is a multidisciplinary product combining knowledge of physics, chemistry, engineering, mathematical, financial, social and other scientific disciplines. It consists, in principle, of three major sub–models: a catastrophe module, an engineering vulnerability module, and an economic multi–agent module.

A catastrophe module simulates a natural phenomenon based on the knowledge of the event and scientific equations and variables describing it. For example, for hurricane model variables are the radius of the maximum winds, or forward speed of the storm. For an earthquake model that simulates the shaking of the ground critical variables are the epicenter location, magnitude of the earthquake, and the Gutenberg–Richter law or attenuation characteristics. For a flood, these are precipitation curves, water discharge, river characteristics, etc. The catastrophe models used in IIASA's case studies are based on Monte Carlo dynamic simulations of geographically explicit catastrophe patterns in selected regions (a discussion of these models is beyond the scope of this chapter but can be found in Amendola et al. 2000; Baranov et al. 2002; Ermoliev et al. 2000b; Rozenberg et al. 2001; Walker 1997). A catastrophe model, in fact, compensates for the lack of historical data on the occurrence of catastrophes in locations where the effects of catastrophes may have never been experienced in the past.

The engineering module is used to estimate the damages that may result from catastrophes. Shaking intensities, duration of standing water, water discharge speed or wind speeds are what engineering modules take from the catastrophe modules to calculate potential damages. The engineering modules use vulnerability curves taking into account the age of the building and the number of storeys, to estimate the damages induced by the simulated disaster.

The economic multi–agent model used in our case studies is a stochastic dynamic welfare growth model (see, e.g., Ermoliev et al. 2000b). This model maps spatial economic losses into gains and losses of agents: central government, a mandatory catastrophe insurance (a catastrophe pool), an investor, "individuals" (cells or regions), producers (farmers), etc., depending on implemented loss mitigating and sharing policy options.

GIS–based modeling of catastrophes and vulnerability coupled with multi–agent models, though still limited in use, is becoming increasingly important: to governments and legislative authorities for better comprehension, negotiation and management of risks; to insurance companies for making decisions on the allocation and values of contracts, premiums, re–insurance arrangements, and the effects of mitigation measures; to households, industries, farmers for risk–based allocation of properties and values. These models are gaining popularity in various scientific communities involved in global change and sustainability research. In the case of the insurance industry, for example, it is possible to simulate different patterns of catastrophes in a region as they may happen in reality and analyze their impacts on the stability of the companies or the industry (Daykin et al. 1994; Ermoliev et al. 2000b; Ermoliev et al. 2000a; Ermolieva et al. 2000).

A catastrophe can ruin many agents if their risk exposures are not appropriate. To design safe catastrophic risk management strategies it is necessary to define location specific feasible decisions based on potential losses generated by a catastrophe model. Some of these decisions reduce the frequencies (likelihood) and magnitudes of catastrophic events (say, land use decisions) and redistribute losses and gains on local and international levels (say, pools, insurance, compensation schemes, credits, borrowing). Different catastrophe scenarios in general, lead to different decision strategies. The number of alternative decisions may be very large. Thus, for a region with only 10 possible sub–locations and 10 alternative sizes of insurance coverage, the number of possible combinations is 10^{10}. The straightforward "if–then" evaluation of all alternatives by calculating the damages of location specific values may easily exceed 100 years.

The important question is how to bypass these limitations of "if–then" analysis and find such combinations of strategies that would be the "best" against all possible catastrophes. By Ermoliev et al. (2000a) it was shown that the search for "robust" optimal decisions can be done by incorporating stochastic spatial adaptive Monte Carlo optimization into catastrophic modeling. This enables the design of desirable robust solutions without evaluating all possible alternatives. Schematically, the model with an embedded optimization procedure is presented in Fig. 3. Starting with some initial setting, policy variables are input into the "catastrophe model". The "catastrophe model" generates catastrophes and induced direct and indirect damages. The efficiency of the policies is evaluated with respect to performance indicators (block "indicators") of the agents, e.g., insurers, insured, governments, etc. If these do not fulfill the requirements, goals and constraints, they are further adjusted in the block "adaptive feedbacks". In this manner it is possible to take into account complex interdependencies between damages at different locations, available decisions and resulting losses and claims. A crucial aspect is the use of appropriate risk indicators (measures), e.g.,

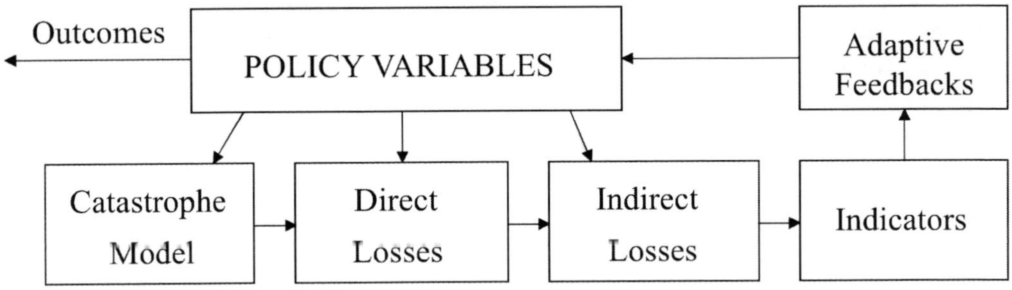

Figure 3. Schematic representation of the models: adaptive Monte Carlo.

to avoid bankruptcies of agents. Catastrophic losses often have multi–mode distributions and therefore the use of mean values (e.g., expected costs and profits) may be misleading. The model described in the next section satisfies these requirements and it emphasizes the need for the collective management of catastrophic risks.

4. Spatial Adaptive Monte Carlo Optimization

The insurance model in Section 2. has a rather simplified illustrative character. In reality, damages and claims depend on geographical patterns of catastrophes, clustering of property values in the region, available mitigation measures and regulations, and the spread of insurance coverage among different locations. For this purpose, the model should be geographically explicit (see Ermoliev et al. 2000b; Ermoliev et al. 2000a; Ermolieva et al. 2000 and the references therein).

A main task in connection with catastrophic risk management is the design of an appropriate loss mitigation and sharing program. A number of crucial questions arise within this analysis, such as: What are optimal ways to alter location–specific risk profiles by modification or/and reinforcement of structural measures such as dikes, reservoirs, irrigation systems, etc? How can the existing situation be adapted, in particular, land use practices, reallocation of capital, etc., to the existing risk profile? What are optimal financial strategies for mitigation and adaptation? Where is the balance between ex–ante "here–and–now" and ex–post "wait–and–see" decisions? Reallocation of properties away from risk prone areas is an important option, but not feasible, however, for many regions (or feasible only within the long–term horizon).

These and other questions emphasize the need for collective efforts in managing catastrophes and involving multiple agents (stakeholders), governments, both local and central, planners, insurers, re–insurers, investors, firms, farmers, and individuals. Heterogeneity of the agents induced by mutually dependent losses from extreme events is a key feature of the integrated catastrophe management model.

The analysis of possible gains and losses of the agents due to different arrangements of the loss sharing program takes into account the frequency and intensity of hazards, the stock of capital at risk, its structural characteristics, and different measures (in particular, engineering, financial) of vulnerability. Evaluation of appropriate structural mitigation and financial loss sharing measures should, in general, take into account the potential synergy of these two sets of actions: the preventive mitigation measures applied today reduce financial losses and adaptation costs tomorrow. Because of the complex interplays of these effects, we now concentrate only on a financial loss sharing program.

The insurance model of Section 2. is modified as follows. The study region is subdivided into sub–regions or locations $j = 1, 2, \ldots, m$. Locations may correspond to a collection of households, a zone with similar seismic activity, to a watershed, etc. They may be constituted by a collection of grid cells for meaningful representation of the simulated patterns of events in space and time. We assume that for each location j an estimation W_j of the property value or "wealth" of this location exists, which includes values of houses, lands, factories, etc.

Suppose that n agents, $i = 1, \ldots, n$, (insurers, governments, re–insurers, investors) are involved in the loss sharing program. They may have contracts with locations and partially cover their losses. Each agent i has an initial fund or a risk reserve R_i^0 that in general depends on magnitudes of catastrophic events. Assume that the planning horizon covers $t = 0, 1 \ldots, T-1$ time intervals. The risk reserve R_i^t at each t is calculated according to the following formula:

$$R_i^{t+1} = R_i^t + \sum_{j=1}^{m} \left[\pi_{ij}^t(q^t) - c_{ij}^t(q^t)\right] - \sum_{j\in\varepsilon_t(\omega_t)} L_j^t(\omega_t) q_{ij}^t, \qquad (1)$$

where $i = 1, 2, \ldots, n$, $q^t = \left\{ q_{ij}^t,\ i = \overline{1,n}, j = \overline{1,m} \right\}$, q_{ij}^t is the coverage of a company i in location j at time t, $\pi_{ij}^t(q^t)$ is the premium from contracts characterized by coverage $\left\{ q_{ij}^t \right\}$ (full coverage of losses corresponds to $q_{ij}^t = 1$), and $c_{ij}^t(q^t)$ are transaction costs or administrative, running or other costs. $L_j^t(\omega_t)$ is the loss (damage) at j caused by a catastrophe ω_t at time t. Random catastrophic events $\omega = (\omega_0, \ldots, \omega_{T-1})$ may affect a random number of different locations. In general, a catastrophic event at time t is modeled by a random subset $\varepsilon_t(\omega)$ of locations j and its magnitude in each j. The losses $L_j^t(\omega_t)$ depend on the event ω_t, mitigation measures (e.g., dikes against flooding or specific building codes in seismic areas), and vulnerability of property values in j.

Variables q_{ij}^t and $\pi_{ij}^t(q^t)$ allow the characterization of the differences in risks at different locations. It is assumed that all agents may cover different fractions of catastrophic losses from the same location. Variables q_{ij}^t interconnect the processes of R_i^t, $i = 1, 2, \ldots, n$ (e.g., $\pi_{ij}^t(q^t)$, $c_{ij}^t(q^t)$ with each other. Inflows of premiums push trajectories of R_i^t up, whereas claims and transactions costs push them down.

In the case of a catastrophe, a location j faces losses (damages) L_j^t. Individuals at this location receive compensation $L_j^t q_{ij}^t$ from company i when such a loss occurs, and pay insurance premiums $\pi_{ij}^t(q^t)$. If W_j^0 is the initial wealth (property value), then the location's j wealth at time $t+1$ equals:

$$W_j^{t+1} = W_j^t + \sum_{i=1}^{n} (L_j^t q_{ij}^t - \pi_{ij}^t(q^t)) - L_j^t, \quad t = 0, 1, \ldots. \tag{2}$$

Equations 1 and (2) represent rather general processes of accumulation. Depending on the interpretation, they describe the accumulation of reserve funds, the dynamics of contamination, or the processes of economic growth with random disturbances (shocks), the reserves of the insurance company at time t, the gross national product of a country or the accumulated wealth of a specific region. In more general cases, when catastrophes may have profound effects on economic growth (can "move" the economy, see, for example, Manne and Richels 1992; Nordhaus 1993), this specification can be generalized to an economic–demographic model (MacKellar and Ermolieva 1999) representing both the movements of individuals and the capital accumulation processes within the economy.

Let us denote the decision variable by a vector x, which includes components of coverage q and feasible mitigation measures. For each insurer (agent) i consider a stopping time τ_i for process $R_i^t(x, \omega)$, i.e., a random variable with integer values $t = \overline{0, T}$. The event $\{\omega : \tau_i = t\}$ with fixed t corresponds to the decision to stop process $W_i^t(x, \omega)$ after time t. Examples of τ_i may be the time of the ruin before a given time T:$\tau_i(x, \omega) = \min\left\{T, \min\left[t : R_i^t(x, \omega) < 0, t > 0\right]\right\}$ (in which case τ_i is a rather complex implicit function of x) or the time of the first catastrophe, $t = \tau$.

Assume that each agent, i, and location, j, maximize their "wealth" at $t = \tau$, i.e., they are concerned with the resilience against possible catastrophes. In general, the notion of wealth at t requires an exact definition (see, e.g., Ginsburg and Keyzer 1997), as it must represent in a sense the whole probability distribution of R_i^τ, W_i^τ. The performance of insurance depends on whether the accumulated fund $\sum_{t=1}^{\tau}\left[\sum_{j=1}^{m}\left[\pi_{ij}^t(q^t) - c_{ij}^t(q^t)\right]\right]$ is able to cover claims $\sum_{j \in \varepsilon_\tau(\omega_\tau)} L_j^\tau(\omega_\tau) q_{ij}^\tau$. Thus, insurers will maximize their wealth, which depends on the (random) balance of income and payments:

$$\vartheta_i^\tau = \sum_{t=1}^{\tau}\left[\sum_{j=1}^{m}\left[\pi_{ij}^t(q^t) - c_{ij}^t(q^t)\right]\right] - \sum_{j \in \varepsilon_\tau(\omega_\tau)} L_j^\tau(\omega_\tau) q_{ij}^\tau.$$

The stability of an insurer is determined by the probability of the event

$$E_1 = \{\vartheta_i^{\mathcal{T}} < 0\}. \tag{3}$$

Individuals (locations) maximize their wealth, which depends on whether the amount of premiums that they pay to the insurer does not exceed the compensation of losses at time $t = \tau$:

$$v_j^{\mathcal{T}} = \sum_{t=0}^{\mathcal{T}} \pi_{ij}^{\mathcal{T}}(q^k) - L_j^{\mathcal{T}}(\omega_{\mathcal{T}})q_{ij}^{\mathcal{T}}.$$

Therefore, the "financial" stability of locations depends on the probability of the event

$$E_2 = \{\nu_i^{\mathcal{T}} < 0\}. \tag{4}$$

Inequalities (3)–(4) define important events, constraining the choice of decision variables. The probability of events (3)–(4), i.e., underpayments to insurers and over–payments by individuals, determine the stability (resilience) of the scheme. This can be expressed in terms of the probabilistic constraint

$$P[E_1, E_2] \leqslant p, \tag{5}$$

where p is a desirable probability threshold of the program's failure (default) that occurs, say, only once in 100 years. Constraint (5) is similar to an insolvency constraint (Ermoliev et al. 2000a), a standard for regulations of the insurance business (see also Section 2.). In stochastic optimization (Ermoliev and Wets 1988; Ermolieva et al. 2000), it is known as the so–called chance constraint. Note, however, that this constraint does not account for the attained values of E_1 and E_2. The main goal in setting up the insurance scheme can now be formulated as the minimization of expected total losses $F(x) = E\sum_{ij}(1 - q_{ij})L_j^{\mathcal{T}}$ including uncovered (un–insured) losses by the insurance scheme subject to chance constraint (5), where vector x, in the most simple example, consists of the components π_{ij} and q_{ij}.

Constraint (5) imposes significant methodological challenges even in cases when $\tau(x)$ does not depend on x and events 3–4 are defined by linear functions of decision variables (see discussion in Ermoliev and Wets 1988, p. 8, and in Ermoliev et al. 2000b; Ermoliev et al. 2000a). This constraint is of "black–and–white" character, i.e., it accounts only for a violation of (3)–(4) but not for the magnitude of violation. There are important connections between the minimization of $F(x)$ subject to highly nonlinear and possibly discontinuous chance constraints (5) and the minimization of convex functions, which have important economic interpretations. Consider the following function:

$$G(x) = F(x) + \alpha\sum_i E\max\{0, \vartheta_i^{\mathcal{T}}\} + \beta\sum_j E\max\{0, \nu_j^{\mathcal{T}}\} \tag{6}$$

where α, β are positive parameters. It is possible to prove (see general results in Ermoliev et al. 2000b; Ermoliev et al. 2000a) that for large enough amount of α, β the minimization of function $G(x)$ generates solutions x with $F(x)$ approaching the minimum of $F(x)$ subject to 5 for any given level p.

The minimization of $G(x)$, as defined by eq. (6), has a simple economic interpretation. Function $F(x)$ comprises expected direct losses associated with the insurance program.

The second term quantifies the expected shortfall of the program to fulfill its obligations; it can be viewed as the expected amount of ex–post borrowing with a fee α needed for this purpose. Similarly, the third term can be interpreted as the expected ex–post borrowing with a fee β needed to compensate over–payments. Obviously, large enough fees α, β will tend to preclude the violation of (3)–(4). Thus, ex–post borrowing with large enough fees allows for a control of the insolvency constraints (5).

In our model, for the adaptive search of optimal robust solutions we apply *stochastic quasi–gradient methods (adaptive Monte Carlo optimization)*. These methods can be used for the maximization of the non–smooth function $G(x)$ by using only sample performance functions $f(q,\pi,\omega)$, $G(x) = Ef(q,\pi,\omega)$,

$$f(q,\pi,\omega) = \sum_{ij}(1-q_{ij})L_j^{\tau}(\omega_{\tau}) + \alpha\sum_i \max\{0, \vartheta_i^{\tau}(\omega_{\tau})\} + \beta\sum_j \max\{0, \nu_j^{\tau}(\omega_{\tau})\}.$$

Detailed descriptions of the method can be found in (Ermoliev and Wets 1988; Ermoliev et al. 2000b; Ermoliev et al. 2000a). Here, we illustrate its application rather schematically only with respect to some components of x, namely, for decisions on contracts $q = \{q_{ij}\}$. A sequence of approximate solutions $q^0, q^1, \ldots$ is generated directly by using statistical estimates (stochastic quasi–gradients for non–smooth function $G(x)$) of grad $W(q,\omega)$ without approximating $W(q)$ by an explicit function. The adaptive search procedure is defined as follows. Let q^0 be an initial guess, and q^k is the approximate solution after k steps. Then

$$q^{k+1} = \Pr j(q^k + \rho_k\xi^k)\,,\, k = 0, 1, \ldots, \tag{7}$$

where $\rho_k \geqslant 0$ is $(q^0, q^1, \ldots q^k)$–measurable random variable ("step–size" multiplier depending on $(q^0, q^1, \ldots q^k)))$, $\xi^k$is $(q^0, q^1, \ldots q^k)$–measurable random vector such that $\left|E\left[\xi^k|q^0, q^1, \ldots q^k\right] - \text{grad}W(q^k)\right| \to 0,\ k \to \infty$. Stochastic quasi–gradients $\xi^k$are often defined at each step $k - 0, 1, \ldots$ by using only one independent sample ω^k The symbol $\Pr j(y)$ defines the projection of y onto a feasible set Q, i.e., it is the point from Q minimizing the distance to y

$$\Pr j(y) = \arg\min\left\{\|z - y\|^2 : z \in Q\right\}.$$

The projection of $q^k + \rho_k\xi^k$ (calculation of q^{k+1}) is a very fast operation when it starts from q^k. The current approximate decision variables $q^k = \{q_{ij}^{kt}\}$ are adaptively adjusted according to feedback (7). Since function $W(q)$ is not concave even for convex $\pi_{ij}^t(\cdot)$, $c_{ij}^t(\cdot)$ (due to, e.g., dependence of τ on x), the random sequence q^k generated according to (7) may not converge to a global solution. The choice of step–size–multipliers ρ_t in (7) satisfies conditions

$$\rho_t \geqslant 0,\ \sum_{t=0}^{\infty}\rho_t = \infty,\ \sum_{t=0}^{\infty}\rho_t^2 < \infty.$$

For example, $\rho_t = C_t/t$, where $0 \leqslant \underline{C}_t \leqslant C_t \leqslant \overline{C}_t < \infty$ ensures the convergence of $\left\{G(q^k)\right\}$ to a local maximum value with a probability of 1 in practically all important cases.

The random adjustment mechanism (7) has the ability to bypass local solutions. Global convergence can be achieved by introducing "shocks" when the sequence q^k shows a steady–state tendency. The important feature of the functions (6) is that for convex $\pi_{ij}^t(q^t)$, $c_{ij}^t(q^t)$ and τ independent of x, this function is concave in contrast to the direct use of (5). This was achieved by a special choice of risk indicators in the definition of (3)–(5).

5. Case Studies: Earthquake Risks Management

In this Section we simplify the model of Section 4. to illustrate its applicability using modified but realistic data from a case study of seismic risks in the Tuscany region of Italy.

The main question in connection with these catastrophes is by whom and in what way should the losses be covered? Until recently, losses from natural catastrophes were mainly absorbed by the victims and their governments (Ermoliev and Wets 1988; Froot 1997; Linnerooth-Bayer and Amendola 2000). The insurance industry (and investors) absorbs only a small portion of the losses. Currently, as losses increase, governments are concerned with escalating costs for disaster prevention, response, compensation to victims, and public infrastructure repair. It is important to create incentives for individuals and local governments to increase their responsibility in dealing with extreme events and their impacts and mitigation. Local governments may be more effective in the evaluation and enforcement of loss–reduction and loss–spreading measures, but this is possible only through location–specific analysis of potential losses, of the mutual interdependencies of these losses, and of the sensitivity of location–specific losses to new land use and other risk management strategies.

An important consideration for national insurance strategies is linking private insurance with mitigation measures to reduce losses. Insurers, however, are reluctant to enter markets that expose them to the risk of bankruptcy. In the USA, for example, many insurers pulled out of catastrophic risk markets in response to their large losses from natural catastrophes in the last decade (ISO 1994). In Italy, a law for integrating insurance in the overall risk management process was proposed only in late 1997 (within the Design of Law 2793: "Measures for the Stabilization of Public Finance"). This opened a debate on various policy options for national insurance strategies. The aim of this Section is to analyze a possible insurance program, which is "robust" against earthquakes and spreads the loss burden among multiple agents (e.g., private insurance, the financial market (contingent credit), the government, and individuals), taking into account their individual goals and constraints with respect to the catastrophes. The program allows for the transfer of some share of the loss via ex–post arrangements (borrowing).

In our example, we use a catastrophe model based on a random earthquake and damage generator (see Amendola et al. 2000; Baranov et al. 2002; Ermoliev et al. 2000b; Rozenberg et al. 2001). Its main idea is the application of the Gutenberg–Richter law connecting the magnitudes of events with the random timing of their occurrence for a given set of seismic faults. The generator is not aimed at prediction, rather its purpose is to create a tool generating potential earthquake scenarios, which can be easily embedded into a stochastic optimization (Adaptive Monte Carlo) model discussed in Section 4. for the analysis of robust strategies. The earthquake and damage generator creates samples from multidimensional damage distributions of catastrophe losses, based on results of modeling geophysical processes, geophysical data and a model of vulnerability of buildings in the pilot region. Geophysical data are given by a map of geo–tectonic structure of the region (Petrini 1995).

Historical data are available as a map of seismic activity in the region and a map of maximum observed macro–seismic activity (`http://www.dstn.pcm.it/ssn/`). Figure 4 presents one of the earthquake scenarios. Specific attenuation characteristics and other data on the region were provided by the Seismic Risk Research Institute (Petrini 1995). The generator, in fact, can be easily adapted to other regions, incorporating different event distributions, non–Poissonian catastrophic processes, as well as micro zoning within modeled locations.

For analyzing of loss management strategies and according to the general model of Section 4., the Tuscany region was subdivided into locations (grid–cells) – cf. Fig. 5 – which were further aggregated into M $\approx$ 300 sub–regions, meaningful for decision making and corresponding to the number of municipalities. For each municipality j the number and types of buildings, their vulnerability, and number of built cubic meters represented the so–called estimate of "wealth" W_j. Simulated in time and space, earthquakes $\omega_0, \ldots, \omega_t$ occurred at different municipalities, inside or outside the region, had random magnitudes and, therefore, affected a random number of municipalities.

The economic losses of destroyed cubic meters of buildings were defined as the cost for their reconstruction. Obviously, the reinforcement of a building's environment would reduce the losses. This fact was adequately reflected in the model, which allowed the interplay between mitigation measures and risk-sharing mechanisms (insurance, re–insurance, financial markets) to be studied.

The risk sharing and spreading scheme analyzed in this chapter involves pooling of risks through mandatory insurance (this may be a pool of companies or the government itself acting as an insurer) based on location–specific exposures, partial compensation to the victims by the central government, and a contingent credit to the pool. This scheme encourages the accumulation of regional capital to better "buffer" against the volatilities of international re–insurance markets. We assumed that the insurance company covers a fraction q_j, $0 \leqslant q_j \leqslant 1$ (e.g., $q_j = 0.75$) of losses. The government compensates a portion ν. Thus, in the case of excessive losses the state could be severely affected. Let L_j^τ be random losses at municipality j at time $t = \tau$ when a catastrophe occurs. The accumulated mutual catastrophe fund at time τ including the proportional compensation $\nu \sum_j L_j^\tau$ by the government amounts to $\tau \sum_j \pi_j + \nu \sum_j L_j^\tau - \sum_j q_j L_j^\tau$. Thus, in this model we assume that the compensation to victims by the government is paid through the mandatory insurance.

The stability of the insurance program depends on whether the accumulated mutual fund together with the government compensation is able to cover claims, i.e., on the probability of event:

$$e_1 = \tau \sum_j \pi_j + \nu \sum_j L_j^\tau - \sum_j q_j L_j^\tau \geqslant 0 \quad . \tag{8}$$

The stability also depends on the willingness of individuals to accept premiums, i.e., on the location–specific probability of over–payments:

$$e_2 = \tau \pi_j - q_j L_j^\tau \geqslant 0, \quad j = 1, \ldots, m. \tag{9}$$

Apart from compensation $\nu \sum_j L_j^\tau$, the government arranges a contingent credit y with a fee φ to improve the stability of the mandatory insurance (pool) by transforming event (8)

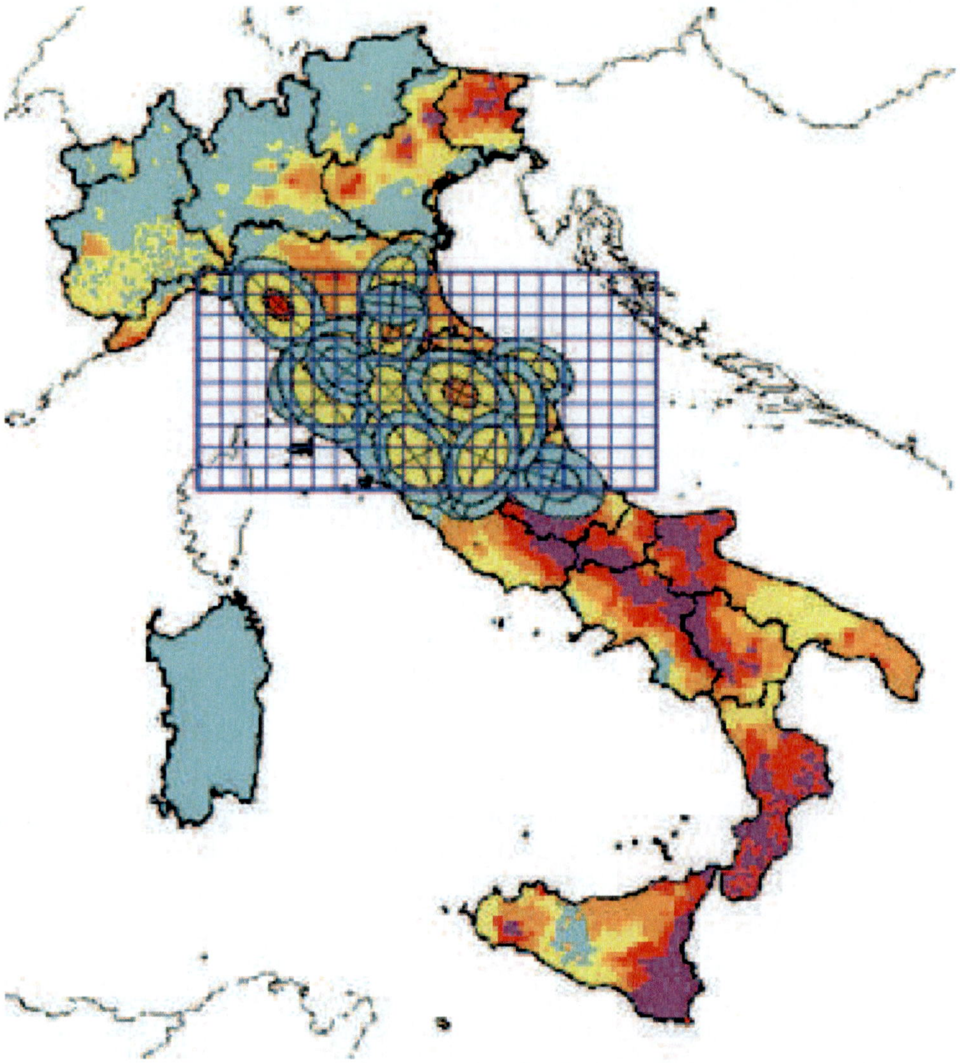

Figure 4. Earthquake generator.

into (10):

$$e_3 = \tau \sum_j \pi_j + \nu \sum_j L_j^\tau - \sum_j q_j L_j^\tau + y - \tau\varphi y \geqslant 0. \tag{10}$$

Constraints (3) and (4) describe the burden sharing within the program. Here, we assume that the mandatory insurance pays the fee $\tau q y$ and receives a credit y, whereas the government repays the credit with the interest rate $\gamma\, y$, $\gamma > 1$. The choice of premiums drives the process of insurance supply–demand: if premiums are too high, (event (9) occurs too often) the willingness to participate in the program will be low. On the other hand, if premiums are not sufficient to guarantee inequality (8) with some acceptable probability, the stability of the mandatory insurance cannot be sustained.

Alternative policy options for the choice of premiums can be proposed by Stakeholders (i.e., insurers, local governments, individuals). Some of them may correspond to the stan-

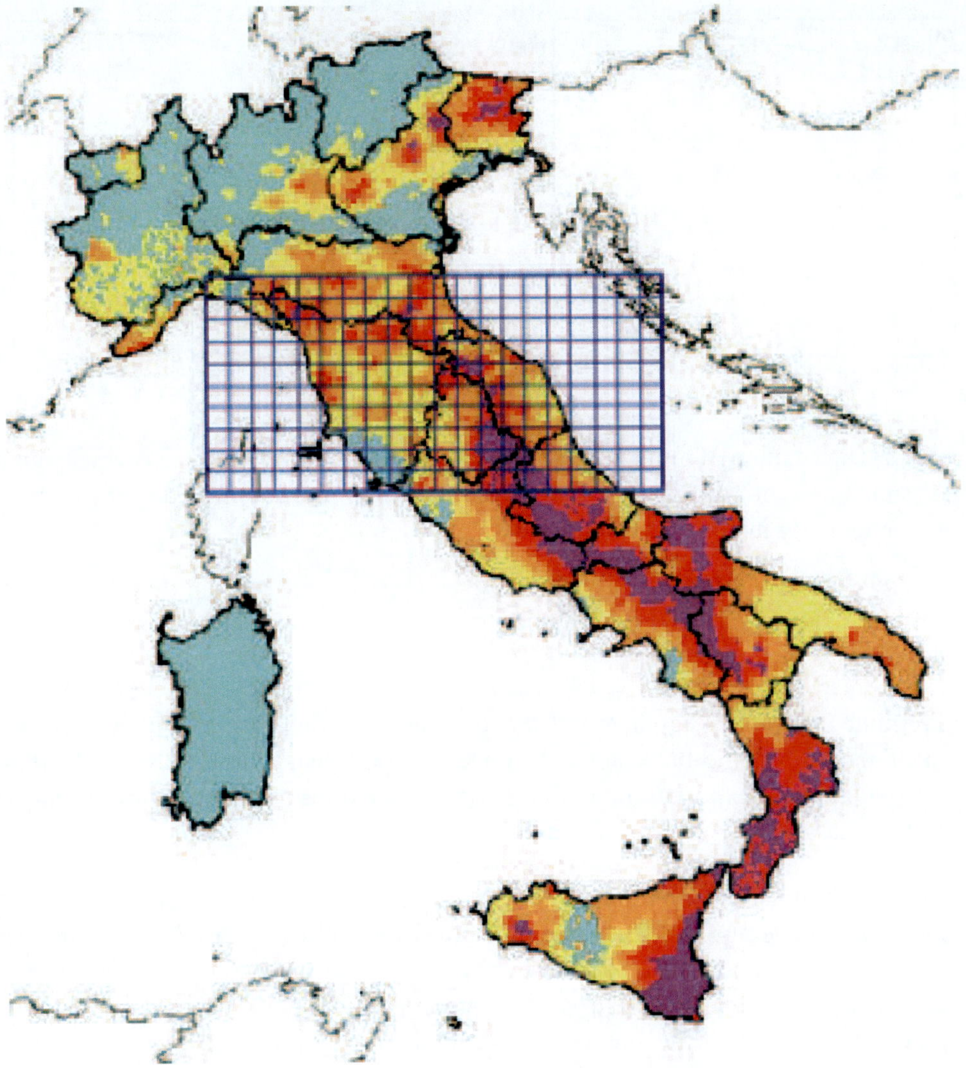

Figure 5. Geographically–explicit subdivision of the Tuscany regions in Italy.

dard actuarial approaches to calculate the premiums based on the expected losses. In the outlined numerical experiments we consider the following three rules:

1. Premiums based on the average damage over all of the municipalities (solidarity principle, making less exposed locations pay premiums equal to those more severely exposed).

2. Location–specific premiums based on average damage in a particular municipality, i.e., risk–based premiums.

The use of average losses may be misleading in the case of heavily tailed distributions that are typical for catastrophic losses. The stochastic optimization risk management model outlined in Section 4. allows calculation of premiums taking into account sustainability indicators of insurers and the state, constraints on individual incomes, willingness to overpay

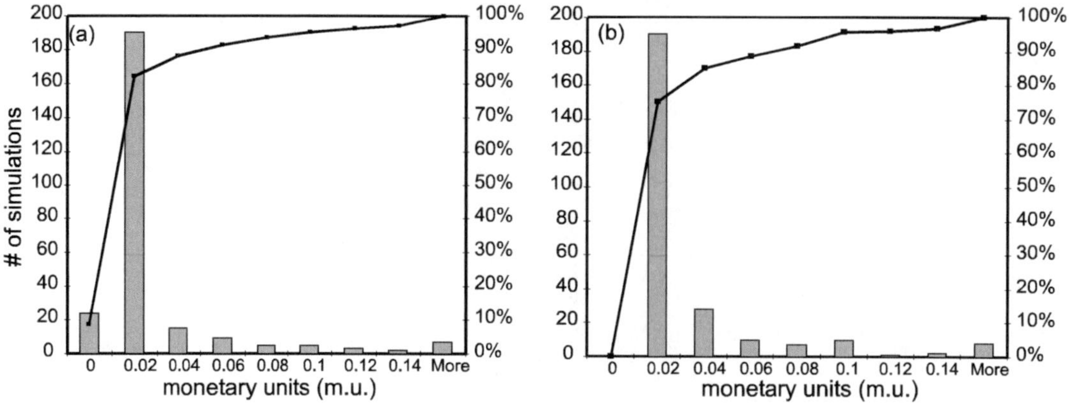

Figure 6. (a) Distribution of municipality specific premiums, textitoption 2 (per m^3 building volume/municipality in %). (b) Distribution of "fair" premiums, *option 3* (per m^3 building volume/municipality in %).

premiums, etc. These model–based robust premiums were stipulated as the third policy option:

3. Premiums that fairly equalize the risk of instability for the insurance company (the insurer may become bankrupt only once in 1 000 years) and the risk of premium overpayment for exposed municipalities (municipalities overpay premiums only once in 100 years).

Besides premiums, the solution of the model also provides optimal policy options on location–specific coverage and the amount of governmental compensation and the contingent credit. Here we present results only relating to premium policies. This is the most interesting case for analyzing catastrophic exposures since optimal robust policies can be significantly different from the standard actuarial approaches. Thus, Figs. 6–7 show considerable differences between options 1, 2 and option 3.

For *option 1*, where the burden of losses is equally distributed over all locations, the simulation of catastrophic losses showed that the annual premium is equal to the flat rate of 0.02 monetary units (m.u.) per cubic meter of building.

For *option 2,* the distribution of municipality specific premiums based on average damage in each municipality (or according to the municipality specific risk) is shown in Fig. 6a. There are a prevailing number of municipalities (about 220) that have to pay 0.02–0.03 m.u., which is close to the flat rate of 0.02, as in option 1. About 20 municipalities are at no risk at all (0 rate). Municipalities that are more exposed to risk have to pay 0.04 and higher rates (more than 50 municipalities).

Figure 7a shows the distribution of the insurers' reserve (cumulated at τ within 50 years) for *options 1, 2* premiums. The probability of insolvency, i.e. when the risk reserve accumulated until the catastrophe is not enough to compensate incurred losses, is also shown. This distribution, in fact, generates the demand for contingent credit. There is a rather high probability of "small" insolvency (values -90, -40 occurred 190 and 90 times out of 500 simulations). High over–payments (more than 500 m.u.) occurred in about 10 per cent of

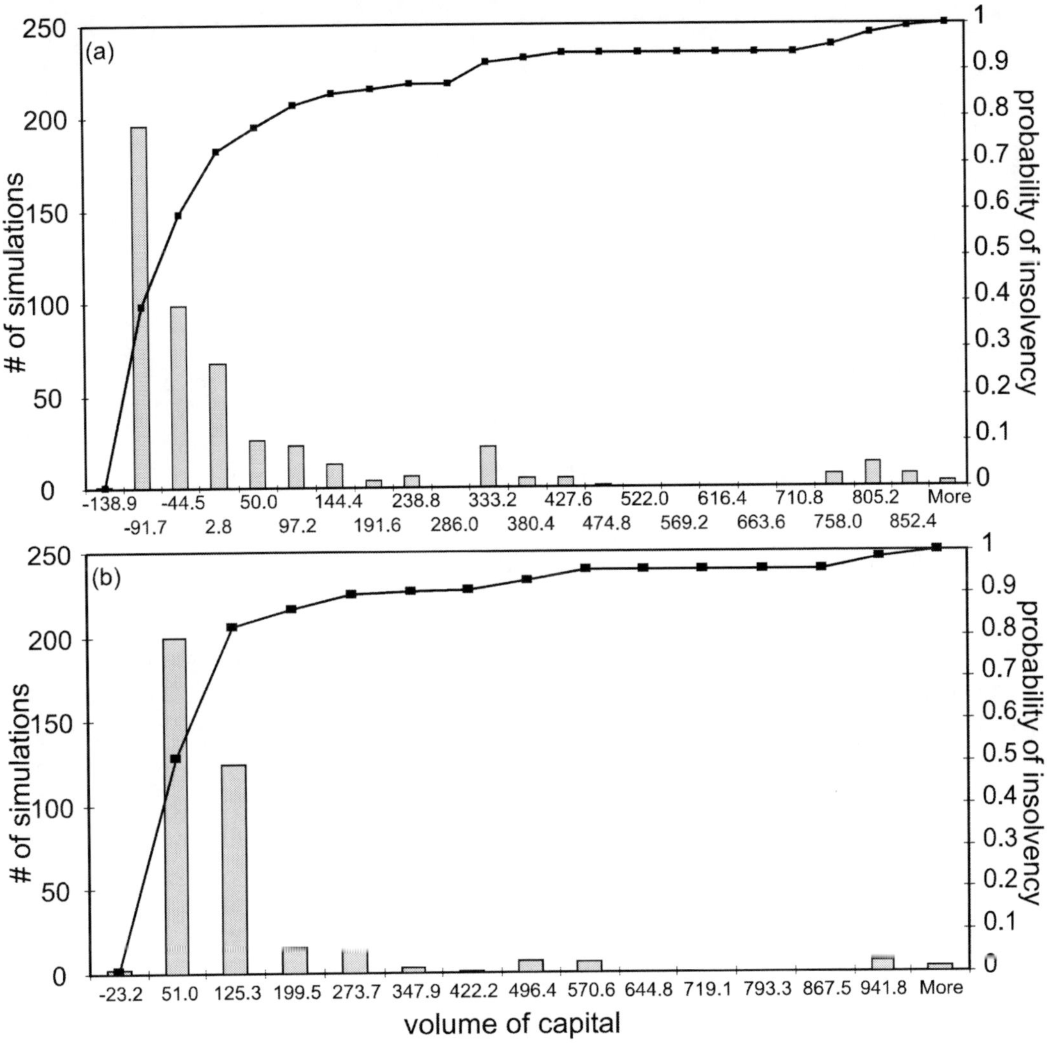

Figure 7. (a) Distribution of insurer's reserve, *options 1, 2* (thousands m.u., 50 years). (b) Distribution of insurers' reserve, *option 3* (thousands m.u., over 50 years).

the simulations. The size of insolvency would represent the cost to the government of covering the losses uncovered by the pool (e.g., by using a possibility to transfer a fraction of the losses to international financial markets, as analyzed in Ermolieva et al. 2000).

Figure 6b shows the distribution of premiums for *option 3*, i.e., robust optimal premiums. According to this principle, most of the municipalities (190) have to pay close to the flat rate of 0.02–0.03 m.u.$/m^3$ of a building. Rates of 0.04 and higher have to be paid by about 100 municipalities. In this case, the highest premium rate is 0.5, which is much lower when compared to the highest rate of 1.2 of option 2. The distribution of the insurer's reserve in Fig. 7b also indicates the improvement of the insurer's stability — the frequency of insolvency is considerably reduced.

Figure 8 provides an illustrative comparison of the three premium options analyzed. For each municipality, it shows the optional premiums to be paid at the flat premium rate

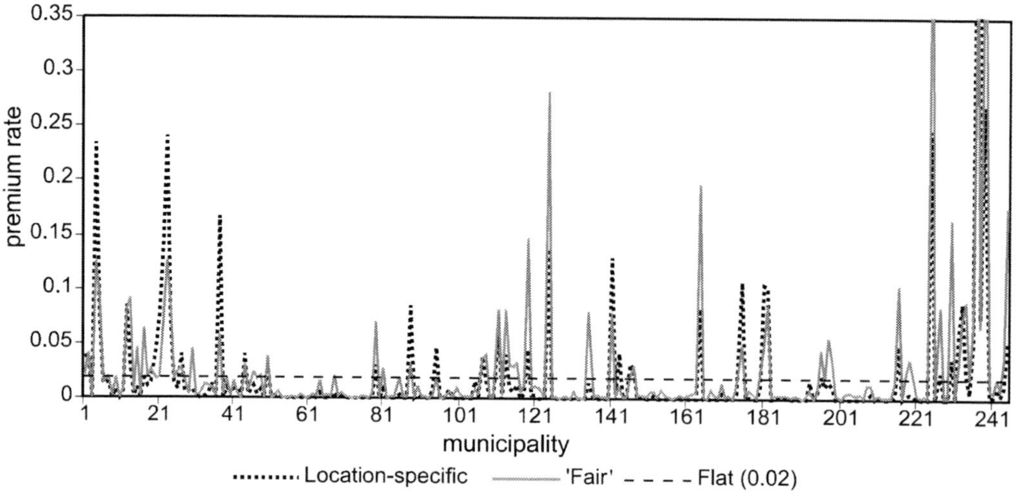

Figure 8. Comparison of options: municipality specific, "fair" and flat (0.02) premiums.

of 0.02, the option 2 municipality specific rate, and the "fair" robust premium of option 3. Many municipalities in all three options have to pay a premium rate, close to the flat rate (0.015–0.03). For quite a number of municipalities in option 2, the rate significantly exceeds the flat rate. For these municipalities, special attention should be given to whether they are able to pay such high premiums. Option 3 allows taking individual constraints on over–payments into account and working out efficient premiums both for the insurer and the municipalities.

6. Conclusion

Managing catastrophic risks is a complex multidisciplinary problem that requires joint efforts of multiple agents and appropriate risk–based approaches to the design of efficient and sustained land use practices, loss sharing and mitigating programs. The risks are characterized by the lack of appropriate knowledge on their occurrence and magnitudes, heavily tailed distributions of losses that come abruptly in time and space. They are rare and hardly predictable (therefore, often unaccounted for), costly and unevenly distributed. They cannot be treated on average, and require specific risk measures. In this Chapter we demonstrate that coping with catastrophes should rely on comprehensive model–based approaches combining natural, engineering, financial and social systems. The model can be regarded as a mitigation tool to analyze the risks and reduce or share them.

The types of models presented here are capable of representing a variety of stakeholder groups in an agent–based setting. They allow the analysis of various ex–ante burden sharing arrangements while paying attention to other measures of the disaster cycle (mitigation, preparedness, response, recovery) and assign responsibilities as well as analyze trade–offs in close cooperation with stakeholders.

In Section 5. we illustrate the applicability of the discussed approach for a seismic prone area. The same type of approach is applicable to a variety of catastrophic risk management situations, e.g., floods, windstorms or even outbreaks of diseases. The key issue in these cases is the specification of catastrophe models and the risk reduction and risk spreading decisions. While the risk spreading (financial) part of the model may be similar for quite different natural and human–made catastrophes, the catastrophe model and the risk reduction (mitigation) measures may be quite different for different case studies. In most cases a key issue is the change of prevailing land use practices, as a causative factor on the one hand, or as a risk–spreading adaptation and risk–reducing mitigation measure on the other, e.g., deforestation, afforestation, spatial patterns of settlements, livestock allocation and densities, etc., towards more resilient, risk–based policies.

References

Amendola, A., Y. Ermoliev, and T. Ermolieva (2000). Earthquake risk management: A case study for an Italian region. In *Proceedings of the Second Euro Conference on Global Change and Catastrophe Risk Management: Earthquake Risks in Europe*, Laxenburg. International Institute for Applied Systems Analysis.

Amendola, A., Y. Ermoliev, T. Ermolieva, V. Gitits, G. Koff, and J. Linnerooth-Bayer (2000). A systems approach to modeling catastrophic risk and insurability. *Natural Hazards Journal* **21**(2-3), 381–393.

Baranov, S., B. Digas, T. Ermolieva, and V. Rozenberg (2002). Earthquake risk management: Scenario generator. Technical Report Interim Report IR-02-025, International Institute for Applied Systems Analysis, Laxenburg.

Borch, K. (1962). Equilibrium in a reinsurance market. *Econometrica* **30**(3), 424–444.

Daykin, C., T. Pentikainen, and M. Pesonen (1994). *Practical Risk Theory for Actuaries. Monographs on Statistics and Applied Probability*, Volume 53. London: Chapman and Hall Ltd.

Ermoliev, Y., T. Ermolieva, G. MacDonald, and V. Norkin (2000a). Insurability of catastrophic risks: The stochastic optimization model. *Optimization Journal* **47**, 51–265.

Ermoliev, Y., T. Ermolieva, G. MacDonald, and V. Norkin (2000b). Stochastic optimization of insurance portfolios for managing exposure to catastrophic risks. *Annals of Operations Research* **99**, 207–225.

Ermoliev, Y. and R. Wets (Eds.) (1988). *Numerical Techniques of Stochastic Optimization: Computational Mathematics*, Berlin: Springer-Verlag.

Ermolieva, T., G. Fischer, and M. Obersteiner (2000). Integrated modeling of spatial and temporal heterogeneity induced by catastrophic events. Technical Report Interim Report IR-03-023, International Institute for Applied Systems Analysis, Laxenburg.

Fischer, G., M. Shah, and H. van Velthuizen (2002). Climate change and agricultural vulnerability. Report commissioned by the United Nations for the Johannesburg Summit, United Nations, Johannesburg. Available on the Internet: *http://www.iiasa.ac.at/Research/LUC/JB-Report.pdf*.

Froot, K. (1997). The limited financing of catastrophe risk: and overview. Technical report, Harvard Business School and National Bureau of Economic Research.

Gilber, C. and C. Gouy (1998). *Flood Response and Crisis Management in Western Europe: A Comparative Analysis*, Chapter Flood Management in France. Berlin: Springer-Verlag.

Ginsburg, V. and M. Keyzer (1997). *The Structure of Applied General Equilibrium Models*. Cambridge: MIT Press.

Grandell, J. (1991). *Aspects of Risk Theory*. Springer Series on Statistics: Probability and Its Applications. New York: Springer-Verlag.

ISO (1994). The impact of catastrophes on property insurance. Technical report, Insurance Service Office (ISO), New York.

Linnerooth-Bayer, J. and A. Amendola (2000). Global change, catastrophic risk and loss spreading. The GENEVA PAPERS on Risk and Insurance 25/2.

MacKellar, L. and T. Ermolieva (1999). The IIASA social security project multiregional economic-demographic growth model: Policy background and algebraic structure. Technical report, International Institute for Applied Systems Analysis, Laxenburg.

Manne, A. and R. Richels (1992). *Buying Greenhouse Insurance: The Economic Costs of CO_2 Emission Limits*. Cambridge: MIT Press.

Milly, P., R. Wetherald, K. Dunne, and T. Delworth (2002). Increasing risk of great floods in changing climate. *Nature* **415**, 512–514.

MunichRe (1999). Climate change and increase in loss trend persistence. Press release, MunichRe, Munich.

Nordhaus, W. (1993). Rolling the DICE: An optimal transition path for controlling greenhouse gases. *Resource and Energy Economics* **15**, 27–50.

NRC (1999). *National Disaster Losses: A Framework for Assessment*. Washington: National Academy Press.

Palmer, T. and J. Raisanen (2002). Quantifying the risk of extreme seasonal precipitation events in a changing climate. *Nature* **415**, 512–514.

Petrini, V. (1995). Pericolosita' sismica e prime valutazioni di rischio in Toscana (seismic hazards and preliminary risk evaluation in Tuscany). Technical report, CNR/IRRS, National Research Council/Seismic Risk Research Institute, Milan.

Prekopa, A. (1995). *Stochastic Programming*. Dordrecht: Kluwer Academic Publishers.

Rozenberg, V., T. Ermolieva, and M. Blizorukova (2001). Modeling earthquakes via computer programs. Interim report IR-01-068., International Institute for Applied Systems Analysis, Laxenburg.

Walker, G. (1997). Current developments in catastrophe modelling. In N. Britton and J. Oliver (Eds.), *Financial Risks Management for Natural Catastrophes*, Brisbane. Griffith University.

In: Risk Management
Editors: B. Jordão and E. Sousa, pp. 327-344

ISBN: 978-1-60876-011-4

Chapter 12

Implicit Safety-Critical Attitudes within Safety Culture

Nicki Marquardt
Leuphana University of Lueneburg, Institute of Experimental Industrial Psychology-LueneLab, Wilschenburcher Weg, Luneburg, Germany

Abstract

Safety culture is a very relevant topic for high reliability organizations. In most models safety culture is defined as being basic assumptions, attitudes or values concerning organizational safety issues. When measuring safety cultures many researchers were primarily focussed on explicit safety-critical attitudes and generally relied on specific survey instruments. However, it is questionable whether self-report measures can capture all aspects of organizational safety culture. This article deals with the relationship between implicit safety-critical attitudes and safety culture. Based on an implicit social cognition approach and conceptual models of safety culture it is asked whether implicit safety-critical attitudes may be a better predictor for the various safety culture indicators compared to explicit attitudes. In this study explicit and implicit safety-critical attitudes of 70 participants working at a German production unit for gearbox manufacturing were measured. The author used the Implicit Association Test (IAT) to measure implicit safety-critical attitudes. Questionnaires were used to assess explicit safety attitudes and various indicators of safety culture. The results of this study show that implicit safety-critical attitudes were superior in the prediction of safety culture indicators on an individual level. Moreover, recommendations for future research in the field of safety culture assessment are made.

Key words: implicit association test (IAT) - implicit attitudes - mental processes - risk awareness - safety culture –

1. Introduction

Over the past 20 years, many researchers have shown rising interest in the topic *safety culture* (Fernández-Muniz, Montes-Perón & Vázquez-Ordás, 2007). For instance, most of the major industrial catastrophes such as the ones in Bhopal, Chernobyl and most recently Texas

City can be traced back to an insufficient safety culture (Baker Panel Report, 2007; INSAG, 1991; Petersen, 1996). Therefore, researchers have attempted to understand the meaning of safety culture and its outstanding role for high-hazard industries (Cox & Cox, 1991; Cox & Flin, 1998; Hale, 2000). In spite of the widespread use of this term, safety culture is a concept lacking a clear definition (Cox & Flin, 1998). Nevertheless, most of the attempted definitions indicate that a safety culture reflects the attitudes, beliefs and assumptions that individuals share on hazards and risks (Clarke, 1998; Cox & Cox, 1991; INSAG, 1991). Moreover, many researchers claim that attitudes are the most comprehensive and useful indicators of a safety culture (Lee, 1994; Williamson, Feyer, Cairns & Biancotti, 1997). However, the absence of a clear definition of safety culture makes determining attitudinal variables more difficult (Harvey, Erdos, Bolam, Kennedy & Gregory, 2002). Attitudes relevant to safety range from *individual responsibility*, *job satisfaction*, to *risk awareness* (Cheyne, Cox, Oliver & Tomas, 1998; Dedobbeleer & Beland, 1991). Apart from the demanding task of analysing relevant contents of safety-critical attitudes, another important but also neglected area of research is evident – the cognitive mode of attitudes.

1.1. Implicit and Explicit Attitudes

In contemporary social psychological research there is a distinction between two different modes of attitude and their cognitive characteristics ((Forgas, Williams & von Hippel, 2003; Greenwald & Banaji, 1995; Kihlstrom, Mulvaney, Tobias & Tobis, 2000; Plessner & Banse, 2001). There are *explicit attitudes*, which "… are expressed evaluative reactions operating on a more conscious level … " (Rowatt, Franklin & Cotton, 2005, p. 30). By contrast, there are also *implicit attitudes*, which can be defined as "… introspectively unidentified (or inaccurately identified) traces of past experience that mediate favourable or unfavourable feelings, thought, or action towards social objects" (Greenwald & Banaji, 1995, p. 8). Wilson, Lindsey & Schooler, (2000) also described implicit attitudes as being evaluations of unknown origin which are activated automatically. Consequently, implicit attitudes are assumed to be evaluations that are, to a great extent, unconscious. However, it is very important to keep in mind that these definitions are not stating this evaluation to be non-conscious, but that behaviour might be mediated by implicit attitudes without conscious awareness of this causal influence (Gawronski, Hofmann & Wilbur, 2005; Rudman, 2004).

Most contemporary models dealing with implicit and explicit attitudes give clear evidence for the two modes' various elements of mental processing. Specifically, implicit attitudes are *quick, intuitive, automatic, relatively effortless, non-conscious*, and *unintentional*. On the contrary, explicit attitudes seem to be *slow, controlled*, compared to implicit attitudes *relatively effortful, conscious*, and *intentional* (Bower & Forgas, 2000; Brewer, 2003; Dienes & Perner, 1996; Dorfman, Shames & Kihlstrom, 1996; Kihlstrom et al., 2000; Perugini, 2005; Smith & DeCoster, 1999; Roberts, 1998; Underwood & Bright, 1996). Furthermore, some models address both forms of attitudes at distinct cognitive processing modes like *bottom-up* and *top-down processing*. Implicit attitudes are described as a top-down processing mode whereas explicit attitudes are assumed to be a bottom-up processing mode (Ajzen & Sexton, 1999; Fazio & Towles-Schwen, 1999). Other models differentiate between *serial* and *parallel processing* modes. (Dorfman et al., 1996). However, most of the dual-process models do not assume that both processes function mutually exclusive. Contemporary dual-process models propose that the two processes generally operate simultaneously rather than alternately (Epstein, 1991; Fazio & Towless-Schwen, 1999; Smith & Decoster, 1999).

1.2. Implicit and Explicit Attitudes within Safety Culture

The basic assertion of this article is that not just explicit attitudes but also implicit attitudes are of essential significance to safety culture. Although this field of research has so far not been thoroughly investigated, there is growing evidence pinpointing the key role of implicit attitudes within safety culture. For instance, Burns, Mearns and McGeorge (2006) were able to develop a model of implicit trust within safety culture by recombining theories of implicit social cognition with models of safety culture. They used the concept of implicit attitudes defined by Greenwald and Banaji (1995) to extend models of safety culture derived from Schein's (1985) theory of organizational culture. In short, Schein (1985) proposed three interconnected levels of culture: observable artefacts, values and basic assumptions. Burns et al. (2006) redefined the basic assumptions in terms of implicit attitudes being the essence of safety culture, whilst explicit attitudes belong to the surface levels of safety culture. Their model of explicit and implicit trust was supported by an empirical study conducted at a UK gas plant. In spite of this model remaining partially elusive due to the ambiguity of the term safety culture, it is a first and valuable approach of enriching models of safety culture with contemporary concepts from implicit social cognition research.

In addition to explicit and implicit trust being components of safety culture, Marquardt and Hoeger (2009) found evidence for the impact of implicit moral attitudes on managerial decision-making. Incorrect decisions made in management often cause latent failures that contribute to organizational incidents and accidents (Reason, 1990). Therefore, implicit attitudes possibly relate to safety culture and its outcome factors.

Implicit processes have proven to have a strong impact on decision-making when conditions such as *high levels of uncertainty*, *complexity*, *consideration of long-term effects of actions*, and *time pressure* prevail (Agor, 1989; Dijksterhuis; 2004; Dijksterhuis & van Olden, 2006; Langhan-Fox & Shirley, 2003; Page, 1993). The MODE model (Fazio, 1990), for instance, proposes that situations with no opportunity to reflect extensively – e.g. due to high mental workload, time pressure or task difficulty – promote the influence of implicit attitudes on behaviour. Consequently, tasks at the "blunt" and "sharp end" of hazardous organizations (Reason, 1990) characterised by these conditions – e.g. in management and operations jobs – should be affected by implicit attitudes.

In addition to theoretical considerations there are also some methodological reasons, which support the key role of implicit attitudes within safety culture. The most common approaches for measuring safety culture apply survey instruments such as questionnaires and interviews (Cox & Cox, 1991; Harvey *et al.*, 2002; Jeffcott, Pidgeon, Weyman & Walls, 2006; Lee, 1994; Williamson *et al.*, 1997). However, survey methods are susceptible to response bias. Results of direct measures as e.g. questionnaires do not only assess participants' explicit attitudes but also include effects of impression management techniques due to socially desirable response (Fazio & Olson, 2003; Greenwald et al., 2000). In contrast, indirect and implicit measures use latency-based methods. Instead of asking directly, implicit measures rely on the automatic activation of attitudes from long-term memory and measure the time it takes an individual to react to attitude-evoking stimuli (Fazio, 2001; Fazio & Olson, 2003; Greenwald et al., 1998). Implicit measures are, thus, much more resistant to artefacts such as response bias than are direct attitude measures (Greenwald, Banaji, Rudman, Farnham, Nosek & Rosier, 2000). Therefore, various levels of safety culture assessment – the *individual, social* and *organizational level* (Wilpert & Fahlbruch, 2003) – could be affected differently by such response biases. Specifically, safety culture aspects on an *individual level* (e.g. inaccurate risk awareness) would be more vulnerable to socially desired responses than factors on *social* (e.g. flaws in communication) or *organizational level would* (e.g. lack of organizational safety commitment). In fact, central aspects of safety culture surveys on an individual level – as e.g. lack of rule compliance, complacency or negligence in safety issues – are very sensitive topics for many workers. Hence, direct measures may not be capable of assessing an individual's safety-critical attitudes validly. On the contrary, faulty safety culture aspects on a social or organizational level may be less vulnerable to response bias. The reason for this is that problems on these two levels cannot be directed at specific individuals. Consequently, more accurate results are likely to be attained using direct measures on these two levels than on the individual one.

Taking these findings into account, it seems convincing that implicit attitudes are an important but neglected issue within safety culture research.

3. Method

The study encompassed a wide range of methods in order to assess the various aspects of safety culture. On one hand direct measures such as questionnaires were used. On the other hand indirect latency-based measures such as the Implicit Association Test (IAT; Greenwald, McGhee & Schwartz, 1998) were applied. Explicit safety-critical attitudes were assessed using a one-item rating scale, while implicit attitudes were measured with a Safety-IAT. Both safety-critical attitudes were used as predictors for other individual, social and organizational level indicators of safety culture – risk awareness, communication and organizational pressure – which were assessed by questionnaire and a task specific safety performance test. Applying theoretical and methodological views would leave the author to assume that implicit attitudes are crucial for the prediction of safety culture aspects on an individual level. As a consequence, general as well as task specific aspects of risk awareness as a safety culture factor were measured on an individual level.

3.1. Participants

Seventy employees from the major German automotive company Volkswagen participated in this study. All employees were shift workers working at a production unit for gearbox manufacturing. Accordingly, all participants belonged to the "sharp end" of the organization. Due to the firms work council's precondition of applying an anonymous survey, personal data such as age, sex and qualification could not be collected. Workers from this department were selected specifically because minor deficiencies in their safety-critical attitudes and behaviour could lead to fatal errors and incidents during the process of production. Moreover, undetected incidents could be the reason for faulty gearboxes, which in turn could lead to devastating car accidents with casualties.

3.2. Implicit Safety-Critical Attitude Measure

The Implicit Association Test (IAT, Greenwald et al., 1998) was used to assess implicit safety-critical attitudes. In general, the IAT measures the strength of association between concepts by timing how long it takes someone to assign valence attributes to words representing distinct target categories. Therefore, the IAT assesses differences in implicit attitudes by measuring the underlying automatic activation of cognitive processes (Aidman & Carroll, 2003). This method includes five timed semantic discrimination tasks (Greenwald et al., 1998): During the first task the participant is presented with a target word on the computer screen and instructed to sort it into one of two possible categories (e.g. I versus workmates) by pressing the designated response key as fast as possible. The second step is also a type of two-category discrimination task in which the participant has to classify valence attributes into two categories (e.g. careful versus careless). As can be seen in figure 1, the third step is to combine the categories of the former two discrimination tasks to be more congruent (e.g. I + careful / workmates + careless) or incongruent (e.g. workmates + careful / I + careless) with available attitudes. During the fourth step, the participants have to do a reverse version of the response assignment for the two target categories. Finally, the fifth step combines the reversed target categories from step four with the unchanged attribute categories from step two. If participants received the congruent combined tasks in step three then they were asked to assign words of the incongruent combined tasks in the fifth step. The underlying assumption of the IAT is that more closely associated target concepts and attributes (e.g. I + careful / workmates + careless) are more quickly processed than lesser associated concepts and attributes (Aidman & Carroll, 2003; Rowatt et al., 2005). As an estimate for the implicit cognitive association between target concept and attribute dimension, an IAT score was computed as a function of the difference of the mean response latencies between the two combined tasks (incongruent combined task - congruent combined task). This difference score between the two critical conditions is called the *IAT effect* (Greenwald et al., 1998).

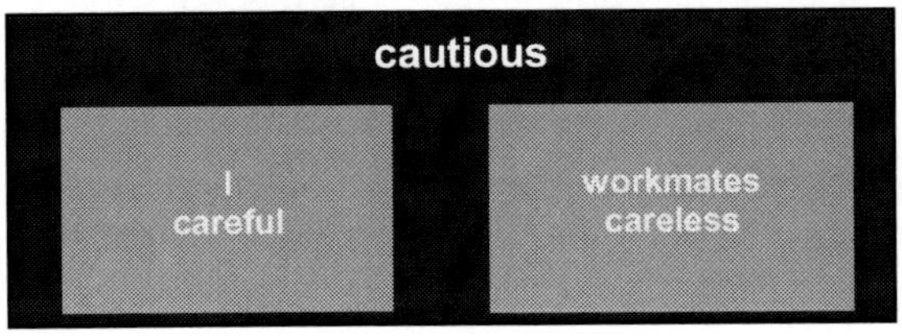

Figure 1. Combined target and attribute categories of the IAT.

3.2.1. Equipment

The IAT was administered on an IBM-compatible desktop computer. During the combined tasks (congruent and incongruent) participants had to randomly sort selected words into the correct target concept category (I versus workmates) or attribute category (careful versus careless). Each practice block (step 1, 2, and 4) had 20 trials and each combined block (step 3 and 5) consisted of 60 trials. Within the combined blocks the first 20 trials were used as practice trials and the subsequent 40 trials were selected as test trials (Greenwald et al., 2003; Nosek, Greenwald & Banaji, 2005). If a participant responded incorrectly the word "error" appeared and remained on the screen until the subject responded correctly. To prevent order effects, the sequence of congruent and incongruent combined tasks was counterbalanced.

3.2.2. Stimuli Development

The target category stimuli were adapted by other IAT studies comparing a self-concept dimension (e.g. I, me, mine) with a contrast category (e.g. others, partner, mates) (Steffens, 2004; Steffens & Schulze König, 2006). The first author generated all the items for the attribute categories. For this twenty safety-critical bipolar attributes, which dealt with safety culture factors as e.g. *responsibility, complacency* or *risk awareness* (Harvey *et al.*, 2002; INSAG, 1991; Lee, 1994) were selected. 84 undergraduate students used these words in a seven-point semantic differential scale in order to assess the safety-critical behaviour of an aero-mechanic in a real case scenario. Based on these ratings a factor analysis (PCA) of all items was performed. The factor analysis yielded five factors with eigenvalues greater than one and 64 % explained variance. The first factor explained more that half of the variance (34%). This factor contained bipolar items such as *careless - careful, unreliable - reliable, imprecise - precise, incautious - cautious, thoughtless - thoughtful* with factor loadings above .50. Cronbach's α was calculated as $\alpha = .80$ for these five items of factor one. Consequently, this factor was interpreted as representing a complacency or carelessness dimension.

3.3. Explicit Safety-Critical Attitude Measure

A questionnaire item was used to assess explicit safety-critical attitudes. To maximize comparability between implicit and explicit attitudes, one item representing the same carelessness dimension as the IAT items was constructed: "My workmates work less careful than I do". A five-point Likert scale with the anchors "agree" and disagree" was applied. The item was included in a safety questionnaire that contained further safety culture aspects. This questionnaire is described in the following section.

3.4. Safety Questionnaire

The assessment tool for the various behavioural and attitudinal factors of safety culture was a questionnaire that included 60 items. These items were consolidated to twelve scales. The items were developed with the help of academic literature, accident reports and human factors practitioners' work experience. Only three out of twelve scales were related to safety culture aspects, whereas the other nine scales referred to general aspects of health, safety and error management at the workplace. Therefore, only the three safety culture scales are reported on in this article. Within this questionnaire five items each were used to reflect aspects of safety culture on an *individual* (lack of risk awareness), *social* (lack of communication) and *organizational* level (organizational pressure). Those scales have been selected due to their eminent role in the safety culture literature (Fernández-Muniz et al. 2007; Harvey *et al.*, 2002; INSAG, 1991; Jeffcott et al., 2006, Lee, 1994). For all items a five-point Likert scale with the anchors "agree" and disagree" was applied.

3.5. Safety Performance Test

As reported in a former section, due to theoretical and methodological reasons, a hypothesis was made that safety culture aspects on an individual level could be crucial for the comparison of the implicit and explicit attitude's predictive validity. As a consequence, an additional more objective indicator for the individual safety culture factor *risk awareness* was used. Therefore, a task specific safety performance test was developed. Task specific questions were generated for assessing the workers' risk awareness according to potential errors in the process of production. Adequate risk awareness often contains attributes such as correct knowledge, perception and judgement of risks as well as the ability to foresee hazards (Fleming et al., 1998; Harvey et al., 2002; Lingard, 2002; Strasson & Fishbein, 1990).

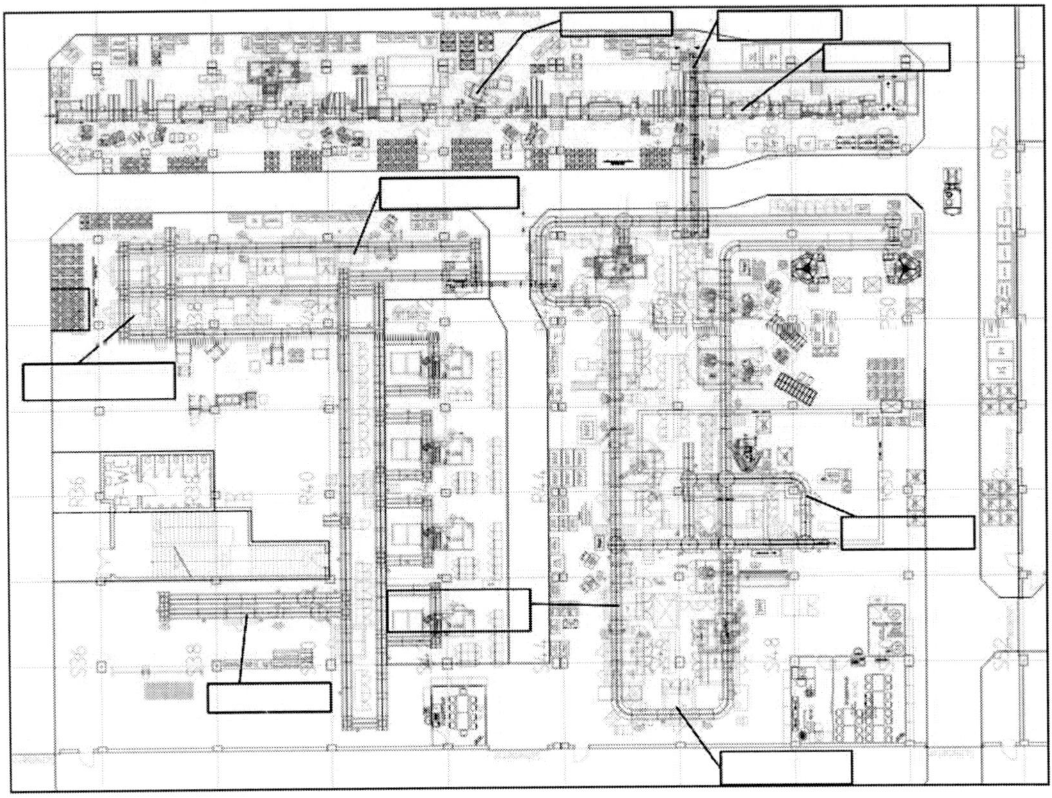

Figure 2. First page of the task specific safety performance test with the layout of the gearbox production process. Participants had to answer four questions to each of the nine workstations.

Therefore, risk awareness is closely related to the concept of situation awareness (Endsley, 1995), well established as a key variable in safety performance (Jones & Endsley, 1996; Stanton, Salmon, Walker, Baber & Jenkins, 2005). The task specific performance test consisted of a layout of the gearbox production process with nine marked workstations (see figure 2).

For each of the nine marked workstations the worker had to answer four open-ended questions, each representing definite indicators of risk awareness: "What type of errors could possibly occur at this stage of the production process?"(*Knowledge about risks*), "What could be the cause for these types of error?" (*Understanding risk causation*), "What are the possible consequences of this error?"(*Anticipation of hazardous events)* and "What kind of suggestions would you make to prevent this error?" (*Development of preventive measures*).

3.6. Design and Procedure

All materials were presented in German. The order of stimuli in the IAT-tasks was randomised. The assignment of participants to sequence of the congruent and incongruent conditions was counterbalanced. The data was collected during the working shifts of the company's three-shift operation. The direct data collection was conducted, in a quiet conference room within the factory, from groups of 15 workers each at the end of every shift. The indirect data from each individual worker was collected in the same quiet conference room within the factory during the shift using an IBM laptop computer.

4. Results

4.1. Data Reduction

Consistent with data reduction procedures described by Greenwald et al. (1998) data from participants that had more than 25 percent errors during their trial phase of the critical tasks, were omitted (n = 7) before initial analyses were conducted (see Penke, Eichstaedt & Asendorf, 2006; Phelps, O´Connor, Cunningham, Funayama, Gatenby, Gore & Banaji, 2000; Rowatt et al., 2005; Svanson, Rudman & Greenwald, 2001). In all, two participants attended the direct but not the indirect data collection phase. In order to calculate the implicit attitude toward the two target concepts (I versus workmates), a scoring algorithm that minimizes the biasing effects of extremely short and long response latencies was used. A measure was calibrated from each respondent's latency variability in order to control artefacts such as individual differences in response speed. The IAT effect measure (D measure) was computed by dividing the mean latency difference, between incongruent and congruent condition, by their overall standard deviation (Greenwald et al., 2003). The resulting value is similar to standardized effect sizes. A high positive value in this study would mean that it is evident that the workers implicitly judged themselves to be more careful (or less careless) than their co-workers. Accordingly, a large IAT effect represents an indicator for a strong implicit association between ones self-concept and safety attributes such as carefulness, reliability or non-complacent behavior.

The department's gearbox engineering specialist rated the qualitative data format of the task specific safety performance tests. Next, the qualitative data was transferred into a quantitative format. This could be achieved by averaging the number of entries for each of the four questions by the number of marked workstations. Hence, the resulting mean for each of the four questions represented a quantitative measure for individual task specific risk awareness.

4.2. Control for Artefacts and Reliability of Implicit Attitude Measure

First of all, the results within the two IAT sequenced conditions (congruent and incongruent task) were compared. There was no order effect within the IAT-tasks ($t_{(59)} = 1.31$; $p = 0.19$). The results also showed no confounding of other variables such as a circadian rhythm, which can sometimes be caused by the three-shift operation ($F(2,58) = 0.18$; $p = 0.84$).

Next, the reliability of the implicit attitude measure was calculated. The reliability, in form of internal consistency, was good (IAT: $\alpha = 0.84$). Internal consistency for the IAT based on correlations between practice trials and test trials of the critical blocks (Greenwald et al., 2003).

4.3. Implicit and Explicit Attitudes and Safety Questionnaire Items

Data for the explicit attitude measure (questionnaire item) revealed a medium value (mean = 2.44; SD = 0.99) of explicitly judging oneself more careful (or careless) that ones co-workers. The IAT latencies (raw latency mean = 912.35 Milliseconds; SD = 419.68 Milliseconds) showed small effect sizes (D = 0.29; SD = 0.34). Values 0.2, 0.5, and 0.8 are considered to represent a small, a medium and a large effect size respectively (Cohen, 1988). The IAT data, thus, indicates a small value, meaning that on an implicit level most workers judge themselves to be only slightly more careful (or less careless) than their co-workers.

After that, the correlation between implicit and explicit attitudes was computed. Neither of them were significantly correlated to each other ($r = 0.12$, $p = 0.35$). This result supports the assumption that both attitude measures assess independent constructs (Greenwald & Banaji, 1995; Lane, Banaji, Nosek & Greenwald, 2007).

Next, three regression analyses were applied to analyse the effect of each attitude on the three safety culture scales measured by the safety questionnaire. Significant relations between attitude measures and questionnaire scales, representing safety culture aspects on an individual, social and organizational level, were observed. The first regression analysis was performed in order to analyse, on an individual level, the unique impact of implicit and explicit attitudes on *risk awareness* as a safety culture factor. The safety culture scale *lack of risk awareness* ($\alpha = 0.65$) represented items in accordance with individual deficiencies in hazard perception, responsibility and rule compliance. The overall regression was – though close to the alpha level of 0.05 – not significant ($R = -0.29$; $F(2, 58) = 2.62$, $p = 0.08$). However, comparing the standardized regression coefficients of both attitudes (implicit attitude: $\beta = -0.29$, $p < 0.01$; explicit attitude: $\beta = -0.04$, $p = 0.77$) revealed that implicit safety-critical attitudes added significantly to the prediction of lack of risk awareness whereas explicit attitudes did not.

Table I. Regression analysis to predict the criterion lack of risk awareness

Variables	R	R^2	F	ß	t (ß)
	-0.29	0.08	2.62*		
Implicit attitude				-0.29	-2.29*
Explicit attitude				-0.04	-0.30

N = 61; * p< 0.05; ** p< 0.01

The purpose of the second regression analysis was to calculate the influence of implicit and explicit attitude on the scale for lack of communication as a social level indicator of safety culture. The scale for *lack of communication* ($\alpha = 0.76$) consisted of items covering social problems such as insufficient sharing of information and dismissing new ideas. As shown in table 2, implicit and explicit attitudes were entered as predictors as had been done for the first regression analysis. Again, overall regression was not significant (R = -0.28; F (2, 58) = 2.44, p = 0.10). However, in contrast to the first regression analysis, implicit attitude did not contribute significantly to the prediction of lack of communication. When again comparing the standardized regression coefficients of both attitudes (implicit attitude: β = -0.04, p = 0.78; explicit attitude: β = -0.28, p < 0.05) the significant larger impact of the explicit attitude on the prediction was revealed.

Table II. Regression analysis for predicting the criterion *lack of communication*

Variables	R	R^2	F	ß	t (ß)
	-0.28	0.08	2.44*		
Implicit attitude				-0.04	-0.28
Explicit attitude				-0.28	-2.21*

N = 61; * p< 0.05; ** p< 0.01

The third regression analysis was used to analyse the effect of both attitudes on the organizational level indicator of safety culture: organizational pressure. The scale for *organizational pressure* ($\alpha = 0.76$) detects deficits on the organizational or managerial level. This scale's items represented issues such as time pressure, safety-costs-trade-offs, and insufficient commitment to safety. As shown in Table 3, implicit and explicit ethical attitudes were entered in the same manner as in the former two regression analyses. Implicit and explicit attitudes contributed significantly to the prediction of organizational pressure (R = -0.44; F (2, 58) = 7.07, p < 0.01). Explicit attitudes, however, revealed a larger effect to the prediction (implicit attitude: β = -0.25, p < 0.05; explicit attitude: β = -0.40, p < 0.01).

Table III. Regression analysis for predicting the criterion *organizational pressure*

Variables	R	R^2	F	ß	t (ß)
	-0.44	0.20	7.07**		
Implicit attitude				-0.25	-2.08*
Explicit attitude				-0.40	-3.36**

N = 61; * p< 0.05; ** p< 0.01

As can be seen in tables 1 to 3, implicit safety critical attitudes revealed significant correlations with items (risk awareness) on an individual level of safety culture. This prediction by the IAT ($\beta = -0.29$; $p < 0.05$) means that workers who implicitly judge themselves to be more careful, reliable and cautious than their colleagues only showed a slight lack in risk awareness. In contrast, explicit safety-critical attitudes did not correlate with this scale. However, explicit safety-critical attitudes were significantly related to social and organizational aspects of safety culture, whereas implicit attitudes showed smaller or no significant correlation. Both scales (for lack of communication and organizational pressure) were significantly related to the explicit safety-critical attitude. Consequently, workers who explicitly evaluated themselves as being less careful than their co-workers reported more failure in communication and organizational pressure within their organization.

4.4. Implicit and Explicit Attitudes and Safety Performance Test Indicators

After revealing the regression analyses of safety-critical attitudes on scales of the safety questionnaire, the prediction of implicit and explicit attitudes on task specific risk awareness measured by the safety performance test was analysed next. The measurement of task specific risk awareness was used as a second and more objective indicator of this individual level safety culture factor. This was important due to the validation of the results of there being a larger effect of implicit attitude on risk awareness as shown in the first regression analysis of the safety questionnaire. Therefore, correlations between the two attitude measures and the safety performance test indicators of risk awareness were calculated. Table 4 presents the results of this analysis.

As in the former regression analyses, there is a significant correlation between implicit attitude and risk awareness. The first indicator of risk awareness, *knowledge of risks,* reflects the task specific knowledge about potential risks which in turn is necessary for adequate cognitive top-down processing in hazard perception (Endsley, 1995; Hoeger, Seidenstucker & Marquardt, 2005; Neisser, 1976). As can be seen in table 4, implicit attitudes correlated significantly to this risk awareness indicator ($r = 0.36$, $p < 0.01$) whereas explicit attitudes did not ($r = 0.16$; $p = 0.23$). The second task specific risk awareness indicator was *understanding of risk causation*. This indicator represents the competence to comprehend risk situations caused by safety rule discrepancies or by mistakes that occur within someone's responsibility, which is important for judging the impact and probability of possible risks. Again, implicit attitudes correlated significantly to this risk awareness indicator ($r = 0.38$, $p < 0.01$), whereas explicit attitudes did not ($r = 0.11$; $p = 0.41$). The third indicator of risk awareness, *anticipation of hazardous events,* reflects the ability to project changes of dynamic processes into the future, which is the cognitive basis for anticipating risky consequences of an action (Endsley, 1995; Jones & Endsley, 1996). Similar to the former two correlations, implicit attitudes correlated significantly to this indicator of risk awareness ($r = 0.33$, $p < 0.05$) whereas explicit attitudes did not ($r = 0.10$; $p = 0.45$). The last indicator of risk awareness was the *development of preventive measures*. This indicator represents the skill to create ideas for proactive countermeasures, which are essential for putting risk awareness into action. Again, implicit attitude correlated significantly with this risk awareness indicator ($r = 0.36$, $p < 0.01$) whereas explicit attitude did not ($r = 0.01$; $p = 0.92$).

Table IV. Correlations between implicit and explicit safety critical attitudes and safety performance test indicators of task specific risk awareness

Indicators of risk awareness	Implicit safety-critical attitude	Explicit safety-critical attitude
Knowledge about risks	0.36**	0.16
Understanding of risk causation	0.38**	0.11
Anticipation of hazardous events	0.33*	0.10
Development of preventive measures	0.36**	-0.01

N = 61; * p< 0.05; ** p< 0.01

Next, a regression analyses was used to analyse the effect of both kinds of attitude on the overall scale value of task specific risk awareness assessed by the safety performance test. The internal consistency of the safety performance test (Cronbach's $\alpha = 0.94$) was based on the mean values of the four indicators. Item-total correlations of the four indicators ranged between 0.78 – 0.95. As can be seen in Table 5, implicit and explicit safety-critical attitude items were entered as predictors of task specific risk awareness. Implicit attitude (IAT) contributed significantly to it's prediction ($R = 0.39$; $F (2, 58) = 5.06$, $p < 0.05$). However, explicit attitude did not prove itself to be a significant addition to the prediction. When again comparing the standardized regression coefficients of both attitudes (implicit attitude: $\beta = 0.37$, $p < 0.01$; explicit attitude: $\beta = 0.06$, $p = 0.61$) the significant larger impact of implicit attitude on the prediction was revealed. Therefore, implicit safety-critical attitude added significantly to the prediction of task specific risk awareness whereas explicit attitude did not.

Table V. Regression analysis for predicting the criterion *task specific risk awareness*

Variables	R	R^2	F	ß	t (ß)
	0.39	0.15	5.06**		
Implicit attitude				0.37	3.05**
Explicit attitude				0.06	0.51

N = 61; * p< 0.05; ** p< 0.01

Apart from the significantly larger effect of implicit attitude on the scale for task specific risk awareness, this scale also significantly correlated with the scale for lack of risk awareness measured by the safety questionnaire ($r = - 0.36$; $p < 0.01$). The other two safety questionnaire scales showed no significant correlation with task specific risk awareness (lack of communication: $r = - 0.20$; $p = 0.11$; organizational pressure: $r = - 0.09$; $p = 0.50$). This is evidence for convergent as well as discriminant validity of these two indicators of risk awareness. Thus, both scales for risk awareness represent similar but also diverse aspects - global and task specific risk awareness – of one safety culture indicator on an individual level.

5. Conclusion

5.1. Discussion of Results

This study outlined the role of implicit and explicit safety-critical attitude within safety culture. In general, the results support the assumption that apart from explicit attitude implicit attitude could also be significantly related to other safety culture aspects. Specifically, implicit attitude significantly predicted individual factors of safety culture measured by the safety questionnaire. The implicit attitude measure (IAT) was significantly related to the safety culture scale for *lack of risk awareness,* which demonstrated individual failures in hazard perception, responsibility and rule compliance. On the contrary, explicit attitude was discovered to have significant correlations with safety culture scales on a social (lack of communication) and organizational (organizational pressure) level. Moreover, implicit attitude significantly correlated with various indicators of risk awareness measured by a task specific safety performance test. All correlations and the regression analysis indicated that the impact of implicit attitude was substantially stronger than the explicit one. Summing up, workers who implicitly judged themselves to be more careful, thoughtful and cautious than their co-workers attained greater values in their task specific risk awareness. On the contrary, workers who responded faster when confronted with the incongruent IAT condition (I + careless / workmates + careful) showed a lack of task specific risk awareness compared to when they were confronted with the congruent condition. Thus, associating oneself more with safety-critical attributes such as careless, unreliable or thoughtless than with the opposite attributes seems to be related to deficiencies in *knowledge of risks, understanding risk causation, anticipation of hazardous results* as well as the ability to *develop preventive measures*. The assessment of explicit safety-critical attitude did not help with the prediction of task specific risk awareness.

5.2. Strengths and Limitations

As in all research, this study has its strengths and limitations. This study was based on previous research on safety culture, which we combined with recent models dealing with implicit social cognition. Unlike other studies in the field of safety culture, this study did not solely rely on self report measures such as questionnaires. The author also applied the Implicit Association Test (IAT), a well-established latency-based method used in experimental cognitive psychology (Fazio & Olson, 2003; Lane et al., 2007; Nosek et al. 2005). The IAT had never been used in the field of safety culture assessment before. As described above, the results indicate that indirect attitude measures such as the IAT can contribute incremental information to the prediction of relevant safety culture indicators. In addition, those measures are more resistant to socially desirable responses than measures of self-report (Greenwald et al., 2000). Actions were also taken in order to improve the ecological validity by using a task specific safety performance test. The use of a safety performance test including a layout with marked workstations taken from the workers work environment combined with task specific questions improves both ecological validity as well as standardizing the respondents stimulus materials and enhancing internal validity.

Despite the strengths, some limitations of the current study, however, are noteworthy. A limitation was the small sample size used in the current study. In order to generalize the findings addressed in the current study more research is needed. Therefore, future studies should extend these results by involving larger samples of workers in hazardous organizations. Nevertheless, the sample size of this study was not smaller than those of similar studies in the field (see Burns et al., 2006).

Also, the explicit safety-critical attitude measure as a single-item scale might imply a somewhat unfair comparison with the more reliable IAT. Thus, a more reliable multi-item scale for measuring explicit safety-critical attitudes (e.g. complacency) must be constructed for further surveys.

Additional methods could be used for measuring implicit attitude so that the risk of having too much of an overlap of the method and the construct can be further minimized (Perugini, 2005). Alternative latency-based methods as e.g. priming tasks can be used to ensure a comprehensive measurement of this construct (see Burns et al., 2006).

Another challenge for future research will be to test further moderating variables (e.g. mental workload, personality factors like conscientiousness, work experience) that could affect the mechanism between implicit safety critical attitude and other safety culture factors such as risk awareness.

5.3. Implications for Safety Culture Assessment

The findings of the current study are tentative but can be linked to various topics of organizational safety culture. Safety culture research aims at fully understanding why individuals behave in a certain way when confronted with safety-critical situations. By answering this question, cognitive science can provide means to develop a more mature safety culture. Specifically, the results of the present study indicate that, on the individual level, implicit attitude could be a better predictor for deficiencies in safety culture aspects whereas explicit attitude seems to contribute more to the prediction on the social and organizational level. There are theoretical and methodological explanations for this result. On one hand there are theoretical views proposing that implicit attitude has shown that it is has a strong impact on other psychological outcomes such as perception and behaviour. This happens especially when situations with no opportunity to reflect extensively – due to high mental workload or time pressure – prevail. Consequently, tasks associated with these conditions are very likely affected by implicit attitude. On the other hand, there are also methodological aspects, which may explain these results. Indirect measures such as the IAT are based on the concept of mental chronometry. Instead of asking directly, indirect measures assess the mental process of attitude activation in milliseconds (Fazio, 2001; Fazio & Olson, 2003; Greenwald et al., 1998). At this level of measuring it is extremely difficult for participants to fake their responses. Consequently, indirect measures such as the IAT are more immune against response bias than direct attitude measures are (Greenwald et al., 2000; Steffens, 2004). In fact, the tendency to fake responses may increase depending on the topic's importance. Specifically, flaws on the individual level of safety culture as e.g. lack of risk awareness, avoidance of individual responsibility or complacency are very critical topics for many workers. Hence, results on direct measures may not appropriately express the workers attitude, beliefs and behaviour. In contrast, faulty safety culture aspects on the social or organizational level could be detected more validly for social and organizational problems would not be attributed to individuals. Therefore, it may be easier for respondents to express their real attitudes and blame others, even the whole organization directly for failings in safety culture. Therefore, indirect measures are a useful addition to common direct safety culture assessment tools such as questionnaires and interviews. While direct measures may be useful for assessing a wide range of safety culture factors on a surface level (Burns et al.,

2006), indirect measures could be adapted to measure deeper levels of critical safety culture aspects, which would otherwise be prone to response bias. Furthermore, the measurement of implicit attitudes could be helpful for evaluating the effectiveness of safety trainings. Implicit measures could be used to assess the degree of internalisation of relevant safety attitudes as induced by a training course. This would be a contribution to a more valid assessment of implicit attitude change within corporate safety culture.

References

Agor, W. H. (1989). *Intuition in Organizations*. Newbury Park CA: Sage Publications.

Aidman, E.V., & Carroll, S.M. (2003). Implicit Individual Differences: Relationships between Implicit Self-Esteem, Gender Identity, and Gender Attitudes. *European Journal of Personality,* **17**, 19-37.

Baker Panel Report (2007). The report of the BP U.S. refineries independent safety review panel, Washington, D.C.

Bower, G. H., & Forgas, J. P. (2000). Affect, Memory, and Social Cognition. In E. Eich, J. F. Kihlstrom, G. H. Bower, J. P. Forgas, P. M. Niedenthal (eds.),*Cognition and Emotion* (pp. 87-157). Oxford: University Press.

Brewer, M. B. (2003). Implicit and Explicit Process in Social Judgment. In J. P. Forgas, K. D. Williams & W. von Hippel (eds.), *Social Judgments: implicit and explicit processes* (pp. 387-395). Cambridge: Cambridge University Press.

Burns, C., Mearns, K., & McGeorge, P. (2006). Explicit and implicit trust within safety culture. *Risk Analysis,* **26**, 1139-1150.

Cheyne, A., Cox, S., Oliver, A., & Tomas, J.M. (1998). Modelling safety climate in the prediction of levels of safety activity. *Work & Stress,* **12**, 255-271.

Cohen, J. (1988). *Statistical power analysis for the behavioural sciences* (2nd ed.). Hillsdale, NJ: Lawrence Erlbaum Associates.

Cox, S. & Cox, T. (1991). The structure of employee attitudes to safety: A European example. *Work & Stress,* **5**, 93-106.

Cox, S., & Flin, R. (1998). Safety culture: Philosopher's stone or man of straw? *Work & Stress,* **12**, 189-201.

Clarke, S. (1998). Safety culture on UK railway network. *Work & Stress,* **12**, 285-292.

Dedobbeleer, N., & Beland, F. (1991). A saftey climate measure for construction sites. *Journal of Safety Research,* **22**, 97-103

Dienes, Z., & Perner, J. (1996). Implicit knowledge in people and connectionist networks. In G. Underwood (ed.), *Implicit Cognition* (pp. 227-253). Oxford: University Press.

Dijksterhuis, A. (2004). Think different: The merits of unconscious thought in preference development and decision making. *Journal of Personality and Social Psychology,* **87**, 586-598.

Dijksterhuis, A., & van Olden, Z. (2006). On the benefits of thinking unconsciously: Unconscious thought can increase post-choice satisfaction. *Journal of Experimental Social Psychology,* **42**, 627-631.

Dorfman, J., Shames, V. A., & Kihlstrom, J. F. (1996). Intuition, incubation, and insight: implicit cognition in problem solving. In G. Underwood (ed.), *Implicit Cognition* (pp. 257-286). Oxford: University Press.

Endsley, M. R. (1995). Toward a Theory of Situation Awarenss in Dynamic Systems. *Human Factors,* **37**(1), 32–64.

Epstein, S. (1991). Cognitive-experiental self-theory: An integrative theory of personality. In R. Curtis (ed.). *The relational self: Theoretical convergences in psychoanalytical, social, and personality psychology* (pp. 111-137). New York: Guilford.

Fazio, R. H. (1990). Multiple processes by which attitudes guide behavior: The MODE model as an integrative framework. In M. P. Zanna (ed.), *Advances in experimental social psychology* (Vol. 23) (pp. 75.109). San Diego: Academic Press.

Fazio, R. H. (2001). On the automatic activation of associated evaluations: An over view. *Cognition and Emotion,* **15** (2), 115-141.

Fazio, R. H. & Olson, M. A. (2003). Implicit Meausures In Social Cognition Research: Their Meaning and Use. *Annual Review of Psychology,* **54**, 297-327.

Fazio, R. H., & Towles-Schwen, T. (1999). The MODE Model of Attitude-Behavior Processes. In S. Chaiken & Y. Trope (eds.), *Dual-process theories in social psychology* (pp. 97-115). New York: Guilford Press.

Fernández-Muniz, B., Montes-Peón, J.M., & Vázquez-Ordás, C.J. (2007). Safety culture: Analysis of the causal relationships between its key dimensions. *Journal of Safety Research,* **38**, 627-641.

Fleming, M., Flin, R., Mearns, K., & Gordon, R. (1998). Risk perceptions of offshore workers on UK oil and gas platforms. *Risk Analysis,* **18**, 103-110.

Forgas, J. P., Williams, K. D., & von Hippel, W. (2003). Responding to the Social World: Explicit and Implicit Processes in Social Judgments. In J. P. Forgas, K. D. Williams & W. von Hippel (eds.), *Social Judgments: implicit and explicit processes* (pp. 1-19). Cambridge: Cambridge University Press.

Gawronski, B., Hofmann, W., & Wilbur, C. J. (2005). Are "implicit" attitudes unconscious? *Consciousness and Cognition,* **15**, 485-499.

Greenwald, A. G., & Banaji, M. R. (1995). Implicit Social Cognition: Attitudes, Self-Esteem, and Stereotypes. *Psychological Review,* **102**, 4-27.

Greenwald, A. G., Banaji, M. R., Rudman, L. A., Farnham, S. D., Nosek, B. A., & Rosier, M. (2000). Prologue to a Unified Theory of Attitudes, Stereotypes, and Self-Concept. In J. P. Forgas, *Feeling and Thinking: The role of affect in social cognition* (pp. 308-330). Cambridge: University Press.

Greenwald, A. G., McGhee, D. E., & Schwartz, J. L. K. (1998). Measuring Individual Differences in Implicit Cognition: The Implicit Association Test. *Journal of Personality and Social Psychology,* **74**, 1464-1480.

Greenwald, A. G., Nosek, B. A., & Banaji, M. R. (2003). Understanding and using the Implicit Association Test: An improved scoring algorithm. *Journal of Personality and Social Psychology,* **85**, 197-216.

Hale, A.R. (2000). Culture's confusions. *Safety Science,* **34**, 1-14.

Harvey, J., Erdos, G. Bolam, H., Cox, M. A. A., Kennedy, J. N. P., & Gregory, D. T. (2002). An analysis of safety culture attitudes in highly regulated environment. *Work & Stress,* **16**, 18-39.

Hoeger, R., Seidenstücker, J., & Marquardt, N. (2005). Mental Models and Attentional Processes in Car Driving. In L. Dorn (ed.), *Driver Behavior and Training II* (pp. 443-449). Aldershot (UK): Ashgate.

International Nuclear Safety Advisory Group – INSAG (1991). *Safety Culture (Saftey Series No. 75-INSAG-4*. Vienna: International Atomic Energy Agency.Jeffcott, S., Pidgeon, N., Weyman, A., & Walls, J. (2006). Risk, Trust, and Saftey Culture in U.K. Train Operating Companies. *Risk Analysis,* **26**, 1105-1121.

Jones, D. G., & Endsley, M. R. (1996). Sources of Situation Awareness Errors in Aviation. *Aviation, Space, and Environmental Medicine,* **67**(6), 507–512.

Kihlstrom, J. F., Mulvaney, S., Tobias, B. A., & Tobis, I. R. (2000). The Emotional Unconscious. In E. Eich, J. F. Kihlstrom, G. H. Bower, J. P. Forgas, P. M.

Niedenthal (eds.), *Cognition and Emotion* (pp. 30-67). Oxford: University Press.

Langhan-Fox, J., & Shirley, D. A. (2003). The nature and measurement of intuition: cognitive and behavioural interests, personality, and experiences. *Creativity Research Journal,* **15**, 207-222.

Lane, K.A., Banaji, M.R., Nosek, B.A., & Greenwald, A.G. (2007). Understanding and using the Implicit Association Test IV: What do we know (so far). In B. Wittenbrink & N.S. Schwatz (Eds.). *Implicit measures of attitudes: Procedures and controversies* (pp. 59-102). New York: Guilford Press.

Lee, T. R. (1994), Employee attitudes – the quintessence of safety culture. Paper presented at the *Third European Seminar on Human Factors in Offshore Safety – Their Importance in Safety Implementation,* Aberdeen, Sept.

Lindgard, H. (2002). The effect of first aid training on Australian construction work's occupational health and safety knowledge and motivation to avoid work-related injuries or illness. *Construction Management and Economics,* **20**, 263-273.

Marquardt, N., & Hoeger, R. (2009). The effect of implicit moral attitudes on managerial decision-making – An Implicit Social Cognition Approach. *Journal of Business Ethics,* **85**, 157-171.

Meagher, B. E. & Aidman, E. V. (2004). Individual differences in implicit and declared self-esteem as predictors of response to negative performance evaluation: Validating Implicit Association Test as a measure of self-attitudes. *International Journal of Testing,* **4**, 19-42.

Neisser, U. (1976). *Cognition and Reality*. San Francisco: Freeman.

Nosek, B. A., Greenwald, A.B., Banaji, M. (2005). Understanding and using the Implicit Association Test II: Method variables and Construct Validity. *Personality and Social Psychology Bulletin,* **31**, 166-180.

Page, J. (1993). Parsons on mathematical intuition. *Mind,* **102**, 247-315.

Penke, L., Eichstaedt, J. & Asendorf, J. B. (2006). Single-attribute Implicit Association Tests (SA-IAT) for the assessment of unipolar constructs. *Experimental Psychology,* **53**, 283-291.

Petersen, D. (1996). *Human Error Reduction and Safety Management*. 3rd ed. Hoboken, N. J.: John Wiley Sons.

Perugini, M. (2005). Predictive models of implicit and explicit attitudes. *British Journal of Social Psychology,* **44**, 29-45.

Phelps, E., O´Connor, K. J., Cunningham, W. A., Funayama, E. S., Gatenby, J. C., Gore, J. C., & Banaji, M. R. (2000). Performance on indirect measures of race evaluation predicts amygdala activation. *Journal of Cognitive Neuroscience,* **12**, 729-738.

Plessner, H., & Banse, R. (2001). Attitude Measurement Using the Implicit Association Test (IAT). *Zeitschrift für Experimentelle Psychologie,* **48**, 82-84.

Reason, J. R. (1990). *Human Error*. New York: Cambridge University Press.

Roberts, P. (1998). Implicit Knowledge and Connectionism: What is the connection? In Kirsner, C. Speelman, M. Maybery, A. O´Brien-Malone, M. Anderson, & C. L.Macleod (eds.), *Implicit and Explicit Mental Processes* (pp. 119-132). New Jersey: Lawrence Erlbaum.

Rowatt, W. C., Franklin, L. M., & Cotton, M. (2005). Patterns and Personality Correlates of implicit and explicit attitudes toward Christians and Muslims. *Journal for the scientific study of religion,* **44**, 29-43.

Rudman, L. (2004). Social justice in our minds, homes, and society: The nature, causes, and consequences of implicit bias. *Social Justice Research,* **17**, 129-142.

Schein, E. (1985). *Organisational Cultur and leadership.* San Francisco: Joessy-Bass.Smith, E. R., & DeCoster, J. (1999). Associative and Rule-Based Processing. – A connectionist interpretation of dual-process models. In S. Chaiken & Y. Trope (eds.), *Dual-process theories in social psychology* (pp. 323-336). New York: Guilford Press.

Stanton, N. A., Salmon, P. M., Walker, G. H., Baber, C., & Jenkins, D. P. (2005). *Human Factors Methods. A practical guide for engineering and design.* Aldershot: Ashgate.

Steffens, M. C. (2004). Is the Implicit Association Test immune to faking? *Experimental Psychology,* **51**, 165-179.

Steffens, M. C., & Schulze König, S. (2006). Predicting spontaneous Big Five behavior with Implicit Association Tests. *European Journal of Psychological Assessment,* **22**;

Strasson, M., & Fishbein, M. (1990). The relation between perceived risk and preventive action: A within-subject analysis of perceived driving risk and intentions to wear seatbelts. *Journal of Applied Social Psychology,* **20**, 1541-1557.

Svanson, J. E., Rudman, L. A., & Greenwald, A. G. (2001). Using the Implicit Association Test to investigate attitute-behavior consistency for stigmatised behavior. *Cognition and Emotion,* **15**, 207-230.

Underwood, G., & Bright, E. H. (1996). Cognition with and without awareness. In G. Underwood (ed.), *Implicit Cognition.* Oxford: University Press.

Williamson, A.M., Feyer, A.M., Cairns, D., & Biancotti, D. (1997). The development of a measure of safety climate: The role of safety perceptions and attitudes. *Safety Science,* **25**, 121-140.

Wilpert, B., & Fahlbruch, B. (2003). Final report on the advanced research and training seminar (ARTS) on workplace safety, system safety and psychology, Singapore, July 13-15, 2002. *International Journal of Psychology,* **38**, 113-118.

Wilson, T. D., Lindsey, S., & Schooler, T. (2000). A model of dual attitudes. *Psychological Review,* **107**, 101-126.

Reviewed by Hans-Rüdiger Pfister
Professor of Work and Engineering Psychology
Department of Business Psychology
Leuphana University of Lueneburg, Germany

In: Risk Management
Editors: B. Jordão and E. Sousa , pp. 345-357
ISBN 978-1-60876-011-4

Chapter 13

HEDGING MISMATCHED CURRENCIES WITH OPTIONS AND FUTURES*

Donald Lien[1,†] ***Maurice K.S. Tse***[2,‡] ***and Kit Pong Wong***[2,§]
[1]Department of Economics, College of Business,
University of Texas at San Antonio, 6900 North Loop 1604 West,
San Antonio, TX 78249-0631, U.S.A
[2]School of Economics and Finance, University of Hong Kong,
Pokfulam Road, Hong Kong

Abstract

This paper develops an expected utility model of an exporting firm in a developing country where currency derivative markets do not exist. The firm faces exchange rate risk exposure to a foreign currency cash flow. To cross-hedge against this risk exposure, the firm uses currency futures and options between the foreign currency and a third currency. Since a triangular parity condition holds among the three given currencies, this available hedging opportunity, albeit incomplete, is proved to be useful in reducing the firm's exchange rate risk exposure. We show that currency options are redundant under two rather restrictive conditions: (i) logarithmic utility functions and/or (ii) independent spot exchange rates. In a more realistic cross-hedging environment, we show that currency options are optimally used by the firm to incompletely span the missing currency futures between the domestic and foreign currencies. We also estimate the benefits of using currency options for cross-hedging purposes. The improvement in hedging effectiveness can be substantial.

JEL classification: F23; F31; D81

Keywords: Options; Futures; Multiple currency risks; Hedging effectiveness

---

*We would like to thank seminar participants at the University of Hong Kong for their helpful comments and suggestions. We also thank Ho Yin Yick for his excellent research assistance.

†E-mail address: dlien@utsa.edu. Tel.: 210-458-7312, fax: 210-458-5837
‡E-mail address: ktse@econ.hku.hk. Tel.: 852-2857-8636, fax: 852-2548-1152.
§E-mail address: kpwong@econ.hku.hk. Tel.: 852-2859-1044, fax: 852-2548-1152.

1. Introduction

Since the collapse of the Bretton Woods Agreement in 1973, exchange rates have become substantially volatile (Meese, 1990), making exchange rate risk management a fact of financial life (Rawls and Smithson, 1990). As documented by Bodnar, Hayt, and Marston (1996, 1998) and Bodnar and Gebhardt (1999), the use of currency forwards, futures, and options is the norm rather than the exception among non-financial corporations.

While currency derivative markets are the hallmark of industrialized countries, they are seldom readily available in less developed countries (LDCs) wherein capital markets are embryonic and foreign exchange markets are heavily controlled. Even if currency forward contracts are available in some LDCs, they are deemed to be forward-cover insurance schemes rather than financial instruments whose prices are freely determined by market forces (Jacque, 1996). Also, in many of the newly industrializing countries of Latin America and Asia Pacific, currency derivative markets are just starting to develop in a rather slow pace (Eiteman, Stonehill, and Moffett, 2001). To indirectly hedge against their exchange rate risk exposure, exporting firms in these countries are obliged to use derivative securities on related currencies. Such an exchange rate risk management technique is referred to as 'cross-hedging.'

The purpose of this paper is to study the hedging decision of an exporting firm in a developing country where currency derivative markets do not exist. We are particularly interested in examining the hedging role of currency options in the context of cross-hedging. To this end, we develop an expected utility model of the exporting firm facing exchange rate uncertainty. There is a third country which has well-developed currency futures and options markets. Since a triangular parity condition holds among the domestic, foreign, and third currencies, this available hedging opportunity, albeit incomplete, remains useful in reducing the firm's exchange rate risk exposure. We show that currency options are redundant under two rather restrictive conditions: (i) logarithmic utility functions and/or (ii) independent spot exchange rates. In a more realistic cross-hedging environment, we show that currency options are optimally used by the firm to incompletely span the missing currency futures between the domestic and foreign currencies. The driving force is the triangular parity condition that gives rise to an exchange rate risk that is multiplicative, thereby non-linear, in nature. This source of non-linearity creates a hedging demand for non-linear currency options, as distinct from that for linear currency futures.

This paper is closest in the spirit of Chang and Wong (2003) who also examine the hedging role of currency options in the context of cross-hedging. The main difference is on how market incompleteness is introduced. In Chang and Wong (2003), no derivative securities exist for the foreign currency but there are currency futures and options between the domestic and third currencies. The degree of incompleteness is less sever in their setting because the hedging instruments are directly related to the domestic currency. The source of non-linearity is shown to be quadratic in nature, which makes the analytical results elegant. In our model, however, the hedging instruments do not involve the domestic currency and the source of non-linearity is of a higher order, thereby complicating the analysis to a great extent.

The rest of the paper is organized as follows. In the next section, we develop an expected utility model of an exporting firm facing multiple currency risks and cross-hedging opportunities. Section 3 derives sufficient conditions under which currency options are never used by the firm. Section 4 shows how the firm can incompletely span the missing currency futures between the domestic and foreign currencies with the available currency options and futures on a third currency. Section 5 offers empirical evidence on the hedging effectiveness of including currency options for cross-hedging purposes. The final section concludes.

2. The Model

Consider a one-period, two-date (0 and 1) model of an exporting firm domiciled in a developing country where currency derivative markets do not exist. At date 0, the firm concludes a transaction in a foreign country, which results in a net foreign currency cash flow, X, to be received at date 1. While the size of X is known with certainty *ex ante*, the firm does not know the then prevailing spot exchange rate at date 1, denoted by $\tilde{S}$, which is expressed in units of the domestic currency per unit of the foreign currency.[1] The firm as such encounters exchange rate risk exposure of $\tilde{S}X$.

To hedge its exchange rate risk exposure, the firm has to rely on a related currency of a third country that has well-developed currency derivative markets. Define $\tilde{S}_1$ as the spot exchange rate of the domestic currency against the third currency at date 1. Likewise, define $\tilde{S}_2$ as the spot exchange rate of the third currency against the foreign currency at date 1. Based on these two spot exchange rates, one can derive the cross-rate of the domestic currency against the foreign currency at date 1 as $\tilde{S}_1\tilde{S}_2$. It follows immediately from the Law of One Price that $\tilde{S} = \tilde{S}_1\tilde{S}_2$. Such a triangular parity condition is depicted in Figure 1.

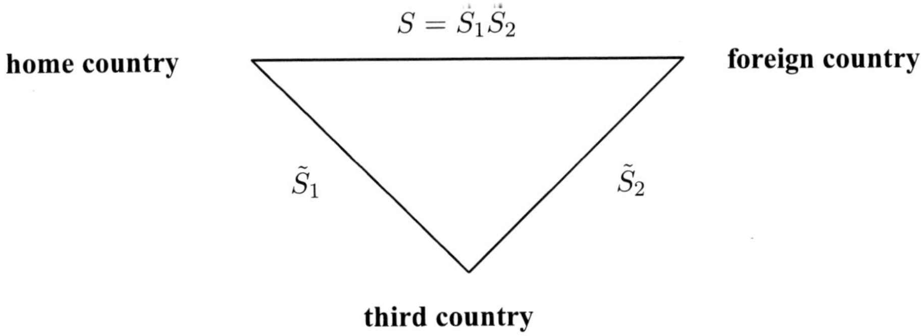

Figure 1. Triangular parity condition.

At date 0, the firm can trade infinitely divisible currency futures and options (calls and puts) that call for delivery of the third currency per unit of the foreign currency at date 1. Without any loss of generality, we restrict the firm to use currency futures and put

[1]Throughout the paper, random variables have a tilde ($\tilde{\ }$) while their realizations do not.

options only.[2] Furthermore, for the pure sake of simplicity, we consider only one strike price, denoted by K, for the currency put options. The strike price, K, is exogenously determined, thereby not a choice variable of the firm.

Let F be the futures price at date 0 and P be the premium on the currency put options, where P is compounded to date 1. To isolate the firm's hedging motive from its speculative motive, it suffices to restrict our attention to the case where the currency futures and put options are perceived as jointly unbiased by the firm. As such, we assume throughout the paper that F equals the expected value of $\tilde{S}_2$ and P equals that of $\max(K - \tilde{S}_2, 0)$.[3]

The firm's date 1 profit denominated in the domestic currency is given by

$$\tilde{\Pi} = \tilde{S}_1\tilde{S}_2 X + \tilde{S}_1(F - \tilde{S}_2)H + \tilde{S}_1[P - \max(K - \tilde{S}_2, 0)]Z, \tag{1}$$

where H and Z are the numbers of the currency futures and put options sold (purchased if negative) by the firm at date 0, respectively. The firm possesses a von Neumann-Morgenstern utility function, $U(\Pi)$, defined over its domestic currency profit, Π, with $U'(\Pi) > 0$ and $U''(\Pi) < 0$, indicating the presence of risk aversion.[4]

The firm is an expected utility maximizer and has to solve the following *ex ante* decision problem at date 0:

$$\max_{H,Z} \mathrm{E}[U(\tilde{\Pi})], \tag{2}$$

where $\mathrm{E}(\cdot)$ is the expectation operator with respect to the firm's subjective joint probability distribution function of $\tilde{S}_1$ and $\tilde{S}_2$, and $\tilde{\Pi}$ is defined in equation (1). The first-order conditions for program (2) are given by

$$\mathrm{E}[U'(\tilde{\Pi}^*)\tilde{S}_1(F - \tilde{S}_2)] = 0, \tag{3}$$

$$\mathrm{E}\{U'(\tilde{\Pi}^*)\tilde{S}_1[P - \max(K - \tilde{S}_2, 0)]\} = 0, \tag{4}$$

where an asterisk (*) indicates an optimal level. The second-order conditions for a maximum are satisfied given risk aversion.

3. Redundancy of Options

Since $F = \mathrm{E}(\tilde{S}_2)$ and $P = \mathrm{E}[\max(K - \tilde{S}_2, 0)]$, we can write equations (3) and (4) as[5]

$$\mathrm{Cov}[U'(\tilde{\Pi}^*)\tilde{S}_1, \tilde{S}_2] = 0, \tag{5}$$

$$\mathrm{Cov}[U'(\tilde{\Pi}^*)\tilde{S}_1, \max(K - \tilde{S}_2, 0)] = 0, \tag{6}$$

---

[2]Because payoffs of any combinations of futures, calls, and puts can be replicated by any two of these three financial instruments, one of them is redundant.

[3]Our intention here is not to impose an ad hoc option pricing theory but to focus on the hedging role of the put currency options.

[4]For privately held, owner-managed firms, risk-averse behavior prevails. Even for publicly listed firms, managerial risk aversion (Stulz, 1984), corporate taxes (Smith and Stulz, 1985), costs of financial distress (Smith and Stulz, 1985), and capital market imperfections (Stulz, 1990; and Froot, Scharfstein, and Stein, 1993) all imply a concave objective function for firms, thereby justifying the use of risk aversion as an approximation. See Tufano (1996) for evidence that managerial risk aversion is a rationale for corporate risk management in the gold mining industry.

[5]For any two random variables, $\tilde{X}$ and $\tilde{Y}$, $\mathrm{Cov}(\tilde{X}, \tilde{Y}) = \mathrm{E}(\tilde{X}\tilde{Y}) - \mathrm{E}(\tilde{X})\mathrm{E}(\tilde{Y})$.

where Cov(·, ·) is the covariance operator with respect to the firm's subjective joint probability distribution function of $\tilde{S}_1$ and $\tilde{S}_2$. Partially differentiating $\mathrm{E}[U'(\tilde{\Pi}^*)\tilde{S}_1|S_2]$ yields

$$\frac{\partial}{\partial S_2}\mathrm{E}[U'(\tilde{\Pi}^*)\tilde{S}_1|S_2] = \mathrm{E}\bigg\{U'(\tilde{\Pi}^*)[1 - R(\tilde{\Pi}^*)]\frac{\partial \tilde{S}_1}{\partial S_2}$$

$$+ U''(\tilde{\Pi}^*)\tilde{S}_1^2\Big[X - H^* - \frac{\partial}{\partial S_2}\max(K - S_2, 0)Z^*\Big]\Big|S_2\bigg\}, \quad (7)$$

where $R(\Pi) = -\Pi U''(\Pi)/U'(\Pi)$ is the Arrow-Pratt measure of relative risk aversion. If $\partial\tilde{S}_1/\partial S_2 \equiv 0$ (i.e., $\tilde{S}_1$ and $\tilde{S}_2$ are independent), or if $R(\Pi) \equiv 1$ for all Π (i.e., $U(\Pi)$ is logarithmic), it is evident from equation (7) that $\mathrm{E}[U'(\tilde{\Pi}^*)\tilde{S}_1|S_2]$ would be invariant to different realizations of $\tilde{S}_2$ when $H^* = X$ and $Z^* = 0$ and thus equations (5) and (6) hold simultaneously.

To see the underlying intuition, consider first the case that the firm's utility function, $U(\Pi)$, is logarithmic. In this case, the objective function of program (2) becomes

$$\mathrm{E}(\ln\tilde{\Pi}) = \mathrm{E}(\ln\tilde{S}_1) + \mathrm{E}\Big\{\ln\{\tilde{S}_2X + (F - \tilde{S}_2)H + [P - \max(K - \tilde{S}_2,\ 0)]Z\}\Big\}.$$

It is evident that $\tilde{S}_1$ does not affect the firm's optimal hedge position and thus the celebrated full-hedging theorem applies (Danthine, 1978; Holthausen, 1979; and Feder, Just, and Schmitz, 1980). Now, consider the case where the two random spot exchange rates, $\tilde{S}_1$ and $\tilde{S}_2$, are independent. When $H = X$ and $Z = 0$, equation (1) implies that $\tilde{\Pi} = \tilde{S}_1FX$. Thus, it follows that equations (5) and (6) hold simultaneously at $H^* = X$ and $Z^* = 0$. In either case, the currency put options are not used by the firm for cross-hedging purposes.

4. Hedging Role of Options

In the previous section, we have shown that currency options are redundant under logarithmic utility functions and/or independent spot exchange rates. However, it is unduly restrictive to assume either condition to hold. In other words, in a more realistic cross-hedging environment, we would expect currency options to be an integral part of the optimal hedge positions of exporting firms in developing countries.

To verify the above conjecture, let us consider the following simple example. Suppose that $\tilde{S}_1 = \overline{S}_1 + \beta\tilde{\theta}$ and $\tilde{S}_2 = \overline{S}_2 + \tilde{\theta}$, where $\overline{S}_i$ is the expected value of $\tilde{S}_i$ ($i = 1, 2$), β is a scalar, and $\tilde{\theta}$ is a zero-mean random variable. Thus, $\tilde{S}_1$ and $\tilde{S}_2$ are perfectly negatively (positively) correlated if $\beta < (>)\ 0$. Let $\tilde{\theta}$ take on three possible values: $-\Theta$ with probability p, 0 with probability $1 - 2p$, and Θ with probability p. Then, we have

$$\tilde{S} = \tilde{S}_1\tilde{S}_2 = (\overline{S}_1 + \beta\tilde{\theta})(\overline{S}_2 + \tilde{\theta}) = \overline{S}_1\overline{S}_2 + (\overline{S}_1 + \beta\overline{S}_2)\tilde{\theta} + \beta\tilde{\theta}^2. \quad (8)$$

Given the assumed three-point probability distribution function of $\tilde{\theta}$, we have $\tilde{\theta}^2 = \Theta[\tilde{\theta} + 2\max(-\tilde{\theta}, 0)]$. Thus, using this fact and equation (8), the exchange rate risk exposure faced by the firm is given by

$$\tilde{S}X = \overline{S}_1\overline{S}_2X + (\overline{S}_1 + \beta\overline{S}_2 + \beta\Theta)\tilde{\theta}X + 2\beta\Theta\max(-\tilde{\theta}, 0)X. \quad (9)$$

Let $K = F$. Since F equals the expected value of $\tilde{S}_2$, we have $F = K = \overline{S}_2$. Then, the payoff of a hedge position, (H, Z), is given by

$$\tilde{V} = (\overline{S}_1 + \beta\tilde{\theta})\{\tilde{\theta}H + [\max(-\tilde{\theta}, 0) - P]Z\}. \tag{10}$$

Given the assumed three-point probability distribution function of $\tilde{\theta}$, we have $\tilde{\theta}^2 = \Theta[\tilde{\theta} + 2\max(-\tilde{\theta}, 0)]$ and $\tilde{\theta}\max(-\tilde{\theta}, 0) = -\Theta\max(-\tilde{\theta}, 0)$. Thus, equation (10) can be written as

$$\tilde{V} = [(\overline{S}_1 + \beta\Theta)H - \beta PZ]\tilde{\theta} + [2\beta\Theta H + (\overline{S}_1 - \beta\Theta)Z]\max(-\tilde{\theta}, 0) - \overline{S}_1 PZ. \tag{11}$$

Inspection of equations (9) and (11) reveals that the firm's exchange rate risk exposure can be completely eliminated by the hedge position, (H^*, Z^*), which satisfies

$$[\overline{S}_1 + \beta\overline{S}_2 + \beta\Theta]X = (\overline{S}_1 + \beta\Theta)H^* - \beta PZ^*, \tag{12}$$

$$2\beta\Theta X = 2\beta\Theta H^* + (\overline{S}_1 - \beta\Theta)Z^*. \tag{13}$$

Solving equations (12) and (13) yields

$$H^* = X - \frac{\overline{S}_1 - \beta\Theta}{2\beta\Theta}Z^*,$$

$$Z^* = -\frac{2\beta^2\overline{S}_2\Theta X}{(\overline{S}_1 - \beta\Theta)(\overline{S}_1 + \beta\Theta) + 2\beta^2 P\Theta}.$$

As long as $\beta \neq 0$, we have $Z^* < 0$. Thus, in order to synthesize a short position of the missing currency futures between the domestic and foreign currencies, a long position of the currency put options between the foreign and third currencies is called for irrespective of whether $\tilde{S}_1$ and $\tilde{S}_2$ are negatively or positively correlated.

In general, complete spanning of the missing currency futures contracts between the domestic and foreign currencies is not feasible. To facilitate the empirical study of hedging effectiveness in the next section, we hereafter restrict our attention to the case where the firm's objective is to minimize the variance of its date 1 domestic currency profit:

$$\min_{H,Z} \mathrm{Var}(\tilde{\Pi}) = \mathrm{E}\{[\tilde{\Pi} - \mathrm{E}(\tilde{\Pi})]^2\}, \tag{14}$$

where $\mathrm{Var}(\cdot)$ is the variance operator with respect to the firm's subjective joint probability distribution function of $\tilde{S}_1$ and $\tilde{S}_2$, and $\tilde{\Pi}$ is defined in equation (1).

The first-order conditions for program (14) are given by

$$\mathrm{Cov}[\tilde{\Pi}^*, \tilde{S}_1(F - \tilde{S}_2)] = 0, \tag{15}$$

$$\mathrm{Cov}\{\tilde{\Pi}^*, \tilde{S}_1[P - \max(K - \tilde{S}_2, 0)]\} = 0. \tag{16}$$

where an asterisk (*) indicates an optimal level.[6] Solving equations (15) and (16) yields

$$\begin{pmatrix} H^* \\ Z^* \end{pmatrix} = -\mathbf{A}^{-1}\mathbf{B}X, \tag{17}$$

[6]The second-order conditions for a minimum are satisfied.

where

$$\mathbf{A} = \begin{pmatrix} \mathrm{Var}[\tilde{S}_1(F - \tilde{S}_2)] & \mathrm{Cov}\{\tilde{S}_1(F - \tilde{S}_2), \tilde{S}_1[P - \max(K - \tilde{S}_2, 0)]\} \\ \mathrm{Cov}\{\tilde{S}_1(F - \tilde{S}_2), \tilde{S}_1[P - \max(K - \tilde{S}_2, 0)]\} & \mathrm{Var}\{\tilde{S}_1[P - \max(K - \tilde{S}_2, 0)]\} \end{pmatrix},$$

$$\mathbf{B} = \begin{pmatrix} \mathrm{Cov}[\tilde{S}_1\tilde{S}_2, \tilde{S}_1(F - \tilde{S}_2)] \\ \mathrm{Cov}\{\tilde{S}_1\tilde{S}_2, \tilde{S}_1[P - \max(K - \tilde{S}_2, 0)]\} \end{pmatrix}.$$

Inspection of equation (17) reveals that Z^* is in general non-zero. However, without specifying the underlying joint probability distribution function of $\tilde{S}_1$ and $\tilde{S}_2$, the sign of Z^* is a priori indeterminate.

When the currency put options are absent (i.e., $Z \equiv 0$), it is easily shown that the firm's optimal futures position, H^0, is given by

$$H^0 = -\frac{\mathrm{Cov}[\tilde{S}_1\tilde{S}_2, \tilde{S}_1(F - \tilde{S}_2)]}{\mathrm{Var}[\tilde{S}_1(F - \tilde{S}_2)]}. \tag{18}$$

The sign of H^0 is opposite to that of $\mathrm{Cov}[\tilde{S}_1\tilde{S}_2, \tilde{S}_1(F - \tilde{S}_2)]$, which is also a priori indeterminate without knowing the functional form of the joint probability distribution function of $\tilde{S}_1$ and $\tilde{S}_2$.

5. Hedging Effectiveness

To empirically evaluate the potential usefulness of cross-hedging with currency options and futures, we assume that $\tilde{S}_1$ and $\tilde{S}_2$ are jointly log-normally distributed:

$$\begin{pmatrix} \ln \tilde{S}_1 \\ \ln \tilde{S}_2 \end{pmatrix} \sim N\left[\begin{pmatrix} \mu_1 \\ \mu_2 \end{pmatrix}, \begin{pmatrix} \sigma_1^2 & \rho\sigma_1\sigma_2 \\ \rho\sigma_1\sigma_2 & \sigma_2^2 \end{pmatrix}\right].$$

Alternatively, we can write $\tilde{S}_1 = \exp(\mu_1 + \sigma_1\tilde{\varepsilon}_1)$ and $\tilde{S}_2 = \exp(\mu_2 + \sigma_2\tilde{\varepsilon}_2)$, where $\tilde{\varepsilon}_1$ and $\tilde{\varepsilon}_2$ are both standard normal random variables with $\mathrm{Cov}(\tilde{\varepsilon}_1, \tilde{\varepsilon}_2) = \rho$. In Appendix A, we prove the following useful result:

$$\mathrm{E}\left(\tilde{S}_1^m\tilde{S}_2^n I_{\{\tilde{S}_2 < K\}}\right) = \exp\left(m\mu_1 + n\mu_2 + \frac{m^2\sigma_1^2}{2} + mn\rho\sigma_1\sigma_2 + \frac{n^2\sigma_2^2}{2}\right) \times \Phi\left(\frac{\ln K - \mu_2}{\sigma_2} - m\rho\sigma_1 - n\sigma_2\right), \tag{19}$$

where $I_{\{\tilde{S}_2 < K\}}$ is the indicator function for the event that $\tilde{S}_2 < K$, and $\Phi(\cdot)$ is the cumulative standard normal distribution function.

Equation (19) can be used repeatedly to express all the moments in equation (17) as functions of the underlying distribution parameters. For example, by setting $m = 0$, $n = 1$, and $K = \infty$ in equation (19), we have

$$F = \mathrm{E}(\tilde{S}_2) = \exp\left(\mu_2 + \frac{\sigma_2^2}{2}\right). \tag{20}$$

Note that

$$P = \mathrm{E}[\max(K - \tilde{S}_2, 0)] = \mathrm{E}\Big[(K - \tilde{S}_2) I_{\{\tilde{S}_2 < K\}}\Big] = K\mathrm{E}\Big(I_{\{\tilde{S}_2 < K\}}\Big) - \mathrm{E}\Big(\tilde{S}_2 I_{\{\tilde{S}_2 < K\}}\Big).$$

The first term on the right-hand side of the above equation corresponds to equation (19) when $m = n = 0$ and the second term to $m = 0$ and $n = 1$. Thus, we have

$$P = K\Phi\Big(\frac{\ln K - \mu_2}{\sigma_2}\Big) - \mathrm{E}(\tilde{S}_2)\Phi\Big(\frac{\ln K - \mu_2}{\sigma_2} - \sigma_2\Big).$$

When $K = \mathrm{E}(\tilde{S}_2)$, the above equation can be further reduced to

$$P = \exp\Big(\mu_2 + \frac{\sigma_2^2}{2}\Big)\Big[1 - 2\Phi\Big(-\frac{\sigma_2}{2}\Big)\Big]. \tag{21}$$

In Appendix B, we report all the variances and covariances contained in equation (17) in terms of the underlying distribution parameters. It is interesting to observe that μ_1 and μ_2, albeit essential for all the relevant moments, do not appear in the ultimate optimal hedge ratios. As such, no information on the means of $\ln \tilde{S}_1$ and $\ln \tilde{S}_2$ is needed for finding the optimal hedge ratios.

The empirical exercise is as follows. We refer to Indonesia as the home country, Taiwan as the foreign country, and the United States as the third country. Thus, $\tilde{S}_1$ is the random spot exchange rate for the Indonesian rupee against the US dollar and $\tilde{S}_2$ is that for the US dollar against the Taiwanese dollar. The foreign currency cash flow, X, is normalized to one unit of the foreign currency so that the firm's hedge position is simply the hedge ratio. The prices of the currency futures and put options with $K = F$ are artificially set equal to equations (20) and (21), respectively. Daily data on spot exchange rates are extracted from *Datastream* for the period from January 1, 1997 to December 31, 2001.

In each year, we substitute the sample variances of $\ln \tilde{S}_1$ and $\ln \tilde{S}_2$ and the sample covariance $\ln \tilde{S}_1$ and $\ln \tilde{S}_1$ into equations (17) and (18), using the results in Appendix B, to compute the firm's optimal cross-hedge ratios, (H^*, Z^*) and H^0, respectively. These results are reported in Table 1.

To compare the performances of using currency options and futures for cross-hedging purposes, we need to estimate the variances of the firm's date 1 domestic currency profit:

$$\mathrm{Var}\{\tilde{S}_1\tilde{S}_2 X + \tilde{S}_1(F - \tilde{S}_2)H + \tilde{S}_1[P - \max(K - \tilde{S}_2, 0)]Z\},$$

for three cases: (i) no hedging (i.e., $H = Z = 0$), (ii) hedging with futures only (i.e., $H = H^0$ and $Z = 0$), and (iii) hedging with options and futures(i.e., $H = H^*$ and $Z = Z^*$). To this end, we compute, each year, three sample variances of the firm's date 1 domestic currency profit using the actual realized spot exchange rates during the year. The first sample variance is based on $H = Z = 0$. The second sample variance is based on $H = H^0$ and $Z = 0$, where H^0 is taken from Table 1. The third sample variance is based on $H = H^*$ and $Z = Z^*$, where $(H^*,\ Z^*)$ is taken from Table 1. These results are reported in Table 2.

As shown in Table 2, using currency options and futures for cross-hedging purposes on average results in variance reductions of about 39% as compared to the no hedging strategy, and about 2% as compared to using currency futures as the sole hedging instrument.

Table 1. Data Description

	1997	1998	1999	2000	2001
Observations	261	261	261	260	261
US Dollar/Taiwanese Dollar					
Mean ($\times 10^{-2}$)	3.49	2.99	3.10	3.21	2.96
Standard Deviation ($\times 10^{-3}$)	1.84	0.81	0.49	0.78	0.84
US Dollar/Indonesian Rupee					
Mean ($\times 10^{-4}$)	3.64	1.04	1.29	1.20	0.98
Standard Deviation ($\times 10^{-5}$)	6.95	2.38	1.28	1.10	0.79
Optimal Cross-Hedge Ratios					
H^0	-2.558	-5.437	-2.583	-1.591	1.020
H^*	-3.342	-6.907	-2.760	-1.714	1.019
Z^*	-1.243	-2.352	-0.329	-0.229	-0.001

This table presents descriptive statistics on the two spot exchange rate series from January 1, 1997 to December 31, 2001. Optimal cross-hedge ratios are computed from equations (17) and (18) in the text.

Table 2. Comparisons of Hedging Effectiveness

	1997	1998	1999	2000	2001
Portfolio Variances					
No Hedging	407	4306	480	398	657
Hedging with Futures only	90.1	1874	381	300	590
Hedging with Futures and Options	81.4	1881	383	295	590
Variance Reductions of Hedging with Options and Futures Compared to:					
No Hedging	80.0%	56.3%	20.2%	25.9%	10.2%
Hedging with Futures only	9.65%	-0.36%	-0.39%	1.43%	0%

This table shows the portfolio variances for three cases: (i) no hedging (i.e., $H = Z = 0$), (ii) hedging with futures only (i.e., $H = H^0$ and $Z = 0$), and (iii) hedging with futures and options (i.e., $H = H^*$ and $Z = Z^*$). The percentage variance reductions of hedging with options and futures over no hedging and hedging with futures only are also given.

Although including currency options in hedge positions may sometimes lower the hedging effectiveness as compared to using currency futures alone, the increase in portfolio variance is almost negligible (less than 0.4%). The potential improvement in hedging effectiveness, however, can be quite substantial (more than 9%). Hence, exporting firms in developing countries should find currency options useful for cross-hedging purposes.

6. Conclusion

In the post-Bretton Woods era, exchange rates have been increasingly volatile, making non-financial firms take exchange rate risk management very seriously. This paper has studied how a risk-averse exporting firm, confronting a foreign currency cash flow but possessing no direct hedging opportunities, can employ derivative securities on a related currency to reduce its exchange rate risk exposure. Currency options play no role as a hedging instrument under two rather restrictive conditions of logarithmic utility functions and/or independent spot exchange rates. In a more realistic cross-hedging environment, we have shown how the firm can use currency options to incompletely replicate the missing risk-sharing contract. The driving force is a triangular parity condition which gives rise to an exchange rate risk that is multiplicative, thereby non-linear, in nature. This source of non-linearity creates a hedging demand for non-linear currency options, as distinct from that for linear currency futures.

Appendix

A. Derivation of Equation (19)

Using the fact that $\tilde{S}_i = \exp(\mu_i + \sigma_i\tilde{\varepsilon}_i)$, $i = 1$ and 2, we have

$$\begin{aligned}
\mathrm{E}\left(\tilde{S}_1^m\tilde{S}_2^n I_{\{\tilde{S}_2<K\}}\right) &= \frac{1}{2\pi\sqrt{1-\rho^2}}\int_{-\infty}^{\infty}\int_{-\infty}^{\frac{\ln K-\mu_2}{\sigma_2}} \exp[m(\mu_1+\sigma_1\varepsilon_1)]\exp[n(\mu_2+\sigma_2\varepsilon_2)] \\
&\quad\times\exp\left[-\frac{\varepsilon_1^2+\varepsilon_2^2-2\rho\varepsilon_1\varepsilon_2}{2(1-\rho^2)}\right]\mathrm{d}\varepsilon_1\,\mathrm{d}\varepsilon_2 \\
&= \frac{1}{2\pi\sqrt{1-\rho^2}}\int_{-\infty}^{\infty}\exp\left[m(\mu_1+\sigma_1\varepsilon_1)-\frac{\varepsilon_1^2}{2(1-\rho^2)}\right] \\
&\quad\times\left\{\int_{-\infty}^{\frac{\ln K-\mu_2}{\sigma_2}}\exp[n(\mu_2+\sigma_2\varepsilon_2)]\exp\left[-\frac{\varepsilon_2^2-2\rho\varepsilon_1\varepsilon_2}{2(1-\rho^2)}\right]\mathrm{d}\varepsilon_2\right\}\mathrm{d}\varepsilon_1 \\
&= \frac{\exp(m\mu_1+n\mu_2)}{2\pi\sqrt{1-\rho^2}}\int_{-\infty}^{\infty}\exp\left\{m\sigma_1\varepsilon_1+\frac{[\rho\varepsilon_1+(1-\rho^2)n\sigma_2]^2-\varepsilon_1^2}{2(1-\rho^2)}\right\} \\
&\quad\times\left\{\int_{-\infty}^{\frac{\ln K-\mu_2}{\sigma_2}}\exp\left\{-\frac{[\varepsilon_2-\rho\varepsilon_1-(1-\rho^2)n\sigma_2]^2}{2(1-\rho^2)}\right\}\mathrm{d}\varepsilon_2\right\}\mathrm{d}\varepsilon_1 \\
&= \frac{1}{\sqrt{2\pi}}\exp\left(m\mu_1+n\mu_2+\frac{m^2\sigma_1^2}{2}+mn\rho\sigma_1\sigma_2+\frac{n^2\sigma_2^2}{2}\right) \\
&\quad\times\int_{-\infty}^{\infty}\exp\left[-\frac{(\varepsilon_1-m\sigma_1-n\rho\sigma_2)^2}{2}\right]\Phi\left[\frac{\frac{\ln K-\mu_2}{\sigma_2}-\rho\varepsilon_1-(1-\rho^2)n\sigma_2}{\sqrt{1-\rho^2}}\right]\mathrm{d}\varepsilon_1
\end{aligned}$$

$$= \frac{1}{\sqrt{2\pi}} \exp\left(m\mu_1 + n\mu_2 + \frac{m^2\sigma_1^2}{2} + mn\rho\sigma_1\sigma_2 + \frac{n^2\sigma_2^2}{2}\right)$$

$$\times \int_{-\infty}^{\infty} \exp\left(-\frac{z^2}{2}\right) \Phi\left(\frac{\frac{\ln K - \mu_2}{\sigma_2} - \rho z - m\rho\sigma_1 - n\sigma_2}{\sqrt{1-\rho^2}}\right) \mathrm{d}z$$

$$= \frac{1}{\sqrt{2\pi}} \exp\left(m\mu_1 + n\mu_2 + \frac{m^2\sigma_1^2}{2} + mn\rho\sigma_1\sigma_2 + \frac{n^2\sigma_2^2}{2}\right)$$

$$\times \mathrm{E}_z\left[\Phi\left(\frac{\frac{\ln K - \mu_2}{\sigma_2} - \rho z - m\rho\sigma_1 - n\sigma_2}{\sqrt{1-\rho^2}}\right)\right], \tag{A.1}$$

where $z = \varepsilon_1 - m\sigma_1 - n\rho\sigma_2$ is a standard normal random variable and $\mathrm{E}_z(\cdot)$ is the expectation operator with respect to $\Phi(z)$. Lemma 1 in Lien (1986) states that

$$\mathrm{E}_z[\Phi(\alpha + \beta z)] = \Phi\left(\frac{\alpha}{\sqrt{1+\beta^2}}\right). \tag{A.2}$$

Using equation (A.2) by setting $\alpha = \frac{\ln K - \mu_2}{\sigma_2} - m\rho\sigma_1 - n\sigma_2$ and $\beta = \frac{\rho}{\sqrt{1-\rho^2}}$, equation (A.1) reduces to equation (19).

B. Derivation of Variances and Covariances

Note that $\mathrm{Var}[\tilde{S}_1(F - \tilde{S}_2)] = \mathrm{E}[\tilde{S}_1^2(F - \tilde{S}_2)^2] - \mathrm{E}[\tilde{S}_1(F - \tilde{S}_2)]^2$, which can be written as

$$\mathrm{E}(\tilde{S}_1^2)F^2 - 2\mathrm{E}(\tilde{S}_1^2\tilde{S}_2)F + \mathrm{E}(\tilde{S}_1^2\tilde{S}_2^2) - \mathrm{E}(\tilde{S}_1)^2F^2 + 2\mathrm{E}(\tilde{S}_1)\mathrm{E}(\tilde{S}_1\tilde{S}_2)F - \mathrm{E}(\tilde{S}_1\tilde{S}_2)^2.$$

Using equation (19) repeatedly, we have

$$\mathrm{Var}[\tilde{S}_1(F - \tilde{S}_2)] = M \times [\exp(\sigma_1^2) - 2\exp(\sigma_1^2 + 2\rho\sigma_1\sigma_2) + \exp(\sigma_1^2 + 4\rho\sigma_1\sigma_2 + \sigma_2^2)$$
$$-1 + 2\exp(\rho\sigma_1\sigma_2) - \exp(2\rho\sigma_1\sigma_2)],$$

where $M = \exp(2\mu_1 + 2\mu_2 + \sigma_1^2 + \sigma_2^2)$. Similarly, we can show that

$$\mathrm{Cov}[\tilde{S}_1\tilde{S}_2, \tilde{S}_1(F - \tilde{S}_2)] = M \times [\exp(\sigma_1^2 + 2\rho\sigma_1\sigma_2) - \exp(\sigma_1^2 + 4\rho\sigma_1\sigma_2 + \sigma_2^2)$$
$$- \exp(\rho\sigma_1\sigma_2) + \exp(2\rho\sigma_1\sigma_2)],$$

$$\mathrm{Var}\{\tilde{S}_1[P - \max(K - \tilde{S}_2, 0)]\} = M \times \left\{\exp(\sigma_1^2)\left[2\Phi\left(\frac{\sigma_2}{2}\right) - 1\right]\left[2\Phi\left(\frac{\sigma_2}{2}\right) - 1 - 2\Phi\left(\frac{\sigma_2}{2} - 2\rho\sigma_1\right)\right]\right.$$
$$+4\exp(\sigma_1^2 + 2\rho\sigma_1\sigma_2)\left[\Phi\left(\frac{\sigma_2}{2}\right) - 1\right]\Phi\left(-\frac{\sigma_2}{2} - 2\rho\sigma_1\right)$$
$$+\exp(\sigma_1^2)\Phi\left(\frac{\sigma_2}{2} - 2\rho\sigma_1\right) + \exp(\sigma_1^2 + 4\rho\sigma_1\sigma_2 + \sigma_2^2)\Phi\left(-\frac{3\sigma_2}{2} - 2\rho\sigma_1\right)$$
$$\left.-\left[2\Phi\left(\frac{\sigma_2}{2}\right) - 1 - \Phi\left(\frac{\sigma_2}{2} - \rho\sigma_1\right) + \exp(\rho\sigma_1\sigma_2)\Phi\left(-\frac{\sigma_2}{2} - \rho\sigma_1\right)\right]^2\right\},$$

$$\mathrm{Cov}\{\tilde{S}_1(F - \tilde{S}_2), \tilde{S}_1[P - \max(K - \tilde{S}_2, 0)]\} = M \times \left\{[\exp(\sigma_1^2) - \exp(\sigma_1^2 + 2\rho\sigma_1\sigma_2)]\left[2\Phi\left(\frac{\sigma_2}{2}\right) - 1\right]\right.$$

$$- \exp(\sigma_1^2)\Phi\Big(\frac{\sigma_2}{2} - 2\rho\sigma_1\Big) + 2\exp(\sigma_1^2 + 2\rho\sigma_1\sigma_2)\Phi\Big(-\frac{\sigma_2}{2} - 2\rho\sigma_1\Big)$$

$$- \exp(\sigma_1^2 + 4\rho\sigma_1\sigma_2 + \sigma_2^2)\Phi\Big(-\frac{3\sigma_2}{2} - 2\rho\sigma_1\Big) - [1 - \exp(\rho\sigma_1\sigma_2)]$$

$$\times\Big[1 - 2\Phi\Big(-\frac{\sigma_2}{2}\Big) - \Phi\Big(\frac{\sigma_2}{2} - \rho\sigma_1\Big) + \exp(\rho\sigma_1\sigma_2)\Phi\Big(-\frac{\sigma_2}{2} - \rho\sigma_1\Big)\Big]\Big\},$$

$$\mathrm{Cov}\{\tilde{S}_1\tilde{S}_2, \tilde{S}_1[P - \max(K - \tilde{S}_2, 0)]\} = M \times \Big\{[\exp(\sigma_1^2 + 2\rho\sigma_1\sigma_2) - \exp(\rho\sigma_1\sigma_2)]\Big[2\Phi\Big(\frac{\sigma_2}{2}\Big) - 1\Big]$$

$$- \exp(\sigma_1^2 + 2\rho\sigma_1\sigma_2)\Phi\Big(-\frac{\sigma_2}{2} - 2\rho\sigma_1\Big) - \exp(2\rho\sigma_1\sigma_2)\Phi\Big(-\frac{\sigma_2}{2} - \rho\sigma_1\Big)\Big\}$$

$$+ \exp(\sigma_1^2 + 4\rho\sigma_1\sigma_2 + \sigma_2^2)\Phi\Big(-\frac{3\sigma_2}{2} - 2\rho\sigma_1\Big) + \exp(\rho\sigma_1\sigma_2)\Phi\Big(\frac{\sigma_2}{2} - \rho\sigma_1\Big),$$

$$\mathrm{Var}(\tilde{S}_1 S_2) = M \times [\exp(\sigma_1^2 + 4\rho\sigma_1\sigma_2 + \sigma_2^2) - \exp(2\rho\sigma_1\sigma_2)].$$

References

Bodnar, G. M., and G. Gebhardt, 1999, "Derivatives Usage in Risk Management by US and German Non-Financial Firms: A Comparative Survey." *Journal of International Financial Management and Accounting* **10**, 153–187.

Bodnar, G. M., G. Hayt, and R. C. Marston, 1996, "1995 Wharton Survey of Derivative Usage by US Non-Financial Firms." *Financial Management* **25**, 113–133.

Bodnar, G. M., G. Hayt, and R. C. Marston, 1998, "1998 Wharton Survey of Financial Risk Management by US Non-Financial Firms." *Financial Management* **27**, 70–91.

Chang, E. C., and K. P. Wong, 2003, "Cross-Hedging with Currency Options and Futures." *Journal of Financial and Quantitative Analysis* **38**, 555-574.

Danthine, J.-P., 1978, "Information, Futures Prices, and Stabilizing Speculation." *Journal of Economic Theory* **17**, 79–98.

Eiteman, D. K., A. I. Stonehill, and M. H. Moffett, 2001, *Multinational Business Finance.* Massachusetts: Addison-Wesley.

Feder, G., R. E. Just, and A. Schmitz, 1980, "Futures Markets and the Theory of the Firm under Price Uncertainty." *Quarterly Journal of Economics* **94**, 317–328.

Froot, K. A., D. S. Scharfstein, and J. C. Stein, 1993, "Risk Management: Coordinating Corporate Investment and Financing Policies," *Journal of Finance* **48**, 1629–1658.

Holthausen, D. M., 1979, "Hedging and the Competitive Firm under Price Uncertainty." *American Economic Review* **69**, 989–995.

Jacque, L. L., 1996, *Management and Control of Foreign Exchange Risk.* Boston: Kluwer Academic Publishers.

Lien, D-.H. D., 1986, "Moments of Ordered Bivariate Log-Normal Distributions." *Economics Letters* **20**, 45–47.

Meese, R., 1990, "Currency Fluctuations in the Post-Bretton Woods Era." *Journal of Economic Perspectives* **4**, 117–134.

Rawls, S. W., and C. W. Smithson, 1990, "Strategic Risk Management." *Journal of Applied Corporate Finance* **1**, 6–18.

Smith, C. W., and R. Stulz, 1985, "The Determinants of Firms' Hedging Policies." *Journal of Financial and Quantitative Analysis* **20**, 391–405.

Stulz, R., 1984, "Optimal Hedging Policies." *Journal of Financial and Quantitative Analysis* **19**, 127–140.

Stulz, R., 1990, "Managerial Discretion and Optimal Financial Policies." *Journal of Financial Economics* **26**, 3–27.

Tufano, P., 1996, "Who Manages Risk? An Empirical Examination of Risk Management Practices in the Gold Mining Industry." *Journal of Finance* **51**, 1097–1137.

INDEX

A

B

C

D

E

G

H

I

J

K

L

M

N

O

P

Q

R

S

T

U

V

W

Z